Dedication

To my mother, for teaching me to read.

Message from the
Publisher

WELCOME TO OUR NERVOUS SYSTEM

Some people say that the World Wide Web is a graphical extension of the information superhighway, just a network of humans and machines sending each other long lists of the equivalent of digital junk mail.

I think it is much more than that. To me the Web is nothing less than the nervous system of the entire planet—not just a collection of computer brains connected together, but more like a billion silicon neurons entangled and recirculating electro-chemical signals of information and data, each contributing to the birth of another CPU and another Web site.

Think of each person's hard disk connected at once to every other hard disk on earth, driven by human navigators searching like Columbus for the New World. Seen this way the Web is more of a super entity, a growing, living thing, controlled by the universal human will to expand, to be more. Yet unlike a purposeful business plan with rigid rules, the Web expands in a nonlinear, unpredictable, creative way that echoes natural evolution.

We created our Web site not just to extend the reach of our computer book products but to be part of this synaptic neural network, to experience, like a nerve in the body, the flow of ideas and then to pass those ideas up the food chain of the mind. Your mind. Even more, we wanted to pump some of our own creative juices into this rich wine of technology.

TASTE OUR DIGITAL WINE

And so we ask you to taste our wine by visiting the body of our business. Begin by understanding the metaphor we have created for our Web site—a universal learning center, situated in outer space in the form of a space station. A place where you can journey to study any topic from the convenience of your own screen. Right now we are focusing on computer topics, but the stars are the limit on the Web.

If you are interested in discussing this Web site, or finding out more about the Waite Group, please send me email with your comments and I will be happy to respond. Being a programmer myself, I love to talk about technology and find out what our readers are looking for.

Sincerely,

Mitchell Waite

Mitchell Waite, C.E.O. and Publisher

200 Tamal Plaza
Corte Madera CA 94925
415 924 2575
415 924 2576 fax

Internet e-mail:
support@waite.com

Website:
http://www.waite.com/waite

CREATING THE HIGHEST QUALITY COMPUTER BOOKS IN THE INDUSTRY

Waite Group Press
Waite Group New Media

Black Art of
Macintosh
Game
Programming

Kevin Tieskoetter

WAITE GROUP PRESS™
A Division of Sams Publishing
CORTE MADERA, CA

PUBLISHER Mitchell Waite
EDITOR-IN-CHIEF Charles Drucker

ACQUISITIONS EDITOR Jill Pisoni

EDITORIAL DIRECTOR John Crudo
MANAGING EDITOR Kurt Stephan
CONTENT EDITOR Lyn Cordell
COPY EDITOR Deirdre McDonald Greene

TECHNICAL REVIEWER Eduard Schwan
PRODUCTION DIRECTOR Julianne Ososke
PRODUCTION MANAGER Cecile Kaufman
DESIGN Sestina Quarequio, Christi Fryday
PRODUCTION Christi Fryday, Karen Johnston
ILLUSTRATIONS Larry Wilson
COVER ILLUSTRATION James Dowlen

© 1996 by The Waite Group, Inc.® Published by Waite Group Press™, 200 Tamal Plaza, Corte Madera, CA 94925

Waite Group Press™ is a division of Sams Publishing.

Waite Group Press™ is distributed to bookstores and book wholesalers by Publishers Group West, Box 8843, Emeryville, CA 94662, 1-800-788-3123 (in California 1-510-658-3453).

Library of Congress Cataloging-in-Publication Data

Tieskoetter, Kevin.
     Black art of Macintosh game programming / Kevin Tieskoetter.
         p.   cm.
     Includes index.
     ISBN 1-57169-059-X
     1. Computer games--Programming. 2. Macintosh (Computer)--Programming.
     QA76.76.C642T54   1995
     794.8'1526--dc20   95-44225
                                                                             CIP

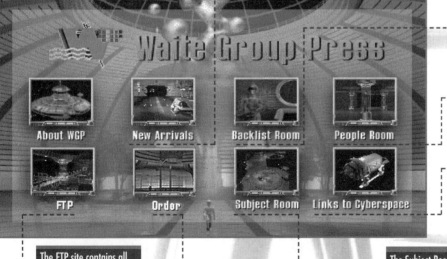

About the Author

Kevin Tieskoetter spent a short time at Drake University in Des Moines, Iowa, and worked in Des Moines at MicroFrontier, Inc., on Color It!, an image processing application for the Macintosh. He is now a software engineer at Specular International, working on products such as InfiniD, a 3D modeling and animation package, and Collage, an image composition tool for graphics professionals. He spends his free time researching methods of procrastinating getting real work done. Regrettably, he does not own a cat, nor is he owned by one.

Table of Contents

Contents

Acknowledgments

As is usual with books, the list of people responsible for the creation of this book extends far beyond the author. I would like to use this page to extend my gratitude to these people.

First of all, I wish to thank the three editors who helped shape my writing into a readable form: Kurt Stephan, Lyn Cordell, and Eduard Schwan. They made it a real pleasure to complete the task, and I look forward to working with them on future projects.

Secondly, I want to thank Drew Cohen for criticism about my writing style and Brendan Donohoe for the excellent models that he created for the final flight simulator.

A portion of the code for the final flight simulator has been carried over from Waite Group Press's *Flights of Fantasy* by Christopher Lampton. The author of this code was Mark Betz—thanks to him for supplying it.

Finally, I have Specular International to thank for the Replicas models that were used for creating some of the sprite shapes that appear here; Lincoln Lydick for some advice in texture mapping; and my family and my friends for their unflagging support during the writing of this book.

Introduction

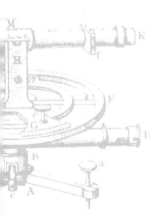

Throughout the history of personal computers, games have flourished. From the advent of the original Adventure, which probably has been ported to more computer platforms than any other program, to modern best-sellers like Civilization and Marathon, game tricks and tips have been constantly traded back and forth. However, the techniques for one genre—true three-dimensional real-time graphics—have always been difficult to come by and if one does find them, it's next to impossible to decipher the code because of all the mathematics involved.

3D games have been incredibly popular for years, typified by best-selling games like DOOM and Marathon, as well the most popular gaming genre, flight simulators. From Spectrum Holobyte's Falcon to Graphic Simulation's Hellcats, F/A-18 Hornet to Parsoft's A-10, flight simulators have captured the attention and imagination of millions of would-be pilots.

Black Art of Macintosh Game Programming will walk you through everything you need to know to create your own three-dimensional game. It will introduce you to the basics of graphics, teach you about techniques of the Macintosh operating system, give you secrets about optimizing your code for the best possible speed, reveal the techniques used for texture-mapped games (you will even be shown how to write your own), detail realistic polygon-graphics techniques, and, in the last chapter, give you the complete source code for a working flight simulator.

You'll learn about the secrets of drawing directly to the screen and bypassing QuickDraw. You'll learn about how to write code for the PowerPC processor and how to maximize its speed potential. And you'll learn about how to take advantage of the Macintosh operating system and how to keep it from getting in your way.

This book also includes discussions about the PowerPC chip's impact on the gaming community. All the source code provided in this book has been tested with the Power Macintosh and has been compiled as native code (but is also compatible with 68020 or better processors).

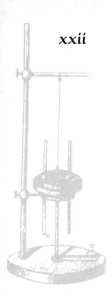

All the code in this book is written in C and can be compiled using the Metrowerks CodeWarrior package or the Symantec C package. This book assumes you have at least basic working knowledge about your compiler (if you don't, both environments provide tutorials to get you up to speed). Project files are included for both environments for each sample program.

The tome you are holding in your hands illustrates several techniques that historically have been difficult or impossible to find in a published book. Among these esoteric tasks are writing directly to the screen, utilizing ultrafast fixed-point arithmetic, optimizing game-specific code for the PowerPC processor, and programming low-level code that will stay compatible with future machines.

For newcomers to Macintosh programming, the first three chapters of this book take you through the steps of using the Macintosh interface and explain the role it plays in games. You will learn the techniques of windows, menus, event loops, and more. From there, you'll learn about two-dimensional sprite graphics, move on to creating the foundation for three-dimensional polygon graphics, and finally graduate to creating a full flight simulator.

I hope you'll find this book and its accompanying collection of software helpful in your quest to create the next killer game.

About the CD-ROM

The accompanying Macintosh CD-ROM contains source code, development tools, and numerous demos of commercial, shareware, and freeware games. The following sections discuss the contents of the CD in greater detail, in addition to giving installation instructions.

Source Code

On the included CD-ROM, you'll find all of the source code detailed in *Black Art of Macintosh Game Programming*. This code is sorted by chapter and is found in the Source Code folder. The source code has been compiled and tested as native Power Macintosh code, but is also compatible with 68020 or better processors. The code is written in C and can be compiled using the Metrowerks CodeWarrior package or the Symantec C package. Project files and compiled applications for each sample program are included for both environments. You will need a minimum of 4MB RAM to run the projects.

Development Tools

Several shareware and demonstration programs that assist in development are provided in the Development Tools folder. Of special note are SpriteWorld, a package that allows you to create sprite animations not unlike those in Invaders; WT, a ray-casting texture-mapped game with full source code; Resourcerer, the world's best resource editor; and Think Reference, an excellent (but unfortunately slightly out-of-date) toolbox reference.

Additionally, you will find bonus tools from Apple Computer in the Apple Tools folder and useful demos of products from Specular and others in the Other Demos folder. Also included on the CD is a special offer from *MacTech,* a Macintosh developer's magazine—a great resource for keeping on the cutting edge of Macintosh programming.

Games

I've also included demos of some of the best available Macintosh commercial games, as well as a representation of some of the best shareware and freeware games. You'll find the commerical games demos in the Game Demos folder; the others are in the Shareware/Freeware Games folder.

Here are some of the highlights:

A-10 Attack! is one of the best flight simulators available for the Macintosh (arguably for any platform) at the time of this writing. A-10's biggest claim to fame is its detailed physics modeling. When you fly the plane, notice how it bounces off the runway on a landing or how debris rolls down the side of a hill. This flight simulator uses a technique called *polygon differencing* when drawing to the screen. Essentially, the simulator draws only the portions of the screen that have changed, which gives it more fluid motion.

Power Pete represents a genre of games that is mainly concentrated on video game platforms such as Nintendo and Sega. It's a refreshing change to see one of these games on the Macintosh, especially one that's so well done.

Spaceward Ho! has been on the Macintosh for a long time and has a cult following. This space-conquest game is a prime example of how to design a game interface.

Troubled Souls is an uplifting example of how a small company can survive. It was designed and written by Randy Reddig, a high school senior. The game is also proof that programmers can make great artists—Randy also created all of the artwork!

Ambrosia has produced several games that have made us all proud to be Macintosh owners. Maelstrom, its first offering, is based on an Asteroids concept, but with radically redesigned artwork and incredible action. In Chiral, you create patterns of molecules at a maddening pace; the game is very addicting. Apeiron is modeled on a game that many of us have spent many a quarter on at the arcades—Centipede—but, of course, with its own little twist. Finally, Swoop is the distant (and much more advanced) cousin of our own Invaders! game.

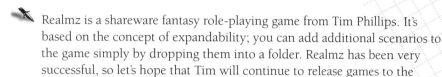 Realmz is a shareware fantasy role-playing game from Tim Phillips. It's based on the concept of expandability; you can add additional scenarios to the game simply by dropping them into a folder. Realmz has been very successful, so let's hope that Tim will continue to release games to the Macintosh community.

Ultima III is a completely rewritten version of the game released by Origin for the Macintosh about 10 years ago. The new version has high-resolution color graphics and has been welcomed with open arms by veteran role-players.

Installation

All the source code presented on the CD-ROM can be installed simply by dragging the Source Code folder onto your hard drive. Allow approximately 10MB of free hard drive space for the source code.

Development tools, demos, and games should also be copied from the CD to your hard drive for best performance, though most items will run directly off the CD. If you encounter performance problems running any item off the CD (or if a program does not run at all), try copying it to your hard drive.

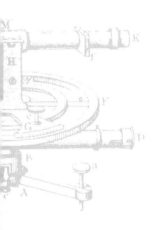

1

Games and the Macintosh

...come trēdi dare lemanovelle ... le quali prmobano ... lalgu
no sgrapi si ... leomēdi ... poni ... sa so grano di bone
forza re nella ma ... la per ma ... tella arsla mano bella pogi qui re
la forza ... piū si omo pib bat.

... elpo ... ...
... ...
... ...

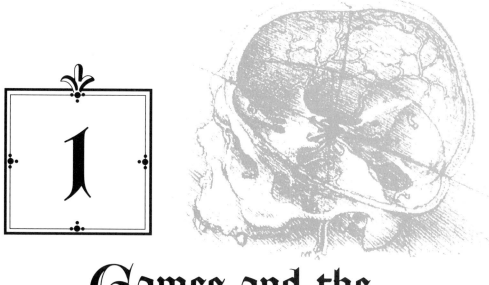

1

Games and the Macintosh

Looking at today's computer games, you might find it hard to imagine that Pong, a game that involved hitting a cube back and forth across the screen, could ever have been state of the art. But it was once the latest rage and it started a revolution in the entertainment industry. Pong soon spawned more games, such as Breakout. And remember Asteroids and Pacman, which both helped establish the computer gaming industry?

All of these early games ran on dedicated hardware. When the personal computer (PC) was introduced, it was simply not powerful enough to play true arcade games. Text-based games, such as the immortal Adventure and the later Zork series, which were translated from their versions on mainframe machines, were more in line with the abilities of PCs.

A major stepping stone for personal computer games was the ancestor to the Macintosh, the Apple II. The Apple II was enormously successful, becoming the de facto standard in schools and gaining great acceptance in the home market. It was powerful enough for some simple arcade games and even had color graphics, a rarity at that time. Over the next few years, hundreds of games found their way onto the computers of every high school, as students discovered something more interesting to do than algebra.

One of these games was Flight Simulator, by Bruce Artwick, and it was radically different from the others of its time. It placed users in the cockpit of a World War I biplane, presenting them with a green field, a river, and two mountains, and let them fly through it all, dogfighting with other planes.

Flight Simulator was one of the first games to use first-person perspective, a concept that has matured into today's "virtual reality", which gives players the same visual perspective a character in the game would have, allowing players to respond as though they were actually a part of the game's world.

Since Flight Simulator, there have been thousands of similar first-person perspective games, both in the flight simulator category (now the most popular type of game on the PC) and in adventure games, such as DOOM or Marathon.

To create an alternate reality, a game must employ three-dimensional graphics and display them on a two-dimensional screen at a speed sufficient to ensure realism. Early games, such as the arcade tank game BattleZone, created graphics using simple lines; more recent machines, using advances in technology, have the advantage of greater horsepower. Today, even the simplest of three-dimensional games uses a technique called *polygon-fill* graphics, that creates solid shapes on the screen. Extensions to polygon-fill graphics such as *gouraud shading* and *texture mapping* also provide more realistic images. A good example of a three-dimensional game that uses polygon-fill graphics is A-10 from Parsoft, as shown in Figure 1-1.

I'll be discussing these topics in later chapters, but first I'll give you the background you'll need to master them. For the benefit of programmers with no graphics programming experience, this chapter provides an overview of the basic concepts of computer

FIGURE 1-1

◎ ◎ ◎ ◎ ◎ ◎

Parsoft's A-10 making a bombing run

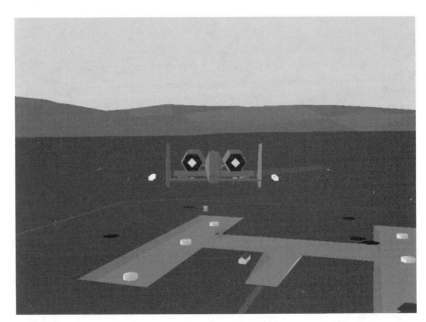

graphics in general and Macintosh graphics in particular. Programmers who have already mastered two-dimensional graphics techniques may wish to skim this chapter, though skipping it entirely is not recommended.

Graphics and Games

At one time, it was possible to publish a major computer game that didn't use graphics. In the 1980s, Infocom, Inc., published a wonderful series of text adventures with no graphics capabilities whatsoever. But in the 1990s, game buyers demand state-of-the-art graphics, even if the visual images have little or nothing to do with the game. (One of the most popular arcade games ever, Spectrum Holobyte's version of Tetris, features background scenes from the former Soviet Union that are completely unrelated to the action of the game.) Great game design and balanced gameplay (i.e., making sure the game is not too hard or too easy) are essential qualities for a top-notch game, of course, but neither can save a game with mediocre graphics from commercial oblivion. Thus, programmers who want to produce games must understand their computer's graphics capabilities.

The Macintosh: Made for Graphics

The Macintosh is an ideal platform for graphics-oriented programs. Unlike most other computers (such as those the Infocom games grew up on), it does not have a text mode. Instead, everything you see on the screen is composed of graphic elements, so the programmer has near complete control over the screen.

Before you begin working with graphics, you should know a little about the history of Macintosh graphics. The methods of controlling what the user sees have remained very similar to those used in the first Macintosh, which was released in 1984. This was the Macintosh 128; it featured a very sharp black-and-white display capable of a resolution of 512 pixels wide and 342 pixels tall on a 9-inch diagonal screen. For the computers of that time, this resolution was fairly impressive, and although the screen was comparatively tiny, its clarity kept it from being difficult to use. However, the fact that it could only display black and white made it a less attractive platform for game developers than other platforms available at the time, such as the Commodore, the Atari, and even the famous Apple II.

Although Apple improved its original Macintosh four times over the next few years, the video system remained exactly the same. The turning point for the Macintosh gaming community came in 1987, when Apple released the Macintosh II. This computer was capable of using a wide variety of screens, but the most common was a 13-inch color monitor, that could display 256 colors at a resolution of 640 by 480 pixels. This display has remained a standard for Macintosh computers, although recent years have seen the popularization of larger displays, including the 16-inch monitor (capable of 832x624 pixels) and the 19-inch monitor (1024x768).

When I say that a monitor has a color depth of 2, 4, 16, or 256 color, I mean that pixels in that many colors can appear together on the screen at one time. If you were to pull out a magnifying glass and count the colors on a screen in 256-color mode, you would find at most 256 colors. (You might find fewer colors, because there is no reason that a programmer has to use all of the colors available.)

Most of the newest machines can display even more colors. Some can reproduce up to 32,000 shades; others can create almost 17 million. Although developers like the idea of taking advantage of the whole capability of today's machines, they must keep in mind that doing so may prevent their software from functioning on older or less expensive computers.

Mapping Color Images

Everything that appears on the screen is composed of tiny dots called *pixels* (short for "pictorial elements"). It is up to the programmer to control these pixels so they present a meaningful image for the user. Fortunately, as you will see later, the pioneers of microcomputers have made this job much easier.

When several pixels are organized in a rectangle, such as the screen, they are collectively called a *bitmap*. In the simplest kind of bitmap, one that represents a video image containing only two colors, the value of each bit in each byte represents the state of a pixel in the image. The zeroes represent pixels set to the background color (white on the Macintosh); the ones represent pixels set to the foreground color (which the Macintosh treats as black). Figure 1-2 shows a two-color bitmap of the letter Z.

This bitmap consists of 8 bytes of data, which would normally be arranged sequentially in the computer's memory. I have displayed it, however, as though the bits in those bytes were arranged in a rectangle, with 8 pixels on a side. Bitmaps are almost always arranged in a rectangular fashion on a video display.

When you work with a 256-color image, 8 bits are used to represent each pixel. This is very handy for graphics programming, because now each pixel fits into 1 byte, which is easy to manipulate. A 256-color picture, although not of photographic quality, can look very impressive. For these reasons, the code that we will work on in this book will be designed for a 256-color display.

The Color Palette

But which 256 colors appear on the screen? That's up to you—the programmer. The collective group of colors that can appear on the screen is called the *color palette*. The Macintosh has a standard color palette referred to as the system palette that is the default for any application to use. It contains a wide variety of colors, that should suit the needs

FIGURE 1-2
◎ ◎ ◎ ◎ ◎ ◎

*A bitmap
representation
of the letter Z*

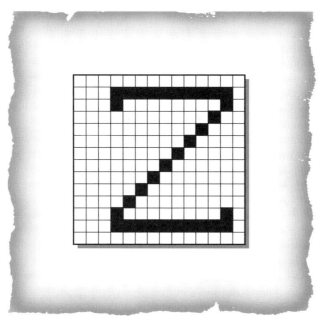

of most programs; these colors are selected from a much larger range, and program-mers who don't want this sample of colors can design a palette of their own. On the Macintosh, the palette is chosen from 16,777,216 different colors, which should include every color you've ever dreamed about.

Each window you see on the Macintosh can have its own color palette. Most use the standard system palette, but some graphics programs may use their own. When a win-dow with a different palette is the active window, the screen colors are redefined to fit this palette. This could really mess up an image on a window in the background, but the operating system automatically redraws background windows so the images look as good as possible. When another window is brought to the front, the colors are remapped to make the front window look its best.

The computer's video circuitry creates colors by adding specific amounts of red, green, and blue together. There are 256 levels of each of these colors available, from 0 (no color, or black) to 255 (the brightest possible shade of that color). To describe a color, you use three numbers in this range, describing the red, blue, and green intensities that togeth-er make up the color. (For instance, the color described by 0,0,0 is pure black; 255,255,255 is pure white. All other shades are between these extremes.)

When 256 of these colors are placed together in a special array, they form a description of each of the colors available on an 8-bit screen. The color in position 0, for example, is equivalent to the bitmap value 00000000, whereas the color in posi-tion 255 is equivalent to the bitmap value 11111111.

For the purposes of future expansion, Apple has created a structure called RGBColor. It consists of three 16-bit integers that describe the red, green, and blue parts of a color. But because the range of a 16-bit integer is between 0 and 65,535, each portion of the color must be expanded before it is placed into this structure. The easiest way to do this is to multiply each color element by 256. Apple has used a 16-bit integer so that in the future, if 17 million colors aren't enough, it will be easy to expand colors to 48 bits of precision (which equates to 281 *trillion* colors).

Creating the Screen Image

Now let's look at how the programmer goes about creating an image on the screen. The Macintosh's video hardware is responsible for generating the signal that is sent to the monitor, but where does it get the contents of the signal?

At the most primitive level, most of the work performed by a computer program involves storing numeric values in memory circuits, retrieving them from those circuits, performing arithmetic operations on them, and putting the result of those operations back into memory circuits. If you program microcomputers in a high-level language such as C, you may not be aware of the degree to which these memory circuits figure into your algorithms because these languages are designed to hide the details of the CPU's interactions with memory.

As you probably know, every memory circuit in the computer has an identifying number called an *address*, which makes it easier for the numeric values stored in that circuit to be retrieved at a later time. If you want to store a number in the computer's memory and retrieve it later, you can store the number in a specific memory address, note that address, and then retrieve that number later from the same address (assuming you haven't turned off the machine or otherwise erased the contents of the memory in the meantime). In fact, this is exactly what you are doing when you use variables in a high-level language such as C. The variable represents a memory address; the statement that assigns a value to the variable stores a numeric value at that address. Of course, you never need to know exactly what memory address the value was stored at; it's the C compiler's job to worry about that. Even assembly language programmers generally give symbolic names to memory addresses and let the assembler worry about what addresses those names represent.

Video Memory

Why is this so important for graphics? Look very closely at your computer screen. In most cases, you'll be able to pick out the individual pixels that make up the image you see. Each of these pixels corresponds to 1 or more bits in computer memory. As I explained earlier, the color mode of your monitor determines how many bits make up each pixel—

in black-and-white mode, each pixel corresponds to 1 bit; in 256-color mode, each pixel takes up 8 bits, or 1 byte. This correlation between the color depth and the number of bits/pixel is expressed by this formula:

colors = 2(bits/pixel)

This formula also explains why black and white games are much faster than color games and why early color games on the Macintosh typically operated in 16-color mode instead of 256-color; the fewer colors the game deals with, the less memory it has to push around to animate the graphics.

On most Macintoshes, the video memory is stored on special chips that are separate from normal RAM (called Video RAM or VRAM) but for others (the IIci and some Power Macintoshes), video memory is just a portion of normal memory. For the programmer, however, it really doesn't make any difference where the video memory is located—it all works the same.

The programmer puts images onto the screen by writing into this area of memory. Every sixtieth of a second the video hardware scans the video memory and converts the contents into a signal. The video display interprets this signal and displays the image. In most cases, even with games, this entire process is done indirectly by using QuickDraw.

QuickDraw: Friend and Enemy of the Game Programmer

One reason the methods of drawing graphics on the Macintosh have remained essentially the same over the years is a part of the Macintosh system software called QuickDraw. This package serves as a layer between the programmer and the hardware.

With the exception of high-speed games and a few other programs that require extra fast animation, everything you see on your Macintosh's screen was created using QuickDraw. Every window, every menu, every dialog was drawn by calling QuickDraw commands, which demonstrates the versatility of this package.

QuickDraw makes it tremendously easy to program graphics applications for the Macintosh, but this convenience comes at a price. Because QuickDraw is very general purpose, it's not always as fast as game programmers would like it to be.

All is not lost, however; should QuickDraw become too slow, it is possible to bypass it and write your own routines. Game programming on the Macintosh involves a balancing act among the issues of speed and compatibility and how much work you are willing to do.

In most cases, the programmer does not need to access QuickDraw directly. For instance, the programmer may use a command from the Menu Manager (an Apple package that handles the menu bar) instead. When the Menu Manager needs to draw a menu, it handles the interaction with QuickDraw to get the job done. Figure 1-3 shows the hierarchy of this system.

QuickDraw is able to decide the best method of writing into video memory and was designed with internal error checking to prevent writing to the wrong area of memory, which could cause the computer to crash. It also offers the advantage of compatibility with future machines—if Apple changes the way video memory is used in a future Macintosh, it will update QuickDraw at the same time to use the new method. Any program that uses QuickDraw will still work fine, but programs that bypass QuickDraw and write directly to the screen will fail.

QuickDraw makes life easier for the programmer and users. It enables the programmer to use graphics devices without knowing the details of how they're made, it ensures that the application will function the same on any current or future Macintosh, and it relieves users of the headaches that come with setting up and configuring software to work with specific graphic devices.

These arguments offer plenty of reasons to not use direct access, but there is one compelling argument in favor of direct access: speed. The super-fast flight simulators of today (Hellcats, F/A-18, and A-10) do not use QuickDraw for everything; in areas where speed is crucial, they use their own specialized routines that write to the video memory. A programmer's decision about when to use QuickDraw and when not to must be weighed carefully. In this book, I'll use several examples that bypass QuickDraw, but in most cases where speed is less critical, I'll use QuickDraw.

Creating the Graphics

In the next few chapters, I explore the tools you'll need to begin creating your own images on the screen. Chapter 2 introduces the Macintosh Toolbox and basic QuickDraw routines, ending in a shape-drawing program. Chapter 3 introduces the Memory Manager, resources, and bitmaps and culminates in a program that opens and displays PICT files.

FIGURE 1-3

◎ ◎ ◎ ◎ ◎ ◎

Interaction between an application and the video hardware

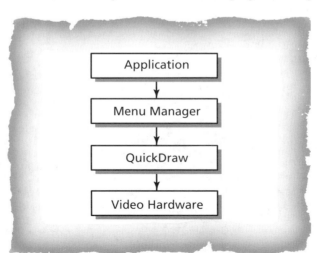

2

Opening the Toolbox: Macintosh Programming Basics

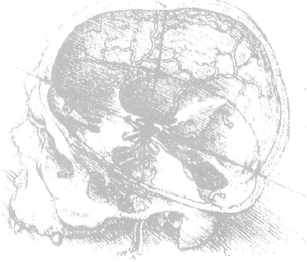

Opening the Toolbox: Macintosh Programming Basics

The tools that are used for creating the Macintosh interface come from the *toolbox*. The toolbox is a library of routines located in the ROM of every Macintosh so it's always available for the programmer's use. The toolbox is also what makes the Macintosh special for development. Not only do all these tools make it easier to create a good interface, they ensure that all Macintosh applications are consistent.

The toolbox consists of about 5,000 functions that you can call from the safety and convenience of your application. These functions are broken down into several *managers;* each manager handles a separate component of the Macintosh. For example, a Menu Manager handles the menu bar at the top of the screen, a Window Manager controls each of the windows, and a Dialog Manager is responsible for each dialog you see. Some of these managers are dependent on others; for example, a dialog is a type of window, so the Dialog Manager frequently makes calls to the Window Manager. Each manager can be thought of as a "black box"—you don't have to know how the manager accomplishes something, only how to give it directions.

Before an application uses the toolbox, it needs to prepare the toolbox for use by initializing the managers it will be calling. An application initializes the managers it will be using by calling a very simple initialization routine. For example, if the application will be using QuickDraw, it has to call QuickDraw's initialization routine, *InitGraf()*. If it will be using windows, it must call *InitWindows()*, and so on.

In this chapter, I introduce QuickDraw, the Window Manager, the Menu Manager, and the Event Manager. Using all of these components, I'll create several simple programs, culminating with one that will draw simple QuickDraw shapes in a window by responding to menu commands.

Building a Window

The window is the first thing most people notice about the Macintosh interface and it's the one they take most for granted. Almost everything you see on the screen is enclosed within a window—your files and folders in the Finder, your workspace in your word processor, or the action occurring in your game.

The Window Manager

You create windows using the Window Manager. This is done through a single call to the toolbox that has the following structure:

```
WindowPtr NewWindow(  Ptr         wStorage,
                      Rect        *boundsRect,
                      Str255      title,
                      Boolean     visible,
                      short       procID,
                      WindowPtr   behind,
                      Boolean     goAwayFlag,
                      long        refCon );
```

The *wStorage* parameter is used to provide the Window Manager a place to store the information necessary for the window. If you pass in NULL, the Window Manager will allocate the space for you—this is usually the preferred way.

The *boundsRect* parameter is a pointer to a variable of type *Rect* that contains the bounding rectangle of the window. The rectangle defines the active area within a window (called the *content area*), but does not include the title bar.

The text contained in the *title* parameter is positioned in the center of the title bar. The text string must be Pascal-style—the first byte must contain the size of the string, followed by the string itself. If you include the string in your code, you must use Pascal notation. To write a string in Pascal notation in the C language, prefix the string with \p; for example \pMy Window. Even if your window does not have a title, you must provide an empty string here. In this case, pass in \p.

The *visible* parameter tells the Window Manager whether or not to display the window on the desktop right away. If you need to set up more things in the window space before you show it or you want to wait until later before drawing the window, pass in FALSE. You can then display the window by calling ShowWindow(), which is another Window Manager toolbox call.

FIGURE 2-1

◎ ◎ ◎ ◎ ◎ ◎

Various window types

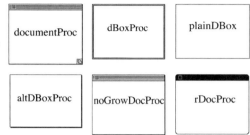

The *procID* parameter is used to create different types of windows. The operating system provides 15 window types, a few of which are shown in Figure 2-1. You can add additional types by writing them or by using windows created elsewhere.

To place the new window behind another window on the screen, pass in the WindowPtr of the existing window for the *behind* parameter. Otherwise, pass in -1 to place the window in front of all windows on the screen or 0 to put it behind the rest of the windows. Because C is expecting a WindowPtr, you must *typecast* (i.e., change the variable type of) the parameter, in the form of (WindowPtr)-1 or (WindowPtr)0.

The *goAwayFlag* parameter allows you to add a close box to the window. Some window styles do not allow a close box; in these cases, this parameter will be ignored. Pass in TRUE to give the window a close box, FALSE for no close box.

Finally, the *refCon* parameter allows you an opportunity to store a value with the window. The use of this field is entirely up to you; the parameter can be useful to provide data abstraction with windows. For example, if your program created several windows, it could store a number in the refCon indicating what it was using this window for. This would provide an easy way of recognizing the window and giving it special treatment if necessary. For example, a game could have a constant defined for the window in which the current scores or character statistics are displayed.

Here is an example of a call to NewWindow:

```
theWindow = NewWindow(  NULL,          /* Let the Window Manager */
                                       /* allocate the memory */
                        bounds,        /* The boundary of the window */
                        title,         /* The window's title */
                        TRUE,          /* We want it visible */
                        dBoxProc,      /* Constant for a standard */
                                       /* window with a title bar */
                        (WindowPtr)-1, /* Place the window in front */
                                       /* of any others */
                        TRUE,          /* Give us a close box */
                        0 );           /* No refCon; we don't need it */
```

Now let's embed the call to NewWindow() in some sample code that brings up a window. This routine is called CreateWindow(); I'll be using it continually throughout this

book. Its only parameter is a rectangle, which defines the window's boundary. It creates a name for the window (which, in this case, will always be My Window), then calls
NewWindow() with those parameters. Finally, it returns WindowPtr (which you'll need
to reference the window in the future) to the calling function.

```
WindowPtr  CreateWindow(Rect  *bounds)
{
  Str255     title = "\pMy Window";  /* Set the window title */
  WindowPtr  theWindow;


  theWindow = NewWindow(  NULL,         /* Let the Window Manager */
                                        /* allocate the memory */
                          bounds,       /* The boundary of the window */
                          title,        /* The window's title */
                          TRUE,         /* We want it visible */
                          dBoxProc,     /* Constant for a standard */
                                        /* window with a title bar */
                          (WindowPtr)-1, /* Place the window in front */
                                        /* of any others */
                          TRUE,         /* Give us a close box */
                          0 );          /* No refCon; we don't need it */

  /* Pass the window pointer back to the caller */
  return theWindow;
}
```

The Event Manager

Most Macintosh applications are based on a design of waiting for the user to do
something and then responding to the user's action. For example, when you're using
your word processor, a vast majority of the time the application is simply waiting for
you to do something, such as type a character or select a menu item. When it's in this
waiting state, it's not processing any information and the CPU is idle or busy handling
some other menial chore, such as blinking the cursor. Figure 2-2 shows the sequence
for Macintosh events.

The underlying flow of an arcade game or simulation is slightly different. Instead
of waiting for the user to do something, a game is constantly doing calculations, updating the screen, or any one of a thousand other tasks. When it gets a chance, it checks
to see if the user has performed any action; if he or she has, it processes that input.

Let's take a closer look at how an application receives and processes events.
Whenever you type a character or click the mouse, the operating system records *what*
the event was, *when* it occurred, and in the case of a mouse event, *where* it happened.
Each of these actions is entered into a first-in-first-out queue, where it remains until
the application retrieves it.

FIGURE 2-2

◎ ◎ ◎ ◎ ◎ ◎

*Macintosh
event sequence*

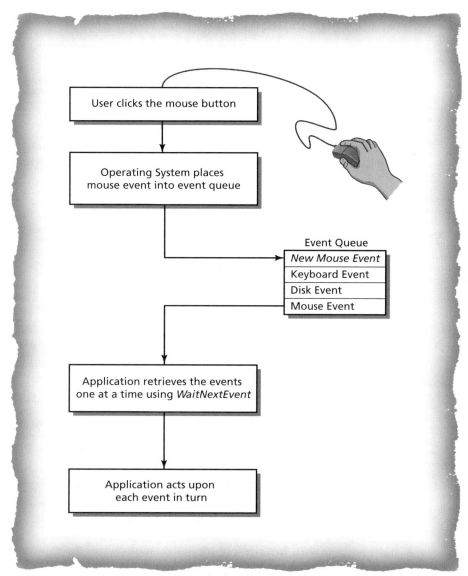

All the application has to do is ask the operating system to tell it about the next event in the queue and then react to it. It does this through an *event loop*, which is basically a normal do…while loop that runs for the entire life of the application.

Event Types

Events can be divided into two categories: those generated as a direct response to a user action and those generated by the operating system. The first type is more important and includes the following:

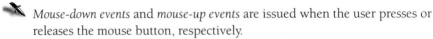 *Mouse-down events* and *mouse-up events* are issued when the user presses or releases the mouse button, respectively.

Keyboard events include *key-down* and *key-up events,* which occur when the user presses and releases a key on the keyboard or keypad; however, key-down and key-up events are not issued when the user presses a modifier key (SHIFT, CONTROL, OPTION, COMMAND, or CAPS LOCK). *Auto-key* events are events that occur repeatedly when the user presses a key and holds it down to make it repeat.

Disk-insert events occur when the user mounts a hard drive or a CD-ROM or inserts a disk into the floppy drive.

Activate events are issued when an inactive window is brought to the front or when the active window is placed behind another. These events generally occur in pairs (i.e., when one window is activated, another is deactivated).

Update events occur when a portion of a window needs to be redrawn. Typically these result from a user action, such as opening, closing, moving, or activating a window.

Event types that are generated by the operating system include the following:

High-level events and *operating system events* are used by the operating system to send messages to the application. These events are commonly used for AppleEvents (high-level events that are sent from application to application).

Null events are used to indicate that there are no waiting events for the application.

The Event Record

The EventRecord is a structure that holds all the information your application needs to react to an event. It consists of

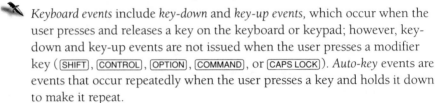 the type of event that occurred;

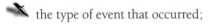 a message about the event (what key was pressed, which window needs updating, and so on);

when the event occurred;

the location of the mouse at that time; and

information about the modifier keys, the mouse button, or the state of the window.

This is the structure of the EventRecord:

```
struct EventRecord {
   short      what;
   Long       message;
   Long       when;
   Point      where;
   short      modifiers;
};
```

The *what* field contains the type of event. After your program receives an event, compare this field (by using the == operator or a switch statement) with the constants for each event (which are outlined in Table 2-1) and call to a routine that will handle the event.

Event	Event Type Constant
Mouse Down	mouseDown
Mouse Up	mouseUp
Key Down	keyDown
Key Up	keyUp
Auto Key	autoKey
Update	updateEvt
Disk Insert	diskEvt
Activate	activateEvt
High Level	kHighLevelEvent
Operating System	osEvt

TABLE 2-1 ◈ *Event type constants*

The *message* field gives the application more specific information about the circumstances of the event. The application should examine this field after determining what kind of event was issued; for some events, this field is undefined. See Table 2-2 for the message field contents generated by different events.

Event	Contents of Message Field
Mouse Down, Mouse Up	Not used
Key Down, Key Up, Auto Key	ASCII character code and key code
Update	Pointer to window that needs updating
Disk Insert	Drive Number and result code
Activate	Pointer to activated window
High Level	Type of high-level event
Operating System	Type of os event

TABLE 2-2 ◈ *Event message field contents*

For keyboard events, the top 8 bits of the message field contain an ASCII code for the key that was pressed and the bottom 8 bits contain a key code. The key code differs from the ASCII code in that each key on the keyboard is bound to a particular code; therefore, the 1 key from the main part of the keyboard has a different key code from the 1 from the numeric keypad, but a w has the same key code as W. See *Inside Macintosh: Toolbox Essentials* for a complete list of Key Codes and ASCII codes.

Update and *activate* events both contain pointers to the target window in the message fields. *Disk insert*, *high level*, and *operating system* events are outside the scope of this book; if you are interested in these events, please consult *Inside Macintosh:Toolbox Essentials*.

When an event is generated, the current *TickCount* is placed in the *when* field of the event record. A *tick* is equal to 1/60th of a second; the TickCount is a measure of how many ticks have occurred since the system started up.

The *where* field contains the screen coordinates of where the mouse was when the event occurred. This field is very important when handling mouse events, but is usually ignored when handling any other type of event.

The *modifiers* field contains the state of the modifier keys when the event occurred. It can be used to determine whether the (SHIFT), (COMMAND), (CONTROL), (OPTION), or (CAPS LOCK) keys were held down or whether the mouse button was pressed. See Figure 2-3 for a diagram of the contents of this field.

The constants used to check the individual parts of the modifiers field are also outlined in Figure 2-3. They can be checked by using the *bitwise and* operator from C ('&'). For example, (event.modifiers & cmdKey) will be zero if the command key was not held down during an event, or nonzero if it was.

Here is an example of how an application might use the modifiers field:

```
if (event.what == keyDown) {    /* a key was pressed */
  if (event.modifiers & cmdKey) {
    /* The command key was held down when the key was pressed */
```

FIGURE 2-3
◉ ◉ ◉ ◉ ◉ ◉
*Bit fields of the
EventRecord
modifiers field*

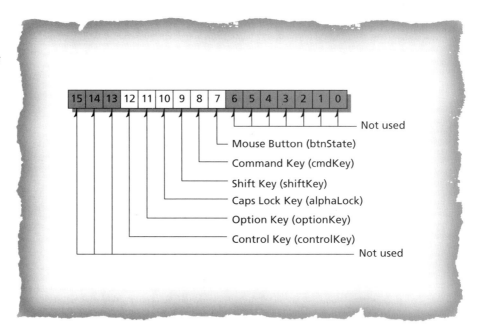

```
    /* Respond to a command-character key event, usually indicating
       the keyboard equivalent of a menu item */
  }
}
```

The WaitNextEvent Call

The most important toolbox call in an application is the one that retrieves each event from the operating system. The call is *WaitNextEvent*; here is its prototype:

```
Boolean  WaitNextEvent(  short       eventMask,
                         EventRecord *theEvent,
                         long        sleep,
                         RgnHandle   mouseRgn );
```

The *eventMask* field contains a 16-bit integer with 1 bit for each event type. If a particular bit is set to 1, the operating system can send that type of event back to the application. (See Figure 2-4 for an illustration of the bits for the eventMask field.)

To aid in the construction of the event mask, Apple has supplied several constants that can be added together to form the integer value. These constants are outlined in Table 2-3, in the Event Mask Constant column.

To create your event mask, all you need to do is add the event mask constants together. For example, if your application only cares about mouse-down, key-down, auto-key, activate, and update events, you would create your event mask like this:

```
eventMask = mDownMask + keyDownMask + autoKeyMask + activMask +
            updateMask.
```

In many cases, however, it is easier to accept every event from the Event Manager and then filter out the events you don't need within your code. This is the most common method used by applications.

The *theEvent* field contains a pointer to an EventRecord, which receives all of the relevant information about the event.

The *sleep* field tells the operating system how many ticks the application is willing to wait for an event. If no events are pending for the application, the operating system will use this time to give other applications a chance to do some work, but it will return control to your application when the time runs out.

If your application needs to regain control immediately, it should pass in a very low number for the sleep field (somewhere between 0 and 10). If it doesn't want to regain control until it receives an important event, it should pass in a very high number (typically 0x7FFFFFFF, the hex notation for the largest possible 32-bit signed number).

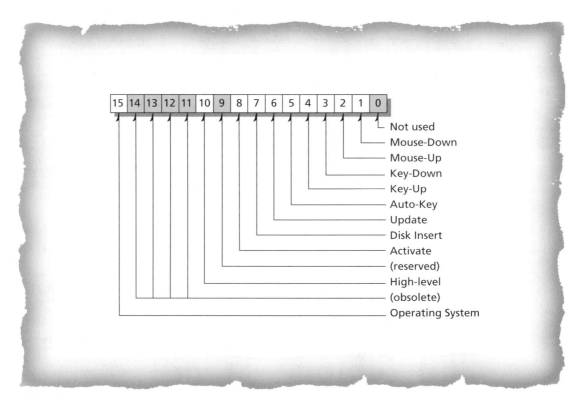

FIGURE 2-4 ◉ *Bit fields of an event mask*

Event	Event Mask Constant	Event Mask Constant Value
All Events	everyEvent	-1
Mouse Down	mDownMask	2
Mouse Up	mUpMask	4
Key Down	keyDownMask	8
Key Up	keyUpMask	16
Auto Key	autoKeyMask	32
Update	updateMask	64
Disk Insert	diskMask	128
Activate	activMask	256
High Level	highLevelEventMask	1024
Operating System	osMask	-32768

TABLE 2-3 ◈ *Event mask constants*

The *mouseRgn* field defines the region of the screen from which the application should *not* receive mouse-moved events. Most of the time, the application does not want to receive any mouse-moved events, in which case it would pass in Null for this parameter. For more information about regions and mouse-moved events, consult the *Inside Macintosh* volumes.

WaitNextEvent returns a Boolean variable. If it is True, a non-null event has been returned. If it is False, the event type is Null.

Putting the Event Loop Together

Now let's look at how you might form an event loop for the window application. Use the *switch* statement from C to provide a way of dispatching events. This makes it very easy to add additional event types in the future. In this example, you care only about mouse-down, key-down, activate, and update events. When an application receives an update event, it needs to tell the operating system that it has taken care of it. It does this by calling two routines: BeginUpdate() and EndUpdate(). BeginUpdate() does the preparation needed for drawing a window; EndUpdate() lets the operating system know that you're finished drawing. Both routines require the WindowPtr of the window you're updating, which can be obtained from the event record's message field. In this first example, there won't be any code between the BeginUpdate and EndUpdate calls because there is nothing to draw in the window.

```
EventRecord      theEvent;
short            eventMask;
short            done = FALSE;     // The loop will continue until
                                   // done is TRUE
Boolean          receivedEvent;

eventMask = everyEvent;

while (!done) {
  receivedEvent = WaitNextEvent(
                    eventMask,    // Which events to mask
                    &theEvent,    // A pointer to our event record
                    0x7FFFFFFF,   // We don't need to receive control
                                  // unless there is a non-null event
                    NULL);        // Don't return mouse-moved events

  if (receivedEvent == TRUE) {
    // We received something other than a NULL event

    switch (theEvent.what) {
      case mouseDown:
        /* Handle mouse down */
        break;

      case keyDown:
        /* Handle key down */
        break;

      case activateEvt:
        /* Handle activate event */
        break;

      case updateEvt:
        BeginUpdate((WindowPtr)theEvent.message);
        EndUpdate((WindowPtr)theEvent.message);
        break;
    }
  }
}
```

The Simple Window Application

Let's use the techniques you just learned to create a very simple application. All it will do is bring up a window and quit when you click the mouse.

For the application, you will be initializing the Window Manager, QuickDraw (you need to initialize QuickDraw, even though you won't be using it directly, because the Window Manager uses it for drawing the window), and the Cursor Manager (so the mouse cursor is changed to an arrow instead of a watch). To initialize these portions of the toolbox, you will make three calls: InitGraf(), InitWindows(), and InitCursor().

The InitWindows() and InitCursor() calls don't require any parameters, but InitGraf(), the routine that initializes QuickDraw, requires a pointer to the application's main port. This pointer is easily obtained from a global structure called *qd*, like this:

```
InitGraf(&qd.thePort);
```

 # The QD Structure

qd is a global variable that stores several parameters that QuickDraw uses to affect your application. These parameters are things like the current port, the current color to use for line drawing, the current cursor, the current random seed, and a pointer to the screen itself.

Start out by declaring the variables you'll need.

```
void main(void)
{
  EventRecord    theEvent;
  short          eventMask;
  short          done = FALSE;
  Boolean        notNullEvent;
  WindowPtr      theWindow;
  Rect           windowBounds;
```

Now initialize QuickDraw, the Window Manager, and the Cursor Manager.

```
/* Initialize everything we need */
InitGraf(&qd.thePort);  // qd.thePort is part of any application
InitWindows();
InitCursor();
```

To set up the windowBounds structure, the toolbox provides a routine called SetRect(). To use it, pass in a pointer to the Rect structure, followed by values for the left, top, right, and bottom, respectively.

```
/* Set up the window boundary */
SetRect(&windowBounds, 20, 40, 200, 220); // you want a 180x180 window
```

Now make use of the CreateWindow() routine defined earlier in this chapter. If you recall, it requires that a pointer to a Rect be passed in and it returns a WindowPtr.

```
/* Create the window */
theWindow = CreateWindow(&windowBounds);
```

Now set up the event mask. Allow the application to receive every possible event, then respond to only those that fit your needs.

```
eventMask = everyEvent;
```

Now you can start the loop. The loop will be executed until done is set to True.

```
while (!done) {
```

Here is the call to WaitNextEvent():

```
notNullEvent = WaitNextEvent(
                eventMask,     // Which events to mask
                &theEvent,     // A pointer to our event record
                0x7FFFFFFF,    // Wait until we receive a
                               // non-null event.
                NULL  );
```

Next, check to see if you received a non-null event.

```
if (notNullEvent == TRUE) {
  // We received something other than a NULL event
```

If so, then figure out what kind of event it was. If it was a mouse-down event, set a flag to indicate the user should quit the application; if it was an update event, make the customary calls to BeginUpdate() and EndUpdate().

```
switch (theEvent.what) {
    case mouseDown:
      // mouse button was clicked, set done to TRUE so we quit
      // on the next pass through the while loop
      done = TRUE;
      break;

    case updateEvt:
      BeginUpdate((WindowPtr)theEvent.message);
      EndUpdate((WindowPtr)theEvent.message);
      break;

    default:
      /* Don't do anything */
      break;
  }
 }
}
```

At this point, the button has been clicked and you are nearly finished with the application. However, there is one detail left to clean up. When the window was created, memory was allocated for its structure. By calling DisposeWindow() before quitting, you free up that memory. This call also erases the window from the screen.

```
DisposeWindow(theWindow);
}
```

The application and the code for this example can be found on your source code disc in the folder Chapter 2:Simple Window π.

Building a Menu

The menu bar is a standard way of receiving input from the user. Menus are commonly used for performing tasks or changing parameters and mainly contain commands that can be used at any time during the program's execution, such as Save, Copy, or Quit. This is in contrast to commands or questions that require the user's immediate attention (such as OK or Cancel buttons) and are placed directly in front of the user in the form of a button or other control.

Your use of the menu bar relies heavily on the Event Manager. As with creating a window, the operating system takes care of most of the work involved in drawing and selecting a menu. All your application needs to do is listen for the mouseDown event and respond to the menu selection.

The Menu Manager

Creating a complete menu bar requires several steps. Each individual menu is first allocated in memory; then the menu items are added one at a time. Once a menu has been constructed, you insert it into the menu bar, at which time it appears at the top of the screen.

Allocating a Menu

To allocate a menu, call NewMenu(), for which the prototype is.

```
MenuHandle  NewMenu(short menuID, Str255 menuTitle);
```

The *menuID* parameter simply holds a number you use to reference the menu internally. When you receive an event from the menu, you will receive this number from the operating system to indicate which menu was selected. Any number between 0 and 32767 is acceptable; negative numbers are reserved for system use. It's a standard convention to number your menus starting at 128. The second parameter you pass to NewMenu is the title for the menu in the form of a pascal string. This routine will give you back a MenuHandle, the internals of which you generally don't need to worry about.

Adding Menu Items

Now that the menu is allocated, you need to start adding items to it. This is accomplished by using AppendMenu(), which adds one or more items to the end of your menu. AppendMenu takes two inputs: the MenuHandle of your menu and a string that contains the items you want to add.

```
void  AppendMenu(MenuHandle  theMenu, Str255 itemText);
```

You have the option of adding one item at a time using multiple calls to AppendMenu or adding several items at once by cramming all of the selections into the input string. To give the routine more than one item, separate items with a semicolon (;). To insert a separator line, pass the string by using (-, and to give the menu a command-key equivalent, use / followed by the character to use for the equivalent.

Here is an example of how to create the standard Edit menu found in most Macintosh applications:

```
MenuHandle    myMenu;

myMenu = NewMenu(128, "\pEdit");
AppendMenu(myMenu, "\pUndo/Z");  /* Add 'Undo' to the menu */
AppendMenu(myMenu, "\p(-");       /* Add a separator line to the menu */
AppendMenu(myMenu, "\pCut/X;Copy/C;Paste/V");/* Add the remaining items*/
```

Updating the Menu Bar

The menu has been created but it has not appeared in the menu bar yet. To add it to the menu bar, call InsertMenu(), as follows:

```
void  InsertMenu(MenuHandle theMenu, short beforeID);
```

The *theMenu* parameter is the MenuHandle of the menu you want to insert; beforeID contains an integer that tells the Menu Manager where to put the new menu in relation to other menus. Pass in 0 to position it at the end of the menu list (to the right of all of the existing menus), or the menuID of an existing menu before which you wish to place it.

Once the menu bar is complete, the next step is to draw the menu bar with DrawMenuBar(), as shown below.

```
void  DrawMenuBar(void);
```

Input from the Menus

When the user chooses an item from the menu, a mouseDown event is generated and sent to the application. You can tell *where* the user clicked by calling FindWindow().

```
short  FindWindow(Point where, WindowPtr *whichWindow);
```

FindWindow() is probably poorly named, because it is used not only for determining which window the user clicked in, but also whether he or she clicked on the menu bar, on the desktop, or in a window belonging to another application.

The *where* parameter is the coordinates of the mouse click (obtained from theEvent.where); the *whichWindow* parameter contains the address of a WindowPtr, indicating which window the mouse click was in. FindWindow() returns a short indicating where the click occurred, which can be compared with the constants listed in Table 2-4.

Constant	Value	Result
inDesk	0	In the desktop (screen background)
inMenuBar	1	In the menubar
inSysWindow	2	In a system window
inContent	3	In the content region of one of the application's windows
inDrag	4	In the drag region of the application's window
inGrow	5	In the size box of the application's window
inGoAway	6	In the close box of the application's window
inZoomIn	7	In the zoom box of a zoomed-out window
inZoomOut	8	In the zoom box of a zoomed-in window

TABLE 2-4 ◈ *FindWindow Constants*

If the mouse click was in a window (i.e., FindWindow returned inContent, inDrag, inGrow, inGoAway, inZoomIn, or inZoomOut), a pointer to that window will be returned in the WindowPtr you pass in.

If you determine that a particular mouseDown event was in the menu, you need to pass the message on to the Menu Manager via MenuSelect(). This routine will take care of drawing the menu, tracking the mouse, and determining which menu item (if any) was chosen.

```
long MenuSelect(Point where);
```

MenuSelect() takes an input of the mouse click point (again, obtained from theEvent.where) and returns a 32-bit-longword telling which menu was used and which item was chosen from that menu.

The high-order 16 bits of this longword provide the menuID of the selected menu. The easiest way to extract this information is by shifting the longword to the right by 16 places (using the C operator—>>); this is functionally equivalent to lopping off the rightmost 16 bits, leaving you with a 16-bit word.

The other 16 bits of the longword provide the menu item that was chosen. To get just the lower 16 bits, lop off the *leftmost* 16 bits, which is done by comparing the longword with a mask. In C, this is written as.

```
menuSelection & 0xFFFF
```

Now that you know which menu item was selected, you can act upon the user's command. The Menu Manager does not dehighlight the menu once an item has been selected. When you select a menu item in an application, the menu remains highlighted until the program has finished the task associated with that menu. When your application finishes with a command, it should call HiliteMenu() and pass in 0 to set the menu bar back to normal. This is the prototype for HiliteMenu():

```
void  HiliteMenu(short menuID);
```

If you want to change the name of an item in a menu, call the toolbox routine SetItem(), as follows:

```
void  SetItem(MenuHandle theMenu, short theItem, Str255 newName);
```

The *theMenu* parameter is the MenuHandle of the menu you want to modify, the *theItem* parameter is the number of the item to change, and *newName* is the new string to use.

The Disappearing Window Application

Now let's pull together the menu routines and build a sample application from them. This application will show a menu bar with the three standard Macintosh menus—Apple, File, and Edit—and one extra menu called Window Controls. None of the menu items in the first three menus will do anything, except for the Quit item in the File menu. The Window Controls menu contains one item that will show or hide a window; the same item will change names, toggling between Show Window and Hide Window.

You'll find the source code for this application on the source code disc under Chapter 2:Window With Menu.

Start out with some constants that define the menuIDs for the menus. By using the C enum{} operator, you are assigning 128 to the first item (the Apple Menu) and consecutive integers to the remaining items (129...131).

```
enum {
  kMENU_Apple = 128,
  kMENU_File,
  kMENU_Edit,
  kMENU_WindowCommands
};
```

This application uses the CreateWindow routine from the first project, with one small change: The window that is created is not drawn immediately. Change the call to NewWindow() like this:

```
WindowPtr  CreateInvisibleWindow(Rect  *bounds)
{
  Str255      title = "\pMy Window";  /* Set the window title */
  WindowPtr   theWindow;


  theWindow = NewWindow(  NULL,
                          bounds,
```

```
                          title,
                          FALSE,        /* We want it invisible */
                          documentProc,
                          (WindowPtr)-1,
                          TRUE,
                          0 );
    /* Pass the window pointer back to the caller */
    return theWindow;
}
```

Next comes the main routine, which does the majority of the work.

```
void main(void)
{
```

First declare the variables.

```
EventRecord    theEvent;
short          eventMask;
short          done = FALSE;
Boolean        notNullEvent;
WindowPtr      theWindow;              // the pointer to our window
Rect           windowBounds;
MenuHandle     appleMenu, fileMenu;    // Here we have all of our
MenuHandle     editMenu, windowMenu;   // menus...
Boolean        visible;                // whether or not the window
                                       // is visible
```

Then do standard initialization.

```
InitGraf(&qd.thePort);/* qd.thePort is part of any application */
InitWindows();
InitCursor();
InitFonts();
InitMenus();
```

Create the window as follows:

```
/* Set up the window boundary, 180x180 pixels in size */
SetRect(&windowBounds, 20, 40, 200, 220);

/* Create an invisible window. It will be shown later */
theWindow = CreateInvisibleWindow(&windowBounds);
visible = FALSE;  /* remember that the window is now invisible */
```

Now you can set up the menu bar:

```
/* Create each of our menus and insert them into the menu bar */
appleMenu = NewMenu(kMENU_Apple, "\p\x14");
                        /* \x14 is C shorthand for the */
                        /* apple character in */
                        /* the chicago font */
AppendMenu(appleMenu, "\pAbout WindowWithMenu ");
AppendMenu(appleMenu, "\p(-"); /* put a gray divider line into */
                          /* the menu */
InsertMenu(appleMenu, 0);      /* add the apple menu to the menu bar */
```

Continued on next page

Continued from previous page

```
fileMenu = NewMenu(kMENU_File, "\pFile");
/* add a series of items at once */
AppendMenu(fileMenu, "\pNew ;Open ;(-;Close;(-;Quit");
InsertMenu(fileMenu, 0);  /* add the file menu to the menu bar */

editMenu = NewMenu(kMENU_Edit, "\pEdit");
AppendMenu(editMenu, "\pUndo;Cut;Copy;Paste;Clear");
InsertMenu(editMenu, 0);

windowMenu = NewMenu(kMENU_WindowControls, "\pWindow Controls");
/* Just one item in this menu */
AppendMenu(windowMenu, "\pShow Window");
InsertMenu(windowMenu, 0);
```

Now that the menus have been defined, you can draw the menu bar.

```
DrawMenuBar();
```

Now enter the main event loop.

```
while (!done) {
  notNullEvent = WaitNextEvent( everyEvent,
                                &theEvent,
                                0x7FFFFFFF,
                                NULL      );
  if (notNullEvent == TRUE) {
    switch (theEvent.what) {
      WindowPtr   hit;
      long        result;
      short       menuHit;
      short       itemHit;
      short       findWindowResult;

      case mouseDown:
```

As you know, a mouseDown event can signify several things: The user could have clicked in one of the application's windows, on the desktop, on another application's windows, or in the menu bar. Use FindWindow to determine exactly where the mouse click took place.

```
/* We received a mousedown event. Check to see where it was */
findWindowResult = FindWindow(theEvent.where, &hit);
if (findWindowResult == inMenuBar) {
```

Here you've found that the click was in the menu bar. Calling MenuSelect will allow the Menu Manager to handle the menu selection.

```
/* It was in the menu bar. Let the Menu Manager take over */
result = MenuSelect(theEvent.where);

/* First check to see if any item was selected at all */
if (result != 0) {
```

You're now left with a 32-bit-longword that has information about which menu was used and which item from that menu was selected. Extract the first word by shifting the longword down by 16 bits.

```
menuHit = result >> 16;
```

Find the lower 16 bits by masking the longword with 0xFFFF (which, when translated to binary, is equivalent to 16 ones).

```
itemHit = result & 0xFFFF;
```

Now compare the menuHit variable with the constants for the menus to discover which menu was chosen from.

```
if (menuHit == kMENU_File) {
```

If the File menu was hit, you only care about one thing: Was the Quit item chosen? If so, set the done flag to True, as follows, so the application terminates when the loop is finished.

```
    if (itemHit == 6) {
      done = TRUE;
    }
  }
```

If the File menu was not hit, check to see if the Window Controls menu was hit.

```
else if (menuHit == kMENU_WindowControls) {
```

There is only one item in this menu, but compare the itemHit against it, because it is good programming form to do so.

```
if (itemHit == 1) {
```

Because the hide/show item was hit, you need to determine whether the window is currently visible and hide it if it is or show it if it isn't. Take this opportunity to change the text of the menu item.

```
      if (visible) {
        /* it is visible; hide it */
        HideWindow(theWindow);

        /* Change the menu text to read "Show Window" */
        SetItem(windowMenu, 1, "\pShow Window");

        /* Remember that the window is not visible */
        visible = FALSE;
      } else {
        /* not visible; show it */
        ShowWindow(theWindow);
```

Continued on next page

Continued from previous page

```
                              /* Change the menu text to read "Hide Window" */
                              SetItem(windowMenu, 1, "\pHide Window");

                              /* Remember that the window is visible */
                              visible = TRUE;
                    }
               }
          }
```

At this point, the menu bar is still highlighted. Calling HiliteMenu will dehighlight it for you.

```
                    /* Un-hilite the menu */
                    HiliteMenu(0);
               }
          }
          break;
```

Now take care of the remainder of the events; in this case, just update events.

```
          case updateEvt:
          {
               /* Update our window if it needs it. */
               BeginUpdate((WindowPtr)theEvent.message);
               EndUpdate((WindowPtr)theEvent.message);
               break;
          }

          default:
               /* Don't do anything */
               break;
          }
     }
}
```

At this point, the program is about to terminate. It's time to call DisposeWindow() to free the memory allocated for the window.

```
     DisposeWindow(theWindow);
}
```

Calling on QuickDraw

I talked briefly about the advantages and disadvantages of using QuickDraw in Chapter 1. Now let's take a closer look at what you can accomplish using QuickDraw. QuickDraw is a complete package designed to assist you in drawing lines, circles, rectangles, and even text to the screen. It completely handles the task of determining which portions of the screen can be drawn into—if you have a window on the screen, you don't want the lines you draw into it to leave their boundary. QuickDraw can also handle the various color depths of the screen and it can take care of drawing into a window that is split between two monitors. Given its extensive capabilities, QuickDraw is remarkably fast and it has many purposes for even the fastest games.

The QuickDraw Package

Whereas most of the rest of the components of the Macintosh toolbox are called managers, QuickDraw doesn't have such a suffix. QuickDraw doesn't have a small, focused task to concentrate on; rather, it is responsible for drawing every bit of graphics you see on the screen. Most of the toolbox relies on QuickDraw to communicate with the user, to such an extent that many programs don't need to access QuickDraw directly. However, most games do not fall in this category.

Let's examine how to tap into QuickDraw directly. In the final part of this chapter, you'll build a simple program that will draw shapes on the screen using some simple QuickDraw commands.

Working with Ports

QuickDraw depends on a concept called the *port*. A port is a rectangular window that is used for drawing into—every window has a port and the screen itself is a port. You can have ports that are partially or even entirely off the screen (which can be a useful concept, as I'll examine later). A port contains information about its size, where its bitmap data is stored, what color to use for drawing into it, which portions are visible on the screen, and several other tidbits. A pointer to a port is called a *GrafPtr*.

Before you begin drawing with QuickDraw, you must tell it which port you want to draw into, which is done with SetPort(). Just pass in the GrafPtr you want to use.

```
void  SetPort(GrafPtr  newPort);
```

Lines, Shapes, and Colors

To draw a line, you must first tell QuickDraw where to start drawing by calling MoveTo(), which takes two inputs—the horizontal and vertical coordinates at which to begin drawing.

```
void  MoveTo(short horizontal, short vertical);
```

A call to LineTo() will draw the line. It also takes two inputs for the ending coordinates of the line.

```
void  LineTo(short horizontal, short vertical);
```

Figure 2-5 shows an example of using MoveTo() and LineTo().

Rectangles are a little easier to draw. Simply define a Rect structure and pass it into FrameRect().

FIGURE 2-5

◎ ◎ ◎ ◎ ◎ ◎

Using MoveTo()
and LineTo()

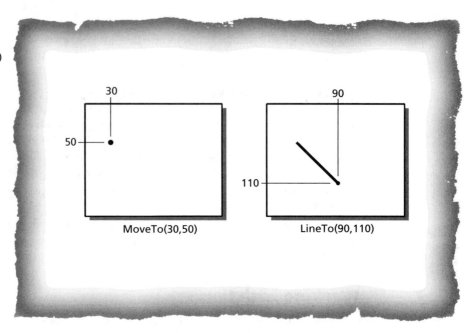

```
void  FrameRect(Rect  *theRectangle);
```

To draw a circle, fill out a Rect structure with the outermost boundaries of the circle and pass it to FrameOval().

```
void  FrameOval(Rect  *ovalBoundary);
```

It is possible to vary the thickness of the lines drawn with these routines by calling PenSize(), which takes two parameters: the width of the pen and the height of the pen. Changing them independently can produce some interesting effects, as shown in Figure 2-6.

The pen's color can be modified through the use of RGBForeColor() and RGBBackColor(). Both of these routines take a structure called RGBColor, shown here:

```
typedef struct {
  unsigned short    red;
  unsigned short    green;
  unsigned short    blue;
} RGBColor ;
```

The prototypes of RGBForeColor and RGBBackColor are.

```
void  RGBForeColor(RGBColor  *foreColor);
void  RGBBackColor(RGBColor  *backColor);
```

If you call RGBForeColor before you draw your shape, it will be drawn in that color. RGBBackColor is used for setting the background color, which is the color that will be filled in when something is erased. Normally, the background color should stay at the default (white).

To change the foreground color to any of eight basic colors (white, black, red, green, blue, cyan, magenta, or yellow) more easily than you can by using RGBForeColor, call ForeColor() and pass it one of the following constants: whiteColor, blackColor, redColor, greenColor, blueColor, cyanColor, magentaColor, or yellowColor. The result is identical to calling RGBForeColor() or RGBBackColor(), with the RGBColor structure filled out with the same values.

```
void  ForeColor(long color);
void  BackColor(long color);
```

Color on the Black-and-White Macintosh

The ForeColor() and BackColor() functions existed long before the first color Macintosh. The old black-and-white Macintosh was capable of handling eight colors even though it couldn't draw them on the screen. The colors were primarily used with the Apple ImageWriter printer, which was capable of printing with a four-color ribbon.

Generating Random Numbers

The final sample program of this chapter uses the same structure you built in the previous program, but it uses components of QuickDraw to draw lines, circles, and rectangles in the window randomly.

FIGURE 2-6

◉ ◉ ◉ ◉ ◉ ◉

Effects of PenSize() on FrameOval() and FrameRect()

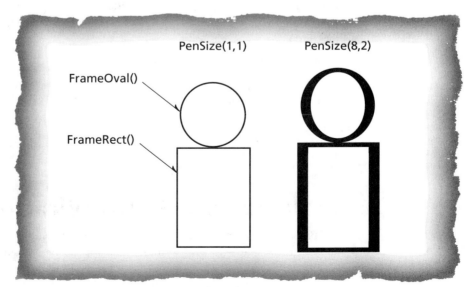

To produce random numbers, use the toolbox routine called Random(). This routine returns a pseudo-random number between -32767 and 32767. What does pseudo-random mean? A computer is not capable of generating truly random numbers; everything it does is based on pure logic and predictability. But it can take a number, apply several mathematical transformations on it, and receive a number that, in human eyes, has no relationship to the original. Random() will take the next number in a series and apply this transformation to it, but the series, by default, is the same every time you run the program. This means that every time your application is used, the same sequence of random numbers will be returned to it, which doesn't make them random at all.

To solve this problem, the application can change the starting value or *seed value* for the random numbers. This seed value is the value on which Random() bases all of its calculations. The application still needs to put a random number into the seed or the results won't be random, but there is a very good solution to this problem. The application has access to the TickCount—a number that represents the number of seconds the computer has been on times 60. Although this number is certainly not random, its precise value is unpredictable enough for your purposes. By placing the TickCount into the random seed, you achieve a satisfactory level of randomness. This only needs to be done once when the application starts up; one seed value produces a whole new sequence of numbers for Random().

```
short  Random(void);
```

A range of -32767 to 32767 isn't always very useful to the application. If you want to draw a random line in a 300x300 window, it's going to be very seldom that Random() produces a usable number. However, because you know the range of the random number and you know the range of numbers you want to get, it's a simple matter of calculation. Instead of writing this in the code every time you want a random number, create a routine called RangedRandom, which takes two parameters—the minimum and maximum numbers you want to get out.

```
short  RangedRandom(long low, long high)
{
  long             range;
  unsigned short   randomNumber;

  range = high - low;
  randomNumber = Random();
  return ((randomNumber * range) / 65535) + low;
}
```

The Shape-Drawing Application

The sample shape-drawing application will create a small window and allow the user to choose several shape-drawing commands from the menu, such as Draw Line,

Draw Rectangle, or Draw Circle. When any of these commands is chosen, the appropriate shape will be drawn using random coordinates.

The shape-drawing application uses the same CreateWindow() routine you designed at the beginning of this chapter. The main() routine is very similar to the one you used in the last program, but the Window Controls menu has been changed to Shape Commands and I've added several new selections.

```
void main(void)
{
```

The variables are very similar to the ones declared in the Window Controls application.

```
EventRecord    theEvent;
  short          eventMask;
  short          done = FALSE;
  Boolean        notNullEvent;
  WindowPtr      theWindow;
  Rect           windowBounds;
  MenuHandle     appleMenu, fileMenu;
  MenuHandle     editMenu, shapeMenu;
```

Initialization is exactly the same.

```
/* Initialize everything we need */
  InitGraf(&qd.thePort);
  InitWindows();
  InitCursor();
  InitFonts();
  InitMenus();
```

Strangely enough, Random() is part of QuickDraw, so the randSeed is part of the qd structure. Here's how you set up the seed for the random number generator:

```
qd.randSeed = TickCount();
```

Make the window for this application slightly larger than the ones from the other samples to allow more space for drawing.

```
/* Set up the window boundary */
  SetRect(&windowBounds, 20, 40, 420, 340);
  /* Create the window */
  theWindow = CreateWindow(&windowBounds);
```

Next, define all of the menus for the application.

```
/* Create each of our menus and insert them into the menu bar */
  appleMenu = NewMenu(kMENU_Apple, "\p\024");
  AppendMenu(appleMenu, "\pAbout Shape Draw ");
  AppendMenu(appleMenu, "\p(-");
  InsertMenu(appleMenu, 0);  /* add the apple menu to the menu bar */
```

Continued on next page

Continued from previous page

```
fileMenu = NewMenu(kMENU_File, "\pFile");
AppendMenu(fileMenu, "\pNew ;Open ;(-;Close;(-;Quit");
InsertMenu(fileMenu, 0);  /* add the file menu to the menu bar */

editMenu = NewMenu(kMENU_Edit, "\pEdit");
AppendMenu(editMenu, "\pUndo;Cut;Copy;Paste;Clear");
InsertMenu(editMenu, 0);

shapeMenu = NewMenu(kMENU_ShapeCommands, "\pShape Commands");
AppendMenu(shapeMenu, "\pClear Window");
AppendMenu(shapeMenu, "\p(-");
AppendMenu(shapeMenu, "\pDraw Line");
AppendMenu(shapeMenu, "\pDraw Rectangle");
AppendMenu(shapeMenu, "\pDraw Circle");
AppendMenu(shapeMenu, "\p(-");
AppendMenu(shapeMenu, "\pChange Pen Color");
AppendMenu(shapeMenu, "\pChange Pen Size");
InsertMenu(shapeMenu, 0);

DrawMenuBar();    /* Now we need to draw our menu */
```

Now define the event mask and enter the main event loop.

```
eventMask = mDownMask + updateEvt;

while (!done) {
  notNullEvent = WaitNextEvent( eventMask,
                                &theEvent,
                                0x7FFFFFFF,
                                NULL  );

  if (notNullEvent == TRUE) {

  switch (theEvent.what) {
    WindowPtr hit;
    long      result;
    short     menuHit;
    short     itemHit;
    short     findWindowResult;

    case mouseDown:
      findWindowResult = FindWindow(theEvent.where, &hit);
      if (findWindowResult == inMenuBar) {
```

When a click occurs in the menu bar, this code will handle it. So far, this application is almost identical to the last program, but now it's time to create something new: the Shape menu.

```
        result = MenuSelect(theEvent.where);

          if (result != 0) {
            menuHit = result >> 16;
            itemHit = result & 0xFFFF;
```

```
            if (menuHit == kMENU_File) {
              if (itemHit == 6) {
              /* Quit was selected */
              done = TRUE;
            }
          } else if (menuHit == kMENU_ShapeCommands) {
```

If the last condition is true, the Shape menu has been clicked on. Because the code for handling the Shape menu is a little large, split that into a separate routine (which I'll examine immediately after this routine).

```
            HandleShapeMenuHit(itemHit, theWindow);
          }
```

Now that the menus have been handled, you can dehighlight the menu bar.

```
  /* Un-hilite the menu */
      HiliteMenu(0);
    }
  }
  break;

  case updateEvt:
  {
```

Despite the fact that this application actually draws something into the window (unlike the previous two applications), it does nothing when it receives an update event. It doesn't keep track of what it has drawn previously, so it would be very difficult to redraw the window (I'll look at ways that you can save the window's contents in Chapter 5).

```
      BeginUpdate((WindowPtr)theEvent.message);
      EndUpdate((WindowPtr)theEvent.message);
      break;
    }

    default:
      /* Don't do anything */
      break;
    }
  }
}

  DisposeWindow(theWindow);
}
```

Now create the code to handle a selection from the Shape menu.

```
void  HandleShapeMenuHit(short whichItem, WindowPtr  theWindow)
{
  short    width, height;
  Rect     windowBounds;
```

Continued on next page

Continued from previous page

```
/* The boundary of the window can be found in theWindow->portRect */
windowBounds = theWindow->portRect;

/* Calculate the width and height of the window */
width = windowBounds.right - windowBounds.left;
height = windowBounds.bottom - windowBounds.top;
```

Before you do any drawing inside the window, you need to set the port to the window. A WindowPtr is functionally equivalent to a GrafPtr, so you don't even need to do any typecasting.

```
SetPort(theWindow);

switch (whichItem) {
```

The first menu item is Clear Window. This is accomplished through a simple procedure called EraseRect(). Pass it the boundary of the window and it'll take care of the rest.

```
case 1:  /* Clear Window */
    EraseRect(&windowBounds);
    break;
```

The second item is a dividing line, so ignore it. The third item is Draw Line, so take random starting x and y positions and random ending x and y positions and draw a line between them.

```
case 3: /* Draw Line */
    {
        short    startX, startY;
        short    endX, endY;

        startX = RangedRandom(  windowBounds.left,
                                windowBounds.right);
        startY = RangedRandom(  windowBounds.top,
                                windowBounds.bottom);

        endX = RangedRandom(windowBounds.left, windowBounds.right);
        endY = RangedRandom(windowBounds.top, windowBounds.bottom);

        /* Move the pen to the starting position */
        MoveTo(startX, startY);

        /* Draw the line to the ending position */
        LineTo(endX, endY);
    }
    break;
```

The rectangle is very similar to the line, but the right edge of the rectangle can't be less than the left edge, so first find the left edge and then make sure the minimum right edge is the same by passing it into RangedRandom().

```
case 4: /* Draw rectangle */
{
  Rect    dstRect;

  dstRect.left = RangedRandom( windowBounds.left,
                               windowBounds.right );
  dstRect.top = RangedRandom( windowBounds.top,
                              windowBounds.bottom );

  dstRect.right = RangedRandom( dstRect.left,
                                windowBounds.right );
  dstRect.bottom = RangedRandom( dstRect.top,
                                 windowBounds.bottom );

  /* Draw the rectangle */
  FrameRect(&dstRect);
}
break;
```

The circle is almost exactly the same as the rectangle, except it includes a call to FrameOval().

```
case 5: /* Draw circle */
  {
    Rect    dstRect;

    dstRect.left = RangedRandom( windowBounds.left,
                                 windowBounds.right );
    dstRect.top = RangedRandom( windowBounds.top,
                                windowBounds.bottom );

    dstRect.right = RangedRandom( dstRect.left,
                                  windowBounds.right );
    dstRect.bottom = RangedRandom( dstRect.top,
                                   windowBounds.bottom);

  /* Draw the circle */
  FrameOval(&dstRect);
  }
  break;
```

The sixth item is also a divider line, so you can ignore it. Menu item 7 changes the pen color, which is done by generating random numbers for each of the color components. Each port has its own pen color, so if you had several windows open, this routine would change the pen color only for the current window.

```
case 7: /* Change the pen color */
{
  RGBColor newColor;
```

Continued on next page

Continued from previous page

```
      newColor.red = RangedRandom(0, 65535);
      newColor.green = RangedRandom(0, 65535);
      newColor.blue = RangedRandom(0, 65535);

      RGBForeColor(&newColor);
    }
    break;
```

The last item will change the pen size; it's similar to changing the pen color. Here the size is limited to 30, but you can change that if you want larger brushes.

```
    case 8: /* Change the pen size */
    {
      short    penSizeX, penSizeY;

      penSizeX = RangedRandom(1, 30);
      penSizeY = RangedRandom(1, 30);

      PenSize(penSizeX, penSizeY);
    }
    break;
  }
}
```

There you have it! You can find all of this code on the source code disc in the Chapter 2 folder under Shape Draw π. Compile the code, run it, and watch what happens when you choose the various menu items from the Shape Commands menu. A sample output image is shown in Figure 2-7.

The next chapter delves more deeply into the toolbox. I'll discuss several more managers on the Macintosh, including the Resource Manager, the Memory Manager, and the File Manager.

FIGURE 2-7

The shape-drawing application

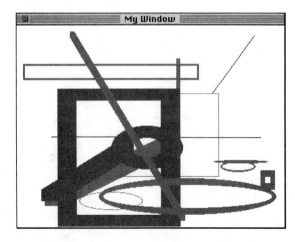

3

More about the Toolbox

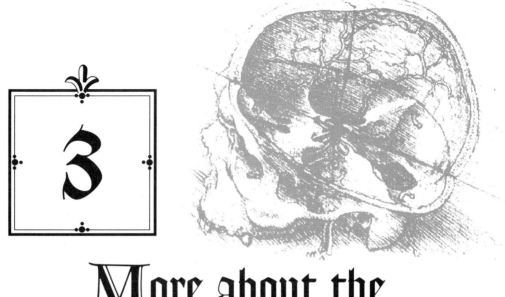

3

More about the Toolbox

In Chapter 2, you learned how to create some of the most essential parts of the Macintosh interface. This chapter concentrates on portions of the toolbox that are less directly related to the interface but are nevertheless very important to the structure of your application. First I'll explore the Memory Manager and explain how the Macintosh handles memory requests. Then I'll look at the Resource Manager and show how you can use ResEdit to create the essential interface elements of your application. Next I'll discuss bitmap and PICT images and explain how they are stored in memory and in files. After that, I'll delve into the File Manager and show you how to open and use the resource and data forks of your files. Finally, you'll create a sample application that opens and displays PICT files.

Getting a Handle on Memory

Memory management with C is very simple: You can either allocate your memory automatically by declaring a variable or allocate it by calling malloc(), which is recommended for a much larger allocation. However, when programming the Macintosh, there are a few more things to think about. The Macintosh has a routine called NewPtr() that is very similar to C's malloc().

```
Ptr  NewPtr(unsigned long size);
```

NewPtr() behaves just the same as malloc() does—pass it the size of the pointer you would like and it gives you back a pointer. When you are finished with a pointer and want to free up its memory, call DisposePtr(), as follows:

```
void    DisposePtr(Ptr thePtr);
```

After you call DisposePtr, the memory allocated for the pointer is marked as free and the pointer is no longer valid. This would be all there is to say about memory management except for one problem: fragmentation. As you're probably aware, when you begin to allocate and dispose of blocks of memory, you will eventually have blocks scattered around in memory with small gaps in between. You can see an example of this concept in Figure 3-1, which shows a diagram of the memory before anything has been allocated and then after three pointers have been created.

Notice that you have 550k of memory free when you begin. After allocating 375k with the pointers, you have a remainder of 175k. When you finish with the second pointer and dispose of it, you have 325k free. You might expect that you could now allocate a 200k pointer, but when you try, the operating system says that you are out of memory. Why? This is because of fragmentation. When you disposed of the second pointer, it left a gap in memory, as shown in Figure 3-2.

Memory must be allocated in contiguous blocks and neither of the blocks of free memory is large enough for the 200k pointer. Because Pointers 1 and 3 directly reference

FIGURE 3-1

◉ ◉ ◉ ◉ ◉ ◉

Pointers being allocated in memory

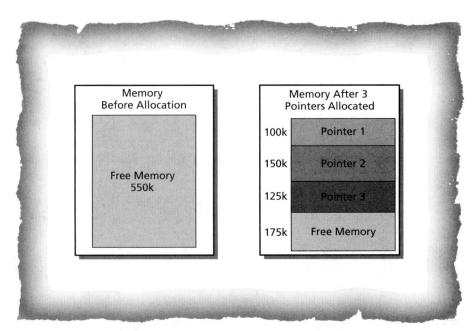

FIGURE 3-2
◎ ◎ ◎ ◎ ◎ ◎
*Fragmented
memory*

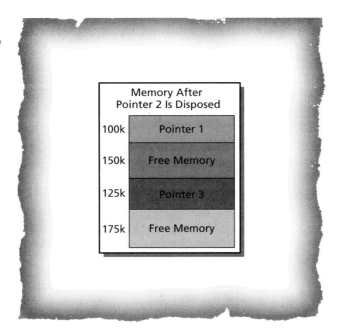

their memory blocks, the third block cannot be shifted up or down in memory to make room for a larger allocation.

Introducing the Handle

To alleviate this problem, the Macintosh operating system has *handles*. A handle is, in the most basic of terms, a pointer to a pointer. Using a pointer, you dereference the pointer to access the data, as in (*myPtr).myData, but if you are using a handle, you double-dereference the handle to access data, which looks like this:

```
(**myHandle).myData
```

A handle allows the Memory Manager to move blocks of memory around to make room for other blocks of memory. Before I examine how a handle accomplishes this task, let's take a look at how this would affect the scenario discussed earlier. As before, allocate three handles to hold the data. When the second handle is disposed, the free memory is again broken into two portions (see Figure 3-3).

Now, however, when we want to allocate another 200k of memory (which I will refer to as Handle 4), the Memory Manager is able to push Handle 3 up to make room for the new block, leaving the full 325k free. Handle 4 is placed just below Handle 3, and everything fits (see Figure 3-4).

FIGURE 3-3

◎ ◎ ◎ ◎ ◎ ◎

Allocating and disposing of handles

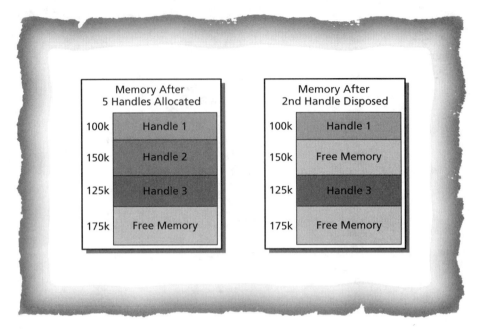

FIGURE 3-4

◎ ◎ ◎ ◎ ◎ ◎

Memory compaction with handles

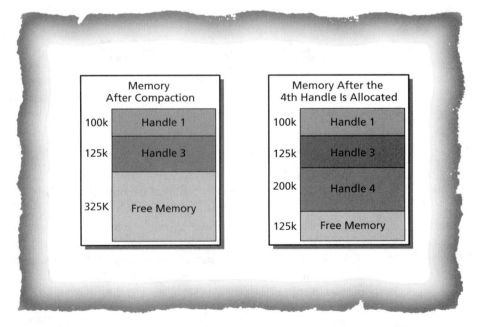

What Goes On behind the Scenes

Remember, a handle is a pointer to a pointer. What makes the handle so useful is that it points into a portion of memory called a *master pointer block*. The master pointer block is a group of pointers that the Memory Manager maintains. This structure enables the Memory Manager to move blocks of memory without the application losing track of where its data is. Figure 3-5 shows the structure of a handle.

The handle points to the second position in the master pointer block, which in the imaginary application starts at memory location 0x0100. The master pointer block then points to the actual data, which in this case is stored at memory location 0x2000.

If the Memory Manager needs to free up more space by compacting memory, it will begin by moving the data block to a different location. This first step would look something like Figure 3-6.

Notice that, at this stage, the master pointer block entry for *myHandle* no longer points to *myData*. The Memory Manager's next task is to update the master pointer block so that the application can again find the data (see Figure 3-7).

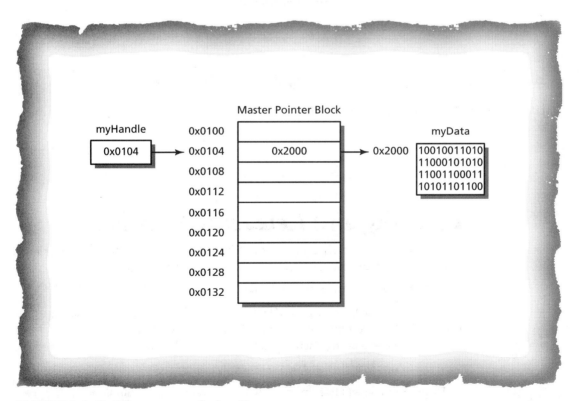

FIGURE 3-5 ◉ *The structure of a handle*

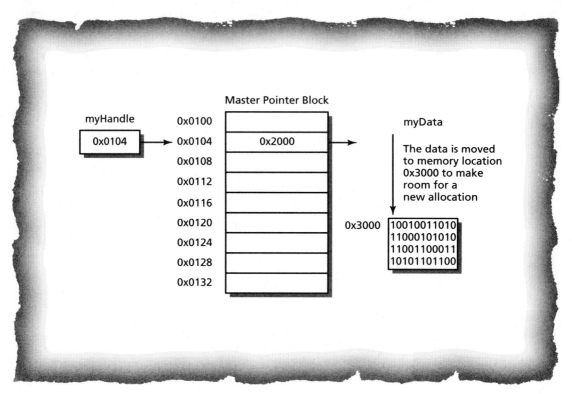

FIGURE 3-6 ◉ *During a memory compaction*

Creating and Releasing Handles

The routines used for creating and destroying handles are very similar to the corresponding routines for pointers. Handles are created by calling NewHandle().

```
Handle  NewHandle(unsigned long size);
```

Just like NewPtr(), you pass NewHandle() the size of the desired handle and it returns the handle. If the resulting handle is Null, the memory allocation failed.

To release the allocated memory, call DisposeHandle().

```
void    DisposeHandle(Handle theHandle);
```

DisposeHandle will free up any memory allocated for the handle.

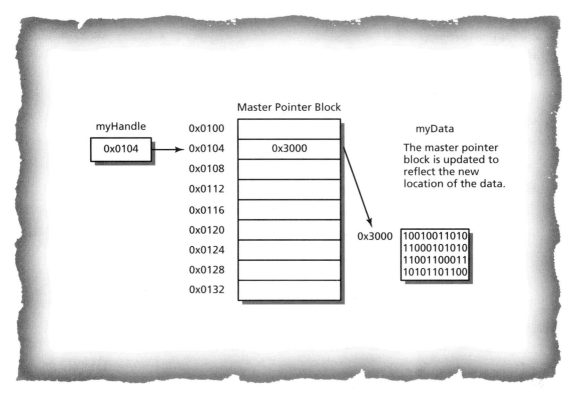

FIGURE 3-7 ◉ *The Memory Manager finishes the compaction*

The Resource Manager

Every file (including applications) on the Macintosh can have two parts: the resource fork and the data fork. The data fork is used for storing raw data in a format determined by the application that created it. The resource fork contains packages of information in a standard format. The packages are called *resources*, each individually numbered and optionally named.

Each resource in the resource fork is assigned a resource "type" that has a four-character signature, such as CODE or ICON (see Figure 3-8). As you might guess, each resource type stores a different kind of data. For example, the PICT resource type stores images. Table 3-1 lists some other resource types.

FIGURE 3-8

◎ ◎ ◎ ◎ ◎ ◎

Structure of a
Macintosh file

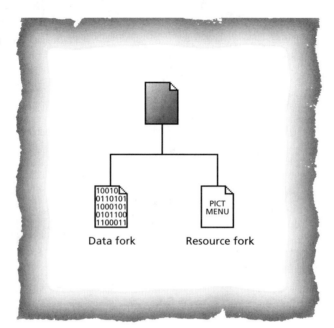

Data fork   Resource fork

Resource	Contents
CODE	Compiled application code
DLOG	Definition for a dialog
ICON	Icons for a file
MENU	Definition for a menu
STR#	Various strings the application might need
WIND	Definition for a window

TABLE 3-1 ◈ *Some resource types*

Using ResEdit

An easy way of looking at the resources stored in a file's resource fork is by using a resource-editing program such as ResEdit (short for Resource Editor) or Resourcerer (an excellent commercial resource editor). A copy of ResEdit should have come with your development environment; if not, it is available through many online services or user groups.

I'm going to take a look at some resources from an application that's on every Macintosh hard drive: SimpleText, which comes with the system software and with a multitude of software packages. Run ResEdit and use it to open a copy of the SimpleText application. A window like the one in Figure 3-9 should appear.

As you can see, some of the resources I talked about earlier are here: the CODE resources, which hold the compiled source code of SimpleText; MENU, which holds the definitions for SimpleText's menus; and the STR# resource, which holds several of the strings SimpleText uses.

Using ResEdit, you can design all of your applications' menus with an easy, Macintosh-style graphical interface. Not only that, you can create icons, dialogs, windows, and even fonts. In this book, I've been defining menus from within the code, mainly so you can see what to expect by looking at the source code. In most cases, you'll define your menus from within ResEdit or a similar resource editor.

Let's try modifying one of SimpleText's menus. Double-click on the MENU icon. This will open a window that shows you all of SimpleText's menus in a graphical format, as in Figure 3-10. Double-click on the first menu listed in the window (the Apple menu). This will open into another window, like the one in Figure 3-11.

Now let's change the menu. Highlight About SimpleText… and change it to About SuperText…. Notice that in the menu bar at the top of your screen, there is an additional Apple menu toward the right side. Pull that menu down and you can see an instant reflection of the new menu.

Close the SimpleText file and save the changes. Now run SimpleText and pull down the Apple menu. You will notice that the menu has changed to About SuperText….

You now have an idea of how easy it is to change the resources in a file. You can create your entire menu bar graphically using ResEdit and then load it while the application is running, which is much easier than designing your menus by hand.

FIGURE 3-9

◎ ◎ ◎ ◎ ◎ ◎

SimpleText opened in ResEdit

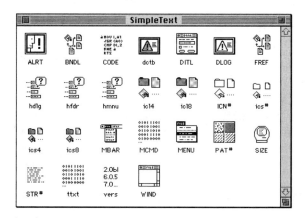

FIGURE 3-10

◉ ◉ ◉ ◉ ◉ ◉

*MENU
resources in
SimpleText*

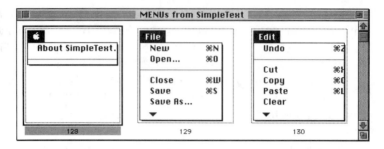

FIGURE 3-11

◉ ◉ ◉ ◉ ◉ ◉

*Editing the
Apple menu
from
SimpleText*

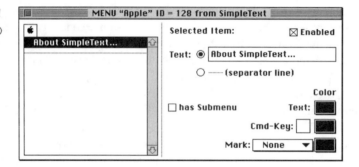

More complicated data can also be stored in the resource fork. For an example of this, open the Sound Rsrc file found in the Chapter 3 folder on the source code disc. Double-click on the snd resource, then choose Try Sound from the snd menu.

Accessing Resources

The toolbox provides several methods of loading resources. The GetResource() routine is the most generic; it can be used to load any type of resource.

```
Handle  GetResource(long resourceType, short resourceID);
```

The *resourceType* parameter is a longword signature telling the Resource Manager which resource type to load. Usually this parameter is typed in literally, for example MENU. The *resourceID* parameter is an integer specifying which ID to load. In the SimpleText example above, the Apple menu had an ID of 128.

GetResource() returns a handle to the specified resource. The way you use this handle depends on the resource type you just loaded.

What if you're not sure what the resource's ID number is? The toolbox provides a procedure called GetIndResource(), short for Get Indexed Resource. Here is how it's used:

```
Handle  GetIndResource(long resourceType, short index);
```

Given an index N, GetIndResource will search through the file and return the Nth resource of that type it finds. The numbering is assigned arbitrarily by the Resource Manager, so calling GetIndResource() with an index of 1 won't necessarily return the lowest ID numbered resource of that type. GetIndResource() is useful when you want to load all the resources of a given type, in which case you can call GetIndResource() sequentially, or when you want to load just one resource of a particular type and you don't care which one you get.

⊚ ResType

The *resourceType* parameter is commonly defined as a ResType instead of a long-word. The conventions for using it are the same.

When you have finished using the resource, call ReleaseResource() to free up the memory used by the resource, as follows:

```
void   ReleaseResource(Handle    resourceHandle);
```

It is important that you keep track of how a handle was allocated. If it was allocated by loading a resource, call ReleaseResource() to free the memory, but if it was created from scratch (such as by calling NewHandle()), you must call DisposeHandle() instead. Mixing up these calls can cause some obscure crashes.

If the resource is of a standard type, such as a WIND or a MENU, the toolbox usually provides a slightly easier way of accessing it. For example, the Menu Manager has a routine called GetMenu(), that takes only one parameter—the resourceID. It also returns a MenuHandle instead of a Handle.

```
MenuHandle    GetMenu(short    menuID);
```

Whenever an application loads a resource, it should check to see if the handle it receives is NULL. If it is, that means the resource could not be loaded and the application should take proper action for error control.

Bitmaps and PICT Files

Bitmapped images are also stored in resources. Icons are stored in the ICON and ICN# (and corresponding color CICN and icl8) resources, black-and-white patterns are stored in PAT# resources, color patterns are stored in ppat resources, and large images (color or black and white) are stored in PICT resources.

The smaller bitmaps (icons and patterns) don't take up much disk space, but because PICT resources can be huge, the amount of storage they use can become a problem. An 8-bit bitmap the size of a typical Macintosh 14-inch monitor can occupy more than 300k by itself. If you have more than a few of these in a file, you'll start having problems with the size of your application. When the Macintosh was first introduced, this problem was much more pronounced; the only storage medium available at the time was a 400k floppy disk, most of which was taken up by the system file. Therefore, Apple's engineers incorporated compression into the PICT resource.

The compression they use is called Run-Length Encoding, or RLE. It is one of the most basic compression algorithms. It does not provide a huge amount of savings except on very simple images, but it is very efficient in terms of speed of encoding and decoding. Fortunately, the system software takes care of the compression and decompression automatically. I'll go into greater detail on RLE compression in Chapter 20, when you build a flight simulator.

The PICT resource can contain much more than just a bitmap. Apple has incorporated a method of storing drawing commands into the PICT format, providing a resolution-independent method of storing and drawing images.

Because of all the complications in the PICT format, you should not try to figure out its data by yourself. Instead, you should allow the operating system to interpret the data and draw the image. This is done through the DrawPicture() routine, which takes two inputs—a PicHandle, which is a handle to a PICT image, and the address of a Rect, which determines where to draw the image.

The rectangle you pass into DrawPicture does not have to have the same dimensions as the original image; if it doesn't, the operating system will scale the image to fit in the requested dimensions. This is very handy for you, but the operating system does a poor job of scaling images and the scaling process does take time, so it's best if the application ensures that the rectangle is the right size, especially if speed is important.

PICT resources used within an application are almost always stored in the resource fork and accessed either by GetResource() or by a special routine for PICT images called GetPicture(), which looks like this:

```
PicHandle    GetPicture(short pictID);
```

GetPicture() takes just one parameter: the resource ID of the PICT you want to load. It passes back a PicHandle, which is the standard format for handling PICT data within an application. The entire format of the PicHandle has not been disclosed by Apple, but you have enough to work with. The PicHandle has a field called *picFrame*, which is a Rect structure defining the boundary of the image. This is useful if you don't already know the dimensions of the image. The other field is *picSize*, which is the size of the image in bytes. However, picSize is defined as a short integer, which can hold a maximum value of 32767. If the PICT were larger than 32k, it would overflow this field, so it is best not to rely on it.

```
typedef struct {
   short      picSize;
   Rect       picFrame;
} Picture, *PicPtr, **PicHandle;
```

An additional method for storing PICT files is typically used by graphics applications saving large images: PICT files can be stored in the data fork of a file. The actual data is stored in exactly the same format that it would be in the resource fork, but it doesn't have the benefits (and problems) associated with the resource structure. The problems associated with using the Resource Manager stem from the fact that it doesn't handle very large resources—anything over 100k—well. Because graphics applications can typically work with 5-megabyte images or even much larger, using the Resource Manager for storing these images would be highly inappropriate. The PICT viewer you will build later in this chapter will deal with PICT images stored in both the resource and data forks; the methods used for reading them are similar.

Using the Macintosh File System

Ever since the Macintosh Plus was introduced, the Macintosh has used a hierarchical method of managing files. This means that files are separated into different directories on the hard drive (or any other storage medium) and you can access a file by specifying its volume, directory, and name. This is similar to the process used on most other platforms, such as UNIX and MS-DOS. Unfortunately, the Macintosh hasn't always used this method and remnants of the old system (used on the Macintosh 128 and 512, when they used 400k disk drives) linger, making things slightly more difficult in some cases.

The toolbox includes several data types that are used for representing files on the hard disk. One of the most convenient to use internally is the FSSpec, shown here:

```
typedef struct FSSpec {
    short       vRefNum;
    long        parID;
    Str63       name;
};
```

The *vRefNum* parameter is a reference number for the volume the file is on (i.e., which hard drive or other medium). The *parID* parameter is the reference for the directory the file is in, and the *name* parameter is a pascal-style string containing the file's name.

It can be very useful for an application to find out its own directory ID and volume reference number; for example, it might need to look for data files in the same directory, or that directory may be the default place where the application saves its own files. With Metrowerks Codewarrior and Think C (version 7 or later), this can be done through calls to two low-memory routines called LMGetSFSaveDisk() and LMGetCurDirStore(). The volume reference number is obtained from the first routine, LMGetSFSaveDisk(), but you must use the negative of this function's result.

```
short    LMGetSFSaveDisk(void);
```

The second routine, LMGetCurDirStore(), returns the directory ID of the application.

```
long    LMGetCurDirStore(void);
```

These two routines are valid when your application starts up, but if you do any file accessing, they may become invalid. Therefore, if you want your application to gain access to its own directory, these two routines should be called when the application starts up and should be stored in a safe location (e.g., a global variable).

Another way of finding a file is to ask the user for one. The easiest way of doing this is to open a standard file dialog (see Figure 3-12). You've undoubtedly seen this dialog thousands of times when using the Macintosh; nearly every application that saves files uses this package or a variation of it. All you need to do is call one function and the operating system will open a window that asks the user to find a file, allows him or her to choose one, closes the window, and returns the selection to your application. The routine, called StandardGetFile(), looks like this:

```
void    StandardGetFile(   FileFilterProcPtr    fileFilter,
                           short                numTypes,
                           SFTypeList           typeList,
                           StandardFileReply    *reply );
```

The *fileFilter* parameter is a pointer to a custom routine that is called when the File Manager wants to know whether or not to show a file in the dialog. You may want to use this parameter if, say, you want to show only files that are smaller than a certain size or files created after a certain date. I won't be using it, so you can disregard it for now.

The second parameter, *numTypes*, is a short that tells the routine how many different file types you want to allow the user to open. One example of this parameter's use is applications that can open graphics files with different formats (like PICT, TIFF, GIF, and JPEG).

The *typeList* parameter is used for listing all the different types to open. SFTypeList is an array of four OSType values; an OSType is a 4-byte longword that contains a file's type. For example, a PICT file has an OSType of PICT, an application has an OSType of APPL, and a text file's OSType is TEXT.

To use *typeList*, fill in the OSTypes you want to open and fill in the number that you listed in the numTypes field (the routine will ignore the rest). If you need to open more than four file types, declare a variable as an array of OSType as large as you need.

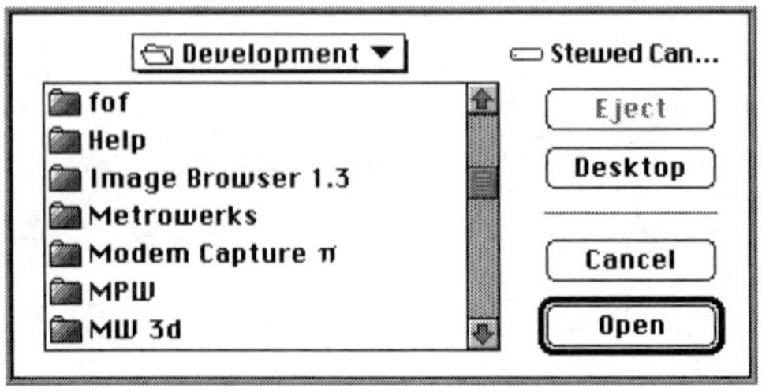

FIGURE 3-12

◎ ◎ ◎ ◎ ◎ ◎

*The standard
get file dialog*

In case you want StandardGetFile to list all of the files it sees, pass in -1 for the numTypes field.

The *reply* parameter is a structure that provides all the information you need about the completion of the StandardGetFile routine. Here is its structure:

```
typedef struct StandardFileReply {
    Boolean      sfGood;
    Boolean      sfReplacing;
    OSType       sfType;
    FSSpec       sfFile;

    ScriptCode   sfScript;

    short        sfFlags;
    Boolean      sfIsFolder;
    Boolean      sfIsVolume;
    long         sfReserved1;
    short        sfReserved2;
};
```

If the user has selected a file and clicked the Open button, sfGood will be True. If sfGood is False, the user has canceled the dialog and the application should *not* open the file.

The *sfReplacing* field is employed only when using StandardPutFile; it does not apply to opening files.

The *sfType* field is the file's type (e.g. PICT or TEXT).

The *sfFile* field is the information about the file's location. This is the most critical information you need from this structure.

The *sfScript* field is used for foreign versions of the operating system, which I won't be dealing with; you can ignore it for now.

The *sfFlags* field provides information about whether the file is invisible, whether or not it is stationary, and other miscellaneous tidbits. It can be ignored for now.

The *sfIsFolder* and *sfIsVolume* fields tell you whether a folder or volume was chosen from the dialog, respectively. They can be disregarded.

The *sfReserved* fields are there so the operating system can expand the functionality of the routines in the future without breaking the current code. These fields should always be ignored.

Opening Files

Now that you know where your file is located, it is a simple matter to open it. When the operating system opens a file, it will return a file reference number (or a resource file reference number for a resource fork), which you will use any time you want to do anything with that file (including close it).

Macintosh and UNIX files

The Macintosh data fork routines are very similar to UNIX's FILE type—many of Unix's operations are mirrored by corresponding Macintosh routines for reading, writing, opening, and closing files. If you are familiar with UNIX, you should feel right at home with Macintosh.

Because each file has two parts (resource fork and data fork), there is a command for opening each half. The data fork is opened by calling HOpen(), outlined here:

```
OSErr   HOpen(   short       vRefNum,
                 Long        dirID,
                 Str255      fileName,
                 SignedByte  permission,
                 short       *refNum);
```

The *vRefNum*, *dirID*, and *fileName* parameters are all obtained from your FSSpec structure containing your file information. The *permission* parameter is a byte defining how you want to open the file: read-only, write-only, read-and-write, or anything you can get. Table 3-2 lists the various constants you need for this field.

Constant	Explanation
fsCurPerm	Read-and-write permission, if available: otherwise just read-only permission
fsRdPerm	Read-only permission
fsWrPerm	Write-only permission
fsRdWrPerm	Read-and-write permission

TABLE 3-2 ◈ *File permission constants*

Pass in a pointer to a short for the *refNum* parameter and HOpen() will use that to return the reference number of the opened file. HOpen() also returns an OSErr, which is a short defining whether the operation completed successfully. A common practice is to compare this result with the constant noErr to ensure success.

The semantics for the resource fork version are almost exactly the same as for the data fork.

```
short   HOpenResFile(   short       vRefNum,
                        Long        dirID,
                        Str255      fileName,
                        SignedByte  permission  );
```

The only real differences are that HOpenResFile() does not return an error; rather, it returns the resource file reference number. If an error does occur, it will return -1, so the application should be sure to check the result before continuing. If the application needs to find out more about the type of error, it can call the routine ResError(), which will return the error code for the last Resource Manager call.

```
OSErr    ResError(void);
```

Table 3-3 shows some of the various types of errors you may receive from the Resource Manager.

Error Type	Error Code	Error Description
nsvErr	-35	No such volume
ioErr	-36	I/O error
tmfoErr	-42	Too many files are open
fnfErr	-43	File not found
opWrErr	-49	File already open with write permission
memFullErr	-108	Not enough memory available
resNotFound	-192	Resource not found
resFNotFound	-193	Resource file not found

TABLE 3-3 ◈ *Common Resource Manager errors*

For a more complete list of resource errors and error codes in general, consult *Inside Macintosh: Toolbox Essentials*.

Reading and Writing Data Forks

The routines for reading and writing to files are very basic and easy to use. I'll deal with data files first because the structure is much more basic.

FSRead() is used for reading from a data fork. It will read data sequentially, starting from the *current position marker*, or mark. The mark is the way the File Manager keeps track of where to read from the file. The mark is set to the beginning of the file when it is opened and it advances every time a byte is read. As you will see later, there are routines for manually changing where the file marker is positioned. Here is the structure:

```
OSErr    FSRead(short fRefNum, long *inOutLength, Ptr buffer);
```

The *fRefNum* parameter is the file reference number (obtained from HOpen), the *inOutLength* parameter is the address of a longword containing the number of bytes to read, and the *buffer* parameter is a pointer to the memory location to read the data into. FSRead() will read the data from the file and return an OSErr if there is a problem.

FSRead() will also place the total number of bytes read in the *inOutLength* parameter, so you can use it to verify that the correct amount of data was received (the total number of bytes read may differ from the number of bytes requested if the File Manager reaches the end of the file).

FSWrite() is the corresponding routine for writing data; it takes the same inputs as FSRead().

```
OSErr    FSWrite(short FRefNum, long *inOutLength, Ptr buffer);
```

The length of the data file can be determined by calling GetEOF(). GetEOF() takes the file reference number and the address of a longword, which it uses to return the size of the data fork of the file in bytes, as follows:

```
OSErr    GetEOF(short fRefNum, long *curEOF);
```

Reading Resource Forks

Before reading from a resource fork, call the toolbox routine UseResFile() to inform the Resource Manager which file to reference.

```
void     UseResFile(short resRefNum);
```

The *resRefNum* parameter is the resource reference number for that file. Now whenever the application requests a resource, this file will be the first one searched. If the resource is not found in that file, the operating system will search any resource files opened before the current file, then the application, and then the system file. If it is not found in any of these files, an error will be returned. When a resource file is opened, it is automatically set as the current resource file, so this routine is not always necessary.

The GetResource() routine, discussed earlier, is the main routine used for getting generic resources. If a more specific routine is available (i.e., GetPicture for loading PICT images), it is recommended that you use it instead.

Writing a Resource

If you want to add a new resource to your file, the way to do so is with AddResource(). This routine will take a handle and attach it to the current resource file. When the resource file is closed, the data will be written to disk. The routine looks like this:

```
void     AddResource(  Handle    data,
                       ResType   resourceType,
                       short     resourceID,
                       Str255    resourceName  );
```

The *data* parameter is a handle to your data, the *resourceType* parameter is the four-character signature of the resource you want to write, the *resourceID* parameter is the desired resource ID number for this data, and the *resourceName* parameter is an optional name for the resource. (If you don't want to name the resource, pass in a blank pascal string—"\p".)

If you have a resource that you have read from the disk but you have changed its data, the best way to write the changed resource back to disk is to call WriteResource(), shown here, which writes the changed data back to disk:

```
void    WriteResource(Handle   resourceHandle);
```

Closing a File

Once you are finished working with your file, you can close it by calling FSClose().

```
OSErr  FSClose(short fileRefNum);
```

The *fileRefNum* parameter is the file reference number you received from HOpen() or HOpenResFile(). It is very important that you don't call FSClose() on a file after it has already been closed. Doing so could potentially wipe out the user's hard drive. To be on the safe side, set your file reference number variable to 0 after closing the file.

If you have loaded any resources from the file, closing the file will release those resources. If you're going to need access to those resources after the file is closed, you need to *detach* them from the file. This causes the Resource Manager to forget that your resource has any relation to the file and turns it into a normal handle. You can detach a resource from its respective file by calling DetachResource(), which looks like this:

```
void  DetachResource(Handle theResource);
```

If you detach a resource, remember to dispose of it when you finish using it. Because the resource has been turned into a normal handle, it can be disposed of by calling DisposeHandle().

The PICT Viewer Application

Now let's bring everything together from this chapter and build another application. This application will open PICT images (both in the data fork and in the resource fork) and display them on the screen. It will have a menu bar with the Apple, File, and Edit menus. The only menu commands I'm going to pay any attention to are the Open, Close, and Quit items from the File menu, which will open an image, close the current image, or quit the program, respectively.

The first routine in the file is the now-familiar CreateWindow() routine. It is identical to the CreateWindow() routine you used in the Shape Drawing and Simple Window programs in Chapter 2.

The next routine is called LoadPicture(). It will open a file, determine whether to read the PICT data from the resource fork or the data fork, and read that data into a new PicHandle. However, I need to provide a bit of explanation before you can get into this routine.

As mentioned in the Bitmaps and PICT Files section of this chapter, the PICT data can be stored in the resource fork or the data fork. A PICT image stored in the data fork is in exactly the same format as one stored in the resource fork, except that because there is no data fork manager, there cannot be multiple images or additional data of any other kind. All the application needs to do is create a new handle the same size as the file (minus the size of the header) and read the PICT data directly into memory.

The header for the PICT data is always 512 bytes long and is usually ignored, so before the data is read, the file position marker must be placed at 512 bytes into the file. From there, it's just a simple call to FSRead() and you have your image!

PICT images stored in the data fork are typically quite large: They can easily be larger than what will fit in memory. If the PICT viewer cannot load an image, it will beep once. It is important that the application remember to do proper error checking so it does not crash under extreme circumstances such as this, especially when such a circumstance could happen frequently.

To make the beep, there is a simple toolbox routine called SysBeep(), shown here:

```
void    SysBeep(short duration);
```

The prototype takes an integer that is used to determine the duration of the beep, but with the newer Macintoshes, this value has no effect. It is common just to pass in a value of 1.

Here, then, is the LoadPicture() routine:

```
/**
 **    LoadPicture()
 **
 **    This routine will open a file, and read the PICT
 **    information from the data fork (if the file's
 **    type is PICT), or from the first PICT resource
 **    it finds. If there is an error, it will set
 **    thePicture to NULL.
 **/
void  LoadPicture( FSSpec      theFile,
                   OSType      fileType,
                   PicHandle   *thePicture  )
{
  short     refNum;    /* The reference number for */
                    /* the file once it's opened */
  PicHandle  theImage = NULL;
  OSErr      theErr;      /* For error checking */

  if (fileType == 'PICT') /* The file's type is PICT, */
          /* so open the data fork */
  {
    /* First declare some variables we will need */
    /* for reading the data fork */
    long    fileSize;
    long    pictSize;
```

```
/* Open the data fork of the file */
theErr = HOpen( theFile.vRefNum,/* Volume Ref Num */
                theFile.parID,  /* Directory ID */
                theFile.name,   /* The file name */
                fsRdPerm,       /* We want read permission */
                &refNum );      /* File reference num */

if (theErr == noErr) {    /* noErr means the */
            /* open was successful */
  /* find the size of the file */
  theErr = GetEOF(refNum, &fileSize);

  if (theErr == noErr) { /* Check for an error again */
  /* PICT data starts 512 bytes into the file, so subtract
   * that from the fileSize to find the size of the pict
   */
    pictSize = fileSize - 512;

    /* Check to make sure the pict data is > 0 */
    if (pictSize > 0) {
  /* Create a new handle for the pict data. NewHandle must
   * be typecast to PicHandle. Since we know how large
   * the pict will be, just pass that size to NewHandle.
   */
      theImage = (PicHandle)NewHandle(pictSize);

  /* Check to make sure the handle returned is not null.
   * If it is, that means the memory allocation failed,
   * which could easily happen if the user tries to load
   * a several-megabyte PICT image (which aren't that
   * uncommon with programs like Photoshop).
   */
      if (theImage != NULL) {
  /* Since the pict data starts at 512 bytes into the file,
   * we must tell the file manager to start reading data
   * at that point, with SetFPos().
   */
        theErr = SetFPos(refNum, fsFromStart, 512);

  /* Check to make sure that SetFPos succeeded */
        if (theErr == noErr) {
  /* Read the pict data from the file into our handle. Since
   * FSRead wants a pointer, not a handle, we dereference the
   * handle before we pass it into the routine. This way, FSRead
   * will place the data directly into our handle.
   */
          theErr = FSRead(refNum, &pictSize, (Ptr)*theImage);
        }
      }
    }
  }
}
```

Continued on next page

Continued from previous page

```
            /* We have to close the data file since we've read
             * everything we  need.
             */
            FSClose(refNum);
        }
    } else {
        /* This is the section for the resource fork. */
        refNum = HOpenResFile(  theFile.vRefNum,/* Volume Ref Num */
                                theFile.parID,  /* Directory ID */
                                theFile.name,   /* The file name */
                                fsRdPerm  );     /* We want 'read' access */
        /* If the refNum is not -1, the file was opened sucessfully. */
        if (refNum != -1) {
            /* Loading a resource is much easier than loading from the
             * data fork. All it takes is one command.
             *
             * GetIndResource('PICT', 1) will load the first
             * PICT resource the resource manager finds in the file.
             */
            theImage = (PicHandle)GetIndResource('PICT', 1);

            /* If we close the file now, the resource will be disposed. To
             * prevent this, detach the resource.
             */
            DetachResource((Handle)theImage);

            /* Close the file since we finished with it */
            FSClose(refNum);
        }
    }


    /* check to see if there were errors */
    if (theErr != noErr) {
      /* There were errors; dispose of the picture
       * if it has been allocated
       */
      if (theImage != NULL) {
        /* If it was a data file, the image was allocated by NewHandle. Use
         * DisposeHandle to deallocate it.
         */
        if (fileType == 'PICT') {
          DisposeHandle((Handle)theImage);
        } else {
          /* If it's a resource file, use ReleaseResource */
          ReleaseResource((Handle)theImage);
        }
        theImage = NULL;
      }
    }


    /* Pass the picture handle back to the calling routine */
```

```
  *thePicture = theImage;

  /* And we're all done! */
  return;
}
```

You can now load the PICT image into memory, but you need a routine that can display the image in a window. This next routine, HandleOpenCommand(), creates a StandardGetFile() open dialog to find out which image to open, calls LoadPicture() to load the image into memory, creates a window with CreateWindow(), and then draws the PICT into the window. Here is the routine:

```
/**
 ** HandleOpenCommand()
 **
 ** Brings up a StandardGetFile dialog, then opens the selected file,
 ** loads the PICT, creates a window for it, and draws it.
 **/
Boolean HandleOpenCommand(void)
{
  SFTypeList          typesToShow;
  StandardFileReply   reply;

  typesToShow[0] = 'PICT';  /* Just show PICT and RSRC files in */
  typesToShow[1] = 'RSRC';  /* the Open dialog. */

  /* Bring up the StandardGetFile dialog */
  StandardGetFile(  NULL,  /* No filtering proc */
                    2,     /* Open 2 types of files */
                    typesToShow,
                    &reply );
  /* check to see if a legitimate file has been chosen... */
  if (reply.sfGood == TRUE) {
    PicHandle    theImage;
    short        fileRefNum;    /* this is the refnum of the file */
                                /* that is opened */
    Rect         imageSize, windowSize;

    /* Call our LoadPicture() routine to load the image */
    LoadPicture(  reply.sfFile,  /* The FSSpec for the file */
                  reply.sfType,  /* The file type */
                  &theImage );

    /* check to see if the routine succeeded */
    if (theImage != NULL) {

      /* Now we must create the window and draw the image into it. */

      /* The size of the PICT is stored in the picFrame field */
      imageSize = (**theImage).picFrame;
```

Continued on next page

Continued from previous page

```
      /* We want to create a window this size */
      windowSize = imageSize;

      /* Offset the window rectangle slightly, because we don't want the
       * window to be created at 0,0 - it would end up being partially
       * underneath the menu bar.
       */
      OffsetRect(&windowSize, 10, 40);

      /* Create the window */
      gPictWindow = CreateWindow(&windowSize);

      /* Set the port to the window */
      SetPort(gPictWindow);

      /* Draw the picture */
      DrawPicture(theImage, &imageSize);

      /* Dispose of the PICT to release it from memory.
       */
      DisposeHandle((Handle)theImage);

      /* If we've gotten to this point, everything worked out fine,
       * so return TRUE.
       */
      return TRUE;
   }
 }


 /* Since TRUE wasn't already returned, something must have gone wrong.
Return
   * FALSE
   */
  return FALSE;
}
```

The main() routine should look very familiar—it is based on the main() routine of the Shape Drawing application reviewed in Chapter 2. The biggest changes are that the menu bar contains only the Apple, File, and Edit menus and there is additional code for dragging windows and for clicking in the close box to close the window. When the PICT Viewer application starts up, the Close menu item from the File menu will be dimmed. When an image is opened, the Close item will become active, and the Open item will be dimmed. This ensures that the user does not try to open more than one image.

For dragging the window, the application uses the toolbox call DragWindow(), outlined here:

```
void    DragWindow(WindowPtr theWindow, Point where, Rect *limitRect);
```

When FindWindow() returns a click on the drag bar of a window, call the DragWindow() routine to allow the Window Manager to reposition the window. The parameters *theWindow* and *where* can be obtained from the event record. The *limitRect* parameter is a rectangle that defines the boundary in which the window can be dragged. Usually, this is the boundary of the entire screen, which can be found in the qd structure as qd.screenBits.bounds.

The other new thing in this main() routine is handling the close box on a window. When the user clicks in the close box, a set of lines appears inside, giving the illusion of the button being pressed. If the user drags the cursor outside of the close box before releasing the mouse button, the action is canceled. Otherwise, the application closes the window. This effect is obtained from a single routine called TrackGoAway(), shown here:

```
Boolean TrackGoAway(WindowPtr theWindow, Point where);
```

The *theWindow* parameter is the WindowPtr returned by FindWindow(); the *where* parameter is the mouse click location obtained from the event record. TrackGoAway() returns a Boolean value indicating TRUE if the user released the mouse button while the cursor was inside the close box, FALSE otherwise.

Here is the main() function for the PICT Viewer application:

```
void main(void)
{
  EventRecord    theEvent;
  short          eventMask;
  short          done = FALSE;
  Boolean        notNullEvent;
  MenuHandle     appleMenu, fileMenu, editMenu;

  /* Initialize everything we need */
  InitGraf(&qd.thePort);    /* qd.thePort is part of any application */
  InitWindows();
  InitCursor();
  InitFonts();
  InitMenus();

  /* Create each of our menus and insert them into the menu bar */
  appleMenu = NewMenu(kMENU_Apple, "\p\024");
  AppendMenu(appleMenu, "\pAbout Pict Viewer ");
  AppendMenu(appleMenu, "\p(-");
  InsertMenu(appleMenu, 0);

  fileMenu = NewMenu(kMENU_File, "\pFile");
  AppendMenu(fileMenu, "\pNew ;Open ;(-;Close;(-;Quit");
  InsertMenu(fileMenu, 0);

  editMenu = NewMenu(kMENU_Edit, "\pEdit");
  AppendMenu(editMenu, "\pUndo;(-;Cut;Copy;Paste;Clear");
  InsertMenu(editMenu, 0);

  DrawMenuBar();    /* Now we need to draw our menu */
```

Continued on next page

Continued from previous page

```
  eventMask = everyEvent;

  gPictWindow = NULL;

  /* Disable the close command from the menu, since there isn't a window
open yet. */
  DisableItem(fileMenu, 4);

  while (!done) {
    notNullEvent = WaitNextEvent(  eventMask,
                                   &theEvent,
                                   0x7FFFFFFF,
                                   NULL);

      if (notNullEvent == TRUE) {    /* We received something other than a
NULL event */

        switch (theEvent.what) {
          WindowPtr    selectedWindow;
          long         result;
          short        menuHit; /* which menu was selected */
          short        itemHit; /* which item from the menu was selected */
          short        findWindowResult;
          Rect         dragRect; /* The area which we'll allow the */
                                 /* window to be dragged in */

          case mouseDown:
            /* We received a mousedown event. Check to see where it was */
            findWindowResult = FindWindow(theEvent.where, &selectedWindow);
            if (findWindowResult == inMenuBar) {
              /* It was in the menu bar. Find what item was selected */
              result = MenuSelect(theEvent.where);

              /* First check to see if any item was selected at all */
              if (result != 0) {
                /* We now need to dissect the
                 * result to find which menu was hit
                 */
                /* Move the upper 16 bits into a word */
                menuHit = result >> 16;

                /* And now we find which item in that menu was selected */
                /* Mask off the bottom 16 bits */
                itemHit = result & 0xFFFF;

                if (menuHit == kMENU_File) {
                  /* an item from the file menu was selected */
                  switch (itemHit) {
                    case 2:
                      /* The Open command was chosen */
                      if (HandleOpenCommand() == TRUE) {
                        /* If HandleOpenCommand returns true, it was */
```

```
                                /* successful. In this case, we want to dim */
                                /* the open command and enable to close */
                                /* command (since we can have only one window */
                                /* open at a time).*/
                                EnableItem(fileMenu, 4);
                                DisableItem(fileMenu, 2);
                            } else {
                        /* The open routine failed, probably either because */
                        /* of a faulty image, or there wasn't enough memory. */
                        /* In this case, beep so the user knows something */
                        /* went wrong. */
                                SysBeep(1);
                            }
                            break;
                        case 4:
                            /* The close command was chosen. Dispose of the */
                            /* window, first checking to make sure that it's */
                            /* not NULL (good programming form). */
                            if (gPictWindow != NULL) {
                                DisposeWindow(gPictWindow);
                                gPictWindow = NULL;

                                /* Now we need to enable the open command and */
                                /* disable the close command. */
                                EnableItem(fileMenu, 2);
                                DisableItem(fileMenu,4);
                            }
                            break;

                        case 6:
                            /* Quit was chosen, so quit the program. */
                            done = TRUE;
                            break;
                    }
                }

        /* Un-hilite the menu */
        HiliteMenu(0);
    }
} else if (findWindowResult == inDrag) {
    /* The user clicked in the drag bar. Allow them to drag it
     * across the screen. First declare the area that we'll allow
     * the dragging to occur in. We'll make this rectangle as
     * large as possible, allowing the window to be dragged
     * anywhere on the monitor.
     */
    SetRect(&dragRect, -32767, -32767, 32767, 32767);
    DragWindow( selectedWindow, /* Obtained from FindWindow */
                theEvent.where, /* Where the user clicked */
                &dragRect);
} else if (findWindowResult == inGoAway) {
    /* The user clicked in the close box. Close the window. */
```

Continued on next page

Continued from previous page

```
                    /* First make sure it's our window they clicked on */
                    if (selectedWindow == gPictWindow) {

                        /* Then call TrackGoAway so the user has an opportunity to
                         * move the mouse out of the close box
                         */
                        if (TrackGoAway(selectedWindow, theEvent.where) == TRUE) {
                          /* Close the window */
                          if (gPictWindow != NULL) {
                            DisposeWindow(gPictWindow);
                            gPictWindow = NULL;

                            /* Enable the open command
                             * and disable the close command
                             */
                            EnableItem(fileMenu, 2);
                            DisableItem(fileMenu,4);
                          }
                        }
                      }
                    }
                    break;

                case updateEvt:
                {
                    /* Update our window if it needs it,
                     * even though we don't draw the contents
                     * back into it.
                     */
                    BeginUpdate((WindowPtr)theEvent.message);
                    EndUpdate((WindowPtr)theEvent.message);
                    break;
                }

                default:
                    /* Don't do anything */
                    break;
            }
          }
        }

    /* If the window is currently open, close it. */
    if (gPictWindow != NULL)
      DisposeWindow(gPictWindow);
}
```

When you run PICT Viewer, choose Open from the File menu. Select an image from the dialog that comes up, and the program will create a new window for that image and display it. Figure 3-13 shows the PICT viewer displaying an image.

FIGURE 3-13

PICT Viewer's flamingo

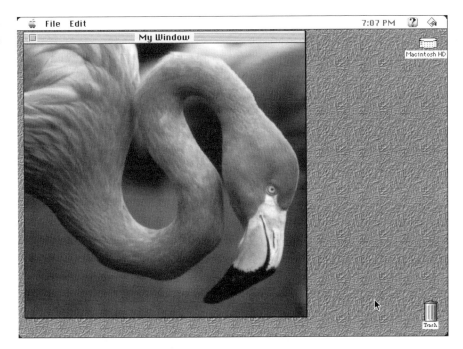

PICT Viewer has a few limitations, most of which can be overcome with a little work.

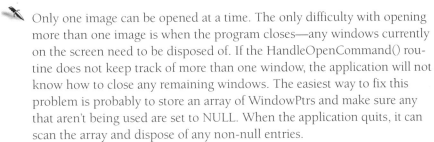 Only one image can be opened at a time. The only difficulty with opening more than one image is when the program closes—any windows currently on the screen need to be disposed of. If the HandleOpenCommand() routine does not keep track of more than one window, the application will not know how to close any remaining windows. The easiest way to fix this problem is probably to store an array of WindowPtrs and make sure any that aren't being used are set to NULL. When the application quits, it can scan the array and dispose of any non-null entries.

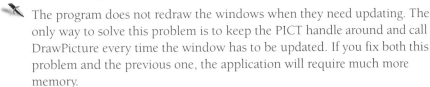 The program does not redraw the windows when they need updating. The only way to solve this problem is to keep the PICT handle around and call DrawPicture every time the window has to be updated. If you fix both this problem and the previous one, the application will require much more memory.

 If the image does not use the system color table, it will not look very good on an 8-bit monitor.

If the image is larger than the monitor, the bottom and right edges will not be on the screen. You could solve this problem by making sure the window that is created is no larger than the screen size (found in qd.screenBits.bounds), then calling DrawPicture() with the smaller destination rectangle. This will force QuickDraw to scale the image to fit the new size. In that case, you may also want to maintain the aspect ratio of the image.

In this chapter, you've learned a great deal about the internal structures of the Macintosh. The next chapter covers the most vital component of 3D graphics animation: mathematics. Mathematics are at the heart of every complex game; a good understanding of the principles is essential for game designers.

4

Mathematics of Art

...ome trsti fione emanotrelle ... ... liquali prnobrano. Laiga
no sgrapo li ... nune come mo e igone o la go granodi Bone
... ong are nella mon e lo per mangiulla ar la manobella pegi ...
aforga a pib ijomo prb val.

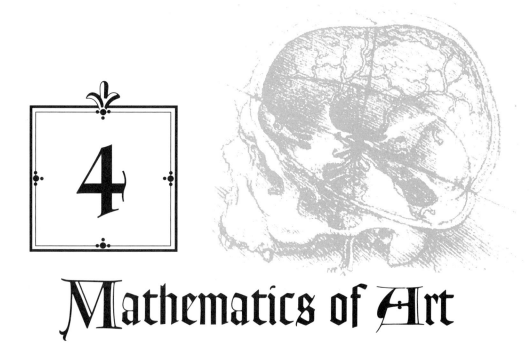

Mathematics of Art

 If you've done some programming, you know that the computer depends on mathematics. Almost any task you want to accomplish will require at least some knowledge of algebra and most of the tricks that are used in the best algorithms are based on some mathematical formula. Graphics animation is especially dependent on algebra or trigonometry.

This doesn't mean the techniques involved in animation have to be difficult. Although there is a great deal to learn about these topics, most of the work has already been done for you by pioneering mathematicians and computer scientists. They have broken down the relationship between math and physical objects into clear formulas, which you take and convert to algorithms.

This chapter covers most of the math you'll need to create the flight simulator. A great deal of effort has been spent to make it as painless as possible. If you're already well versed in mathematics, much of the information presented here may be familiar. I'll be discussing coordinate systems, geometry, and a little bit of linear algebra.

Cartesian Coordinates

In Chapter 1, I referred to the computer screen as being a collection of pixels laid out in a two-dimensional array. In Chapter 2, you created an application that draws shapes using this array. These pixels are organized using a method that is a slightly modified version of the Cartesian coordinate system.

THE BIRTH OF THE CARTESIAN COORDINATE SYSTEM

Legend has it that the 17th-century French philosopher and mathematician René Descartes was lying in bed one day watching a fly buzz around the ceiling when he conceived the coordinate system that bears a Latinized version of his name. It occurred to Descartes that the position of the fly at any given instant could be described with three numbers, each representing the insect's position relative to some fixed point. Later, he expanded this idea to include two-dimensional points on a plane, the positions of which could be described with two numbers for any given point. He included the idea in a long appendix to a book published in 1637. Despite being tucked away in the back of another book, Descartes' method of representing points on a plane and in a space by numeric coordinates launched a new branch of mathematics, combining features of geometry and algebra, known today as analytic geometry.

The Cartesian Plane

You're probably already familiar with the Cartesian coordinate system. It is introduced in any high school geometry class and it's an essential part of trigonometry. The Cartesian coordinate system is simple, elegant, and very useful in certain kinds of computer graphics. Because three-dimensional animation is one of the areas in which it is essential, I am going to review it in some detail.

Any number can be regarded as a point on a line. In geometry, a line (a theoretical concept that doesn't necessarily exist in the "real" world) consists of an infinite number of points. It is also infinitely divisible, meaning that no matter how small the segment you choose from that line, there are an infinite number of points along that segment.

The system of real numbers is very similar to the concept of a line. Real numbers, roughly speaking, are numbers that can have fractional values, commonly represented by decimal points (The C data type *float* corresponds to the concept of a real number). Like a line, real numbers have an infinite range and therefore are infinitely divisible.

Thus on any geometrical line (which, as you will recall, is infinitely long), you can find a point that corresponds to every real number. Because it is difficult to imagine an infinite line (and impossible to draw one), we make do with an approximation, like the one in Figure 4-1. This line, rather like a ruler, has been marked off at intervals to denote the integers—that is, the whole numbers—from -5 to 5, with tick marks in between

FIGURE 4-1

◎ ◎ ◎ ◎ ◎ ◎

A horizontal line segment from -5 to 5

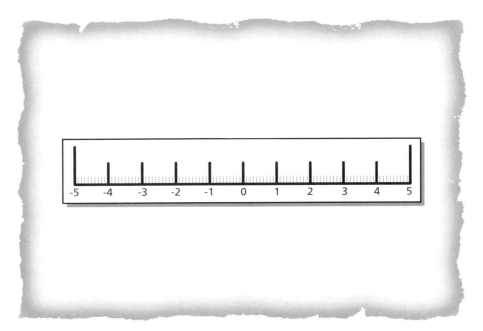

to denote tenths of a number. This concept is introduced in geometry classes as number lines; you can locate points on the line such as 5, 4.7, -2.1, and so forth.

These points are represented by tick marks—between each tick mark, more precise fractions are represented such as 3.46 or 0.045. In practice, if you started dividing the line up finely, you would surpass the resolution of the printer's ink used to inscribe it onto the page. So when we say that all these points are on the line, we are speaking theoretically. But on a perfect, theoretical, geometric line, there is a point corresponding to every real number.

Geometry Meets Algebra

It was Descartes' genius to see that this correspondence between points on a line and a number allowed mathematicians to treat geometric concepts—that is, concepts involving points, lines, planes, three-dimensional space, and so forth—as numbers.

The line represents a single dimension, but it does not always have to be horizontal. It is helpful to take the line and place it vertically, as in Figure 4-2. In traditional mathematics, coordinates on a vertical line increase as they go up, but in computer science, they are reversed. This is an important concept to remember, as it can sometimes cause confusion, especially when you are trying to convert a mathematical formula into an algorithm.

Both the horizontal and vertical lines are one-dimensional—any point on the line can be represented by a single real number. This is very simple, but it does not provide for

FIGURE 4-2

A vertical line
segment

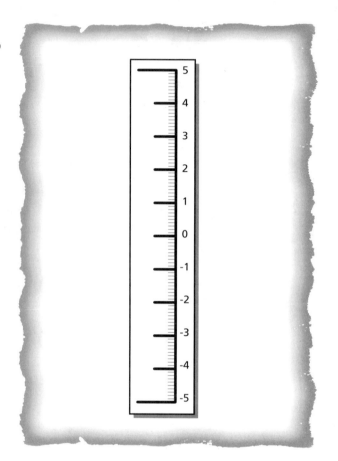

very interesting shapes. However, if you combine the two lines to create two dimensions, you have a plane. In the Cartesian plane, the standard way of representing geometric shapes, the two lines cross at the 0 coordinate, as illustrated in Figure 4-3.

Not only does every real number have a corresponding point on both of these lines, but every pair of real numbers has a corresponding point on the Cartesian plane upon which these points are situated. For instance, the pair of numbers (-3, 2) corresponds to the point on the plane that is aligned with the -3 tick on the horizontal line and the 2 tick on the vertical line, as in Figure 4-4. Just as on a line, you can represent decimal fractions on the two-dimensional plane. Figure 4-5 shows the number pair (2.3, -1.6). By convention, the first number of the number pair refers to a point along the horizontal line, and the second number refers to a point along the vertical line.

Just as there are an infinite number of points on a line, there are an infinite number of points on a plane, each of which can be described by using a pair of numbers.

FIGURE 4-3

◎ ◎ ◎ ◎ ◎ ◎

The Cartesian plane

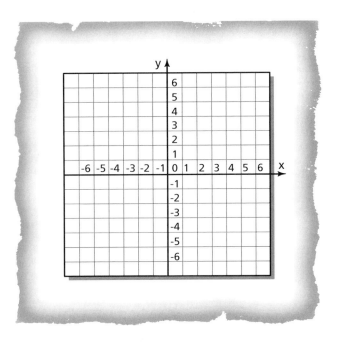

FIGURE 4-4

◎ ◎ ◎ ◎ ◎ ◎

Point (-3, 2) on the Cartesian plane

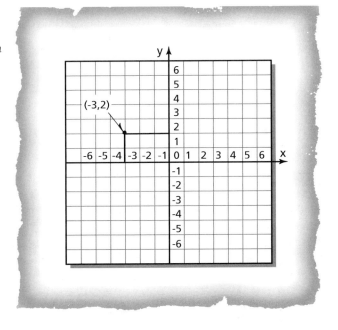

FIGURE 4-5

◎ ◎ ◎ ◎ ◎ ◎

Point (2.3, -1.6)
on the
Cartesian plane

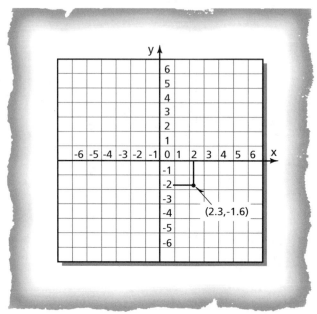

A pair of numbers that corresponds to a point on the Cartesian plane is called a *coordinate pair,* or just *coordinates.*

Using a pair of coordinates, it was possible for Descartes to give a precise numerical description of vague geometrical concepts. Not only can a point be described by a coordinate pair, but a line segment can be described by two pairs of coordinates, representing the endpoints of the line. The line in Figure 4-6, for instance, extends from the coordinate (2,2) to the coordinate (4,4). Thus this line can be described by the coordinate pairs (2,2) and (4,4). Other shapes can also be described numerically, as you'll see in a moment.

The two number lines used to establish the position of points on the plane are called the *axes.* For historical reasons, coordinate pairs are commonly represented by the variables x and y, as in (x,y). For this reason, the coordinates themselves are frequently referred to as x,y *coordinates.* The first (horizontal) coordinate of the pair is known as the x *coordinate* and the second (vertical) coordinate is known as the y *coordinate.* It follows that the horizontal axis (the one used to locate the position of the x coordinate) is referred to as the x *axis* and the vertical axis is known as the y *axis.* The two axes always cross at the zero point; because all points are numbered relative to this (0,0) point, it is called the *origin* of the coordinate system.

FIGURE 4-6

◎ ◎ ◎ ◎ ◎ ◎

A line from
(2,2) to (4,4)

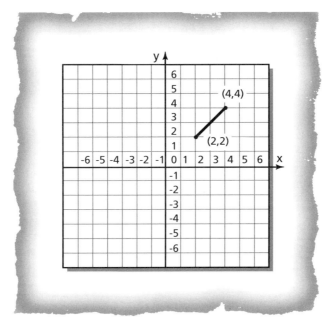

Coordinates on the Computer

The surface of the computer display is a plane and the graphics that you draw on it are made up of pixels—the points—on that plane. There aren't an infinite number of pixels on the display—on most Macintosh monitors, there are just over 300,000—but the video display is still a good approximation of the Cartesian plane. Any position on the display can be specified by a pair of coordinates.

This is the most common method of specifying the location of pixels. Although you can place the Cartesian axes anywhere on (or off) the display, it is common to regard the line of pixels at the top of the display as the x axis and the line of pixels running down the left side of the display as the y axis, as shown in Figure 4-7. This puts the origin of the coordinate system in the upper-left corner of the display. Thus the pixel in that corner is said to be at coordinates (0,0). However, the programming convention is to orient the y axis of the computer display upside-down relative to a standard Cartesian y axis, with numbers growing larger going down the axis. This convention arose because it corresponds to the way the addresses of pixels in video RAM grow larger going down the display. As you'll see in a moment, orienting the coordinates in this manner simplifies the task of calculating the location in RAM of a specific pixel on the display.

FIGURE 4-7

ⓞ ⓞ ⓞ ⓞ ⓞ ⓞ

The computer
screen on the
Cartesian plane

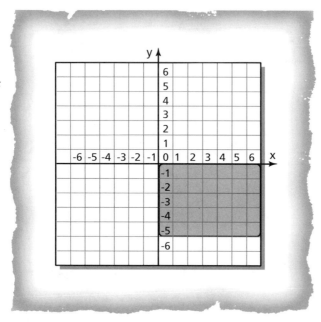

Coordinates to Pixels

If the coordinates of the pixel in the upper-left corner of the display are (0,0), then the coordinates of the pixel in the lower-right corner of the standard Macintosh 14-inch display are (639, 479). Note that, because we start with coordinates (0,0) rather than (1,1), the coordinates at the opposite extremes of the display are one short of the actual number of pixels in the horizontal and vertical directions. All other pixels on the display are at coordinates between those extremes. The black pixel in Figure 4-8, for instance, is at coordinates (217,77)—that is, it's located 217 pixels from the left edge of the display and 77 pixels from the top.

In the previous chapter, you used this coordinate system to create windows and draw shapes. When you created a window, two coordinate pairs—defining a rectangle—were used to determine where the window would be positioned and what size it would be. The first pair defined the upper-left corner of the rectangle, whereas the second pair defined the lower-right corner. These two pairs were placed in a Rect structure, like this one:

```
typedef struct {
  short top;
  short left;
  short bottom;
  short right;
} Rect;
```

FIGURE 4-8

◉ ◉ ◉ ◉ ◉ ◉

*One pixel on
the computer
screen*

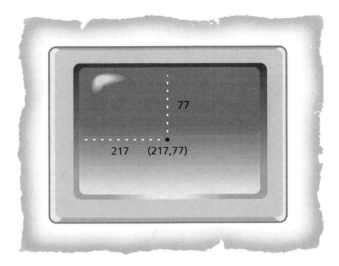

The toolbox has another structure, called a point. A point is a pair of integers indicating a horizontal (x) and a vertical (y) position.

```
typedef struct {
  short v;
  short h;
} Point;
```

The system of regarding the upper-left corner of the screen as coordinate pair (0,0) is known as *global coordinates*. However, when you are drawing into individual windows on the screen, each window has its own coordinate system. In these coordinates, the pair (0,0) corresponds to the upper-left corner of the window, not the screen. This coordinate system is known as *local coordinates*.

This system, although initially confusing, has many advantages. When you draw something on the screen, most of the time it is being drawn within a window. In this case, you want to position whatever you're drawing relative to the window, not to the screen itself. An illustration of local and global coordinates and the difference between drawing a shape in the two coordinate systems is shown in Figure 4-9. The window is located at the global coordinates (150,160). Any shape drawn within the window will be drawn relative to the window's local coordinates, which begin at (0,0) at the upper-left corner of the window.

Because the window is situated at the global coordinates (150,160), you can use this to translate any local coordinates to global coordinates by adding 150 to the x position

FIGURE 4-9

◎ ◎ ◎ ◎ ◎ ◎

*The relationship
between local
and global
coordinates*

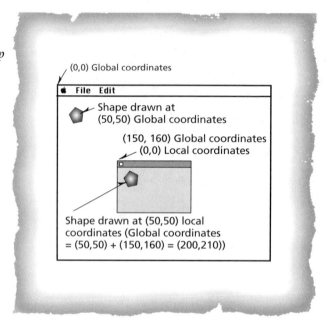

and 160 to the y position. The toolbox has a function that will do this translation for you, called LocalToGlobal().

```
void LocalToGlobal(Point *pt);
```

All you need to do is pass the address of a point to LocalToGlobal() and the function will do the translation. However, you must be sure that the port is set to the correct window (the window that the point is local to) before calling this routine so that the system knows which window's coordinate system to use.

The toolbox also supplies the opposite routine, GlobalToLocal(). This routine translates a point in global coordinates to coordinates local to the current window.

```
void GlobalToLocal(Point *pt);
```

How Images Are Stored

If you've ever worked with a painting or image-processing program such as Photoshop, you know that bitmapped images come in many varieties. One of the primary distinctions that can be made between various types of images is whether they are *direct color* or *indexed color*. For direct color images, exact color values are stored for each pixel, usually consisting of 16 or 24 bits of information per pixel. Images stored in this fashion are called 16-bit or 24-bit images, respectively. This allows a huge range of color (over 32,000 for a 16-bit image and over 16 million for a 24-bit image), but there is a catch: The information takes up a huge amount of space. For example, a 640x480 24-bit image takes up almost a megabyte of storage space.

An indexed color image, on the other hand, stores an index value for each pixel, typically using 2, 4, or 8 bits per pixel. In addition, a *color table* is stored with the image. The color table contains a color value for every possible pixel value. When it comes time to display the image, the table is consulted to find the correct color for each index. If a pixel has a value of 100, QuickDraw looks at the 100th entry of the color table and retrieves that color value. Indexed color images are limited to a far smaller range of colors—256 colors for 8-bit images—but they require a great deal less space for storage. The same 640x480 image in 8-bit color requires only 300k for storage.

Almost all Macintoshes sold today are capable of displaying 8-bit color and many are capable of producing 16- or 24-bit color. Because of the smaller memory requirements, 8-bit color images are displayed much more quickly, so I use the 8-bit format in this book. A majority of games use the 8-bit color mode, but some games that do not have much high-speed animation can take advantage of 16- or 24-bit color levels, which produce much more realistic looking images.

The actual data in a bitmap is stored sequentially in memory, row by row, as shown in Figure 4-10. Because memory is not designed in a grid as the screen is, you must use a simple formula for finding the memory location for a particular pixel. In the most general case, you would multiply the width of the image with the y coordinate, add the x coordinate and then add that to the beginning address of the bitmap, as follows:

```
memory_location = base_address + (y_coordinate * width) + x_coordinate;
```

This only works with 8-bit images, because each pixel corresponds to 1 byte in memory. Unfortunately, images stored on the Macintosh are a little more complicated. To have optimum speed, processors must align data with certain boundaries in memory. On most 68k-based Macintoshes, these boundaries are even multiples of 2 bytes. Therefore, a 68k processor can access the memory location 1000 much more quickly than it can access memory location 1001. On PowerPC processors, the boundary has been changed to every 4 bytes; it may change again in the future.

To allow its operations to work as quickly as possible, QuickDraw begins each row of an image on at least a 4-byte boundary. If your image is not an even multiple of the boundary size, there will be some space left over at the end of each row, as shown in Figure 4-11. As you can see, the previous formula won't work any more because the width of each row in memory is not the same as the width of the image. There is, however, an easy solution to this problem. QuickDraw will store a value called rowBytes, which tells you just how many bytes make up one row of pixels. Instead of multiplying the y coordinate by the width of the image, multiply it by the rowBytes value, and then add the x coordinate.

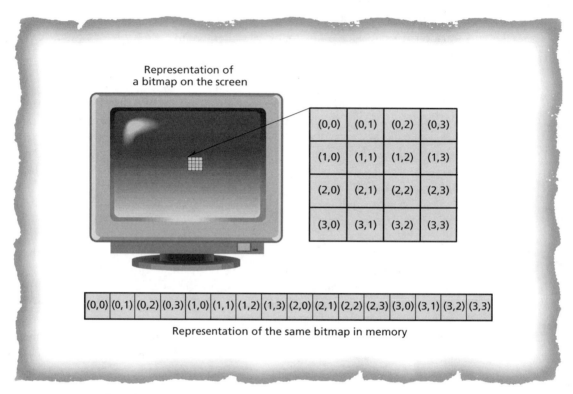

FIGURE 4-10 ◉ *A bitmap on the screen and in memory*

```
memory_location = base_address +
                  (y_coordinate * rowBytes) +
                  x_coordinate;
```

The PixMap Structure

A QuickDraw structure you will be working with a great deal in this chapter is the PixMap. It is the Macintosh's structure for a color bitmap and you need to be able to access its internal structure for fast animation. Below is a portion of the PixMap structure—the actual structure is much longer, but you won't be using most of the fields. This is just to familiarize you with the most important portions.

```
typedef struct {
  Ptr        baseAddr;
  short      rowBytes;
  Rect       bounds;
  short      pixelType;
  short      pixelSize;
  CTabHandle pmTable;
} PixMap, *PixMapPtr, **PixMapHandle;
```

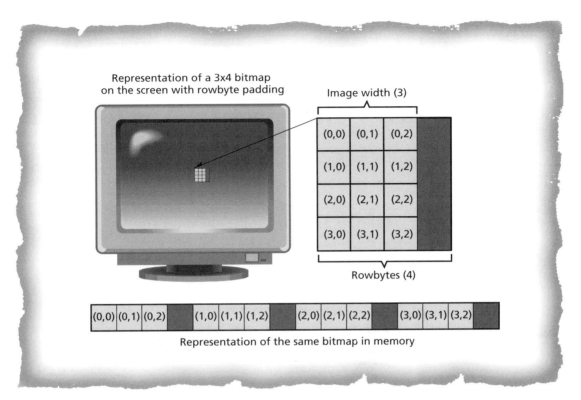

Representation of a 3x4 bitmap
on the screen with rowbyte padding

Image width (3)

Rowbytes (4)

Representation of the same bitmap in memory

FIGURE 4-11 ◉ *A bitmap with rowbyte padding*

You can find the complete listing for the PixMap structure in QuickDraw.h, which is included with your compiler.

baseAddr is the address of the beginning of the bitmapped image. Although you should know that this field is here, you should never access it directly. Instead, use the toolbox call GetPixBaseAddr(), as shown here:

```
Ptr GetPixBaseAddr(PixMapHandle pm);
```

GetPixBaseAddr() will return a pointer to the image; it should be used to ensure future compatibility.

rowBytes is an integer indicating how many bytes make up one row of the image. The top 2 bits of the rowBytes field are used internally by QuickDraw, so you must mask them off to ensure you get the correct rowBytes value. The masking value to use is 0x3FFF.

bounds is simply a Rect defining the size of the Pixmap. Typically, the top and left coordinates will be 0, but not always.

pixelType tells you whether the image is stored as direct color or indexed color. A value of 0 indicates indexed color; a value of 16 indicates direct color.

pixelSize is how many bits are used for each pixel. For the examples you will be using, the image will always use 8 bits per pixel, giving you 256 colors.

pmTable is the color table that is used for translating the pixel values of indexed color images into colors for the screen.

Using the PixMap Structure to Access the Image

Let's construct an example of how to access the image data using the PixMap structure. Before using the PixMap, you must call LockPixels() to ensure the integrity of the data.

```
void LockPixels(PixMapHandle pm);
```

Once you are finished with the PixMap, call UnlockPixels() to allow the Memory Manager to deal with it more efficiently.

```
void UnlockPixels(PixMapHandle pm);
```

Listing 4-1 is a code example that will change the color of a specific pixel in a PixMap.

Listing 4-1 *Changing a pixel's color in a PixMap*

```
void  SetPixMapPixel(PixMapHandle pm, Point location, short color)
{
  short    rowBytes;
  Ptr      imageDataAddress;
  Ptr      pixelAddress;
  Rect    pixMapBounds;

  /* First make sure that the pixel location is within the
   * boundary of the pixmap. If it isn't, just return to the caller.
   */
  pixMapBounds = (**pm).bounds;

  if ((location.h < pixMapBounds.left) ||
      (location.h > pixMapBounds.right) ||
      (location.v < pixMapBounds.top) ||
      (location.v > pixMapBounds.bottom)) {
      return;
  }

  /* This routine will not work for anything but an 8-bit
   * color pixmap. Return if it is anything but that.
   */
  if ((**pm).pixelSize != 8)
    return;

  /* We need to make the location point local to the
   * pixmap. To do this, just subtract the pixmap
   * bounds top and left from the point. Usually, the
   * bounds will be centered at (0,0) anyway, but this
   * is just to be sure.
```

```
 */
location.h -= pixMapBounds.left;
location.v -= pixMapBounds.top;

/* Lock the pixmap down so we can start accessing it */
LockPixels(pm);

/* Get the rowBytes and mask off the top 2 bits */
rowBytes = (**pm).rowBytes & 0x3FFF;

/* Get the address of the pixmap data */
imageDataAddress = GetPixBaseAddr(pm);

/* Find the address of the pixel we want to change */
pixelAddress = imageDataAddress +
            (location.h * rowBytes) +
            location.v;

/* Set that pixel. We typecast 'color' to an unsigned char
 * because we need an 8-bit color, and color is not signed.
 */
*pixelAddress = (unsigned char)color;

/* We are done. Unlock the pixmap before we return. */
UnlockPixels(pm);

return;
}
```

Moving the Origin

Although it is customary to put the origin of the screen's coordinate system at the upper-left corner of the display (or the current window), it is not always desirable to do so. In fact, later you will move the origin to several different positions on the display, including the center. Nonetheless, it is simpler to calculate screen positions based on an origin in the upper-left corner, so you'll need to translate back and forth between the two systems (similar to when you move between global and local coordinates). You'll perform the calculations concerning the positions of the objects on the screen with the origin located at coordinates (XORIGIN, YORIGIN) relative to the upper-left corner of the display or window, where XORIGIN and YORIGIN are predefined constants. In effect, you are creating a virtual coordinate system separate from the system normally used to specify coordinates on the display. Figure 4-12 shows the difference between the virtual system and the usual system.

To translate these virtual coordinates back into screen coordinates (i.e., coordinates with the origin in the upper-left corner of the display), use the following formula:

```
screen_x = virtual_x + XORIGIN;
screen_y = virtual_y + YORIGIN
```

FIGURE 4-12
◎ ◎ ◎ ◎ ◎ ◎

*The relationship
between the
virtual screen
coordinate
system and the
"real" screen
coordinate
system*

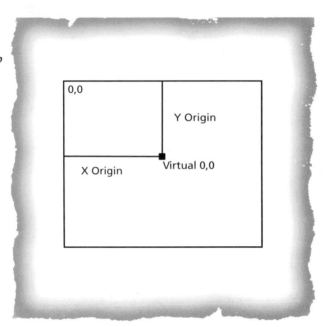

You'll see this formula pop up several times in the chapters to come.

Accessing Multiple Pixels

Most of the time, you will not be setting 1 pixel at a time—if games used this method, we'd still be playing Pong (the first home video game). If you want to draw a horizontal line, you could calculate the address of the first point, plot the pixel, add one to the point, calculate the address again, plot the pixel, and so on. It would be much easier, however, to take advantage of the structure of images in memory. To move right by 1 pixel, all you need to do is add one to the address; to move left, just subtract one. And because the rowBytes value holds the offset to the next row, to move vertically just add or subtract the rowBytes value from the address.

You'll be using this method extensively when you start to design your own drawing routines; it's a good way to extract speed from the machine.

Into the Third Dimension

So far, I've spoken only of two-dimensional coordinate systems. But this book is about three-dimensional computer graphics, so it's time to add a dimension and take a look at three-dimensional coordinate systems.

First, however, a fundamental question: What do I mean when I refer to a dimension? Without getting technical, a dimension can be defined as a way in which a line can be perpendicular (i.e., at right angles) to other lines. On the surface of a sheet of paper, you can draw two lines that are perpendicular to each other, as in Figure 4-13. Thus the surface of the paper is two-dimensional (actually, it is a close representation of a two-dimensional object—two-dimensional objects cannot exist in a three-dimensional world); in geometric terms, it is a plane. If you could draw lines in space, you could draw three lines perpendicular to one another. Thus space is three dimensional. Although you can't draw in space, you can demonstrate this to yourself by holding three pencils in your hand and arranging them so that each is perpendicular to each other.

In a Cartesian coordinate system, the axes represent the dimensions—that is, the ways in which lines can be perpendicular to one another. After all, each coordinate axis is always perpendicular to all other coordinate axes. In a two-dimensional coordinate system, there are two axes (x and y), one for each dimension. In a three-dimensional coordinate system, there are three axes—a fact that René Descartes well understood.

If the story about Descartes and the fly is true, then the philosopher/mathematician must have invented three-dimensional coordinate systems before he invented the two-dimensional kind. Descartes realized that the position of the fly at any instant could be measured—in theory, at least—relative to an origin somewhere in space. But it would

FIGURE 4-13
◎ ◎ ◎ ◎ ◎ ◎
Two mutually
perpendicular
lines

be necessary to use three numbers to measure the position of the fly, not two as with the position of a point on a plane, because there are three directions in which the fly can move relative to the origin. These directions are sometimes called height, width, and depth, although the terms seem arbitrary. We can refer to them as the three dimensions of space.

To plot the position of the fly, a *coordinate triple* is required. When the fly is at the origin, it is at coordinates (0,0,0). If it then buzzes off 5 units in the x direction it moves to coordinates (5,0,0). A motion of 7 units in the y direction takes the fly to coordinates (5,7,0). After a move of 2 units in the third direction—which, to stay in sequence, I'll call the z direction—the fly will wind up at coordinates (5,7,2). Of course, most flies don't zip around with such neat regard for coordinate axes. More likely, the fly went straight from coordinates (0,0,0) to coordinates (5,7,2) in a single spurt of flight, then meandered off in a different direction altogether, possibly straight into Descartes' cup of tea.

You can't draw a three-dimensional coordinate system on a sheet of paper, but you can devise such systems in your mind. And, as you'll see in Chapter 10, you can create them on the computer. In a three-dimensional coordinate system, you typically call the three axes x, y, and z. The x and y axes correspond to the x and y axes of a two-dimensional graph, whereas the z axis becomes a depth axis, running into and out of the traditional two-dimensional graph, as shown in Figure 4-14. In Chapter 10, I'll look at ways to make the axes of the three-dimensional graph correspond to directions in our real three-dimensional world.

FIGURE 4-14

ⓞ ⓞ ⓞ ⓞ ⓞ ⓞ

Three-dimensional Cartesian axes

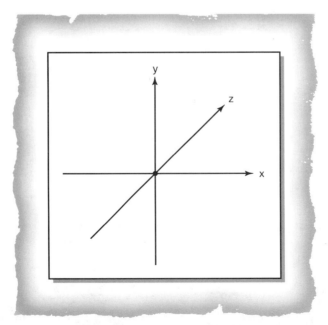

Shapes, Solids, and Coordinates

I showed earlier that you could use two-dimensional coordinates to describe geometric concepts such as points and lines. You can also use two-dimensional coordinates to describe shapes, such as triangles, squares, circles, and even arbitrary polygons (i.e., many-sided shapes). And you can use three-dimensional coordinates to describe three-dimensional solids, such as cubes, pyramids, and spheres. In fact, you needn't stop with simple shapes. You can use coordinate systems to describe just about any shape or solid that can occur in the real world, including rocks, trees, mountains, or even human beings, though some of these shapes are easier to describe than others. Because this is going to be an important topic throughout the rest of this book, let's see just how you would go about creating this kind of coordinate representation.

From describing a line with two coordinate pairs representing the line's endpoints, it takes only a little leap of imagination to extend this concept to describe any shape that can be constructed out of line segments—triangles (Figure 4-15a), squares (Figure 4-15b), even polygons of arbitrary complexity (Figure 4-15c). Any shape made out of an unbroken series of line segments can be represented as a series of *vertices*. In geometry, a vertex is a point at which two lines intersect, though I'll use the term more loosely here to include endpoints of lines as well. Because vertices are points in space, they can be described by their coordinates. Thus the square in Figure 4-16 could be

FIGURE 4-15a

◎ ◎ ◎ ◎ ◎ ◎

Coordinates for a triangle

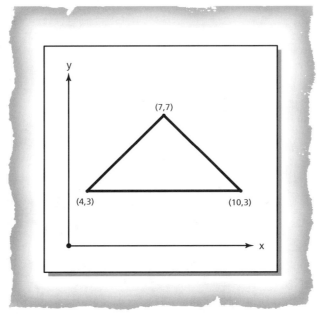

FIGURE 4-15b

◎ ◎ ◎ ◎ ◎ ◎

*Coordinates for
a square*

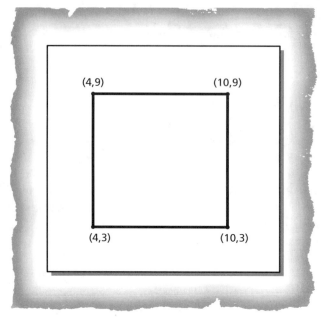

FIGURE 4-15c

◎ ◎ ◎ ◎ ◎ ◎

*An arbitrary
polygon*

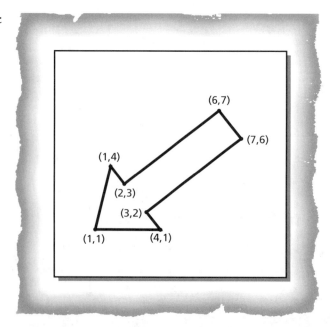

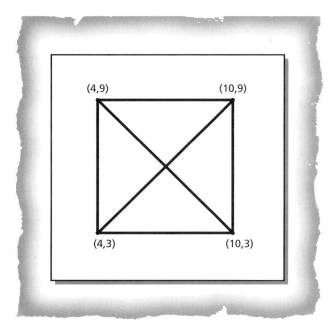

described by the coordinates of its vertices: (4,9), (4,3), (10,3), and (10,9). I'll use this scheme to describe two-dimensional shapes in Chapter 9.

   Not all shapes are made out of a continuous, unbroken series of line segments; consider the square with an X inside it shown in Figure 4-16, for instance. Although all the lines in this shape touch one another, they cannot be drawn with a continuous line. If you doubt this, try drawing this shape without lifting your pencil from the paper or retracing a previously drawn line. A more versatile system for storing shapes that would take such awkward (but quite common) cases into account would consist of two lists: a list of the coordinates of the vertices and a list of the lines that connect them. The list of vertex coordinates for Figure 4-16 would look exactly like Figure 4-15(b). The list of lines could consist simply of pointers to the entries in the vertex descriptor list, indicating which vertices in the list represent the endpoints of a given line: (0,1), (1,2), (2,3), (3,0), (0,2), and (1,3). This tells you that the first line in the shape connects vertex 0 (the first vertex in the last paragraph) with vertex 1, the second line in the shape connects vertex 1 and vertex 2, and so forth. I'll use this scheme for describing shapes in Chapter 11.

Three-Dimensional Vertices

Describing a three-dimensional shape made up of line segments is done in exactly the same manner as describing two-dimensional shapes, except that a third coordinate must be included when describing each vertex so that the vertex's location in the z dimension can be pinpointed. Although it's difficult to do this on a sheet of paper, it's easy to imagine it. Figure 4-17 shows a cube made up of line segments within a three-dimensional coordinate system.

Shapes made out of line segments aren't especially realistic, but all of these concepts can be extended to drawing more complex shapes. You might wonder, though, how something like a circle or sphere can be described as a series of vertices connected by line segments. Wouldn't the number of vertices required to describe such a shape be prohibitively large, perhaps even infinite?

Although this is true, there are two approaches you can take to describe such shapes within a coordinate system. One is to approximate the shape through relatively small line segments. How small should the line segments be? That depends on how realistic the drawing is intended to be and how much time you can spend on mathematical calculations relating to those vertices. For instance, a square can be thought of as a *very* rough approximation of a circle using 4 line segments. An octagon, which uses 8 line segments, is a better approximation of a circle (see Figure 4-18a), but a hexadecagon, with 16 line segments, is even better (Figure 4-18b). As far as realism is concerned, the more line segments the better, but there are memory and performance considerations, especially when you are storing and processing the vertex and line segment information in a computer.

FIGURE 4-17

◎ ◎ ◎ ◎ ◎ ◎

A cube in the three-dimensional coordinate system

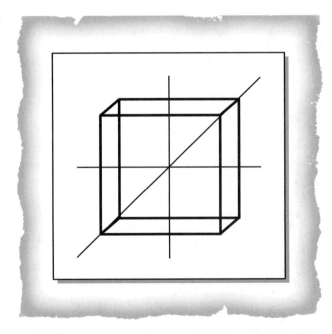

FIGURE 4-18a

◉ ◉ ◉ ◉ ◉ ◉

A circle approximated with 8 line segments

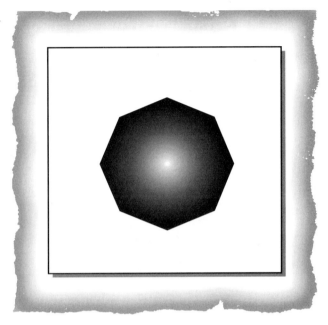

FIGURE 4-18b

◉ ◉ ◉ ◉ ◉ ◉

A circle approximated with 16 line segments

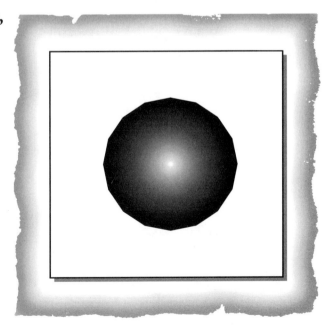

Graphing Equations

Descartes came up with an alternative method of describing shapes such as circles and spheres, one that is nicely suited to microcomputer graphics, even though Descartes developed it three-and-a-half centuries before the advent of electronic computers. Descartes realized that coordinate systems such as the one that now bears his name could be used to graph the results of algebraic equations; the resulting graphs often took on familiar (and not so familiar) geometric shapes. This means that you can also describe shapes—in theory, any shape at all—as algebraic equations. If you ever took an algebra course, you probably remember a thing or two about graphing equations (for better or for worse).

Algebra deals with equations—symbolic statements about the relationships between different values—in which certain values are unknown or variable. These equations resemble the assignment statements found in all computer programming languages, but instead of assigning a value to a variable, they assert that the value of one variable bears a certain relationship to the value of one or more other variables. The resemblance between algebraic equations and assignment statements can be confusing, both to students of algebra and to students of programming, so I'll dwell for a moment on the difference.

Here is a familiar algebraic equation:

```
x = y
```

The letters x and y represent numeric quantities of unknown value. And yet, though you do not know what the values of these numeric quantities are, you do know something important about the *relationship* between these two values. You know that they are the same. Whatever the value of y is, x has the same value, and vice versa. Thus, if y is equal to 2, then x is also equal to 2. If y is equal to 324.218, then x is equal to 324.218.

In C, on the other hand, the statement

```
x = y;
```

would be an assignment statement. It would assign the value of the variable y to the variable x. After this assignment, the algebraic equation x = y would be true, but it wouldn't necessarily be true before this assignment statement. The difference between an algebraic equation and assignment statement, then, is that the algebraic equation asserts that a relationship *is* true, whereas the assignment statement *makes* it true.

Here's another familiar algebraic equation:

```
x = 2y
```

This tells us that the value of x is two times the value of y. If y is equal to 2, then x is equal to 4. If y is equal to -14, then x is equal to -28.

Solving the Equation

Determining the value of x based on y is called *solving the equation*. Every time you solve an equation with two variables in it, you produce a pair of numbers—the value of x and the value of y. By treating these pairs of numbers as Cartesian coordinates you can depict them as points on a two-dimensional Cartesian plane, thus *graphing the equation*. The graph of the equation x = y is shown in Figure 4-19. The equation has been solved for four values of y—0, 1, 2, and 3—producing the coordinate pairs (0,0), (1,1), (2,2), and (3,3). These coordinates have been graphed and connected by lines. The lines, however, are not an arbitrary part of the graph. They represent additional solutions of the equation for noninteger (i.e., fractional) values of y as well, such as 1.2, 2.7, and 0.18. All solutions of the equation between 0 and 3 fall somewhere on this line. There's no way you could work out all of these fractional solutions because there's an infinite number of them, but the graph shows these solutions anyway as points on an infinitely divisible line.

Similarly, the equation x = 2y produces a line when it is graphed, but the line has a different angle, or slope, from the line produced in the equation x = y. (I'll talk more about the slope of the line in Chapter 9) For any straight line that you can draw on a

FIGURE 4-19
◎ ◎ ◎ ◎ ◎ ◎
A graph of the equation x = y

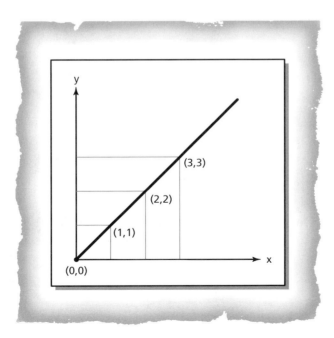

graph, there is an equation that will produce that line when graphed. That equation is called, logically enough, the *equation of the line*.

Not all equations produce straight lines, however. For the purposes of game programming, the more interesting equations are those that produce curves because curves are so difficult to represent using line segments. For some purposes, though not for all, it's more efficient to represent a curve with an equation: Solving an equation for various values can take quite a bit of time, even for a computer, so it's often faster to approximate a curve with line segments.

Fractals

One type of shape called a *fractal* is often easier to produce using equations than by storing vertices and line segments simply because of the difficulty in storing such a shape in the computer's memory. You've probably run across this term before—"fractals" has recently become a buzzword in both mathematics and computer programming.

A fractal—the term was coined by the mathematician Benoit Mandelbrot—is a shape that possesses the quality of *self-similarity*. This means that the shape is built up of smaller versions of itself; these smaller versions of the shape are in turn built up of still smaller versions of the shape.

A tree, for instance, is a kind of fractal shape. A tree is made up of branches, which resemble tiny trees. A branch in turn is made up of twigs, which resemble tiny branches. Because it possesses this self-similarity at several orders of magnification, a tree is said to be fractal.

Many other shapes found in nature are essentially fractal. A jagged shoreline, for instance, has pretty much the same quality of jaggedness whether it's viewed from a satellite orbiting 200 miles overhead, from an airplane 20,000 feet above, or by a person sitting on a hilltop overlooking the shore. The human circulatory system consists of a hierarchy of branching arteries and veins that is pretty much identical at several levels of size. A mountain has an irregular faceted appearance that resembles that of the large and small rocks that make it up. And so forth.

If you want to duplicate three-dimensional nature within the computer, it will be necessary to create fractal shapes. Why? Because fractals provide the maximum amount of realistic detail for a minimum amount of stored data. Instead of storing every vertex in every polygon in a mountain, you can store a fractal equation that will generate an infinite number of mountainlike shapes—and can do so at any level of detail. Similarly, instead of storing every twist and turn of a river or coastline, you can store a fractal equation that can generate a near infinite number of rivers and coastlines. Alternatively, you can use fractal algorithms to generate in advance shapes that would be difficult to encode by hand and then store the data generated by the algorithm in your program, just as you store the data for the other shapes you need.

Transformations

In this book, I'll represent two-dimensional and three-dimensional shapes as vertices connected by line segments. (Actually, I'll use line segments in the early chapters, then graduate to connecting vertices with colored polygons to create greater realism in later chapters.) And I'll develop routines that will draw those shapes at specific coordinate positions on the video display. If I'm going to animate these objects, however, it's not enough to create and display them. I must also be able to manipulate them, to change their position on the display, even to rotate the shapes into brand new positions. In the language of 3D graphics, I am going to *transform* the images.

One of the many advantages of being able to define a shape as a series of numbers is that you can perform mathematical operations on those numbers to your heart's content. Many generations of mathematicians and computer programmers have worked out the mathematical operations necessary for performing most of the transformations that you might wish to perform on three-dimensional objects.

You could perform quite a few such transformations, but I will concentrate on three: translating, scaling, and rotating. (Actually, when performed on three-dimensional objects, there are *five* transformations because 3D rotation consists of three separate operations, as you will see.) *Scaling* means changing the size of an object, *translating* refers to moving an object from one place to another within the coordinate system, and *rotating* refers to rotating an object around a fixed point, through a specified axis, within the coordinate system. These are operations you will perform in the programs developed in later chapters; the formulas for performing them are widely known. It's a simple matter to include these formulas in a computer program. Making the computer code based on these formulas work quickly and accurately is another matter, one that I'll talk about at greater length in later chapters. Note that in all the formulas that follow, it is assumed that the objects are represented by a list of coordinate pairs or triples representing all vertices within the object.

Translating

Translation is the easiest of these three transformations you'll undertake, and the one the microcomputer is best equipped to perform without clever optimization. It involves adding values to the coordinates of the vertices of an object. To move a two-dimensional object from its current location to another coordinate position, perform the following C operation on each vertex within the object:

```
new_x = x + tx;
new_y = y + ty;
```

where x and y are the current coordinates of the vertex, *new_x* and *new_y* are the translated coordinates, *tx* is the distance you wish to move the vertex in the x dimension, and *ty* is the distance you wish to move the vertex in the y dimension. For instance, if you wish to move a vertex by 7 coordinate positions in the x dimension and 5 coordinate positions in the y dimension, perform these operations:

```
new_x = x + 7;
new_y = y + 5;
```

By performing these operations on all of the vertices in an object, you will obtain a new set of vertices representing the translated object. You will have "moved" the object to a new location within the coordinate system. (At this point, of course, the object exists only as a set of numbers within the computer's memory and it is only the changes in these numbers that indicate the object has "moved." I'll deal with the actual details of drawing and animating the object in Chapter 9.)

Translating an object in three dimensions works the same way, except that you add a z translation value to the z coordinate to move it in the z dimension:

```
new_z = z + tz;
```

Scaling

Scaling an object is no more difficult than translating it from the programmer's point of view, though it may take the processor of a computer slightly longer to accomplish because scaling involves a multiplication operation. (Multiplication is somewhat more time consuming than addition.) To scale an object, simply multiply all of the coordinates of a vertex by a *scaling factor*. For instance, to double the size of an object, multiply every coordinate of every vertex by two. Actually, I am using the term "double" very loosely here. This operation doubles the distance between vertices, which would have the effect of quadrupling the area of a two-dimensional object and increasing the volume of a three-dimensional object by a factor of eight! To triple the size of an object, multiply every coordinate by three. To cut the size of an object in half, multiply every coordinate by 0.5. Here is a general formula for scaling the x,y coordinates of the vertex in a two-dimensional object:

```
new_x = scaling_factor * x;
new_y = scaling_factor * y;
```

For a three-dimensional object, the z coordinate of each vertex must also be scaled:

```
new_z = scaling_factor * z;
```

Rotating on X, Y, and Z

Rotation is more complex than translating and scaling because it involves the use of the *sine* and *cosine* trigonometric functions. If you're not familiar with trigonometry, don't worry. You don't need to understand how the rotation formulas work to use them. You don't even need to know how to perform the sine and cosine operations, because these functions are included with your compiler. To access them, you need only place the statement *#include <math.h>* at the beginning of your program. Alas, these functions tend to be a bit on the slow side, but they'll suffice for demonstrating three-dimensional rotations in the next several chapters. Eventually, you'll develop your own high-speed trigonometric functions.

As mentioned earlier, 3D rotation consists of three distinct operations, one for each axis. Before I discuss the rotation formulas, let's take a look at what I mean when I say you are going to rotate an object. When you hold an object in your hands—this book, for instance—you can rotate it into any position that you wish. At the moment, you are presumably holding the book open with the pages facing toward you and the text right-side-up. It would be a simple matter for you to turn the book so that the text is upside down, as in Figure 4-20a, though that would make it a bit difficult to read. Or you could turn the book so that the front and back covers are facing you instead of the pages. When you perform this latter rotation, you could do it in one of two different ways: by grabbing the sides of the book and rotating it sideways, as in Figure 4-20b, or by holding the top and bottom and rotating it head over heels, as in Figure 4-20c. Each of these rotations takes place, roughly speaking, around a point somewhere in the middle of the book, which I'll call the center of the rotation. And each of these rotations takes place around one of the three axes of a three-dimensional Cartesian coordinate system.

FIGURE 4-20a

◎ ◎ ◎ ◎ ◎ ◎

Rotating the book upside down

FIGURE 4-20b

⊙ ⊙ ⊙ ⊙ ⊙ ⊙

Rotating the book sideways

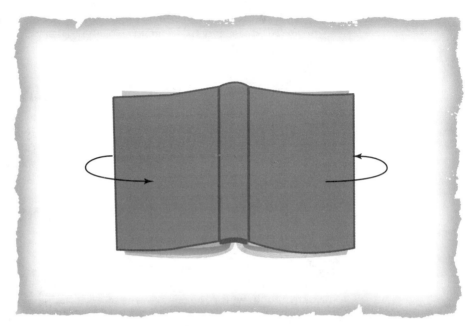

FIGURE 4-20c

⊙ ⊙ ⊙ ⊙ ⊙ ⊙

Rotating the book head over heels

The Virtual Book

To understand what the previous section means, imagine you're not holding a real book but a virtual book, made up of a series of points in a three-dimensional Cartesian coordinate system. The x axis of your virtual book's coordinate system runs horizontally across the pages, the y axis runs vertically up and down the pages, and the z axis runs straight out of the middle of the book toward the tip of your nose (see Figure 4-21). When you rotate the book so that the text turns upside down, you are rotating it around the z axis, almost as though the book were a wheel and the z axis was its axle.

Similarly, when you rotate the book head over heels, you are rotating it around the book's y axis. And when you rotate it from side to side, you are rotating it around the book's x axis. (For you pilots out there, rotation on the x axis is equivalent to pitch, rotation on the y axis is equivalent to yaw, and rotation around the z axis is equivalent to roll.)

Just as there are three ways for a line to be perpendicular to another line in a three-dimensional world, so there are three possible rotations that an object can make in three dimensions—and you've just tried them all on this book. The three rotations are known as the *x-axis rotation*, the *y-axis rotation*, and the *z-axis rotation*.

A two-dimensional shape—that is, a shape defined within a two-dimensional coordinate system—can only make one kind of rotation: z-axis rotations. Ironically, this is the only type of rotation that does *not* change the z coordinate of any of the vertices

FIGURE 4-21

◎ ◎ ◎ ◎ ◎ ◎

Axes of the virtual book

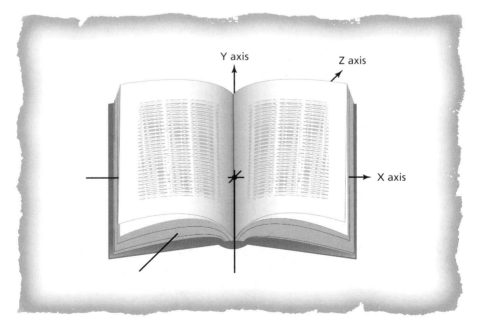

in an object. Because the z coordinate of a two-dimensional object is always zero, it cannot be changed and thus other types of rotations, which do change the z coordinate, are impossible in two dimensions.

Degrees vs. Radians

Before you can perform calculations involving the rotation of objects, you must have some way of measuring rotations. Because rotated objects move in a circular motion, the obvious unit for measuring rotations is a *degree*. Because there are 360 degrees in a circle, an object rotated through a full circle is said to have been rotated 360 degrees. When you rotated this book so that the text was upside down, you rotated it 180 degrees around the z axis. If you had stopped halfway through this motion, you would have rotated it 90 degrees around the z axis.

Mathematicians, however, do not like to use degrees as a unit of angular measure. Degrees are an arbitrary unit developed by ancient astronomers and mathematicians who were laboring under the misapprehension that the year was 360 days long. Thus, the degree was supposedly the angular distance that the earth rotated in a day (or the angular distance that the stars rotated around the earth in a day). Modern mathematicians prefer to use a unit of angular measure that actually has something to do with the mathematical properties of a circle. The unit they favor is the *radian*, which is a distance around the circumference of a circle equal to the circle's radius. Most readers will recall the relationship of a circle's diameter to its circumference is 3.14159..., better known as *pi*. Because the radius is half the diameter, there are 2pi, or roughly 6.28, radians, in the circumference of a circle. Figure 4-22 shows how the degree and radians systems can both describe a circle. When you rotate this book 360 degrees, you are rotating it 6.28 radians.

The truth is, it doesn't matter which of these units you use to measure the rotation of an object, as long as the sine and cosine routines that you are using are designed to handle that type of unit. The sine and cosine functions that are supplied with your compiler are written to handle radians, so that's the unit of measure I will use in the early chapters of this book. Later, when you design your own ways of calculating sine and cosine, I will use degrees because that was the method most of us were taught and I can represent them more precisely using integers.

Rotation Formulas

Now that you have a unit of measure for object rotations, let's look at the formulas for performing those rotations. Because you'll be constructing objects out of vertices (and the lines and polygons that connect those vertices), you'll rotate objects by rotating vertices. Because a vertex is nothing more than a point in space that can be represented by a trio of Cartesian coordinates, you'll create rotational formulas in terms of those coordinates. In effect, a rotational formula is a mathematical formula that, when

FIGURE 4-22

◎ ◎ ◎ ◎ ◎ ◎

*A full circle
consists of 360
degrees or 6.28
radians*

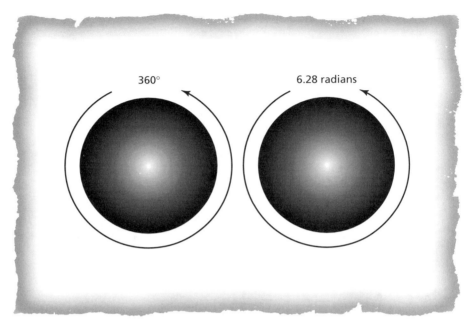

applied to the coordinates of a point in space, will tell you the new coordinates of that point after it has been rotated by a given number of degrees on one of the three axes around the origin (0,0,0).

The best known and most widely applicable of these formulas is the one that rotates vertices around the z axis because it is the only one needed for rotating two-dimensional shapes. Here is the formula for rotating the vertex of an object, or any other point, around the origin of the coordinate system on the z axis:

```
new_x = x * cos(z_angle) - y * sin(z_angle);
new_y = y * cos(z_angle) + x * sin(z_angle);
```

where x and y are the x and y coordinates of the vertex before the rotation, *z_angle* is the angle (in radians) through which you wish to rotate the object through its z axis, and *new_x* and *new_y* are the x and y coordinates of the rotated object. (The z coordinate is not changed by the rotation.) The *cos()* and *sin()* functions calculate the cosine and sine of the angle, respectively. The center of rotation for this formula is always the origin of the coordinate system, which is why I defined the origin of the rotating virtual book as the book's center, because that greatly simplifies calculating the rotation of the book using this formula (and the formulas that follow). To rotate an object around the origin of the coordinate system, you must perform these calculations on the coordinates of all the vertices that define that object.

Unlike a two-dimensional object, a three-dimensional object can also rotate on its x axis and its y axis. Here is the formula for rotating an object around the origin of the coordinate system on the x axis:

```
new_y = y * cos(x_angle) - z * sin(x_angle);
new_z = y * sin(x_angle) + z * cos(x_angle);
```

Note that the x axis is not changed by this rotation.

Here is the formula for rotating an object around the origin of the coordinate system on the y axis:

```
new_z = z * cos(y_angle) - x * sin(y_angle);
new_x = z * sin(y_angle) + x * cos(y_angle);
```

By performing all of these operations on all of the coordinates of all of the vertices of an object, you obtain a brand new set of coordinates that describes the object after it has been rotated by *x_angle* on the x axis, *y_angle* on the y axis, and *z_angle* on the z axis.

Matrix Algebra

If you have a lot of vertices in an object — or, even worse, more than one object — it's going to take a lot of calculations to scale, translate, and rotate the coordinates of all of the vertices of those objects. Because the ultimate goal is to perform all of these operations in real time while animating three-dimensional objects on the computer video display, you might wonder if there's enough time to perform all these calculations.

The existance of several games on the market that accomplish this task indicates that there must be a way. But the operations must be optimized, and there is a method of combining all five operations—scaling, translation, x rotation, y rotation, and z rotation—into one simple operation.

The key to this is matrix arithmetic, and it's not as intimidating as it may sound. Matrix arithmetic is a mathematical system for performing arithmetic operations on matrices, which are roughly equivalent to the numeric array structures offered by most programming languages. Matrix operations can be substituted for most standard mathematical operations. Usually you don't want to do this, because the matrix operations are a bit more complicated (and therefore time consuming) than standard operations. But matrix operations have one great advantage over standard operations. Several matrix operations can be *concatenated*—combined—into a single operation. Thus you can use matrix operations to reduce the five transformations into a single master transformation.

Building Matrices

Matrices are usually presented as a collection of numbers arranged in rows and columns, like this:

```
1   2   3   4
5   6   7   8
9  10  11  12
```

This particular matrix has three rows and four columns and thus is referred to as a 3x4 matrix. In C, you could store such a matrix as a 3x4 array of type *float*, like this:

```
float matrix[3][4] = {
  1, 2, 3, 4,
  5, 6, 7, 8,
  9,10,11,12
};
```

If a 3x4 array-called matrix has already been declared but not yet initialized, it can be initialized to the matrix above with this series of assignment statements:

```
matrix[0][0] = 1; matrix[0][1] = 2;
matrix[0][2] = 3; matrix[0][3] = 4;
matrix[1][0] = 5; matrix[1][1] = 6;
matrix[1][2] = 7; matrix[1][3] = 8;
matrix[2][0] = 9; matrix[2][1] = 10;
matrix[2][2] = 11; matrix[2][3] = 12;
```

The three coordinates that describe a three-dimensional vertex can be regarded as a 1x3 matrix—a matrix with one row and three columns. For instance, the coordinate triple (x,y,z) is equivalent to the 1x3 matrix.

```
x   y   z
```

A matrix with only one row or only one column has a special name. It is called a *vector*. To scale, translate, or rotate the coordinates in a vector, multiply them by a special kind of matrix called a *transformation matrix*.

Multiplying Matrices

How do you multiply a vector by a matrix? Let's take two vectors and a matrix declared in C:

```
float oldVector[1][3];
float newVector[1][3];
float matrix[3][3];
```

Now visualize the three components of *oldVector* as x, y, and z. The components of *newVector* are nx, ny, and nz and the components of *matrix* are a, b, c, d, e, f, g, h, and i, as shown in Figure 4-23.

To calculate nx (which is the representation of newVector[0][0]), use the formula.

```
nx = x * a + y * b + z * c
```

which translates into C code as:

FIGURE 4-23

ⓐ ⓐ ⓐ ⓐ ⓐ ⓐ

*A vector to be
multiplied with
a matrix*

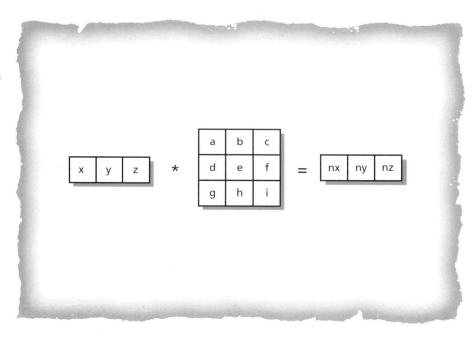

```
newVector[0][0] = oldVector[0][0] * matrix[0][0] +
                  oldVector[0][1] * matrix[0][1] +
                  oldVector[0][2] * matrix[0][2];
```

This is shown in Figure 4-24. Calculating ny is similar, except now multiply the *oldVector* components with the second row of the matrix.

FIGURE 4-24

ⓐ ⓐ ⓐ ⓐ ⓐ ⓐ

Calculating nx

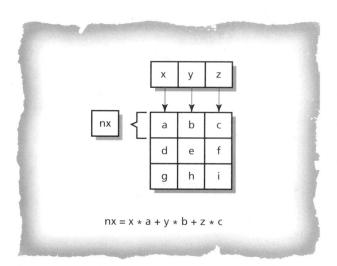

$$nx = x * a + y * b + z * c$$

```
ny = x * d + y * e + z * f
```
which in C is
```
newVector[0][1] = oldVector[0][0] * matrix[1][0] +
                  oldVector[0][1] * matrix[1][1] +
                  oldVector[0][2] * matrix[1][2];
```

This part is shown in Figure 4-25. The last portion is just the same; this time you are multiplying by the last row of the matrix (illustrated in Figure 4-26).

FIGURE 4-25
◎ ◎ ◎ ◎ ◎ ◎
Calculating ny

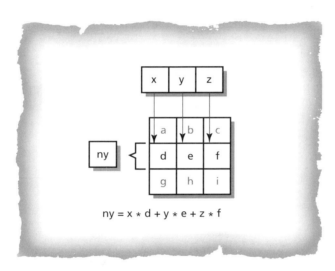

FIGURE 4-26
◎ ◎ ◎ ◎ ◎ ◎
Calculating nz

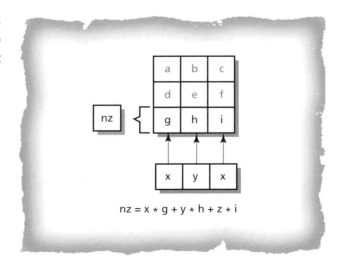

```
nz = x * g + y * h + z * i
```

which in C is

```
newVector[0][2] = oldVector[0][0] * matrix[2][0] +
                  oldVector[0][1] * matrix[2][1] +
                  oldVector[0][2] * matrix[2][2];
```

As it happens, you'll be mostly multiplying 1x4 vectors and 4x4 matrices (rather than 1x3 vectors and 3x3 matrices) in this book. Why? Because the translation matrix (the one that will actually move the object in the x, y, and z coordinates) has to be 4x4 instead of 3x3 (this is because a translation can't be accomplished through a multiplication, unlike scaling and rotation, and the extra matrix term can be used for addition). The vectors must also have four terms in order to multiply them by the larger matrix. This means you will need to add an extra element to the coordinate triples, turning them into coordinate quadruples. This extra element will always be equal to 1 and is there only to make the math come out right. Thus, when you are working with matrices, the coordinate vectors will take the form (x, y, z, 1). This fourth "coordinate" will never actually be used outside of matrix multiplication. The transformation matrices with which you will be multiplying this vector will all be 4x4 matrices. Here's a second code fragment that will multiply a 4x4 matrix called *matrix* by a 1x4 vector called *oldVector* and leave the result in a 1x4 vector called *newVector*. The only real change that has been made is that there are now four steps and one more term to multiply by.

```
newVector[0][0] = oldVector[0][0] * matrix[0][0] +
                  oldVector[0][1] * matrix[0][1] +
                  oldVector[0][2] * matrix[0][2] +
                  oldVector[0][3] * matrix[0][3];
newVector[0][1] = oldVector[0][0] * matrix[1][0] +
                  oldVector[0][1] * matrix[1][1] +
                  oldVector[0][2] * matrix[1][2] +
                  oldVector[0][3] * matrix[1][3];
newVector[0][2] = oldVector[0][0] * matrix[2][0] +
                  oldVector[0][1] * matrix[2][1] +
                  oldVector[0][2] * matrix[2][2] +
                  oldVector[0][3] * matrix[2][3];
newVector[0][3] = oldVector[0][0] * matrix[3][0] +
                  oldVector[0][1] * matrix[3][1] +
                  oldVector[0][2] * matrix[3][2] +
                  oldVector[0][3] * matrix[3][3];
```

Now let's take a look at the transformation matrices that can be used to translate, scale, and rotate a set of coordinates. When the following 4x4 matrix is multiplied by a 1x4 coordinate vector, the product vector is equivalent to the coordinate vector scaled by a scaling factor of sf.

```
sf  0   0   0
0   sf  0   0
0   0   sf  0
0   0   0   1
```

This is called a *scaling matrix*. If you want to get even fancier, you can scale by a different factor along each of the x, y, and z axes, using this matrix:

```
sx  0   0   0
0   sy  0   0
0   0   sz  0
0   0   0   1
```

where sx scales along the x axis, sy scales along the y axis, and sz scales along the z axis. Thus, if we wish to make an object twice as tall but no larger in the other dimensions, we would set the sy factor to 2 and the sx and sz factors to 1.

You can also perform translation with matrices. The following matrix will move a coordinate vector by the translation factors of tx, ty, and tz:

```
1   0   0   0
0   1   0   0
0   0   1   0
tx  ty  tz  1
```

This is called a *translation matrix*.

Three Kinds of Rotation Matrices

You can perform all three kinds of rotation with matrices. The following matrix will rotate a coordinate vector by za degrees on the z axis:

```
cos(za)   sin(za)  0        0
-sin(za)  cos(za)  0        0
0         0        1        0
0         0        0        1
```

The following matrix will rotate a coordinate vector by xa degrees on the x axis:

```
1         0         0         0
0         cos(xa)   sin(xa)   0
0         -sin(xa)  cos(xa)   0
0         0         0         1
```

The following matrix will rotate a coordinate vector by ya degrees on the y axis:

```
cos(ya)   0         -sin(ya)  0
0         1         0         0
sin(ya)   0         cos(ya)   0
0         0         0         1
```

When you want to perform several of these transformations on the vertices of one or more objects, you can initialize all of the necessary matrices, multiply the matrices together (i.e., concatenate them), and then multiply the master concatenated matrix by each vertex in the object or objects.

Multiplying two matrices together is a bit more difficult than multiplying a vector and a matrix. Basically, you take the first matrix and break it into four vectors by separating out each column. Then multiply each of these vectors with the second matrix, resulting in four new vectors. The first vector forms the first column, the second vector forms the second column, and so on to create the new matrix. Here is a code fragment that will do this:

```
for (int i = 0; i < 4; i++)
  for (int j = 0; j < 4; j++) {
    newmatrix[i][j] = 0;
    for (k = 0; k < 4; k++)
      newmatrix[i][j] += matrix1[k][j] * matrix2[i][k];
  }
```

In addition to the transformations given above, there is one more special matrix. This is a matrix that, when multiplied by another matrix, will leave that matrix unchanged. This matrix is called the *identity matrix*, and it looks like this:

```
1   0   0   0
0   1   0   0
0   0   1   0
0   0   0   1
```

You'll learn more about the uses of the identity matrix when you start incorporating matrices in games.

Floating-Point Math

Before I leave this discussion of useful mathematics, let's look at how the computer handles math operations. As you're probably aware, the C language (and the Macintosh extensions of the C language) offers several numeric data types. For your purposes, the most important of these are the *short* type and the *float* type. Numeric data declared as *short* consists of whole numbers in the range of -32768 to 32767. Numeric data declared as *float*, which is short for floating point, includes fractional numbers as well as integers, and in a much greater range. You can also define short as type *unsigned short*, which gives a range of numbers from 0 to 65536 and use *double* in place of float, giving more precision.

The mathematical operations performed in three-dimensional animation programs usually require floating-point data types because they use fractional values. The functions that C uses to perform mathematical operations on floating-point data can be quite slow, however, on machines that don't have a math coprocessor (the PowerPC has a math coprocessor built into the chip). Nonetheless, by way of illustration, I'll use the float data type in many of the early programs that demonstrate three-dimensional transformations and animation, because it is the easiest solution for now. In later chapters, I will investigate some methods for increasing the speed.

In this chapter, I've covered almost all of the mathematics operations you'll need for 2D and 3D graphics, including coordinates, bitmaps, and transformations. In the next chapter, I'll dive into one form of graphics you'll be using for games called *sprites*.

Sprite Animation

come trovle fare le manovelle e le quali provabano li alçe
e grave pesi intorne le maniera a gene so fagograno di bone
organi nellamo defa per manovella aefa manovella pergi quin
aforça e pie stomo pribibot.

5

Sprite Animation

If you know how motion pictures work, then you already understand the basic principles of computer animation. Figure 5-1 illustrates a strip of motion picture film that consists of a series of frames, each containing a small picture. When these still pictures are projected on a white screen in a series, they give the impression of motion.

But where did this motion come from? There's obviously no motion in the still frames that make up the strip of film. Yet somehow we perceive motion when we see these same frames projected on a screen. The motion, in fact, is in our minds. Each of the still pictures on the strip of motion picture film is slightly different from the previous one. When the strip is projected on a screen our minds interpret these differences as continuous motion, when in fact what we are seeing is a sequence of still pictures.

For instance, the film in Figure 5-1 shows a figure walking from left to right across the frame. In the first frame, the figure is near the left edge of the frame. In the second, it is nearing the center, and in the fourth, it is at the right.

If we were to view this film on a projection screen, it would appear that the figure was gliding smoothly from one side of the screen to the other, whereas the figure is in fact moving across the screen in discrete jumps. Our minds, which expect to see continuous movement, fill in the blanks in the sequence. We see motion where no motion actually exists.

FIGURE 5-1

◎ ◎ ◎ ◎ ◎ ◎

A strip of motion picture film depicting a person walking left to right

Motion Pictures for the Computer Screen

You have already drawn motionless bitmaps on the screen using the PICT Viewer application you built in Chapter 3. In this chapter, you will learn how to make those static images move.

Just like on a movie projection screen, computer animation is produced on a frame-by-frame basis. We draw a series of slightly changing images in rapid succession to show that something is moving on the screen.

If you've ever played with a home video game system such as Sega or Nintendo, you will notice that, besides the scrolling of the background, most of the motion on the screen is limited to small bitmap images known as *sprites*. A sprite can consist of several different images that are used when animating that object. For example, in Sega's Sonic the Hedgehog, the main character can be seen running, jumping, rolling, and getting zapped by mutants. Each of these actions requires several bitmap images, all of which are stored as one sprite.

Even though the older home video game systems are several times less powerful than a Macintosh, you would find it difficult to create the same speed of a sprite-based game like Sonic on even a 68040 Macintosh. This is because video game systems use dedicated graphics chips that give them blazing performance for sprites with little effort from the CPU. These chips, however, only provide the speed enhancement for sprite-based games, which is why you won't see a game like F/A-18 Hornet on a 16-bit game console. Newer games systems, such as 3DO, have processing power comparable to the newer Macintoshes, so this situation will most likely change.

Even though the Macintosh does not have the dedicated hardware for sprites, it is possible to create a game that uses sprites on a Macintosh. Many popular shareware games use sprite technology to create a fast, smooth arcade experience, such as the classic Maelstrom from Ambrosia Software (shown in Figure 5-2). In this chapter, you'll be creating several routines to create and draw sprites. You'll then use these routines to build a sprite animation of a man walking across the screen.

FIGURE 5-2

◉ ◉ ◉ ◉ ◉ ◉

The popular shareware game Maelstrom from Ambrosia software

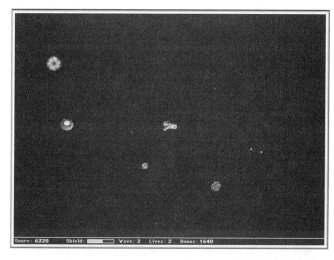

Bitmaps in Motion

At its most basic level, a sprite is a rectangular bitmap image, just like the PICT images that the PICT Viewer program used. A sprite bitmap is generally quite small. As you can see from a game like Sonic the Hedgehog, each sprite takes up a very small portion of the screen. The reason for this is that the larger the sprite, the longer it takes to animate it, so a program that has many large sprites will be significantly slower than one with small sprites.

In this chapter, you will be using medium-sized sprites (relatively speaking). The walking man image is 90x60 pixels and uses the standard 256-color system palette. Figure 5-3 shows an example of one of these images. This image is part of a sequence of images composing the sprite, which are all stored together in one PICT resource.

Of course, the image that you see in Figure 5-3 is represented in the computer's memory as a bitmap. As with any 8-bit bitmap, each pixel is represented by a single byte corresponding to an entry in a color table. This particular image is arranged in a rectangle that is 60 pixels wide and 90 pixels tall. Thus the bitmap for this image consists of 60x90 or 5,400 bytes.

A moment ago, I said that animation is a matter of putting a sequence of images on the screen and changing each image in such a way that they seem to move. You don't have to change the whole image for each frame of the animation, just the part or parts that move. With sprite animation, the part that moves is usually just the sprite. So only the sprite itself has to change from frame to frame. The easiest way to animate a sprite is to draw the sprite in one position, leave it there for a fraction of a second, then erase

it, and draw it in a new location. By doing this repeatedly, the sprite will seem to move across the screen.

Erasing the sprite is the tricky part. Usually, you will want to animate the sprite against a detailed background and you must be careful not to erase the background along with the sprite. Unfortunately, the background is obliterated by the actual act of drawing the sprite onto the screen. The trick is to keep a copy of the entire background in memory and then when you want to erase the sprite, just copy that portion of the background onto the screen. Thus the background stays whole and the sprite disappears.

Graphical Worlds

When you use QuickDraw to draw a picture or a shape, you must first tell it which port you want to draw to, using SetPort(). Up to now, the port that we've been using corresponds to a window on the screen. Thus when the shape or picture is drawn, it shows up on the display. However, you don't always want to draw directly on the screen. It may seem strange to draw an image that doesn't show up on the display, but it is very useful for games. In this case, it is useful because you need to have a copy of the entire background image in memory so you can properly erase the sprite. This image is called an *offscreen bitmap*.

To facilitate the use of offscreen bitmaps, the Macintosh has a structure called a GWorld. A GWorld encapsulates everything that is necessary for creating, maintaining, and disposing of an offscreen bitmap (although a GWorld could also be used onscreen). The bitmap is rectangular and can be of any size up to 4096 pixels square, provided enough memory is available. A GWorld is created by calling NewGWorld().

```
OSErr  NewGWorld(  GWorldPtr       *offscreenGWorld,
                   short           pixelDepth,
                   Rect            *bounds,
                   CTabHandle      colorTable,
                   GDHandle        aGDevice,
                   unsigned long   flags );
```

The *offscreenGWorld* parameter receives the new GWorld when it is allocated.

The *pixelDepth* parameter is the color depth for the new offscreen. For games, 8-bit is the most common mode, but you can also use 1-bit (for black and white), 2-bit (4 colors), 4-bit (16 colors), 16-bit (thousands of colors), or 24-bit (millions of colors).

The *bounds* parameter defines the size of the new GWorld. Usually, a GWorld will have the top, left coordinates at 0,0, but this is not necessary. You must be careful when creating large GWorlds, as they use up memory quickly.

The *colorTable* parameter is used if you want to use a different color table. If you want to use the system's color table, just pass in Null for this parameter.

The *aGDevice* parameter is used only if you have a particular graphics device you want to use for the GWorld, such as a monitor or a printer. You almost always use Null for this parameter as well.

The *flags* parameter is used if you want to give the GWorld some special characteristics, such as using the system heap for its memory or allowing it to be disposed of if the application runs out of memory. Because you don't need any of these features, pass a 0 for this parameter.

NewGWorld() will return an OSErr value. It is very important to check this value to ensure that the allocation was successful. Because GWorlds are commonly very large, there is a fair chance that a call to NewGWorld() will fail because there isn't enough memory available.

Creating the Offscreen Image

Once the GWorld is allocated, it is a relatively simple matter to draw an image into it.

1. Obtain a handle to the offscreen bitmap from the GWorld (called a PixMapHandle).

2. Lock that bitmap.

3. Set the port to the GWorld.

4. Use QuickDraw commands to draw into the GWorld.

5. Set the port back to the screen.

6. Unlock the bitmap.

Let's look at these steps more closely.

Obtaining the PixMapHandle

The GWorld structure holds a PixMapHandle, which is a handle to the PixMap structure discussed in Chapter 4. There are basically two ways to obtain the PixMapHandle from the GWorld. The first method is to reference the PixMap field directly from the GWorld, like this:

```
PixMapHandle    myPixMap;
myPixMap = myGWorld->portPixMap;
```

The second method is to call a routine named GetGWorldPixMap() like this:

```
PixMapHandle    GetGWorldPixMap(GWorldPtr offscreenGWorld);
```

All you need to do is pass it your GWorld and it will return the GWorld's PixMapHandle.

The first method will not work on any machine that does not have Color QuickDraw installed, which essentially means any 68000 Macintosh (Plus, SE, Powerbook 100). Any Macintosh that has a 68020 or better processor will handle this method just fine (including the black-and-white Macintoshes, such as the Powerbook 150).

To ensure compatibility, Apple created the Toolbox routine GetGWorldPixMap(). This routine was intended to function on any Macintosh, color or not. Unfortunately, in many versions of QuickDraw, this routine doesn't work due to a bug in the system software. The bug was fixed with 32-bit QuickDraw version 1.3 (which is installed internally with System 7).

So you're left with a small problem. Either you can reference the field directly, which will fail on some older Macintoshes, or you can call GetGWorldPixMap(), which will fail on the older System versions. If you design your game to only run under System 7, you're probably safer with the second method, GetGWorldPixMap(). However, if your game will only run on color Macintoshes, the first method is preferable. If your game will use both restrictions, the GetGWorldPixMap() method is probably best, and because the code I'm using in this book is restricted to newer System 7 Macintoshes, that's the method I'll use.

Locking the PixMapHandle

The offscreen image for the GWorld is stored in a handle. It would be disastrous if the Memory Manager shifted the location of the handle while QuickDraw is drawing into the offscreen bitmap—the QuickDraw routines wouldn't know that the PixMap had moved and would begin to trash memory. To prevent this from happening, call LockPixels().

```
Boolean  LockPixels(PixMapHandle pm);
```

LockPixels() will return a Boolean value indicating whether or not it was successful. Unless you are allowing QuickDraw to dispose of the GWorld when there isn't enough memory (by using the *flags* parameter of NewGWorld), LockPixels() won't fail.

Setting the Port to the GWorld

Changing the current port to the GWorld is very similar to using SetPort() before you draw into a window, but it is done using a routine called SetGWorld(). SetGWorld() takes one more parameter, a Graphic Device Handle, or GDHandle.

```
void SetGWorld(CGrafPtr port, GDHandle gdh);
```

Pass in the GWorldPtr of your offscreen bitmaps for the *port* parameter—a GWorldPtr is the same as a CGrafPtr (i.e., a port) as far as QuickDraw is concerned.

A graphic device is QuickDraw's representation of a monitor, a printer, or an offscreen buffer. When you call NewGWorld(), a new device is automatically created. This device is held within the GWorldPtr, so it is unnecessary to pass it in separately to the routine. However, it is necessary to use it when changing the port back to the monitor. So how do you obtain the monitor's device handle? The answer is to call GetGWorld() before calling SetGWorld().

```
void GetGWorld(CGrafPtr *port, GDHandle *gdh);
```

GetGWorld() will give you the exact parameters you're going to need to set the port back to the screen. Call it before you use SetGWorld(); then when you're done with the GWorld, you will already have the original settings, to which you can return.

Drawing into the GWorld

From this point until you return the port to its original settings, any QuickDraw command you use will affect the GWorld instead of the screen. You can also use the QuickDraw calls to change the pen size, change the pen color, or any other similar operation. If you use QuickDraw to draw a shape outside of the GWorld's boundary (which was defined by *bounds* when you called NewGWorld()), the drawing will be clipped to the boundary of the GWorld.

Returning the Port to the Screen

This step involves calling SetGWorld() with the values you received when you called GetGWorld() earlier, which returns QuickDraw to the state it was in previous to using the GWorld.

Unlocking the PixMapHandle

When finished using the GWorld, unlock the PixMapHandle again to allow the Memory Manager to operate more efficiently. This is done with a simple call to UnlockPixels().

```
void UnlockPixels(PixMapHandle pm);
```

Showing the Offscreen Bitmap

At this point, you have a bitmapped image in memory. It is now possible to transfer all or a portion of the image into another GWorld or to the screen through the use of the toolbox routine CopyBits(). CopyBits() is perhaps the most complex and powerful routine in the toolbox, yet it is easy to use. To gain maximum performance, however, a knowledge of its operation is required. I will examine optimizing the use of CopyBits() in Chapter 12.

In its most basic form, CopyBits() is designed for copying bitmap images from one location to another. Depending on the conditions of the source and destination bitmaps, however, CopyBits() can do several things while it is copying. Here is a partial list:

➤ Scale the image.

➤ Change the color depth of the image (e.g., from 8-bit to 4-bit or 4-bit to 8-bit).

➤ Copy a nonrectangular portion of the image.

➤ Make the white areas of the image transparent.

➤ Blend two images together.

Of these features, you will be using only one—making the white areas of the image transparent. Here is the prototype for CopyBits():

```
void    CopyBits(  BitMap      *srcImage,
                   BitMap      *destImage,
                   Rect        *srcRect,
                   Rect        *destRect,
                   short       transferMode,
                   RgnHandle   maskRegion  );
```

The *srcImage* and *destImage* parameters are both pointers to bitmaps. Because the PixMapHandle type you are already familiar with is a handle, you can dereference it to obtain a PixMapPtr. Typecast the PixMapPtr to a Bitmap* (i.e., a BitMapPtr) before sending it to CopyBits(). CopyBits() is intelligent enough to recognize that it received a pointer to a PixMap instead of a BitMap. You can use a window on the screen for the *destImage* parameter by passing it a pointer to the window's *portBits* field, such as &myWindow–>portBits. You'll see examples of this later.

srcRect is the portion of the source image you want to copy. It can be the entire size of the source image or just a portion. *destRect* is the area of the destination bitmap you want to copy the source image into. If *srcRect* and *destRect* are not the same size, CopyBits will scale the source image to fit. This scaling is handy, but the quality has been sacrificed to make it faster. Still, it is adequate for most game purposes.

transferMode indicates to CopyBits() how the source image should be combined with the destination. Table 5-1 shows some of the modes that can be used with CopyBits(). The full list can be found in *Inside Macintosh: Imaging* from Apple Computer (Addison-Wesley, 1991).

The ditherCopy mode can be combined with any of the others by adding them together, but otherwise use just one of these constants. The only ones you will be using in this chapter are srcOr (which is the fastest mode) and transparent (so the sprite doesn't have a white box around it is when placed over the background).

The last parameter, *maskRegion,* is used for copying a nonrectangular portion of the source image. You can ignore this parameter for now because I won't be using it in this book (CopyBits() is significantly slower when using a mask region).

Transfer Mode	Effect
srcCopy	Overwrites the background entirely
srcOr	Overwrites where the source image is black
srcXor	Inverts where source is black
srcBic	Changes destination to white where the source is black
notSrcCopy	Inverts source, then transfers with srcCopy
notSrcOr	Inverts source, then transfers with srcOr
notSrcXor	Inverts source, then transfers with srcXor
notSrcBic	Inverts source, then transfers with srcBic
blend	Blends the source and destination together
transparent	Overwrites the background, except where the source is white
ditherCopy	Dithers the source image if copying into a bitmap with fewer colors

TABLE 5-1 ◈ *CopyBits() modes*

Just like when drawing into a GWorld, if you are copying to or from a GWorld, the GWorld's PixMapHandle must be locked by using LockPixels(). Once the copy is completed, the PixMapHandle may be unlocked again.

When you are through using the GWorld, a simple call to DisposeGWorld() will free up the memory it uses.

```
void DisposeGWorld(GWorldPtr offscreenGWorld);
```

The GWorld's PixMapHandle should be unlocked before calling DisposeGWorld().

The Walking Sprites

The sprite bitmaps we are creating are all stored together in one image. This image is placed into a GWorld and is connected to the sprite structure. All of the left-walking bitmaps are placed into the first row, the right-walking bitmaps are in the second row, and the bitmap for standing still is in the third row, as shown in Figure 5-4.

Every time the program draws a sprite, it uses an index value to determine which image in the series is appropriate to draw. It then increments the index, indicating that the next image in the series should be drawn next. After it has drawn all of the images in the current sequence, it starts again with the first.

With the sprite images and the background in their separate GWorlds (see Figure 5-5), you can use them for some simple animation. When the application starts up, a window is created that is the same size as the background image. The entire window is then filled with the background. Using the transparent mode of CopyBits, the

FIGURE 5-4

◎ ◎ ◎ ◎ ◎ ◎

The Walking Man animation strip

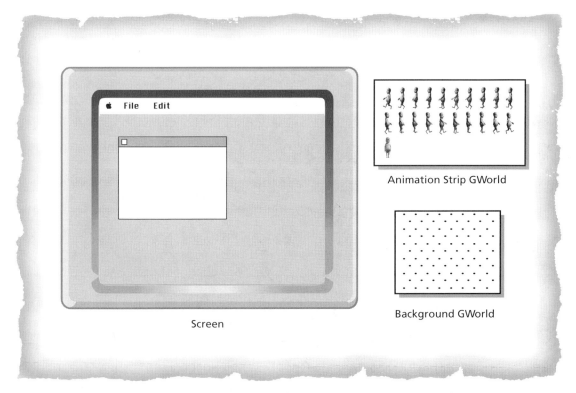

FIGURE 5-5 ◎ *The offscreen buffers for the sprite images and the background*

sprite can then be drawn onto the background. When the sprite moves, the location the sprite used to occupy is copied over by the background (which effectively erases the sprite) and the sprite is drawn into its new location. This provides the animation that you want, but there is a problem. There is a fraction of a second between the time that the sprite is erased and it is drawn again. This delay is long enough to cause a phenomenon called *flickering* that it is very distracting for the user. To alleviate this problem, you are going to use a third GWorld. This buffer will be large enough to encompass where the sprite was for the last frame and where it will be for this frame. The buffer is painted over using the background image, and then the sprite is drawn onto it. When the buffer is copied to the screen, it replaces the old sprite and draws the new one at the same time, giving a smooth transition.

This sequence is seen in Figures 5-6a through 5-6f. In Figure 5-6a, you see the sprite on the screen that needs updating. A rectangle is calculated that holds both the current position of the sprite and the new position (Figure 5-6b). A temporary GWorld of the same size is created (Figure 5-6c). The background image is copied into the temporary GWorld (Figure 5-6d), then the next sprite is copied into the GWorld (Figure 5-6e). The temporary GWorld is then copied onto the screen (Figure 5-6f).

During the animation, a new GWorld is being created and disposed of for every frame. If you were attempting to optimize the program to gain the best performance, this method would need to be improved. However, because this is such a simple animation, you can get good frame rates despite the less-than-optimal methods.

FIGURE 5-6a
◉ ◉ ◉ ◉ ◉ ◉
The old sprite in the window

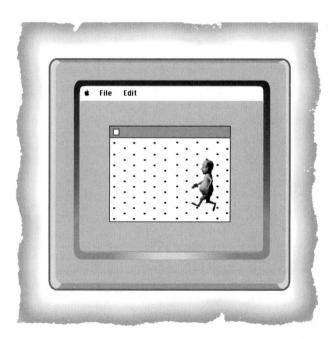

FIGURE 5-6b

◎ ◎ ◎ ◎ ◎ ◎

A bounding box is calculated

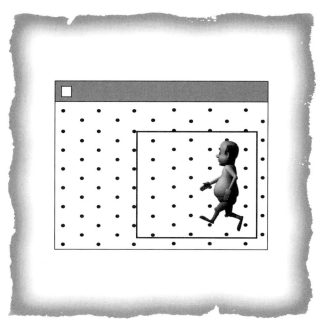

FIGURE 5-6c

◎ ◎ ◎ ◎ ◎ ◎

A temporary GWorld is created using the bounding box for the size

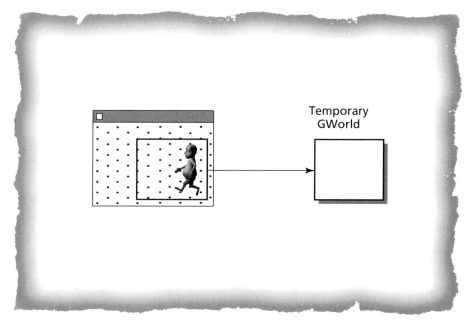

FIGURE 5-6d

◉ ◉ ◉ ◉ ◉ ◉

The temporary GWorld is filled with the background image

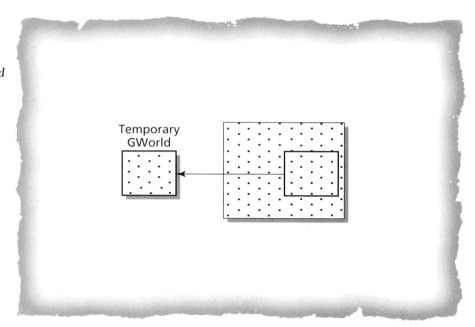

FIGURE 5-6e

◉ ◉ ◉ ◉ ◉ ◉

The next sprite is copied from the animation strip into the temporary GWorld

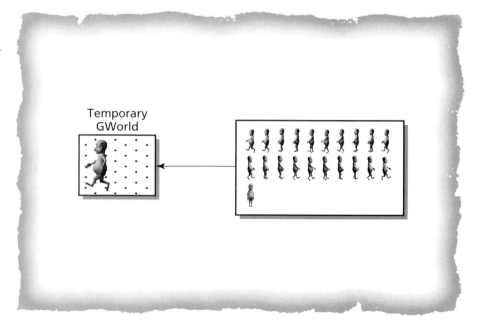

FIGURE 5-6f

ⓐ ⓐ ⓐ ⓐ ⓐ ⓐ

*The temporary
GWorld is
copied to the
screen,
completing
the process*

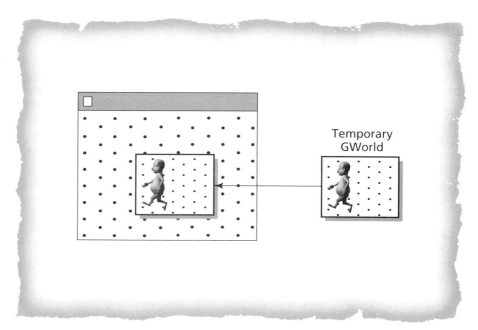

A Structure for Sprites

You now have enough information to create a structure for your sprites. This sprite structure holds almost all of the information pertaining to the sprite, such as the GWorld
containing the sprite images, the number of sprite images, and the position and size
of each sprite. You need to define three constants for the sprite's actions. These constants are used to determine whether the sprite is moving left or right or standing still.
These constants and structures can be found in Sprites.h on the source code disc in the
Chapter 5 folder.

```
enum {
  kSpriteWalkingLeft,
  kSpriteStandingStill,
  kSpriteWalkingRight
};

typedef struct {
  short      movingLeftImages;
  short      movingRightImages;
  short      staticImages;

  short      spriteAction;
```

Continued on next page

Continued from previous page

```
/* spriteAction is one of kSpriteWalkingLeft, kSpriteWalkingRight,
 * or kSpriteStandingStill.
 */
short      currentImageIndex;
/* currentImageIndex is the index of the last sprite
 * image shown.
 */

GWorldPtr  spriteSequenceImage;

short      width, height;
/* width and height are the size of the sprite */
short      x, y;
/* x and y  are the current screen coordinates */
/* of the sprite */
} Sprite, *SpritePtr;
```

Sprite Manipulation

You now need some routines for manipulating the sprites. All of the routines you're about to look at can be found on the source code disc in the file named Sprite Utilities.c.

Initializing a New Sprite

The first routine (Listing 5-1) in Sprite Utilities.c is one that will initialize a new sprite, load the appropriate animation strip, put it in a new GWorld, and fill out the new sprite's fields. This routine takes advantage of the GWorld routines discussed in this chapter.

Listing 5-1 *Initializing a new sprite*

```
OSErr  NewSprite( Sprite     *sprite,
                  short      width,
                  short      height,
                  short      numOfMovingLeftImages,
                  short      numOfMovingRightImages,
                  short      numOfStaticImages,
                  short      imageResID  )
{
  GWorldPtr    newOffscreenBuffer;
  Rect         bounds;
  OSErr        err;
  GDHandle     saveDevice;
  CGrafPtr     savePort;
  PicHandle    spritePict;
  short        imageWidth, imageHeight;

  /* Load the sprite's image sequence from the resource fork */
  spritePict = GetPicture(imageResID);

  /* Check for an error */
```

```
      if (spritePict == NULL) {
        err = ResError();
        /* ResError() returns the current resource error */
        return err;
      }

      /* Get the bounds for the sprite's image sequence. */
      bounds = (**spritePict).picFrame;

      /* The image has to be at least as wide as each sprite image's
       * width times the number of sprites for each sequence.
       */
      imageWidth = bounds.right - bounds.left;
      if ((imageWidth < width * numOfMovingLeftImages) ||
          (imageWidth < width * numOfMovingRightImages) ||
          (imageWidth < width * numOfStaticImages))
      {
        /* If the image isn't big enough, something went wrong.
         * Return a generic error.
         */
        return -1;
      }


      /* The image's height must be at least as large as the
       * individual sprite's images * 3 (since there are 3
       * rows of sprites in the offscreen for walking left,
       * right, and standing still).
       */
      imageHeight = bounds.bottom - bounds.top;
      if (imageHeight < height * 3) {
        return -1;
      }



      err = NewGWorld( &newOffscreenBuffer,
                  8,     /* we use an 8-bit palette (256 colors) */
                  &bounds,
                  NULL,  /* use the system color table for now */
                  NULL,  /* no GDevice */
                  0 );   /* no special flags */

    /* check for an error */
    if (err == noErr) {
     /* We now want to draw the image sequence into the offscreen gworld */

      /* Get the current port and device and save them */
      GetGWorld(&savePort, &saveDevice);

      /* Set the port to the offscreen gworld */
      SetGWorld(newOffscreenBuffer, NULL);

      /* Now our quickdraw commands will work on the offscreen buffer. */
```

Continued on next page

Continued from previous page

```
        DrawPicture(spritePict, &bounds);

        /* And set the port back to the screen */
        SetGWorld(savePort, saveDevice);

        /* We can now release the PICT resource */
        ReleaseResource((Handle)spritePict);

        /* Fill out the structure for the sprite */
        sprite->movingLeftImages = numOfMovingLeftImages;
        sprite->movingRightImages = numOfMovingRightImages;
        sprite->staticImages = numOfStaticImages;

        /* The sprite starts out standing still. */
        sprite->spriteAction = kSpriteStandingStill;
        sprite->currentImageIndex = 0;

        sprite->spriteSequenceImage = newOffscreenBuffer;
        sprite->width = width;
        sprite->height = height;
        sprite->x = 0;
        sprite->y = 0;
    }

    /* We're all done. If there was an error, return the proper code.
     */

    return err;
}
```

Moving the Sprite

MoveSpriteTo() and OffsetSprite() change the position of the sprite. These routines do
not, however, redraw the sprite.

```
/**
 **   MoveSpriteTo()
 **
 **   Places the sprite at a particular x,y position. Does not draw the
 **   sprite.
 **/
void  MoveSpriteTo(SpritePtr  sprite, short x, short y)
{
    sprite->x = x;
    sprite->y = y;
}


/**
 **   OffsetSprite()
 **
 **   Offsets the relative sprite location by the coordinates given.
```

```
**   Does not draw the sprite.
**/
void  OffsetSprite(SpritePtr  sprite, short xOffset, short yOffset)
{
  sprite->x = sprite->x + xOffset;
  sprite->y = sprite->y + yOffset;
}
```

Drawing the Sprite on the Screen

The next routine, DrawSpriteToWindow(), copies the sprite directly to the screen. Although you don't use this routine when animating the sprite, it is useful if you need to redraw the window from scratch or for drawing the sprite when the program first starts up. This routine (Listing 5-2) tests to make sure that the sprite is in the window—if it isn't, it doesn't bother to draw it.

Listing 5-2 *The DrawSpriteToWindow( ) routine*

```
/**
**   DrawSpriteToWindow()
**
**   Draws the sprite on the window provided using its own internal
**   position.
**/
void  DrawSpriteToWindow(SpritePtr  sprite, WindowPtr  dstWindow)
{
  GWorldPtr       spriteGWorld;
  PixMapHandle    srcPixmap;
  Rect            spriteRect;
  Rect            srcRect, dstRect;
  Rect            windowRect;
  short           xImagePos, yImagePos;

  /* Extract some of the essential information from the input structures
*/
  spriteGWorld = sprite->spriteSequenceImage;
  srcPixmap = GetGWorldPixMap(spriteGWorld);
  windowRect = dstWindow->portRect;

  /* It is OK if the sprite is partially
   * off the window. However, if the sprite is entirely off the
   * window, we don't bother copying it, so we can save time. We don't
   * return an error for this condition, since it's no big deal...
   */
  dstRect.left = sprite->x;
  dstRect.top = sprite->y;
  dstRect.right = sprite->x + sprite->width;
  dstRect.bottom = sprite->y + sprite->height;

  if ((dstRect.left > windowRect.right) ||
    (dstRect.right < windowRect.left) ||
```

Continued on next page

Continued from previous page

```
    (dstRect.top > windowRect.bottom) ||
    (dstRect.bottom < windowRect.top))
  {
    /* In this case, the sprite is entirely off the window. Just
     * drop out of this routine without doing anything.
     */
    return;
  }

  /* Now calculate where on the sprite's animation sequence
   * image the proper sprite lies...
   */

  /* Calculate which row the image is in based on the sprite's action */
  if (sprite->spriteAction == kSpriteWalkingLeft)
    yImagePos = 0;
  else if (sprite->spriteAction == kSpriteWalkingRight)
    yImagePos = 1;
  else if (sprite->spriteAction == kSpriteStandingStill)
    yImagePos = 2;

  /* Now calculate which image along that row to take */
  xImagePos = sprite->currentImageIndex;

  /* Fill out the rectangle based on these positions */
  srcRect.left = xImagePos * sprite->width;
  srcRect.right = (xImagePos + 1) * sprite->width;
  srcRect.top =  yImagePos * sprite->height;
  srcRect.bottom = (yImagePos + 1) * sprite->height;

  /* Prepare to do the copy */

  LockPixels(srcPixmap);

  SetPort(dstWindow);

  /* Perform the copy */
  CopyBits( (BitMap *)*srcPixmap,
            (BitMap *)&dstWindow->portBits,
            &srcRect,
            &dstRect,
            transparent,
            NULL );

  /* Unlock the pixmap */
  UnlockPixels(srcPixmap);
}
```

Drawing the Sprite on a GWorld

The last routine (Listing 5-3) in SpriteUtilities.c is DrawSpriteToOffscreen(). This routine is used to draw the sprite onto the temporary GWorld before it is drawn on the screen. It is very similar to DrawSpriteToWindow. The main differences to note are that both the source and destination PixMapHandles must be locked down before CopyBits() is called and you use SetGWorld() to set the port to the destination GWorld and back to the screen. Also notice that GetGWorld() is called beforehand to remember the current port settings.

Listing 5-3 *The DrawSpriteToOffscreen() routine*

```
/**
**    DrawSpriteToOffscreen()
**
**    Draws the sprite on the image provided using its own internal
**    position. This routine will only work for drawing to an offscreen
**    gworld.
**/
void  DrawSpriteToOffscreen(SpritePtr  sprite, GWorldPtr  offscreenImage)
{
  GWorldPtr     spriteGWorld;
  PixMapHandle  srcPixmap;
  PixMapHandle  dstPixmap;
  Rect          srcRect;
  Rect          dstRect;
  Rect          offscreenImageBounds;
  GDHandle      saveDevice;
  CGrafPtr      savePort;
  short         xImagePos, yImagePos;

  /* Extract some of the essential information from the input structures
*/
  spriteGWorld = sprite->spriteSequenceImage;
  srcPixmap = GetGWorldPixMap(spriteGWorld);
  dstPixmap = GetGWorldPixMap(offscreenImage);
  offscreenImageBounds = (**dstPixmap).bounds;

  /* It is OK if the sprite is partially
   * off the window. However, if the sprite is entirely off the
   * window, we don't bother copying it, so we can save time. We don't
   * return an error for this condition, since it's no big deal...
   */
  dstRect.left = sprite->x;
  dstRect.top = sprite->y;
  dstRect.right = sprite->x + sprite->width;
  dstRect.bottom = sprite->y + sprite->height;

  if ((dstRect.left > offscreenImageBounds.right) ||
    (dstRect.right < offscreenImageBounds.left) ||
    (dstRect.top > offscreenImageBounds.bottom) ||
    (dstRect.bottom < offscreenImageBounds.top))
  {
    /* In this case, the sprite is entirely off the image. Just
     * drop out of this routine without doing anything.
     */
```

Continued on next page

Continued from previous page

```
    return;
  }

  /* Now calculate where the proper sprite lies on its
   * animation image
   */

   /* Calculate which row the image is in based on the sprite's action */
  if (sprite->spriteAction == kSpriteWalkingLeft)
    yImagePos = 0;
  else if (sprite->spriteAction == kSpriteWalkingRight)
    yImagePos = 1;
  else if (sprite->spriteAction == kSpriteStandingStill)
    yImagePos = 2;

  /* Now calculate which image along that row to take */
  xImagePos = sprite->currentImageIndex;

  /* Fill out the rectangle based on these positions */
  srcRect.left = xImagePos * sprite->width;
  srcRect.right = (xImagePos + 1) * sprite->width;
  srcRect.top =  yImagePos * sprite->height;
  srcRect.bottom = (yImagePos + 1) * sprite->height;

  /* Prepare to do the copy */

  LockPixels(srcPixmap);
  LockPixels(dstPixmap);

  GetGWorld(&savePort, &saveDevice);
  SetGWorld(offscreenImage, NULL);

  /* Perform the copy */
  CopyBits( (BitMap *)*srcPixmap,
            (BitMap *)*dstPixmap,
            &srcRect,
            &dstRect,
            transparent,
            NULL );

  SetGWorld(savePort, saveDevice);

  /* Unlock the pixmap */
  UnlockPixels(srcPixmap);
  UnlockPixels(dstPixmap);
}
```

The Walking Man Routines

Now let's look at some code that's more specific to the walking man animation. The code for PrepareSprites can be found in SpriteAnimation.c in the Chapter 5 folder on the source code disc.

Creating the Sprites

The first routine, PrepareSprites() (Listing 5-4), simply calls NewSprite() with the pre-defined information for the animation, then moves the sprite to its starting position. This information contains the sprite width and height, the number of images for each of the sprite's actions, and the resource ID for the animation strip.

Listing 5-4 The PrepareSprites( ) routine

```
#define kSpriteWidth          60
#define kSpriteHeight         90
#define kNumOfMovingSprites   10
#define kNumOfStaticSprites   1
#define kSpriteSpeed          3   /* pixels moved per frame */
#define kSpriteStartingXPos   250 /* starting x pos of the sprite */
#define kSpriteStartingYPos   250 /* starting y pos of the sprite */
#define kPICT_AnimationStrip  128
/**
 **   PrepareSprites()
 **
 **   Initializes all of the sprites and retrieves the graphics from
 **   the animation strip
 **/
OSErr   PrepareSprites(void)
{
  OSErr      err = noErr; /* noErr is defined by the toolbox to be 0 */

  /* All this function has to do is call NewSprite, which will do
   * all of the work!
   */

  err = NewSprite( &gWalkmanSprite,
                   kSpriteWidth,
                   kSpriteHeight,
                   kNumOfMovingSprites,
                   kNumOfMovingSprites,
                   kNumOfStaticSprites,
                   kPICT_AnimationStrip );

  MoveSpriteTo(&gWalkmanSprite, kSpriteStartingXPos,
kSpriteStartingYPos);

  return err;
}
```

Creating the Background

The next routine, PrepareBackgroundImage() (Listing 5-5), loads the PICT for the background and copies it into a new GWorld. This is so you can copy out portions of it later, plus it's much faster to copy from a GWorld than it is to call DrawPicture(). This routine will use up about 200k of memory for the background's GWorld.

Listing 5-5 *The PrepareBackgroundImage() routine*

```
#define kPICT_Background       129
/**
 **   PrepareBackgroundImage()
 **
 **   Creates the background GWorld and fills it with the
 **   PICT background image.
 **/
OSErr  PrepareBackgroundImage(void)
{
  PicHandle       backgroundPICT;
  Rect            pictBounds;
  PixMapHandle    backgroundPixmap;
  GDHandle        saveDevice;
  CGrafPtr        savePort;
  OSErr           err = noErr;


  /* Load the pict from the resource */
  backgroundPICT = GetPicture(kPICT_Background);

  /* Check for an error. GetPicture() is a resource
   * manager routine, and its error codes can be
   * found by calling ResError().
   */
  if (backgroundPICT == NULL) {
    err = ResError();
    return err;
  }

  /* Find the size of the background image */
  pictBounds = (**backgroundPICT).picFrame;

  /* Create the offscreen image for the background */
  err = NewGWorld( &gBackgroundGWorld,
                   8,
                   &pictBounds,
                   NULL,
                   NULL,
                   0  );

  if (err != noErr)
    return err;

  /* Draw the PICT into the offscreen image */
  GetGWorld(&savePort, &saveDevice);
  SetGWorld(gBackgroundGWorld, NULL);

  DrawPicture(backgroundPICT, &pictBounds);

  SetGWorld(savePort, saveDevice);
```

```
/* Now we can release the PICT resource — we don't
 * need it any longer.
 */
ReleaseResource((Handle)backgroundPICT);

return err;
}
```

Drawing the Walking Man Image Using a Temporary GWorld

You now need a routine that will handle the animation of the sprite. This routine is called MoveCurrentSprite(); it will use a temporary GWorld to composite the sprite onto the background before moving it to the screen, eliminating flicker. This routine is also responsible for incrementing the sprite's image index, which is used to calculate which frame to draw next and to calculate the current position of the sprite. Every time this routine is called, the sprite will be moved a certain distance depending on which direction it is facing.

There are two calls to CopyBits() within this routine. The first copies the relevant portion of the background image into the temporary GWorld; the second copies the temporary GWorld to the screen. There is a third call to CopyBits() buried in the call to DrawSpriteToOffscreen(), which places the current sprite on a temporary GWorld. You will notice, however, that the two calls to CopyBits() within this routine use the *srcCopy* mode, whereas the previous calls you looked at used *transparent*. This is because the *transparent* mode is necessary only when copying the sprite over a background image. When you copy the composited image to the screen, you are actually replacing that part of the window, so the simpler (and faster) *srcCopy* mode suffices. Listing 5-6 shows this routine.

Listing 5-6 *The MoveCurrentSprite() routine*

```
/**
 **  MoveCurrentSprite()
 **
 **  Changes the position of the sprite on the screen and redraws
 **  the sprite. This routine generates a temporary GWorld to hold
 **  the moving sprite composited onto the background. The temporary
 **  GWorld is large enough to hold both the place the
 **  sprite _was_ and the position that it _will be_.
 **/
OSErr  MoveCurrentSprite(WindowPtr  dstWindow)
{
  Rect           windowBounds;
  Rect           spriteBounds;
  GWorldPtr      temporaryBuffer;
  PixMapHandle   tempBufferPixmap;
  PixMapHandle   backgroundPixmap;
```

Continued on next page

Continued from previous page

```
OSErr        err;
GDHandle     saveDevice;
CGrafPtr     savePort;
short        distanceMoved;

/* Move the sprite according to its facing */
if (gWalkmanSprite.spriteAction == kSpriteWalkingLeft)
  distanceMoved = -kSpriteSpeed;
else if (gWalkmanSprite.spriteAction == kSpriteWalkingRight)
  distanceMoved = kSpriteSpeed;
else
  distanceMoved = 0;

/* Make sure we're not moving the sprite off the screen */
windowBounds = dstWindow->portRect;
if ((gWalkmanSprite.x + distanceMoved) < windowBounds.left) {
  distanceMoved = windowBounds.left - gWalkmanSprite.x;
}

if ((  gWalkmanSprite.x +
    gWalkmanSprite.width +
    distanceMoved  ) > windowBounds.right) {
  distanceMoved = windowBounds.right -
                  gWalkmanSprite.width -
                  gWalkmanSprite.x;
}


OffsetSprite(&gWalkmanSprite, distanceMoved, 0);

/* We're going to create a temporary gworld
 * and then dispose of it when we finish. This temporary
 * gworld will be the size of the sprite plus the distance that
 * it moved during this frame.
 */

spriteBounds.left = gWalkmanSprite.x;
spriteBounds.right = spriteBounds.left + gWalkmanSprite.width;
spriteBounds.top = gWalkmanSprite.y;
spriteBounds.bottom = spriteBounds.top + gWalkmanSprite.height;

if (distanceMoved < 0)
  /* If the sprite moved to the left, we need to expand the right
   * edge of the buffer to erase where the sprite used to be
   */
  spriteBounds.right -= distanceMoved;
else
  /* Otherwise, update the left edge of the buffer */
  spriteBounds.left -= distanceMoved;

/* Increment the sprite's image index */
gWalkmanSprite.currentImageIndex++;
```

```
/* We need to check to see if we've advanced the sprite's
 * image index past the end of the animation sequence. Since
 * each action sequence can have a different number of
 * images, we must take this into account
 */
if (gWalkmanSprite.spriteAction == kSpriteWalkingLeft)
  if (gWalkmanSprite.currentImageIndex >=
      gWalkmanSprite.movingLeftImages)
    gWalkmanSprite.currentImageIndex = 0;

if (gWalkmanSprite.spriteAction == kSpriteWalkingRight)
  if (gWalkmanSprite.currentImageIndex >=
      gWalkmanSprite.movingRightImages)
    gWalkmanSprite.currentImageIndex = 0;

if (gWalkmanSprite.spriteAction == kSpriteStandingStill)
  if (gWalkmanSprite.currentImageIndex >= gWalkmanSprite.staticImages)
    gWalkmanSprite.currentImageIndex = 0;


err = NewGWorld( &temporaryBuffer,
                 8,
                 &spriteBounds,
                 NULL,
                 NULL,
                 0 );
if (err)
  return err;

/* Get the temporary offscreen's pixmap */
tempBufferPixmap = GetGWorldPixMap(temporaryBuffer);
backgroundPixmap = GetGWorldPixMap(gBackgroundGWorld);

/* Lock the pixmaps for both offscreens */
LockPixels(tempBufferPixmap);
LockPixels(backgroundPixmap);

/* Copy the relevant portion of the background into
 * the temporary offscreen buffer.
 */

GetGWorld(&savePort, &saveDevice);
SetGWorld(temporaryBuffer, NULL);

CopyBits( (BitMap *)*backgroundPixmap,
          (BitMap *)*tempBufferPixmap,
          &spriteBounds,
          &spriteBounds,
          srcCopy,
          NULL );

SetGWorld(savePort, saveDevice);
```

Continued on next page

Continued from previous page

```
UnlockPixels(tempBufferPixmap);
UnlockPixels(backgroundPixmap);

/* The next step is to draw the sprite into the temporary
 * offscreen. Fortunately, we already have a routine to
 * do this.
 */
DrawSpriteToOffscreen(&gWalkmanSprite, temporaryBuffer);

/* All that's left to do is draw the temporary buffer to the
 * window.
 */
LockPixels(tempBufferPixmap);

SetPort(dstWindow);

CopyBits( (BitMap *)*tempBufferPixmap,
          (BitMap *)&dstWindow->portBits,
          &spriteBounds,
          &spriteBounds,
          srcCopy,
          NULL );

UnlockPixels(tempBufferPixmap);

/* Now just dispose of the temporary offscreen buffer */
DisposeGWorld(temporaryBuffer);

return err;
}
```

Handling Input from the Keyboard

The next routine is called whenever the user presses a key. It determines what direction the sprite is currently facing and, if necessary, changes it. It uses constants for the keys that are currently defined as the left and right arrow keys. If you prefer to use different keys for input, feel free to change these constants. Chapter 6 fully explains key codes and supplies the key codes for the entire keyboard.

```
#define kMoveLeftKeyCode      0x7B    /* Left-arrow key */
#define kMoveRightKeyCode     0x7C    /* Right-arrow key */

/**
 **   HandleKeyInput()
 **
 **   Uses a key input to change a sprite's direction.
 **/
void  HandleKeyInput(short  theKey)
{
  if (theKey == kMoveLeftKeyCode) {
    /* The left arrow was pressed. If the sprite is moving
```

```
     * right, change it to stationary mode. If it is currently
     * stationary, change it to 'walking-left' mode.
     */
    if (gWalkmanSprite.spriteAction == kSpriteWalkingRight) {
      gWalkmanSprite.spriteAction = kSpriteStandingStill;
    } else if (gWalkmanSprite.spriteAction == kSpriteStandingStill) {
      gWalkmanSprite.spriteAction = kSpriteWalkingLeft;
    }
  } else if (theKey == kMoveRightKeyCode) {
    /* The right arrow was pressed. If the sprite is moving
     * left, change it to stationary mode. If it is currently
     * stationary, change it to 'walking-right' mode.
     */
    if (gWalkmanSprite.spriteAction == kSpriteWalkingLeft) {
      gWalkmanSprite.spriteAction = kSpriteStandingStill;
    } else if (gWalkmanSprite.spriteAction == kSpriteStandingStill) {
      gWalkmanSprite.spriteAction = kSpriteWalkingRight;
    }
  }
}
```

Redrawing Everything

The last routine in SpriteAnimation.c is one that is used for redrawing the entire window—first drawing the background, then drawing the sprite over the top. Because this routine isn't used while animating but just when the window needs updating, it doesn't use a temporary GWorld—it just draws everything directly to the window.

```
/**
 **   RedrawEntireWindow()
 **
 **   Refreshes the entire window - background, sprite, and all.
 **/
void  RedrawEntireWindow(WindowPtr  theWindow)
{
  PixMapHandle    backgroundPixmap;
  Rect            windowBounds;

  /* Draw the entire background */
  windowBounds = theWindow->portRect;
  backgroundPixmap = GetGWorldPixMap(gBackgroundGWorld);

  LockPixels(backgroundPixmap);
  SetPort(theWindow);

  CopyBits(  (BitMap *)*backgroundPixmap,
             (BitMap *)&theWindow->portBits,
             &windowBounds,
             &windowBounds,
             srcCopy,
             NULL  );
```

Continued on next page

Continued from previous page

```
UnlockPixels(backgroundPixmap);

/* Draw the sprite onto the window */
DrawSpriteToWindow(&gWalkmanSprite, theWindow);
}
```

The main() Routine

The last source file, Walkman.c (which can be found on the source code disc), contains two routines. The first is the familiar CreateWindow() routine and the second is main(). You are already familiar with most of the contents of main(). The first portion of the routine is used for initializing the toolbox, the sprites, and the background image. The main event loop simply looks for keyboard and update events. The keyboard events are sent to HandleKeyInput() and whenever an update event is received, it redraws the entire main window.

Whenever a Null event is received, the sprite is redrawn. Because faster machines tend to get Null events more frequently, a timing limit is added. This limit ensures that the animation is not drawn more than once every 1/12 of a second (although this can be changed by modifying the timing value used). If the application receives a Null event and it drew the sprite less than 1/12 of a second ago, it will do nothing. Otherwise, it redraws the sprite.

If this time limit were removed, your computer would redraw the sprite as quickly as it could. If you are running a slower Macintosh (such as one with a 68030 processor), there would be little or no change in the animation speed, but on a Power Macintosh, the difference would be very distinct. Although this may seem advantageous, not limiting the speed of your game may make it unplayable on the next generation of Macintoshes because it runs too fast. Listing 5-7 shows the main() routine.

Listing 5-7 *The main() routine*

```
void main(void)
{
    WindowPtr      mainWindow;
    EventRecord    theEvent;
    short          eventMask;
    short          done = FALSE;
    Boolean        notNullEvent;
    Rect           windowRect;
    OSErr          err;
    long           currentTickCount;
    long           lastTickCount = 0;

    /* Initialize everything we need */
    InitGraf(&qd.thePort);    /* qd.thePort is part of any application */
    InitWindows();
    InitCursor();
```

```
eventMask = everyEvent;

/* Create a window that is 512x384 pixels large */
SetRect(&windowRect, 0, 0, 512, 384);

/* Offset the window rect so that the window does not appear
 * under the menu bar.
 */
OffsetRect(&windowRect, 20, 50);

mainWindow = CreateWindow(&windowRect);

/* Initialize the sprite routines */
err = PrepareSprites();

if (err == noErr) {
  /* Load the sprite background image */
  err = PrepareBackgroundImage();
}

if (err != noErr) {
  /* There was an error in the sprite routines.
   * Terminate the program.
   */
  SysBeep(1);
  ExitToShell();
}


RedrawEntireWindow(mainWindow);

while (!done) {
  /* In this case, we want to receive null events as well as keyDown
   * and mouseDown, so we set the sleep value to a low number (in
   * this case, 10), since we want other applications to have a chance
   * to do some processing).
   */
  notNullEvent = WaitNextEvent( eventMask,
                                &theEvent,
                                10,
                                NULL);

  switch (theEvent.what) {
    WindowPtr    selectedWindow;
    short        findWindowResult;
    short        keyCode;

    case keyDown:
      /* Process a key event. A key code is stored in bits 8-15
       * of the message field, so use the Macintosh toolbox
       * constant for masking it.
       */
      keyCode = theEvent.message & keyCodeMask;
```

Continued on next page

Continued from previous page

```
        /* Shift the bits in keyCode down so they take up the lower
         * 8 bits of the word
         */
        keyCode >>= 8;

        /* Allow the sprite routines to process the input */
        HandleKeyInput(keyCode);

        /* Update the sprite */
        MoveCurrentSprite(mainWindow);
        break;


    case mouseDown:
        /* We received a mousedown event. Check to see where it was */
        findWindowResult = FindWindow(theEvent.where, &selectedWindow);
        if (findWindowResult == inDrag) {
            /* The user clicked in the drag bar. Allow them to drag it
             * across the screen.
             */
            DragWindow(  selectedWindow,
                         theEvent.where,
                         &qd.screenBits.bounds);
        } else if (findWindowResult == inGoAway) {
            /* The user clicked in the close box. Close the window. */

            /* First make sure it's our window they clicked on */
            if (selectedWindow == mainWindow) {

                /* Then call TrackGoAway so the user has an opportunity to
                 * move the mouse out of the close box
                 */
                if (TrackGoAway(selectedWindow, theEvent.where) == TRUE) {
                    /* Clicking the GoAway box in this application will cause
                     * it to quit. Set the done flag to TRUE so this happens.
                     */
                    done = TRUE;
                }
            }
        }
        break;

    case updateEvt:
    {
        BeginUpdate((WindowPtr)theEvent.message);

        /* Update the window to show the sprite */
        if ((WindowPtr)theEvent.message == mainWindow)
            RedrawEntireWindow(mainWindow);

        EndUpdate((WindowPtr)theEvent.message);
        break;
    }
```

```
      default:
        /* We want to allow the sprite to animate itself here. Call
         * the MoveCurrentSprite routine.
         * We implement a delay structure so that the routine is not
         * called more than once every 5 ticks (1/12 of a second).
         *
         * If you want to see the maximum speed your computer can
         * handle, change the 5 to 0.
         */
        currentTickCount = TickCount();

        if ((currentTickCount - lastTickCount) > 5) {
          lastTickCount = currentTickCount;
          MoveCurrentSprite(mainWindow);
        }
        break;
    }
  }

  /* Close the main window. */
  if (mainWindow != NULL)
    DisposeWindow(mainWindow);
}
```

Meet the Animated Gentleman

When you run the Walking Man application, the program initializes itself and you see the walking man sprite in the center of the screen. Press the left or right arrow keys to make him move. This particular sprite was raytraced using Infini-D from Specular International. The individual frames were then placed into the animation sequence.

▨ QUICKTIME COMPRESSION

To fill the entire window, a background image of the same size was needed. An image of such size would normally use up almost 200k of disk space. Because of the limited size of the media supplied with this book, this was much too large. The normal compression built into PICT files would not work effectively on a color image, but there is another method. When the user has QuickTime installed, it is possible to use a highly efficient method of compression within PICT files. The algorithm used is called JPEG, but PICT files compressed in this manner are referred to as QuickTime PICTs.

Using this form of compression, the 200k image was compressed to 27k. A little bit of quality was lost, but it's fine for these demonstration purposes. Loading a QuickTime PICT is no different from loading any other type of PICT—the operating system handles everything. The only caveat is that the user must have QuickTime installed on his or her system.

To create a QuickTime PICT, it is necessary to have an application that can save PICT images into the resource fork. For the Walking Man application, Adobe Photoshop was used.

This particular animation is not fast enough to be used in an arcade game. The biggest reason is that using the transparent mode with CopyBits() is about five times slower than using the srcCopy mode. You can get around this problem either by not using a background image (in which case you could use CopyBits' srcCopy mode) or by writing your own transparent copying routine. The second method is significantly more difficult, because CopyBits() is already very efficient. I will examine this method in later chapters. For the arcade game in Chapter 8, however, I will go the easier route—not using a background image.

In the next chapter, I will examine other methods of getting input from the user, including an alternate method of looking for keyboard input and a method of tracking the mouse position.

6

Talking to the Computer

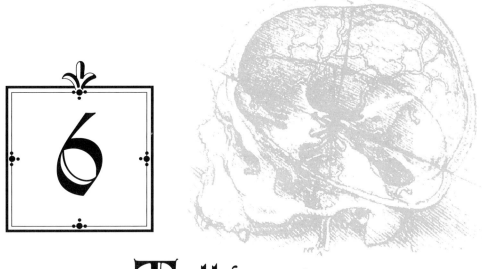

6

Talking to the Computer

In Chapter 5, you animated a sprite using keyboard input received via WaitNextEvent().
This chapter will demonstrate additional methods of obtaining input from the keyboard,
the mouse, and the most game-oriented input device, the joystick.

Obtaining input from the user is a very important part of a game. You must take care
that obtaining input does not use up significant resources or your game will end up wasting most of its time figuring out what the player wants to do.

To use what you learn in the first half of this chapter, you're going to improve the
walking man animation created in Chapter 5. The new walking man animation you created will respond directly to key presses, the mouse, and a joystick.

Where Did the Mouse Go?

Perhaps the easiest input device to track is the mouse. Whenever you need to check
its position, simply call GetMouse().

```
void GetMouse(Point *location);
```

GetMouse() returns the current location of the mouse in local coordinates. Local coordinates are useful if you are attempting to determine whether the user has clicked on

157

an object in a particular window. If you are tracking the movement of an object across the entire screen (e.g., if the user is controlling the movement of the walking man sprite with the mouse), global coordinates are more useful. To convert a local coordinate to a global one, use the LocalToGlobal() routine introduced in Chapter 4.

The state of the mouse button can also be determined by calling Button(). Button() will return TRUE if the mouse button is down or FALSE if it is up.

```
Boolean Button(void);
```

The point obtained from GetMouse() will always be within the boundary of the monitor(s). Therefore, machines with large monitors will return a greater range of values when GetMouse() is called. If you are writing a game that, for example, rotates the view faster as the cursor gets farther from the center of the screen, it is important to consider the *ratio* of the cursor's position to the screen size. For example, if the user has a monitor with a 640x480 resolution and the mouse is at location (600, 440), the cursor will show up almost at the bottom-right edge of the screen. However, if the user has a monitor with a higher resolution (e.g. 1600x1200), that same mouse coordinate would indicate a position in the middle of the screen.

The best way to handle this situation is to divide the mouse coordinate by the screen size, providing a value between 0 and 1 indicating the relative position of the mouse. You can't use integer division for this task, however, because a fractional number cannot be represented by an integer. Typecast the mouse location to a *float* before performing the division and the result will have enough precision to be acceptable. Here is a routine that will do this:

```
void GetMouseRelativePosition(float *xPosition, float *yPosition)
{
  Rect    screenRectangle;
  Point   mouseLoc;
  short   screenWidth, screenHeight;

  /* Obtain the mouse position */
  GetMouse(&mouseLoc);

  /* Convert the position to global coordinates */
  LocalToGlobal(&mouseLoc);

  /* Get the screen size */
  screenRectangle = qd.screenBits.bounds;

  screenWidth = screenRectangle.right - screenRectangle.left;
  screenHeight = screenRectangle.bottom - screenRectangle.top;

  /* Calculate the relative location */
  *xPosition = (float)mouseLoc.h / (float)screenWidth;
  *yPosition = (float)mouseLoc.v / (float)screenHeight;
}
```

Keyboard Input

Most arcade games react to a keypress and continue that action until the key is released. It is possible to make a game react this way using WaitNextEvent() by beginning an action when the game receives a keyDown event and stopping the action when it receives a keyUp event. This method has many problems, however. First of all, using the event loop structure can be awkward for the flow of an arcade game. Generally, the best way for an arcade game to operate is for it to check which keys are being pressed at any given time. If a game uses the event queue, it will be receiving the keyboard events in sequence. This means that by the time the game receives a keyDown event, the event may be a half second old or even older, which is certainly not fast enough for an action game.

Not only is an event queue likely to provide old events, simply calling WaitNextEvent() consumes a lot of processing time. When WaitNextEvent() is called, any other applications that are running have an opportunity to perform some tasks. Although this is advantageous for a multitasking computer, action games generally want to get as much CPU time as possible.

If you stop calling WaitNextEvent() altogether, the user will not be able to switch to another application while running the game and any applications operating in the background will be frozen until the game is finished. Although this situation is unacceptable to many users, a number of games do exactly that. Marathon is a good example; while playing Marathon, the user cannot use any other application and any work that was being done in the background is halted until the user stops playing.

Another solution is to call WaitNextEvent() occasionally, such as two or three times a second, and gain keyboard input through the other means presented in this chapter. This allows background operations to continue (albeit slowly, but good enough for, say, a modem download) while the application retains most of its speed. This is the approach I'll be taking for many of the games you'll create in this book.

The GetKeys() Alternative

A toolbox function called GetKeys() will tell you the state of all the keys on the keyboard. GetKeys() returns the status of the keyboard in a structure called KeyMap. KeyMap is defined in C as an array of four longwords which corresponds to 128 bits. However, the individual bits are not organized as longwords, but rather as 16 bytes. The distinction between 4 longwords and 16 bytes is very important. On the Macintosh, an array of four longwords is arranged in memory so the top (most significant) bit of each longword is in the lowest memory space, as illustrated in Figure 6-1. An array of 16 bytes is also arranged so that the most significant bit of each byte is in the lowest address. However, when compared to four longwords, each byte of the longwords seems reversed, as in Figure 6-2.

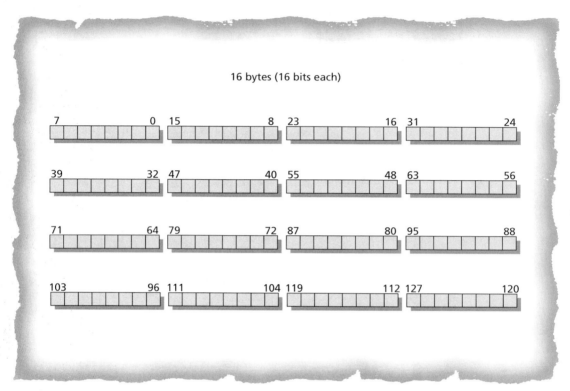

FIGURE 6-1 ◉ *The KeyMap structure*

BIG ENDIAN PROCESSORS

Any processor that organizes data with its most significant bit in the lowest address is called *big endian*. All 68000-based computers (including the Macintosh and Amiga line) are big endian. Intel processors (8086, 80286, 80386, 80486, Pentium, etc.), on the other hand, are *little endian*. On little endian machines, the bytes are not reversed. The PowerPC processor can be switched between big endian and little endian, but the Macintosh operating system is always in big endian mode.

Each bit in the KeyMap structure represents one key and because the Macintosh extended keyboard contains 104 keys (not including the power button, which is not included in the KeyMap structure), there is barely enough space in the structure to represent the entire keyboard.

```
void  GetKeys(KeyMap theKeys);
```

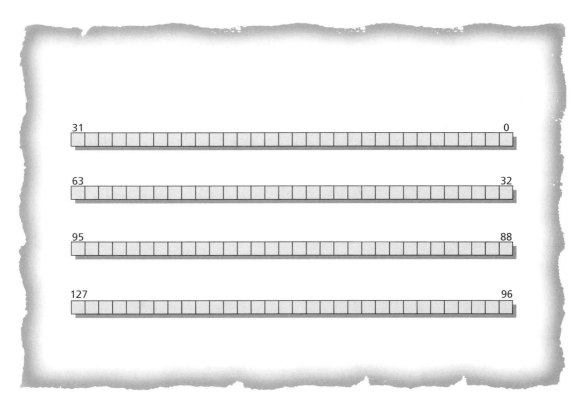

FIGURE 6-2 ◉ *Array of four longwords arranged in memory*

Breaking the Key Code

To determine the state of a specific key, it is necessary to know the corresponding key code. A diagram of the key codes for the Macintosh extended keyboard is shown in Figure 6-3. Most keyboards contain the same or fewer keys than the extended keyboard, so you should be able to obtain all of the keys you need from this diagram even if you use a different keyboard. All the key codes listed in this diagram are in hexadecimal.

The key code indicates which bit of the KeyMap holds the status of that key. For example, the key code for q is 0x0C, or 12 in decimal format. This means that the 12th bit of the KeyMap holds the state of the Q key, as shown in Figure 6-4.

In C, you normally use the & operator to test a particular bit of a variable. However, because the KeyMap bits are not organized in a linear sequence, you must break the KeyMap structure down into individual bytes. Once you have done that, you can use the & operator to test the individual bits.

FIGURE 6-3

*Key codes on
an extended
keyboard*

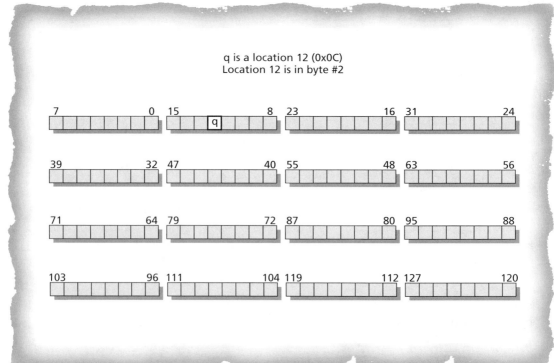

q is a location 12 (0x0C)
Location 12 is in byte #2

FIGURE 6-4 ⊙ *Location of q in a KeyMap*

The definition of the GetKeys() routine requires that an array of four longwords be sent into it. However, you want to access the data as individual bytes. To do this, you can declare an array of 16 bytes (which can be declared by using the C data type *unsigned char*) and then typecast to an array of longwords when GetKeys() is called.

```
unsigned char    ourKeyMap[16];
GetKeys((unsigned long *)ourKeyMap);
```

Once you have the key map data, you need to determine which of the 16 bytes contains the bit you're looking for. To do this, simply divide the key code by 8. Because the range of key codes is between 0 and 127 and C always rounds down when doing integer division, you will be left with a number between 0 and 15.

```
keyMapIndex = ourKeyMap[keyCode / 8];
```

In the example above, the bit corresponding to the q key (with a key code of 12) would be in byte number 2.

The next step is to determine which bit of this byte contains the information you're looking for. At this point, you want to know the remainder from dividing the key code by 8. C provides an operation for determining this called *mod*. The mod symbol is %; it is used in the same way as the multiplication and division symbols. The individual bit can be determined by using the mod operator:

```
bitToCheck = keyCode % 8;  /* compute the individual bit to check.*/
```

Now you know which bit in the byte contains the key status. The next step is to use the & operator to determine whether that bit is on or off. For the example here, you need to check bit 4 of the byte (because 12 % 8 is 4). You can do this in one of two ways. The first method is to create a byte with a 1 in bit 4 and then use it to mask the key map longword. The other method is to *shift* the key map byte to the right by 4 places, using the C >> operator. This will leave the status of the q key at the first bit, where you can mask it with a value of 1. This technique is illustrated in Figure 6-5.

The first method may sound more natural, but it is actually more involved. The second method, shown here, is more efficient.

```
isKeyPressed = (keyMapIndex >> bitToCheck) & 0x01;
```

Now let's look at the complete code for this function.

```
Boolean  IsKeyPressed(short keyCode)
{
  unsigned char       ourKeyMap[16];
  long                keyMapIndex;
  Boolean             isKeyPressed;
  short               bitToCheck;

  GetKeys((unsigned long*)ourKeyMap);
  /* Find which longword the key is located in */
  keyMapIndex = ourKeyMap[keyCode / 8];
```

Continued on next page

Continued from previous page

```
/* Compute the individual bit to check */
bitToCheck = keyCode % 8;
/* Calculate the status of the individual key */
isKeyPressed = (keyMapIndex >> bitToCheck) & 0x01;

return isKeyPressed;
}
```

Directly Supporting Joysticks

For many years, the game hardware manufacturers ignored the Macintosh platform almost entirely. The only joystick available until about 1993 was the MouseStick by Advanced Gravis. The MouseStick is a very good joystick, but until recently it was also a very expensive one. Fortunately, quite a few joysticks for the Macintosh have been introduced in the last few years, including the ThrustMaster FCS and the CH FlightStick Pro.

These joysticks allow the user to emulate the mouse or certain keys on the keyboard. This feature allows a joystick to work with any Macintosh game, even if the game does not have built-in support for it. However, either the game programmer or the user must use the joystick's software to configure the stick for the game.

Writing your game to support a joystick directly will eliminate the need to create any configuration files and it may give your game better response when using the joystick. In this section, I explain how to support two of the more popular Macintosh joysticks directly: the Gravis MouseStick and the ThrustMaster system. The code contained in this chapter for the Gravis MouseStick and the ThrustMaster was obtained from the respective manufacturers and is included with their permission.

FIGURE 6-5

◎ ◎ ◎ ◎ ◎ ◎

Masking off q in a byte

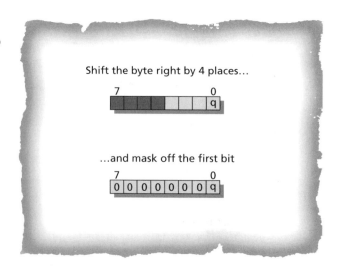

ADB Drivers

Both of the joysticks I'll be discussing here use low-level calls to the ADB Manager, which handles the interactions between any devices on the ADB port (keyboards, mice, and in this case joysticks) and the operating system. When the Macintosh starts up, it scans all of the devices on the ADB port and assigns an address from 1 to 16 to each of them. This address may change every time the computer is restarted, so the software cannot depend on a device being at any particular position.

To locate a particular device, you can scan through all of the possible ADB addresses and get information about each device. Determining whether a device is the one you're looking for depends on how the device is made; each joystick manufacturer has a different method of checking this that they generally provide free of charge to developers. Let's look at the interfaces provided by ThrustMaster for its three-piece flight system and by Gravis for its MouseStick II.

The ThrustMaster Interface

The ThrustMaster system can consist of more than just a joystick. A full ThrustMaster setup comprises a joystick, a throttle control, and a rudder control. All these devices are read through the same interface.

A pointer to the ThrustMaster joystick information is obtained using this routine:

```
#include "ThrustMaster.h"
ThrustMasterInfoPtr    GetThrustMasterInfoPtr()
{
  // Return a pointer to the "optional data area" of the
  // ThrustMaster device.
  // Returns a nil pointer if the device is not found on the bus.

  OSErr         resultCode;
  char          assignedADBAddress;
  ADBDataBlock  adbGetInfo;

  for ( assignedADBAddress = 1;
        assignedADBAddress < 16;
        assignedADBAddress++)
  {
    resultCode = GetADBInfo (&adbGetInfo, assignedADBAddress);
    if (resultCode == noErr) {
      if (adbGetInfo.origADBAddr == tmOriginalAdbAddress &&
        adbGetInfo.devType      == tmHandlerId)
      {
        return (ThrustMasterInfoPtr) adbGetInfo.dbDataAreaAddr;
      }
    }
  }
}
```

Continued on next page

Continued from previous page

```
// The Thrustmaster joystick was not found
return NULL;
}
```

This code will find out whether there is a ThrustMaster joystick on the ADB port. If there is, it will return a pointer to a data area controlled by the ThrustMaster drivers. Any time the joystick is moved or a button is pressed, this data will be updated immediately. All the application needs to do is check the contents of this memory when it wants the current state of the joystick. Listing 6-1 shows the structure of this memory.

Listing 6-1 *The ThrustMaster data area*

```
typedef struct  {
  // Calibrated position data from device(s)
    char           roll;       // -127 (left) ...+127 (right)
    chart          pitch;      // -127 (forward/down) ...+127 (back/up)
    unsigned char  thrust;     // 0 (back) ...255 (forward)
    char           yaw;        // -127 (left) ...+127 (right)
  // Throttle button bits:
    short          rockerDown :1;    // 0 (open), 1 (closed)
    short          rockerUp   :1;
    short          button1    :1;
    short          button2    :1;
    short          button3    :1;
    short          button5    :1;
    short          button6    :1;
    short          button4    :1;
  // Stick button bits:
    short          pinkey     :1;
    short          thumbLow   :1;
    short          trigger    :1;
    short          thumbHigh  :1;
    short          hatLeft    :1;
    short          hatRight   :1;
    short          hatDown    :1;
    short          hatUp      :1;
  // Padding to 8 bytes (max adb register size)
    char           reserveByte1;
    char           reserveByte2;
  // Device structure version number
    char           version;
  // This byte is cleared by the driver each time new
  // data is acquired and calibrated
    char           notNew;
  // Device attachment indicators
    char           throttleAttached;
    char           rudderAttached;
  // Mousing stuff
    char           mouseDefeated;
  // Private Stuff
```

```
long            dontTouch;
long            fini;
} ThrustMasterInfoStruct, *ThrustMasterInfoPtr;
```

The *roll* field is the current left/right position of the joystick. Any negative number indicates the joystick is being pulled to the left; any positive number means it is being pulled to the right. *Pitch* indicates forward and back movement (forward is negative, back is positive).

If the user has a throttle control attached, the *thrust* field will indicate its current setting; the rudders affect the *yaw* parameter.

The MouseStick Interface

The MouseStick has its own unique qualities. Although the MouseStick interface does not include a throttle or rudder pedals, it allows the user to connect two MouseSticks at the same time. This way one stick can be used for normal flight control while the other can be used for something like throttle or gun positioning. Despite the added stick, the interface isn't really any more complex than ThrustMaster's.

The routine for gaining access to the MouseStick's data area is almost identical to ThrustMaster's. The biggest difference is in the way the routine identifies the MouseStick.

```
#include "MouseStick.h"
MouseStickInfoPtr  GetMouseStickDriverInfo()
{
  ADBDataBlock          adbGetInfo;
  MouseStickInfoPtr     vars;
  short                 x, numADB;
  char                  found = false;

  numADB = CountADBs();
  for (x = 1; x <= numADB; x++)
  {
    GetADBInfo(&adbGetInfo,GetIndADB(&adbGetInfo,x));
    vars = (MouseStickInfoPtr)adbGetInfo.dbDataAreaAddr;
    if (vars != nil && vars->signature == 0x4A656666)
      return(vars);
  }
  return (nil);
}
```

The MouseStick's data area has a few less fields than the ThrustMaster's (but, then, the MouseStick has fewer buttons than the ThrustMaster), as shown in Listing 6-2.

Listing 6-2 *The MouseStick data area*

```
typedef struct
{
  long      signature;              /* MouseStick signature */
```

Continued on next page

Continued from previous page

```
char      private1[18];
short     numSticksConnected;    /* how many sticks are available */
char      private2[22];

    /* STICK 1 INFO */
short     stick1_xIn;            /* absolute stick position */
short     stick1_yIn;            /* absolute stick position */
Byte      stick1_buttons;        /* button states */
Byte      private3;
short     stick1_xOut;           /* adjusted cursor position */
short     stick1_yOut;           /* adjusted cursor position */
char      stick1_old;            /* true if device is an old mousestick */
char      private4;
char      stick1_on;             /* pad is on or off */
char      private5;
char      stick1_cursorCouple;   /* true if stick should move cursor */
char      stick1_appAware;       /* is driver switching sets? */
char      private6[152];

    /* STICK 2 INFO */
short     stick2_xIn;            /* absolute stick position */
short     stick2_yIn;            /* absolute stick position */
Byte      stick2_buttons;        /* button states */
Byte      private7;
short     stick2_xOut;           /* adjusted cursor position */
short     stick2_yOut;           /* adjusted cursor position */
char      stick2_old;            /* true if device is an old mousestick */
char      private8;
char      stick2_on;             /* pad is on or off */
char      private9;
char      stick2_cursorCouple;   /* true if stick should move cursor */
char      stick2_appAware;       /* is driver switching sets? */
char      private10[152];

} *MouseStickInfoPtr;
```

The range of values produced by the movement of the stick is significantly larger with the MouseStick than it is with the ThrustMaster. Both the *xIn* and *yIn* values can range from approximately -600 to 600 (depending on how well the stick has been calibrated; the actual range could be a little more or a little less than that).

The status of the MouseStick buttons is contained as individual bits in the *stick1_buttons* and *stick2_buttons* fields. Bit 0 contains the state of button 1, bit 1 corresponds to button 2, and so on. Because there are five buttons on the MouseStick, bits 5 through 7 are not used. The values of the bits are reversed from what you might expect, however. A value of 0 means the button is pressed, a value of 1 means the button is up.

Improving the Walking Man Animation

Now you're going to add several improvements to the Walking Man application. The new application, called Walking Man 2, will have a menu bar with the standard Apple, File, and Edit menus plus one additional menu: Input. The Input menu will allow the user to select the form of input for the animation. It will have six choices: Keyboard, Mouse Absolute to Screen, Mouse Absolute to Window, Mouse Relative, ThrustMaster Joystick, and MouseStick Joystick, as you can see in Figure 6-6.

When the keyboard option is selected, the sprite will walk to the left or to the right while the left or right arrow keys is being held down. When no keys are being pressed, the sprite will stand still.

Mouse Absolute to Screen means that if, for example, the mouse is one-third of the way from the left edge of the screen, the sprite will walk one-third of the way across the window. If the mouse is at the left edge of the monitor, the sprite will walk to the left edge of the window.

Mouse Absolute to Window means that the sprite will always walk to the same horizontal position as the mouse. This method is very similar to the previous one (Mouse Absolute to Screen) and the two methods share most of the same code.

Mouse Relative divides the screen into three horizontal sections. If the mouse is in the left third of the screen, the sprite begins walking left and will continue until the mouse moves out of the left section. While the mouse is in the middle third of the screen, the sprite stands still; if the mouse moves to the right third, the sprite begins to walk to the right.

ThrustMaster Joystick and MouseStick Joystick enable these joysticks to control the walking man's movement directly. The joysticks determine only the direction in which the sprite is moving, not the speed.

FIGURE 6-6

◎ ◎ ◎ ◎ ◎ ◎

The Input menu

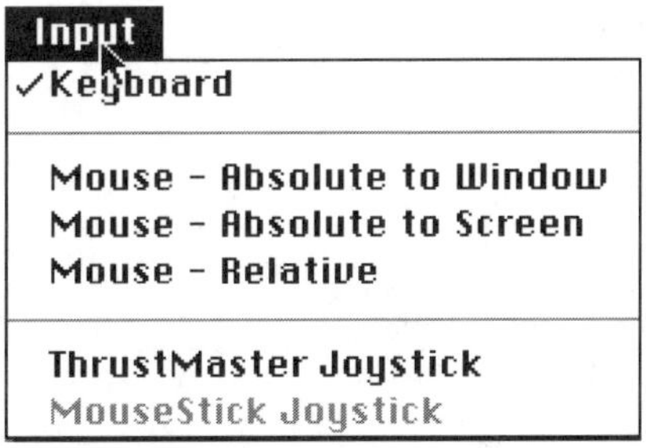

Checking Menu Items

There is one new concept introduced in this example application: putting a check mark next to menu items. You can see an example of checking a menu item in the Finder. Just select a file and pull down the Label menu. One of the items in the menu will have a check mark next to it.

A single toolbox call will check or uncheck a menu; it is called CheckItem().

```
void CheckItem(MenuHandle theMenu, short theItem, Boolean checkIt);
```

theMenu is the MenuHandle of the menu you want to use, *theItem* is the ID of the item to modify, and *checkIt* indicates whether to check or uncheck the item.

A common way to ensure the proper items are checked is to go through the entire menu, uncheck everything, and then check just the item(s) you want.

The Walking Man 2 Code

Two routines have been changed from the original Walking Man application, four routines have been added, and one routine has been removed.

The two routines that were modified are main() and MoveCurrentSprite(). The only events that are acted upon are mouseDown and updateEvent. All of the keyboard input is handled through calls to GetKeys().

The Main() Routine

Main() has been modified to call the WaitNextEvent() routine once every 5 ticks (5/60 or 1/12 of a second). Main() also now creates a menu bar and initializes the joysticks. If one or both of the joysticks is not found, the appropriate menu item will be dimmed. Listing 6-3 is the main() routine from Walking Man 2.

Listing 6-3 *The Walking Man 2 main() routine*

```
void main(void)
{
   WindowPtr        mainWindow;
   EventRecord      theEvent;
   short            eventMask;
   short            done = FALSE;
   Boolean          notNullEvent;
   Rect             windowRect;
   OSErr            err;
   MenuHandle       appleMenu, fileMenu;
   MenuHandle       editMenu, inputMenu;
   long             currentTickCount;
   long             lastWaitNextEventCall = 0;
   long             lastMoveCurrentSpriteCall = 0;
```

```
short               inputMethod = kKeyboardInput;

/* Initialize everything we need */
InitGraf(&qd.thePort);     /* qd.thePort is part of any application */
InitWindows();
InitCursor();

eventMask = everyEvent;

/* Create each of our menus and insert them into the menu bar */
appleMenu = NewMenu(kMENU_Apple, "\p\024");
AppendMenu(appleMenu, "\pAbout Walking Man ");
AppendMenu(appleMenu, "\p(-");
InsertMenu(appleMenu, 0);

fileMenu = NewMenu(kMENU_File, "\pFile");
AppendMenu(fileMenu, "\pNew ;Open ;(-;Close;(-;Quit");
InsertMenu(fileMenu, 0);

editMenu = NewMenu(kMENU_Edit, "\pEdit");
AppendMenu(editMenu, "\pUndo;Cut;Copy;Paste;Clear");
InsertMenu(editMenu, 0);

inputMenu = NewMenu(kMENU_Input, "\pInput");
AppendMenu(inputMenu, "\pKeyboard");
AppendMenu(inputMenu, "\p(-");
AppendMenu(inputMenu, "\pMouse - Absolute to Window");
AppendMenu(inputMenu, "\pMouse - Absolute to Screen");
AppendMenu(inputMenu, "\pMouse - Relative");
AppendMenu(inputMenu, "\p(-");
AppendMenu(inputMenu, "\pThrustMaster Joystick");
AppendMenu(inputMenu, "\pMouseStick Joystick");
InsertMenu(inputMenu, 0);

/* Put a check beside the 'keyboard' item */
CheckItem(inputMenu, kINPUT_Keyboard, TRUE);

DrawMenuBar();     /* Now we need to draw our menu */

/* Initialize the ThrustMaster and MouseStick info pointers.
 * If either of these joysticks is not connected, NULL
 * will be returned. We then dim the menu item for that
 * joystick.
 */
gThrustMasterInfo = GetThrustMasterInfoPtr();
gMouseStickInfo = GetMouseStickDriverInfo();

/* Check to see if these joysticks are connected */
if (gThrustMasterInfo == NULL) {
  DisableItem(inputMenu, kINPUT_ThrustMaster);
}
```

Continued on next page

Continued from previous page

```
  if (gMouseStickInfo == NULL) {
    DisableItem(inputMenu, kINPUT_MouseStick);
  }


  /* Create a window that is 512x384 pixels large. This window is the
   * same size as the 12" RGB monitor, but since some of the 12" screen
   * is taken up by the menu bar and the window border, the window
   * won't fit on that screen. This window size is best for a 640x480
   * monitor (the most common size).
   */
  SetRect(&windowRect, 0, 0, 512, 384);

  /* Offset the window rect so that the window does not appear
   * under the menu bar.
   */
  OffsetRect(&windowRect, 20, 50);

  mainWindow = CreateWindow(&windowRect);

  /* Initialize the sprite routines */
  err = PrepareSprites();

  if (err == noErr) {
    /* Load the sprite background image */
    err = PrepareBackgroundImage();
  }

  if (err != noErr) {
    /* There was an error in the sprite routines.
     * Terminate the program.
     */
    SysBeep(1);
    ExitToShell();
  }

  RedrawEntireWindow(mainWindow);

  while (!done) {
    currentTickCount = TickCount();

    /* If it has been long enough since we last called WaitNextEvent(),
     * go ahead and call it again.
     */
    if (  (currentTickCount - lastWaitNextEventCall) >=
          kWaitNextEventDelay)
    {
      lastWaitNextEventCall = currentTickCount;
      /* We want to regain control from WaitNextEvent() rather quickly
       * so we set the sleep value to a low number.
       */
      notNullEvent = WaitNextEvent( eventMask,
```

```
                                                &theEvent,
                                                0,
                                                NULL);

            switch (theEvent.what) {
              WindowPtr    selectedWindow;
              short        findWindowResult;
              short        menuHit;  /* which menu was selected */
              short        itemHit;
              case mouseDown:
                /* We received a mousedown event. Check to see where it was */
                findWindowResult = FindWindow(theEvent.where, &selectedWindow);
                if (findWindowResult == inDrag) {
                  /* The user clicked in the drag bar. Allow them to drag it
                   * across the screen.
                   */
                  DragWindow(  selectedWindow,
                               theEvent.where,
                               &qd.screenBits.bounds);
                } else if (findWindowResult == inGoAway) {
                  /* The user clicked in the close box. Close the window. */

                  /* First make sure it's our window they clicked on */
                  if (selectedWindow == mainWindow) {

                    /* Then call TrackGoAway so the user has an opportunity to
                     * move the mouse out of the close box
                     */
                    if (TrackGoAway(selectedWindow, theEvent.where) == TRUE) {
                      /* Clicking the GoAway box in this application will cause
                       * it to quit. Set the done flag to TRUE so this happens.
                       */
                      done = TRUE;
                    }
                  }
                } else if (findWindowResult == inMenuBar) {
                  long  result;

                  /* It was in the menu bar. Find what item was selected */
                  result = MenuSelect(theEvent.where);

                  /* First check to see if any item was selected at all */
                  if (result != 0) {
                    /* We now need to dissect the result to */
                    /* find which menu was hit */
                    /* Move the upper 16 bits into a word */
                    menuHit = result >> 16;

                    /* And now we find which item in that menu was selected */
                    /* Mask off the bottom 16 bits */
                    itemHit = result & 0xFFFF;
```

Continued on next page

Continued from previous page

```
          if (menuHit == kMENU_File) {
            /* An item from the file menu was selected */
            /* The only item in the file menu we care about is
             * 'quit'
             */
            if (itemHit == kFILE_Quit)
              done = TRUE;
          } else if (menuHit == kMENU_Input) {
            short    i;
            /* Change the input method based on the constants
             * defined in Sprite Animator.h
             */
            if (itemHit == kINPUT_Keyboard)
              inputMethod = kKeyboardInput;
            else if (itemHit == kINPUT_MouseAbsoluteWindow)
              inputMethod = kAbsoluteWindowInput;
            else if (itemHit == kINPUT_MouseAbsoluteScreen)
              inputMethod = kAbsoluteScreenInput;
            else if (itemHit == kINPUT_MouseRelative)
              inputMethod = kRelativeInput;
            else if (itemHit == kINPUT_ThrustMaster)
              inputMethod = kThrustMaster;
            else if (itemHit == kINPUT_MouseStick)
              inputMethod = kMouseStick;

            /* Uncheck all of the menu items */
            for (i = 1; i <= kINPUT_MouseStick; i++) {
              CheckItem(inputMenu, i, FALSE);
            }

            /* Check the current input method */
            CheckItem(inputMenu, itemHit, TRUE);
          }
        }

        /* Un-hilite the menu */
        HiliteMenu(0);
      }
      break;

    case updateEvt:
    {
      BeginUpdate((WindowPtr)theEvent.message);

      /* Update the window to show the sprite */
      if ((WindowPtr)theEvent.message == mainWindow)
        RedrawEntireWindow(mainWindow);

      EndUpdate((WindowPtr)theEvent.message);
      break;
```

```
       }
     }
   }

  /* Allow the sprite-drawing portion to act. MoveCurrentSprite now
   * handles its own keyboard input.
   *
   * We implement a delay structure so that the routine is not
   * called more than once every 5 ticks (1/12 of a second).
   *
   * If you want to see the maximum speed your computer can
   * handle, change the 5 to 0.
   */
  currentTickCount = TickCount();

  if ((currentTickCount - lastMoveCurrentSpriteCall) >= 5) {
    lastMoveCurrentSpriteCall = currentTickCount;
    MoveCurrentSprite(mainWindow, inputMethod);
  }
}

/* Close the main window. */
if (mainWindow != NULL)
  DisposeWindow(mainWindow);
}
```

The MoveCurrentSprite() Function

The MoveCurrentSprite() function for Walking Man 2 is responsible for handling all
input from the keyboard and the mouse. It takes one more parameter, *inputMethod,* which
indicates which menu item is selected. The *inputMethod* can be one of the following constants: kKeyboardInput, kAbsoluteWindowInput, kAbsoluteScreenInput, or kRelativeInput.

To keep the routine a manageable size, MoveCurrentSprite delegates the responsibility for input to a new routine called ProcessInput(). ProcessInput() returns the current
sprite action (kSpriteWalkingLeft, kSpriteWalkingRight, or kSpriteStandingStill).
MoveCurrentSprite() then checks to see if that action is different from what the sprite
did during the previous frame. If it is, the image index is reset to 0.

Only the first few lines of the new MoveCurrentSprite() routine are shown here. The
rest of the routine remains unchanged.

```
/**
 **  MoveCurrentSprite()
 **
 **  Checks the keyboard or mouse for input, then animates the
 **  sprite based on that.
 **  This routine generates a temporary GWorld to hold
 **  the moving sprite composited onto the background. The temporary
 **  GWorld is large enough to hold both the place that the
 **  sprite _was_ and the position that it _will be_
```

Continued on next page

Continued from previous page

```
**/
OSErr  MoveCurrentSprite(WindowPtr  dstWindow, short inputMethod)
{
  Rect          windowBounds;
  Rect          spriteBounds;
  GWorldPtr     temporaryBuffer;
  PixMapHandle  tempBufferPixmap;
  PixMapHandle  backgroundPixmap;
  OSErr         err;
  GDHandle      saveDevice;
  CGrafPtr      savePort;
  short         distanceMoved;
  short         movingDirection;

  /* Check for input and get the sprite's current action based on that */
  movingDirection = ProcessInput(dstWindow, inputMethod);

  /* If the sprite changed its direction, reset the sprite's image index
   * to zero.
   */
  if (movingDirection != gWalkmanSprite.spriteAction) {
    gWalkmanSprite.spriteAction = movingDirection;
    gWalkmanSprite.currentImageIndex = 0;
  }
```

The ProcessInput() Routine

Three new routines for Walking Man 2 have already been shown—IsKeyPressed(), GetThrustMasterInfoPtr(), and GetMouseStickDriverInfo(). The last new routine used in Walking Man 2 is ProcessInput(); it is called by MoveCurrentSprite(). ProcessInput() reads the mouse, the keyboard, or a joystick (depending on the current input method) and then translates that information into an action for the sprite.

For keyboard input, ProcessInput() calls IsKeyPressed() for each of the two action keys (left arrow and right arrow). If it finds that one of these keys is pressed, it returns the corresponding direction for the sprite.

If one of the mouse input methods is being used, ProcessInput() will read the mouse position (using GetMouse()) and then use one of the methods outlined earlier to determine a direction for the sprite.

If a joystick is being used for input, only the current x position of the stick will be read. If the joystick is within the left third of its range, the sprite will walk to the left. If the stick is within the right third of its range, the sprite will walk to the right. A good improvement upon this method would be to vary the speed of the sprite depending on the extent of the joystick.

Listing 6-4 shows the code for ProcessInput().

Listing 6-4 *The ProcessInput() routine*

```
/**
** ProcessInput()
**
** Handles keyboard, mouse, or joystick input and returns the current
** direction of the sprite's movement.
**/
short  ProcessInput(WindowPtr theWindow, short inputMethod)
{
  short      movingDirection = kSpriteStandingStill;
  Point      mouseLoc;

  /* Check for input based on the inputMethod */
  if (inputMethod == kKeyboardInput) {
    /* Check for keyboard input */
    if (IsKeyPressed(kMoveLeftKeyCode)) {
      movingDirection = kSpriteWalkingLeft;
    } else if (IsKeyPressed(kMoveRightKeyCode)) {
      movingDirection = kSpriteWalkingRight;
    }
  } else {
    /* The input is based on the mouse. */
    GetMouse(&mouseLoc);

    /* Handle the mouse input differently depending on the mode */
    if ((inputMethod == kAbsoluteWindowInput) ||
      (inputMethod == kAbsoluteScreenInput)) {
      short    currentSpriteLeftEdge;
      short    currentSpriteRightEdge;
      short    mouseHorizLoc;

      /* If the input is relative to the screen, scale its position
       * to the width of the window before continuing. This segment
       * of code is the only difference between absolute window
       * and absolute screen positioning.
       */
      if (inputMethod == kAbsoluteScreenInput) {
        short    windowWidth, screenWidth;
        float    screenToWindowRatio;
        /* First convert the mouse position to global (screen)
         * coordinates.
         */
        LocalToGlobal(&mouseLoc);

        /* Find the width of the screen and that of the window */
        windowWidth = theWindow->portRect.right -
                      theWindow->portRect.left;
        screenWidth = qd.screenBits.bounds.right -
                      qd.screenBits.bounds.left;

        /* Calculate the ratio between the screen's width and the
```

Continued on next page

Continued from previous page

```
     * window's width.
     */
    screenToWindowRatio = (float)windowWidth / (float)screenWidth;

    /* Convert the mouse's 'h' location to be in the same range
     * as the window. We don't bother converting the 'v' location
     * because the sprite only moves left and right.
     */
    mouseLoc.h *= screenToWindowRatio;
}

currentSpriteLeftEdge = gWalkmanSprite.x;
currentSpriteRightEdge = gWalkmanSprite.x + gWalkmanSprite.width;
mouseHorizLoc = mouseLoc.h;

/* We must check to see if the sprite is 'close enough'
 * to the mouse. If we didn't, the sprite would constantly
 * be changing directions to match the mouse (since it
 * moves several pixels per frame)
 */
if (currentSpriteLeftEdge - mouseHorizLoc > kSpriteSpeed) {
  /* The mouse is to the left of the sprite */
  movingDirection = kSpriteWalkingLeft;
} else if (mouseHorizLoc - currentSpriteRightEdge > kSpriteSpeed) {
  /* The mouse is to the right of the sprite */
  movingDirection = kSpriteWalkingRight;
} else {
  movingDirection = kSpriteStandingStill;
}
} else if (inputMethod == kRelativeInput) {
  /* Move the sprite based on whether the mouse is close
   * to the left edge or close to the right edge of the
   * screen. This method involves a process similar to
   * kAbsoluteScreenInput in that the mouse position must
   * be translated into screen coordinates.
   */
  short    screenWidth;
  short    oneThirdOfScreenWidth;

  /* First convert the mouse position to global (screen)
   * coordinates.
   */
  LocalToGlobal(&mouseLoc);

  /* Calculate the width of the screen */
  screenWidth = qd.screenBits.bounds.right -
                qd.screenBits.bounds.left;

  /* We divide the screen into three vertical segments. If the mouse
   * is in the first (leftmost) segment, the sprite will be moving
   * to the left. If the mouse is in the middle, the sprite will be
   * standing still, and if the mouse is in the third segment, the
```

❖❖❖❖❖ *Talking to the Computer*   **179**

```
      * sprite will be moving right.
      */
    oneThirdOfScreenWidth = screenWidth / 3;

    if (mouseLoc.h < oneThirdOfScreenWidth) {
      /* Leftmost segment */
      movingDirection = kSpriteWalkingLeft;
    } else if (mouseLoc.h < (oneThirdOfScreenWidth * 2)) {
      /* Middle segment */
      movingDirection = kSpriteStandingStill;
    } else {
      movingDirection = kSpriteWalkingRight;
    }
  } else if (inputMethod == kThrustMaster) {
    /* The only ThrustMaster parameter we are using is 'roll'.
     * Roll is calibrated to be from -127 to 127. We are going
     * to break this range up into three equal segments. Values
     * less than -42 will move the sprite left, and values
     * greater than 42 will move the sprite to the right.
     */

    if (gThrustMasterInfo->roll < -42) {
      movingDirection = kSpriteWalkingLeft;
    } else if (gThrustMasterInfo->roll > 42) {
      movingDirection = kSpriteWalkingRight;
    } else {
      movingDirection = kSpriteStandingStill;
    }
  } else if (inputMethod == kMouseStick) {
    /* The MouseStick support is very similar to that of the
     * ThrustMaster, except that the range is much larger,
     * -600 to 600, so the cutoff points will be at
     * -200 and 200.
     */
    if (gMouseStickInfo->stick1_xIn < -200) {
      movingDirection = kSpriteWalkingLeft;
    } else if (gMouseStickInfo->stick1_xIn > 200) {
      movingDirection = kSpriteWalkingRight;
    } else {
      movingDirection = kSpriteStandingStill;
    }
  }
}
return movingDirection;
}
```

Using Walking Man 2

When Walking Man 2 starts up, the input method will default to the keyboard, as you can see in Figure 6-7. One of the first things you will notice is that when you press one of the arrow keys, the sprite will move only as long as the key is held down. This form of input is more like that used in arcade games than using WaitNextEvent(), like you did for the walking man animation in Chapter 5.

Experiment with the mouse modes until you understand how they work. The various modes are important for different types of games—flight simulators tend to use the relative mode, whereas a game like Space Invaders might use the absolute to screen mode.

Up until now, I've been focusing on the visual part of arcade games, but in the next chapter, I will examine another very important feature—sound. After all, where would a good arcade game be without the sound of blaster fire or the roar of jet engines?

FIGURE 6-7

◎ ◎ ◎ ◎ ◎ ◎

The walking man in action

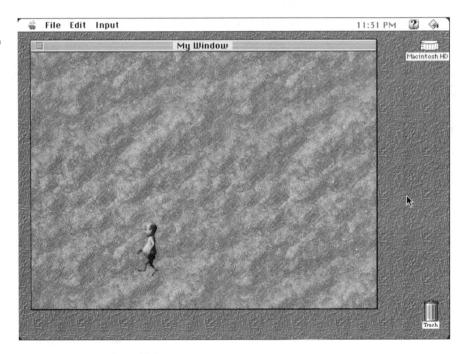

7

Listening to the Computer

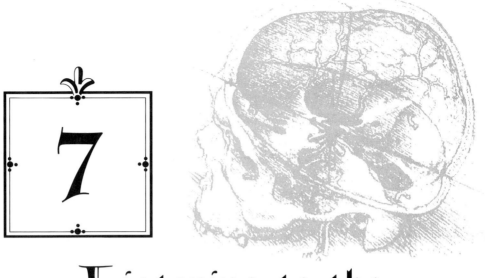

7

Listening to the Computer

So far, I have touched upon two of the three basic parts of any game: graphics and user input. The third, sound, is equally as important. There are two basic kinds of game sounds: sound effects, such as an explosion or the whine of a race car engine, and music, which is usually used to set a mood.

In this chapter, you'll learn how to create *asynchronous* sound effects. Asynchronous means that the effects play while your application continues to execute, as opposed to *synchronous* sound, where you must wait for the sound to finish before you can resume the game. Asynchronous sound is absolutely necessary for games because the sound effects have to match up with the action occurring on-screen.

This chapter will also show you how to create a sound that loops continually. This is great for background music or for a perpetual sound effect, such as an airplane's engines. In addition, you can switch between different continuous sounds, allowing you to have several themes of music and vary them as the player's situation changes.

Your game can create music with a MIDI sound package. Such a package stores *samples* of musical instruments (which are very short segments of their sound, frequently a half-second or less), then creates music by playing the samples back at varying rates and tempos using a preprogrammed script. Two popular formats for such music are the Amiga-born MOD file and the QuickTime 2.0 package. Although I won't be covering MIDI music in this book, you can look at *Inside Macintosh: QuickTime* for a discussion of that.

A third way to create your music soundtrack doesn't involve using the CPU at all. Some modern games that ship on a CD-ROM store their musical tracks as normal compact disc audio tracks, which any compact disc player can read. While playing the game, these CDs tell the CD-ROM player to start playing a particular musical track; they don't need to worry about it again until the track ends. The advantage of this method is that the sound quality is much better than most computers can produce (and still have time to animate a game) and CPU time is conserved, improving the speed of the game. The disadvantages are that the entire game must reside on the hard drive (because the CD-ROM can't be accessed for data while it's playing a musical track) and playing musical tracks off of a CD-ROM disc won't work if the CD-ROM drive is external (unless the user has speakers connected to the drive). Despite the disadvantages, some PC games are using this approach; a few Macintosh games are likely to follow in the future.

Components of Sound

Figure 7-1 shows a representation of the most simple kind of sound wave—a sine wave. As you can see, the sine wave consists of two elements: amplitude, which is the height of the wave and controls how much energy the sound has (i.e., how loud it is), and frequency, which is how tightly packed each peak of the wave is and provides the sound's pitch.

Frequency is measured in *hertz*, which is the number of sound wave peaks passing through a particular point in 1 second. The farther the peaks are from one another, the lower the frequency and the lower the pitch of the sound. The human ear under ideal conditions can detect frequencies between 15 hertz and 20,000 hertz (or 20 *kilohertz*).

FIGURE 7-1

◉ ◉ ◉ ◉ ◉ ◉

A sine wave

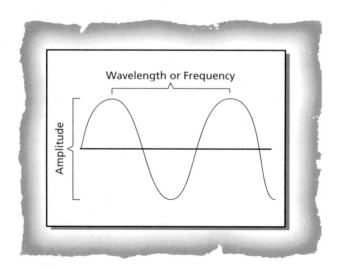

The Sound of Sine

If you were to convert the sine wave in Figure 7-1 into a sound, you would hear a continuous tone. The pitch of that tone would depend on how quickly each hump of the wave was played.

In general, sine waves produce relatively pleasant tones. This is because there is a smooth transition between each curve peak and thus the sound is soft. If you would like to hear an example for yourself, check out the 1000hz sound created from a sine wave on the source code disc under Chapter 7:1000 hz sine wave.

Sawtooth Waves and Square Waves

What would happen to a sound if there wasn't the smooth transition between each peak? Figure 7-2 shows one such wave. Each peak is connected with a straight line instead of a curve, which has the effect of making the sound harsher than the sine wave. An example of a *sawtooth wave* can be heard by double-clicking on the file Chapter 7:1000hz sawtooth wave.

A third type of wave is called a *square wave*. As shown in Figure 7-3, a square wave doesn't have any transition between each peak. The effect is a very severe sound, guaranteed to strike a nerve.

Complex Sounds

If I represent sounds that you hear every day in wave form, you'll see a pattern similar to the previous three waves (see Figure 7-4). In fact, every sound you hear is composed

FIGURE 7-2

◎ ◎ ◎ ◎ ◎ ◎

A sawtooth wave

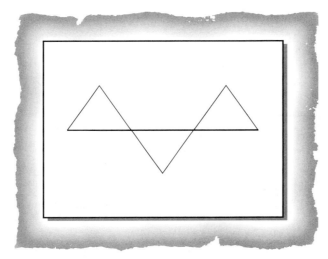

FIGURE 7-3

◎ ◎ ◎ ◎ ◎ ◎

A square wave

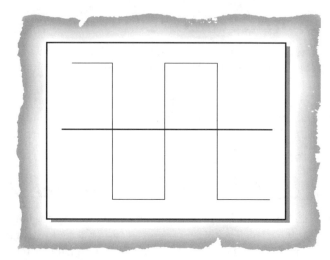

FIGURE 7-4

◎ ◎ ◎ ◎ ◎ ◎

*A complex
sound wave*

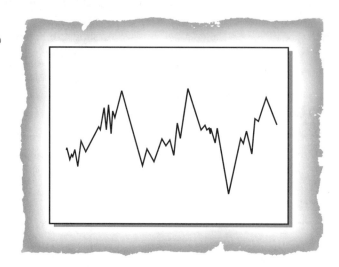

of some number of the basic waves jumbled together in a single wave. For these games, you'll be using complex sounds to make the action more interesting.

Modern Equipment and Sound

The sound you experience is waves of compressed air. The frequency of the sound is defined by the physical distance between each compression; the amplitude (volume) of the sound comes from the energy within each wave. Thus it is possible to generate sound waves by having some way of compressing air at a particular interval and strength.

The speakers in your stereo system and your computer do this by vibrating a paper or plastic cone at various frequencies. Every time the cone moves out, a compression is created (equivalent to the top of the sine wave). When the cone moves in, a drop in air pressure is created (the bottom of the wave). This is shown in Figure 7-5. If the cone vibrates 1,000 times a second, it creates a 1,000 hertz (or one kilohertz) sound.

A Computer's Representation of Sound

For simple sounds, it would be easy for a computer to represent the sound as a continuous wave. For example, to produce the sine wave you heard earlier, it could remember the sound as the sin() function repeated 1000 times a second.

For more complex sounds, however, the computer would have to generate enormous formulas that would require massive amounts of disk space and processor time to interpret. Instead, the computer converts the sound into a digital format. The sound wave is measured at regular intervals along its length and each measured value is stored as a number. This process is called *sampling*. Later, when the sound is played back, these numbers are converted back into a sound wave by the appropriate hardware.

When a sound is sampled, a certain amount of quality is lost. This is because the sound wave, being analog, has infinite precision. The computer cannot take an infinite number of samples, so it has to settle for some specific precision. This rate is called

FIGURE 7-5

◉ ◉ ◉ ◉ ◉ ◉

A loudspeaker producing sound

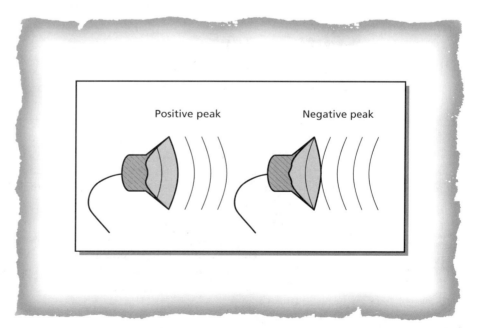

Positive peak   Negative peak

the *sampling rate*, and different rates are used for various purposes. For example, a compact disc samples at a rate of approximately 44,000 samples per second. But for a sound sample that doesn't require much quality, such as a person's voice over a telephone, a rate of about 7,000 samples per second will suffice.

The amount of data used for each sample also makes a big difference in the sound quality. For example, until recently, the Macintosh used an 8-bit value for each sample (which is said to be an 8-bit sound). This provides good sound quality for almost anything a computer needs to do, but it is not sufficient for professional sound output. For a compact disc, 16 bits are used for each sample. It hasn't been necessary to use any more than 16-bit sound because the human ear has limitations on the details it can distinguish.

Digital sound can consume huge amounts of space. If you were to record sounds for your game at CD quality, it would take 44,000 samples per second at 16 bits per sample. This equates to 86k per second, or over 5 megabytes per minute, and that's not even using stereo sound! If the game shipped on a CD-ROM (which can hold approximately 600 megabytes), you could store sound at this quality, but you would still be using a large portion of CPU time just to play the sound.

Most games today use a sampling rate of either 22,000 or 11,000 samples per second and 8-bit sound, which only uses 22k or 11k of space per second, respectively. Although this is significantly less than CD-quality, the quality is sufficient for games.

The Sound Manager can compress sounds so they consume less memory and drive space. However, this compression results in the loss of some sound quality, and the results are less than spectacular for music. It's primary use lies in lower fidelity sounds, such as speech, so you won't be using it in the code you develop in this chapter.

Synthesizers

As discussed earlier, the Macintosh can handle two types of sounds: sounds comprising the basic sound waves (sine, sawtooth, and square) and digital sounds. The Sound Manager provides three different packages, or *synthesizers*, designed for these sounds.

The first synthesizer is the *square-wave synthesizer*; it can play a sequence of sounds, each composed of three factors: pitch (i.e., frequency), volume (i.e., amplitude), and duration. As you might have guessed from its name, the square-wave synthesizer is not capable of generating sine waves, but it can be used to generate smooth sound by using several commands to fade sound in and out quickly. The simple beep provided with System 7 uses the square-wave synthesizer.

The second synthesizer is called the *wave-table synthesizer*. The wave-table synthesizer produces sound based on a description of a single wave cycle. The single wave cycle is then repeated over and over (based on the frequency of the sound). The wave description is called the *wave table*; it consists of a sequence of bytes that represent the amplitude at that point in the cycle. A sine wave can be represented using a wave table, as shown in Figure 7-6.

FIGURE 7-6

◉ ◉ ◉ ◉ ◉ ◉

*A wave table
representation
of a sine wave*

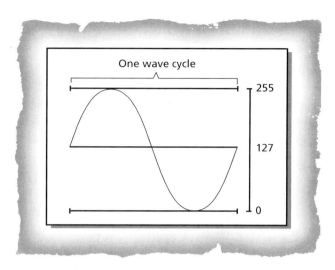

Each byte of the wave table is a value between 0 and 255. A value of 127 represents an amplitude of 0; the largest possible amplitude is 255 and the smallest is 0.

The last synthesizer is the one you should be most concerned with. It is called the *sampled sound synthesizer* and it is capable of playing back digitized sound samples. The sample program in this chapter will use the sampled sound synthesizer exclusively.

Sound Channels

Every sound the Macintosh plays is piped through a *sound channel*. A sound channel is the Sound Manager's way of keeping track of a set of sound commands. Each sound channel is created separately and is capable of playing one sound at a time. If your particular application needs to play more than one sound at a time, it should create as many channels as it needs. Of course, the more channels you use, the more CPU power will be required.

To create a new sound channel, use SndNewChannel():

```
OSErr  SndNewChannel( SndChannelPtr *newChannel,
                      short          synth,
                      long           initializationOption,
                      ProcPtr        userRoutine );
```

Pass in the address of a SndChannelPtr to *newChannel* to receive the new channel. *synth* is the ID of the synthesizer you want to use for this channel. Each channel can use only one synthesizer, and the three synthesizers are represented with one of these constants provided by the Sound Manager: squareWaveSynth, waveTableSynth, or sampledSynth. If you want the Sound Manager to decide which synthesizer is best for each sound, just pass in 0 for this parameter.

initializationOption can be used to specify specific initialization commands to the synthesizer. You won't be using any of these commands in this chapter so you can ignore this parameter for now by passing in 0.

userRoutine provides you with a way of having the Sound Manager call your code when certain conditions are met. In the code examples that follow, you'll tell the Sound Manager to call this routine whenever it is finished playing a sound. The routine that the Sound Manager calls is known as a *callback routine*; these routines are used quite often throughout the toolbox.

Callback Routines

In every case that the toolbox defines a callback routine, you will be able to find a template describing how to set up your routine in the Apple header files included with your compiler. In the case of SndNewChannel(), your callback routine is described in Sound.h and must be defined like this:

```
pascal void MySndCallBackFunction( SoundChannelPtr theSoundChannel,
                                   SndCommand      *infoRecord );
```

The specific name of the function (MySndCallBackFunction) and the names of the parameters (*theSoundChannel* and *infoRecord*) can be anything you like, but otherwise the function must be defined in exactly the same way. In this case, the function must take inputs of a SoundChannelPtr and a SndCommand.

When the Sound Manager calls your callback function, it will pass the function these two parameters—a SoundChannelPtr and a SndCommand structure. The SoundChannelPtr is the channel that needs attention and the SndCommand structure holds the callback command. I'll look at the SndCommand structure in more detail later on.

The Pascal Keyword

You might notice that the callback function was defined using the Pascal keyword. This doesn't mean that your routine is written in Pascal—it just means that your routine will read parameters in the same way that Pascal does. Pascal and C pass parameters to functions differently: Pascal pushes parameters onto the stack from left to right—which means the first parameter defined in a function is the first one onto the stack. C passes parameters in the opposite order, that is, from right to left.

The original Macintosh Toolbox is written in Pascal, so all callback functions must be written to receive parameters in the same way that a Pascal function would. Using the Pascal keyword does not affect how your routine functions in any other way.

PowerPC Procedure Pointers

The PowerPC computer introduces one more level of complexity to using callback functions. As you are probably aware, the Power Macintosh can use two types of code: PowerPC code and 68k code (the 68k code gets executed in an emulation mode). Before calling a function, the Power Macintosh must know whether it is calling a PowerPC function or a 68k function. When you compile an application for the PowerPC, this is entirely taken care of for you—the compiler tells the processor that it is using PowerPC code. However, when the toolbox uses a callback function on a PowerPC, it doesn't automatically know if that routine is in PowerPC or 68k code. You must manually indicate the kind of routine it is when specifying the callback.

The method used for telling the Power Macintosh about a routine is called a *universal procedure pointer* (or UPP). The only time you need to create a UPP is when you need to call a routine through a procedure pointer. In this book, you will only need UPPs for toolbox callback functions.

Along with every callback definition, Apple includes a routine that will take a pointer to your procedure and create a UPP specifically for that toolbox call. In the case of the SndNewChannel() procedure, that routine would be NewSndCallBackProc().

```
SndCallBackUPP NewSndCallBackProc(ProcPtr soundCallBackProc);
```

Here is an example of how you could call SndNewChannel() using UPP:

```
err = SndNewChannel(  &newChannel,
                      0, /* Let the sound manager decide
                         * which synth to use */
                      0, /* No special commands for
                         * the synth */
                      NewSndCallBackProc(SoundIsFinishedCallBack));
                      /* This is to let it know which routine
                       * should be called when the sound is
                       * finished.
                       */
```

When this code is compiled for a 68k Mac, the call to NewSndCallBackProc is ignored because 68k Macs don't need to use UPPs. However, it is still a good idea to use them in case you want to compile for the PowerPC in the future.

Synchronous Sound

Let's look at how to get the computer to play sounds. The first method I'll look at is synchronous sound, which is the most basic method of playing sounds. When an application calls a routine in the Sound Manager to play a sound synchronously, it will not regain control until the sound has finished playing. This method of playback is handy for many simple tasks, such as beeping to let the user know that a task is done, or for a sound effect accompanying a still image. Although it does not have much use in arcade games, synchronous sound is good to learn about because asynchronous sound is simply an extension of synchronous sound.

The most basic routine to use for sound playback is SndPlay().

```
OSErr SndPlay(  SndChannelPtr    channel,
                SndListHandle    soundHandle,
                Boolean          asynchronous );
```

The *channel* parameter of SndPlay() is used to tell the Sound Manager to use a particular channel for playing the sound. If you want the Sound Manager to create a new channel for playing this sound, pass in NULL for this parameter.

The sounds played by SndPlay() are SND (sound) resources that were previously loaded using GetResource(). (Because each resource type must have four characters, the signature for the sound resource contains a space.) If you open a System 7 sound file using ResEdit, you will notice that there is a SND resource. SND resources are treated like any other resource.

The asynchronous parameter is used to play sounds asynchronously. Because you are just playing sounds synchronously for now, pass in FALSE for this parameter.

The following code will load a SND resource from the resource fork and play it synchronously using SndPlay(). This code can also be found on your source code disc under Chapter 7:Synchronous Sound.

```
void main(void) {
  SndListHandle     theSound;

  /* Load the sound resource */
  theSound = (SndListHandle)GetResource('snd ', 100);

  if (theSound != NULL) {
  . SndPlay(  NULL,      /* Let the sound manager allocate
                          * a new channel for this sound.
                          */
              theSound, /* The sound to play */
              FALSE);   /* Play it synchronously */
  }
}
```

When you double-click on the application, an explosion sound (SND resource ID #100) will be loaded into memory and played synchronously before the program quits.

Asynchronous Sound

The next step is to play sound asynchronously. This allows you to play sounds while doing a complex animation and to play multiple sounds at the same time. Each asynchronous sound must have its own channel while it is playing. However, once the sound has finished playing, the channel is free for any other sound. You can open a channel just before playing a sound and then close it when we are finished or you can allocate a few channels when the program starts up and share them among several different sounds. The first method involves a little more overhead, because it takes a bit of CPU time to open and close a channel. If you don't play sounds very often in your application, this method would be preferable because each channel will consume a certain amount of CPU time while it is open. Closing a channel also frees up those resources for other applications that may be running.

The second method, allocating a channel and leaving it open, works well for games. Although there is a constant minor CPU drain, it is less than the cost of opening new sound channels every time there is another sound effect. The second method is the one I'll be using throughout this book.

Has the Sound Finished?

You need a way to detect when the sound has finished playing. Because you send sound to the Sound Manager and then continue before the sound is finished, you can't send another sound to that channel before the first one has finished playing (if you did, either the sound currently playing would be cut off or the new sound wouldn't start until the current sound had completed).

This is where the callback routines become handy. Tell the Sound Manager to call a function in the code when the sound has finished playing. You have to be careful when constructing the callback routine because you don't know when it will be called—code in some other part of the game will be running when suddenly it is interrupted and the callback routine is executed.

Code that is used this way is said to be called at *interrupt time*. A routine that is called at interrupt time must be careful not to change the state of the processor, or the code that is being interrupted may crash. As you saw in Chapter 3, there are some cases in which the Memory Manager will move memory around—functions that are called at interrupt time must not do anything that would cause this to happen. As it happens, a good deal of the routines in the toolbox can cause memory to move and so they are off limits. Information on whether a particular routine moves memory can be found in the plethora of *Inside Macintosh* volumes.

There is one more catch: The routine that is called at interrupt time cannot access any of the application's global variables (this includes static variables within the function) without doing some special tricks that involve juggling the A5 register whenever entering or leaving the callback routine. This restriction has been removed on the Power Macintosh, but because you want your code to work on the 68k, you still have to follow this rule.

Sending Signals

So what *can* this routine do? You need to send a message back to the rest of the application saying that the sound has finished playing. Because you can't use global variables (or call any routine that uses global variables), this may seem impossible. But Apple has provided a way to get information back and forth.

You might have noticed that the callback routine takes two parameters—a sound channel and a structure called a SndCommand. Here is the format of that structure:

```
typedef struct {
  unsigned short  cmd;
  short           param1;
  long            param2;
} SndCommand;
```

The SndCommand structure is used whenever you want to place a sound command into a sound channel. Sound commands can do a variety of things, such as changing the frequency, volume, or duration of a sound. The only thing you'll be using sound commands for in this chapter is telling the Sound Manager to execute the callback function when the current sound has finished playing.

To issue a sound command, fill out a SndCommand structure with the particular command and its parameters, if it has any (all of these commands and their parameters are documented in *Inside Macintosh: Sound*). In the case of the callback command, the two parameters have a special meaning.

Whenever the callback routine is called, it will receive the exact SndCommand structure you used to define the command in the first place. The *cmd* field is always going to be callBackCmd (a constant defined by Apple), but you can use anything you want for *param1* and *param2*.

So *param1* and *param2* are used for sending information to the callback routine. But because they're not sent back to the application, what good are they? The *param2* field is a longword, just large enough to store an address. All you need to do is to store the address of a global variable in this field. It is illegal for a callback routine to access a global variable directly, but it *is* legal to access the global variable *indirectly*.

Figure 7-7 shows this entire process in detail.

Creating the Asynchronous Sound

Let's look at the code you would use for these steps. The first thing you need to do is to create a sound channel, which you saw earlier in the chapter. It is at this point that you tell the Sound Manager which callback routine to use.

The second step is to call SndPlay(). Give it the same parameters you gave it when using synchronous sound, except that you don't have the option of passing in NULL for the channel. The channel must be allocated prior to calling SndPlay() and it cannot be disposed of before the sound is finished playing. If you wait until the program quits before disposing of sound channels, you should be fine in this respect.

The next step is to issue the callBackCmd to the Sound Manager. When the Sound Manager finishes the sound, it will execute the callBackCmd using the callback

FIGURE 7-7

◉ ◉ ◉ ◉ ◉ ◉

The asynchronous sound callback sequence of events

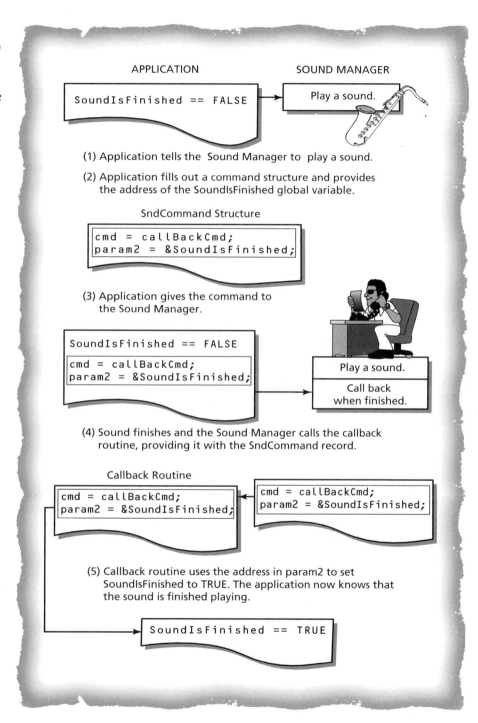

APPLICATION   SOUND MANAGER

```
SoundIsFinished == FALSE
```
Play a sound.

(1) Application tells the Sound Manager to play a sound.

(2) Application fills out a command structure and provides the address of the SoundIsFinished global variable.

SndCommand Structure

```
cmd = callBackCmd;
param2 = &SoundIsFinished;
```

(3) Application gives the command to the Sound Manager.

```
SoundIsFinished == FALSE

cmd = callBackCmd;
param2 = &SoundIsFinished;
```

Play a sound.

Call back when finished.

(4) Sound finishes and the Sound Manager calls the callback routine, providing it with the SndCommand record.

Callback Routine

```
cmd = callBackCmd;
param2 = &SoundIsFinished;
```

```
cmd = callBackCmd;
param2 = &SoundIsFinished;
```

(5) Callback routine uses the address in param2 to set SoundIsFinished to TRUE. The application now knows that the sound is finished playing.

```
SoundIsFinished == TRUE
```

function. The function to use for sending commands to the Sound Manager is SndDoCommand().

```
OSErr  SndDoCommand(    SndChannelPtr   channel,
                        SndCommand      *command,
                        Boolean         async );
```

Every command is associated with a channel. Because a sound channel is actually a first-in-first-out queue, the command will be executed once everything already in the channel has finished executing (in this case, a sound being played).

You have already seen the SndCommand structure. It is in here that you place the specific command and its parameters (in this case, you use the callBackCmd and a pointer to your isSoundFinished variable).

If you set *async* to FALSE, your program's execution will stop until the command you just added is finished. If you do this, it will negate any advantage of asynchronous sound, but it does have its advantages (such as waiting for commands to finish before exiting the application). Most of the time, you'll pass TRUE for this parameter.

Now let's look at a simple program that will load a sound resource and play it asynchronously.

Asynchronous Sound Player

The first thing you'll need is a global variable for checking the status of the current sound:

```
Boolean isSoundFinished;
```

The main() routine loads the sound, creates a new channel, plays the sound, and tells the Sound Manager to call SoundIsFinishedCallBack() when it is finished. It then continually checks the status of isSoundFinished before exiting the application in an empty while() loop. Listing 7-1 shows this process.

Listing 7-1 *Loading and playing a sound resource asynchronously*

```
void main(void) {
  SndListHandle   theSound;
  SndChannelPtr   soundChannel;
  OSErr           err;

  /* Load the sound resource */
  theSound = (SndListHandle)GetResource('snd ', 100);

  /* Quit if there was an error loading the sound */
  if (theSound == NULL)
    ExitToShell();

  /* Create the sound channel */
  soundChannel = NULL;  /* It is important to set the
                         * sound channel to NULL before
```

```
                              * allocating it with SndNewChannel!
                              */
        err = SndNewChannel( &soundChannel,
                        0, /* Let the sound manager decide
                            * which synth to use */
                        0, /* No special commands for
                            * the synth */
                        NewSndCallBackProc(SoundIsFinishedCallBack));
                        /* This is to let it know which routine
                         * should be called when the sound is
                         * finished.
                         */

    /* Test for errors */
    if ((err != noErr) || (soundChannel == NULL))
      ExitToShell();

    /* Play the sound */
    SndPlay( soundChannel,/* Use our new channel */
             theSound,    /* The sound to play */
             TRUE);       /* Play it asynchronously */

    if (err == noErr) {
      /* Now send a command to this sound channel to
       * call us back when this sound is finished.
       * This is so we can dispose of this sound channel
       * and leave it free for other programs
       */
      SndCommand    soundCommand;

      isSoundFinished = FALSE;
      soundCommand.cmd = callBackCmd;

      /* Send in the address of the isSoundFinished
       * boolean value. When the callback is invoked,
       * it will change this boolean value to TRUE,
       * letting us know the sound is finished.
       *
       * The param1 and param2 fields are provided for
       * our own use - we can put any values we like into
       * them. Since param1 is defined as a short, we'll
       * use param2 to pass in the address.
       */
      soundCommand.param2 = (long)&isSoundFinished;

      /* Send the command to the Sound Manager. */
      err = SndDoCommand( soundChannel,   /* use the same channel */
                          &soundCommand,  /* our sound command */
                          FALSE);         /* don't wait for it to finish */
    }

    /* Wait until the sound is done before quitting */
```

Continued on next page

Continued from previous page
```
while (isSoundFinished == FALSE)
{
  /* Do nothing */
}
}
```

The final part you need is the callback routine. It looks like Listing 7-2.

Listing 7-2 *The SoundIsFinishedCallBack( ) routine*

```
/**
**    SoundIsFinishedCallBack()
**
**    This routine is called when a sound is finished playing. It will
**    mark that channel as 'finished'. This routine cannot call any
**    function that can move memory!
**
**    All callback routines used by the toolbox must be declared as
**    Pascal.
**/
pascal void  SoundIsFinishedCallBack(  SndChannelPtr theSoundChannel,
                                        SndCommand *infoRecord)
{
  Boolean    *sndIsFinishedPtr;
  /* The infoRecord that has been provided has a field that points to
   * isSoundFinished. Our only task in this routine is to change that
   * entry to TRUE, indicating that the sound is finished playing. If
   * this were a normal routine, we could just use global variables
   * directly. However, this routine is called at interrupt time, and any
   * routine called this way cannot use any global variables without
   * going through a few tricks. For such a simple task, this
   * method is better.
   *
   * First extract the Boolean pointer from the information record. The
   * param2 field of the record is defined as a long, so we must
   * typecast it to a (Boolean *).
   */
  sndIsFinishedPtr = (Boolean *)infoRecord->param2;

  /* Set the isSoundFinished global */
  *sndIsFinishedPtr = TRUE;
}
```

Using the Asynchronous Player

Double-clicking on the asynchronous sound application will play the explosion sound just as the synchronous sound player did. In fact, in this limited capacity, you won't notice any difference between the two applications (because the player doesn't have anything to do while playing the sound anyway). This example illustrates how to create asynchronous sounds, not what you can do with them. The final application will illustrate some of the applications of asynchronous sound.

Continuous Sound

I've now covered all the aspects of sound for games except for the background music or continuous sound effects, like the whine of an engine. In this section I'll focus on background music. Music can play a large role in setting the mood of the game. In a space combat game like Wing Commander or X-Wing, the musical sequences change depending on whether or not the player is engaged in combat. The normal music is relaxing, whereas the combat music is upbeat and designed to get your heart pumping. In role-playing games like Might and Magic, the music changes, for example, when the party enters a dungeon or it is attacked by orcs or goblins.

Just as in a movie, music in computer games is used to manipulate the mood of the player. An excellent example of this is the software titles created by LucasArts Entertainment. If you own a copy of X-Wing or TIE Fighter, play it through a few battles and listen closely to the music. There is a musical theme for almost every occurrence—a new ship entering the area, killing a ship, achieving your mission goals, even failure. All of these small touches go toward making a great game.

Playing the Music

The routines you will use for playing the music are similar to the asynchronous sound routines, except a bit more complicated. You need a mechanism that will constantly feed the Sound Manager new information to play without leaving gaps. Fortunately, the Sound Manager has just the package you need.

The method you'll be using for continuous background sound is called *double buffering*. Essentially, you will be setting up two buffers of equal size into which you will pump sound information.

The Sound Manager will play all of the information in one of the buffers. When it finishes, it will instantly switch to the second buffer and begin to use that data. While the second buffer is being consumed, the Sound Manager will tell the application to refill the first buffer. If the buffers are large enough, by the time the Sound Manager finishes with the second buffer, the first one will be filled with fresh information. This process continues indefinitely until you decide to stop the sound, as shown in Figure 7-8.

Sound Headers

Unfortunately, to use double buffers, you must dig down to a lower level in the Sound Manager. You will be feeding raw sound data to the Sound Manager, unlike the neat package found in a sound resource.

In every sound resource, there is a *sound header* at the beginning, followed by the data. There are two approaches you can take to getting at the data. The first is to make some assumptions about every sound you will be playing. These assumptions are then hard-coded into the source code and you strip the headers off of the sounds by hand.

FIGURE 7-8

The double-
buffering
process

(1) Application creates two
    sound buffers of equal size.

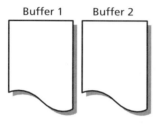

(2) Application fills both
    sound buffers.

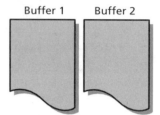

(3) Application sends buffers to
    Sound Manager. The Sound
    Manager begins to play the
    data in Buffer1.

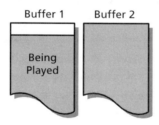

(4) Sound Manager finishes
    with Buffer 1, starts on
    Buffer 2. It also asks the
    application to refill Buffer 1.

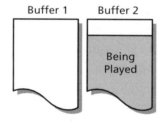

(5) Application refills buffer 1
    with fresh data and tells
    the Sound Manager it
    is ready.

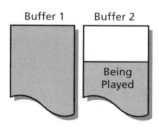

(6) Sound Manager finisher
    with Buffer 2 and goes
    back to Buffer 1. Application
    is asked to refill Buffer2.

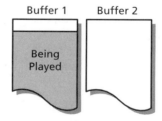

This method has a big disadvantage: It is difficult to change the sounds you use (every time the sound is changed, you must remember to strip the data off). This may not seem like a big deal, but when you reach the end of the development cycle of a product, you end up changing things like this quite often (or worse...forgetting to!). The other disadvantage is that if you change the sound format (like the sample rate or even the length of the sound), you must change the code at the same time and recompile.

The second method is to make the code smart about the sounds it will be using. The code will do the work of stripping off the sound header, learning about the format of the sound at the same time. This technique requires a little more work when writing the code to begin with, but it will pay off in the long run. This is the method that will be used in this book.

Figure 7-9 shows the format of the sound header. Here is a breakdown of what the contents mean.

- Sound format: Sounds can be Type 1 or Type 2. Type 2 sounds have a little less information and they are obsolete. You will deal only with Type 1 sounds.

- Number of synths: How many synthesizers are used to play this sound. You're only going to use sounds that use one sampled-sound synthesizer, so this field should always be 1.

- First synth ID: Because you are only using sampled-synth sounds, this field should always be 5 (the value of the sampleSynth constant).

- First synth options: Any special options to use for this synthesizer. Ignore this field.

- Number of sound commands: How many commands are used to play this sound. This value will determine how much space in the header is consumed by sound commands (8 bytes per command).

- Sound commands: Following the number of sound commands field is a series of sound commands. Ignore the commands used by the sound, but to get to the rest of the data, you need to jump over them. Each sound command is 8 bytes, so you know you need to skip (number of sound commands * 8) bytes.

- Offset to sound info: This tells the Sound Manager where to find the rest of the sound info. It is generally 0, indicating that this info is immediately following, so just ignore it.

- Number of bytes in the sample: This is an important field. It tells you how large the sound is, which is important when you start looping the sound.

- Sound sample rate: This is also important. It tells you how many samples/second are used for this sound. Any sample rate can be used for double buffering, but you need to use this value when creating the buffers.

FIGURE 7-9

◎ ◎ ◎ ◎ ◎ ◎

The format of a SND resource

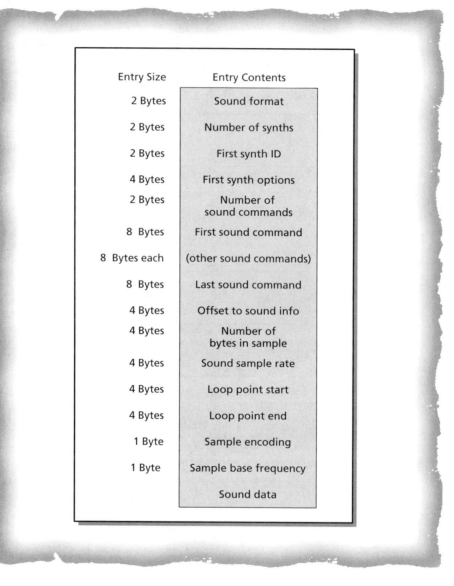

Entry Size	Entry Contents
2 Bytes	Sound format
2 Bytes	Number of synths
2 Bytes	First synth ID
4 Bytes	First synth options
2 Bytes	Number of sound commands
8 Bytes	First sound command
8 Bytes each	(other sound commands)
8 Bytes	Last sound command
4 Bytes	Offset to sound info
4 Bytes	Number of bytes in sample
4 Bytes	Sound sample rate
4 Bytes	Loop point start
4 Bytes	Loop point end
1 Byte	Sample encoding
1 Byte	Sample base frequency
	Sound data

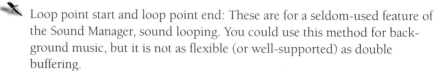 Loop point start and loop point end: These are for a seldom-used feature of the Sound Manager, sound looping. You could use this method for background music, but it is not as flexible (or well-supported) as double buffering.

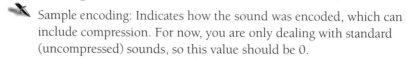 Sample encoding: Indicates how the sound was encoded, which can include compression. For now, you are only dealing with standard (uncompressed) sounds, so this value should be 0.

Base frequency: The pitch used to record the sound. Don't worry about this field either.

 Sound data: This is the data that you need to access.

As you can see, the only fields you want to check are the Number of bytes in sample and Sample rate fields. However, you also need to look at the Number of sound commands field to know how many bytes to skip.

Skipping the Sound Header

Let's build some sample code to use for removing the header from a sound. This code assumes the sound handle is theSoundHandle and it is already loaded from the disk. Because you are going to be using the internal data of the handle, it must be locked down before you begin to dissect it.

At the end of this code segment, soundPtr will point directly at the beginning of the sound data, where you can use it for the double buffer. You will also know what the sample rate and the total size of this sound is. This is shown in Listing 7-3.

Listing 7-3 *Removing the header from a sound*

```
short          numberOfSoundCommands;
long           soundCommandSize;
Ptr            soundPtr;

/* SoundSize and sampleRate contain the only information
 * from the sound header that we want to keep
 */
long           soundSize;
long           sampleRate;

/* First lock down the sound handle - we're going to be
 * messing with its contents, so we can't let it move
 * around in memory.
 */
HLock(theSoundHandle);

/* Dereference the sound handle so we just have a pointer
 * to the beginning of the sound header
 */
soundPtr = *theSoundHandle;

/* Skip over the first 10 bytes of the sound header. These
 * 10 bytes consist of the format, number of synths, synth
 * resource ID, and synth options.
 */
soundPtr += 10;
```

Continued on next page

Continued from previous page

```
/* The next 2 bytes of the header is the 'Number of
 * Sound Commands'. Each command uses 8 bytes, so
 * we can use it to skip over all of the sound commands.
 */
numberOfSoundCommands = *(short *)soundPtr;

/* Now move the pointer past those two bytes */
soundPtr += 2;

/* Calculate how much space is being used for
 * the sound commands.
 */
soundCommandSize = numberOfSoundCommands * 8;

/* Skip over the sound commands. */
soundPtr += soundCommandSize;

/* soundPtr is now positioned approximately halfway
 * into the header. There is some important data
 * at this point, some of which we need, some we don't.
 *
 * The rest of the header consists of an offset
 * to the data (which we don't need), the size of
 * this sound (which we need), the sample rate
 * of the sound (which we need), and 10 more bytes
 * of other information (which we don't need).
 *
 * Grab the information we need, skip the stuff we
 * don't need.
 */

/* The offset to the data - 4 bytes - we don't need it. */
soundPtr += 4;

/* The sound size - 4 bytes - we need this */
soundSize = *(long*)soundPtr;
soundPtr += 4;

/* The sound sample rate - 4 bytes - we need this. */
soundSize = *(long*)soundPtr;
soundPtr += 4;

/* An extra 10 bytes, which we don't need */
soundPtr += 10;
```

Fill'er Up

Just as with asynchronous sounds, the Sound Manager uses callback routines to ask the sound buffers to be refilled. In this case, the prototype for the callback routine must look like this:

```
pascal void FillSoundBuffers(   SndChannelPtr        soundChannel,
                                SndDoubleBufferPtr doubleBuffer  );
```

The *soundChannel* parameter is the channel that the sound is playing under. *doubleBuffer*, however, is a structure that looks like this:

```
typedef struct {
    long      dbNumFrames;
    long      dbFlags;
    long      dbUserInfo[2];
    char      dbSoundData[1];
} SndDoubleBuffer;
```

The *dbNumFrames* field indicates how many bytes of sound remain in this buffer. When your callback routine is executed, this value will always be 0 (because the routine is called when the buffer is empty).

The *dbFlags* field is the status of the buffer. The only 2 bits you need to worry about are the first (which indicates whether the buffer is ready to be used) and the third (which is used to tell the Sound Manager that this is the last buffer to play). These 2 bits have respective constants: dbBufferReady and dbLastBuffer. The rest of the bits of this field are used by the Sound Manager, so do not disturb them.

The *dbUserFlags* fields are two longwords you can use for passing data into your callback routine. Because this callback is also issued at interrupt time, it has to follow the same restrictions as the asynchronous sound callback. You'll use one of these longwords for passing in the address of a structure and ignore the other.

The *dbSoundData* field is the beginning of the double-buffer data. The double-buffer record is variable-sized, and all of the data after the dbUserInfo fields is for the sound. This is the area you will copy the sound data into.

Next you'll build the structure you'll be passing into the callback routine. You need to have access to several bits of information:

 How large the sound is (in bytes)

 A pointer to the beginning of the sound data

 How many bytes you've already copied into the buffer

✄ A flag used to tell the callback routine to stop copying data; this flag will be set by the main application when it is finished with the sound

Here is the definition for that structure:

```
typedef struct {
    long      soundBytesTotal;
    Ptr       soundDataBegin;
/* soundBytesTotal is the size of each sound we can switch between,
 * and soundDataBegin is an array of pointers to the beginning
 * of each sound.
 */
```

Continued on next page

Continued from previous page

```
    long      soundBytesCopied;
/* soundBytesCopied is how much of the current sound has already
 * been copied into the sound buffer. The next time the buffer
 * needs to be refilled, this is where we'll start to pull the
 * data from.
 */

    Boolean    die;
/* If die is set to true, don't continue copying sound data -
 * instead, signal to the Sound Manager that we're done.
 */
} PrivateSoundData, *PrivateSoundDataPtr;
```

The callback function will use this data to copy the sound data into the buffer. It uses *soundBytesCopied* to keep track of where it last left off copying, and will continue from there. It uses a toolbox routine called BlockMove() to copy the data.

```
void   BlockMove( Ptr  srcPtr, Ptr destPtr, long byteCount );
```

The *srcPtr* parameter is where to copy from, the *destPtr* parameter is where to copy to, and the *byteCount* parameter is the number of bytes to copy. Ironically, BlockMove() is one of the few toolbox routines that will *not* cause the Memory Manager to rearrange memory, so it is safe to use at interrupt time.

Listing 7-4 shows the code for a buffer-filling routine.

Listing 7-4 *The buffer-filling routine*

```
pascal void FillSoundBuffers(  SndChannelPtr       theChannel,
                               SndDoubleBufferPtr  doubleBuffer)
{
  PrivateSoundDataPtr    ourPrivateData;
  long                   bytesToCopy;
  long                   sizeOfCurrentSound;
  Ptr                    currentSoundDataPtr;

  /* Get access to our private data */
  ourPrivateData = (PrivateSoundDataPtr)doubleBuffer->dbUserInfo[0];

  /* Retrieve the size of the current sound */
  sizeOfCurrentSound = ourPrivateData->soundBytesTotal;

  /* Calculate how many bytes remain to be copied into the buffer */
  bytesToCopy = sizeOfCurrentSound - ourPrivateData->soundBytesCopied;

  /* Check to see if the data that remains to be copied is larger
   * than the whole sound buffer. If so, just copy enough to fill
   * the buffer.
   */
  if (bytesToCopy > kSoundBufferSize)
    bytesToCopy = kSoundBufferSize;
```

```
/* Calculate a pointer to the beginning of the
 * sound data to be copied
 */
currentSoundDataPtr = ourPrivateData->soundDataBegin +
                      ourPrivateData->soundBytesCopied;

/* Copy the sound data into the buffer */
BlockMove ( currentSoundDataPtr,
            &doubleBuffer->dbSoundData[0],
            bytesToCopy );

/* Let the Sound Manager know how much data we just
 * put into the buffer
 */
doubleBuffer->dbNumFrames = bytesToCopy;

/* Tell the Sound Manager that the buffer is ready to use */
doubleBuffer->dbFlags = (doubleBuffer->dbFlags) | dbBufferReady;

/* Update our soundBytesCopied marker */
ourPrivateData->soundBytesCopied += bytesToCopy;

/* Check to see if we've copied the entire sound. If so, set
 * the data pointer back to the beginning of the sound.
 * Also check to see if we've been told to quit playing.
 */
if (ourPrivateData->soundBytesCopied == sizeOfCurrentSound)
{

  if (ourPrivateData->die) {
    /* We've been told to stop playing, so let the sound manager
     * know not to continue playing after it finishes with this
     * buffer.
     */
    doubleBuffer->dbFlags = (doubleBuffer->dbFlags) | dbLastBuffer;
  } else {
    ourPrivateData->soundBytesCopied = 0;
  }
}
return;
}
```

Starting the Process

The next code segment I'll look at will actually start the double-buffering process. The Sound Manager routine for this is called SndPlayDoubleBuffer():

```
OSErr  SndPlayDoubleBuffer( SndChannelPtr            theChannel,
                            SndDoubleBufferHeaderPtr bufferParams );
```

The key structure for this task is the SndDoubleBufferHeader. This structure holds all of the information the Sound Manager needs to start a buffered sound and keep it running. Here is the definition for the structure:

```
typedef struct {
  short                   dbhNumChannels;
  short                   dbhSampleSize;
  short                   dbhCompressionID;
  short                   dbhPacketSize;
  Fixed                   dbhSampleRate;
  SndDoubleBufferPtr      dbhBufferPtr[2];
  SndDoubleBackProcPtr    dbhDoubleBack;
} SndDoubleBufferHeader, *SndDoubleBufferHeaderPtr;
```

The *dbhNumChannels* field is the total number of channels required for this sound. This code you're only dealing with single-channel sounds, so set this field to 1.

The *dbhSampleSize* field is the size of each individual sound sample. The sample sizes supported are 8-bit and 16-bit. To operate efficiently on older machines, use 8-bit sounds.

The *dbhCompressionID* field is the ID number of the compression algorithm used for this sound. For uncompressed sounds (which you'll be using), pass in 0 for this parameter.

The *dbhPacketSize* field is the packet size for the compression algorithm. If you're using uncompressed sounds, set this to 0.

The *dbhSampleRate* field is the number of samples/second for the sound. You obtained this value when parsing the sound header.

The *dbhBufferPtr* field is an array of two SndDoubleBuffers, which you are responsible for allocating (the SndDoubleBuffer structure was described earlier, when I explained the FillDoubleBuffer() callback routine). The SndDoubleBuffer must be large enough for the entire buffer, plus some space for the header. I'll look at how to allocate this space shortly.

The *dbhDoubleBack* field is the UPP for your FillDoubleBuffer routine. In this case, the UPP is created by using a routine called NewSndDoubleBackProc().

When creating the double buffer, you need to know how much space to allocate for it. Space must be allocated not only for the fields of the structure but also for the sound buffer itself. Here is a formula for calculating this size:

```
soundBufferStructSize = sizeof(SndDoubleBuffer) + kSoundBufferSize;
```

The sizeof() function will return the space required by the record as it is declared. Once you have determined this size, you can allocate the buffer:

```
SndDoubleBufferPtr      doubleBuffer
doubleBuffer = (SndDoubleBufferPtr) NewPtrClear(soundBufferStructSize);
```

NewPtrClear() works the same way that NewPtr() does, except it also initializes the area it allocates to 0.

You now have enough information to allocate the double buffer header. Listing 7-5 shows some sample code that will do just that.

Listing 7-5 *Allocating the double buffer header*

```
SndDoubleBufferHeader   doubleBufHeader;
PrivateSoundData        privateSoundInfo;

/* Begin preparations for calling the sound double buffer routines.
 * Start by initializing our private sound data area.
 */

/* Initialize our private data area */
privateSoundInfo.soundBytesTotal = soundSize;
privateSoundInfo.soundDataBegin = soundPtr;
privateSoundInfo.soundBytesCopied = 0;
privateSoundInfo.die = FALSE;

/* Now move on to initializing the 'double buffer header' */

/* Only one channel (mono sound) */
doubleBufHeader.dbhNumChannels = 1;
/* We're working with 8-bit sounds */
doubleBufHeader.dbhSampleSize = 8;
/* The sound is not compressed */
doubleBufHeader.dbhCompressionID = 0;
/* dbhPacketSize doesn't matter for non-compressed sounds */
doubleBufHeader.dbhPacketSize = 0;
/* The sample rate for our sounds */
doubleBufHeader.dbhSampleRate = soundSampleRate[0];
/* Give it the procedure pointer for our call-back routine
 * (after converting it to a UniversalProcPtr for the PowerPC
 */
doubleBufHeader.dbhDoubleBack = NewSndDoubleBackProc(FillSoundBuffers);

/* Now initialize both of the double-buffer buffers and put
 * them both into the double-buffer header.
 */
for (i = 0; i < 2; i++) {
  SndDoubleBufferPtr    doubleBuffer;

  /* Allocate the space for this buffer */
  doubleBuffer = (SndDoubleBufferPtr)NewPtrClear(
                    sizeof(SndDoubleBuffer) + kSoundBufferSize);

  /* We shouldn't run out of memory here, because we're allocating
   * such a small block of memory, but check anyway to be
   * sure.
```

Continued on next page

Continued from previous page

```
     */
    if (doubleBuffer == NULL) {
      err = MemError();
      return err;
    }


    /* No data is in the buffer yet */
    doubleBuffer->dbNumFrames = 0;
    /* No status flags (status flags are used to indicate
     * the buffer is ready to use, or that we're done using
     * the buffer).
     */
    doubleBuffer->dbFlags = 0;
    /* Put our data into the user-info area. By doing
     * this, we'll have access to this data when the
     * Sound Manager calls our FillSoundBuffers()
     * routine. They supply us with two longwords to
     * put our data into, but we only need one.
     */
    doubleBuffer->dbUserInfo[0] = (long)&gOurSoundInfo;

    /* Call FillSoundBuffers() to fill this buffer with
     * the waiting sound data.
     */
    FillSoundBuffers(theSoundChannel, doubleBuffer);

    /* Put this buffer into the 'double-buffer header' so
     * the Sound Manager has access to it.
     */
    doubleBufHeader.dbhBufferPtr[i] = doubleBuffer;
  }

  /* We're finished setting everything up. Give the double buffer
   * information to the Sound Manager, and it'll handle playing
   * the sound and calling our FillSoundBuffers() routine when
   * it needs more data.
   */
  err = SndPlayDoubleBuffer(theSoundChannel, &doubleBufHeader);
```

The Continuous Sound Player

You've now seen all the steps required to start a continuous sound. Now let's build a complete set of routines you can call to handle the music for your games. The code will look very similar to what I just discussed except it will have a few more capabilities.

Because an important aspect of computer game music is the ability to switch between different musical themes depending on the situation of the player, let's add this feature to what you're creating. The code will be based on some maximum number of "themes" you can switch among. When the buffer is allocated, all of these sounds will be loaded into memory. When the game needs to change the theme, it can call a routine that will set a flag to this effect. The next time the music loops around, this flag will be detected and the new theme will begin playing. This will result in a delay between when the new theme is specified and when it starts playing, but it allows the music to transition in the same spot always. Otherwise, the current music would cut out in midbeat and the new theme would start, which could prove to be very disharmonious.

The private data area will need to be expanded to encompass these changes. *soundBytesTotal* and *soundDataBegin* have both been changed to arrays to hold information about each theme and fields have been added to keep track of the current theme, which theme to play next, and how many themes have been allocated. This is how the new PrivateSoundData structure looks:

```
typedef struct {
    long              soundBytesTotal[kMaximumThemes];
    Ptr               soundDataBegin[kMaximumThemes];
/* soundBytesTotal is the size of each sound we can switch between,
 * and soundDataBegin is an array of pointers to the beginning
 * of each sound.
 */

        short         themesAllocated;
/* themesAllocated is the total number of themes loaded and
 * ready to be used (always less than or equal to kMaximumThemes).
 */

    long              soundBytesCopied;
/* soundBytesCopied is how much of the current sound has already
 * been copied into the sound buffer. The next time the buffer
 * needs to be refilled, this is where we'll start to pull the
 * data from.
 */

        short         currentTheme;
/* currentTheme is which sound we're currently playing from the
 * buffer.
 */
        short         nextThemeToPlay;
/* nextThemeToPlay is the number of the theme to play when this
 * one is finished.
 */

        Boolean       die;
/* If die is set to true, don't continue copying sound data -
 * instead, signal to the Sound Manager that we're done.
 */
} PrivateSoundData, *PrivateSoundDataPtr;
```

You're also going to keep track of several items in global variables. For example, the private sound data cannot be declared locally to the StartContinuousSound() routine because that data would cease to exist once that routine returned. Here is the global variable declaration:

```
/**
 **  Globals
 **
 **/
static SndChannelPtr          gContinuousSoundChannel;
static Handle                 gSoundDataArray[kMaximumThemes];
static PrivateSoundData       gOurSoundInfo;
static SndDoubleBufferHeader  gDoubleBufHeader;
```

StartContinuousSound

I have already discussed almost all of StartContinuousSound, but a few changes have been made for the extra themes. StartContinuousSound takes parameters for the resource ID of the first theme, how many themes there are, and which theme to begin playing first. The sequence of events for this routine looks like this:

✦ Load all of the sounds.

✦ Create the new sound channel.

✦ Strip off the headers for all of the sounds.

✦ Initialize the private data area.

✦ Initialize the double-buffer header.

✦ Initialize each double buffer.

✦ Invoke SndPlayDoubleBuffer().

At this point, the routine returns (Listing 7-6) and the Sound Manager begins to play the sound. It will continue until the program quits or a routine is called to kill the sound (which I'll demonstrate later).

Listing 7-6 *The StartContinuousSound routine*

```
OSErr  StartContinuousSound( short   firstSoundResourceID,
                             short   numberOfSounds,
                             short   initialSound  )
{
  short          i;
  OSErr          err;
  long           soundSampleRate[kMaximumThemes];

  /* Limit the number of sounds to the kMaximumThemes constant
   * previously defined.
   */
  if (numberOfSounds > kMaximumThemes)
    numberOfSounds = kMaximumThemes;
```

```
/* Load each sound into memory */
for (i = 0; i < numberOfSounds; i++) {
  gSoundDataArray[i] = GetResource('snd ', firstSoundResourceID + i);

  /* Check for failure */
  if (gSoundDataArray[i] == NULL) {
    return ResError();
  }

  /* Lock the sound down */
  MoveHHi(gSoundDataArray[i]);
  HLock(gSoundDataArray[i]);
}

/* Create a new channel for the sound. */
gContinuousSoundChannel = NULL;
err = SndNewChannel(&gContinuousSoundChannel, sampledSynth, 0, NULL);

/* Each sound resource has some essential information about that
 * sound at the beginning of its data, called a 'sound header'.
 * Following this header is the actual sound data. For double
 * buffering, the Sound Manager wants only the sound data, not
 * the header, so we have to remove this header. Unfortunately,
 * all sound headers are not the same length, so we have to
 * remove the header in a few steps.
 *
 * There is also a little bit of information contained in the
 * header that we want access to.
 */
for (i = 0; i < numberOfSounds; i++) {
  short           numberOfSoundCommands;
  long            soundCommandSize;
  Ptr             soundPtr;
  long            soundSize;

  /* Set a pointer to the beginning of the sound resource.
   * This pointer will soon be advanced to the middle of the
   * sound header information, then entirely past the sound
   * header, and onto the start of the sound data.
   */
  soundPtr = *gSoundDataArray[i];

  /* Skip over the first 10 bytes of the sound header. These
   * 10 bytes consist of the format, number of synths, synth
   * resource ID, and synth options.
   */
  soundPtr += 10;

  /* The next 2 bytes of the header is the 'Number of
   * Sound Commands'. Each command uses 8 bytes, so
   * we can use it to skip over all of the sound commands.
```

Continued on next page

Continued from previous page

```
*/
numberOfSoundCommands = *(short *)soundPtr;

/* Now move the pointer past those two bytes */
soundPtr += 2;

/* Calculate how much space is being used for
 * the sound commands.
 */
soundCommandSize = numberOfSoundCommands * 8;

/* Skip over the sound commands. */
soundPtr += soundCommandSize;

/* soundPtr is now positioned approximately halfway
 * into the header. There is some important data
 * at this point, some of which we need, some we don't.
 *
 * The rest of the header consists of an offset
 * to the data (which we don't need), the size of
 * this sound (which we need), the sample rate
 * of the sound (which we need), and 10 more bytes
 * of other information (which we don't need).
 *
 * Grab the information we need, skip the stuff we
 * don't need.
 */

/* The offset to the data - 4 bytes - we don't need it. */
soundPtr += 4;

/* The sound size - 4 bytes - we need this */
soundSize = *(long*)soundPtr;
soundPtr += 4;

/* The sound sample rate - 4 bytes - we need this. */
soundSampleRate[i] = *(long*)soundPtr;
soundPtr += 4;

/* An extra 10 bytes, which we don't need */
soundPtr += 10;

/* We now have the soundPtr pointing directly at the sound
 * data. Now initialize this part of our private data
 * area.
 */
gOurSoundInfo.soundBytesTotal[i] = soundSize;
gOurSoundInfo.soundDataBegin[i] = soundPtr;
}

/* Finish up initializing our private data area */
gOurSoundInfo.soundBytesCopied = 0;
gOurSoundInfo.currentTheme = initialSound;
```

```
    gOurSoundInfo.die = FALSE;
    gOurSoundInfo.nextThemeToPlay = initialSound;
    gOurSoundInfo.themesAllocated = numberOfSounds;

    /* Begin preparations for calling the sound double buffer routines.
     * Start by initializing the 'double buffer header'.
     */

    /* Only one channel (mono sound) */
    gDoubleBufHeader.dbhNumChannels = 1;
    /* We're working with 8-bit sounds */
    gDoubleBufHeader.dbhSampleSize = 8;
    /* The sound is not compressed */
    gDoubleBufHeader.dbhCompressionID = 0;
    /* dbhPacketSize doesn't matter for non-compressed sounds */
    gDoubleBufHeader.dbhPacketSize = 0;
    /* The sample rate for our sounds */
    gDoubleBufHeader.dbhSampleRate = soundSampleRate[0];
    /* Give it the procedure pointer for our call-back routine
     * (after converting it to a UniversalProcPtr for the PowerPC
     */
    gDoubleBufHeader.dbhDoubleBack =
                NewSndDoubleBackProc(FillSoundBuffers);

    /* Now initialize both of the double-buffer buffers and put
     * them both into the double-buffer header.
     */
    for (i = 0; i < 2; i++) {
      SndDoubleBufferPtr    doubleBuffer;

      /* Allocate the space for this buffer */
      doubleBuffer = (SndDoubleBufferPtr)NewPtrClear(
                                  sizeof(SndDoubleBuffer) +
                                  kSoundBufferSize );

      /* We shouldn't run out of memory here, because we're allocating
       * such a small block of memory, but check anyway to be
       * sure.
       */
      if (doubleBuffer == NULL) {
        err = MemError();
        return err;
      }

      /* No data is in the buffer yet */
      doubleBuffer->dbNumFrames = 0;
      /* No status flags (status flags are used to indicate
       * the buffer is ready to use or that we're done using
       * the buffer).
       */
      doubleBuffer->dbFlags = 0;
      /* Put our data into the user-info area. By doing
```

Continued on next page

Continued from previous page

```
       * this, we'll have access to this data when the
       * Sound Manager calls our FillSoundBuffers()
       * routine. They supply us with two longwords to
       * put our data into, but we only need one.
       */
      doubleBuffer->dbUserInfo[0] = (long)&gOurSoundInfo;

      /* Call FillSoundBuffers() to fill this buffer with
       * the waiting sound data.
       */
      FillSoundBuffers(gContinuousSoundChannel, doubleBuffer);

      /* Put this buffer into the 'double-buffer header' so
       * the Sound Manager has access to it.
       */
      gDoubleBufHeader.dbhBufferPtr[i] = doubleBuffer;
   }

   /* We're finished setting everything up. Give the double buffer
    * information to the Sound Manager, and it'll handle playing
    * the sound and calling our FillSoundBuffers() routine when
    * it needs more data.
    */
   err = SndPlayDoubleBuffer(  gContinuousSoundChannel,
                               &gDoubleBufHeader  );

   return err;
}
```

New FillSoundBuffers

The FillSoundBuffers() routine hasn't changed too much with the addition of multiple themes. The main difference is some extra code to check to see if the sound theme has changed when the sound ends. Listing 7-7 shows this routine.

Listing 7-7 *The FillSoundBuffers() routine*

```
/**
 **    FillSoundBuffers()
 **
 **    This routine is called by the Sound Manager (and in one place in
 **    our own code) in order to refill the buffers when they are empty.
 **    Since we are playing our sound continuously, our routine will
 **    keep looping around whenever it finishes with the sound.
 **
 **    If the sound theme changes, the sound will start to be taken from
 **    the new sound source as soon as the current one is finished
 **/
pascal void FillSoundBuffers(  SndChannelPtr       theChannel,
                               SndDoubleBufferPtr  doubleBuffer)
{
```

```
PrivateSoundDataPtr    ourPrivateData;
long                   bytesToCopy;
long                   sizeOfCurrentSound;
Ptr                    currentThemeDataPtr;
short                  currentTheme;

/* Get access to our private data */
ourPrivateData = (PrivateSoundDataPtr)doubleBuffer->dbUserInfo[0];

/* Retrieve the size of the current sound */
sizeOfCurrentSound =
    ourPrivateData->soundBytesTotal[ourPrivateData->currentTheme];

/* Calculate how many bytes remain to be copied into the buffer */
bytesToCopy = sizeOfCurrentSound - ourPrivateData->soundBytesCopied;

/* Check to see if the data that remains to be copied is larger
 * than the whole sound buffer. If so, just copy enough to fill
 * the buffer.
 */
if (bytesToCopy > kSoundBufferSize)
  bytesToCopy = kSoundBufferSize;

/* Retrieve the current theme */
currentTheme = ourPrivateData->currentTheme;

/* Calculate a pointer to the beginning of the
 * sound data to be copied
 */
currentThemeDataPtr = ourPrivateData->soundDataBegin[currentTheme] +
                    ourPrivateData->soundBytesCopied;

/* Copy the sound data into the buffer */
BlockMove ( currentThemeDataPtr,
            &doubleBuffer->dbSoundData[0],
            bytesToCopy );

/* Let the Sound Manager know how much data we
 * just put into the buffer
 */
doubleBuffer->dbNumFrames = bytesToCopy;

/* Tell the Sound Manager that the buffer is ready to use */
doubleBuffer->dbFlags = (doubleBuffer->dbFlags) | dbBufferReady;

/* Update our soundBytesCopied marker */
ourPrivateData->soundBytesCopied += bytesToCopy;

/* Check to see if we've copied the entire sound. If so, set
 * the data pointer to the beginning of the next sound
 * (which can either be the same sound, or a new one).
 * Also check to see if we've been told to quit playing.
```

Continued on next page

Continued from previous page

```
  */
if (ourPrivateData->soundBytesCopied == sizeOfCurrentSound)
{
  if (ourPrivateData->die) {
    /* We've been told to stop playing, so let the sound manager
     * know not to continue playing after it finishes with this
     * buffer.
     */
    doubleBuffer->dbFlags = (doubleBuffer->dbFlags) | dbLastBuffer;
  } else {
    short    newTheme;

    newTheme = ourPrivateData->nextThemeToPlay;
    ourPrivateData->soundBytesCopied = 0;
    ourPrivateData->currentTheme = newTheme;
  }
}
return;
}
```

Changing the Theme and Stopping the Music

You now have the two routines you need for playing the music. The only things you need now are routines for changing the current theme and for stopping the music entirely.

Changing the current theme is easy—just change the entry in the private sound data area and the next time the sound loops, FillSoundBuffer() will notice the change and react accordingly.

```
/**
 **    ChangeCurrentTheme()
 **
 **    Causes the current sound being played to change to a new one
 **    when it finishes. (Range of 0..numOfThemes-1)
 **/
void  ChangeCurrentTheme(short newTheme)
{
  /* Check to see if the new theme is valid */
  if ((newTheme >= 0) &&
    (newTheme < gOurSoundInfo.themesAllocated))
  {
  gOurSoundInfo.nextThemeToPlay = newTheme;
  }
}
```

Stopping a continuous sound is a very similar process to stopping an asynchronous sound. If you want to stop the sound immediately, just dispose of the sound channel.

If you want to be a little more graceful about it and allow the current sound to reach the loop point before dying, change the *die* flag in your private data area. When the sound is exhausted, FillSoundBuffers() will tell the Sound Manager to stop playing.

After setting the *die* flag, you must wait until the sound finishes before disposing of the sound channel. The Sound Manager allows you to do this through a routine called SndChannelStatus():

```
OSErr  SndChannelStatus(  SndChannelPtr   theChannel,
                          short           statusLength,
                          SCStatusPtr     theStatus );
```

This routine is a little odd in that you must pass it a status structure plus the size of that structure. Apple has designed it this way so that it can add more information to the SCStatus structure without breaking all of the existing code. All you need to do is pass *sizeof(SCStatus)* for *statusLength*.

The only field of *theStatus* you care about is scChannelBusy, which will be True until the sound has finished playing.

After the sound has terminated and the sound channel has been disposed of, you need to unlock and dispose of all the sound handles you loaded in StartContinuousSound(). You also need to dispose of both sound buffers before returning. Listing 7-8 shows the code.

Listing 7-8 *The StopContinuousSound() routine*

```
/**
 **    StopContinuousSound()
 **
 **    Terminates the current continuous sound. If stopImmediately
 **    is true, the sound will stop in mid-play. Otherwise, the
 **    routine will wait until this iteration of the sound is
 **    finished. This routine also deallocates any memory used
 **    by this package.
 **/
void  StopContinuousSound(Boolean stopImmediately)
{
  short  i;

  /* Check to see whether or not to wait for the sound to
   * finish.
   */
  if (stopImmediately) {
    /* To kill the sound immediately, just close the
     * sound channel
     */
    SndDisposeChannel(gContinuousSoundChannel, TRUE);
  } else {
    SCStatus     Stats;
    OSErr        err;
```

Continued on next page

Continued from previous page

```
    /* Set the flag to stop the sound */
    gOurSoundInfo.die = TRUE;

    /* Monitor the sound channel until the sound has stopped */
    do {
      err = SndChannelStatus ( gContinuousSoundChannel,
                               sizeof(SCStatus),
                               &Stats );
    } while ((Stats.scChannelBusy == TRUE) && (err == noErr));

    /* Now that the sound has finished, dispose of the channel */
    SndDisposeChannel(gContinuousSoundChannel, TRUE);
  }

  /* Unlock each of the sounds and dispose of them */
  for (i = 0; i < gOurSoundInfo.themesAllocated; i++) {
    HUnlock(gSoundDataArray[i]);
    DisposeHandle(gSoundDataArray[i]);
  }
  /* Dispose of the buffer memory */
  DisposePtr((Ptr)gDoubleBufHeader.dbhBufferPtr[0]);
  DisposePtr((Ptr)gDoubleBufHeader.dbhBufferPtr[1]);
}
```

There you have it! You now have all the routines necessary for creating background music for your games. When you create your sound resources, be sure they are 8-bit, uncompressed, and all at the same sample rate. Put them in consecutive resource IDs and then call StartContinuousSound(). Everything else is taken care of.

Multiple Asynchronous Sounds

Later in this chapter, you will create a sample program to demonstrate the capabilities of asynchronous and continuous sounds. First, however, you will add some capabilities to the asynchronous sound player created earlier in this chapter. It is very beneficial for a game to be able to have several asynchronous sounds playing at once, so you will make this possible using the asynchronous sound player.

Another feature that you'll add is priorities. This is my own little invention and is not part of the toolbox. When each sound is played, it is given a priority. If the asynchronous sound player is given a new sound to play but there are no free channels, it will compare the new sound's priority with those of the currently playing sounds. If it finds a sound currently playing that has a lower priority, it will replace it with the new sound. This allows you to assign a high priority to sounds that are critical to the user, such as the main character getting injured, and a lower priority to less important sounds, like those of opening doors. Sound priorities are defined in Async Sound.h:

```
enum {
        kSndPriorityLow,
        kSndPriorityMedium,
        kSndPriorityHigh,
        kSndPriorityUrgent
};
```

The first change is to the global variables—each of them has been changed to an array, representing each sound channel I've allocated. One new array has also been added for sound priorities:

```
SndChannelPtr    gSoundChannelArray[kMaximumSoundChannels];
Boolean          gSoundChannelPlaying[kMaximumSoundChannels];
short            gSoundPriority[kMaximumSoundChannels];
```

kMaximumSoundChannels is an arbitrary value I've decided upon for the most sound channels that can be in use at one time. Four channels are generally sufficient and don't drain too much from the CPU, so that's the value I'll be using. Feel free to modify it to experiment.

New InitializeAsyncSoundPlayer

This routine hasn't changed much from the previous version. A loop has been added to initialize all of the sound channels.

```
void  InitializeAsyncSoundPlayer(void)
{
  short          i;
  OSErr          err;
  SndChannelPtr  newChannel;

  for (i = 0; i < kMaximumSoundChannels; i++) {
    gSoundChannelPlaying[i] = FALSE;
    gSoundPriority[i] = 0;

    newChannel = NULL;
    err = SndNewChannel( &newChannel,
                         0, /* Let the sound manager decide
                            * which synth to use */
                         0, /* No special commands for
                            * the synth */
                         NewSndCallBackProc(SoundIsFinishedCallBack));
                           /* This is to let it know which routine
                            * should be called when the sound is
                            * finished.
                            */
    gSoundChannelArray[i] = newChannel;
  }
}
```

New PlayAsyncSound

PlayAsyncSound() is now responsible for locating an empty sound channel. If it does-
n't find one, it will check to see if it can displace a currently playing sound that has a
lower priority. If every sound that is playing has a higher priority, it will just return without playing a sound. Listing 7-9 shows this routine.

Listing 7-9 The new PlayAsyncSound( ) routine

```
/**
**   PlayAsyncSound()
**
**   Finds a free sound channel, allocates it, and plays a sound
**   asynchronously. If it can't find a free channel (i.e. there are
**   already 4 sounds playing), it will check to see if any of the
**   sounds currently playing has a lower priority than this one.
**   If so, it will kill that sound and replace it.
**/
OSErr  PlayAsyncSound(SndListHandle theSound, short priority)
{
  short    i;
  short    channelToUse = -1;
  OSErr    err = noErr;

  /* Scan for free sound channels */
  for (i = 0; i < kMaximumSoundChannels; i++) {
    if (gSoundChannelPlaying[i] == FALSE) {
      /* Found a free channel */
      channelToUse = i;
    }
  }

  /* If we didn't find a free channel, start checking the sound
   * priorities. Find the lowest priority sound playing, then
   * check to see if this sound has a higher priority.
   */
  if (channelToUse == -1) {
    short  lowestPriorityChannel = 32767;
    short  whichChannel = -1;

    for (i = 0; i < kMaximumSoundChannels; i++) {
      if (gSoundPriority[i] < lowestPriorityChannel) {
        lowestPriorityChannel = gSoundPriority[i];
        whichChannel = i;
      }
    }

    /* Check to see if the lowest priority channel has a lower
     * priority than the new sound
     */
    if (lowestPriorityChannel < priority) {
```

```
    SndCommand      soundCommand;
    /* This sound has a higher priority, so kill the currently
     * playing sound.
     */

    soundCommand.cmd = quietCmd;
    SndDoImmediate(gSoundChannelArray[whichChannel], &soundCommand);
    channelToUse = whichChannel;
  }
}

/* If we found a channel to use, then allocate it and send our
 * sound into it.
 */
if (channelToUse != -1) {
  SndChannelPtr    newChannel = NULL;

  newChannel = gSoundChannelArray[channelToUse];

  if (err == noErr) {


    err = SndPlay( newChannel,    /* use our new channel */
                   theSound,      /* our sound to play */
                   TRUE  );       /* Play it asynchronously */
    if (err == noErr) {
      /* Now send a command to this sound channel to
       * call us back when this sound is finished.
       * This is so we can dispose of this sound channel
       * and leave it free for other programs
       */
      SndCommand      soundCommand;

      gSoundChannelPlaying[channelToUse] = TRUE;
      gSoundPriority[channelToUse] = priority;
      soundCommand.cmd = callBackCmd;

      /* Send in the address of the gSoundChannelPlaying
       * boolean value. When the callback is invoked,
       * it will change this boolean value to FALSE,
       * letting us know the sound is finished.
       *
       * The param1 and param2 fields are provided for
       * our own use - we can put any values we like into
       * them. Since param1 is defined as a short, we'll
       * use param2 to pass in the address.
       */
      soundCommand.param2 = (long)&gSoundChannelPlaying[channelToUse];

      /* Send the command to the Sound Manager. */
      err = SndDoCommand(newChannel, &soundCommand, FALSE);
    }
```

Continued on next page

Continued from previous page

```
      }
    }
    return err;
}
```

Asynchronous Sound Utility Routines

I have one new routine for the expanded asynchronous sound player that will return the number of sounds currently playing. This may be useful if the game needs to gauge how much sound activity is occurring.

```
/**
 **   HowManySoundsArePlaying()
 **
 **   Returns a number (from 0..kMaximumSoundChannels) indicating how
 **   many sounds are now being played.
 **/
short  HowManySoundsArePlaying(void)
{
  short  numSoundsPlaying = 0;
  short  i;

  for (i = 0; i < kMaximumSoundChannels; i++) {
    if (gSoundChannelPlaying[i] == TRUE)
      numSoundsPlaying += 1;
  }

  return numSoundsPlaying;
}
```

The last routine you need for this package is one that will dispose of all the sound channels and free up the allocated memory. CleanUpSounds() will do just this and it allows the option of stopping the current sounds immediately or waiting until they finish before eliminating the sound channels.

```
/**
 **   CleanUpSounds()
 **
 **   Disposes of all of the sound channels. If stopImmediately is
 **   false, the sounds will be allowed to finish before their channels
 **   are destroyed, but otherwise they will be killed immediately.
 **   Be sure to use this routine just before your application quits! It's
 **   very important that an application release its sound channels
 **   before terminating.
 **/
void  CleanUpSounds(Boolean stopImmediately)
{
  short  i;

  for (i = 0; i < kMaximumSoundChannels; i++) {
    if (gSoundChannelArray[i] != NULL) {
      SndDisposeChannel(gSoundChannelArray[i], stopImmediately);
```

```
        gSoundChannelArray[i] = NULL;
      }
    }
  }
```

The Complete Package

You now have all the routines you need for the asynchronous sound player. All of the asynchronous sound routines can be found on the source code disc in Chapter 7:Async Sound.c; you'll be using that file throughout the remainder of the book.

Testing the Sounds

All that remains to be done in this chapter is to test the new sound routines. To do this, you'll build a tiny shell that will produce a cacophonous symphony: Three asynchronous sounds will play at the same time, and a continuous sound will start in the background. The three sounds that are included on the source code disk consist of a symphony of Canadian geese, the tolling of a bell tower, and the sound of waves on a shore.

There are also three themes provided for the continuous sound. The theme that the application starts out with is the sound of a sonar. The second is a thunderstorm, and the third is an airplane's engine (which you'll also be using when you create the flight simulator).

The user can switch between asynchronous sounds by typing q, w, or e and between the continuous themes by typing a number (1, 2, or 3). There is a delay before the new theme begins playing because the current sound must finish first. The user may also quit the application by pressing ESC. Listing 7-10 shows the routine.

Listing 7-10 *Testing the new sound routines*

```
void main(void)
{
  SndListHandle  sndHandle[kNumOfAsyncSounds];
  short          i;
  OSErr          err;
  Boolean        quit;

  /* Initialize the asynchronous sound player */
  InitializeAsyncSoundPlayer();

  err = StartContinuousSound(  kFirstContinuousSoundRsrcID,
                               kNumOfContinousSounds,
                               0 );
  if (err)
    ExitToShell();
```

Continued on next page

```
Continued from previous page
  for (i = 0; i < kNumOfAsyncSounds; i++) {
    /* Get the next sound to play */
    sndHandle[i] = (SndListHandle)GetResource('snd ',
kFirstAsyncSoundRsrcID + i);

    /* Play it with a priority of 0 (since they all have
     * the same priority, a new sound will never kill
     * a sound already playing)
     */
    err = PlayAsyncSound(sndHandle[i], i);
  }

  quit = FALSE;

  while (!quit) {
    /* Check to see if we should change the current continuous sound */
    if (IsKeyPressed(0x12))  /* '1' key */
      ChangeCurrentTheme(0);
    if (IsKeyPressed(0x13))  /* '2' key */
      ChangeCurrentTheme(1);
    if (IsKeyPressed(0x14))  /* '3' key */
      ChangeCurrentTheme(2);

    /* Check to see if we should play another async sound */
    if (IsKeyPressed(0x0C)) /* 'q' key */
      err = PlayAsyncSound(sndHandle[0], kSndPriorityMedium);
    if (IsKeyPressed(0x0D)) /* 'w' key */
      err = PlayAsyncSound(sndHandle[1], kSndPriorityMedium);
    if (IsKeyPressed(0x0E)) /* 'e' key */
      err = PlayAsyncSound(sndHandle[2], kSndPriorityMedium);

    if (IsKeyPressed(0x35))  /* 'esc' key */
      quit = TRUE;
  }

  /* Stop the continuous sound from playing */
  StopContinuousSound(TRUE);

  /* We're done sending the sounds to the player. Now deinitialize
   * the sound player. Also allow the currently playing
   * sounds to finish before disposing the channels and quitting.
   */
  CleanUpSounds(TRUE);
}
```

You now have the tools you need for playing sound effects and background music. Because the routines are in their own separate files, it is easy to add them to any project and access their capabilities. You'll be using these two files for sound effects and background music throughout the rest of the book, including in the next chapter, where you will create an alien invasion arcade game complete with sprite animation and sound effects!

8

Invaders!

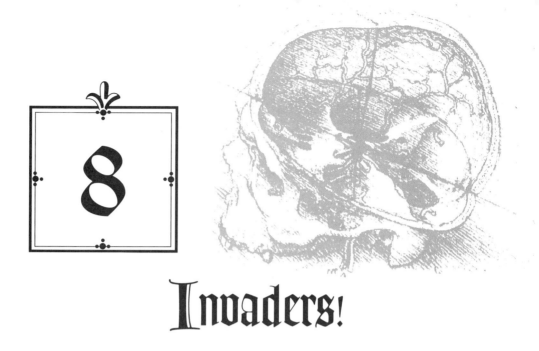

8

Invaders!

It's time for your first real game. I've already discussed each of the elements you will need for it: the Macintosh Toolbox, input, sprites, and sound. This simple game is similar to early home video game systems. The player controls a spaceship that can move left or right along the bottom of the window. Several alien spaceships travel back and forth across the top, dropping down slightly each time they reach the edge of the screen. The player can fire missiles at the invaders and the invaders drop bombs on the player. If the invaders reach the bottom of the screen or the player is hit by a bomb, the game ends.

I'll call the game Invaders!; it is based on the enhanced Walking Man application that you built in Chapter 6. Many of the routines are unchanged, but some of them must go through changes.

Enhancing the Sprites

In the Walking Man animation, the sprites had images for moving right, moving left, and standing still. For the Invaders! game, these actions will work fine but one additional sequence is required: explosions. The explosions will consist of a sequence of images, just like the other animations. The explosion images are stored as the last row in the animation strip. This also requires another field in the sprite structure indicating how many explosion images are in the strip:

```
short        explodingImages;
```

The invaders can move to the left and right but they are never stationary. The way the sprite code is written now, it will always look in the first row for the left-moving sprites, the second row for the right-moving sprites, and the third row for the stationary ones. If you add a third image type (explosions), it will look in the fourth row for them. Because there are no stationary invader images, it would be wasteful to leave the third row empty. To solve this problem, you're going to add another few fields to the sprite structure. These fields will hold indices for the locations of the sprite images. For example, *movingLeftRow* indicates which row holds the images for the left-moving animation.

```
short        movingLeftRow, movingRightRow;
short        standingStillRow, explodingRow;
```

You also need a way of remembering the status of the sprite. A sprite can have one of three states: active, exploding, or destroyed. These states are defined by the following constants:

```
enum {
  kSpriteActive,
  kSpriteExploding,
  kSpriteDestroyed
};
```

The last addition to the sprite structure is the status of the sprite:

```
short        spriteStatus;
```

Listing 8-1 is the complete new sprite structure.

Listing 8-1 *The new sprite Structure*

```
typedef struct {
  short        movingLeftImages;
  short        movingRightImages;
  short        staticImages;
  short        explodingImages;

  /* spriteAction is one of kSpriteMovingLeft, kSpriteMovingRight,
   * or kSpriteStandingStill.
   */
  short        spriteAction;
  /* currentImageIndex is the index of the last sprite
   * image shown.
   */
  short        currentImageIndex;

  /* spriteStatus is one of the constants 'kSpriteActive',
   * 'kSpriteExploding', or 'kSpriteDestroyed'.
   */
```

```
    short       spriteStatus;

    /* These variables tell us which row to look for a particular image
     * sequence. This allows us to use the same row for two different
     * sprite actions or to not have any images for a particular action
     * (indicated by a value of -1).
     */
    short       movingLeftRow, movingRightRow;
    short       standingStillRow, explodingRow;

    GWorldPtr   spriteSequenceImage;

    short       width, height;   /* The size of the sprite */
    short       x, y;            /* Current screen coordinates */
                                 /* of the sprite */
} Sprite, *SpritePtr;
```

The NewSprite() Function

A little additional code is required in the NewSprite() function to initialize the new sprite fields. *explodingImages, movingLeftRow, movingRightRow, standingStillRow,* and *explodingRow* are all fields obtained from new parameters for the function, whereas *spriteStatus* is always initialized to kSpriteActive. The remainder of the function is largely unchanged from the original NewSprite() function (see Listing 8-2).

Listing 8-2 *The NewSprite() function*

```
/**
 **   NewSprite
 **
 **   Allocates the storage for a sprite and loads its animation strip
 **   into a GWorld.
 **/
OSErr  NewSprite( Sprite     *sprite,
                  short      width,
                  short      height,
                  short      numOfMovingLeftImages,
                  short      numOfMovingRightImages,
                  short      numOfStaticImages,
                  short      numOfExplodingImages,
                  short      movingLeftRowIndex,
                  short      movingRightRowIndex,
                  short      staticRowIndex,
                  short      explodingRowIndex,
                  short      imageResID  )
{
    GWorldPtr   newOffscreenBuffer;
    Rect        bounds;
    OSErr       err;
    GDHandle    saveDevice;
    CGrafPtr    savePort;
```

Continued on next page

Continued from previous page

```
PicHandle      spritePict;
short          imageWidth, imageHeight;
short          totalRows;

/* Load the sprite's image sequence from the resource fork */
spritePict = GetPicture(imageResID);

/* Check for an error */
if (spritePict == NULL) {
  err = ResError();
  return err;
}

/* Get the bounds for the sprite's image sequence. */
bounds = (**spritePict).picFrame;

/* The image has to be at least as wide as each sprite image's
 * width times the number of sprites for each sequence.
 */
imageWidth = bounds.right - bounds.left;
if ((imageWidth < width * numOfMovingLeftImages) ||
    (imageWidth < width * numOfMovingRightImages) ||
    (imageWidth < width * numOfStaticImages) ||
    (imageWidth < width * numOfExplodingImages))
{
  /* If the image isn't big enough, something went wrong.
   * Return a generic error.
   */
  return -1;
}

/* Check to see how many rows we have (by finding the largest
 * row index), and make sure the image is tall enough to
 * contain all of them.
 */
totalRows = 0;

if (movingLeftRowIndex > totalRows)
  totalRows = movingLeftRowIndex;

if (movingRightRowIndex > totalRows)
  totalRows = movingRightRowIndex;

if (staticRowIndex > totalRows)
  totalRows = staticRowIndex;

if (explodingRowIndex > totalRows)
  totalRows = explodingRowIndex;

imageHeight = bounds.bottom - bounds.top;
if (imageHeight < height * (totalRows + 1)) {
  /* The image isn't large enough, so something went wrong.
   * Return a generic error.
```

```
      */
      return -1;
  }


  err = NewGWorld( &newOffscreenBuffer,
                   8,  /* we use just an 8-bit palette (256 colors) */
                   &bounds,
                   NULL,  /* use the system color table for now */
                   NULL,
                   0  );

/* check for an error */
if (err == noErr) {
  /* We now want to draw the image sequence into the
   * offscreen gworld
   */

  /* Get the current port and device and save them */
  GetGWorld(&savePort, &saveDevice);

  /* Set the port to the offscreen gworld */
  SetGWorld(newOffscreenBuffer, NULL);

  /* Now our quickdraw commands will work on the offscreen buffer. */
  DrawPicture(spritePict, &bounds);

  /* And set the port back to the screen */
  SetGWorld(savePort, saveDevice);

  /* We can now release the PICT resource */
  ReleaseResource((Handle)spritePict);

  /* Fill out the structure for the sprite */
  sprite->movingLeftImages = numOfMovingLeftImages;
  sprite->movingRightImages = numOfMovingRightImages;
  sprite->staticImages = numOfStaticImages;
  sprite->explodingImages = numOfExplodingImages;

  /* Fill out the row indices */
  sprite->movingLeftRow = movingLeftRowIndex;
  sprite->movingRightRow = movingRightRowIndex;
  sprite->standingStillRow = staticRowIndex;
  sprite->explodingRow = explodingRowIndex;

  /* The sprite starts out standing still. */
  sprite->spriteAction = kSpriteStandingStill;
  sprite->currentImageIndex = 0;

  sprite->spriteSequenceImage = newOffscreenBuffer;
  sprite->width = width;
  sprite->height = height;
  sprite->x = 0;
```

Continued on next page

Continued from previous page

```
    sprite->y = 0;

    /* The sprite is active */
    sprite->spriteStatus = kSpriteActive;
  }

  /* We're all done. If there was an error, return the proper code.
   */

  return err;
}
```

Drawing the Explosion

The routine in Sprite Utilities.c designed to draw the sprite, DrawSpriteToOffscreen(), requires small modifications to display the explosions.

In the walking man animations of Chapters 5 and 6, when this routine had to decide which image sequence was needed, it would look at the *spriteAction* field of the sprite. If the sprite was moving left, it would use the first row of the animation strip; if it moved right, the second row would be used, and so on.

In the invaders code, the specific row is determined by using the row indices defined for the sprite structure in the previous section. The sprite can also now be exploding, in which case the image is taken from *explodingRow*. Here is the code to accomplish this:

```
/* Calculate which row the image is in based on the sprite's action */
if (sprite->spriteStatus == kSpriteExploding)
  yImagePos = sprite->explodingRow;
else if (sprite->spriteAction == kSpriteMovingLeft)
  yImagePos = sprite->movingLeftRow;
else if (sprite->spriteAction == kSpriteMovingRight)
  yImagePos = sprite->movingRightRow;
else if (sprite->spriteAction == kSpriteStandingStill)
  yImagePos = sprite->standingStillRow;
```

The remaining two functions in this file, MoveSpriteTo() and OffsetSprite(), are unchanged.

The Player vs. the Invaders

For this game, you're going to use two different types of sprites: invader sprites and ship sprites. Several invader sprites will be on the screen at the same time; they all share the same animation strip. Their movements are automated by the computer so their drawing routines do not need to check for input.

The ship sprite is controlled by the player—there is only one on the screen at a time and it has the same input options that the enhanced Walking Man program did. The ship sprite has image sequences for three movement modes (left, right, and still) as well as an explosion. The invaders have only two movement modes (left and right), plus an explosion. Each movement mode has 8 frames and the explosion consists of 3 frames. The invader's animation strip is shown in Figure 8-1 and the ship's is shown in Figure 8-2. Like the walking man's sprite images, the ship and invader sprites were raytraced using Specular's Infini-D software.

Because of the differences between the ship sprites and the invader sprites, they each have their own routines for handling movement and drawing. Sprite Animator.c, which used to hold all of these routines, now handles initializing the sprites and loading the background image. The specific routines for the ship and invaders are on the source code disc in the Chapter 8 folder under Ship Sprite.c and Invader Sprites.c, respectively.

✸ SOURCE CODE ORGANIZATION

It's very important to give some thought to how you organize your code. Related routines that work together to accomplish a task should be kept in the same file and the file should have a logical name. This helps you find your routines faster, minimizes having to recompile all of your source code, and can help make bugs easier to track down. It also makes it easier to use a set of routines for another game. A little time invested while writing your code will save you a lot of headaches down the road.

FIGURE 8-1

◎ ◎ ◎ ◎ ◎ ◎

The invaders animation strip

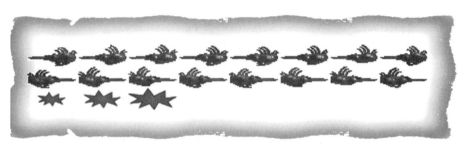

FIGURE 8-2

◎ ◎ ◎ ◎ ◎ ◎

The ship animation strip

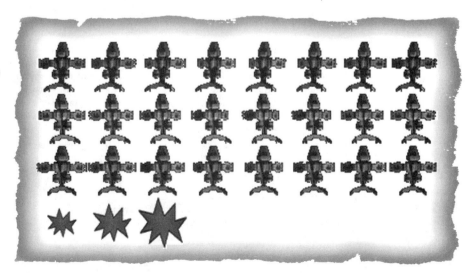

Invader Sprites

The creation of the invader sprites must be handled slightly differently than that of the walking man sprite. The NewSprite() function will create a new GWorld for the animation strip every time it is called. If you have 15 invaders (the default value) and you call NewSprite() for each of these sprites, you will end up allocating 15 GWorlds, all with identical content. Because each animation strip consumes 28k of memory, you would be using over 400k just for the sprite images. Obviously this is wasteful; invader sprites can all share the same GWorld.

The invader sprite initialization routine (InitializeInvaderSprites()) builds each of the invader sprites individually. Because the code for loading the GWorld is rather long and it has already been implemented in NewSprite(), InitializeInvaderSprites() won't repeat it. Instead, it calls NewSprite() once, allowing it to initialize a "dummy" sprite. The only thing it wants from the dummy sprite is its spriteSequenceImage field.

Once it has the animation strip GWorld, InitializeInvaderSprites() fills out the fields of each of the invader sprites, positioning them in a grid. The invaders are positioned so that there are 5 pixels between each of them (determined by the constant kSpaceBetweenInvaders).

Because all of the invaders are always moving in the same direction, it is convenient to keep track of their movement with a global variable:

```
static short    gCurrentInvaderDirection;
```

Part of the job of InitializeInvaderSprites() is to set *gCurrentInvaderDirection* to kSpriteMovingRight (because the invaders always start out at the upper-left-hand corner of the screen). Listing 8-3 shows the code.

Listing 8-3 *The InitializeInvaderSprites() routine*

```
/**
 **   InitializeInvaderSprites()
 **
 **   Sets up each individual invader sprite. The invader sprites
 **   all share the same image. NewSprite() will attempt to
 **   allocate an animation strip for every sprite, which won't
 **   work for us. But we can call NewSprite() once to
 **   have it load the animation strip, copy that information into
 **   all of the sprites, then change just the information that
 **   varies between each sprite.
 **
 **/
OSErr  InitializeInvaderSprites(void)
{
  short    currentSprite;
  short    currentVSprite, currentHSprite;
  short    currentVPosition, currentHPosition;
```

```
Sprite    starterSprite;
OSErr     err = noErr;
short     imageIndex;

currentSprite = 0;
currentVSprite = 0;
currentHSprite = 0;

/* Initialize the starter sprite */
err = NewSprite( &starterSprite,
                 kInvaderWidth,
                 kInvaderHeight,
                 kNumOfMovingInvaderSprites,
                 kNumOfMovingInvaderSprites,
                 kNumOfStaticInvaderSprites,
                 kNumOfExplodingInvaderSprites,
                 kInvaderLeftRow,
                 kInvaderRightRow,
                 kInvaderStaticRow,
                 kInvaderExplodingRow,
                 kPICT_InvaderAnimationStrip  );

/* All of the invaders start out moving to the right */
starterSprite.spriteAction = kSpriteMovingRight;

/* Now copy that information to each invader sprite, then
 * customize some of its data.
 */
for (  currentSprite = 0;
       currentSprite < kNumOfInvaders;
       currentSprite++)
{
  gInvaderSprites[currentSprite] = starterSprite;

  /* Set the sprite's position */
  currentHPosition = currentHSprite *
                     (kInvaderWidth + kSpaceBetweenInvaders);
  currentVPosition = currentVSprite *
                     (kInvaderHeight + kSpaceBetweenInvaders);

  MoveSpriteTo(  &gInvaderSprites[currentSprite],
                 currentHPosition,
                 currentVPosition          );

  /* Find the position of the next sprite */
  currentHSprite += 1;
  if (currentHSprite == kNumOfHorizInvaders) {
    currentHSprite = 0;
    currentVSprite += 1;
  }
```

Continued on next page

Continued from previous page

```
    /* Randomize the starting image for this invader sprite. */
    imageIndex = RangedRandom(0, kNumOfMovingInvaderSprites-1);
    gInvaderSprites[currentSprite].currentImageIndex = imageIndex;
  }

  gCurrentInvaderDirection = kSpriteMovingRight;

  return err;
}
```

Moving the Invaders

The next thing you need is a routine to animate the invader sprites. The invaders are entirely computer controlled, so it isn't necessary to include any of the input routines that you'll be using for the player's ship. The invaders will move across the screen, turning around and dropping down whenever they reach the edge. If any invader reaches the bottom, the player loses the game.

So the invaders know when to turn around, you must calculate a rectangle that encompasses all of the invaders. Only the active (or exploding) invaders are included in this rectangle so, for example, if the player eliminates the entire left-hand column of invaders, the remaining invaders will have to fly farther before turning around. Listing 8-4 is a code segment that determines whether or not the invaders should be turned around.

Listing 8-4 *Animating the invaders*

```
    /* Determine the direction that the invader sprites are moving now. */
    movingDirection = gCurrentInvaderDirection;

    /* Calculate the bounding rectangle around all of the remaining
     * invaders (ignore those that have been destroyed)
     */
    spriteBounds.left = spriteBounds.top = 10000;
    spriteBounds.right = spriteBounds.bottom = -1000;

    for ( currentInvader = 0;
          currentInvader < kNumOfInvaders;
          currentInvader++    )
    {
      /* Is the sprite still alive? */
      if (gInvaderSprites[currentInvader].spriteStatus != kSpriteDestroyed)
      {
        /* Set the sprite's left/right bounds */
        if (spriteBounds.left > gInvaderSprites[currentInvader].x)
          spriteBounds.left = gInvaderSprites[currentInvader].x;
        if (spriteBounds.right <
            gInvaderSprites[currentInvader].x + kInvaderWidth)
          spriteBounds.right =
```

```
                 gInvaderSprites[currentInvader].x + kInvaderWidth;

      /* Set the sprite's top/bottom bounds */
      if (spriteBounds.top > gInvaderSprites[currentInvader].y)
        spriteBounds.top = gInvaderSprites[currentInvader].y;
      if (spriteBounds.bottom <
          gInvaderSprites[currentInvader].y + kInvaderHeight)
        spriteBounds.bottom =
          gInvaderSprites[currentInvader].y + kInvaderHeight;
    }
  }

  /* Determine the window size */
  windowBounds = dstWindow->portRect;

  /* We can now determine whether the sprites are close enough to either
   * side of the window to warrant turning them back.
   */
  if (movingDirection == kSpriteMovingLeft) {
    /* See if the sprites are too close to the left side of the window */
    if (spriteBounds.left - windowBounds.left < kInvaderSpeed) {
      /* Change the sprite direction */
      movingDirection = kSpriteMovingRight;
    }
  } else {
    /* See if the sprites are too close to the right
     * side of the window
     */
    if (windowBounds.right - spriteBounds.right < kInvaderSpeed) {
      /* Change the sprite direction */
      movingDirection = kSpriteMovingLeft;
    }
  }
```

The invaders are also capable of dropping missiles on the player. The chance of dropping a missile is determined by the constant kChanceToDropMissile: The chance of an invader dropping a missile on any given turn is 1 in kChanceToDropMissile. The higher the constant, the less frequent the drops. The default value you'll be using for kChanceToDropMissile is 100, so each invader has a 1 in 100 chance of dropping a missile each frame.

The missiles are handled by a separate file called Missiles.c. MoveInvaderSprites() calls FireInvaderMissile() whenever an invader drops a missile. I'll cover the missile routines a little later in this chapter.

If an invader sprite is currently exploding, MoveInvaderSprites() will also check to see if the explosion sequence has finished. If so, it will mark that sprite as destroyed.

As you can see (Listing 8-5), MoveInvaderSprites() has quite a few tasks to complete, but it is fairly straight forward. It bears a close resemblance to MoveSprites() in the Walking Man application.

Listing 8-5 *The MoveInvaderSprites( ) routine*

```
/**
**    MoveInvaderSprites()
**
**    Animates all of the invader sprites, moving them across the screen,
**    or down one row if they have reached the edge. If any sprite reaches
**    the bottom of the screen, 'gameOver' will return TRUE.
**/
OSErr   MoveInvaderSprites(WindowPtr  dstWindow, Boolean  *gameOver)
{
  Rect          windowBounds;
  Rect          spriteBounds;
  Rect          gworldBounds;
  GWorldPtr     temporaryBuffer;
  GWorldPtr     backgroundImage;
  PixMapHandle  tempBufferPixmap;
  PixMapHandle  backgroundPixmap;
  OSErr         err;
  GDHandle      saveDevice;
  CGrafPtr      savePort;
  short         movingDirection;
  short         currentInvader;
  short         horizontalMovement, verticalMovement;

  /* Start by assuming that the invaders have not landed. */
  *gameOver = FALSE;

  /* Determine the direction that the invader sprites are moving now. */
  movingDirection = gCurrentInvaderDirection;

  /* Calculate the bounding rectangle around all of the remaining
   * invaders (ignore those that have been destroyed).
   */
  spriteBounds.left = spriteBounds.top = 10000;
  spriteBounds.right = spriteBounds.bottom = -1000;

  for (    currentInvader = 0;
           currentInvader < kNumOfInvaders;
           currentInvader++    )
  {
    if (gInvaderSprites[currentInvader].spriteStatus != kSpriteDestroyed)
    {
      if (spriteBounds.left > gInvaderSprites[currentInvader].x)
        spriteBounds.left = gInvaderSprites[currentInvader].x;
      if (spriteBounds.right <
          gInvaderSprites[currentInvader].x + kInvaderWidth)
        spriteBounds.right =
          gInvaderSprites[currentInvader].x + kInvaderWidth;

      if (spriteBounds.top > gInvaderSprites[currentInvader].y)
        spriteBounds.top = gInvaderSprites[currentInvader].y;
```

```
      if (spriteBounds.bottom <
          gInvaderSprites[currentInvader].y + kInvaderHeight)
        spriteBounds.bottom =
          gInvaderSprites[currentInvader].y + kInvaderHeight;
  }
}

/* Determine the window size */
windowBounds = dstWindow->portRect;

/* We can now determine whether the sprites are close enough to either
 * side of the window to warrant turning them back.
 */
if (movingDirection == kSpriteMovingLeft) {
  /* See if the sprites are too close to the left side of the window */
  if (spriteBounds.left - windowBounds.left < kInvaderSpeed) {
    /* Change the sprite direction */
    movingDirection = kSpriteMovingRight;
  }
} else {
  /* See if the sprites are too close to the right
   * side of the window.
   */
  if (windowBounds.right - spriteBounds.right < kInvaderSpeed) {
    /* Change the sprite direction */
    movingDirection = kSpriteMovingLeft;
  }
}

/* Calculate how far each invader is moving this turn. If they did not
 * change direction, they will move a distance of
 * kInvaderSpeed. If they hit the edge, they will move
 * down by a factor of kInvaderHeight.
 */
if (movingDirection == gCurrentInvaderDirection) {
  if (movingDirection == kSpriteMovingRight)
    horizontalMovement = kInvaderSpeed;
  else
    horizontalMovement = -kInvaderSpeed;
  verticalMovement = 0;
} else {
  horizontalMovement = 0;
  verticalMovement = kInvaderHeight;
}

gCurrentInvaderDirection = movingDirection;

/* Check to see if the invaders are close to the bottom
 * of the window. If so, the game is over - the player loses. In
 * this case, we'll define 'close' as twice the invader sprite's
 * height.
 */
```

Continued on next page

Continued from previous page

```
if (  (windowBounds.bottom -  spriteBounds.bottom) <
      kInvaderHeight * 2  )
{
  *gameOver = TRUE;
  return noErr;
}


/* Update each sprite's position, then randomly let them drop missiles.
 */
for (    currentInvader = 0;
         currentInvader < kNumOfInvaders;
         currentInvader++) {
  if (gInvaderSprites[currentInvader].spriteStatus == kSpriteActive) {
    OffsetSprite(  &gInvaderSprites[currentInvader],
                    horizontalMovement,
                    verticalMovement  );

    /* Check to see if this invader drops a missile */
    if (RangedRandom(0, kChanceToDropMissile) == 0) {
      /* Activate a missile */
      FireInvaderMissile(
            gInvaderSprites[currentInvader].x + (kInvaderWidth / 2),
            gInvaderSprites[currentInvader].y + kInvaderHeight  );
    }
  }
}


/* We're going to create a temporary gworld
 * and then dispose of it when we finish. It will be used
 * to merge the sprite and background images before
 * copying them onto the screen. This temporary
 * gworld will be the size of the bounding rectangle we
 * calculated earlier, plus the distance that the
 * sprites moved for this frame.
 */

gworldBounds = spriteBounds;

if (horizontalMovement < 0) {
  /* Expand the left side of the bounds (add them because
   * horizontalMovement is negative).
   */
  gworldBounds.left += horizontalMovement;
} else {
  /* Expand the right side. */
  gworldBounds.right += horizontalMovement;
}
/* Expand the bottom bounds */
gworldBounds.bottom += verticalMovement;


/* Create the temporary gworld and check for errors */
```

```
              err = NewGWorld( &temporaryBuffer,
                               8,
                               &gworldBounds,
                               NULL,
                               NULL,
                               0 );
              if (err)
                return err;

              /* Find the GWorldPtr for the background. The background
               * GWorld is stored in the Sprite Animation.c file as a global.
               * Another way of handling this is to make the background GWorld
               * global directly accessible to other files (by declaring
               * it as 'extern' in Sprite Animation.h). However, that way
               * makes it a little more confusing to follow.
               */
              backgroundImage = GetBackgroundGWorld();

              /* Get the pixmaps from both offscreens */
              tempBufferPixmap = GetGWorldPixMap(temporaryBuffer);
              backgroundPixmap = GetGWorldPixMap(backgroundImage);

              /* Lock the pixmaps for both offscreens */
              LockPixels(tempBufferPixmap);
              LockPixels(backgroundPixmap);

              /* Copy the relevant portion of the background into
               * the temporary offscreen buffer.
               */

              GetGWorld(&savePort, &saveDevice);
              SetGWorld(temporaryBuffer, NULL);

              CopyBits(   (BitMap *)*backgroundPixmap,
                          (BitMap *)*tempBufferPixmap,
                          &gworldBounds,
                          &gworldBounds,
                          srcCopy,
                          NULL );

              SetGWorld(savePort, saveDevice);

              UnlockPixels(tempBufferPixmap);
              UnlockPixels(backgroundPixmap);

              /* The next step is to draw the invader sprites (that are active)
               * into the temporary offscreen. Loop through all of the sprites,
               * update their animation indices, and draw them. Also take
               * this opportunity to update the individual sprite's moving direction
               * and to determine whether any invaders have finished exploding
               * (in which case we mark them as 'destroyed').
               */
```

Continued on next page

Continued from previous page

```
for (    currentInvader = 0;
         currentInvader < kNumOfInvaders;
         currentInvader++) {
  /* Update the image index no matter whether the sprite is
   * alive or not. If the sprite is alive or exploding,
   * we want it to increment, and if it is dead, incrementing
   * this value doesn't hurt anything.
   */
  gInvaderSprites[currentInvader].currentImageIndex += 1;

  /* Check to see if the invader is alive */
  if (gInvaderSprites[currentInvader].spriteStatus == kSpriteActive) {
    if (  gInvaderSprites[currentInvader].currentImageIndex >=
        kNumOfMovingInvaderSprites  )
    {
      /* Index went beyond the end, so wrap it back to the beginning */
      gInvaderSprites[currentInvader].currentImageIndex = 0;
    }

    gInvaderSprites[currentInvader].spriteAction =
        gCurrentInvaderDirection;

    DrawSpriteToOffscreen(  &gInvaderSprites[currentInvader],
                            temporaryBuffer);
  } else if (gInvaderSprites[currentInvader].spriteStatus ==
          kSpriteExploding) {
    /* If the invader's status is kInvaderHit and
     * it has finished exploding,  change it to
     * kInvaderDestroyed. Otherwise, it is still displaying
     * its explosion images, so draw it to the screen.
     */
    if (gInvaderSprites[currentInvader].currentImageIndex >=
        kNumOfExplodingInvaderSprites)
      gInvaderSprites[currentInvader].spriteStatus = kSpriteDestroyed;
    else
      DrawSpriteToOffscreen(  &gInvaderSprites[currentInvader],
                              temporaryBuffer);
  }
}

/* All that's left to do is draw the temporary buffer to the
 * window.
 */
LockPixels(tempBufferPixmap);

SetPort(dstWindow);

CopyBits(  (BitMap *)*tempBufferPixmap,
           (BitMap *)&dstWindow->portBits,
           &gworldBounds,
           &gworldBounds,
           srcCopy,
           NULL );
```

```
UnlockPixels(tempBufferPixmap);

/* Now just dispose of the temporary offscreen buffer */
DisposeGWorld(temporaryBuffer);

return err;
}
```

Ship Sprites

You now have invaders crawling across the screen dropping missiles. Let's give the player a chance to fight back. The first step is to initialize the ship sprite, which is the responsibility of InitializeShipSprite(). This routine is almost unchanged from the PrepareSprites() routine of the Walking Man animation except for the addition of the new parameters to NewSprite(). The ship sprite is then moved to its default starting position.

```
/**
 **   InitializeShipSprite()
 **
 **   Creates a new ship sprite and passes it back to the
 **   caller. This routine is called once at startup time by
 **   PrepareSprites() in Sprite Animator.c.
 **
 **   Although this code is small and could just be put directly
 **   into PrepareSprites(), I'm putting it here to
 **   separate the routines specific to the ship sprite. It's
 **   a matter of code organization.
 **/
OSErr  InitializeShipSprite(void)
{
  OSErr    err = noErr;


  err = NewSprite( &gShipSprite,
                   kShipWidth,
                   kShipHeight,
                   kNumOfMovingShipSprites,
                   kNumOfMovingShipSprites,
                   kNumOfStaticShipSprites,
                   kNumOfExplodingSprites,
                   kShipMovingLeftIndex,
                   kShipMovingRightIndex,
                   kShipStaticIndex,
                   kShipExplodingIndex,
                   kPICT_ShipAnimationStrip  );

  MoveSpriteTo(&gShipSprite, kShipStartingXPos, kShipStartingYPos);

  return err;
}
```

Moving the Ship

The ship animation routine, MoveShip(), depends on the player's input to avoid the invaders' missiles and to fire missiles of its own. Again, this routine bears a close resemblance to its parent routine, MoveCurrentSprite(). The two main distinctions are how it handles the player firing missiles and the ship exploding.

Like MoveCurrentSprite(), this routine determines the ship's movement by calling ProcessInput() periodically. However, ProcessInput() has been modified to return a value indicating whether or not the player fired a missile this turn. If so, a routine in Missiles.c is called to create the new missile.

A delay has been added for calling ProcessInput(). The ProcessInput() routine used in earlier chapters could, on a fast machine, be called several hundred times a second. This is not only a wasteful use of computer resources, but when the player pressed the fire key, the routine would register a missile launch every time it was called. All the player's missiles would be launched within a fraction of a second.

The last major modification to the routine is for the explosion images; MoveShip() handles it in a fashion similar to the way MoveInvaderSprite() does (see Listing 8-6).

Listing 8-6 *The MoveShip( ) routine*

```
/**
**   MoveShip()
**
**   Checks the keyboard or mouse for input, then animates the
**   ship based on that.
**   This routine generates a temporary GWorld to hold
**   the moving sprite composited onto the background. The temporary
**   GWorld is large enough to hold both the place that the
**   sprite _was_ and the position that it _will be_.
**/
OSErr  MoveShip(WindowPtr  dstWindow, short inputMethod)
{
    Rect            windowBounds;
    Rect            spriteBounds;
    GWorldPtr       temporaryBuffer;
    GWorldPtr       backgroundGWorld;
    PixMapHandle    tempBufferPixmap;
    PixMapHandle    backgroundPixmap;
    OSErr           err;
    GDHandle        saveDevice;
    CGrafPtr        savePort;
    short           distanceMoved;
    short           movingDirection;
    Boolean         shipFiredMissile;
    long            thisTickCount;

    /* If it's been long enough since we last checked for input (and the
     * ship hasn't been destroyed), do it now.
     */
```

```
if (gShipSprite.spriteStatus == kSpriteActive) {
  thisTickCount = TickCount();

  if (thisTickCount - gLastCheckTickCount > kInputProcessingDelay) {
    movingDirection = ProcessInput(  dstWindow,
                                     inputMethod,
                                     &shipFiredMissile);

    if (shipFiredMissile)
      /* Use missile position from the center of the ship */
      FireShipMissile(gShipSprite.x + (kShipWidth / 2));

    /* If the sprite changed its direction, reset the sprite's
     * image index to zero.
     */
    if (movingDirection != gShipSprite.spriteAction) {
      gShipSprite.spriteAction = movingDirection;
      gShipSprite.currentImageIndex = 0;
    }
    gLastCheckTickCount = thisTickCount;
  }
}

/* Move the sprite according to its direction */
if (gShipSprite.spriteAction == kSpriteMovingLeft)
  distanceMoved = -kShipSpeed;
else if (gShipSprite.spriteAction == kSpriteMovingRight)
  distanceMoved = kShipSpeed;
else
  distanceMoved = 0;

/* Make sure we're not moving the sprite off the screen */
windowBounds = dstWindow->portRect;
if ((gShipSprite.x + distanceMoved) < windowBounds.left) {
  distanceMoved = windowBounds.left - gShipSprite.x;
}

if ((  gShipSprite.x +
       gShipSprite.width +
       distanceMoved  ) > windowBounds.right) {
  distanceMoved = windowBounds.right -
                  gShipSprite.width -
                  gShipSprite.x;
}


OffsetSprite(&gShipSprite, distanceMoved, 0);

/* We're going to create a temporary gworld
 * and then dispose of it when we finish. This temporary
 * gworld will be the size of the sprite plus the distance that
 * it moved during this frame.
 */
```

Continued on next page

Continued from previous page

```
spriteBounds.left = gShipSprite.x;
spriteBounds.right = spriteBounds.left + gShipSprite.width;
spriteBounds.top = gShipSprite.y;
spriteBounds.bottom = spriteBounds.top + gShipSprite.height;

if (distanceMoved < 0)
  /* If the sprite moved to the left, we need to expand the right
   * edge of the buffer to erase where the sprite used to be.
   */
  spriteBounds.right -= distanceMoved;
else
  /* Otherwise, update the left edge of the buffer */
  spriteBounds.left -= distanceMoved;

/* Increment the sprite's image index */
gShipSprite.currentImageIndex++;

/* If the ship has been hit, check to see if it has finished exploding.
 * If so, change its status to kSpriteDestroyed.
 */
if (gShipSprite.spriteStatus == kSpriteExploding) {
  if (gShipSprite.currentImageIndex >= gShipSprite.explodingImages)
    gShipSprite.spriteStatus = kSpriteDestroyed;
} else {
  /* The ship hasn't been hit, so check to see if the image sequence
   * is ready to be looped around.
   */
  if (gShipSprite.spriteAction == kSpriteMovingLeft)
  {
    if (gShipSprite.currentImageIndex >= gShipSprite.movingLeftImages)
      gShipSprite.currentImageIndex = 0;
  }
  else if (gShipSprite.spriteAction == kSpriteMovingRight)
  {
    if (gShipSprite.currentImageIndex >= gShipSprite.movingRightImages)
      gShipSprite.currentImageIndex = 0;
  }
  else if (gShipSprite.spriteAction == kSpriteStandingStill) {
    if (gShipSprite.currentImageIndex >= gShipSprite.staticImages)
      gShipSprite.currentImageIndex = 0;
  }
}

err = NewGWorld( &temporaryBuffer,
                 8,
                 &spriteBounds,
                 NULL,
                 NULL,
                 0 );
if (err)
  return err;
```

```
/* Get the background image's GWorldPtr */
backgroundGWorld = GetBackgroundGWorld();

/* Get the temporary offscreen's pixmap */
tempBufferPixmap = GetGWorldPixMap(temporaryBuffer);
backgroundPixmap = GetGWorldPixMap(backgroundGWorld);

/* Lock the pixmaps for both offscreens */
LockPixels(tempBufferPixmap);
LockPixels(backgroundPixmap);

/* Copy the relevant portion of the background into
 * the temporary offscreen buffer.
 */

GetGWorld(&savePort, &saveDevice);
SetGWorld(temporaryBuffer, NULL);

CopyBits( (BitMap *)*backgroundPixmap,
          (BitMap *)*tempBufferPixmap,
          &spriteBounds,
          &spriteBounds,
          srcCopy,
          NULL  );

SetGWorld(savePort, saveDevice);

UnlockPixels(tempBufferPixmap);
UnlockPixels(backgroundPixmap);

/* The next step is to draw the sprite into the temporary
 * offscreen. Fortunately, we already have a routine to
 * do this.
 */
DrawSpriteToOffscreen(&gShipSprite, temporaryBuffer);

/* All that's left to do is draw the temporary buffer to the
 * window.
 */
LockPixels(tempBufferPixmap);

SetPort(dstWindow);

CopyBits( (BitMap *)*tempBufferPixmap,
          (BitMap *)&dstWindow->portBits,
          &spriteBounds,
          &spriteBounds,
          srcCopy,
          NULL  );

UnlockPixels(tempBufferPixmap);
```

Continued on next page

Continued from previous page

```
/* Now just dispose of the temporary offscreen buffer */
DisposeGWorld(temporaryBuffer);

return err;
}
```

Fire Away!

Now that you have the invaders and the player's defending ship, the third element required for the game is missiles. When a missile is being fired, a MissileInfo structure is filled out, which holds information on the missile's position and whether it's active:

```
typedef struct {
  Boolean    active;
  short      hPosition;
  short      vPosition;
} MissileInfo;
```

A fixed number of missiles can be active at the same time. The defaults are set to three player missiles and eight invader missiles—these constants can be changed to examine the effects on gameplay.

Each missile must be tracked and updated, just like a ship, so you need a record for each one. These records are stored in two global arrays, each with enough elements to support the maximum number of missiles allowed:

```
MissileInfo  gShipMissiles[kMaxShipMissiles];
MissileInfo  gInvaderMissiles[kMaxInvaderMissiles];
```

It is necessary to initialize the missiles before using them. All the initialization routine does is set the active flag of each missile to FALSE, as shown here:

```
/**
 ** InitializeMissiles()
 **
 ** Initializes the fields of the two MissileInfo structs.
 ** The only thing that needs initializing is the 'active'
 ** field.
 **/
void  InitializeMissiles(void)
{
  short    mIndex;

  /* Initialize the ship missile info */
  for (mIndex = 0; mIndex < kMaxShipMissiles; mIndex++)
  {
    gShipMissiles[mIndex].active = FALSE;
  }

  /* Initialize the invader missile info */
  for (mIndex = 0; mIndex < kMaxInvaderMissiles; mIndex++)
```

```
  {
    gInvaderMissiles[mIndex].active = FALSE;
  }
}
```

You've already seen references to the two routines that create a missile—FireShipMissile() and FireInvaderMissile(). The routines are similar; I'll look at FireShipMissile() first.

The first thing FireShipMissile() does is examine each of the available missile slots looking for one that's available. If it finds one, it fills out the structure. The only parameter to FireShipMissile() is the horizontal position of the ship—the vertical position is always the same because the ship cannot move vertically. Here is the routine:

```
/**
 **   FireShipMissile()
 **
 **   Starts a ship missile. Returns TRUE if there was an
 **   available missile, FALSE otherwise.
 **/
Boolean  FireShipMissile(short shipHLocation)
{
  short    missileToUse;
  short    mIndex;

  /* See if there's a free missile we can use. */

  missileToUse = -1; /* Set missileToUse to a bogus value */
  for (mIndex = 0; mIndex < kMaxShipMissiles; mIndex++)
  {
    if (gShipMissiles[mIndex].active == FALSE) {
      missileToUse = mIndex;
    }
  }

  /* If we didn't find a free missile, return FALSE */
  if (missileToUse == -1)
    return FALSE;

  /* Fill out the missileInfo structure with our info */
  gShipMissiles[missileToUse].active = TRUE;
  gShipMissiles[missileToUse].hPosition = shipHLocation;
  gShipMissiles[missileToUse].vPosition = kShipMissileVStart;

  return TRUE;
}
```

Invader Missiles

Very few changes are necessary for FireInvaderMissile(). You're now searching through the other missile array, and because the invaders change position both horizontally and vertically, there is now a parameter for each coordinate. Here's the code:

```
/**
**   FireInvaderMissile()
**
**   Starts an invader missile. Returns TRUE if there was an
**   available missile, FALSE otherwise.
**/
Boolean  FireInvaderMissile(short invaderHLoc, short invaderVLoc)
{
  short     missileToUse;
  short     mIndex;

  /* See if there's a free missile we can use. */

  missileToUse = -1; /* Set missileToUse to a bogus value */
  for (mIndex = 0; mIndex < kMaxInvaderMissiles; mIndex++)
  {
    if (gInvaderMissiles[mIndex].active == FALSE) {
      missileToUse = mIndex;
    }
  }

  /* If we didn't find a free missile, return FALSE */
  if (missileToUse == -1)
    return FALSE;

  /* Fill out the missileInfo structure with our info */
  gInvaderMissiles[missileToUse].active = TRUE;
  gInvaderMissiles[missileToUse].hPosition = invaderHLoc;
  gInvaderMissiles[missileToUse].vPosition = invaderVLoc;

  return TRUE;
}
```

Moving the Missiles

The next routine that's necessary is one to animate each of the missiles and determine if there has been a hit. This routine is called UpdateAllMissiles() and it moves the invader and ship missiles separately. It calls other routines to test for hits and for drawing each missile.

Even though the missile is drawn as a white rectangle, animating it is still a little tricky. As the missile moves up (or down, in the case of the invaders' missiles), the background image has to be replaced. UpdateAllMissiles() doesn't do the drawing, but it passes the pixmap of the background image to the routine that does. Listing 8-7 shows the routine.

Listing 8-7 *The UpdateAllMissiles() routine*

```
/**
**   UpdateAllMissiles()
**
**   Draws the missiles on the screen and tests for collision
```

```
**   with opposing objects. It will also handle destruction of
**   invaders.
**/
void  UpdateAllMissiles(WindowPtr dstWindow)
{
  short          mIndex;
  GWorldPtr      backgroundGWorld;
  PixMapHandle   backgroundPixMap;
  MissileInfo    *missileRef;
  Rect           windowRect;

  /* Get the background gworld and pixmap, then lock it
   * down.
   */
  backgroundGWorld = GetBackgroundGWorld();
  backgroundPixMap = GetGWorldPixMap(backgroundGWorld);
  LockPixels(backgroundPixMap);

  /* Set the port to the window */
  SetPort(dstWindow);

  /* Get the window's boundary */
  windowRect = dstWindow->portRect;

  /* First handle the invader missiles and see if the
   * player has been destroyed.
   */
  for (mIndex = 0; mIndex < kMaxInvaderMissiles; mIndex++)
  {
    if (gInvaderMissiles[mIndex].active == TRUE) {
      /* Obtain a pointer to this missile info. This
       * allows us to access the information more
       * efficiently, because if we didn't use this
       * method, we would be constantly indexing
       * into an array, which is slower.
       */
      missileRef = &gInvaderMissiles[mIndex];

      /* Move the missile's position */
      missileRef->vPosition += kMissileSpeed;

      /* Check for collision */
      DetectShipCollision(missileRef);

      /* Check to see if the missile has gone off the bottom
       * of the screen. If it has, deactivate it. We still go
       * through the drawing stuff, because we need to redraw
       * the background.
       */
      if (missileRef->vPosition > windowRect.bottom) {
        missileRef->active = FALSE;
      }
```

Continued on next page

Continued from previous page

```
    DrawMissile( backgroundPixMap,
                 dstWindow,
                 missileRef,
                 kMissileSpeed );
  }
}

/* Now handle the player's missiles */
for (mIndex = 0; mIndex < kMaxShipMissiles; mIndex++)
{
  if (gShipMissiles[mIndex].active == TRUE) {
    missileRef = &gShipMissiles[mIndex];

    /* Move the missile's position */
    missileRef->vPosition -= kMissileSpeed;

    /* Check for collision */
    if (DetectInvaderCollision(missileRef)) {
      missileRef->active = FALSE;
    }

    /* Check to see if the missile has gone off the top
     * of the screen. If it has, deactivate it. We still go
     * through the drawing stuff, because we need to redraw
     * the background.
     */
    if (missileRef->vPosition < windowRect.top) {
      missileRef->active = FALSE;
    }

    DrawMissile( backgroundPixMap,
                 dstWindow,
                 missileRef,
                 -kMissileSpeed );
  }
 }
}
```

It's necessary to pass the missile speed to DrawMissile() so it knows whether to redraw the background above or below the missile. If the missile speed is negative, the missile is moving up; if it's positive, the missile is moving down.

DrawMissile() doesn't do anything surprising. It calculates a rectangle representing the missile and then calls the toolbox routine EraseRect() to draw it onto the screen. EraseRect() is a handy way to fill a rectangle with the current background color (which is normally white).

Once the missile has been drawn, DrawMissile() finds the area of the screen that was just vacated by the missile. It then uses CopyBits() to redraw that portion of the background, as shown in Listing 8-8.

Listing 8-8 The DrawMissile() routine

```
/**
 ** DrawMissile()
 **
 ** Draws the missile and replaces the background area that it
 ** erased as it flew by. 'distanceMoved' is required because
 ** the routine must know which portion of the background to
 ** replace.
 **/
static void  DrawMissile( PixMapHandle    background,
                          WindowPtr       dstWindow,
                          MissileInfo     *mInfo,
                          short           distanceMoved  )
{
  Rect       missileRect;
  Rect       backgroundCopyRect;

  /* We want to draw the missile. Calculate the
   * bounding rectangle for the missile.
   */
  missileRect.left = mInfo->hPosition;
  missileRect.right = missileRect.left +
                      (kMissileWidth - 1);
  missileRect.bottom = mInfo->vPosition;
  missileRect.top = missileRect.bottom -
                    (kMissileHeight - 1);

  /* Now figure out the area that the missile
   * left behind it. This is so we can copy
   * the background image back into this area
   * and erase the old missile.
   */
  backgroundCopyRect = missileRect;
  if (distanceMoved > 0) {
    backgroundCopyRect.bottom = missileRect.top;
    backgroundCopyRect.top = missileRect.top - distanceMoved;
  } else {
    backgroundCopyRect.top = missileRect.bottom;
    backgroundCopyRect.bottom = missileRect.bottom - distanceMoved;
  }
  /* Now copy that background area onto the image,
   * erasing the old missile.
   */

  CopyBits( (BitMap *)*background,
            (BitMap *)&dstWindow->portBits,
            &backgroundCopyRect,
            &backgroundCopyRect,
            srcCopy,
            NULL  );
```

Continued on next page

Continued from previous page
```
  /* Draw the missile onto the window at its new position.
   * For now, our missiles are just white rectangles (which work
   * pretty well, and are very fast to draw). A white
   * rectangle is drawn by using EraseRect().
   */
  EraseRect(&missileRect);
}
```

Collision Detection

Two routines called by UpdateAllMissiles() haven't been described yet. They are routines for detecting a collision between a missile and an invader or the player's ship. The routines are called DetectShipCollision() and DetectInvaderCollision(). They are not in the Missiles.c file, because they need access to the sprite structures. DetectShipCollision() is in Ship Sprite.c and DetectInvaderCollision() is in Invader Sprites.c, both of which are in the Chapter 8 folder on the source code disc.

DetectShipCollision() is a simple routine. It checks the position of the missile against the bounds of the ship sprite. If it finds the missile inside the ship boundary, it marks the ship sprite's status as kSpriteExploding. It then plays an asynchronous explosion sound using the sound routines outlined in Chapter 7.

Both collision routines return TRUE if a hit is detected, which allows UpdateAllMissiles() to deactivate that missile. Here is DetectShipCollision():

```
/**
 **   DetectShipCollision()
 **
 **   Returns TRUE if this missile hits the player's ship,
 **   plus updates the ship's status.
 **/
Boolean  DetectShipCollision(MissileInfo  *mData)
{
  SndListHandle  explosionSound;

  /* If the ship has already been destroyed, there's no
   * point in checking to see if it has been hit again.
   */
  if (gShipSprite.spriteStatus == kSpriteActive) {
    if(  (mData->hPosition >= gShipSprite.x) &&
         (mData->hPosition <= gShipSprite.x + kShipWidth) &&
         (mData->vPosition >= gShipSprite.y) &&
         (mData->vPosition <= gShipSprite.y + kShipHeight) )
    {
      gShipSprite.spriteStatus = kSpriteExploding;
      gShipSprite.currentImageIndex = 0;

      /* Insert an explosion sound to play now */
      explosionSound = (SndListHandle)GetResource('snd ', 128);
      PlayAsyncSound(explosionSound, kSndPriorityHigh);
```

```
        return TRUE;
    }
  }
  return FALSE;
}
```

DetectInvaderCollision() (Listing 8-9) has to check the missile against all of the active invaders, but is otherwise identical to DetectShipCollision().

Listing 8-9 The DetectInvaderCollision() routine

```
/**
 **  DetectInvaderCollision()
 **
 **  Given a missile, this routine detects whether it has collided with
 **  an invader ship, and if so, destroys that ship. Returns TRUE if
 **  there was a collision, FALSE if not.
 **/
Boolean  DetectInvaderCollision(MissileInfo  *mData)
{
  short       invaderIndex;
  Boolean       invaderDestroyed = FALSE;
  SndListHandle  explosionSound;

  for (invaderIndex = 0; invaderIndex < kNumOfInvaders; invaderIndex++)
  {
    if (gInvaderSprites[invaderIndex].spriteStatus == kSpriteActive)
    {
      if( (mData->hPosition >=
             gInvaderSprites[invaderIndex].x) &&
        (mData->hPosition <=
           gInvaderSprites[invaderIndex].x + kInvaderWidth) &&
        (mData->vPosition >=
           gInvaderSprites[invaderIndex].y) &&
        (mData->vPosition <=
           gInvaderSprites[invaderIndex].y + kInvaderHeight) )
      {
        /* The invader has been destroyed. Update both the invader status
         * array AND the invader's sprite. Also reset the image index
         * to 0 so all of the explosion images are shown.
         */
        gInvaderSprites[invaderIndex].spriteStatus = kSpriteExploding;
        gInvaderSprites[invaderIndex].currentImageIndex = 0;
        invaderDestroyed = TRUE;

        /* Insert an explosion sound to play now */
        explosionSound = (SndListHandle)GetResource('snd ', 128);
        PlayAsyncSound(explosionSound, kSndPriorityMedium);
      }
    }
  }
  return invaderDestroyed;
}
```

The Invaders! main() Function

Like many of the routines in this project, the main() function is a slightly modified version of the one used in the Walking Man application in Chapter 6. The menu items and window are exactly the same, as are most of the initializations and the main event loop.

Here are the steps followed by main():

- Initialize the toolbox.
- Initialize the asynchronous sound player.
- Create the menus and draw the menu bar.
- Initialize the joysticks.
- Initialize the sprites.
- Initialize the missiles.
- Initialize the background image.
- Draw the background.
- Enter the main event loop.
- Call WaitNextEvent occasionally and process the results.
- Move the ship.
- Move the invader sprites.
- Update the missiles.
- Check to see if the game is over (either the ship has been destroyed or the invaders have reached the bottom).
- If the game has ended, display the Game Over message and wait for a mouse click.
- Quit the application.

Listing 8-10 is the complete routine.

Listing 8-10 *The complete Invaders! main() routine*

```
void main(void)
{
    WindowPtr       mainWindow;
    EventRecord     theEvent;
    short           eventMask;
    short           done = FALSE;
    Boolean         notNullEvent;
    Rect            windowRect;
    OSErr           err;
    MenuHandle      appleMenu, fileMenu;
```

```
MenuHandle      editMenu, inputMenu;
long            currentTickCount;
long            lastWaitNextEventCall = 0;
long            lastMoveCurrentSpriteCall = 0;
short           inputMethod = kKeyboardInput;
Boolean         gameOver;

/* Initialize everything we need */
InitGraf(&qd.thePort);    /* qd.thePort is part of any application */
InitWindows();
InitCursor();

/* Initialize the async sound player */
InitializeAsyncSoundPlayer();

eventMask = everyEvent;

/* Create each of our menus and insert them into the menu bar */
appleMenu = NewMenu(kMENU_Apple, "\p\024");
AppendMenu(appleMenu, "\pAbout Invaders! ");
AppendMenu(appleMenu, "\p(-");
InsertMenu(appleMenu, 0);

fileMenu = NewMenu(kMENU_File, "\pFile");
AppendMenu(fileMenu, "\pNew ;Open ;(-;Close;(-;Quit");
InsertMenu(fileMenu, 0);

editMenu = NewMenu(kMENU_Edit, "\pEdit");
AppendMenu(editMenu, "\pUndo;Cut;Copy;Paste;Clear");
InsertMenu(editMenu, 0);

inputMenu = NewMenu(kMENU_Input, "\pInput");
AppendMenu(inputMenu, "\pKeyboard");
AppendMenu(inputMenu, "\p(-");
AppendMenu(inputMenu, "\pMouse - Absolute to Window");
AppendMenu(inputMenu, "\pMouse - Absolute to Screen");
AppendMenu(inputMenu, "\pMouse - Relative");
AppendMenu(inputMenu, "\p(-");
AppendMenu(inputMenu, "\pThrustMaster Joystick");
AppendMenu(inputMenu, "\pMouseStick Joystick");
InsertMenu(inputMenu, 0);

/* Put a check beside the 'keyboard' item */
CheckItem(inputMenu, kINPUT_Keyboard, TRUE);

DrawMenuBar();    /* Now we need to draw our menu */

/* Initialize the ThrustMaster and MouseStick info pointers.
 * If either of these joysticks is not connected, NULL
 * will be returned. We then dim the menu item for that
 * joystick.
 */
```

Continued on next page

Continued from previous page

```
gThrustMasterInfo = GetThrustMasterInfoPtr();
gMouseStickInfo = GetMouseStickDriverInfo();

/* Check to see if these joysticks are connected */
if (gThrustMasterInfo == NULL) {
  DisableItem(inputMenu, kINPUT_ThrustMaster);
}

if (gMouseStickInfo == NULL) {
  DisableItem(inputMenu, kINPUT_MouseStick);
}

/* Create a window that is 512x384 pixels large */
SetRect(&windowRect, 0, 0, 512, 384);

/* Offset the window rect so that the window does not appear
 * under the menu bar.
 */
OffsetRect(&windowRect, 20, 50);

mainWindow = CreateWindow(&windowRect);

/* Initialize the sprite routines */
err = PrepareSprites();

/* Initialize the missiles. This routine can't fail. */
InitializeMissiles();

if (err == noErr) {
  /* Load the sprite background image */
  err = PrepareBackgroundImage();
}

if (err != noErr) {
  /* There was an error in the sprite routines.
   * Terminate the program.
   */
  SysBeep(1);
  ExitToShell();
}

DrawBackground(mainWindow);

while (!done) {
  currentTickCount = TickCount();

  /* If it has been long enough since we last called WaitNextEvent(),
   * go ahead and call it again.
   */
  if ((currentTickCount - lastWaitNextEventCall) >=
      kWaitNextEventDelay)
  {
```

```
              lastWaitNextEventCall = currentTickCount;
              /* We want to regain control from WaitNextEvent() rather quickly
               * so we set the sleep value to a low number.
               */
              notNullEvent = WaitNextEvent( eventMask,
                                            &theEvent,
                                            0,
                                            NULL);

              switch (theEvent.what) {
                WindowPtr    selectedWindow;
                short        findWindowResult;
                short        menuHit;
                short        itemHit;

                case mouseDown:
                  /* We received a mousedown event. Check to see where it was */
                  findWindowResult = FindWindow(theEvent.where, &selectedWindow);
                  if (findWindowResult == inDrag) {
                    /* The user clicked in the drag bar. Allow them to drag it
                     * across the screen.
                     */
                    DragWindow( selectedWindow,
                                theEvent.where,
                                &qd.screenBits.bounds);
                  } else if (findWindowResult == inGoAway) {
                    /* The user clicked in the close box. Close the window. */

                    /* First make sure it's our window they clicked on */
                    if (selectedWindow == mainWindow) {

                      /* Then call TrackGoAway so the user has an opportunity to
                       * move the mouse out of the close box
                       */
                      if (TrackGoAway(selectedWindow, theEvent.where) == TRUE) {
                        /* Clicking the GoAway box in this application will cause
                         * it to quit. Set the done flag to TRUE so this happens.
                         */
                        done = TRUE;
                      }
                    }
                  } else if (findWindowResult == inMenuBar) {
                    long  result;

                    /* It was in the menu bar. Find what item was selected */
                    result = MenuSelect(theEvent.where);

                    /* First check to see if any item was selected at all */
                    if (result != 0) {
                      /* We now need to dissect the result to
                       * find which menu was hit.
                       * Move the upper 16 bits into a word.
```

Continued on next page

Continued from previous page

```
                        */
                    menuHit = result >> 16;

                    /* And now we find which item in that menu was selected */
                    /* Mask off the high word, leaving just the low word */
                    itemHit = result & 0xFFFF;

                    if (menuHit == kMENU_File) {
                      /* An item from the file menu was selected */
                      /* The only item in the file menu we care about is
                       * 'quit.'
                       */
                      if (itemHit == kFILE_Quit)
                        done = TRUE;
                    } else if (menuHit == kMENU_Input) {
                      short    i;
                      /* Change the input method based on the constants
                       * defined in Sprite Animator.h.
                       */
                      if (itemHit == kINPUT_Keyboard)
                        inputMethod = kKeyboardInput;
                      else if (itemHit == kINPUT_MouseAbsoluteWindow)
                        inputMethod = kAbsoluteWindowInput;
                      else if (itemHit == kINPUT_MouseAbsoluteScreen)
                        inputMethod = kAbsoluteScreenInput;
                      else if (itemHit == kINPUT_MouseRelative)
                        inputMethod = kRelativeInput;
                      else if (itemHit == kINPUT_ThrustMaster)
                        inputMethod = kThrustMaster;
                      else if (itemHit == kINPUT_MouseStick)
                        inputMethod = kMouseStick;

                      /* Uncheck all of the menu items */
                      for (i = 0; i < kINPUT_MouseStick; i++) {
                        CheckItem(inputMenu, i, FALSE);
                      }

                      /* Check the current input method */
                      CheckItem(inputMenu, itemHit, TRUE);
                    }
                  }

                  /* Un-hilite the menu */
                  HiliteMenu(0);
                }
                break;

              case updateEvt:
              {
                BeginUpdate((WindowPtr)theEvent.message);

                /* Update the window to show the sprite */
```

```
        if ((WindowPtr)theEvent.message == mainWindow)
          DrawBackground(mainWindow);

        EndUpdate((WindowPtr)theEvent.message);
        break;
    }
  }
}

/* Allow the sprite-drawing portion to act. MoveCurrentSprite now
 * handles its own keyboard input.
 *
 * We implement a delay structure so that the routine is not
 * called more than once every 5 ticks (1/12 of a second).
 *
 * If you want to see the maximum speed your computer can
 * handle, change the 5 to 0.
 */
currentTickCount = TickCount();

if ((currentTickCount - lastMoveCurrentSpriteCall) >= 5) {

  MoveShip(mainWindow, inputMethod);

  MoveInvaderSprites(mainWindow, &gameOver);

  UpdateAllMissiles(mainWindow);
}

/* Check to see if the game has ended. */
if (IsShipActive() == FALSE || gameOver) {
  /* The ship has been destroyed. Put a 'game over' message
   * in the middle of the screen and wait until the player
   * clicks the mouse.
   */
  PicHandle    gameOverPic;
  Rect         picBounds;
  short        picLocationX, picLocationY;
  short        picWidth, picHeight;

  gameOverPic = GetPicture(kGameOverPictID);
  picBounds = (**gameOverPic).picFrame;

  /* Calculate the pic's width and height */
  picWidth = picBounds.right - picBounds.left;
  picHeight = picBounds.bottom - picBounds.top;

  /* We want to draw the picture so its
   * center is in the middle of the window. To
   * do this, we must determine what the upper-left-hand
   * corner of the pict will be.
   */
```

Continued on next page

Continued from previous page

```
        picLocationX = ((mainWindow->portRect.right -
                       mainWindow->portRect.left) / 2) - (picWidth / 2);
        picLocationY = ((mainWindow->portRect.bottom -
                       mainWindow->portRect.top) / 2) - (picHeight / 2);

        /* Now set up the pic's drawing boundary. */
        picBounds.left = picLocationX;
        picBounds.right = picLocationX + picWidth;
        picBounds.top = picLocationY;
        picBounds.bottom = picLocationY + picHeight;

        /* Set the port to the window */
        SetPort(mainWindow);

        /* Draw the picture */
        DrawPicture(gameOverPic, &picBounds);

        /* Wait until the player clicks the mouse */
        while (Button() == FALSE) {
          /* do nothing. */
        }

        /* Signal to quit the game */
        done = TRUE;
      }
    }

  /* Close the main window. */
  if (mainWindow != NULL)
    DisposeWindow(mainWindow);
}
```

A Few Remaining Routines

Only a few routines are left to be discussed, all residing in Sprite Animator.c on the source code disc. Sprite Animator.c now holds four routines: PrepareSprites(), PrepareBackgroundImage(), DrawBackground(), and GetBackgroundGWorld(). PrepareBackgroundImage() is unchanged from the Walking Man animation, so there is no need to show it here.

PrepareSprites() merely calls the two sprite initialization routines already created: InitializeShipSprite() and InitializeInvaderSprites().

```
/**
 **  PrepareSprites()
 **
 **  Initializes the ship sprite and each of the invaders.
 **/
OSErr  PrepareSprites(void)
{
```

```
OSErr       err = noErr;

/* NewShipSprite will initialize all of the data for our ship.
 */

err = InitializeShipSprite();

/* NewInvaderSprites will initialize all of our invaders.
 */
if (!err)
  err = InitializeInvaderSprites();

return err;
}
```

DrawBackground() copies the entire background GWorld into the window. It's used when the window needs updating. The sprites are redrawn the next time through the event loop.

```
/**
 **   DrawBackground()
 **
 **   Draws the background image into the window.
 **/
void  DrawBackground(WindowPtr  theWindow)
{
  PixMapHandle    backgroundPixmap;
  Rect            windowBounds;

  /* Draw the entire background */
  windowBounds = theWindow->portRect;
  backgroundPixmap = GetGWorldPixMap(gBackgroundGWorld);

  LockPixels(backgroundPixmap);
  SetPort(theWindow);

  CopyBits(  (BitMap *)*backgroundPixmap,
             (BitMap *)&theWindow->portBits,
             &(**backgroundPixmap).bounds,
             &windowBounds,
             srcCopy,
             NULL );

  UnlockPixels(backgroundPixmap);
}
```

The last routine, GetBackgroundGWorld(), returns a pointer to the background GWorld. This routine is used by the sprite and missile files to gain access to the background. Another approach you could have taken is to make the background GWorld variable external (*extern*) to the file (as opposed to *static*), but the approach used here is a little cleaner as far as code organization goes. It's also a matter of preference on your part.

```
/**
**   GetBackgroundGWorld()
**
**   Returns the background image GWorld.
**/
GWorldPtr  GetBackgroundGWorld(void)
{
  return gBackgroundGWorld;
}
```

Two remaining routines have been referenced but haven't been described: CreateWindow() and RangedRandom(). Both are outlined in previous chapters (you've been using CreateWindow() since Chapter 2; RangedRandom() was introduced in Chapter 3). You can find these routines on the source code disc in Invaders.c and Misc Utils.c, respectively.

Playing the Game

When you run the game, you will see a screen similar to Figure 8-3. You can move the ship sprite back and forth using any of the input methods and fire a missile using the space bar, the mouse button, or the trigger on your joystick. Figure 8-4 shows a successful hit on one of the invaders, bringing you one step closer to victory. If your ship is hit by an invader missile, it will explode and a Game Over message will appear, as shown in Figure 8-5. If that happens, click the mouse to quit the program.

This sample game is a good basis for a sprite-based arcade game. You've probably already thought of several possible improvements. Among those that might come to mind are:

- Detect when all of the invaders have been eliminated and end the game.
- Increase levels of difficulty after the first wave has been eliminated.
- Add different numbers of invaders. This improvement can be tricky in that the space for the invaders is determined at compile time. If you want to have increasing numbers of invaders, you must allocate enough space for the maximum possible invaders, then make partial use of the array in the earlier levels.
- Vary the speed of the invaders or the player's ship. These constants are found at the top of Invader Sprites.c and Ship Sprite.c.
- Add more animation images.
- Keep track of the score.
- Add multiple "lives" for the player.

FIGURE 8-3

⊚ ⊚ ⊚ ⊚ ⊚ ⊚

The Invaders! game

FIGURE 8-4

⊚ ⊚ ⊚ ⊚ ⊚ ⊚

The end of an invader

FIGURE 8-5

*A premature
end for the
player*

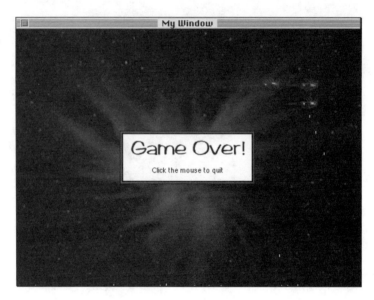

Using Invaders! as a foundation, you're on your way to creating some great games! Countless top-10 arcade games, such as Centipede, Asteroids, and Lemmings, are based on this simple 2D sprite style

In the next chapter, I'm going to approach graphics in a different fashion. Instead of using bitmaps like the sprites, I'm going to start describing images as points and lines. This is necessary before you take the leap to three-dimensional graphics, because all 3D graphics are based upon mathematics. Once you have the techniques of points and lines mastered, you'll be well on the way to creating three-dimensional masterpieces.

9

Wireframe Graphics

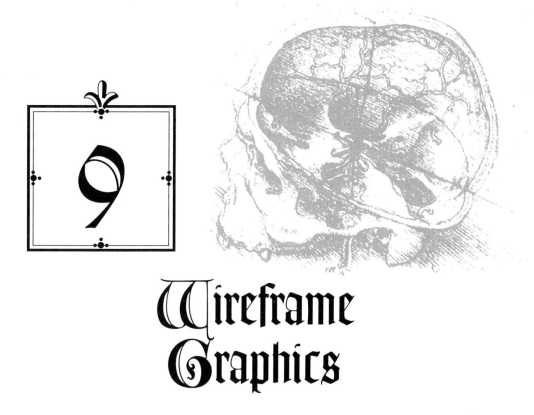

9

Wireframe Graphics

It's time to examine another way of describing graphic images. Up to now, I've defined a picture in terms of rows and columns of individual pixels, known as bitmapped graphics. For games, bitmaps are useful for still images (such as those used in Myst or 7th Guest) or for situations where there aren't many variations of each element (e.g., sprite-based games such as Maelstrom, Apeiron, or your own Invaders! game).

However, bitmapped graphics are not ideal for all types of games. In a flight simulator, for example, you can view any object (such as the enemy aircraft) from an almost infinite number of positions. It would be highly impractical to create a bitmapped image for every single viewing angle of an object—the memory requirements would be enormous. A more practical solution is the use of polygon-based objects.

SPRITE-BASED 3D GAMES

A few games on the market do use bitmapped images for views of three-dimensional objects, such as the first few games in the Wing Commander series or 3D Astro Chase. These games do not have images for *every* angle that the user can see an object from, but instead they take a series of images from a few dozen angles and store them in look-up tables. When the player moves around an object, he or she sees the object "jumping" to a new orientation. The result is not smooth, but it works adequately, especially for space games.

Polygon-Based Objects

Instead of attempting to predict (and draw an image for) every angle of an object, you can store a basic description of it and create the images on the fly. The description, or *model*, that you keep consists of points (or *vertices*), lines (or *vectors*), and polygons. Through mathematical operations, you can rotate the model to whatever orientation you want to view it at (called a *transformation*), then draw it to the screen (a process called *rendering*). Because the player's computer must do all of this work in real time while the game is running, there are severe limits on the quality of the graphics produced.

The rendering process determines the quality of the animation produced. In general, the faster the rendering technique, the lower the quality it produces. In this chapter I'll discuss the fastest and crudest rendering method, *wireframe*. Wireframe graphics are produced by playing "connect the dots" with the vertices of the model. As Figure 9-1 shows, the result is a relatively unrealistic image; however, this technique formed the basis of the earliest three-dimensional arcade games such as BattleZone and Tron.

Wireframe graphics are not widely used nowadays because most personal computers are capable of performing some of the more realistic techniques and competition demands the best available. However, it is useful to learn about this method because it forms the basis for several current techniques, which I'll mention briefly here before going on to explore wireframe graphics in detail.

Polygon-Fill Graphics

Polygon-fill graphics, which I'll discuss in Chapter 11, expand upon wireframe graphics by filling each face of the model with a solid color. A simple extension to polygon-fill

FIGURE 9-1

◎ ◎ ◎ ◎ ◎ ◎

Wireframe rendering of a biplane

graphics is called *flat shading*; it involves changing the color of a polygon based on its angle to a light source. Although the process of calculating the color of a polygon for flat shading is simple, greater difficulty comes in finding a color in an 8-bit color palette to use for the polygon.

Most of today's flight simulators (F/A-18 Hornet, Hellcats over the Pacific, A-10) use flat shading, but faster processors have encouraged experimentation with more realistic methods. Figure 9-2 shows an example of flat shading.

Gouraud Shading

Gouraud shading is another technique that is beginning to gain popularity. It creates a smooth-looking object by blending the edges of a polygon with the edges of its neighbors using a process called *interpolation*. It calculates the colors of the vertices using the same methods as flat shading, but given the greater range of colors, using gouraud shading with an 8-bit color palette is even more difficult. You can see an example of gouraud shading in Figure 9-3.

Texture Mapping

Texture mapping has been used in many popular games such as DOOM and Marathon. It is a hybrid between bitmap and polygon graphics, and it can be used to get realistic images relatively quickly. It works by using mathematical transformations to calculate each polygon in a scene, then distorting a two-dimensional image to fit it to the same shape. I'll talk more about texture mapping in Chapter 19.

FIGURE 9-2

◎ ◎ ◎ ◎ ◎ ◎

Polygon-fill rendering of a biplane

FIGURE 9-3

◎ ◎ ◎ ◎ ◎ ◎

Gouraud-shading rendering of a biplane

Ray Tracing and Beyond

Ray tracing is one of the most realistic rendering methods available. It works by casting thousands of rays from the camera (viewport) onto objects in the scene. A path is traced until the ray reaches an object in the world. This method allows features such as reflections and shadows, providing an almost lifelike illustration. Although the images that are produced can be incredible, each frame can take hours to render—obviously far too computationally intensive for real-time games on today's computers. Games that use prerendered scenes, such as Myst, can afford to use ray tracing. After all, because the scenes only need to be rendered once, what does it matter if they take hours to create on the programmer's machine? A ray-traced image is shown in Figure 9-4. Notice the reflective properties of the biplane engine, a result that can be obtained only from ray tracing.

Techniques are still being developed that are even more realistic than ray tracing, one of which is called *radiosity*. These methods require many times more computational power to render than ray tracing, with scenes taking a matter of days instead of hours. There may come a day, however, when real-time games can make use of these approaches.

Wireframe Graphics

As mentioned earlier, wireframe graphics are created by taking a series of vertices and connecting them with straight lines. Although this method is not in widespread use today, it was very popular in the early arcade games because it requires relatively

FIGURE 9-4

◎ ◎ ◎ ◎ ◎ ◎

Ray-traced image of a biplane

little computational power to render. You can still find good examples of this technique in some nostalgic arcades that feature games such as Tempest, Star Wars, or the original Asteroids. A more recent example is the original Spectre by Velocity.

Drawing Wires

Just as it provides routines for drawing rectangles and circles, the toolbox also has routines for drawing lines. Using these routines requires two steps: positioning QuickDraw's pen at the starting coordinate and then drawing a line to the ending coordinate.

Positioning the QuickDraw pen is done using one of two functions. The first is called MoveTo(), and it places the pen at a specific coordinate:

```
void  MoveTo(short horizLoc, short vertLoc);
```

horizLoc and *vertLoc* are the local coordinates of the new pen position. The second routine, called Move(), positions the pen *relative* to where it is now:

```
void   Move(short horizDistance, short vertDistance);
```

horizDistance is the distance to move the pen horizontally and *vertDistance* is the vertical offset.

The functions used for drawing a line are LineTo() and Line(). Similar to MoveTo() and Move(), these functions draw a line either to a specific screen position or to a position relative to the current pen location:

```
void  LineTo(short horizLoc, short vertLoc);
void  Line(short horizDistance, short vertDistance);
```

LineTo() and Line() also change the pen location, so you can form a polygon by calling MoveTo() once and LineTo() or Line() several times, like this:

```
/* Commands to draw a triangle */
MoveTo(100, 280);
LineTo(400, 280);
LineTo(250, 30);
LineTo(100, 280);
```

These lines of code will draw a triangle from the coordinate (100,280) to (400, 280) to (250,30) and back to (100,280). Figure 9-5 shows the results. I've provided a sample program using this code under the name of MoveTo/LineTo Demo in the Chapter 9 folder on the source code disc.

Bresenham's Algorithm

Although QuickDraw provides routines for drawing lines, you're going to write your own. This implementation, in its unoptimized form, will be about 30 percent faster than LineTo(). It's not that this algorithm is faster than the toolbox's (in fact, LineTo() uses the same algorithm), but you can make some assumptions about the pixmap you're drawing into, which will make this version's implementation slightly smaller than LineTo(). The reason for writing your own routine is not mainly for speed—the concepts presented in this algorithm will be used later, when you start drawing solid polygons.

The process of drawing lines with your own routines is quite involved and has several limitations; among them is the fact that, to use this algorithm, we need to use an offscreen GWorld. You also need to write *directly* into the GWorld, a procedure I'll examine soon.

FIGURE 9-5

◎ ◎ ◎ ◎ ◎ ◎

Output from the MoveTo/LineTo application

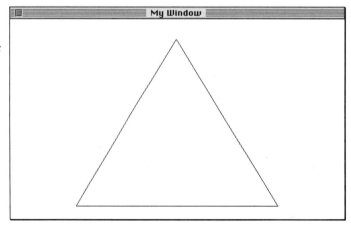

An algorithm for drawing lines is not as trivial as you might expect. The one that you'll be using was invented by a man named Bresenham in the mid-1960s. It is probably the most widely used line-drawing algorithm today and it will suit your purposes well.

The difficulties behind drawing lines on the computer screen stem from the fact that you are trying to display a line defined in real numbers with infinite precision on a screen defined in an integer (nonfractional) system. Thus a computer screen cannot precisely display a line (unless it is exactly horizontal or vertical). Figure 9-6 shows a line that does not fit into the screen's pixel matrix. The line passes directly through the middle of some pixels, yet barely touches others. The difficulty lies in determining which of those pixels should be lit. Figure 9-7 shows the same line approximated with pixels. Notice that the line appears to be stair-stepping—if you look closely at any sloping line on a computer screen, you'll notice this effect. The phenomena is known as aliasing.

Techniques that eliminate the aliasing effect (called *antialiasing*), are used primarily in graphics packages that do not depend on real-time animation. However, these techniques are very time consuming and the resulting precision is not always necessary for games.

The Slope of a Line

To draw a line, it is important to know what its *slope* is. The slope is a fraction indicating the line's angle; it's defined as the ratio between the change in y and the change in x.

FIGURE 9-6

◎ ◎ ◎ ◎ ◎ ◎

A line through the pixels on a computer screen

FIGURE 9-7

◎ ◎ ◎ ◎ ◎ ◎

*The line
approximated
with pixels*

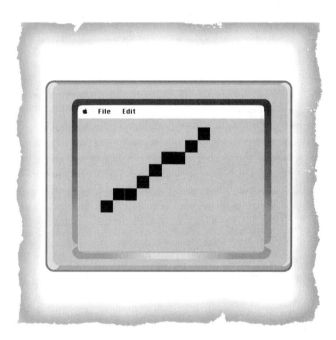

Given two coordinate pairs (x1, y1) and (x2, y2), this ratio can be expressed with the following C expression:

```
slope = (y2 - y1) / (x2 - x1);
```

There are two special cases of lines: horizontal and vertical. To illustrate the properties of these lines, let's look at two examples.

A horizontal line running from (0, 10) to (10, 10) has a slope of 0 / 10, or 0. A vertical line from (10, 0) to (10, 10) has a slope of 10 / 0, which is undefined (because you can't divide a number by 0). If you attempt to calculate the slope of a vertical line, your program will crash (because a processor generates an error if you attempt a division by 0).

Because the special-case lines are simple to draw, I'll show you a more interesting example. Figure 9-8 shows a line from (1,5) to (4,11). The change in x is 3, and the change in y is 6, which leaves us with a slope of (6 / 3), or 2.

Knowing the slope of the line allows you to draw it on the screen easily. The slope tells you how far the line moves vertically for every unit of horizontal movement. A line with a slope of 2 means that you'll draw 2 pixels vertically, move to the right by 1 pixel, draw 2 more pixels vertically, and so on until the entire line has been drawn. Figure 9-9 shows the line drawn on the pixel matrix.

What happens, however, if the line has a negative slope? Or what if its slope is fractional? This is where line-drawing algorithms start to get interesting.

FIGURE 9-8

◎ ◎ ◎ ◎ ◎ ◎

A line from (1, 5) to (4, 11) has a slope of 2

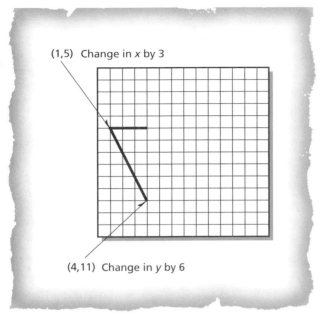

(1,5)   Change in *x* by 3

(4,11)   Change in *y* by 6

FIGURE 9-9

◎ ◎ ◎ ◎ ◎ ◎

The same line drawn with pixels

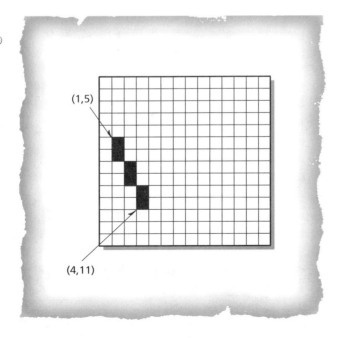

(1,5)

(4,11)

Every line can be drawn by incrementing one coordinate, either x or y, once for each pixel in the line. If the absolute value of the slope is less than 1, then the x coordinate is the one that is incremented for every pixel. If the slope is greater than 1, the y coordinate is used. If the slope is precisely 1, the line is perfectly diagonal and it doesn't matter which coordinate is used.

But when is the second coordinate incremented? In the case of horizontal and vertical lines, the second coordinate is never incremented; in the case of diagonal lines, the second coordinate is incremented every time the first is. For other types of lines, deciding when the second coordinate is incremented is the heart of the algorithm.

For the purposes of Bresenham's algorithm, lines come in two varieties: those that have slopes greater than 1 and those that have slopes less than 1. You can allow diagonal lines (lines with a slope equal to 1) to fall into either category.

For lines with slopes greater than 1 (or smaller than -1), the y coordinate is changing more rapidly than the x coordinate. This means you can allow y to be changed every time through the loop and change x only when you need to. If you are drawing a line with a slope between -1 and 1, just reverse the coordinates (change x every time through the loop and y only when necessary). Because you have two distinct possibilities that are handled in different manners, Bresenham's algorithm is divided into two distinct parts. The first part handles the case where the line's slope is between -1 and 1 and the second part handles every other case.

You must then calculate how often you want to advance the second coordinate. Bresenham accomplished this through the use of an *error term*. The error term is an integer used in such a way as to simulate a fraction. At the beginning of the function, the change in x (referred to as dx, or delta x) and the change in y (referred to as dy, or delta y) are calculated. The two values are compared to determine the type of line. If dx is greater than dy, the slope is less than 1 and x is the primary coordinate. If dy is greater than dx, the slope is greater than 1.

When the loop begins, the error term is set to zero. If you are incrementing in the x direction, you add dy to the error term. If the error term is still smaller than dy, the y coordinate is not incremented and you continue through the loop, adding dy to the error term each time. Once the error term is greater than or equal to dx, you know it's time to increment the y coordinate. Once you do that, you subtract dx from the error term and begin the process again.

This process automatically handles vertical and horizontal lines. If the line is horizontal, dy will be zero. If dy is zero, the error term will never get as large as dy and you will never increment the y coordinate. If the line is vertical, the opposite is true: dx is zero and the line will never be incremented in the x direction.

Drawing Directly to a GWorld

Because you're replacing a QuickDraw routine with your own, it is necessary to draw directly into a GWorld. To perform the drawing, you need to obtain two parameters from the GWorld's PixMapHandle: the beginning address of the pixel data and the rowbytes that make up each row of the pixmap.

Once you have these two parameters, you can draw anywhere within the GWorld. The rowbyte value was discussed in Chapter 4: It is the number of bytes that make up each row of the image. To find the address of any particular pixel on an 8-bit GWorld, use the following formula:

```
pixel_address = base_address + (y * row_bytes) + x;
```

The pixel can then be changed by dereferencing the pixel address and assigning a color value to it:

```
*pixel_address = color;
```

Another way to obtain the address of a pixel is to use an offset. This method breaks the previous formula into two parts. The first part calculates how far you need to look into the pixel data for the pixel, which is the offset. To obtain the pixel address, add the offset to the base address:

```
offset = (y * row_bytes) + x;
pixel_address = base_address + offset;
```

Although this method is a little more complicated, it has its advantages in that, to reference adjacent pixels, you need only increment or decrement the offset. Remember that if you move to the left or right, offset is changed by 1, but to move up or down, you should add or subtract the rowbytes value.

The other advantage of using the offset value is that you can change the color of the pixel in one step by referencing the base address as if it were an array, like this:

```
base_address[offset] = color;
```

Using an offset value is not the fastest method, but it'll do for now.

Obtaining the Base Address and Rowbytes

As you saw in Chapter 4, the rowbytes value is obtained by dereferencing the PixMapHandle, looking at its rowbytes value, and masking it with 0x3FFF, like this:

```
rowBytes = (**myPixMapHandle).rowBytes & 0x3FFF;
```

The base address of the pixmap is merely a pointer to its upper-left pixel and is obtained by calling GetPixBaseAddr(). The routine returns a pointer to the first pixel of the pixmap.

```
Ptr  GetPixBaseAddr(PixMapHandle thePixMap);
```

It is important to remember to lock the pixmap before calling GetPixBaseAddr() and not to unlock it until you are finished drawing into it. As soon as the pixmap has been unlocked, the base address should be considered invalid. If you want to do more drawing at a later time, lock the pixmap and call GetPixBaseAddr() again. The rowbytes value, however, will stay valid as long as you don't change the pixmap size (something that's not usually done).

The Bresenham Line-Drawing Algorithm

The line-drawing routine you'll be using is based on Bresenham's algorithm and it takes seven parameters: the x and y of the starting and ending points, the pixmap base address, the pixmap rowbytes, and the desired color of the line. The base address and rowbyte values are copied into local variables because this speeds up the code a little bit. Another thing to note is that the rowbyte and pixel offset values are both declared as *unsigned long*. Because you know for a fact that neither of these variables could legitimately be negative, declaring them as *unsigned* makes the code a little clearer (see Listing 9-1).

Listing 9-1 *The line-drawing routine*

```
void BresenhamLine( short         x1,
                    short         y1,
                    short         x2,
                    short         y2,
                    Ptr           pixMapPtr,
                    unsigned long theRowBytes,
                    unsigned char color  )
{
  short         dx, dy;
  short         xDirection, yDirection;
  short         i;
  Ptr           basePtr;
  unsigned long rowBytes;
  long          rowOffset;
  unsigned long pixelOffset;
  short         error_term;


    /* Copy the parameters to local variables for speed */
    basePtr = pixMapPtr;
    rowBytes = theRowBytes;

    /* Calculate the x and y distances for this line (and make sure that
     * they are absolute values - i.e., larger than or equal to zero).
     */
    dx = x2 - x1;
    if (dx < 0)
      dx = -dx;
```

```
dy = y2 - y1;
if (dy < 0)
  dy = -dy;

/* Calculate the horizontal direction of the line (i.e., are
 * we moving left or right?).
 */
if (x2 - x1 < 0) {
  xDirection = -1;
} else if (x2 - x1 > 0) {
  xDirection = 1;
} else {
  xDirection = 0;
}

/* Calculate the vertical direction of the line (i.e., are we moving
 * up or down?).
 */
if (y2 - y1 < 0) {
  yDirection = -1;
  rowOffset = -rowBytes;  /* Subtract rowBytes to move up a line */
} else if (y2 - y1 > 0) {
  yDirection = 1;
  rowOffset = rowBytes;  /* Add rowBytes to move down a line */
} else {
  yDirection = 0;
  rowOffset = 0;        /* We aren't moving up or down */
}

/* Initialize the error term */
error_term = 0;

/* Calculate where the first pixel will be placed */
pixelOffset = (y1 * rowBytes) + x1;

/* Begin the drawing loop */
if (dx > dy)  /* If we're moving farther in x than y... */
{
  for (i = 0; i <= dx; i++) /* Start counting off in x */
  {
    /* Set this pixel */
    basePtr[pixelOffset] = color;

    /* Move the pixelOffset 1 pixel left or right (depending
     * on which direction the line is being drawn)
     */
    pixelOffset += xDirection;

    /* Check to see if we need to move the pixelOffset
     * in the y direction.
     */
```

Continued on next page

Continued from previous page

```
      error_term += dy;

      if (error_term > dx) {  /* If so... */
        /* Reset the error term */
        error_term -= dx;

        /* Move the pixelOffset 1 pixel up or down */
        pixelOffset += rowOffset;
      }
    }
  } else {
    /* This portion of the routine takes care of the condition
     * where the line is more vertical than horizontal.
     * It is very similar to the previous case, with just a
     * few variables swapped around.
     */
    for (i = 0; i <= dy; i++) {
      /* Set this pixel */
      basePtr[pixelOffset] = color;

      /* Move the pixelOffset in the y direction */
      pixelOffset += rowOffset;

      /* Check to see if we're ready to move horizontally */
      error_term += dx;

      if (error_term > dy) {  /* If so... */
        /* Reset the error term */
        error_term -= dy;

        /* Move the pixelOffset to the left or right */
        pixelOffset += xDirection;
      }
    }
  }
}
```

Bresenham Triangles

Let's look at a program that uses the line-drawing routine you just built. This application is similar to the one that used the MoveTo() and LineTo() calls—in fact, the output is identical. However, the new program is a little more complicated. It creates a GWorld, erases it, and gains access to the rowbytes and base address parameters of the pixmap. It is then able to call the line-drawing routines.

After the triangle has been drawn, the program will use CopyBits() to display it in the window and wait for a mouse click before it quits (see Listing 9-2). You'll find the source code for this program under the name Bresenham Triangles in the Chapter 9 folder on the source code disc.

Listing 9-2 *The Bresenham triangles routine*

```
void main(void)
{
  Rect            windowRect;
  Rect            gworldRect;
  WindowPtr       mainWindow;
  GWorldPtr       offscreenGWorld;
  PixMapHandle    offscreenPixMap;
  unsigned long   rowBytes;
  Ptr             pixmapBaseAddress;
  OSErr           err;
  GWorldPtr       savePort;
  GDHandle        saveDevice;

  /* Initialize everything we need */
  InitGraf(&qd.thePort);
  InitWindows();
  InitCursor();

  /* Create a window that is 500x300 pixels large */
  SetRect(&windowRect, 0, 0, 500, 300);

  /* We want our gworld to be the same size */
  gworldRect = windowRect;

  /* Offset the window rect so that the window does not appear
   * under the menu bar.
   */
  OffsetRect(&windowRect, 20, 40);

  mainWindow = CreateWindow(&windowRect);

  SetPort(mainWindow);

  /* Create the offscreen GWorld */

  err = NewGWorld( &offscreenGWorld,
                   8,
                   &gworldRect,
                   NULL,
                   NULL,
                   0  );

  if (err)  /* Quit if there was an error */
    ExitToShell();

  /* Erase the GWorld */

  GetGWorld(&savePort, &saveDevice);
  SetGWorld(offscreenGWorld, NULL);
```

Continued on next page

Continued from previous page

```
  EraseRect(&gworldRect);

  SetGWorld(savePort, saveDevice);

  /* Find the GWorld's PixMapHandle */

  offscreenPixMap = GetGWorldPixMap(offscreenGWorld);

  /* Lock the pixmap */
  LockPixels(offscreenPixMap);

  /* Get a pointer to the pixmap data */
  pixmapBaseAddress = GetPixBaseAddr(offscreenPixMap);

  /* Find the pixmap rowbytes (remember to mask off the top 2 bits!) */
  rowBytes = (**offscreenPixMap).rowBytes & 0x3FFF;

  /* Draw the triangle into the GWorld */
  BresenhamLine( 100, 280,  /* draw from x = 100, y = 280... */
                 400, 280,  /* ...to x = 400, y = 280. */
                 pixmapBaseAddress,
                 rowBytes,
                 0xFF  );  /* Draw in black (255) */

  BresenhamLine( 400, 280,  /* draw from x = 400, y = 280... */
                 250, 30,   /* ...to x = 250, y = 30. */
                 pixmapBaseAddress,
                 rowBytes,
                 0xFF  );  /* Draw in black (255) */

  BresenhamLine( 250, 30,   /* draw from x = 250, y = 30... */
                 100, 280,  /* ...to x = 100, y = 280. */
                 pixmapBaseAddress,
                 rowBytes,
                 0xFF  );  /* Draw in black (255) */

  /* Copy the gworld to the screen */
  CopyBits( (BitMap *)*offscreenPixMap,
            (BitMap *)&mainWindow->portBits,
            &gworldRect,
            &gworldRect,
            srcCopy,
            NULL  );

  /* Wait until the user clicks before quitting */
  while (!Button())
  {
    /* Do nothing */
  }
}
```

Descriptions of the Objects

In a complicated arcade game, it simply isn't feasible to hard-code the coordinates of each shape into the program. Instead, you're going to create data structures for each shape. For the first time since the introduction of the principles presented in Chapter 4, you're going to make extensive use of them, employing mathematical operations to define and modify objects.

The models you use will be formed using the Cartesian coordinate system. The model consists of several vertices defined in Cartesian space (using two or three coordinates for each point, depending on whether the object is two- or three-dimensional). For wireframe rendering, the points are connected by lines and then drawn to the screen.

The data structures you are creating are relatively simple. I'll expand upon these structures in later chapters as I introduce new concepts. Here's a definition for a simple two-dimensional wireframe shape:

```
/* 2D Shape Data Structures: */

typedef struct {
  short  x, y;
} Vertex2D;


typedef struct {
  unsigned char  color;
  short          numOfVertices;
  Vertex2D       *vertex;
} Shape2D;
```

Vertex2D simply holds the x and y coordinates of one vertex of the shape. The Shape2D structure holds the color of the shape, how many vertices it holds, and a pointer to the first element of an array of vertices.

Here is how you might initialize a vertex array and shape data for an object, in this case a triangle:

```
Vertex2D  triangleVertexArray[] = {
  100,  280,           /* First Vertex */
  400,  280,           /* Second Vertex */
  250,  30             /* Third Vertex */
};

Shape2D    triangleShape = {
  255,                 /* Color (Black) */
  3,                   /* Number of vertices */
  triangleVertexArray  /* Pointer to vertex array */
};
```

A Shape-Drawing Routine

You are now able to create a routine that will draw any shape using the Bresenham line-drawing routine. The routine is simple: It loops through each vertex of the shape, grabs the current vertex and the next vertex, and draws a line between them. When it reaches the last vertex, it draws a line between that one and the first vertex.

```
/**
 **   DrawShape()
 **
 **   Draws a shape, using the Bresenham line-drawing routine,
 **   onto the provided pixmap.
 **/
void   DrawShape( Shape2D        shape,
                  Ptr            pixMapPtr,
                  unsigned long  rowBytes )
{
  short    i;
  short    p2;

  /* Loop through each vertex in the shape: */
  for (i = 0; i < shape.numOfVertices; i++)
  {
    /* Find the offset of the next vertex */
    p2 = i + 1;

    /* Check to see if p2 should wrap around to 0 */
    if (p2 == shape.numOfVertices)
      p2 = 0;

    /* Draw this line */
    BresenhamLine( shape.vertex[i].x, shape.vertex[i].y,
                   shape.vertex[p2].x, shape.vertex[p2].y,
                   pixMapPtr,
                   rowBytes,
                   shape.color );
  }
}
```

Sample Shape Program

Listing 9-3 is the main function of a simple program that will use the shape-drawing routines to create a triangle.

Listing 9-3 *The shape drawing routine*

```
Vertex2D   triangleVertexArray[] = {
   100,  280,             /* First Vertex */
   400,  280,             /* Second Vertex */
   250,   30              /* Third Vertex */
};
```

```
Shape2D    triangleShape = {
  255,                    /* Color (Black) */
  3,                      /* Number of vertices */
  triangleVertexArray     /* Pointer to vertex array */
};

void main(void)
{
  Rect            windowRect;
  Rect            gworldRect;
  WindowPtr       mainWindow;
  GWorldPtr       offscreenGWorld;
  PixMapHandle    offscreenPixMap;
  unsigned long   rowBytes;
  Ptr             pixmapBaseAddress;
  OSErr           err;
  GWorldPtr       savePort;
  GDHandle        saveDevice;

  /* Initialize everything we need */
  InitGraf(&qd.thePort);
  InitWindows();
  InitCursor();

  /* Create a window that is 500x300 pixels large */
  SetRect(&windowRect, 0, 0, 500, 300);

  /* We want our gworld to be the same size */
  gworldRect = windowRect;

  /* Offset the window rect so that the window does not appear
   * under the menu bar.
   */
  OffsetRect(&windowRect, 20, 40);

  mainWindow = CreateWindow(&windowRect);

  SetPort(mainWindow);

  /* Create the offscreen GWorld */

  err = NewGWorld( &offscreenGWorld,
                   8,
                   &gworldRect,
                   NULL,
                   NULL,
                   0 );

  if (err)  /* Quit if there was an error */
    ExitToShell();

  /* Erase the GWorld */
```

Continued on next page

Continued from previous page

```
GetGWorld(&savePort, &saveDevice);
SetGWorld(offscreenGWorld, NULL);

EraseRect(&gworldRect);

SetGWorld(savePort, saveDevice);

/* Find the GWorld's PixMapHandle */

offscreenPixMap = GetGWorldPixMap(offscreenGWorld);

/* Lock the pixmap */
LockPixels(offscreenPixMap);

/* Get a pointer to the pixmap data */
pixmapBaseAddress = GetPixBaseAddr(offscreenPixMap);

/* Find the pixmap rowbytes (remember to mask off the top 2 bits!) */
rowBytes = (**offscreenPixMap).rowBytes & 0x3FFF;


/* Draw the shape */
DrawShape(triangleShape, pixmapBaseAddress, rowBytes);


/* Copy the gworld to the screen */
CopyBits( (BitMap *)*offscreenPixMap,
          (BitMap *)&mainWindow->portBits,
          &gworldRect,
          &gworldRect,
          srcCopy,
          NULL );

/* Wait until the user clicks before quitting */
while (!Button())
{
  /* Do nothing */
}
}
```

The source code for the shape drawing program is named Shape Drawing on the source code CD-ROM.

Shape Transformation

In this section, the math from Chapter 4 really starts to come in handy. Now that you have your shape, it would be useful to be able to translate, rotate, or scale it. As you may recall, translation refers to changing the location of the shape, rotation changes the orientation of the shape, and scale changes the size and proportions of the shape.

Local Coordinates

Until now, all the shapes have been defined in terms of their window coordinates. Although this allows you to draw the shape without any further calculations, it won't work if you want to perform any mathematical transformations. While the shape is being transformed it needs to be defined in coordinates local to the shape. This is different from local and global screen coordinates—an object drawn in a window is *local to the window*; while doing transformations, you'll be working in coordinates *local to the shape*. Before the shape is drawn, however, its coordinates will be translated into ones local to the window. Thus, you have three sets of coordinates: global, local to the window, and local to the shape. For the sake of clarity, window-local coordinates will be referred to as *window coordinates* and shape-local coordinates will be referred to as *shape coordinates*.

Using a shape-local coordinate system, you could describe a triangle with the vertices (-10, 10), (0, -10), and (10, 10), relative to a local origin at the center of the triangle, as shown in Figure 9-10. If you wanted to place the triangle on the screen, you would need to translate the shape coordinates to window coordinates. This is done with a value called the *shape origin*. The shape origin indicates where the shape is drawn in window coordinates. To translate a shape from shape coordinates to window coordinates, you add the shape origin to each of the shape's vertices.

FIGURE 9-10

◉ ◉ ◉ ◉ ◉ ◉

A triangle defined in shape coordinates

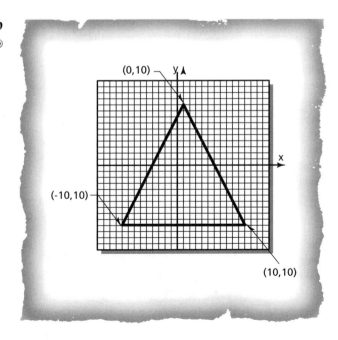

Coordinate Precision

Because its coordinates are stored as integers, every time a shape is scaled or rotated, there may be some loss of precision. For example, rotating a shape by 10 degrees 36 times will almost certainly not give you the original shape. This is a problem inherent to integer calculations and there are only two ways around it. The first method is to use floating-point calculations. You will still lose some precision, but it will happen much more slowly. The second method is to apply the transformations to the original coordinates continually. In this case, to rotate a shape by 10 degrees 36 times, the rotations would have to be cumulative. The first rotation would be by 10 degrees, the second by 20 degrees, the third by 30 degrees, and so on. This is the method you'll be using here. Because you need to preserve the original coordinates of the shape before you do any transformations, you need to make a copy of those coordinates. You'll store the copy in the vertex structure along with everything else.

New Vertex Fields

It will be useful to add a few parameters to the Vertex2D structure. Vertex2D will now consist of three coordinate pairs: shape coordinates, transformed coordinates, and window coordinates. An additional parameter will also be added to the Shape2D structure—the shape origin. Here are the new structures:

```
typedef struct {
  short         lx, ly;    /* Shape coordinates */
  short         tx, ty;    /* Transformed coordinates */
  short         sx, sy;    /* Window coordinates */
} Vertex2D;


typedef struct {
  unsigned char  color;
  short          numOfVertices;
  Vertex2D       *vertex;
  short          originX, originY;
} Shape2D;
```

Manipulating the shape will now occur in three steps:

1. Copy the shape coordinates to the transformed coordinates.

2. Apply the transformations to the shape.

3. Translate the shape from the transformed coordinates to window coordinates.

Let's look at the two routines that translate between the different coordinates in the vertex structure. The first routine is very simple—it just copies the lx and ly fields to the tx and ty fields:

```
/**
 **   BeginTransformation()
 **
 **   Copies the shape coordinates to the transformed
 **   coordinates. This is in preparation for doing
 **   some sort of transformation to the object.
 **/
void  BeginTransformation(Shape2D  *theShape)
{
  short    i;

  for (i = 0; i < theShape->numOfVertices; i++) {
    theShape->vertex[i].tx = theShape->vertex[i].lx;
    theShape->vertex[i].ty = theShape->vertex[i].ly;
  }
}
```

Next you need a routine that will translate a shape from transformed coordinates to window coordinates. It loops through each vertex and adds the shape's origin to the tx and ty fields.

```
/**
 **   ShapeToWindowCoordinates()
 **
 **   Translates a shape to window coordinates.
 **/
void  ShapeToWindowCoordinates(Shape2D *theShape)
{
  short    i;

  /* Loop through each vertex of the shape */
  for (i = 0; i < theShape->numOfVertices; i++) {
    /* Translate this vertex */
    theShape->vertex[i].sx = theShape->vertex[i].tx +
                             theShape->originX;
    theShape->vertex[i].sy = theShape->vertex[i].ty +
                             theShape->originY;
  }
}
```

Moving Shapes

Let's look at the first mathematical transformation—shape translation. All that a translation does is change the origin of the shape. When the shape is translated into window coordinates, it will appear in the new location. Here is a routine that translates a shape:

```
/**
 **   TranslateShape()
 **
 **   Moves a shape by a distance of dx and dy.
 **/
```

Continued on next page

Continued from previous page
```
void  TranslateShape(Shape2D *theShape, short dx, short dy)
{
  theShape->originX += dx;
  theShape->originY += dy;
}
```

Scaling Shapes

As discussed in Chapter 4, scaling a shape involves multiplying the shape coordinates by a scaling factor, like this:

```
vertice.tx *= scalingX;
vertice.ty *= scalingY;
```

You can change the proportions of the shape by setting scalingX and scalingY to different values. Most of the time, however, you will want to scale the shape evenly. A routine to scale a shape needs to apply the scaling factor to each of its vertices.

```
/**
 **   ScaleShape()
 **
 **   Scales a shape by the scaleFactor.
 **/
void  ScaleShape(Shape2D *theShape, float scaleFactor)
{
  short    i;

  /* Loop through each vertex of the shape */
  for (i = 0; i < theShape->numOfVertices; i++) {
    /* Translate this vertex */
    theShape->vertex[i].tx *= scaleFactor;
    theShape->vertex[i].ty *= scaleFactor;
  }
}
```

The *scaleFactor* parameter is defined as *float* so you have the capability of using a fractional scaling factor to reduce the shape's size.

Rotating a Shape

Shape rotation requires trigonometry, namely the use of the sine and cosine functions. In Chapter 4, you saw how this is done; now it's time to apply those concepts to these shapes. If you recall, a two-dimensional rotation is done like this:

```
newX = oldX * cos(angle) - oldY * sin(angle);
newY = oldX * sin(angle) + oldY * cos(angle);
```

Putting that formula into a function provides this routine:

```
/**
 **   RotateShape()
 **
```

```
**   Rotates a shape by the provided angle. The angle is expressed
**   in radians.
**/
void  RotateShape(Shape2D *theShape, float angle)
{
  short    i;
  short    x, y;

  /* Loop through each vertex of the shape */
  for (i = 0; i < theShape->numOfVertices; i++) {
    /* Store rotated coordinates in temporary variables */
    x = theShape->vertex[i].tx * cos(angle) -
      theShape->vertex[i].ty * sin(angle);
    y = theShape->vertex[i].tx * sin(angle) +
      theShape->vertex[i].ty * cos(angle);

    /* Transfer the temporary variables into the shape */

    theShape->vertex[i].tx = x;
    theShape->vertex[i].ty = y;
  }
}
```

A Scaling and Rotation Sample Program

It should now be relatively simple to create a sample program that can do shape transformation. This program will take the triangle (now defined in shape coordinates) and animate it spinning around while growing and shrinking. The animation speed isn't too bad, but it's not fast enough for a real game. You'll still need to do several optimizations.

The application has a simple loop for erasing the GWorld, changing the rotation and scaling values, transforming the shape, and copying it onto the screen (Listing 9-4). One thing to note is that you're dealing with radians for the angle unit because the trigonometric functions can't deal with angles measured in degrees. The triangle definition also has been updated to use the new shape structure. The source code for this program is in a folder called Shape Transformation on the source code disc.

Listing 9-4 *The shape transformation routine*

```
/* Data for a Triangle */

Vertex2D  triangleVertexArray[] = {
  -80,   80,    0,  0,  0,  0,       /* First Vertex */
   80,   80,    0,  0,  0,  0,        /* Second Vertex */
    0,  -100,   0,  0,  0,  0        /* Third Vertex */
};
```

Continued on next page

Continued from previous page

```
Shape2D      triangleShape = {
  255,            /* Color (Black) */
  3,              /* Number of vertices */
  250, 150,         /* Origin */
  triangleVertexArray     /* Pointer to vertex array */
};

/**
 ** main()
 **
 **/
void main(void)
{
  Rect            windowRect;
  Rect            gworldRect;
  WindowPtr       mainWindow;
  GWorldPtr       offscreenGWorld;
  PixMapHandle    offscreenPixMap;
  unsigned long   rowBytes;
  Ptr             pixmapBaseAddress;
  OSErr           err;
  GWorldPtr       savePort;
  GDHandle        saveDevice;
  float           angle;
  float           scale;
  Boolean         scaleIncreasing;

  /* Initialize everything we need */
  InitGraf(&qd.thePort);
  InitWindows();
  InitCursor();

  /* Create a window that is 500x300 pixels large */
  SetRect(&windowRect, 0, 0, 500, 300);

  /* We want our gworld to be the same size */
  gworldRect = windowRect;

  /* Offset the window rect so that the window does not appear
   * under the menu bar.
   */
  OffsetRect(&windowRect, 20, 40);

  mainWindow = CreateWindow(&windowRect);

  SetPort(mainWindow);

  /* Create the offscreen GWorld */

  err = NewGWorld(  &offscreenGWorld,
                    8,
                    &gworldRect,
```

```
                    NULL,
                    NULL,
                    0  );

   if (err)  /* Quit if there was an error */
     ExitToShell();

   /* Find the GWorld's PixMapHandle */

   offscreenPixMap = GetGWorldPixMap(offscreenGWorld);

   /* Lock the pixmap */
   LockPixels(offscreenPixMap);

   /* Get a pointer to the pixmap data */
   pixmapBaseAddress = GetPixBaseAddr(offscreenPixMap);

   /* Find the pixmap rowbytes (remember to mask off the top 2 bits!) */
   rowBytes = (**offscreenPixMap).rowBytes & 0x3FFF;

   /* Start the rotation off at 0 and scale at 1 */
   angle = 0.0;
   scale = 1.0;
   scaleIncreasing = FALSE;

   /* Wait until the user clicks before quitting */
   while (!Button())
   {
     /* Erase the GWorld */

     GetGWorld(&savePort, &saveDevice);
     SetGWorld(offscreenGWorld, NULL);

     EraseRect(&gworldRect);

     SetGWorld(savePort, saveDevice);

     /* Fiddle with the rotation value */
     angle += 0.1;

     /* If the angle has passed 2PI (6.28 radians, or 360 degrees),
      * reset it.
      */
     if (angle > 6.28)
       angle -= 6.28;

     /* Change the scale value */
     if (scaleIncreasing) {
       scale += 0.1;

       if (scale > 1) {
         scale = 1;
```

Continued on next page

Continued from previous page

```
      scaleIncreasing = FALSE;
    }
  } else {
    scale -= 0.1;

    if (scale < 0.1) {
      scale = 0.1;
      scaleIncreasing = TRUE;
    }
  }

  /* Prepare the shape for rotation & scaling */
  BeginTransformation(&triangleShape);

  /* Rotate the shape */
  RotateShape(&triangleShape, angle);

  /* Scale the shape */
  ScaleShape(&triangleShape, scale);

  /* Translate it to screen coordinates */
  ShapeToWindowCoordinates(&triangleShape);

  /* Draw the shape */
  DrawShape(triangleShape, pixmapBaseAddress, rowBytes);


  /* Copy the gworld to the screen */
  CopyBits( (BitMap *)*offscreenPixMap,
            (BitMap *)&mainWindow->portBits,
            &gworldRect,
            &gworldRect,
            srcCopy,
            NULL );
  }
}
```

Matrix Mathematics

One of the ways you can speed up animations is by using matrices for calculations. When I discussed matrix math in Chapter 4, I mentioned that matrix math is faster because it allows you to combine, or *concatenate*, math operations. Although using matrix mathematics won't speed up the rotating triangle program much, it will become a larger factor in later applications.

To work with matrices, the vertex structure must be changed once again. An additional term must be added to each coordinate system. This term is included only to get the matrix math to work correctly. It is ignored by the drawing routines and it is always set to 1 before working with matrices.

```
typedef struct {
  short  lx, ly, lt;    /* Shape coordinates */
  short  tx, ty, tt;    /* Transformed coordinates */
  short  sx, sy, st;    /* Window coordinates */
} Vertex2D;
```

When you define your shape, initialize the lt, tt, and st fields to 1. For example, here is the new definition for the triangle shape:

```
Vertex2D  triangleVertexArray[] = {
  -80,  80,   1,  0,  0,  1,  0,  0,  1,  /* First Vertex */
   80,  80,   1,  0,  0,  1,  0,  0,  1,  /* Second Vertex */
    0, -100,  1,  0,  0,  1,  0,  0,  1,  /* Third Vertex */
};
```

In Chapter 4, I examined the matrices for three-dimensional transformations. In this case, however, you're using two-dimensional shapes. Here are the matrices for the same functions:

translation:

```
1              0              0
0              1              0
xTrans         yTrans         1
```

scaling:

```
scaleFactor    0              0
0              scaleFactor    0
0              0              1
```

rotation:

```
cos(angle)     -sin(angle)    0
sin(angle)     cos(angle)     0
0              0              1
```

The rotation and translation matrices can easily be combined into the following matrix:

```
cos(angle)     -sin(angle)    0
sin(angle)     cos(angle)     0
xTrans         yTrans         1
```

Combining this matrix and the scaling matrix is a little more difficult, so it will be done using the matrix multiplication loop.

An added benefit of using one routine to do all the transformations is that the same routine can also translate the object to window coordinates. In fact, the transformation fields of the Vertex2D function (tx, ty, and tt) are no longer being used. They're still there, however, because you'll use them again at some point in the future.

The shape transform function replaces five functions: BeginTransformation(), ShapeToWindowCoordinates(), TranslateShape(), ScaleShape(), and RotateShape(). At the present time, it's not terribly efficient, but you'll worry about that later. Listing 9-5 shows this function.

Listing 9-5 *The shape transform function*

```
void  TransformShape( Shape2D  *theShape,
                      float     scaleFactor,
                      short     xTrans,
                      short     yTrans,
                      float     angle  )
{
    float    mainMatrix[3][3];  /* main transform matrix */
    float    scaleMatrix[3][3];  /* Scaling matrix */
    float    rotMatrix[3][3];  /* Rotation & transform matrix */
    short    i,j,k;

    /* Initialize the scaling matrix */
    scaleMatrix[0][0] = scaleFactor;
    scaleMatrix[0][1] = 0;
    scaleMatrix[0][2] = 0;

    scaleMatrix[1][0] = 0;
    scaleMatrix[1][1] = scaleFactor;
    scaleMatrix[1][2] = 0;

    scaleMatrix[2][0] = 0;
    scaleMatrix[2][1] = 0;
    scaleMatrix[2][2] = 1;

    /* Initialize rotation and translation matrix */
    rotMatrix[0][0] = cos(angle);  /* Rotation */
    rotMatrix[0][1] = -sin(angle);
    rotMatrix[0][2] = 0;

    rotMatrix[1][0] = sin(angle);  /* Rotation */
    rotMatrix[1][1] = cos(angle);
    rotMatrix[1][2] = 0;

    /* The translation portion also includes moving the object to the
     * window coordinates.
     */
    rotMatrix[2][0] = xTrans + theShape->originX;
    rotMatrix[2][1] = yTrans + theShape->originY;
    rotMatrix[2][2] = 1;

    /* Multiply the two matrices together to get
     * the concatenated transform matrix.
     */
    for (i = 0; i < 3; i++) {
      for (j = 0; j < 3; j++) {
        /* Initialize this entry to 0 */
        mainMatrix[i][j] = 0;

        for (k = 0; k < 3; k++) {
          mainMatrix[i][j] += scaleMatrix[i][k] *
```

```
                              rotMatrix[k][j];
            }
          }
        }

        /* Transform the shape with the new matrix */
        for (i = 0; i < theShape->numOfVertices; i++) {
          /* Declare some temporary variables */
          short   temp0, temp1, temp2;

          /* Multiply against the matrix */
          temp0 = theShape->vertex[i].lx * mainMatrix[0][0] +
              theShape->vertex[i].ly * mainMatrix[1][0] +
              mainMatrix[2][0];

          temp1 = theShape->vertex[i].lx * mainMatrix[0][1] +
              theShape->vertex[i].ly * mainMatrix[1][1] +
              mainMatrix[2][1];

          temp2 = theShape->vertex[i].lx * mainMatrix[0][2] +
              theShape->vertex[i].ly * mainMatrix[1][2] +
              mainMatrix[2][2];

          /* Put the results directly into the shape's
           * window coordinates.
           */
          theShape->vertex[i].sx = temp0;
          theShape->vertex[i].sy = temp1;
          theShape->vertex[i].st = temp2;
      }
    }
```

The example program doesn't need to be changed much to use the new transformation methods. Instead of calling several routines to transform the shape and translate it to window coordinates, it requires only one call to TransformShape(). This source code is named Shapes w/matrices on the source code CD-ROM. Listing 9-6 shows this routine.

Listing 9-6 *The shapes with matrices routine*

```
void main(void)
{
  Rect          windowRect;
  Rect          gworldRect;
  WindowPtr     mainWindow;
  GWorldPtr     offscreenGWorld;
  PixMapHandle  offscreenPixMap;
  unsigned long rowBytes;
  Ptr           pixmapBaseAddress;
  OSErr         err;
  GWorldPtr     savePort;
```

Continued on next page

Continued from previous page

```
GDHandle      saveDevice;
float         angle;
float         scale;
Boolean       scaleIncreasing;

/* Initialize everything we need */
InitGraf(&qd.thePort);
InitWindows();
InitCursor();

/* Create a window that is 500x300 pixels large */
SetRect(&windowRect, 0, 0, 500, 300);

/* We want our gworld to be the same size */
gworldRect = windowRect;

/* Offset the window rect so that the window does not appear
 * under the menu bar.
 */
OffsetRect(&windowRect, 20, 40);

mainWindow = CreateWindow(&windowRect);

SetPort(mainWindow);

/* Create the offscreen GWorld */

err = NewGWorld( &offscreenGWorld,
                 8,
                 &gworldRect,
                 NULL,
                 NULL,
                 0  );

if (err)  /* Quit if there was an error */
  ExitToShell();


/* Find the GWorld's PixMapHandle */

offscreenPixMap = GetGWorldPixMap(offscreenGWorld);

/* Lock the pixmap */
LockPixels(offscreenPixMap);

/* Get a pointer to the pixmap data */
pixmapBaseAddress = GetPixBaseAddr(offscreenPixMap);

/* Find the pixmap rowbytes (remember to mask off the top 2 bits!) */
rowBytes = (**offscreenPixMap).rowBytes & 0x3FFF;

/* Start the rotation off at 0 and scale at 1 */
angle = 0.0;
```

```
scale = 1.0;
scaleIncreasing = FALSE;

/* Wait until the user clicks before quitting */
while (!Button())
{
  /* Erase the GWorld */

  GetGWorld(&savePort, &saveDevice);
  SetGWorld(offscreenGWorld, NULL);

  EraseRect(&gworldRect);

  SetGWorld(savePort, saveDevice);

  /* Fiddle with the rotation value */
  angle += 0.1;

  /* If the angle has passed 2PI (6.28 radians, or 360 degrees),
   * reset it.
   */
  if (angle > 6.28)
    angle -= 6.28;

  /* Change the scale value */
  if (scaleIncreasing) {
    scale += 0.1;

    if (scale > 1) {
      scale = 1;
      scaleIncreasing = FALSE;
    }
  } else {
    scale -= 0.1;

    if (scale < 0.1) {
      scale = 0.1;
      scaleIncreasing = TRUE;
    }
  }

  /* Do all of the object's transformations */
  TransformShape( &triangleShape,
                  scale,
                  0, /* No translation */
                  0,
                  angle );

  /* Draw the shape */
  DrawShape(triangleShape, pixmapBaseAddress, rowBytes);


  /* Copy the gworld to the screen */
```

Continued on next page

Continued from previous page

```
CopyBits(  (BitMap *)*offscreenPixMap,
           (BitMap *)&mainWindow->portBits,
           &gworldRect,
           &gworldRect,
           srcCopy,
           NULL  );
  }
}
```

Moving On

The concepts presented in this chapter will go far in helping you create three-dimensional games. Perhaps the most important concept to know when working with polygon-based graphics is matrix mathematics. What you have learned here is the basis for every 3D game or 3D graphics package on the market today, and it's really not all that complicated.

I encourage you to experiment with what you've learned in this chapter. One thing to be very careful of is not letting any of the shapes go off the edge of the screen. Because you have not implemented clipping functions yet, and you are drawing directly into the GWorlds, if you write outside the pixmap boundary, you are writing into random memory, which will likely cause your machine to crash.

Clipping is one of the niceties that you gave up when you implemented your own functions to replace those in QuickDraw. In Chapter 16, you'll be writing your own clipping routine.

The next thing to do is to step into the third dimension—the final result of the next chapter will be spinning three-dimensional shapes!

Three-Dimensional Graphics

pome tutti fare la manouilla . di quali pruduono . l'alza
o grap. si . uue li muu lle me . gen. fo . alo grano di bono
org. are nella mo . r lo per maggu tu della manouilla pugi gua
a forza . c piu i l omo piu . di uali .

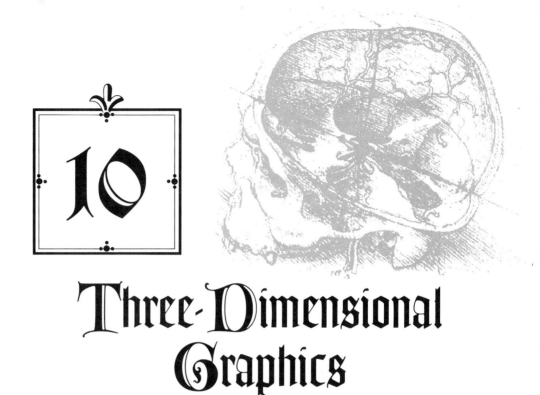

10

Three-Dimensional Graphics

Many of the most popular computer games are based on three-dimensional graphics. In the Macintosh community, some of the great early 3D games include Colony, Flight Simulator, and a version of Star Wars. More recent creations include several games that have been mentioned in previous chapters—Marathon, F/A-18 Hornet, and Hellcats Over the Pacific.

There are quite a few things to keep track of when creating 3D graphics, but overall it is not a difficult task. The math is relatively simple and most of the work programmers invest in 3D graphics is concentrated in optimization. This chapter will show you how to create three-dimensional animations.

The z Coordinate

When working in two dimensions, you had two coordinates: x and y. The third dimension also requires its own coordinate, called z. Whereas the x and y coordinates are typically used to describe width and height respectively, the z coordinate usually describes depth. This corresponds to the computer screen, where x describes the horizontal axis, y describes the vertical axis, and z describes an imaginary axis leading *into* the screen. Figure 10-1 illustrates this 3D coordinate system. Computer screens are two-dimensional, which is what makes 3D graphics more complicated than their 2D counterparts. You can't directly show depth on a computer screen, so the trick is to show the *illusion* of depth.

Artists have been using these techniques for centuries. In fact, you may have used the same techniques in an elementary school art class. The effect is called *perspective* drawing and it involves tricking the human eye into thinking there is depth where there really isn't any.

To have 3D graphics, you need to describe your shapes in three dimensions. To do this, you'll have to create a new vertice structure called Vertex3D. Because I'm describing depth, I'll use the term z. Here is the definition for Vertex3D:

```
typedef struct {
  short lx, ly, lz, lt;    /* Shape coordinates */
  short tx, ty, tz, tt;    /* Transformed coordinates */
  short sx, sy, st;        /* Window coordinates */
} Vertex3D;
```

Because the s coordinates (sx, sy, and st) describe the position of the shape on the screen, there is no need for a z term. By the time the shape is drawn onto the screen, the z coordinate will have been discarded.

A Recipe for 3D

Before I go into the details of manipulating and displaying 3D shapes, it will be helpful if I present an overview of all of the steps involved. This list includes only the ingredients that are introduced in this chapter—I'll expand on it in later chapters as you learn more. Here are the basic steps required to use 3D graphics:

- Define the object in 3D shape coordinates.
- Create transformation matrices.
- Transform the shape.
- Convert the shape from transformed to world coordinates.
- Project the shape, which converts it to screen coordinates.
- Draw the shape.

I discussed how to define a 2D object in Chapter 9. The process of defining a 3D shape is very similar but some changes to the shape structure are required. These modifications will be introduced when I talk about world coordinates (so that all of the changes are introduced at once).

Let's look at the second and third steps. For the transformations, you're going to be using matrices similar to those reviewed in Chapter 9 but they have been expanded to encompass all three dimensions.

FIGURE 10-1
◎ ◎ ◎ ◎ ◎ ◎
*The 3D
coordinate
system*

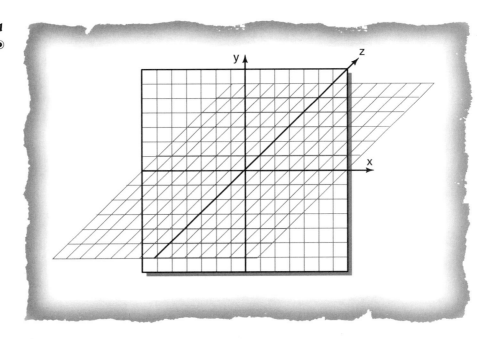

Three-Dimensional Transformations

Three-dimensional transformations are slightly more complicated than the two-dimensional ones you've been working with. For translating and scaling, the changes are simple: One more coordinate is added to the formulas. However, there are now three rotation formulas. As discussed in Chapter 4, with the addition of a third dimension, objects can be rotated around one of three axes: x, y, or z.

The matrices for 3D transformations are understandably larger than those for 2D transformations. The matrices now consist of four rows and four columns: one each for x, y, and z, plus the extra t coordinate discussed in Chapter 4.

3D Translating

Translating in the third dimension is easy—just add x, y, and z terms to each coordinate of the shape. The 3D translation matrix is a simple extension of the 2D version:

```
1        0        0        0
0        1        0        0
0        0        1        0
xTrans   yTrans   zTrans   1
```

3D Scaling

Scaling is also simple. An additional z term has been added to the 2D version:

```
xScale   0        0        0
0        yScale   0        0
0        0        zScale   0
0        0        0        1
```

3D Rotation

The only rotation you've worked with until now has been 2D rotation. The type of rotations you were applying to 2D shapes was rotation about the z axis. The z axis, remember, can be imagined as a line extending through the screen of the display perfectly perpendicular to the surface of the display. An object rotating about the z axis is not rotating in the z dimension; in fact, that is the only dimension it *isn't* rotating in. An object rotating about the z axis is rotating in the x and y dimensions, which are the only dimensions available to a two-dimensional shape. Figure 10-2 shows an object being rotated about the z axis.

FIGURE 10-2

Rotating an object about the z axis

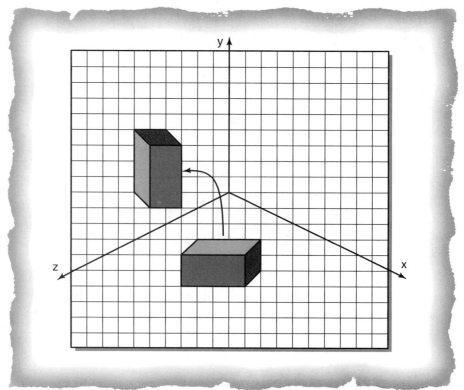

Three-dimensional objects can also rotate about the x and y axes, providing two new formulas. Rotating an object about the x axis moves it in the y and z dimensions, whereas rotating about the y axis moves in the x and z dimensions. Figure 10-3 shows an example of an object rotating about the x axis; Figure 10-4 shows it rotating about the y axis.

Let's take a look at the matrices used for these rotations. Here is a 3D version of the z rotation used in Chapter 9:

```
cos(za)  sin(za)  0     0
-sin(za) cos(za)  0     0
0        0        1     0
0        0        0     1
```

Rotation about the x and y axes simply involves rearranging the terms a bit. Here is the matrix for the x axis:

```
1        0        0        0
0        cos(xa)  sin(xa)  0
0        -sin(xa) cos(xa)  0
0        0        0        1
```

FIGURE 10-3

◎ ◎ ◎ ◎ ◎ ◎

Rotating an object about the x axis

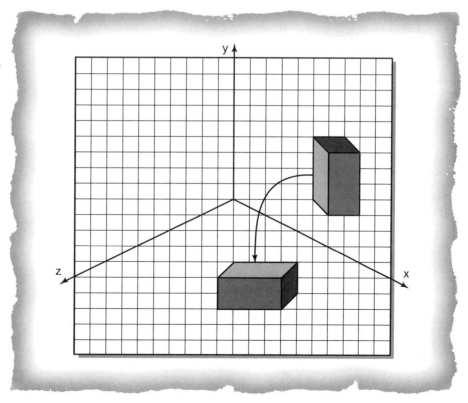

FIGURE 10-4

◎ ◎ ◎ ◎ ◎ ◎

Rotating an object about the y axis

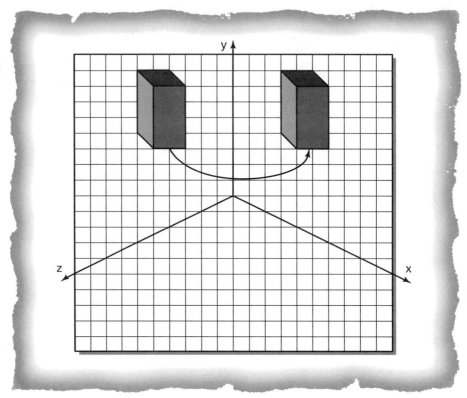

The matrix for rotating the y axis looks like this:

```
cos(ya)    0      -sin(ya)    0
0          1      0           0
sin(ya)    0      cos(ya)     0
0          0      0           1
```

Incremental Matrices

In Chapter 9, all the transformations were done through a single routine. This is handy if you're always going to have to rotate, translate, and scale the object. However most of the time, you're going to want to use only one or two of these transformations at a time. In light of this, I'm going to break the transformation process into separate routines for each operation.

When I introduced matrices in Chapter 4, I mentioned that transformations applied to matrices are cumulative. If you apply several transformations to a matrix and then use that matrix to transform a shape, you will get the same result as applying each of those transformations directly to the shape.

It is important to remember that the order in which the transformations are applied makes a big difference. For example, applying a transformation and then a rotation to a shape will achieve a very different result than applying the rotation first.

Figure 10-5a shows a 2D triangle centered on the origin. If you transform the triangle to a different location, you get a result like the one in Figure 10-5b. Because rotations

FIGURE 10-5a

◎ ◎ ◎ ◎ ◎ ◎

A 2D triangle defined in local coordinates (a) shown after a translation (b) and after a translation and a rotation (c)

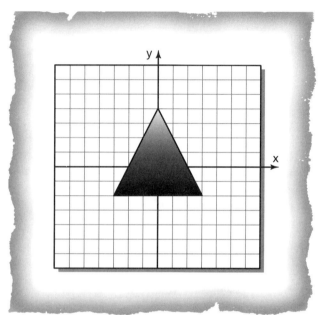

FIGURE 10-5b

◎ ◎ ◎ ◎ ◎ ◎

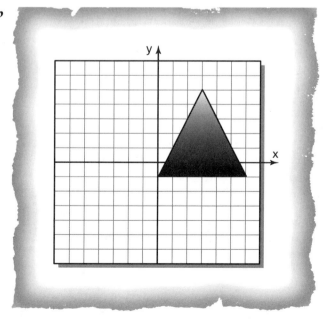

FIGURE 10-5c

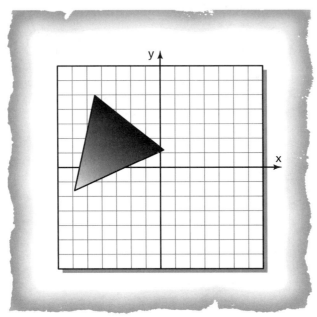

are based around the origin of the coordinate system, rotating the triangle will give you something like Figure 10-5c.

If you take the same triangle and first rotate it as shown in Figure 10-6a, then translate it, you get a result like the one shown in Figure 10-6b. As you can see, the results are quite different.

Most of the time, you want to rotate shapes around their centers, so rotations generally should be done first. When using 3D shapes, you want to rotate objects around the z axis first, then the x, and lastly the y.

The next transformation you usually want to perform is scaling, followed finally by a translation.

Matrix Initialization

The *identity matrix* is a special matrix that you will find useful in your transformations. This matrix does not change any other matrix with which it is multiplied; in this sense, it is functionally similar to the integer 1. Its elements are all 0 except for a diagonal row (i.e., [0,0], [1,1], [2,2] and [3,3]), which is initialized to 1. The routine InitMatrix(), shown here, creates an identity matrix.

FIGURE 10-6a

◉ ◉ ◉ ◉ ◉ ◉

The same triangle shown after a rotation (a) and after a rotation and translation (b)

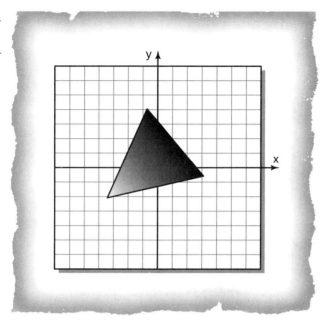

FIGURE 10-6b

◉ ◉ ◉ ◉ ◉ ◉

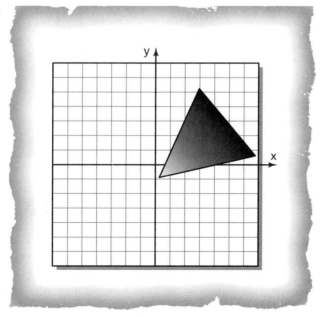

```
/**
**   InitMatrix()
**
**   Initializes a matrix to the Identity Matrix.
**/
void   InitMatrix(float matrix[4][4])
{
  matrix[0][0] = 1; matrix[0][1] = 0;
  matrix[0][2] = 0; matrix[0][3] = 0;

  matrix[1][0] = 0; matrix[1][1] = 1;
  matrix[1][2] = 0; matrix[1][3] = 0;

  matrix[2][0] = 0; matrix[2][1] = 0;
  matrix[2][2] = 1; matrix[2][3] = 0;

  matrix[3][0] = 0; matrix[3][1] = 0;
  matrix[3][2] = 0; matrix[3][3] = 1;
}
```

Matrix Multiplication

As you'll recall from Chapter 9, matrices are concatenated by multiplying them together. Because you need to concatenate matrices quite often, here is a routine specifically for that purpose.

```
/**
**   MultiplyMatrix()
**
**   Concatenates matrix1 and matrix2 and returns the result
**   in matrix3
**/
void  MultiplyMatrix(  float matrix1[4][4],
                       float matrix2[4][4],
                       float matrix3[4][4]  )
{
  float  i,j,k;

  for (i = 0; i < 4; i++) {
    for (j = 0; j < 4; j++) {
      matrix3[i][j] = 0;
      for (k = 0; k < 4; k++) {
        matrix3[i][j] += matrix1[i][k] * matrix2[k][j];
      }
    }
  }
}
```

Copying a Matrix

Another function you'll find useful is one that will copy a matrix. I'll call it CopyMatrix().

```
/**
 ** CopyMatrix()
 **
 ** Copies srcMatrix to dstMatrix.
 **/
void  CopyMatrix(  float srcMatrix[4][4],
                   float dstMatrix[4][4]  )
{
  short  i, j;

  for (i = 0; i < 4; i++) {
    for (j = 0; j < 4; j++) {
      dstMatrix[i][j] = srcMatrix[i][j];
    }
  }
}
```

Creating the Transformation Matrices

The goal here is to create a master transformation matrix—a matrix that, when applied to a shape, will change its scale, rotation, and position at the same time. The first thing you do is to initialize a blank matrix by calling InitMatrix(). Then pass that matrix to each of the matrix transformation routines in the order you want them to occur (which will typically be rotation, scale, and translation).

Each transformation routine will fill out a matrix with its particular operation and then call MultiplyMatrix() to concatenate its matrix with your master matrix. In the case of the rotation routines, each one has to concatenate three matrices with the master matrix.

After you've called the transformation routines you need, you're left with the master matrix, which you apply to your shape.

Let's examine the matrix transformation routines in detail. The first is the translation matrix routine. You'll notice that a temporary matrix is used to store the result of the matrix multiplication. This is because the matrix multiplication routine can't handle the case when its output matrix is the same as either of its input matrices. To get around this, use a temporary matrix and then copy the result back into the input matrix.

```
/**
 ** TranslateMatrix()
 **
 ** Applies a translation to the input matrix.
```

Continued on next page

Continued from previous page

```
**/
void TranslateMatrix(  float  inputMatrix[4][4],
                       short  xTrans,
                       short  yTrans,
                       short  zTrans  )
{
  float  transMatrix[4][4];
  float  tempMatrix[4][4];

  /* Set transMatrix to a translation matrix */
  transMatrix[0][0] = 1; transMatrix[0][1] = 0;
  transMatrix[0][2] = 0; transMatrix[0][3] = 0;

  transMatrix[1][0] = 0; transMatrix[1][1] = 1;
  transMatrix[1][2] = 0; transMatrix[1][3] = 0;

  transMatrix[2][0] = 0; transMatrix[2][1] = 0;
  transMatrix[2][2] = 1; transMatrix[2][3] = 0;

  transMatrix[3][0] = xTrans; transMatrix[3][1] = yTrans;
  transMatrix[3][2] = zTrans; transMatrix[3][3] = 1;

  /* Concatenate the translation matrix with the
   * input matrix.
   */
  MultiplyMatrix(inputMatrix, transMatrix, tempMatrix);

  /* Copy the temp matrix back into the input matrix */
  CopyMatrix(tempMatrix, inputMatrix);
}
```

The scaling function is very similar. You could use a different scaling value for each axis, but for your needs, assume that the object will be scaled evenly.

```
/**
 **   ScaleMatrix()
 **
 **   Applies a scaling to the input matrix.
 **/
void ScaleMatrix(  float  inputMatrix[4][4],
                   float  scalingFactor  )
{
  float  scaleMatrix[4][4];
  float  tempMatrix[4][4];

  /* Set scaleMatrix to a scaling matrix */
  scaleMatrix[0][0] = scalingFactor; scaleMatrix[0][1] = 0;
  scaleMatrix[0][2] = 0; scaleMatrix[0][3] = 0;

  scaleMatrix[1][0] = 0; scaleMatrix[1][1] = scalingFactor;
  scaleMatrix[1][2] = 0; scaleMatrix[1][3] = 0;
```

```
scaleMatrix[2][0] = 0; scaleMatrix[2][1] = 0;
scaleMatrix[2][2] = scalingFactor; scaleMatrix[2][3] = 0;

scaleMatrix[3][0] = 0; scaleMatrix[3][1] = 0;
scaleMatrix[3][2] = 0; scaleMatrix[3][3] = 1;

/* Concatenate the scaling matrix with the
 * input matrix.
 */
MultiplyMatrix(inputMatrix, scaleMatrix, tempMatrix);

/* Copy the temp matrix back into the input matrix */
CopyMatrix(tempMatrix, inputMatrix);
}
```

Rotation is a little more complicated. This routine is actually performing three different transformations at once. To avoid copying over any critical data, you need to use two temporary matrices, but the rotation matrix can be reused. Because it makes good sense for a flight simulator, order the rotations as y, x, and z, as shown in Listing 10-1.

Listing 10-1 *The RotateMatrix() routine*

```
/**
 **   RotateMatrix()
 **
 **   Applies x,y, and z rotations to the input matrix.
 **/
void  RotateMatrix(  float   inputMatrix[4][4],
                     float   xRot,
                     float   yRot,
                     float   zRot  )
{
  float   rotMatrix[4][4];
  float   tempMatrix1[4][4];
  float   tempMatrix2[4][4];

  /* We want to apply all three rotations to the inputMatrix,
   * in the order of z, y, and x. In order to accomplish all of
   * these transformations, we have to use two temporary matrices
   * and copy between them.
   */

  /* Set rotMatrix to the y rotation matrix */
  rotMatrix[0][0] = cos(yRot); rotMatrix[0][1] = 0;
  rotMatrix[0][2] = -sin(yRot); rotMatrix[0][3] = 0;

  rotMatrix[1][0] = 0; rotMatrix[1][1] = 1;
  rotMatrix[1][2] = 0; rotMatrix[1][3] = 0;

  rotMatrix[2][0] = sin(yRot); rotMatrix[2][1] = 0;
  rotMatrix[2][2] = cos(yRot); rotMatrix[2][3] = 0;
```

Continued on next page

Continued from previous page

```
  rotMatrix[3][0] = 0; rotMatrix[3][1] = 0;
  rotMatrix[3][2] = 0; rotMatrix[3][3] = 1;

  /* Concatenate rotMatrix with inputMatrix */
  MatrixMultiply(inputMatrix, rotMatrix, tempMatrix1);

  /* Set rotMatrix to the x rotation matrix */
  rotMatrix[0][0] = 1; rotMatrix[0][1] = 0;
  rotMatrix[0][2] = 0; rotMatrix[0][3] = 0;

  rotMatrix[1][0] = 0; rotMatrix[1][1] = cos(xRot);
  rotMatrix[1][2] = sin(xRot); rotMatrix[1][3] = 0;

  rotMatrix[2][0] = 0; rotMatrix[2][1] = -sin(xRot);
  rotMatrix[2][2] = cos(xRot); rotMatrix[2][3] = 0;

  rotMatrix[3][0] = 0; rotMatrix[3][1] = 0;
  rotMatrix[3][2] = 0; rotMatrix[3][3] = 1;

  /* Concatenate rotMatrix with tempMatrix1 */
  MatrixMultiply(tempMatrix1, rotMatrix, tempMatrix2);

  /* Set rotMatrix to the z rotation matrix */
  rotMatrix[0][0] = cos(zRot); rotMatrix[0][1] = sin(zRot);
  rotMatrix[0][2] = 0; rotMatrix[0][3] = 0;

  rotMatrix[1][0] = -sin(zRot); rotMatrix[1][1] = cos(zRot);
  rotMatrix[1][2] = 0; rotMatrix[1][3] = 0;

  rotMatrix[2][0] = 0; rotMatrix[2][1] = 0;
  rotMatrix[2][2] = 1; rotMatrix[2][3] = 0;

  rotMatrix[3][0] = 0; rotMatrix[3][1] = 0;
  rotMatrix[3][2] = 0; rotMatrix[3][3] = 1;

  /* Concatenate rotMatrix with tempMatrix2 */
  MatrixMultiply(tempMatrix2, rotMatrix, tempMatrix1);

  /* Copy the temp matrix back into the input matrix */
  CopyMatrix(tempMatrix1, inputMatrix);
}
```

Transforming the Shape

The shape transformation routine is relatively simple (see Listing 10-2). It takes each vertice of the shape and runs it through a master transformation matrix, leaving the result in the shape's transformed coordinates.

Listing 10-2 The TransformShape3D() routine

```
/**
 **   TransformShape3D()
 **
 **   Takes a shape's local coordinates and transforms them
 **   with the provided transformation matrix, placing
 **   the result in the tx,ty,tz, and tt fields of the
 **   vertices.
 **/
void  TransformShape3D( Shape3D  *theShape,
                        float  transformMatrix[4][4]  )
{
  short    i;

  /* Transform the shape with the new matrix */
  for (i = 0; i < theShape->numOfVertices; i++) {
    /* Declare some temporary variables */
    short  temp0, temp1, temp2, temp3;

    /* Multiply against the matrix */
    temp0 = theShape->vertex[i].lx * transformMatrix[0][0] +
            theShape->vertex[i].ly * transformMatrix[1][0] +
            theShape->vertex[i].lz * transformMatrix[2][0] +
            transformMatrix[3][0];

    temp1 = theShape->vertex[i].lx * transformMatrix[0][1] +
            theShape->vertex[i].ly * transformMatrix[1][1] +
            theShape->vertex[i].lz * transformMatrix[2][1] +
            transformMatrix[3][1];

    temp2 = theShape->vertex[i].lx * transformMatrix[0][2] +
            theShape->vertex[i].ly * transformMatrix[1][2] +
            theShape->vertex[i].lz * transformMatrix[2][2] +
            transformMatrix[3][2];

    temp3 = theShape->vertex[i].lx * transformMatrix[0][3] +
            theShape->vertex[i].ly * transformMatrix[1][3] +
            theShape->vertex[i].lz * transformMatrix[2][3] +
            transformMatrix[3][3];


    /* Put the results into the shape's
     * transformed coordinates
     */
    theShape->vertex[i].tx = temp0;
    theShape->vertex[i].ty = temp1;
    theShape->vertex[i].tz = temp2;
    theShape->vertex[i].tt = temp3;
  }
}
```

World Coordinates

So far, every shape you've created has been defined in two coordinate systems: the position of the shape relative to its origin and the position of the shape relative to the window (the transformed coordinates portion of the Vertex3D structure is just a modified version of the shape coordinates). This works fine when you're dealing with only one shape at a time, but when you start using 3D graphics, there will be times when you'll need to look at all of the shapes in relation to one another. This is especially true when some shapes are behind others or are not even visible on the screen. To make this possible, you're going to create one more coordinate system called *world coordinates*. World coordinates will be used to bridge the transformed and screen coordinates to organize objects efficiently.

The world coordinate system, like the new shape coordinate system, is three dimensional (the screen coordinate system remains two dimensional). When a shape is created, it exists in shape coordinates, like the sphere and cube shown in Figure 10-7 a and b. At this point, you don't know *where* the cube is relative to the sphere. It could be beside, behind, or even inside it—you can't tell. After the shapes have been transformed, they are translated into three-dimensional world coordinates. At this point, you can observe the actual location of each shape, as shown in Figure 10-8, and see that the cube is above the sphere.

FIGURE 10-7a

⊚ ⊚ ⊚ ⊚ ⊚ ⊚

A sphere (a) and a cube (b) defined in shape coordinates

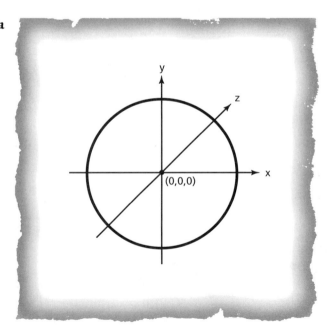

FIGURE 10-7b

◎ ◎ ◎ ◎ ◎ ◎

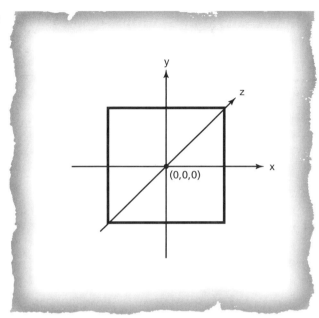

FIGURE 10-8

◎ ◎ ◎ ◎ ◎ ◎

The sphere and cube defined in the world coordinate system

3D Shape Structures

Because of the new coordinate system, you need to modify the Vertex3D structure once again. For this coordinate system, use the prefix w:

```
typedef struct {
  short  lx, ly, lz, lt;    /* Shape coordinates */
  short  tx, ty, tz, tt;    /* Transformed coordinates */
  short  wx, wy, wz, wt;    /* World coordinates */
  short  sx, sy, st;        /* Window coordinates */
} Vertex3D;
```

In Chapter 9, you were able to create a shape by describing each of its vertices in the order they would be connected. Previously, to draw the object, all you had to do was loop through each of the vertices and draw lines between them. This method works fine if you have a shape that can be drawn with one continuous line, as many 2D shapes can.

This method breaks down quickly when dealing with 3D shapes. A cube, for example, cannot be drawn with a continual line without duplicating some of the vertices. It *would* be possible to continue using the old method and just allow some of the vertices to be duplicated in the shape definition, but that would be inefficient.

In the new shape structure, you're going to continue to have a list of all the vertices of the shape; however, instead of assuming the order in which the lines are connected, you're going to define a second array of a structure called VertexConnect. This array tells you which of the vertices are connected so you know where to draw the lines. Here is the definition of VertexConnect:

```
typedef struct {
  short    begin, end;
} VertexConnect;
```

The *begin* and *end* fields correspond to indices to the *vertice* array in the Shape structure. For example, if a particular VertexConnect record had values of 0 and 2 for begin and end, you would know that you needed to draw a line between vertex[0] and vertex[2] of the shape (keep in mind that vertex[0] would indicate the *first* vertice and vertex[2] is the *third*, because arrays in C begin at element 0).

Figure 10-9 shows a cube that has been defined as a series of vertices. Each of the eight vertices shown would be stored in the Vertex3D array. In the VertexConnect array, 12 vertex pairs would be stored; in the example shown, the pairs would be (0,1), (1,2), (2,3), (3,0), (4,5), (5,6), (6,7), (7,4), (0,4), (1,5), (2,6), and (3,7). It doesn't really make any difference in what order you store the vertex pairs.

In Chapter 9, you used the *origin* field of the shape to define how the shape could be translated between shape coordinates and screen coordinates. I'm going to redefine

FIGURE 10-9

◉ ◉ ◉ ◉ ◉ ◉

A 3D cube defined as eight vertices

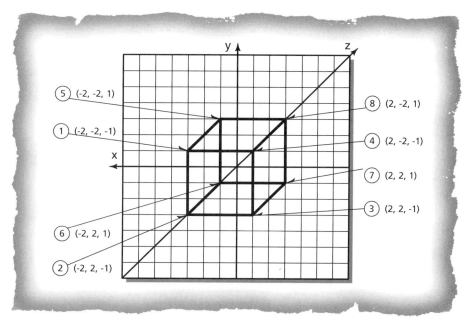

the purpose of this field. Instead of using it to convert to screen coordinates, you're now going to use it to translate into world coordinates. And like the shape and world coordinates, it requires a third field, called *originZ*.

The new shape structure, which encompasses all of these changes, is called Shape3D.

```
typedef struct {
  unsigned char    color;
  short            numOfVertices;
  short            numOfLines;
  short            originX, originY, originZ;
  Vertex3D         *vertex;
  VertexConnect    *shapeLines;
} Shape3D;
```

With all the new vertex fields, it becomes a little more complicated to describe shapes directly in the code; I'll introduce a better method in Chapter 11. For now, however, continue to use the old method. Listing 10-3 is a cube defined using these new structures.

Listing 10-3 *Defining a cube with new vertex fields*

```
Vertex3D  cubeVertexArray[] = {
  -80,  80,   -80,  1,
    0,   0,    0,   1,
```

Continued on next page

Continued from previous page

```
      0,    0,    0,    1,
      0,    0,    1,        /* Vertex 0 */
     80,   80,  -80,   1,
      0,    0,    0,    1,
      0,    0,    0,    1,
      0,    0,    1,        /* Vertex 1 */
     80,  -80,  -80,   1,
      0,    0,    0,    1,
      0,    0,    0,    1,
      0,    0,    1,        /* Vertex 2 */
    -80,  -80,  -80,   1,
      0,    0,    0,    1,
      0,    0,    0,    1,
      0,    0,    1,        /* Vertex 3 */
    -80,   80,   80,   1,
      0,    0,    0,    1,
      0,    0,    0,    1,
      0,    0,    1,        /* Vertex 4 */
     80,   80,   80,   1,
      0,    0,    0,    1,
      0,    0,    0,    1,
      0,    0,    1,        /* Vertex 5 */
     80,  -80,   80,   1,
      0,    0,    0,    1,
      0,    0,    0,    1,
      0,    0,    1,        /* Vertex 6 */
    -80,  -80,   80,   1,
      0,    0,    0,    1,
      0,    0,    0,    1,
      0,    0,    1         /* Vertex 7 */
};

VertexConnect  cubeVertexConnections[] = {
    0, 1,
    1, 2,
    2, 3,
    3, 0,
    4, 5,
    5, 6,
    6, 7,
    7, 4,
    0, 4,
    1, 5,
    2, 6,
    3, 7
};

Shape3D    cubeShape = {
    255,                  /* Color (Black) */
    8,                    /* Number of vertices */
```

```
    12,                    /* Number of lines */
    0, 0, 320,             /* Origin */
    cubeVertexArray,       /* Pointer to vertex array */
    cubeVertexConnections  /* Pointer to connections array */
};
```

Converting into World Coordinates

It's a simple matter to convert the shape to world coordinates. All that needs to be done is to loop through all of the vertices and add the *origin* (*originX*, *originY*, and *originZ*) values to each of the transformed coordinates (tx, ty, and tz). Here is the code for ShapeToWorldCoordinates().

```
/**
 **   ShapeToWorldCoordinates()
 **
 **   Translates a shape from its transformed coordinates
 **   to world coordinates.
 **/
void  ShapeToWorldCoordinates(Shape3D  *theShape)
{
    short    i;
    short    shapeOriginX, shapeOriginY, shapeOriginZ;
    Vertex3D *vertexRef;

    /* Copy the shape's origin coordinates into local variables
     * for speed and code clarity
     */
    shapeOriginX = theShape->originX;
    shapeOriginY = theShape->originY;
    shapeOriginZ = theShape->originZ;

    for (i = 0; i < theShape->numOfVertices; i++) {
        /* Obtain a pointer to the current vertex. This allows
         * us to reference this particular vertex more efficiently,
         * instead of indexing through the shape vertex array each
         * time.
         */
        vertexRef = &theShape->vertex[i];

        vertexRef->wx = vertexRef->tx + shapeOriginX;
        vertexRef->wy = vertexRef->ty + shapeOriginY;
        vertexRef->wz = vertexRef->tz + shapeOriginZ;
    }
}
```

The Screen in 3D Space

Now that you have your objects in world coordinates, you'll need to find a way to convert them to screen coordinates. This process is the heart of all 3D graphics: regrettably, it is not as simple as adding an *origin* field to each vertex.

The objects you want to display now exist in the same coordinate system. If you are writing a flight simulator, you have an airplane, a runway, the airport control tower, and possibly a few buildings and mountains. Since you can look at the objects from any direction (e.g., you can look at the world as if you were sitting in the airplane's cockpit or you can look at your airplane from the perspective of the control tower), how do you translate these objects to points on the computer screen?

What you have to do is imagine the computer screen as an invisible two-dimensional rectangular window somewhere in the world. If you want to look out of the cockpit of the airplane, you position the invisible window right in front of the airplane, facing outward.

This window can be placed *anywhere* in the world facing in any direction. Once its location has been decided, you can imagine standing behind the window and looking through it. You can calculate what is visible through this imaginary window and use that to draw the image on the screen.

Figure 10-10 shows the airport and the imaginary window, which has been placed immediately in front of the plane. The field of view extends from the window in a cone

FIGURE 10-10

An airport with the view placed directly in front of the airplane

shape: anything that falls within this field is potentially visible on the screen. Figure 10-11 shows the image that would be constructed from this world using that window.

Perspective Viewing

When an object moves away from you, it appears to get smaller. In the same way, two parallel lines, when viewed at an angle, will appear to grow closer together the farther away from you they are. A good example of this is railroad tracks. If you stand on railroad tracks (first making sure there's no coming train!) and look down them toward the horizon, you will notice that the tracks appear to come together in the distance, as in Figure 10-12.

The reason for this is your field of view, which covers approximately a 120° angle. When you examine an object very closely (about 1 foot from your eyes), your field of view covers about 2 feet side to side. However, when you look at something that is a mile away, your field of view can cover much more distance—several miles or more. Because you view everything in the same way, regardless of its distance, objects that are far away appear smaller. If you want to experience this, go outside and choose a good-sized object (such as a house) that's a few hundred feet away (see Figure 10-13). As you begin to walk toward it, notice that it takes up more of your field of view (see Figure 10-14). If you get close enough, you won't be able to see anything else without

FIGURE 10-11

⊚ ⊚ ⊚ ⊚ ⊚ ⊚

The view from the cockpit of the airplane

FIGURE 10-12

◎ ◎ ◎ ◎ ◎ ◎

Railroad tracks appear to converge in the distance

turning your head. If you then walk backwards, the object will look smaller and smaller (see Figure 10-15) until eventually you won't be able to see it anymore.

To create convincing 3D computer graphics, you must simulate this phenomena. The farther an object is from the screen (represented by its z coordinate), the smaller it must appear. This technique is called *projection*: the easiest way to accomplish this is to take each vertex's x and y coordinates and divide them by the z coordinate, like this:

```
newX = vertexX / vertexZ;
newY = vertexY / vertexZ;
```

This formula assumes that all z coordinates will be greater than 0. It is especially important to ensure that you never try to project an object that has a z coordinate of 0—you would be trying to divide by zero, which is mathematically impossible and will cause your game to crash.

This particular formula will give you a perspective view of your world, but the perspective would be far too great; it would be equivalent to a very wide field of view, far wider than your eyes can see. An object 10 units away from the origin would be reduced to 1/10 of its original size, and objects would quickly be reduced to nothing as they moved away from the screen.

FIGURE 10-13
◎ ◎ ◎ ◎ ◎ ◎
A view of a house

FIGURE 10-14
◎ ◎ ◎ ◎ ◎ ◎
A closer view of the house

FIGURE 10-15

◎ ◎ ◎ ◎ ◎ ◎

The house at a distance

To counter this problem, reduce the rate at which the coordinates diminish. You want to achieve a field of view of about 120°—equivalent to your own. This can be done by multiplying the original x and y values by a constant before dividing them by z:

```
newX = (vertexX * kDistanceConstant) / vertexZ;
newY = (vertexY * kDistanceConstant) / vertexZ;
```

A typical range for the distance constant is between 200 and 400.

Moving to Screen Coordinates

You now have enough information to convert an object from world to screen coordinates. In later chapters, when you're dealing with clipping and moving the views—processes that are quite a bit more involved—you'll need more information, but this will do for now.

For this chapter, you're always going be put the middle of the imaginary window on the (0,0,0) origin of the world facing down the z axis. This allows you to view the world without doing any additional transformations. (You'll learn about viewing transformations in Chapter 17.)

Without doing viewing transformations, the function to convert shapes to screen coordinates is quite simple. It loops through all the vertices of the object and applies the projection formula to each of them. This leaves the shape centered around the screen's origin. Because you want the shape in the middle of the window, translate it by adding half of the window's size (a predefined constant) to each vertex. Listing 10-4 is the ProjectShape() function.

Listing 10-4 The ProjectShape() routine

```
/**
**   ProjectShape()
**
**   Converts each vertex of a shape to screen coordinates. The
**   shape must have been transformed before calling this function.
**/
void  ProjectShape(Shape3D *theShape)
{
  Vertex3D      *vertexRef;
  short         i;

  /* We don't need to pay any attention to what order the vertices
   * are connected, since that's irrelevant for projection.
   */
  for (i = 0; i < theShape->numOfVertices; i++)
  {
    /* Obtain a pointer to the current vertex. This allows
     * us to reference this particular vertex more efficiently,
     * instead of indexing through the shape vertex array each
     * time.
     */
    vertexRef = &theShape->vertex[i];

    /* Project the vertex */
    vertexRef->sx = (vertexRef->tx * kDistanceConstant) / vertexRef->tz;
    vertexRef->sy = (vertexRef->ty * kDistanceConstant) / vertexRef->tz;

    /* Translate the vertex to screen coordinates */
    vertexRef->sx += kHalfWindowWidth;
    vertexRef->sy += kHalfWindowHeight;
  }
}
```

If you take the 3D cube in Figure 10-9, move a few units down the z axis (because you can't project a shape with a z coordinate less than or equal to 0), and project it using ProjectShape(), you will get a shape like the one in Figure 10-16. As you can see, the vertices that are farther in the distance are closer to the middle of the screen, giving a feeling of perspective. This basic formula for achieving perspective is probably used in every 3D computer program available today.

FIGURE 10-16

ⓐ ⓐ ⓐ ⓐ ⓐ ⓐ

*A cube
projected onto
screen
coordinates*

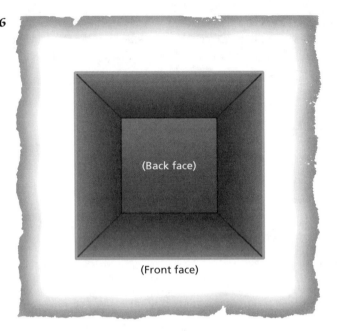

(Back face)

(Front face)

Drawing the Shape

The shape-drawing routine has to be modified to handle the new shape structure. Instead of looping through each vertex of the shape, it now loops through the VertexConnect array. Each time through the loop, it grabs the beginning and ending vertex for that line and draws it using the Bresenham algorithm. You must be careful not to let this routine draw outside of the pixmap boundary, which would probably cause the application to crash.

```
/**
 **    DrawShape()
 **
 **    Draws a shape, using the Bresenham line-drawing routine,
 **    onto the provided pixmap
 **/
void   DrawShape(  Shape3D        shape,
                   Ptr            pixMapPtr,
                   unsigned long  rowBytes  )
{
  short    i;

  /* Loop through each vertex in the shape: */
  for (i = 0; i < shape.numOfLines; i++)
```

```
{
  short  beginVertex, endVertex;

  /* Draw this line */
  beginVertex = shape.shapeLines[i].begin;
  endVertex = shape.shapeLines[i].end;

  BresenhamLine( shape.vertex[beginVertex].sx,
                 shape.vertex[beginVertex].sy,
                 shape.vertex[endVertex].sx,
                 shape.vertex[endVertex].sy,
                 pixMapPtr,
                 rowBytes,
                 shape.color  );
  }
}
```

3D Cube Application

To demonstrate the techniques presented in this chapter, you're going to build an application that displays a spinning 3D cube. You have all the routines you need for processing the 3D data, so the only thing left is the main() routine.

For this demonstration, you'll be using the 3D cube data that was outlined earlier. You'll be scaling and rotating the cube around the x and y axes, a process that requires four calls: InitMatrix(), ScaleMatrix(), RotateMatrix(), and TransformShape3D(). The cube is then converted to world coordinates, projected into screen coordinates, and drawn into the GWorld, as shown in Listing 10-5.

Listing 10-5 *The spinning 3D cube routine*

```
/**
 ** main()
 **
 **/
void main(void)
{
  Rect              windowRect;
  Rect              gworldRect;
  WindowPtr         mainWindow;
  GWorldPtr         offscreenGWorld;
  PixMapHandle      offscreenPixMap;
  unsigned long     rowBytes;
  Ptr               pixmapBaseAddress;
  OSErr             err;
  GWorldPtr         savePort;
  GDHandle          saveDevice;
  float             xAngle, yAngle;
  float             scale;
```

Continued on next page

Continued from previous page

```
Boolean          scaleIncreasing;
float            transformMatrix[4][4];

/* Initialize everything we need */
InitGraf(&qd.thePort);
InitWindows();
InitCursor();

/* Create a window that is 500x300 pixels large */
SetRect(&windowRect, 0, 0, 500, 300);

/* We want our gworld to be the same size */
gworldRect = windowRect;

/* Offset the window rect so that the window does not appear
 * under the menubar.
 */
OffsetRect(&windowRect, 20, 40);

mainWindow = CreateWindow(&windowRect);

SetPort(mainWindow);

/* Create the offscreen GWorld */

err = NewGWorld( &offscreenGWorld,
                 8,
                 &gworldRect,
                 NULL,
                 NULL,
                 0  );

if (err)  /* Quit if there was an error */
  ExitToShell();


/* Find the GWorld's PixMapHandle */

offscreenPixMap = GetGWorldPixMap(offscreenGWorld);

/* Lock the pixmap */
LockPixels(offscreenPixMap);

/* Get a pointer to the pixmap data */
pixmapBaseAddress = GetPixBaseAddr(offscreenPixMap);

/* Find the pixmap rowbytes (remember to mask off the top 2 bits!) */
rowBytes = (**offscreenPixMap).rowBytes & 0x3FFF;

/* Start the rotations off at 0 and scale at 1 */
xAngle = 0.0;
```

```
yAngle = 0.0;
scale = 1.0;
scaleIncreasing = FALSE;

/* Wait until the user clicks before quitting */
while (!Button())
{
  /* Erase the GWorld */

  GetGWorld(&savePort, &saveDevice);
  SetGWorld(offscreenGWorld, NULL);

  EraseRect(&gworldRect);

  SetGWorld(savePort, saveDevice);

  /* Fiddle with the rotation values */
  xAngle += 0.1;
  yAngle += 0.15;

  /* If either angle has passed 2PI (6.28 radians, or 360 degrees),
   * reset it.
   */
  if (xAngle > 6.28)
    xAngle -= 6.28;

  if (yAngle > 6.28)
    yAngle -= 6.28;

  /* Change the scale value */
  if (scaleIncreasing) {
    scale += 0.04;

    if (scale > 1) {
      scale = 1;
      scaleIncreasing = FALSE;
    }
  } else {
    scale -= 0.04;

    if (scale < 0.1) {
      scale = 0.1;
      scaleIncreasing = TRUE;
    }
  }

  /* Initialize our transformation matrix */
  InitMatrix(transformMatrix);

  /* Apply the rotations to the matrix */
  RotateMatrix(transformMatrix, xAngle, yAngle, 0);
```

Continued on next page

Continued from previous page

```
/* Apply the scale to the matrix */
ScaleMatrix(transformMatrix, scale);

/* Transform the shape */
TransformShape3D(&cubeShape, transformMatrix);

/* Convert the shape to world coordinates */
ShapeToWorldCoordinates(&cubeShape);

/* Project the shape into screen coordinates */
ProjectShape(&cubeShape);

/* Draw the shape */
DrawShape(cubeShape, pixmapBaseAddress, rowBytes);

/* Copy the gworld to the screen */
CopyBits( (BitMap *)*offscreenPixMap,
          (BitMap *)&mainWindow->portBits,
          &gworldRect,
          &gworldRect,
          srcCopy,
          NULL );
}
}
```

Double-clicking on the 3D Cube application will bring up a window with the animated cube and clicking the mouse will exit. Although the cube is reasonably fast on a 68040 Macintosh (and quite speedy on a PowerPC), it is by no means optimized. If it seems really slow, make sure your monitor is set to 256 colors—because we are copying from an 8-bit GWorld to the screen, it helps speed greatly if the operating system doesn't have to remap the colors.

You've now seen what it takes to create three-dimensional graphics on a 2D computer screen. The process involves several steps, but overall it isn't terribly difficult. By experimenting with the shape definition fields, you can create almost any wireframe object you like. But when was the last time you played a flight simulator that was based on wireframe graphics? In the next chapter, you're going to learn how to create much more realistic images using a newer technique: polygon-fill graphics.

11

Polygon-Fill Graphics

come tutti sono le manouelle . . . . le quali pruobano . lalza
no a gran pesi . . . sono le mini . . . . e . . senesse . . fa e grano di bone
forza e nella mano . . e . fa per . . . nella . . . la manouelle pegi . quan
la forza . a . piu . . uomo . . pub . . . bri .

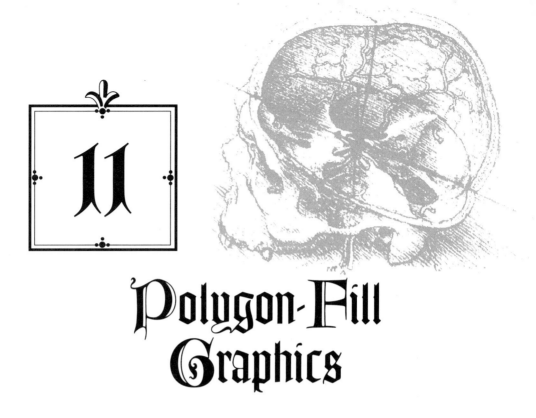

11

Polygon-Fill Graphics

Wireframe graphics may have been good enough for arcade games of the 1980s, but they don't take advantage of today's faster machines. In this chapter, I'll examine a newer method of rendering polygons called *polygon-fill graphics*. With this technique, you can draw polygons as solid objects, improving the look of your objects significantly.

I'll also show you a method of storing objects on disk instead of defining them in your code. This will allow you to define objects a little easier and to use better memory management techniques.

Polygons

I'm about to start treating shapes a little differently. In fact, I'm going to do away with the concept of "shapes" and replace it with two new categories: polygons and objects. A *polygon* is a flat shape composed of three or more vertices. It is very important that the vertices of a polygon form a flat plane (a property known as *coplanar*).

An *object* consists of several connected polygons. It also contains a list of all of the vertices to be used by those polygons, similar to the Vertex3D list that a shape uses.

In the object and polygon structures, you're going to start using fixed-sized arrays instead of the pointers used in Chapters 9 and 10. This method does have a few disadvantages: You'll be wasting some memory and you'll have a little less freedom in how large you can make your objects; however, you will be able to allocate objects more easily. Only one pointer is needed for each object. Without fixed-sized arrays, 10 or more pointers could be allocated for every object. If you had a database of 100 objects (entirely conceivable in a flight simulator), you'd be using 1,000 pointers instead of the 100 that would be allocated using fixed-sized arrays. In the Macintosh memory environment, manipulating 1,000 pointers would slow everything down.

To use fixed arrays, you have to decide how many polygons and vertices an object can have and how many vertices can be in a polygon. For the next several chapters, I'll be using some values that will give you enough flexibility to create moderately complex objects: 50 vertices per object, 20 polygons per object, and 4 vertices per polygon. If you want to change these values, they are defined as constants in Objects.h in the Chapter 11 folder on the source code disc:

```
#define kMaximumVertices   50
#define kMaximumPolys       20
#define kMaxPolygonSize      4
```

Now let's take a look at the new polygon structure:

```
typedef struct {
        short                   numOfVertices;
        unsigned char           color;
        Vertex3D                *polyVertex[kMaxPolygonSize];
} Polygon3D;
```

The main thing to note about this structure is that you have an array of pointers to vertices. I'll discuss this feature shortly.

Here is the new object structure:

```
typedef struct {
  short         numOfVertices;
  short         numOfPolygons;
  short         originX, originY, originZ;
  Vertex3D      vertex[kMaximumVertices];
  Polygon3D     polygon[kMaximumPolys];
} Object3D;
```

The object stores both an array of vertices and an array of polygons. The polygons store an array of *pointers* to vertices. These point directly at specific vertices from the object's list, as illustrated in Figure 11-1.

This new method permits you to reference the polygon's vertices more efficiently. It also allows you to pass only the polygon into a function; because the polygon knows where its vertices are, the vertex list doesn't need to be passed separately.

FIGURE 11-1
◎ ◎ ◎ ◎ ◎ ◎
*A polygon
points directly
to the vertices it
uses*

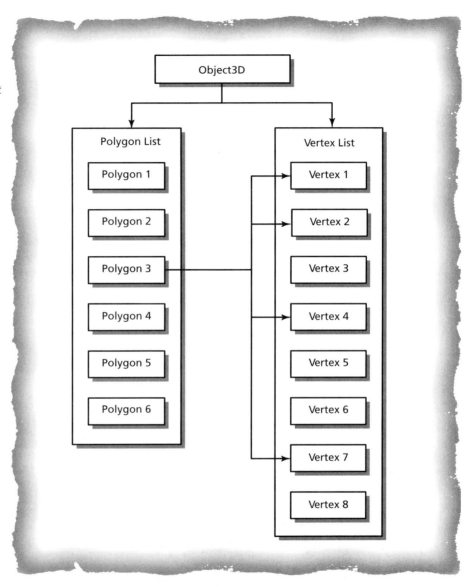

This object structure will consume 1,910 bytes for each object you define, or about 1.8 megabytes for a 1,000 object database. That's manageable, especially for developing a method of loading just the portions of the database from disk that you need at any given time.

Polygon-Fill Drawing

Drawing routines are designed to handle just polygons. A higher-level routine will take the objects, break them down into polygons, and pass them to the drawing routines. A polygon-drawing routine that can handle a polygon with any number of sides and any angles is extremely complex and not terribly fast, so it isn't well suited to a fast game. I'm going to put some restrictions on the polygons you'll be drawing to keep the drawing code at a reasonable complexity and speed.

The first restriction is that a polygon has to be *convex*. A convex polygon is one that has no internal angles greater than 180°, as opposed to a *concave* polygon. Figure 11-2 shows convex and concave polygons.

There is an easy way to determine whether a polygon is convex or concave. Attempt to draw a straight line through the polygon that touches more than two of its sides. If you are able to do this, the polygon is concave. If every line touches exactly two sides, the polygon is convex, and if any line touches only one side, you don't have a polygon (every vertex of a polygon must be connected to exactly two other vertices). Figure 11-3 shows three lines drawn through a concave polygon. Although two of the

FIGURE 11-2

◎ ◎ ◎ ◎ ◎ ◎

Convex (a) and concave (b) polygons

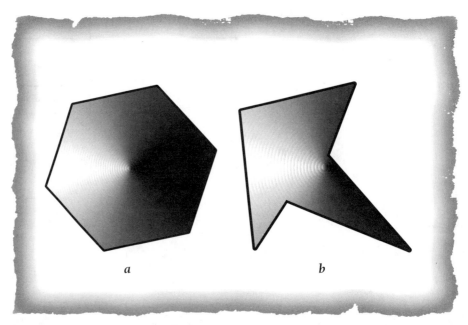

a   *b*

lines touch only two sides each, one of the lines touches four sides, indicating a concave polygon.

Because it is much more difficult to draw concave polygons, probably every 3D computer game in existence draws only convex polygons. In fact, many games limit themselves to drawing only triangles (which are *always* convex) because any possible shape can be approximated by drawing a number of triangles. Defining a polygon as a triangle also assures you that it is flat. I'm going to allow polygons to be defined using either three or four sides, so if you create any four-sided polygons, you must make sure to follow these rules.

By allowing only convex polygons, I'm not really limiting you—if you need a concave polygon, you can just define it as two or more convex polygons—Figure 11-4 shows the concave polygon from Figure 11-3 drawn as two convex polygons.

The second restriction is a little easier to get along with—every polygon must define its vertices counterclockwise. This rule allows the game to figure out which side of a polygon is on the *outside*. It can also make drawing a little easier, but it means that a polygon really has only one side—if you take a polygon and rotate it, you will only be able to see it when it's facing towards you. If you need a two-sided polygon, just define two polygons using the same vertices in reverse order.

The Polygon-Fill Algorithm

The algorithm you'll use for drawing polygons is based on Bresenham's line-drawing algorithm, which you used in the previous two chapters. Essentially, you'll be drawing the

FIGURE 11-3

◎ ◎ ◎ ◎ ◎ ◎

Testing to see if a polygon is concave

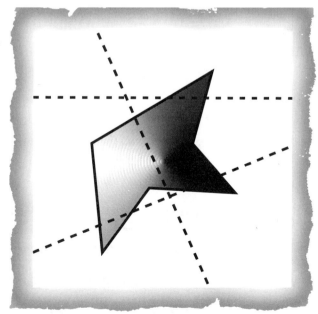

FIGURE 11-4

ⓞ ⓞ ⓞ ⓞ ⓞ ⓞ

Using two convex polygons to create a concave polygon

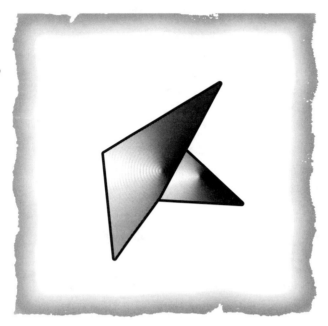

polygon as a wireframe, then filling in the space between the wires with horizontal lines. You'll use Bresenham's algorithm to figure out the starting and ending positions of each horizontal line, but the actual process of drawing the line is simple.

Here is an outline of the algorithm you'll use to draw the polygon (Figure 11-5 presents this process as a flowchart):

1. Determine which vertex is at the top of the polygon (i.e., has the smallest y coordinate).

2. Determine the next vertex to the right of the top vertex.

3. Determine the next vertex to the left of the top vertex.

4. Use Bresenham's algorithm to calculate the points on both lines.

5. Draw a horizontal line to connect each vertical increment on these lines.

6. Whenever a line ends at a vertex, find the next vertex to the left or right from that vertex and repeat steps 4 through 6.

7. Stop when the bottom of the polygon has been reached.

The Polygon-Fill Function

The function for drawing the polygon is called PolygonFillDrawPolygon() , which is a mouthful, but each of the polygon-rendering modes (including wireframe, which is now called WireframeDrawPolygon()) is named similarly and placed in PolygonRender.c.

FIGURE 11-5

◉ ◉ ◉ ◉ ◉ ◉

*The flowchart
for the polygon-
fill algorithm*

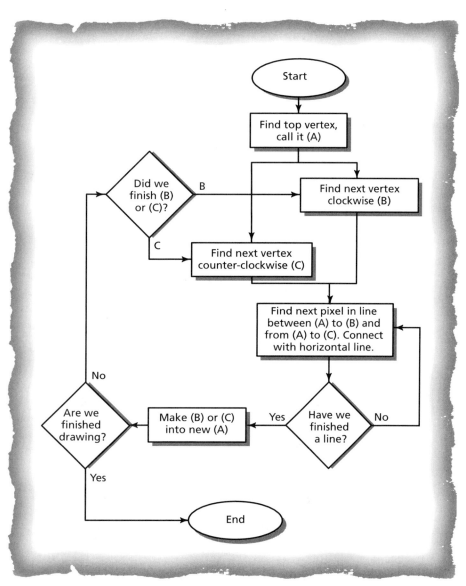

This allows you to switch between rendering modes easily and makes it possible for you to allow the user to set a preference as to his or her desired mode.

Preparation

The polygon-draw routine requires quite a few parameters. Many of the parameters are similar to those used in the wireframe routine in Chapter 10, but they have been doubled up, because you're going to be running two Bresenham line-drawing routines at once. Here are the variables specifically relating to the polygon sides:

```
short    dx1, dx2;      /* x length of sides */
short    dy1, dy2;      /* y length of sides */
short    topVertex;
short    edgeCount;      /* Edges remaining to draw */

/* These variables define which two segments (1 & 2) we're
 * drawing between. start1 and end1 are the starting and
 * ending indices of line #1, xStart1, yStart1, xEnd1,
 * and yEnd1 are the coordinates of line #1. Each of these
 * has a counterpart for line #2.
 */
short    start1, end1;
short    xStart1, yStart1;
short    xEnd1, yEnd1;
short    start2, end2;
short    xStart2, yStart2;
short    xEnd2, yEnd2;
```

More variables will be defined as you start working your way down the polygon, but you'll need these for setting it up. The variable to note at this point is *edgeCount*, which is the number of edges that remains to be drawn. At the beginning of the routine, this value is initialized to the number of vertices in the polygon:

```
edgeCount = polygon->numOfVertices;
```

The first step of the algorithm is to find out which vertex is on top (i.e., has the lowest y value). This is a relatively simple process that involves scanning each of its vertices:

```
/* Figure out which vertex is at the top of the polygon */
{
  short  minVertexY;

  /* Start by assuming the first vertex is on top */
  topVertex = 0;
  minVertexY = polygon->polyVertex[0]->sy;

  /* loop through all of the vertices */
  for (i = 1; i < polygon->numOfVertices; i++) {
    /* Check to see if this vertex is higher
     * than the current one.
     */
    if (polygon->polyVertex[i]->sy < minVertexY) {
      /* It is. Remember it for later */
      topVertex = i;
      minVertexY = polygon->polyVertex[i]->sy;
    }
  }
}
```

At this point, set the two lines to start at the top vertex. At the same time, put the vertex's coordinates into local variables so you can access them easily later on:

```
/* Find the starting and ending vertices for the first
 * two edges
 */
start1 = topVertex;
start2 = topVertex;  /* They both start from the same vertex */
xStart1 = polygon->polyVertex[start1]->sx;
yStart1 = polygon->polyVertex[start1]->sy;
xStart2 = polygon->polyVertex[start2]->sx;
yStart2 = polygon->polyVertex[start2]->sy;
```

The next step of the algorithm is to grab the vertices to the right and left of the top vertex (the terms *right* and *left* are not used literally here—because the polygon is defined in a counterclockwise fashion, the right vertex is obtained by looking at the top vertex minus one, and the left vertex is obtained by adding one):

```
/* Get the end of vertex 1 - check for wrap */
end1 = start1 - 1;
if (end1 < 0)
  end1 = polygon->numOfVertices - 1;
xEnd1 = polygon->polyVertex[end1]->sx;
yEnd1 = polygon->polyVertex[end1]->sy;

/* Get the end of vertex 2 */
end2 = start2 + 1;
if (end2 == polygon->numOfVertices)
  end2 = 0;
xEnd2 = polygon->polyVertex[end2]->sx;
yEnd2 = polygon->polyVertex[end2]->sy;
```

Scanning from Top to Bottom

The setup is now done and you're ready to start working your way down the polygon. Because you're going to repeat this loop until you're out of edges to draw, a *while* loop is handy here:

```
while (edgeCount > 0) {  /* Draw until we're out of edges.*/
```

You need several more variables to handle the scanning. Many of these variables determine which direction you're drawing and how to get to the next pixel of the line. They also include two *errorTerm* values from Bresenham's algorithm:

```
short    errorTerm1, errorTerm2;
long     pixelOffset1, pixelOffset2;
short    xUnit1, yUnit1;
short    xUnit2, yUnit2;
```

Continued on next page

Continued from previous page

```
short     count1, count2;
short     length;
long      lineStart, lineEnd;
```

Some of these new variables need to be initialized now. Set up the two pixelOffset values, both of which are offsets into the pixmap. Also initialize the error terms to 0:

```
/* Set up the offsets for both edges */
pixelOffset1 = (rowBytes * yStart1) + xStart1;
pixelOffset2 = (rowBytes * yStart2) + xStart2;

/* Initialize error terms */
errorTerm1 = errorTerm2 = 0;
```

The next step is to find the lengths of the two line segments, which you'll store in dx and dy. If dx is negative, the line is moving to the left. In this case, make dx positive and set *xUnit* to -1 (otherwise, it's set to 1). Now whenever you need to change the x coordinate of the line, just add *xUnit* to it.

Because you're working your way down the polygon, dy can only be positive, so there's no need to negate it.

```
/* If the line is going to the left, set the
 * xUnit to -1 and make dx positive
 */
if (dx1 < 0) {
  dx1 = -dx1;
  xUnit1 = -1;
} else {
  xUnit1 = 1;
}

/* Do the same for edge 2 */
dx2 = xEnd2 - xStart2;
if (dx2 < 0) {
  dx2 = -dx2;
  xUnit2 = -1;
} else {
  xUnit2 = 1;
}

/* Find the y length of the edges */
dy1 = yEnd1 - yStart1;
yUnit1 = rowBytes;

dy2 = yEnd2 - yStart2;
yUnit2 = rowBytes;
```

Drawing the Edges

The actual drawing of the edges is the tricky part. When drawing a line with Bresenham's algorithm, you have two distinct possibilities: The line can have a slope greater than or less than 1 and the algorithm can have a separate code snippet to handle each case. In the polygon routine, you can have four cases because you have two lines (see Table 11-1).

	Edge 1	Edge 2
Case #1	Slope < 1	Slope < 1
Case #2	Slope < 1	Slope >= 1
Case #3	Slope >= 1	Slope < 1
Case #4	Slope >= 1	Slope >= 1

TABLE 11-1 ❖ *Line Slopes in the polygon routine*

Handling all four cases is what makes the code so large—a significant part of each case is duplicated. I'm only going to examine one of the cases here, because the principles involved in all four sections can be seen in one. Let's take a look at case 2, where edge 1 has a slope less than 1 and edge 2 has a slope greater than or equal to 1.

Counting Off the Pixels

To begin with, you'll need to count off the pixels so you know when you are finished with one of the edges. The number of pixels to be plotted is simply the difference between the starting and ending coordinates in the dimension you're incrementing. If you're incrementing on the x coordinate, it will be the x difference. If you're incrementing in the y coordinate, it will be the y difference. In the example I've chosen, it will be both the x difference for edge 1 and the y difference for edge 2:

```
/* Increment edge 1 on x and edge 2 on y.*/
count1 = dx1;
count2 = dy2;
```

This segment of code will continue executing until one or both of these edges has finished, so the actual drawing will be done in a *while* loop:

```
/* Draw until one of the edges is done */
while (count1 && count2) {
```

Now let's find the next point on edge 1 so you can draw a horizontal line from that point to the next point on edge 2. This maneuver is a bit tricky because edge 1 is being incremented on the x coordinate. This means the x coordinate can be incremented several times before the y coordinate is incremented, which makes it difficult to determine exactly when you should draw the horizontal line. If you draw it every time the x coordinate is incremented, you may end up drawing several horizontal lines on top of each other, which would waste a lot of time. Instead, continue incrementing the x coordinate until it is time to increment the y coordinate and then draw the horizontal line from edge 1 to edge 2.

But what if you're dealing with the left edge and x is being incremented in the positive (right) direction? If you wait until the y coordinate is about to be incremented, you'll miss a few pixels on the edge of the polygon. To guard against this possibility, set a pixel every time the x coordinate is incremented. When you draw the horizontal line, you may well draw over the top of these pixels, but the redundancy will be minor (however, it is a place to remember when you try to optimize this routine).

Looping until y Increments

The upshot of all this is that you will be calculating the next point (or points) on edge 1 in a loop that will continue until the y coordinate is about to be incremented. The y coordinate is incremented when the value of *errorTerm1* is greater than or equal to dx1, so make this condition the criterion for terminating the loop:

```
while ((errorTerm1 < dx1) && (count1 > 0)) {
```

Then subtract 1 from *count1* (indicating that you just incremented x). After that, position yourself at the next pixel by adding *xOffset1* to both *pixelOffset1* and *xStart1*:

```
count1--;  /* Count off this pixel */
pixelOffset1 += xUnit1;  /* Point to next pixel */
xStart1 += xUnit1;
```

To determine whether it's time to increment the y coordinate, add dy1 to *errorTerm1*. If it's not time yet to draw the horizontal line, plot a pixel:

```
/* Increase the error term */
errorTerm1 += dy1;

/* Check to see if we're ready to move in y */
if (errorTerm1 < dx1) {
  /* Nope, we're not ready yet. Plot a pixel for
   * this line
   */
  pixMapPtr[pixelOffset1] = polygon->color;
 }
}
```

When the innermost *while* loop finishes, it's time to increment the y coordinate of edge 1, which means that *errorTerm1* must be reset so the process can start over again. As in Bresenham's algorithm, this is done by subtracting dx1:

```
/* Reset the error term.*/
errorTerm1 -= dx1;
```

That's it for edge 1—at least for now. Now it's time to deal with edge 2. Because you're working with case 2, edge 2 is being incremented on the y coordinate, which is actually a little easier. You don't need to worry about missing any pixels when you draw the horizontal line. Incrementing edge 2 is simply a matter of adding dx2 to *errorTerm2* and checking to see if it's time to move in the x coordinate yet. If it is, reset *errorTerm2* and add *xUnit2* to *pixelOffset2* and *xStart2*. Finally, decrement *count2* to indicate you've moved down one line and continue to the routine that draws the horizontal line:

```
errorTerm2 += dx2;  /* Increment error term */

/* Check to see if it's time to move in the x
 * direction. If so, reset the error term
 * and increment the pixelOffset
 */
if (errorTerm2 >= dy2) {
  errorTerm2 -= dy2;
  pixelOffset2 += xUnit2;
  xStart2 += xUnit2;
}
count2--;
```

Drawing the Line

Now it's time to draw the horizontal line between edge 1 and edge 2. This is perhaps the easiest part of the entire algorithm. The first thing to do is figure out the starting and ending pixels of the line and then use a *for()* loop to draw the line:

```
/* Draw a line from edge 1 to edge 2.
 * Find the length of the line:
 */
length = pixelOffset2 - pixelOffset1;
if (length < 0) {  /* If negative... */
  length = -length;  /* make it positive */
  lineStart = pixelOffset2;
  lineEnd = pixelOffset1;
} else {
  lineStart = pixelOffset1;
  lineEnd = pixelOffset2;
}

for (i = lineStart; i <= lineEnd; i++) {
  pixMapPtr[i] = polygon->color;
}
```

Now that the line has been drawn, advance the two offset variables to the next line so you can start everything over again. To do so, add the *rowBytes* value (*yUnit1* and *yUnit2*) to the offset and 1 to the *yStart* values:

```
/* Advance to next line */
pixelOffset1 += yUnit1;
yStart1++;
pixelOffset2 += yUnit2;
yStart2++;
```

Moving to the Remaining Edges

At this point, one or both of the segments has run out of lines to draw, so you need to give the routine the next segment (or terminate if all of the segments have been drawn). First check to see whether edge 1 has terminated:

```
/* An edge is done. Start another edge, if there are any remaining.*/
if (count1 == 0) {
```

If so, decrement *edgeCount*:

```
/* Edge 1 is complete. Decrement the edgecount.*/
 edgeCount--;
```

Then turn the ending vertex of edge 1 into the starting vertex:

```
/* Make the ending vertex into the starting vertex.*/
start1 = end1;
```

Now grab a new ending vertex by subtracting 1 and checking for wrap:

```
/* Get a new ending vertex.*/
end1 -= 1;

/* Check to see if this vertex wraps to the beginning.*/
if (end1 < 0) {
  end1 = polygon->numOfVertices-1;
}
```

As you did at the beginning of the routine, you need to fill in the *xEnd* and *yEnd* fields for this edge:

```
/* Get the x & y of the new ending vertex */
xEnd1 = polygon->polyVertex[end1]->sx;
yEnd1 = polygon->polyVertex[end1]->sy;
```

You don't have to get the *xStart* and *yStart* values because, in drawing the line, they've already been set to the proper values.

The edge checking is repeated for the second edge, after which the algorithm goes back to the start of its main loop. When *edgeCount* reaches 0, the function terminates.

The Complete Function

Listing 11-1 is the polygon-fill routine in its entirety.

Listing 11-1 *The polygon-fill routine*

```
/**
 **   PolygonFillDrawPolygon()
 **
 **   Draw a polygon with a solid color
 **/
void  PolygonFillDrawPolygon(   Polygon3D       *polygon,
                                Ptr             pixMapPtr,
                                unsigned long   rowBytes  )
{
  long      i;
  short     dx1, dx2;     /* x length of sides */
  short     dy1, dy2;     /* y length of sides */
  short     topVertex;
  short     edgeCount;    /* Edges remaining to draw */

  /* These variables define which two segments (1 & 2) we're
   * drawing between. start1 and end1 are the starting and
   * ending indices of line #1, xStart1, yStart1, xEnd1,
   * and yEnd1 are the coordinates of line #1. Each of these
   * has a counterpart for line #2.
   */
  short     start1, end1;
  short     xStart1, yStart1;
  short     xEnd1, yEnd1;
  short     start2, end2;
  short     xStart2, yStart2;
  short     xEnd2, yEnd2;

  edgeCount = polygon->numOfVertices;

  /* Figure out which vertex is at the top of the polygon */
  {
    short  minVertexY;

    /* Start by assuming the first vertex is on top */
    topVertex = 0;
    minVertexY = polygon->polyVertex[0]->sy;

    /* loop through all of the vertices */
    for (i = 1; i < polygon->numOfVertices; i++) {
      /* Check to see if this vertex is higher
```

Continued on next page

Continued from previous page

```
           * than the current one.
           */
         if (polygon->polyVertex[i]->sy < minVertexY) {
           /* It is. Remember it for later */
           topVertex = i;
           minVertexY = polygon->polyVertex[i]->sy;
         }
       }
     }

     /* Find the starting and ending vertices for the first
      * two edges
      */
     start1 = topVertex;
     start2 = topVertex;   /* They both start from the same vertex */
     xStart1 = polygon->polyVertex[start1]->sx;
     yStart1 = polygon->polyVertex[start1]->sy;
     xStart2 = polygon->polyVertex[start2]->sx;
     yStart2 = polygon->polyVertex[start2]->sy;

     /* Get the end of vertex 1 - check for wrap */
     end1 = start1 - 1;
     if (end1 < 0)
       end1 = polygon->numOfVertices - 1;
     xEnd1 = polygon->polyVertex[end1]->sx;
     yEnd1 = polygon->polyVertex[end1]->sy;

     /* Get the end of vertex 2 */
     end2 = start2 + 1;
     if (end2 == polygon->numOfVertices)
       end2 = 0;
     xEnd2 = polygon->polyVertex[end2]->sx;
     yEnd2 = polygon->polyVertex[end2]->sy;

     /* Our setup is done. Start the drawing */

     while (edgeCount > 0) {  /* Draw until we're out of edges */
       short    errorTerm1, errorTerm2;
       long     pixelOffset1, pixelOffset2;
       short    xUnit1, yUnit1;
       short    xUnit2, yUnit2;
       short    count1, count2;
       short    length;
       long     lineStart, lineEnd;

       /* Set up the offsets for both edges */
       pixelOffset1 = (rowBytes * yStart1) + xStart1;
       pixelOffset2 = (rowBytes * yStart2) + xStart2;

       /* Initialize error terms */
       errorTerm1 = errorTerm2 = 0;
```

```
/* If the line is going to the left, set the
 * xUnit to -1 and make dx positive
 */
if (dx1 < 0) {
  dx1 = -dx1;
  xUnit1 = -1;
} else {
  xUnit1 = 1;
}

/* Do the same for edge 2 */
dx2 = xEnd2 - xStart2;
if (dx2 < 0) {
  dx2 = -dx2;
  xUnit2 = -1;
} else {
  xUnit2 = 1;
}

/* Find the y length of the edges */
dy1 = yEnd1 - yStart1;
yUnit1 = rowBytes;

dy2 = yEnd2 - yStart2;
yUnit2 = rowBytes;

/* Use one of four different methods for drawing between
 * these edges
 */
if (dx1 > dy1) {  /* Edge 1 slope is < 1 */
  if (dx2 > dy2) {  /* Case 1 */
    /* Edge 2 slope is < 1 */
    /* Figure out how many pixels to draw in each edge */
    count1 = dx1;
    count2 = dx2;

    /* Draw until one of the edges is done */
    while (count1 && count2) {
      /* Draw the wireframe portion of the line
       * until we're ready to jump down a pixel
       */

      while ((errorTerm1 < dx1) && (count1 > 0)) {
        count1--;   /* Count off this pixel */
        pixelOffset1 += xUnit1;  /* Point to next pixel */
        xStart1 += xUnit1;

        /* Increase the error term */
        errorTerm1 += dy1;

        /* Check to see if we're ready to move in y */
        if (errorTerm1 < dx1) {
```

Continued on next page

Continued from previous page

```
                /* Nope, we're not ready yet. Plot a pixel for
                 * this line
                 */
                pixMapPtr[pixelOffset1] = polygon->color;
          }
        }
        /* Reset the error term */
        errorTerm1 -= dx1;

        /* Now do the same thing to edge 2 */

        while ((errorTerm2 < dx2) && (count2 > 0)) {
          count2--;        /* Count off this pixel */
          pixelOffset2 += xUnit2;  /* Point to next pixel */
          xStart2 += xUnit2;

          /* Increase the error term */
          errorTerm2 += dy2;

          /* Are we ready to move in y? */
          if (errorTerm2 < dx2) {
            /* We're not ready yet. Plot a pixel */
            pixMapPtr[pixelOffset2] = polygon->color;
          }
        }

        /* Reset the error term */
        errorTerm2 -= dx2;

        /* Draw the line from edge 1 to edge 2 */

        length = pixelOffset2 - pixelOffset1;
        if (length < 0) {  /* If negative... */
          length = -length;  /* make it positive */
          lineStart = pixelOffset2;
          lineEnd = pixelOffset1;
        } else {
          lineStart = pixelOffset1;
          lineEnd = pixelOffset2;
        }

        for (i = lineStart; i <= lineEnd; i++) {
          pixMapPtr[i] = polygon->color;
        }

        /* Advance to next line */
        pixelOffset1 += yUnit1;
        yStart1++;
        pixelOffset2 += yUnit2;
        yStart2++;
      }
    } else {  /* Case 2 */
      /* Edge 2 slope is >= 1 */
```

```
/* Increment edge 1 on x and edge 2 on y */
count1 = dx1;
count2 = dy2;

/* Draw until one of the edges is done */
while (count1 && count2) {
  /* Draw the wireframe portion of the line
   * until we're ready to jump down a pixel
   */

  while ((errorTerm1 < dx1) && (count1 > 0)) {
    count1--;  /* Count off this pixel */
    pixelOffset1 += xUnit1;  /* Point to next pixel */
    xStart1 += xUnit1;

    /* Increase the error term */
    errorTerm1 += dy1;

    /* Check to see if we're ready to move in y */
    if (errorTerm1 < dx1) {
      /* Nope, we're not ready yet. Plot a pixel for
       * this line
       */
      pixMapPtr[pixelOffset1] = polygon->color;
    }
  }
  /* Reset the error term */
  errorTerm1 -= dx1;

  /* Now handle edge 2 */

  errorTerm2 += dx2;  /* Increment error term */

  /* Check to see if it's time to move in the x
   * direction. If so, reset the error term
   * and increment the pixelOffset
   */
  if (errorTerm2 >= dy2) {
    errorTerm2 -= dy2;
    pixelOffset2 += xUnit2;
    xStart2 += xUnit2;
  }
  count2--;

  /* Draw a line from edge 1 to edge 2.
   * Find the length of the line:
   */
  length = pixelOffset2 - pixelOffset1;
  if (length < 0) {  /* If negative... */
    length = -length;  /* make it positive */
    lineStart = pixelOffset2;
    lineEnd = pixelOffset1;
```

Continued on next page

Continued from previous page

```
          } else {
            lineStart = pixelOffset1;
            lineEnd = pixelOffset2;
          }

          for (i = lineStart; i <= lineEnd; i++) {
            pixMapPtr[i] = polygon->color;
          }

          /* Advance to next line */
          pixelOffset1 += yUnit1;
          yStart1++;
          pixelOffset2 += yUnit2;
          yStart2++;
        }
      }
    } else{
      /* Edge 1 slope is >= 1 */
      if (dx2 > dy2) {  /* Case 3 */
        /* Edge 2 slope is < 1 */

        /* Increment edge 1 on y and edge 2 on x */
        count1 = dy1;
        count2 = dx2;

        /* Draw until one edge is done */
        while (count1 && count2) {
          /* Process edge 1 */

          /* Initialize edge 1 errorterm */
          errorTerm1 += dx1;

          /* If it's time to move in the x dimension, reset
           * error term and move offset to the next pixel
           */
          if (errorTerm1 >= dy1) {
            errorTerm1 -= dy1;
            pixelOffset1 += xUnit1;
            xStart1 += xUnit1;
          }

          count1--;

          /* Handle the second edge */

          while ((errorTerm2 < dx2) && (count2 > 0)) {
            count2--;       /* Count off this pixel */
            pixelOffset2 += xUnit2;  /* Point to next pixel */
            xStart2 += xUnit2;

            /* Increase the error term */
            errorTerm2 += dy2;
```

```
                /* Are we ready to move in y? */
                if (errorTerm2 <= dx2) {
                  /* We're not ready yet. Plot a pixel */
                  pixMapPtr[pixelOffset2] = polygon->color;
                }
              }

              /* Reset the error term */
              errorTerm2 -= dx2;

              /* Draw the line from edge 1 to edge 2 */
              length = pixelOffset2 - pixelOffset1;
              if (length < 0) {  /* If negative... */
                length = -length;  /* make it positive */
                lineStart = pixelOffset2;
                lineEnd = pixelOffset1;
              } else {
                lineStart = pixelOffset1;
                lineEnd = pixelOffset2;
              }

              for (i = lineStart; i <= lineEnd; i++) {
                pixMapPtr[i] = polygon->color;
              }

              /* Advance to next line */
              pixelOffset1 += yUnit1;
              yStart1++;
              pixelOffset2 += yUnit2;
              yStart2++;
            }
          } else {  /* Case 4 */
            /* Edge 2 slope >= 1. Increment edge 1
             * and edge 2 on y
             */
            count1 = dy1;
            count2 = dy2;

            /* Draw until one edge is done */

            while (count1 && count2) {
              /* Handle edge 1 */

              /* Initialize edge 1 errorterm */
              errorTerm1 += dx1;

              /* If it's time to move in the x dimension, reset
               * error term and move offset to the next pixel
               */
              if (errorTerm1 >= dy1) {
                errorTerm1 -= dy1;
                pixelOffset1 += xUnit1;
```

Continued on next page

Continued from previous page

```
            xStart1 += xUnit1;
        }

        count1--;

        /* Now handle edge 2 */

        errorTerm2 += dx2;    /* Increment error term */

        /* Check to see if it's time to move in the x
         * direction. If so, reset the error term
         * and increment the pixelOffset
         */
        if (errorTerm2 >= dy2) {
          errorTerm2 -= dy2;
          pixelOffset2 += xUnit2;
          xStart2 += xUnit2;
        }
        count2--;

        /* Draw a line from edge 1 to edge 2.
         * Find the length of the line:
         */
        length = pixelOffset2 - pixelOffset1;
        if (length < 0) {  /* If negative... */
          length = -length;  /* make it positive */
          lineStart = pixelOffset2;
          lineEnd = pixelOffset1;
        } else {
          lineStart = pixelOffset1;
          lineEnd = pixelOffset2;
        }
        for (i = lineStart; i <= lineEnd; i++) {
          pixMapPtr[i] = polygon->color;
        }

        /* Advance to next line */
        pixelOffset1 += yUnit1;
        yStart1++;
        pixelOffset2 += yUnit2;
        yStart2++;
      }
    }
  }

  /* An edge is done. Start another edge, if there are any remaining */
  if (count1 == 0) {
    /* Edge 1 is complete. Decrement the edgecount */
    edgeCount--;

    /* Make the ending vertex into the starting vertex */
    start1 = end1;
```

```
            /* Get a new ending vertex */
            end1 -= 1;

            /* Check to see if this vertex wraps to the beginning */
            if (end1 < 0) {
              end1 = polygon->numOfVertices-1;
            }

            /* Get the x & y of the new ending vertex */
            xEnd1 = polygon->polyVertex[end1]->sx;
            yEnd1 = polygon->polyVertex[end1]->sy;
          }

        if (count2 == 0) {
          /* Edge 2 is complete. Decrement the edge count */
          edgeCount -= 1;

          /* Make ending vertex 2 into starting vertex 2 */
          start2 = end2;

          /* Get a new ending vertex */
          end2++;

          /* Check to see if this vertex wraps to the beginning */
          if (end2 == polygon->numOfVertices) {
            end2 = 0;
          }

          /* Get the x & y of new ending vertex */
          xEnd2 = polygon->polyVertex[end2]->sx;
          yEnd2 = polygon->polyVertex[end2]->sy;
        }
      }
    }
```

3D Object Routines

Because you have redesigned the object structure, you'll need to make some modifications to the existing routines for transforming, projecting, and drawing objects. All these altered routines are in a file called Objects.c in the Chapter 11 folder on the source code disc.

For most of the routines, the changes are simple; merely substitute Object3D for Shape3D and rename a few of the fields. Other routines must be more heavily modified because the polygons are directly pointing to their vertices.

Because they don't directly modify any part of the objects, the matrix routines are entirely unchanged.

TransformObject3D()

The object transformation routine hasn't changed much (Listing 11-2). Mainly, it has been renamed to TransformObject3D() and it now takes an Object3D as parameter.

Listing 11-2 *The TransformObject3D() routine*

```
/**
**   TransformObject3D()
**
**   Takes a object's local coordinates and transforms them
**   with the provided transformation matrix, placing
**   the result in the tx,ty,tz, and tt fields of the
**   vertices.
**/
void  TransformObject3D(  Object3D  *theObject,
                          float     transformMatrix[4][4]  )
{
  short   i;
  short   numOfVertices;

  numOfVertices = theObject->numOfVertices;

  /* Transform the object's vertices with the matrix */
  for (i = 0; i < numOfVertices; i++) {
    /* Declare some temporary variables */
    short    temp0, temp1, temp2, temp3;
    Vertex3D *vertexRef;

    /* Get a pointer to the current vertice */
    vertexRef = &theObject->vertex[i];

    /* Multiply against the matrix */
    temp0 = vertexRef->lx * transformMatrix[0][0] +
            vertexRef->ly * transformMatrix[1][0] +
            vertexRef->lz * transformMatrix[2][0] +
            transformMatrix[3][0];

    temp1 = vertexRef->lx * transformMatrix[0][1] +
            vertexRef->ly * transformMatrix[1][1] +
            vertexRef->lz * transformMatrix[2][1] +
            transformMatrix[3][1];

    temp2 = vertexRef->lx * transformMatrix[0][2] +
            vertexRef->ly * transformMatrix[1][2] +
            vertexRef->lz * transformMatrix[2][2] +
            transformMatrix[3][2];

    temp3 = vertexRef->lx * transformMatrix[0][3] +
            vertexRef->ly * transformMatrix[1][3] +
```

```
        vertexRef->lz * transformMatrix[2][3] +
        transformMatrix[3][3];


    /* Put the results into the vector's
     * transformed coordinates
     */
    vertexRef->tx = temp0;
    vertexRef->ty = temp1;
    vertexRef->tz = temp2;
    vertexRef->tt = temp3;
  }
}
```

ObjectToWorldCoordinates()

The routine that translates an object into world coordinates hasn't changed much either. It now takes an Object3D as input instead of a Shape3D:

```
/**
 **   ObjectToWorldCoordinates()
 **
 **   Translates an object from its transformed coordinates
 **   to world coordinates.
 **/
void  ObjectToWorldCoordinates(Object3D  *theObject)
{
  short     i;
  short     objectOriginX, objectOriginY, objectOriginZ;
  Vertex3D  *vertexRef;

  /* Copy the shape's origin coordinates into local variables
   * for speed and code clarity
   */
  objectOriginX = theObject->originX;
  objectOriginY = theObject->originY;
  objectOriginZ = theObject->originZ;

  for (i = 0; i < theObject->numOfVertices; i++) {
    /* Obtain a pointer to the current vertex. This allows
     * us to reference this particular vertex more efficiently,
     * instead of indexing through the shape vertex array each
     * time.
     */
    vertexRef = &theObject->vertex[i];

    vertexRef->wx = vertexRef->tx + objectOriginX;
    vertexRef->wy = vertexRef->ty + objectOriginY;
    vertexRef->wz = vertexRef->tz + objectOriginZ;
  }
}
```

ProjectObject()

ProjectObject() is the last routine from Objects.c that has changed. Like the two previous routines, it now takes an Object3D as input:

```
/**
 **   ProjectObject()
 **
 **   Converts each vertex of an object to screen coordinates. The
 **   object must be in world coordinates before calling this function.
 **/
void  ProjectObject(Object3D *theObject)
{
  Vertex3D    *vertexRef;
  short       i;

  /* We don't need to pay any attention to what order the vertices
   * are connected, since that's irrelevant for projection.
   */
  for (i = 0; i < theObject->numOfVertices; i++)
  {
    /* Obtain a pointer to the current vertex. This allows
     * us to reference this particular vertex more efficiently,
     * instead of indexing through the shape vertex array each
     * time.
     */
    vertexRef = &theObject->vertex[i];

    /* Project the vertex */
    vertexRef->sx = (vertexRef->wx * kDistanceConstant) / vertexRef->wz;
    vertexRef->sy = (vertexRef->wy * kDistanceConstant) / vertexRef->wz;

    /* Translate the vertex to screen coordinates */
    vertexRef->sx += kHalfWindowWidth;
    vertexRef->sy += kHalfWindowHeight;
  }
}
```

Object Drawing

I mentioned earlier that there is a new way of drawing objects. With the new method, an object is passed to a routine called DrawObject(), along with a constant to indicate which method to use for rendering it. DrawObject() then breaks the object down into polygons and calls the proper routine for rendering. This allows you to mix different rendering modes in the same scene or to change modes on the fly.

When drawing an object, you must take something else into consideration. Any solid object at any one time will, on the average, have about half its polygons facing *away* from the user because they are on the back side of the object. These polygons are called *backface polygons* and they don't need to be drawn. In fact, if they were drawn, they would mess up the frontfacing polygons, unless you had a way of ensuring the backfacing polygons were drawn first.

This problem is a part of a larger issue called *hidden surface removal*, a major consideration in three-dimensional graphics. In fact, it is so important that an entire chapter of this book (Chapter 15) is devoted to it. For now, I'll look at how to deal with backfacing polygons (which is all I'll need to do until you start having multiple objects in your scenes).

Backface Removal

The direction that a polygon is facing can be determined by running the polygon through a formula based on its *cross product* and *dot product* (both algebraic equations that are applied to vectors). This formula is entirely dependent on the fact that you're defining objects in a counterclockwise fashion. If the result is less than zero, the polygon faces you; if it is greater than zero, it faces away.

```
/**
 **   BackfacePolygon()
 **
 **   Processes a polygon and finds out whether it is facing towards
 **   the screen or away. Returns TRUE if it is facing away (which means
 **   don't draw it), or FALSE if it is facing the screen.
 **/
Boolean  BackfacePolygon(Polygon3D *thePolygon)
{
  Vertex3D  *v0,*v1,*v2;
  long      x1, x2, x3, y1, y2, y3, z1, z2, z3;
  long      c;

  /* Get pointers to the first three vertices of the polygon */
  v0 = thePolygon->polyVertex[0];
  v1 = thePolygon->polyVertex[1];
  v2 = thePolygon->polyVertex[2];

  /* Pull out the individual terms of the vertices and convert
   * them to longwords.
   */
  x1 = v0->wx; x2 = v1->wx; x3 = v2->wx;
  y1 = v0->wy; y2 = v1->wy; y3 = v2->wy;
  z1 = v0->wz; z2 = v1->wz; z3 = v2->wz;

  /* Calculate the dot product of the polygon */
  c=(  x3 * ((z1 * y2) - (y1 * z2)) +
       y3 * ((x1 * z2) - (z1 * x2)) +
       z3 * ((y1 * x2) - (x1 * y2)));

  /* If c is positive, the polygon is facing away from the screen */
```

Continued on next page

Continued from previous page

```
  if (c > 0)
    return TRUE;
  else
    return FALSE;
}
```

DrawObject()

The DrawObject() routine checks to see if a polygon is backfacing. If it isn't, the polygon will be drawn using the specified rendering method. The polygon is dispatched using a switch() statement, allowing you to easily add more rendering methods later.

```
/**
**   DrawObject()
**
**   Draws an object using one of the available rendering modes.
**/
void  DrawObject( Object3D      *object,
                  short         renderingMode,
                  Ptr           pixMapPtr,
                  unsigned long rowBytes )
{
  short      numOfPolygons;
  short      currentPolygon;
  Polygon3D  *polyRef;

  numOfPolygons = object->numOfPolygons;

  /* Loop through each polygon */
  for (  currentPolygon = 0;
         currentPolygon < numOfPolygons;
         currentPolygon++) {
    /* Get a pointer to the current polygon */
    polyRef = &object->polygon[currentPolygon];

    /* If this polygon is backfacing, don't draw it.
     */
    if (!BackfacePolygon(polyRef)) {

      /* Figure out what rendering mode to use for this polygon */
      switch (renderingMode) {

        case kRender_Wireframe:  /* Wireframe rendering */
          WireframeDrawPolygon(polyRef, pixMapPtr, rowBytes);
          break;

        case kRender_PolygonFill:
          PolygonFillDrawPolygon(polyRef, pixMapPtr, rowBytes);
          break;
      }
    }
  }
}
```

Wireframe Object Drawing

Because you worked so hard to get your original wireframe object, I'm not going to toss out wireframe rendering as one of your choices (as you can see in the DrawObject() routine). The wireframe-drawing routine has to go through some larger changes to handle the new Object3D structure because the polygons now have access to their vertices, but it is still a simple routine:

```
/**
 ** WireframeDrawPolygon()
 **
 ** Draws a polygon, using the Bresenham line-drawing routine,
 ** onto the provided pixmap
 **/
void  WireframeDrawPolygon(  Polygon3D      *polygon,
                            Ptr            pixMapPtr,
                            unsigned long  rowBytes  )
{
  short    i, p2;

  /* Loop through each vertex in the shape: */
  for (i = 0; i < polygon->numOfVertices; i++)
  {
    Vertex3D  *beginVertex;
    Vertex3D  *endVertex;

    /* Find the index of the next vertex, looping around
     * to the beginning if you have to
     */
    p2 = i+1;

    if (p2 >= polygon->numOfVertices)
      p2 = 0;

    /* Get pointers to the beginning and ending vertices */
    beginVertex = polygon->polyVertex[i];
    endVertex = polygon->polyVertex[p2];

    /* Draw this line */
    BresenhamLine( beginVertex->sx,
                   beginVertex->sy,
                   endVertex->sx,
                   endVertex->sy,
                   pixMapPtr,
                   rowBytes,
                   polygon->color );
  }
}
```

Defining Objects

The only step that remains to have a solid polygon object on the screen is the actual definition of the object. In Chapters 9 and 10, you defined the object by hand in the code; but with every revision of the shape structure, you had to add more fields (most of which you didn't really need to define at that point). It would be tedious at best to define 1,000 objects for a flight simulator in that fashion, and if you had to change the object structure after they all had been created it would be utterly disastrous. It would also be inefficient to define them as globals in the code because they would be occupying space on the stack instead of on the heap, where data belongs.

For these reasons, I'm going to create a new method of storing objects. They are going to be stored in resources on disk, where you can load them as needed and easily change them without affecting code (you can also change the object structure without hurting the objects).

The objects will not be stored on disk the same way they are in memory. There are several reasons for this: First, you don't have to store everything on disk that you need in memory; for example, you don't need to store the transformed or world coordinate fields of each vertex because these values are generated on the fly. The second reason is that you can change the object format without affecting the objects you've already created. The final reason is that different computers align data differently.

Before I go on, let me clarify the last point. The 68k line of processors functions most efficiently when you access data that is aligned on 2-byte boundaries. This means that reading a longword from memory location 0x1000 is going to takes less time than reading it from memory location 0x1001 (in fact, on the 68000 processor, reading from odd addresses generates an error). On the 68k processor, your compiler will align all of its structures so their components fit within 2-byte boundaries. For example, look at the following structure:

```
typedef struct {
  char    aByte;
  long    aLongword;
} myStruct;
```

A compiler would set up this structure so that *aByte* would have an offset of 0, but *aLongword* would be located 2 bytes into the structure. This means that, even though you defined the first field to take 1 byte of space, the compiler has allocated 2 bytes.

On the PowerPC processor, 2-byte boundaries are no longer used—The PowerPC is optimized to access memory on 4-byte boundaries. So for the structure you just looked at, 4 bytes would be allocated for *aByte*.

The effect of this change is completely transparent to the programmer. All you have to do is access the structure directly (e.g., myStruct.aByte or myStruct.aLongword). The compiler will figure out what to do.

These behaviors only start to become a problem when you begin to save structures directly to disk. If you save the myStruct structure to a resource on a 68k machine and then read it in on a PowerPC, the fields would be completely messed up—the data for *aLongword* would begin 2 bytes into the structure instead of 4 bytes, as the PowerPC expects.

There are a few ways around this. First, you can tell the compiler to define its PowerPC structures as it would on a 68k, with 2-byte boundaries. Although this works, it generates a huge performance penalty for the PowerPC chip, especially on the 603 and later.

The second method is to tell the 68k compiler to generate structures as though it were a PowerPC, that is, with 4-byte boundaries. This works fine, with no performance penalty on either side (except that the 68k version will use a little more memory than it used to, but that's no big deal). This isn't the *best* solution, however, because what happens if Apple introduces a machine in the future that performs best on an *8-byte* boundary?

The best solution is to not save these structures directly to disk. Instead, when reading or writing the structure, process each field one at a time. For your code, you only have to worry about reading data, so you'll read in a structure from disk (which has *not* been aligned to any particular processor's needs), parse it, and fill in the structure.

The Structure on Disk

Before you look at reading the object, you need to define how it's going to be stored on the disk. The layout will look similar to the one you're using for our objects, but it won't have as many fields. This structure allows variable-length fields for holding as many vertices and polygons as you like, but it is important to respect the limits defined earlier (50 vertices/object, 20 polygons/object, and 4 vertices/polygon).

Here is the resource polygon structure:

```
2 bytes: # of vertices in the object
for each vertice {
  2 bytes: x
  2 bytes: y
  2 bytes: z
}

2 bytes: # of polygons in the object
for each polygon {
  2 bytes: color of the polygon
  2 bytes: # of vertices in the polygon
  for each vertice in the polygon {
    2 bytes: vertice index (0-based)
  }
}

2 bytes: x origin of the object
2 bytes: y origin of the object
2 bytes: z origin of the object
```

Resource Templates

Now, you could go and type all this information in raw data form for each of the objects, but that would be time consuming and error prone. Fortunately, ResEdit gives you a very handy way of creating these objects called a *resource template*. If you open a resource such as a dialog (DLOG) or menu (MENU), you'll get a graphical editor for it. This editor is, in some ways, similar to a template. A template will structure resource data so that when you open it, you aren't presented with raw hexadecimal data, but rather a list of fields.

The first step is to create a template for your objects. Open up ResEdit and create a new resource file. Select Create New Resource from the Resource menu ⌘-K.

A dialog box like the one in Figure 11-6 will appear asking what kind of resource you want to create. A template is resource type TMPL, so type that (make sure it's all uppercase) and click OK.

A window similar to the one in Figure 11-7 will appear. It is now time to start filling in the fields of the template. Unfortunately, the template creation process is not very intuitive—it involves typing several codes for the field type and a label for each field.

Click on the 1) ***** that you see in the window. Select Insert New Field(s) from the Resource menu and two fields will appear — Label and Type, as in Figure 11-8. You can now define the first field of the structure.

The field types are defined as four-character abbreviations and there are quite a few choices. You're only going to use a few of these, as listed in Table 11-2. The rest of the codes can be found in *ResEdit Reference* from Apple Computer (pp. 91-94).

Field Type	Definition
DWRD	Decimal word (2-bytes signed)
OCNT	Word count (put this before a list)
LSTC	Start of a counted list
LSTE	End of a counted list

TABLE 11-2 ◈ *Resource template field types*

FIGURE 11-6

◉ ◉ ◉ ◉ ◉ ◉

Selecting the TMPL resource type

Select New Type

| 3Dob |
| actb |
| acur |
| ADBS |
| aedt |
| ALRT |
| APPL |

TMPL|

OK

Cancel

The LSTC and LSTE types do not correspond to values you type; rather these are fields that indicate to ResEdit when it should begin and end a list, which is similar to an array in C. Also, when defining an object, you won't need to type values for 0CNT fields; ResEdit will automatically count the items you create.

Let's look at how to arrange these to create a template. Start with a 0CNT field for the number of vertices you'll be defining; enter 0CNT (that's a zero, not an O) into the Type field, and "Num of verts" into the Label field (you want to keep the name short or ResEdit will tend to mess up the formatting).

On to the next field. Click on 2) ***** and select Insert New Field(s) from the Resource menu. The next field is the start of the vertex list. It is named Vertex and the type is LSTC.

The next three fields are the components of the vertex: x, y, and z. Each has a type of DWRD. The list is ended by a field of type LSTE. At this point, your template definition should look like the one in Figure 11-9.

The remaining template items are Num of Polys (0CNT), Polygon (LSTC), Color (DWRD), Polygon Verts (0CNT), Polygon Vertex (LSTC), Vertex Index (DWRD),

FIGURE 11-7

◎ ◎ ◎ ◎ ◎ ◎

The blank template

FIGURE 11-8

◎ ◎ ◎ ◎ ◎ ◎

Creating the first fields of the object template

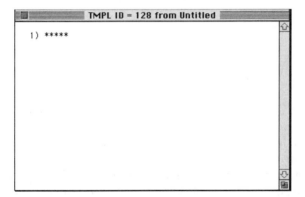

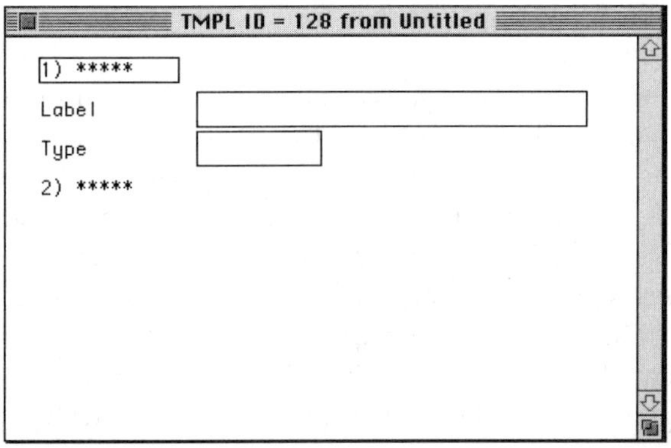

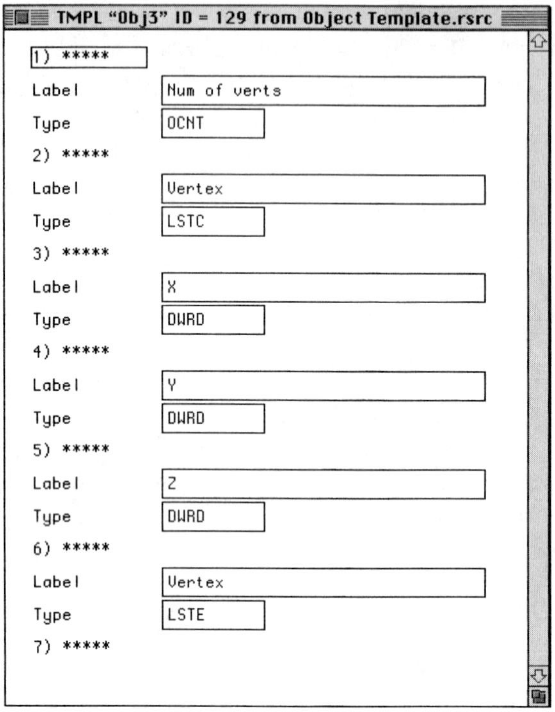

FIGURE 11-9

◎ ◎ ◎ ◎ ◎ ◎

The first part of the object template defined

Polygon Vertex (LSTE), Polygon (LSTE), Origin X (DWRD), Origin Y (DWRD), and Origin Z (DWRD).

You'll find the completed template in Object Template.rsrc in the Chapter 11 folder on the source code disc.

When you are finished defining the template, it is necessary to tell ResEdit which resource type the template applies to. Close the template window, then choose your new template from the list you see. Select Get Resource Info from the Resource menu and you'll see a window similar to the one in Figure 11-10. Type Obj3 into the Name field and close the window.

Your template is finished and you can now create objects using it. To test it out, close the TMPL list window, then select Create New Resource from the Resource menu. Type in Obj3 and click OK. A window like the one in Figure 11-11 appears, giving you a list of the fields of your structure. You can now start defining your object.

The new object doesn't have any vertices yet. To create each vertex, click on 1) Vertex and select Insert New Field(s) from the Resource Menu. Each time you do this, another vertex will be added to the vertex list.

When you are finished typing in the values for each vertex, it is time to start creating the polygons. Click on 1) Polygon and insert a new field. Type in the polygon color

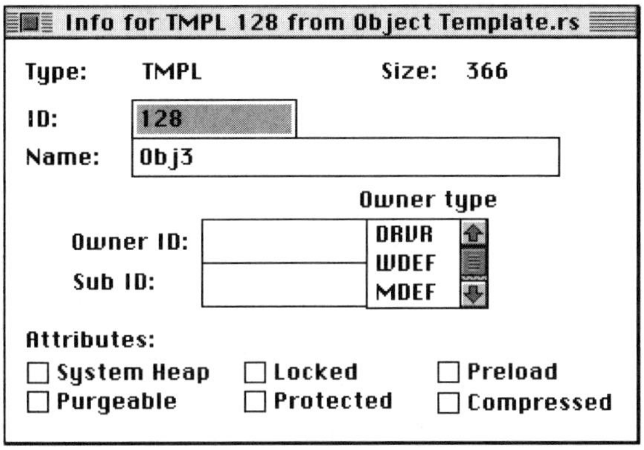

FIGURE 11-10

◎ ◎ ◎ ◎ ◎ ◎

Naming the
TMPL resource

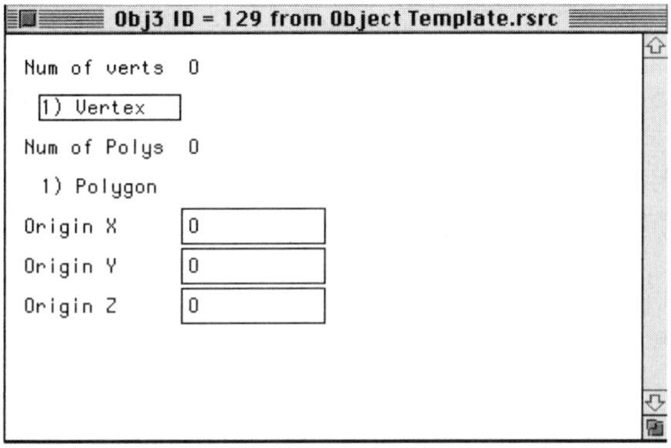

```
┌──────────────────────────────────────────────┐
│ ▣▤ Info for TMPL 128 from Object Template.rs ▤│
├──────────────────────────────────────────────┤
│  Type:    TMPL            Size:   366          │
│                                                │
│  ID:     ▣128▣                                 │
│  Name:   │Obj3                        │        │
│                                                │
│                          Owner type            │
│                         ┌──────────┬─┐         │
│         Owner ID:       │ DRUR     │⬆│         │
│                         ├──────────┤ │         │
│         Sub ID:         │ WDEF     │ │         │
│                         │ MDEF     │⬇│         │
│                         └──────────┴─┘         │
│  Attributes:                                   │
│  ☐ System Heap   ☐ Locked     ☐ Preload        │
│  ☐ Purgeable     ☐ Protected  ☐ Compressed     │
└──────────────────────────────────────────────┘
```

FIGURE 11-11

◎ ◎ ◎ ◎ ◎ ◎

Creating a new
object using the
Obj3 template

```
┌──────────────────────────────────────────────┐
│ ▣▤   Obj3 ID = 129 from Object Template.rsrc ▤│⬆
├──────────────────────────────────────────────┤
│  Num of verts   0                              │
│  ┌──────────┐                                  │
│  │1) Vertex │                                  │
│  └──────────┘                                  │
│  Num of Polys   0                              │
│    1) Polygon                                  │
│  Origin X    │0              │                 │
│  Origin Y    │0              │                 │
│  Origin Z    │0              │                 │
│                                                │
│                                               ⬇│
└──────────────────────────────────────────────┘
```

(a value from 0 to 255, which I'll cover shortly) and then create each of the polygon vertices.

Although this method of creating objects is not as exciting as, say, creating them in a 3D modeling program, it'll do for now. When you start writing your blockbuster game, you can write a utility that will convert an object from the file format of your favorite 3D package into this format.

In the Object Template.rsrc file, you'll find an object that has already been defined—it's the cube that you were working with in previous chapters. Although you can experiment with creating your own objects with this template, don't invest too much time in doing so; in later chapters, you'll be making some additions to the template that will be incompatible with your objects.

The System Color Palette

Right now, the Color field of the template is a little puzzling. The color can be any value between 0 and 255, but what do those values mean? With 8-bit graphics, the color table can be anything you want it to be, but for this book, I've been using the *system color table*—the Macintosh's default palette for colors.

Because the pages of this book are not printed in color, you'll have to refer to the source code disc for a file named System Color Table in the Chapter 11 folder. This file is a PICT image that can be opened using SimpleText or the PICT Viewer application you created in Chapter 3.

The color table file contains all 256 system colors. When you find the color you want to use, refer to the number at the top of the column and to the number to the left of the row. Add them together to get the index of your color.

Reading in Object Resources

It's now necessary to write the routines that will read in the object data and parse through it. Although the data you've created is not aligned on 4-byte boundaries, you don't care about the speed penalties; you're only reading an object in once and it doesn't take that long anyway. Once the data has been read and parsed, it is put into the correctly aligned Object3D structure. These routines are all in a file called Object Rsrc.c, which is used exclusively for dealing with object resources.

The main routine for dealing with object resources is LoadObjectFromRsrc(). It takes a resource ID for an input and returns a pointer to an Object3D. The first thing that LoadObjectFromRsrc() does is load the object resource handle with a simple call to GetResource(). After checking to see if the resource has been loaded correctly, it creates a new object through a simple call to NewPtr(), like this:

```
newObject = (Object3D *)NewPtr(sizeof(Object3D));
```

LoadObjectFromRsrc() then locks the resource handle and dereferences it to make parsing a little easier, like this:

```
/* Lock the resource handle */
HLock(objectResourceHandle);

/* Dereference the handle into a pointer */
resourceData = *objectResourceHandle;
```

For parsing the data from the resource handle, three routines read a byte, a word, and a longword, respectively. To keep track of that last byte of the data that has been read, LoadObjectFromRsrc() defines a variable called resourceDataOffset. This offset is passed into each of the parsing routines; those routines automatically increment it, ensuring that no data will be read twice. I'll look at these parsing routines in a bit.

LoadObjectFromRsrc() also makes use of a toolbox call that you haven't seen before. It is a function that is used primarily to aid in debugging programs; when it is encountered, it breaks into MacsBug and displays a string. Obviously, you wouldn't want to call this function during the normal execution of your program, but it is useful to alert the user (in this case, usually the programmer) of an abnormal condition. The routine is called DebugStr():

```
void    DebugStr(Str255 theString);
```

It can be used by simply passing in a Pascal-style string, like this:

```
DebugStr("\pI just encountered a problem!");
```

In LoadObjectFromResource(), it is used to indicate that the object has too many vertices or polygons.

As LoadObjectFromRsrc() parses the data from the resource handle, it places the data into the new object one field at a time. Once all the data has been read, the resource handle is unlocked and released and the new object is passed back to the function that called it. Listing 11-3 shows the code.

Listing 11-3 *The LoadObjectFromRsrc() routine*

```
/**
**   LoadObjectFromRsrc()
**
**   Fetches an object from a 'obj3' resource, converts it
**   to a Object3D type, processes the object, and sends
**   it back.
**/
Object3D * LoadObjectFromRsrc(short resourceID)
{
  Object3D     *newObject;
  short        numOfVertices;
  short        numOfPolygons;
  short        currentVertice;
  short        currentPolygon;
  Handle       objectResourceHandle;
  long         resourceDataOffset;
  Ptr          resourceData;

  /* Load the resource from the disk */
  objectResourceHandle = GetResource('Obj3', resourceID);

  /* Check to make sure the resource was loaded correctly */
  if (objectResourceHandle == NULL)
    return NULL;

  /* Allocate memory for the new object */
  newObject = (Object3D *)NewPtr(sizeof(Object3D));

  /* Lock the resource handle */
  HLock(objectResourceHandle);
```

Continued on next page

Continued from previous page

```
/* Dereference the handle into a pointer */
resourceData = *objectResourceHandle;

/* Initialize the offset. This offset indicates the last
 * byte of the resource data that we've read. The data
 * parsing routines will automatically increase this
 * value as they read the data.
 */
resourceDataOffset = 0;

/* Begin reading from the object data. The first word
 * of the data is the number of vertices in the object.
 */
numOfVertices = ReadDataWord(resourceData, &resourceDataOffset);

/* Make sure that the object does not have too many vertices */
if (numOfVertices > kMaximumVertices) {
  DebugStr("\pThe resource data has too many vertices. Increase
kMaximumVertices if you want to load this object.");
  return NULL;
}

newObject->numOfVertices = numOfVertices;

/* Read all of the vertices in */
for ( currentVertice = 0;
      currentVertice < numOfVertices;
      currentVertice++)
{
  short    verticeX, verticeY, verticeZ;

  verticeX = ReadDataWord(resourceData, &resourceDataOffset);
  verticeY = ReadDataWord(resourceData, &resourceDataOffset);
  verticeZ = ReadDataWord(resourceData, &resourceDataOffset);

  /* Put this vertex into the object */
  newObject->vertex[currentVertice].lx = verticeX;
  newObject->vertex[currentVertice].ly = verticeY;
  newObject->vertex[currentVertice].lz = verticeZ;
  newObject->vertex[currentVertice].lt = 1;
}

/* Read the number of polygons in the object */
numOfPolygons = ReadDataWord(resourceData, &resourceDataOffset);

/* Make sure the object doesn't have too many polygons */
if (numOfVertices > kMaximumPolys) {
  DebugStr("\pThe resource data has too many polygons. Increase
kMaximumPolys if you want to load this object.");
  return NULL;
}
```

```
newObject->numOfPolygons = numOfPolygons;

/* Read all of the polygons in */
for (  currentPolygon = 0;
       currentPolygon < numOfPolygons;
       currentPolygon++)
{
  short       numOfPolygonVerts;
  short       currentPolygonVert;
  Polygon3D  *polygonRef;

  /* Obtain a pointer to the current polygon in the new object */
  polygonRef = &newObject->polygon[currentPolygon];

  /* Read the polygon color */
  polygonRef->color = ReadDataWord(resourceData, &resourceDataOffset);

  /* Read the number of vertices in this polygon */
  numOfPolygonVerts = ReadDataWord(resourceData, &resourceDataOffset);

  /* Make sure that this polygon doesn't have too many vertices */
  if (numOfPolygonVerts > kMaxPolygonSize) {
    DebugStr("\pThe resource data has too many vertices in a polygon.
Increase kMaxPolygonSize if you want to load this object.");
    return NULL;
  }

  polygonRef->numOfVertices = numOfPolygonVerts;

  /* Read each of the vertices */
  for (  currentPolygonVert = 0;
         currentPolygonVert < numOfPolygonVerts;
         currentPolygonVert++  )
  {
    short    vertexIndex;
    Vertex3D *vertexPtr;

    vertexIndex = ReadDataWord(resourceData, &resourceDataOffset);

    /* Verify that the vertex index is valid */
    if (vertexIndex >= numOfVertices) {
      DebugStr("\pOne of the polygon vertex indices is invalid.");
      return NULL;
    }

    /* Find a pointer to this vertex and put it into the polygon */
    vertexPtr = &newObject->vertex[vertexIndex];
    polygonRef->polyVertex[currentPolygonVert] = vertexPtr;
  }

  /* We're done with the polygon - we'll calculate the polygon
```

Continued on next page

Continued from previous page

```
    * normal later.
    */
  }

  /* Read the origin of the object */
  newObject->originX = ReadDataWord(resourceData, &resourceDataOffset);
  newObject->originY = ReadDataWord(resourceData, &resourceDataOffset);
  newObject->originZ = ReadDataWord(resourceData, &resourceDataOffset);

  /* We're done reading the object. Unlock the data handle and release
   * the resource.
   */
  HUnlock(objectResourceHandle);
  ReleaseResource(objectResourceHandle);

  /* Return the new object */
  return newObject;
}
```

Data Parsing

The resource data is parsed by calling one of three specific routines: ReadDataByte(), ReadDataWord(), or ReadDataLong(). These routines take 1, 2, or 4 bytes out of the data, respectively, and advance the offset value by that amount. You might have noticed that LoadObjectFromRsrc() calls only ReadDataWord—all the object information is stored as 16-bit values. The other two routines are presented here because, as the object definition evolves, you'll need to have the capability of reading more than just a word at a time.

Each of the routines takes the data pointer, adds the offset value to it, and then type-casts it to a (char *), (short *), or (long *), depending on the type of data it wants to extract. This typecasting tells the compiler that, when dereferenced, the pointer should produce a byte, word, or longword respectively.

The routine then dereferences the pointer, increments the offset, and passes the result back to the routine that called it.

Here is the routine for reading a byte from a data pointer:

```
/**
 ** ReadDataByte()
 **
 ** Grabs a byte from the supplied data pointer, increments
 ** the data offset, and returns the obtained data.
 **/
char  ReadDataByte(Ptr data, long *currentOffset) {
  Ptr     offsetData;
  char    readByte;

  /* Create a pointer that is pointing directly at the
   * byte we want to read
```

```
    */
    offsetData = data + *currentOffset;

    /* Dereference that pointer to get our byte */
    readByte = *(char *)offsetData;

    /* We read 1 byte, so increment the offset by 1 */
    *currentOffset += 1;

    return readByte;
}
```

There are just two differences between ReadDataByte() and ReadDataWord(): The pointer is typecast to a *(short *)* instead of a *(char *)* and the offset is incremented by 2 in ReadDataWord().

```
/**
 ** ReadDataWord()
 **
 ** Grabs a word from the supplied data pointer, increments
 ** the data offset, and returns the obtained data.
 **/
short  ReadDataWord(Ptr data, long *currentOffset) {
  Ptr    offsetData;
  short  readWord;

  /* Create a pointer that is pointing directly at the
   * word we want to read
   */
  offsetData = data + *currentOffset;

  /* Dereference that pointer to get our byte */
  readWord = *(short *)offsetData;

  /* We read 2 bytes, so increment the offset by 2 */
  *currentOffset += 2;

  return readWord;
}
```

Finally, ReadDataLong() typecasts the data pointer to a (long *) and increments the offset by 4:

```
/**
 ** ReadDataLong()
 **
 ** Grabs a longword from the supplied data pointer, increments
 ** the data offset, and returns the obtained data.
 **/
long  ReadDataLong(Ptr data, long *currentOffset) {
  Ptr    offsetData;
```

Continued on next page

Continued from previous page

```
long    readLongword;

/* Create a pointer that is pointing directly at the
 * longword we want to read
 */
offsetData = data + *currentOffset;

/* Dereference that pointer to get our byte */
readLongword = *(long *)offsetData;

/* We read 4 bytes, so increment the offset by 4 */
*currentOffset += 4;

return readLongword;
}
```

Polygon-Fill Application

You now have all the elements necessary to build a sample application of a 3D object rendered with the new polygon-fill algorithm. Because you are now storing objects in the resource fork, you don't need to write out the object data by hand. The data (a cube) is loaded into memory, rotated, projected, and finally drawn using the new DrawObject() routine. The rendering technique can be changed simply by passing a different constant to DrawObject(). The only two techniques you've created so far are wireframe and polygon fill. Here are the constants for those modes:

```
enum {
        kRender_Wireframe,
        kRender_PolygonFill
};
```

Overall, the main() function is very similar to the one used for the wireframe spinning cube as shown in Listing 11-4.

Listing 11-4 *The polygon-fill spinning cube routine*

```
void main(void)
{
  Rect            windowRect;
  Rect            gworldRect;
  WindowPtr       mainWindow;
  GWorldPtr       offscreenGWorld;
  PixMapHandle    offscreenPixMap;
  unsigned long   rowBytes;
  Ptr             pixmapBaseAddress;
  OSErr           err;
  GWorldPtr       savePort;
```

```
GDHandle      saveDevice;
float         xAngle, yAngle;
float         transformMatrix[4][4];
Object3D      *theObject;

/* Initialize everything we need */
InitGraf(&qd.thePort);
InitWindows();
InitCursor();

/* Create a window that is 500x300 pixels large */
SetRect(&windowRect, 0, 0, 500, 300);

/* We want our gworld to be the same size */
gworldRect = windowRect;

/* Offset the window rect so that the window does not appear
 * under the menubar.
 */
OffsetRect(&windowRect, 20, 40);

mainWindow = CreateWindow(&windowRect);

SetPort(mainWindow);

/* Create the offscreen GWorld */

err = NewGWorld(  &offscreenGWorld,
                  8,
                  &gworldRect,
                  NULL,
                  NULL,
                  0 );

if (err)  /* Quit if there was an error */
  ExitToShell();

/* Find the GWorld's PixMapHandle */

offscreenPixMap = GetGWorldPixMap(offscreenGWorld);

/* Lock the pixmap */
LockPixels(offscreenPixMap);

/* Get a pointer to the pixmap data */
pixmapBaseAddress = GetPixBaseAddr(offscreenPixMap);

/* Find the pixmap rowbytes (remember to mask off the top 2 bits!) */
rowBytes = (**offscreenPixMap).rowBytes & 0x3FFF;

/* Read the resource in from disk */
```

Continued on next page

Continued from previous page

```
  theObject = LoadObjectFromRsrc(128);

  /* Test for failure */
  if (theObject == NULL) {
    ExitToShell();
  }

  /* Start the rotations off at 0 and scale at 1 */
  xAngle = 0.0;
  yAngle = 0.0;

  /* Wait until the user clicks before quitting */
  while (!Button())
  {
    /* Erase the GWorld */

    GetGWorld(&savePort, &saveDevice);
    SetGWorld(offscreenGWorld, NULL);

    EraseRect(&gworldRect);

    SetGWorld(savePort, saveDevice);

    /* Fiddle with the rotation values */
    xAngle += 0.1;
    yAngle += 0.15;

    /* If either angle has passed 2PI (6.28 radians, or 360 degrees),
     * reset it.
     */
    if (xAngle > 6.28)
      xAngle -= 6.28;

    if (yAngle > 6.28)
      yAngle -= 6.28;

    /* Initialize our transformation matrix */
    InitMatrix(transformMatrix);

    /* Apply the rotations to the matrix */
    RotateMatrix(transformMatrix, xAngle, yAngle, 0);

    /* Transform the shape */
    TransformObject3D(theObject, transformMatrix);

    /* Convert the shape to world coordinates */
    ObjectToWorldCoordinates(theObject);

    /* Project the shape into screen coordinates */
    ProjectObject(theObject);
```

```
/* Draw the shape */
DrawObject(  theObject,
             kRender_PolygonFill,
             pixmapBaseAddress,
             rowBytes  );

/* Copy the gworld to the screen */
CopyBits(  (BitMap *)*offscreenPixMap,
           (BitMap *)&mainWindow->portBits,
           &gworldRect,
           &gworldRect,
           srcCopy,
           NULL  );
    }
}
```

Figure 11-12 shows a screenshot of the polygon-fill sample application. The polygon-fill rendering presented in this chapter is the same technique used in most 3D computer games today. However, although the algorithms you've been using are fast enough for a simple spinning cube, if you tried to use them for an environment that included hundreds of polygons, they would quickly prove to be inadequate.

Any 3D game depends on fast animation to produce a realistic environment. In the next chapter I will concentrate on techniques to improve the speed of code dramatically.

FIGURE 11-12

◎ ◎ ◎ ◎ ◎ ◎

The spinning polygon-fill cube in action

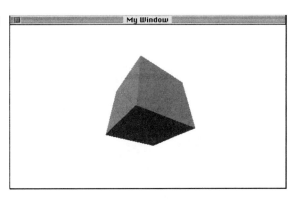

Optimization

12

Optimization

Up until now, you've been building the basis for a 3D game engine suitable for an arcade game or a flight simulator. However, the code that's been introduced lacks a characteristic necessary for any amazing computer game: speed. Few things are more annoying than having your game become slow and jerky just as that zombie is about to have your guts for dinner, or to have your flight simulator stall just as the enemy MiG fires a heat-seeker up your tail.

That's why I'm going to discuss techniques for optimizing the performance of your code in this and the following two chapters. This chapter covers the general methods of optimization—methods that have been used by computer scientists for decades. Chapter 13 discusses ways to get the most out of QuickDraw and how to write your own routines to extract everything possible from the Macintosh's graphics hardware. Chapter 14 focuses on Apple's PowerPC chip and ways to optimize your code especially for the RISC architecture.

The first thing to remember about optimizing your code (a.k.a., the first cardinal rule of software optimization) is to *get it working*. When you're first writing a routine to complete a task, don't worry about how slow it's going to be. Just focus on how to get it done; once that's accomplished, optimizing becomes relatively easy.

However, once your function is finished and you can see how performs, it's time to move on to the second rule of optimization.

The Profiler

The second rule of software optimization is to *use a profiler*. A *profiler* is a tool that measures how long your program spends in each of its functions. With this information, you know which routines are the most expensive and where you should spend your time optimizing.

There are two main types of profilers: *passive profilers* and *active profilers*. The difference is in how the profiler detects the functions being used.

A passive profiler is external to the target application—the target's source code doesn't need to be recompiled to be profiled. The passive profiler watches the application running and periodically (hundreds of times a second) checks the application's program counter (PC) and records where it points to.

When the application has terminated, the passive profiler will compile the samples it has gathered and attempt to figure out which functions were being accessed the most. The result is fairly accurate, but may be skewed when profiling very small functions. The main advantage of a passive profiler is that source code is not necessary.

Active profilers add code to each of the functions of the target application. As the application runs, data is collected every time a function is called or returns, and the data is written out as the application terminates. Because the active profiler works internally to the application, the profiling must be compiled directly with the source code.

Active profilers do not require an external application to monitor the target, although the Metrowerks compiler has an application designed to view the profiling data that was output from the target. Each compiler has its own way of activating the profiler and interpreting its statistics.

In this chapter, I'm going to look at the profilers of the two main development environments you're using: Metrowerks and Think C. Both profilers produce more or less the same results, but their interfaces are significantly different. Both profilers are turned on from within the compiler's preferences dialog and are activated by calling a few functions as your application starts up. Both of them also require you to add another library to your project.

The way they differ is in how the results of the profiling are presented. Think C writes the profiling results to a text file, which any standard text-editing program (such as SimpleText or the Think editor itself) can read.

The results of the Metrowerks profiling are saved in a special file that can only be processed by the MW Profiler application. As you will see shortly, this output is similar to Think's profiler, but the data can be viewed a little more interactively than the output from Think C.

Let's take a look at what you need to do to apply these profilers to the polygon-fill cube. Because each environment has a different method for invoking the profiler and it would be a real pain to keep track of two separate source files, take advantage of conditional compilation. Conditional compilation involves the use of the *#ifdef*, *#else*, and *#endif* compiler directives. If you want to write code that is used only in Metrowerks, define it like this:

```
#ifdef __MWERKS__
   ....code....
#endif
```

Code that is compiled only for Think C is written like this:

```
#ifdef THINK_C
   ....code....
#endif
```

Conditional compilation allows you to mix code for both environments within the same source file. First I'll look at what's required to use the Metrowerks profiler.

Initializing the Metrowerks Profiler

To compile your code using the profiler in Metrowerks, open the Metrowerks preferences dialog and select the Processor panel. From there, check the box labeled Generate Profiler Calls. Next, include either the Profiler68k.lib or ProfilerPPC.lib file in your project, depending on whether you're compiling your code for the 68k or the PowerPC.

In the main() function, activate the profiler by calling a function provided by Metrowerks named ProfilerInit():

```
pascal OSErr ProfilerInit( ProfilerCollectionMethod  method,
                           ProfilerTimeBase          timeBase,
                           short                     numFunctions,
                           short                     stackDepth  );
```

The *method* parameter tells the profiler how detailed a report you want. It can be one of two constants: collectDetailed and collectSummary. The detailed report will show you the order in which each function was called, allowing you to track some esoteric problems, whereas the summary gives you only the timing of each of your functions. You're just going to be using the summary here, but feel free to experiment with the detailed version if you like.

The *timeBase* parameter defines the precision the profiler will use when timing the code. The most precise method will give you the most accurate results, but it will also generally be the slowest. You can choose from five constants for this parameter. *ticksTimeBase* gives a resolution of 60 counts per second. It is the most inaccurate, but doesn't require much overhead. *timeMgrTimeBase* counts by microseconds, but is significantly slower than *ticksTimeBase*. This method is especially slow on a Power Macintosh (because the microsecond timer is emulated on the Power Macintosh). *microsecondsTimeBase* gives the same resolution as *timeMgrTimeBase*, but is faster (although still very slow on a Power Macintosh). *PPCTimeBase* uses the timing facilities present in the PowerPC chip, so it isn't available on a 68k machine. It is very accurate and has low overhead. If you're not sure which method to use, pass in *bestTimeBase*, which allows the profiler to select the best method for your machine. Metrowerks recommends that you use *bestTimeBase*.

The *numFunctions* parameter tells the profiler the maximum number of functions that exist in your program; *stackDepth* indicates how many functions deep the stack can get over the course of the program. The larger these values are, the more memory will be necessary for the profiler, but if you use values that are too small, the profiler is likely to crash. If in doubt, a value of 200 for each is usually more than sufficient.

Let's look at a sample call to the Metrowerks profiler. You can use a preprocessor variable called __profile__ to check if the profiler option is turned on in the preferences. This allows you to turn the profiler on and off without changing your code in case you need to profile the code again in the future. Also check to make sure the code is being compiled by Metrowerks before issuing the call:

```
#ifdef __MWERKS__    /* If we're using the metrowerks compiler... */
#if __profile__
  /* Initialize the metrowerks profiler */
  ProfilerInit(collectSummary, bestTimeBase, 100, 20);
#endif
#endif
```

Terminating the Metrowerks Profiler

When your application has finished, it needs to make one last call to the profiler to force it to save the statistics to disk. In Metrowerks, this function is called ProfilerDump():

```
OSErr ProfilerDump(StringPtr filename);
```

All you need to do is provide a file name to save the data into. The file will be saved in the same directory as the application.

After dumping the profiler statistics, call ProfilerTerm() to stop the profiler from collecting data:

```
void ProfilerTerm(void);
```

Here's a code fragment that accomplishes both tasks:

```
#ifdef __MWERKS__
#if __profile__
        /* Dump out the profiler data to a file */
        ProfilerDump("\pOptimization Profiler Info");

        /* Stop the profiler */
```

```
        ProfilerTerm();
#endif
#endif
```

Initializing the Think C Profiler

Invoking the Think C profiler involves a similar process. Include profile.h in your main source file so you have access to Think C's profiler functions. The profiler initialization function is called InitProfile(), and it's defined like this:

```
void  InitProfile(short numFunctions, short stackDepth);
```

The two parameters function just the same as they do for the Metrowerks profiler. Think C 8 and later versions of Think C 7 support only Ticks for a time base (1/60th of a second).

In Think C, after the profiler has been initialized, you must create a file to be used for the profiler output (otherwise, the results will be displayed on the screen). Instead of going through the Macintosh method of creating a file (which is more involved than necessary), you can take a shortcut by calling an ANSI C function named freopen(). This function opens a new text file in the same directory as the application, as shown here:

```
freopen("Optimization TC Report", "w", stdout);
```

The first parameter is the name of the file, whereas the other two indicate that the file is to be opened for writing and that the standard C output is to be redirected to this file. If you'd like more information about this function, any standard C reference manual will provide a detailed description.

Just as with Metrowerks, you can test to see whether the Think C profiler is active or not by checking the preprocessor variable __option(profile).

```
#ifdef THINK_C    /* If we're using the Think C compiler... */
#if __option(profile)
  /* Initialize the Think C profiler */
  InitProfile(100, 20);

  /* Open a file for the Think C profile output to go into */
 freopen("Optimization TC Report", "w", stdout);
#endif
#endif
```

You must also include the Think C library profile in your project.

Terminating the Think C Profiler

The data from the Think C profiler is automatically written to disk when the application quits. If you want to write the data at an earlier point, make a simple call to DumpProfile():

```
void DumpProfile(void);
```

This call forces the profiler to write its statistics to the optimization file you created earlier. Here is a fragment to accomplish this:

```
#ifdef THINK_C    /* If we're using the Think C compiler... */
#if __option(profile)
  /* Dump the profile statistics */
  DumpProfile();
#endif
#endif
```

Profiling the Polygon-Fill Cube

To illustrate the optimization techniques of this chapter, I'm going to use the polygon-fill application you created in the last chapter. In addition to adding the profiler initialization code I just talked about, you're going to add a gauge with which you can measure progress—you're going to have the program calculate how many frames per second it is displaying.

To do this, you need to keep track of two values: how many ticks have elapsed since the program started and how many frames the program has displayed so far. Then divide the frames by the ticks, multiply by 60 (because there are 60 ticks per second), and you have the frames per second (fps).

Then convert the fps number to a text string so you can display it on the screen. Fortunately, the Macintosh toolbox has a function to do this, called NumToString():

```
void NumToString(long theNum, Str255 theString);
```

Next, set the pen location to where you want the text drawn (using MoveTo()); then draw it using a function called DrawString():

```
void  DrawString(Str255 theString);
```

Here is a code segment that calculates the fps and displays it on the screen:

```
  Str255    fpsText;

  /* Increment the framecount, calculate fps and draw
   * it on the screen
   */
  framesSoFar += 1;
```

```
thisTickCount = TickCount();
framesPerSecond = ((float)framesSoFar /
                  (float)(thisTickCount - originalTickCount)) * 60;

/* Convert that fps number into text so we can show it */
NumToString(framesPerSecond, fpsText);

/* Draw the string */
MoveTo(10, 30);
DrawString(fpsText);
```

I've made one more change to the application. Instead of calling CopyBits() directly from the main() function, I've moved it into a new function. This change is necessary
because the profiler cannot track calls to the toolbox that come from the main function. It allows you to observe the cost of using CopyBits. The new function looks like
this:

```
/**
 **   CopyOntoScreen()
 **
 **   Copies an offscreen pixmap to the window. This has been
 **   broken off to its own routine so its speed can be measured.
 **/
void  CopyOntoScreen( PixMapHandle  offscreen,
                      WindowPtr     mainWindow,
                      Rect          bounds  )
{
  CopyBits( (BitMap *)*offscreen,
            (BitMap *)&mainWindow->portBits,
            &bounds,
            &bounds,
            srcCopy,
            NULL );
}
```

Once you've added all the profiler support code to your application and compiled
it, all you need to do is run your program and let it work for a few minutes. During the
course of executing, the profiler will be timing each function call; when the application finishes, this information will be written to a file.

Let's see what the profiler tells us. For the experiments in this chapter, the profil-
ings have been run on a Quadra 700 with a 25Mhz 68040 processor. The profiles on
your particular machine will differ, particularly if you're using a PowerPC. And of course
the fps values will also be different.

With the unoptimized version of the polygon-fill cube, the Quadra 700 achieves approximately 22 frames per second (in 8-bit color). I'll use this value to see how successful
you are in fine-tuning this program throughout this and the next two chapters.

Profiling Results from Metrowerks

Once your application has finished running, double-click on the profiling file that has been created, Optimization Profiler Info. The Metrowerks profiler application will be launched and you will see a window like the one in Figure 12-1.

The first column lists each of the functions that were called over the course of the application's life. The second column, Count, lists how many times each function was called. In Figure 12-1, 341 frames are displayed, because CopyOntoScreen() was called 341 times, as were several other functions. You can see that BackfacePolygon() was called six times per frame (which makes sense, because there are six polygons in the cube) and MatrixMultiply() was called four times per frame.

The next column, Only, gives the total amount of time spent executing code in a particular function. This does not include any time spent in any routines *called* by this function. The % column following Only breaks the times down into percentages of the total time. As you can see, the biggest resource hog was CopyOntoScreen(), using 51 percent of the total resources! Copying from an offscreen buffer has always been one of the bottlenecks of game writing and it's a topic I'll cover in the next chapter. For this chapter, I'm going to work on improving the other 49 percent of the application.

The next largest consumer is PolygonFillDrawPolygon(), with 24.3 percent of the resources, which is not surprising because it is one of the most complex routines in the application. The next is MatrixMultiply(), consuming 10.5 percent of the resources, which may seem surprising because it's such a simple function. I'll talk about why it's so slow shortly. The only other major time consumer is TransformObject3D(), which takes up less than 10 percent of the execution time.

The next two columns of the report indicate how much time is spent in each function *plus* the time spent in any routine that it calls. These columns indicate that

---

Optimization Profiler Info

Method: Summary   Timebase: Microseconds   Saved at: 12:27:25 AM 6/8/95   Overhead: 672.323

Function Name	Count	Only	%	+Children	%	Average	Maximum	Minimum	S
CopyOntoScreen	341	5206.053	51.0	5206.053	51.0	15.267	16.053	14.617	
PolygonFillDrawPolygon	711	2477.430	24.3	2477.430	24.3	3.484	7.386	0.299	
MatrixMultiply	1023	1070.860	10.5	1070.860	10.5	1.047	1.593	0.479	
TransformObject3D	341	1001.527	9.8	1001.527	9.8	2.937	4.600	2.316	
RotateMatrix	341	343.363	3.4	1416.246	13.9	1.007	1.507	0.485	
DrawObject	341	96.050	0.9	2579.142	25.3	0.282	0.774	0.001	
BackfacePolygon	2046	5.662	0.1	5.662	0.1	0.003	0.312	0.000	
CopyMatrix	341	2.023	0.0	2.023	0.0	0.006	0.320	0.000	
ProjectObject	341	1.816	0.0	1.816	0.0	0.005	0.615	0.000	
ObjectToWorldCoordinates	341	0.956	0.0	0.956	0.0	0.003	0.297	0.000	
InitMatrix	341	0.842	0.0	0.842	0.0	0.002	0.275	0.000	

FIGURE 12-1 ◉ *The results from profiling the original application*

DrawObject() takes quite a bit of this time, which is not surprising because it calls both PolygonFillDrawPolygon() *and* BackfacePolygon(). Still, though, CopyOntoScreen is the major time hog.

The next three columns indicate how much time is spent in each routine on the average and the minimum and maximum timings. The main use of these columns is to provide an easy way of telling how much you've improved the speed of a particular routine.

Next I'll look at the results you can get from the Think C profiler.

Profiling Results from Think C

The profiling results from Think C are a little more sparse. You can open the file that is saved with any text editor (such as SimpleText). Figure 12-2 shows an example of the output you'll obtain from Think C.

As you can see, the Think C profiler shows information on the average, minimum, and maximum timings of each routine, the percentage of time being spent in each, and how many times each routine was called. One of the first things you should notice is that, although their rank is still pretty much the same, the exact percentages vary from the Metrowerks version. This is because there are some operations the Think compiler can optimize better than the Metrowerks version, and vice versa. The differences are minor, however, and are not enough to really affect your game's overall speed.

Interpreting the Profile

Earlier, I listed the major time consumers in the application: CopyOntoScreen(), PolygonFillDrawPolygon(), MatrixMultiply(), and TransformObject3D(). This gives you a good idea of where to concentrate your optimization efforts. The fast turnaround time

FIGURE 12-2

◎ ◎ ◎ ◎ ◎ ◎

The results of profiling the application using Think C

Optimization TC Report					
Function	Minimum	Maximum	Average	%	Entries
BackfacePolygon	0	1	0	0	1728
CopyMatrix	0	1	0	0	288
CopyOntoScreen	0	1	0	51	288
DrawObject	0	1	0	0	288
InitMatrix	0	0	0	0	288
MatrixMultiply	0	1	0	8	864
ObjectToWorldCoordinates	0	0	0	0	288
PolygonFillDrawPolygon	0	1	0	26	601
ProjectObject	0	0	0	0	288
RotateMatrix	0	1	0	2	288
TransformObject3D	0	1	0	9	288

of today's compilers allows you to test every change you make individually to find out if each one helps or hurts performance.

The first routines I'm going to look at deal with the matrices and math. Because it's so complicated, I won't touch the PolygonFillDrawPolygon() until the end of the chapter.

Floating-Point Coprocessors

Some Macintoshes are built with a special chip in them called a *math coprocessor* (also known as an FPU, or *floating-point unit*). This coprocessor can do floating-point calculations several times more quickly than the CPU can, but your code must be specially compiled to take advantage of it. All PowerPC processors have an FPU built in, as do 68040 processors. A Macintosh with a 68LC040 processor does not have an FPU; those with a 68020 or 68030 may have an external FPU.

If you're compiling code for the PowerPC, it *always* takes advantage of the FPU (because the FPU is always present), but if you compile code for the 68k, you have to turn on an option in the preferences dialog. 68k code compiled for an FPU will not function on a processor that doesn't have an FPU.

Let's take a look at how to take advantage of an FPU. (If you have a PowerPC or a 68k processor without an FPU, you can ignore this section.) The first thing to do is turn on the 68881 flag in your project's preferences dialog. Then, if you are using Metrowerks, you must replace the ANSI libraries with libraries compiled for a coprocessor. (I'll be using the library named ANSI (2i/F) C.68k.Lib.)

After you recompile all of the files in the project and run the application, you get the profiling results. Let's look at what happened.

The frame rate of the program went up to 25 frames per second—not bad for a 2-minute fix. If you compare the profiler results (shown in Figure 12-3) with the statistics from the original program, you will see that the average time to complete MatrixMultiply() dropped from 1.05 to 0.133—that's almost eight times as fast! Other math-intensive functions such as TransformObject3D() and RotateMatrix() also experienced speed boosts, but they were not as dramatic.

Fixed-Point Mathematics

It looks like utilizing an FPU in your code will provide good performance for a game. However, if you require an FPU, you alienate a large portion of Macintosh owners (well over 50 percent of 68k machines sold do *not* have math coprocessors, especially those sold into homes). It's also not fast *enough*. Fortunately, games have the "luxury" of sacrificing precision in favor of speed. Because it doesn't matter much if a few pixels are slightly out of place in a high-speed game, you can use mathematical methods that deliver speeds *better* than those obtained with an FPU, even on non-FPU machines.

FIGURE12-3

◎ ◎ ◎ ◎ ◎ ◎

The profile from the FPU version of the application

Function Name	Count	Only	%	+Children	%	Average	Maximum	Minimum
CopyOntoScreen	341	5214.338	61.6	5214.338	61.6	15.291	15.978	14.823
PolygonFillDrawPolygon	711	2478.342	29.3	2478.342	29.3	3.486	7.426	0.298
TransformObject3D	341	340.681	4.0	340.681	4.0	0.999	1.435	0.584
RotateMatrix	341	196.282	2.3	334.892	4.0	0.576	1.021	0.079
MatrixMultiply	1023	137.880	1.6	137.880	1.6	0.135	0.438	0.000
DrawObject	341	90.230	1.1	2573.708	30.4	0.265	0.602	0.000
BackfacePolygon	2046	5.542	0.1	5.542	0.1	0.003	0.306	0.000
ProjectObject	341	1.859	0.0	1.859	0.0	0.005	0.305	0.000
ObjectToWorldCoordinates	341	1.319	0.0	1.319	0.0	0.004	0.302	0.000
CopyMatrix	341	0.730	0.0	0.730	0.0	0.002	0.312	0.000
InitMatrix	341	0.623	0.0	0.623	0.0	0.002	0.281	0.000

Optimization Profiler Info — Method: Summary Timebase: Microseconds Saved at: 12:29:41 AM 6/8/95 Overhead: 664.282

This technique is called *fixed-point mathematics*; it involves using integer values to *simulate* fractional numbers. Integer calculations are much faster than floating-point calculations (at least on the 68k processor—I'll talk about how it affects the PowerPC processor in Chapter 14).

The concept is simple—you take an integer number (generally a longword) and break it up into an integer part and a fractional part. How many bits to allocate to each half is up to you. The more bits you allocate to the integer portion, the larger range you'll have for your number, but the less you'll have left for the fractional portion. Essentially, you're taking a 32-bit integer value and putting an imaginary decimal point somewhere in the middle. If you put the decimal point in the middle (16 bits for integer, 16 bits for fraction), the resulting fixed-point number has a range of -32,768 to 32,767.999985 and can hold a number as small as 0.000015. If you instead allocate 24 bits to the integer and 8 bits to the fraction, you get a range of -8,388,608 to 8388607.996094 that can store a number as small as 0.003906. You're starting to lose accuracy here, but it's good enough for a video game, so this is the size you'll be using. It is commonly expressed as 24.8 fixed-point math.

The Format of Fixed-Point Numbers

Let's look at how a fixed-point number is formatted in memory. In Figure 12-4, a 32-bit longword has been divided into 24 bits of integer and 8 bits of fraction. The number stored there is 6734.031250 (it's difficult to get nice round numbers using fixed point), or 0x001A4E08 in hexadecimal. Because a fixed-point number is stored in a single 32-bit value, the C bitshift operators (<< and >>) will prove to be very valuable.

The fixed-point number is declared as a normal longword—the only difference is how you treat it:

```
Long    myFixedPointVar;
```

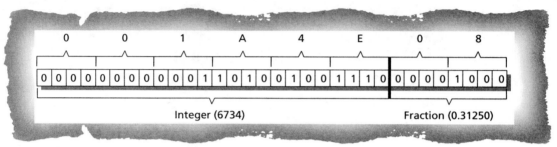

FIGURE 12-4 ◉ *A 24.8 fixed-point number*

This method could get confusing because you can't easily tell whether a particular variable is a fixed-point number or not. However, you can declare a new variable type that, although it does not affect the actual operation of the variable, makes it easier to identify it as fixed-point:

```
typedef long  Fixed24;
```

Declare fixed-point variables like this:

```
Fixed24  fix1, fix2, fix3;
```

Apple has also defined a type called Fixed, but you won't use it for declaring variables because this Fixed type is assumed to be 16.16 (16 bits of integer and 16 bits of fraction).

You can convert an integer into a fixed-point number by using the bitshift operator. Here is how you can create a 24.8 fixed-point number from an integer:

```
fix1 = myInteger << 8;
```

If you want to convert a floating-point number to a fixed-point number, multiply it by 256 (you can't bitshift a floating-point number, and multiplying by 256 gives the same effect as bitshifting my 8). Here is how you might do this:

```
fix1 = myFloatingPoint * 256;
```

Mathematics Using Fixed-Point Numbers

Addition and subtraction of fixed-point numbers are no different than that of normal integers. The only thing to keep in mind is that both numbers in the addition or subtraction must be fixed-point numbers:

```
fix3 = fix1 + fix2;
fix3 = fix1 - fix2;
```

Multiplication and division are more complicated, however. Multiplying two fixed-point numbers produces a fixed-point number that has *twice* as many fractional bits. This is analogous to multiplying decimal numbers:

```
   384.56
x    3.83
   115368
  3076480
 11536800
1472.8648
```

Similarly, here is a multiplication between two 24.8 fixed-point numbers (in binary), each holding a value of 1:

```
    000000000000000000000100000000    /* 1 as a 24.8 fixed number */
x   000000000000000000000100000000    /* The same number */
    000000000000010000000000000000    /* The resulting 16.16 with a */
                                       /* loss of 8 bits off the left */
                                       /* edge */
```

After multiplying two 24.8 fixed-point numbers, you are left with a 16.16 fixed-point number. To get back to a 24.8 number, you must shift the number to the right by 8 places:

```
fix3 = fix1 * fix2; /* fix3 is now 16.16 */
fix3 = fix3 >> 8;    /* fix3 is changed back to 24.8 */
```

This phenomenon brings up concerns about loss of data when two numbers are multiplied. When two 24.8 numbers are multiplied together, you have to ensure that the result will fit in a 16.16 number. Because you have 16 bits of integer precision remaining, you can only multiply numbers whose product is less than 32768 (2^{16}).

Division presents similar problems. When a 24.8 number is divided by another 24.8 number, the entire fractional portion disappears—you are left with a normal integer number. Although this may be fine if you're not worried about losing all of your fractional precision, there is a way you can avoid it. If you shift the numerator to the left by 8 places *before* you do the division (i.e., turn it into a 16.16 number), the result will be a 24.8 fixed-point number.

If you plan on dividing several numbers by the same value, it may be advantageous to create a reciprocal of the denominator first and then multiply that by the numerator, like this:

```
fix2 = ((long)1 << 16) / fix2; /* Find the reciprocal of fix2 */
fix3 = fix1 * fix2; /* Multiply fix1 and fix2 */
fix3 = fix3 >> 8;    /* Convert fix3 back to a 24.8 */
```

You may notice that when you convert 1 to a 16.16 number, you typecast it to a long. If you didn't do that, the compiler would assume that the value 1 is a 16-bit value and when the variable is shifted, it will overflow.

In the course of designing your game, you're going to have to be aware of the limitations of fixed-point mathematics, but that shouldn't be too much of a problem. In any case, the benefits will far outweigh the difficulties.

Mixing Fixed-Point Numbers and Integers

Although it may seem complicated, mixing fixed-point numbers and integers in calculations is easy. A 24.8 fixed-point number multiplied by an integer results in another 24.8 number! Similarly, a 24.8 number divided by an integer also results in a 24.8 number. Look at this multiplication for example:

```
    00000000000000000000000100000000    /* 1 as a 24.8 fixed number */
  x 00000000000000000000000000000001    /* 1 as an integer */
    00000000000000000000000100000000    /* The result is a 24.8
                                          * fixed-point number  */
```

This method makes some multiplication and division tasks extremely easy and there is no loss in precision.

Reaping the Benefits of Fixed-Point Mathematics

Let's examine how to incorporate fixed-point math into an application. Almost all the changes will occur in Objects.c and Object.h because I want to focus on the matrix routines. You can examine all of these changes in the folder named Optimization 2 on the source code disc.

A new file has been added to the project called Fixed.h. At this point, this file just contains the Fixed24 typedef mentioned earlier. Each of the matrices has been redesigned to look like this:

```
Fixed24  matrix[4][4];
```

Let's examine the matrix utility routines first. InitMatrix() has been changed so that it's placing fixed-point numbers into the new matrix by shifting 1 to the left by eight places. Because the resulting number (256) fits in 16 bits, there is no need to typecast the number to a longword before shifting it.

```
/**
 ** InitMatrix()
```

```
**
**  Initializes a matrix to the Identity Matrix.
**/
void   InitMatrix(Fixed24 matrix[4][4])
{
  matrix[0][0] = 1 << 8; matrix[0][1] = 0;
  matrix[0][2] = 0; matrix[0][3] = 0;

  matrix[1][0] = 0; matrix[1][1] = 1 << 8;
  matrix[1][2] = 0; matrix[1][3] = 0;

  matrix[2][0] = 0; matrix[2][1] = 0;
  matrix[2][2] = 1 << 8; matrix[2][3] = 0;

  matrix[3][0] = 0; matrix[3][1] = 0;
  matrix[3][2] = 0; matrix[3][3] = 1 << 8;
}
```

The MatrixMultiply() routine has been modified to shift the multiplication result to the right by eight places after the multiplication:

```
/**
**  MatrixMultiply()
**
**  Concatenates matrix1 and matrix2 and returns the result
**  in matrix3
**/
void  MatrixMultiply(  Fixed24 matrix1[4][4],
                       Fixed24 matrix2[4][4],
                       Fixed24 matrix3[4][4]  )
{
  short   i,j,k;

  for (i = 0; i < 4; i++) {
    for (j = 0; j < 4; j++) {
      matrix3[i][j] = 0;
      for (k = 0; k < 4; k++) {
        /* Do the multiplication and shift the result back into
         * a 24.8 fixed-point number
         */
        matrix3[i][j] += (matrix1[i][k] * matrix2[k][j]) >> 8;
      }
    }
  }
}
```

The routine to apply a matrix to an object hasn't changed much. Because the object's coordinates are defined as integers, multiplying them by a 24.8 fixed-point number will result in a 24.8 number. Simply shifting to the right by eight places brings you back to an integer, as shown in Listing 12-1.

Listing 12-1 *Applying a matrix to an object*

```
/**
 **   TransformObject3D()
 **
 **   Takes a object's local coordinates and transforms them
 **   with the provided transformation matrix, placing
 **   the result in the tx,ty,tz, and tt fields of the
 **   vertices.
 **/
void  TransformObject3D(  Object3D  *theObject,
                          Fixed24    transformMatrix[4][4]  )
{
  short    i;
  short    numOfVertices;

  numOfVertices = theObject->numOfVertices;

  /* Transform the object's vertices with the matrix */
  for (i = 0; i < numOfVertices; i++) {
    /* Declare some temporary variables */
    short      temp0, temp1, temp2, temp3;
    Vertex3D  *vertexRef;

    /* Get a pointer to the current vertex */
    vertexRef = &theObject->vertex[i];

    /* Multiply against the matrix. The vertices are integers,
     * not fixed-point, so we can do straight multiplication
     * and shift the result back when we're done.
     */
    temp0 = (vertexRef->lx * transformMatrix[0][0] +
             vertexRef->ly * transformMatrix[1][0] +
             vertexRef->lz * transformMatrix[2][0] +
             transformMatrix[3][0]) >> 8;

    temp1 = (vertexRef->lx * transformMatrix[0][1] +
             vertexRef->ly * transformMatrix[1][1] +
             vertexRef->lz * transformMatrix[2][1] +
             transformMatrix[3][1]) >> 8;

    temp2 = (vertexRef->lx * transformMatrix[0][2] +
             vertexRef->ly * transformMatrix[1][2] +
             vertexRef->lz * transformMatrix[2][2] +
             transformMatrix[3][2]) >> 8;

    temp3 = (vertexRef->lx * transformMatrix[0][3] +
             vertexRef->ly * transformMatrix[1][3] +
             vertexRef->lz * transformMatrix[2][3] +
             transformMatrix[3][3]) >> 8;

    /* Put the results into the vector's
```

```
      * transformed coordinates
      */
    vertexRef->tx = temp0;
    vertexRef->ty = temp1;
    vertexRef->tz = temp2;
    vertexRef->tt = temp3;
  }
}
```

You have to be careful when using the translation matrix routine to convert the translation factor to an 24.8 fixed-point number. Because you can't assume that the result of the shift will still fit in a 16-bit value, the routine must typecast the number to *long* before changing it:

```
/**
 **   TranslateMatrix()
 **
 **   Applies a translation to the input matrix.
 **/
void  TranslateMatrix( Fixed24   inputMatrix[4][4],
                       short     xTrans,
                       short     yTrans,
                       short     zTrans  )
{
  Fixed24   transMatrix[4][4];
  Fixed24   tempMatrix[4][4];

  /* Set transMatrix to a translation matrix */
  transMatrix[0][0] = 1 << 8; transMatrix[0][1] = 0;
  transMatrix[0][2] = 0; transMatrix[0][3] = 0;

  transMatrix[1][0] = 0; transMatrix[1][1] = 1 << 8;
  transMatrix[1][2] = 0; transMatrix[1][3] = 0;

  transMatrix[2][0] = 0; transMatrix[2][1] = 0;
  transMatrix[2][2] = 1 << 8; transMatrix[2][3] = 0;

  transMatrix[3][0] = ((long)xTrans) << 8;
  transMatrix[3][1] = ((long)yTrans) << 8;
  transMatrix[3][2] = ((long)zTrans) << 8;
  transMatrix[3][3] = 1 << 8;

  /* Concatenate the translation matrix with the
   * input matrix.
   */
  MatrixMultiply(inputMatrix, transMatrix, tempMatrix);

  /* Copy the temp matrix back into the input matrix */
  CopyMatrix(tempMatrix, inputMatrix);
}
```

The scaling matrix routine still takes a floating-point number as input. The first thing it does is convert it to a fixed-point number. This makes it easier to call this routine and the performance penalty is negligible. To convert the float to a fixed-point number, the routine multiplies by 256 instead of shifting (shifting floating-point values is illegal):

```
/**
 **    ScaleMatrix()
 **
 **    Applies a scaling to the input matrix.
 **/
void  ScaleMatrix(  Fixed24   inputMatrix[4][4],
                    float     scalingFactor  )
{
  Fixed24   scaleMatrix[4][4];
  Fixed24   tempMatrix[4][4];
  Fixed24   fixedScalingFactor;

  /* Create the fixed-point scaling factor */
  fixedScalingFactor = scalingFactor * 256;

  /* Set scaleMatrix to a scaling matrix */
  scaleMatrix[0][0] = scalingFactor; scaleMatrix[0][1] = 0;
  scaleMatrix[0][2] = 0; scaleMatrix[0][3] = 0;

  scaleMatrix[1][0] = 0; scaleMatrix[1][1] = scalingFactor;
  scaleMatrix[1][2] = 0; scaleMatrix[1][3] = 0;

  scaleMatrix[2][0] = 0; scaleMatrix[2][1] = 0;
  scaleMatrix[2][2] = scalingFactor; scaleMatrix[2][3] = 0;

  scaleMatrix[3][0] = 0; scaleMatrix[3][1] = 0;
  scaleMatrix[3][2] = 0; scaleMatrix[3][3] = 1 << 8;

  /* Concatenate the scaling matrix with the
   * input matrix.
   */
  MatrixMultiply(inputMatrix, scaleMatrix, tempMatrix);

  /* Copy the temp matrix back into the input matrix */
  CopyMatrix(tempMatrix, inputMatrix);
}
```

Like the matrix scaling routine, RotateMatrix() takes three floating-point values for the rotation parameters. It then passes these values directly into the cos() and sin() routines and converts the result into a fixed-point number. Besides the use of fixed-point numbers, there is an additional improvement to RotateMatrix()—it now calls cos() and sin() only once for each rotation value instead of twice, as it did before. This optimization alone will create a big gain in time.

In the next section, you'll improve RotateMatrix() again, but Listing 12-2 shows what it looks like using fixed-point math.

Listing 12-2 *RotateMatrix() using fixed-point math*

```
/**
 ** RotateMatrix()
 **
 ** Applies x,y, and z rotations to the input matrix.
 **/
void  RotateMatrix(  Fixed24  inputMatrix[4][4],
                     float    xRot,
                     float    yRot,
                     float    zRot  )
{
  Fixed24  rotMatrix[4][4];
  Fixed24  tempMatrix1[4][4];
  Fixed24  tempMatrix2[4][4];
  Fixed24  xSin, xCos;
  Fixed24  ySin, yCos;
  Fixed24  zSin, zCos;

  /* Create fixed-point versions of each rotation trig function */
  xSin = sin(xRot) * 256;
  xCos = cos(xRot) * 256;
  ySin = sin(yRot) * 256;
  yCos = cos(yRot) * 256;
  zSin = sin(zRot) * 256;
  zCos = cos(zRot) * 256;

  /* We want to apply all three rotations to the inputMatrix,
   * in the order of y, x, and z. In order to accomplish all of
   * these transformations, we have to use two temporary matrices
   * and copy between them.
   */

  /* Set rotMatrix to the y rotation matrix */
  rotMatrix[0][0] = yCos; rotMatrix[0][1] = 0;
  rotMatrix[0][2] = -ySin; rotMatrix[0][3] = 0;

  rotMatrix[1][0] = 0; rotMatrix[1][1] = 1 << 8;
  rotMatrix[1][2] = 0; rotMatrix[1][3] = 0;

  rotMatrix[2][0] = ySin; rotMatrix[2][1] = 0;
  rotMatrix[2][2] = yCos; rotMatrix[2][3] = 0;

  rotMatrix[3][0] = 0; rotMatrix[3][1] = 0;
  rotMatrix[3][2] = 0; rotMatrix[3][3] = 1 << 8;

  /* Concatenate rotMatrix with inputMatrix */
  MatrixMultiply(inputMatrix, rotMatrix, tempMatrix1);

  /* Set rotMatrix to the x rotation matrix */
```

Continued on next page

Continued from previous page

```
rotMatrix[0][0] = 1 << 8; rotMatrix[0][1] = 0;
rotMatrix[0][2] = 0; rotMatrix[0][3] = 0;

rotMatrix[1][0] = 0; rotMatrix[1][1] = xCos;
rotMatrix[1][2] = xSin; rotMatrix[1][3] = 0;

rotMatrix[2][0] = 0; rotMatrix[2][1] = -xSin;
rotMatrix[2][2] = xCos; rotMatrix[2][3] = 0;

rotMatrix[3][0] = 0; rotMatrix[3][1] = 0;
rotMatrix[3][2] = 0; rotMatrix[3][3] = 1 << 8;

/* Concatenate rotMatrix with tempMatrix1 */
MatrixMultiply(tempMatrix1, rotMatrix, tempMatrix2);

/* Set rotMatrix to the z rotation matrix */
rotMatrix[0][0] = zCos; rotMatrix[0][1] = zSin;
rotMatrix[0][2] = 0; rotMatrix[0][3] = 0;

rotMatrix[1][0] = -zSin; rotMatrix[1][1] = zCos;
rotMatrix[1][2] = 0; rotMatrix[1][3] = 0;

rotMatrix[2][0] = 0; rotMatrix[2][1] = 0;
rotMatrix[2][2] = 1 << 8; rotMatrix[2][3] = 0;

rotMatrix[3][0] = 0; rotMatrix[3][1] = 0;
rotMatrix[3][2] = 0; rotMatrix[3][3] = 1 << 8;

/* Concatenate rotMatrix with tempMatrix2 */
MatrixMultiply(tempMatrix2, rotMatrix, tempMatrix1);

/* Copy the temp matrix back into the input matrix */
CopyMatrix(tempMatrix1, inputMatrix);
}
```

The Fixed-Point Spinning Cube

Incorporating all of these changes into the program produces a cube that's faster than the one you created using the FPU. At this point, the speed increase is not huge—you're still getting about 25 fps. However, looking at the profiling results shown in Figure 12-5, you can see the benefits much more clearly.

The most obvious speed increase has been in TransformObject3D(). In the non-FPU version, this routine took, on average, 2.95 milliseconds. The FPU version improved this significantly, reducing the time to 1.03 milliseconds. The fixed-point version reduced this number to 0.11 microseconds, an improvement of over nine times from the FPU version and 26 times from the non-FPU version!

The dramatic improvement in this routine stems from the numerous multiplications it performs. The other matrix routines, however, aren't quite as impressive; their

Function Name	Count	Only.	%	+Children	%	Average	Maximum	Minimum	S
CopyOntoScreen	259	3958.672	62.6	3958.672	62.6	15.284	15.889	14.980	
PolygonFillDrawPolygon	541	1895.247	30.0	1895.247	30.0	3.503	7.480	0.297	
RotateMatrix	259	244.470	3.9	364.545	5.8	0.944	1.358	0.696	
MatrixMultiply	777	119.795	1.9	119.795	1.9	0.154	0.483	0.000	
DrawObject	259	71.874	1.1	1970.070	31.1	0.278	0.645	0.000	
TransformObject3D	259	29.383	0.5	29.383	0.5	0.113	0.403	0.000	
BackfacePolygon	1554	3.072	0.0	3.072	0.0	0.002	0.304	0.000	
ProjectObject	259	2.073	0.0	2.073	0.0	0.008	0.302	0.000	
InitMatrix	259	0.843	0.0	0.843	0.0	0.003	0.277	0.000	
ObjectToWorldCoordinates	259	0.687	0.0	0.687	0.0	0.003	0.311	0.000	
CopyMatrix	259	0.280	0.0	0.280	0.0	0.001	0.280	0.000	

Optimization Profiler Info — Method: Summary   Timebase: Microseconds   Saved at: 6:01:18 PM 8/26/95   Overhead: 499.869

FIGURE 12-5 ◉ *The profiling results after using fixed-point arithmetic*

speed has remained fairly constant with the FPU version. When you compare these routines with the non-FPU version (which is more fair, because the fixed-point version of the application does not require an FPU), you can start to feel proud of yourself. The MultiplyMatrix() routine went from 1.04 milliseconds and 10.8 percent of the resources to 0.15 milliseconds and a mere 1.9 percent of CPU time! RotateMatrix() didn't improve much, but that's because you're still using expensive trigonometric functions. Let's see what you can do to fix that.

Look-up Tables

Look-up tables are based on a fairly simple concept: What if you were to create a huge table of numbers representing all of the possible results of cos() and sin()? OK, it would be impossible to include *all* of the possible results, but what if you broke it down into a specific number of results, say 360? Giving the table 360 entries would leave a result for all 360 degrees of an angle, and that's more than precise enough for our purposes.

The table is easy to create. Just initialize an array of the desired size and then call sin() and cos() for each of the entries. You don't need to worry about optimizing the table-creation routine, because it is only used once.

Store the look-up tables in two global variables, accessible anywhere in the application, named gSinTable[] and gCosTable[]:

```
Fixed24 gSinTable[360];
Fixed24 gCosTable[360];
```

Here is the function to initialize the look-up table:

```
/**
**   InitializeSinCosTable()
**
**   Sets the initial values for each of the entries of the sin and
**   cos tables.
**/
void  InitializeSinCosTable(void)
{
  short     i;
  float     radians;
  float     sinResult, cosResult;

  for (i = 0; i < 360; i++) {
    radians = i * kDegreesToRadians;

    sinResult = sin(radians);
    cosResult = cos(radians);

    gSinTable[i] = sinResult * 256;
    gCosTable[i] = cosResult * 256;
  }
}
```

When a function needs to find the result of a sin() or cos() function, all it needs to do is index the table. For example, instead of calling cos(xRot), index the array like this: gCosTable[xRot]. Listing 12-3 shows the RotateMatrix() routine, optimized to take advantage of look-up tables.

Listing 12-3 *The optimized RotateMatrix() routine*

```
/**
**   RotateMatrix()
**
**   Applies x,y, and z rotations to the input matrix.
**/
void  RotateMatrix(  Fixed24     inputMatrix[4][4],
                     short       xRot,
                     short       yRot,
                     short       zRot  )
{
  Fixed24   rotMatrix[4][4];
  Fixed24   tempMatrix1[4][4];
  Fixed24   tempMatrix2[4][4];
  Fixed24   xSin, xCos;
  Fixed24   ySin, yCos;
  Fixed24   zSin, zCos;

  /* Create fixed-point versions of each rotation trig function */
  xSin = gSinTable[xRot];
```

```
xCos = gCosTable[xRot];
ySin = gSinTable[yRot];
yCos = gCosTable[yRot];
zSin = gSinTable[zRot];
zCos = gCosTable[zRot];

/* We want to apply all three rotations to the inputMatrix,
 * in the order of y, x, and z. In order to accomplish all of
 * these transformations, we have to use two temporary matrices
 * and copy between them.
 */

/* Set rotMatrix to the y rotation matrix */
rotMatrix[0][0] = yCos; rotMatrix[0][1] = 0;
rotMatrix[0][2] = -ySin; rotMatrix[0][3] = 0;

rotMatrix[1][0] = 0; rotMatrix[1][1] = 1 << 8;
rotMatrix[1][2] = 0; rotMatrix[1][3] = 0;

rotMatrix[2][0] = ySin; rotMatrix[2][1] = 0;
rotMatrix[2][2] = yCos; rotMatrix[2][3] = 0;

rotMatrix[3][0] = 0; rotMatrix[3][1] = 0;
rotMatrix[3][2] = 0; rotMatrix[3][3] = 1 << 8;

/* Concatenate rotMatrix with inputMatrix */
MatrixMultiply(inputMatrix, rotMatrix, tempMatrix1);

/* Set rotMatrix to the x rotation matrix */
rotMatrix[0][0] = 1 << 8; rotMatrix[0][1] = 0;
rotMatrix[0][2] = 0; rotMatrix[0][3] = 0;

rotMatrix[1][0] = 0; rotMatrix[1][1] = xCos;
rotMatrix[1][2] = xSin; rotMatrix[1][3] = 0;

rotMatrix[2][0] = 0; rotMatrix[2][1] = -xSin;
rotMatrix[2][2] = xCos; rotMatrix[2][3] = 0;

rotMatrix[3][0] = 0; rotMatrix[3][1] = 0;
rotMatrix[3][2] = 0; rotMatrix[3][3] = 1 << 8;

/* Concatenate rotMatrix with tempMatrix1 */
MatrixMultiply(tempMatrix1, rotMatrix, tempMatrix2);

/* Set rotMatrix to the z rotation matrix */
rotMatrix[0][0] = zCos; rotMatrix[0][1] = zSin;
rotMatrix[0][2] = 0; rotMatrix[0][3] = 0;

rotMatrix[1][0] = -zSin; rotMatrix[1][1] = zCos;
rotMatrix[1][2] = 0; rotMatrix[1][3] = 0;
```

Continued on next page

Continued from previous page

```
    rotMatrix[2][0] = 0; rotMatrix[2][1] = 0;
    rotMatrix[2][2] = 1 << 8; rotMatrix[2][3] = 0;

    rotMatrix[3][0] = 0; rotMatrix[3][1] = 0;
    rotMatrix[3][2] = 0; rotMatrix[3][3] = 1 << 8;

    /* Concatenate rotMatrix with tempMatrix2 */
    MatrixMultiply(tempMatrix2, rotMatrix, tempMatrix1);

    /* Copy the temp matrix back into the input matrix */
    CopyMatrix(tempMatrix1, inputMatrix);
}
```

Because you are now measuring angles in degrees rather than radians, the main() function must be changed to reflect this. Otherwise, these are the only changes necessary to the project. The look-up table version of the cube application can be found in the Optimization 3 folder on the source code disc.

Compiling and running the application shows that you're up to 27 frames per second. The profiler results (shown in Figure 12-6), however, show the massive benefits to the RotateMatrix() routine. Its timing went from 0.923 milliseconds to 0.186 milliseconds, an improvement of almost five times.

Look-up tables have many more uses—some examples are tables for multiplying or dividing a small range of numbers or for graphical transformations. In fact, some programmers claim there is nothing that cannot be optimized by using look-up tables. Although this may or may not be true, it *is* something to consider.

There is one caveat about look-up tables. Although a function can check for an input that is out of bounds or invalid, a look-up table cannot. If you use look-up tables, you *must* ensure that you do not try to access values that are not in the table.

Optimization Profiler Info								
Method : Summary Timebase : Microseconds Saved at : 6 :15 :43 PM 8/26/95 Overhead : 1471.695								
Function Name	Count	Only	%	+Children	%	Average	Maximum	Minimum
CopyOntoScreen	774	11841.058	64.6	11841.058	64.6	15.299	16.109	14.584
PolygonFillDrawPolygon	1619	5647.709	30.8	5647.709	30.8	3.488	7.819	0.000
MatrixMultiply	2322	375.728	2.1	375.728	2.1	0.162	0.639	0.000
DrawObject	774	199.251	1.1	5859.778	32.0	0.257	0.686	0.000
RotateMatrix	774	144.190	0.8	522.986	2.9	0.186	0.582	0.000
TransformObject3D	774	85.250	0.5	85.250	0.5	0.110	0.427	0.000
BackfacePolygon	4644	13.076	0.1	13.076	0.1	0.003	0.330	0.000
ProjectObject	774	6.293	0.0	6.293	0.0	0.008	0.322	0.000
CopyMatrix	774	3.326	0.0	3.326	0.0	0.004	0.425	0.000
ObjectToWorldCoordinates	774	1.053	0.0	1.053	0.0	0.001	0.318	0.000
InitMatrix	774	0.920	0.0	0.920	0.0	0.001	0.272	0.000

FIGURE 12-6 ◉ *The profiling results after implementing look-up tables in the application*

Unrolling Loops

Loop unrolling is a very general optimization that can be applied to almost any application. Consider the following code example:

```
for (i = 0; i < 1000; i++) {
  array[i] = i;
}
```

When this code is compiled on a 68k Macintosh, the resulting assembly code spends two instructions assigning i to *array[i]*, but four instructions handling the loop. At least half, if not three-quarters, of the CPU's time is spent handling just the overhead of the loop; the rest is spent performing the actual task.

You could eliminate the process of looping by writing:

```
array[0] = 0;
array[1] = 1;
array[2] = 2;
...
array[999] = 999;
```

But who wants to write all that out by hand? After all, that's why you have the convenient loop structures of C. Instead of discarding the loop entirely, you can *unroll* it. This process increases the number of instructions executed every time through the loop in trade for executing the loop fewer times. Here's what the fragment would look like if you unrolled it five times:

```
for (i = 0; i < 1000; i += 5) {
  array[i] = i;
  array[i+1] = i+1;
  array[i+2] = i+2;
  array[i+3] = i+3;
  array[i+4] = i+4;
}
```

Unrolling loops can, in some cases, make a loop two or three times faster, but there is a limit. Modern CPUs have an on-chip memory cache; when the CPU accesses code and data from within that cache, it is faster by an order of magnitude. As you unroll the loop farther and farther, you'll start to notice less performance gain, until eventually, when the instructions no longer fit within the cache, your peformance will actually start to drop. In general, you only need to unroll a loop by between four and ten instructions to get the best results.

Let's incorporate loop unrolling into the code. The best routine to apply this principle to is MatrixMultiply(). This routine has three nested loops of four passes each, so the innermost instruction is executed 64 times. By unrolling the innermost loop entirely, there are only 16 iterations.

Unrolling the loop allows you to make a few other optimizations. First of all, instead of indexing the matrix3 array each time a multiplication is done, you can store the result in a temporary variable. Additionally, instead of shifting the 16.16 result of a multiplication back to a 24.8 number immediately, you can wait until all of the fixed-point numbers have been added up and then do just one shift. This is legal because all the fixed-point numbers you're adding are the same type.

```
/**
 **   MatrixMultiply()
 **
 **   Concatenates matrix1 and matrix2 and returns the result
 **   in matrix3
 **/
void  MatrixMultiply(  Fixed24 matrix1[4][4],
                       Fixed24 matrix2[4][4],
                       Fixed24 matrix3[4][4]  )
{
  short  i,j;
  Fixed24  temporaryFixed;

  for (i = 0; i < 4; i++) {
    for (j = 0; j < 4; j++) {
      /* Do the multiplication and store it in a temporary
       * variable
       */
      temporaryFixed = (matrix1[i][0] * matrix2[0][j]);
      temporaryFixed += (matrix1[i][1] * matrix2[1][j]);
      temporaryFixed += (matrix1[i][2] * matrix2[2][j]);
      temporaryFixed += (matrix1[i][3] * matrix2[3][j]);

      /* Shift the result back by 8 places */
      temporaryFixed = temporaryFixed >> 8;

      /* Store the result in the matrix */
      matrix3[i][j] = temporaryFixed;
    }
  }
}
```

This relatively minor optimization improves the speed of MatrixMultiply() from 0.168 milliseconds to 0.076 milliseconds. That's over a two times improvement, which is important because this routine is called so often. You'll find the code from this optimization in the Optimization 4 folder on the source code disc.

Incrementing Pointers

Indexing into an array can be a relatively expensive operation. The processor must fetch the address of the array, multiply its element size by your offset, add it to the array address, and then dereference it. If you are accessing an array in a tight loop, this can be a major source of speed loss.

If you access the array in a linear fashion (e.g., element 1, element 2, element 3, etc), there is a much more efficient method. Before you enter your loop, create a pointer that is pointing at the first element of the array, like this:

```
short   myArray[1000];
short   *arrayPtr;

arrayPtr = array;
for (i = 0; i < 1000; i++) {
```

Then every step through the loop, dereference and increment the pointer in one step, like this:

```
  *arrayPtr++ = i;
```

This statement puts the value of *i* into the address pointed to by *arrayPtr*, and then increments *arrayPtr* to point at the next element of the array. This little technique can give you massive speed enhancements and it's useful in many settings. It'll play a major role when you optimize the polygon-fill routine.

Bitshift Operations

The bitshift operations (<< and >>) have been used in several places throughout the code presented in this book (including the fixed-point mathematics introduced in this chapter), mainly for the purpose of moving around the bits of a variable. You probably already know that you can use multiplication and division as a replacement for bitshifting (multiplication for shifting left, division for shifting right).

With a few limitations, you can also use bitshifting as a substitute for multiplication or division. Take a simple multiplication, for example:

```
myVariable *= 2;
```

You can rewrite this line to use a bitshift operator, like this:

```
myVariable = myVariable << 1;
```

or, alternatively, like this:

```
myVariable <<= 1;
```

The catch is, you can only multiply by a power of 2 (because shifting by *n* places is equivalent to multiplying by 2^n). However, if you need to multiply by a value that is *not* a power of 2, you can break it down into several bitshifts added together. For example, take this multiplication:

```
myVariable *= 52;
```

Although 52 is not a power of 2, you can break it down into a shift by 5 (equivalent to multiplying by 32) plus a shift by 4 (a multiply by 16), plus a shift by 2 (a multiply by 4). The resulting instruction would look like this:

```
myVariable = (myVariable << 5) + (myVariable << 4) + (myVariable << 2);
```

Although this seems cumbersome, it actually produces the correct result faster than direct multiplication. Because it is obviously not as clear as the original, it should only be used in cases where speed is *absolutely* critical (in this case, you should also use comments liberally to explain what you're doing).

You can also do division using bitshifting. Like multiplication, it must be done using powers of 2:

```
myVariable = myVariable >> 1; /* Equivalent to dividing by 2 */
```

Shifting with LSL vs. ASL: The Inside Scoop

A bit of interesting trivia affects the bitshift operator. When processing a left shift (multiplication), the C compiler will use the LSL instruction (or the equivalent for the PowerPC processor). LSL stands for logical shift left; it takes all the bits of a variable and moves them to the left, setting the rightmost bit to 0. This operation is equivalent to a multiplication.

However, when the C compiler comes across a right shift, if it uses a LSR (logical shift right) operation, the *leftmost* bit will be set to 0. If you were working with unsigned numbers, this wouldn't cause a problem, but if you had a number like -2 (represented as 1111111111111110 in binary), an LSL instruction would produce 0111111111111111, or 32767. Fortunately, there is another instruction the C compiler can use: ASL, or arithmetic shift left. This operation preserves the leftmost bit, so it would produce 1111111111111111, or -1, the proper result.

Unfortunately, the C standard doesn't specify which operation should be used for a right shift. However, like most C compilers on the market, every major Macintosh C compiler (including Metrowerks, Think C, and MPW C), uses the ASL operator. Thus you're safe from this problem, but it's something you should be aware of if you're looking at other platforms or compilers.

There is one problem with using the right bitshift operator for division. If you divide negative numbers, it can give you a slightly different result than using the division operator. When the processor divides a negative number, it rounds the result up, or toward 0. When it uses the bitshift operator, it rounds the number down. Thus, if you use the right bitshift on a negative odd number, the result will be one less than normal. For most games, accuracy isn't all that critical so the difference is not usually a problem, but you should be aware of it.

Based on some sample tests compiled in Metrowerks, using the left bitshift instead of a multiplication yields almost a 10 times performance gain on a 68040, whereas the right bitshift is almost 20 times as fast as an integer division. Although this balance may vary significantly on different configurations, you can be confident that a bitshift is faster than the equivalent arithmetic operation.

If you go through your program and change all of your multiplies to bitshifts, it is possible that you won't see any speed-up. This is because most compilers are smart enough to convert a multiplication into a bitshift automatically (as long as the multiplication is by a power of 2). However, the compiler will not usually convert divisions into bitshifts, particularly if you're using signed values (because they're not always entirely equivalent).

Bitshift operations can be applied only to integer numbers. For floating-point values, you will have to stick with the normal methods of multiplication and division.

Miscellaneous Optimization Tips

Now let's look at some general rules and smaller changes that can be used to tweak the most critical portions of your code. Most of the speed enhancements suggested here are rather minor, but they can make a difference in the middle of a tight loop. As with the other optimizations, don't bother to use these unless you really need the best possible speed.

Optimize Prudently

Only optimize a routine if it's really going to speed up the entire program. And if you do optimize, don't turn it into a complete mess, like this:

```
a = (*c >> a) * (&(d++))->e;
```

What does that line of code do? I don't know, and you won't be able to figure it out either when you come back to it to fix a bug.

Contrary to what most programmers seem to think, adding comments to your code does not slow it down. Comments optimize the speed with which you can fix bugs in your code or reuse it for some other purpose in the future. Also, eliminating white space and making your code *look* compact does absolutely nothing for its performance. Long, descriptive variable names do not hurt the performance of your code, either. If your code is not clear enough to debug, it's useless.

The Best Optimization Is a New Algorithm

The first step when attempting to optimize your code is to examine just how you're achieving a task. Often another approach will make better use of the computer's resources. Although other optimization techniques might gain you a twofold or fourfold performance gain, by using a different algorithm, you might realize a ten- or twentyfold increase. Once you're confident that you're using the best algorithm you can think of, proceed with the other optimization techniques.

Global Variables Are Slow

If you use global variables in your function, don't access them inside of a tight loop. Instead, at the beginning of the routine, copy them into a local variable. If you change the value, copy it back into the global variable before leaving the routine.

Pass Pointers instead of Large Structures

If you need to call a routine and pass it a large structure, instead pass it the address of that structure (using the & operator). Any variables you pass into a function are copied onto the stack; if the structure is large, it will not only use quite a bit of stack space, it will waste time copying that information.

Use the register Keyword, but Sparingly

When declaring your local variables, you can add the keyword register to its definition, like this:

```
register long    myImportantVariable;
```

Using the register keyword tells the compiler that, if possible, it should allocate a register specifically for this variable. If the compiler has run out of registers, it can ignore the keyword, so this doesn't guarantee that the variable will be in a register. If a variable is in a register, the CPU can access it much more quickly than it could if the variable was on the stack. The compiler usually does a good job of deciding which variables are accessed most often and therefore should be given a register, but sometimes giving your compiler this hint can enhance your function's speed.

However, if it turns out that you're wrong about how often this variable is accessed, you can actually impair the speed of your program. In general, it is best to leave the register allocation up to the compiler, but if you do decide to use the register keyword, profile the function to make sure that you made it faster.

Access Data Linearly if Possible

When you're accessing data from memory, it is much faster if you can access it linearly. For example, look at this simple loop that assigns data to a two-dimensional array:

```
for (i = 0; i < 1000; i++) {
  for (j = 0; j < 1000; j++) {
    myArray[j][i] = i * j;
  }
}
```

This loop will access the array as myArray[0][0], myArray[1][0], myArray[2][0], etc. In memory, however, the array is stored as myArray[0][0], myArray[0][1], myArray[0][2], and so on, so the loop is accessing memory locations 1000 elements apart every time through!

Simply rewriting the loop to access the elements in the opposite order would speed it up immensely:

```
for (i = 0; i < 1000; i++) {
  for (j = 0; j < 1000; j+=) {
    myArray[i][j] = i * j;
  }
}
```

The reason for this is that the CPU has a cache between it and the main memory banks. If data accesses are happening in one part of memory, an entire chunk will get loaded into the cache, where it can be accessed much faster.

Take Advantage of Locality

This tip is very similar to the last one. When organizing your code, put similar functions together in the same file. Also, if a function can be called only by other functions in the same file, it can sometimes help to declare the function as *static*, like this:

```
static short myFunction(void)
{
   return 1;
}
```

A function declared as static cannot be accessed from outside that source code file, which can sometimes help the compiler when it generates its jump tables.

Use malloc() for Small Memory Allocations

The Macintosh toolbox provides a function called NewPtr() for allocating blocks of data. However, NewPtr() can be slow and it doesn't perform well if you start to allocate a lot of pointers. The standard C function, malloc(), is handy for this task. malloc() is more efficient when dealing with many small allocations and it has the advantage of being portable to other platforms as well.

Use while() and Count Backwards

Instead using a for() loop and incrementing a variable to accomplish a task a certain number of times, you can use a while() loop and decrement a variable each time, like this:

```
count = 100;
while (count--) {
  do_my_stuff();
}
```

Using the while() loop reduces the work the CPU must complete each time through the loop.

Optimizing PolygonFillDrawPolygon()

Two functions on the profiler report are taking up most of the time. PolygonFillDrawPolygon() takes approximately 25 percent of the CPU time right now, while CopyOntoScreen() takes about 65 percent (on a 25Mhz 68040; your mileage may vary). Although PolgyonFillDrawPolygon() is already fairly fast, you can squeeze out a little more performance using new optimization techniques.

One of the first things you might notice is that every time a pixel is accessed, the pixMapPtr is treated like an array:

```
pixMapPtr[pixelOffset1] = polygon->color;
```

These lines are fairly time critical, so anything you can do to speed them up should be worth it. First of all, you can turn *pixelOffset1* into a pointer that points directly at its pixel just by adding the *pixMapPtr* address to it. The best place to do this is when the pixel offsets are being calculated in the first place:

```
/* Set up the offsets for both edges */
pixelPtr1 = (rowBytes * yStart1) + xStart1 + pixMapPtr;
pixelPtr2 = (rowBytes * yStart2) + xStart2 + pixMapPtr;
```

This calculation can also safely be moved outside of the main loop because it only needs to be calculated once for each side.

The other part of optimizing the pixel plotting statement is to stop dereferencing the polygon structure every time you need to access the polygon's color. Instead, store the polygon's color in a local variable when the function starts, like this:

```
polygonColor = polygon->color;
```

The modified statement looks like this:

```
*pixelOffset1 = polygonColor;
```

Another good area to optimize is the loop for drawing the horizontal line for the polygon:

```
length = pixelOffset2 - pixelOffset1;
if (length < 0) {        /* If negative... */
  length = -length;      /* make it positive */
  lineStart = pixelOffset2;
  lineEnd = pixelOffset1;
} else {
  lineStart = pixelOffset1;
  lineEnd = pixelOffset2;
}
for (i = lineStart; i <= lineEnd; i++) {
  pixMapPtr[i] = polygon->color;
}
```

This could be considered the innermost loop of the polygon-fill function and the CPU spends quite a bit of time here. As in the previous optimization, you can access the pixels directly instead of through an array, but here you can go even further. Instead of using a for() loop, set *i* to the line length and count backwards using a while() loop. You can also set up a temporary pointer to the first pixel and dereference and increment it in one step each time through the loop (a very fast operation).

```
length = (pixelPtr2 - pixelPtr1)+1;
if (length < 0) {        /* If negative... */
  length = -length;      /* make it positive */
```

Continued on next page

Continued from previous page
```
  linePixelPtr = pixelPtr2;
} else {
  linePixelPtr = pixelPtr1;
}

while (length--)
  *linePixelPtr++ = polygonColor;
```

There is one more area of this function that is a little slow. Here is an example:

```
/* Get the x & y of new ending vertex */
xEnd2 = polygon->polyVertex[end2]->sx;
yEnd2 = polygon->polyVertex[end2]->sy;
```

As you can see, you're dereferencing the polygon every time you want access to its vertices. You can streamline this operation by declaring a local variable that holds a pointer to this list:

```
Vertex3D  **polyVertexList;
```

Here is how to initialize the variable:

```
polyVertexList = polygon->polyVertex;
```

Then each time you need to access a polygon vertex, you can use the local polyVertexList, like this:

```
/* Get the x & y of new ending vertex */
xEnd2 = polyVertexList[end2]->sx;
yEnd2 = polyVertexList[end2]->sy;
```

Although this doesn't produce a huge speedup, it doesn't hurt the code's readability, so keep it.

Listing 12-4 is the complete optimized polygon-fill routine. You'll find it in the Poly Render.c file located in the Optimization 5 folder on the source code disc.

Listing 12-4 The optimized polygon-fill routine

```
/**
**    PolygonFillDrawPolygon()
**
**    Draw a polygon with a solid color
**/
void  PolygonFillDrawPolygon(  Polygon3D      *polygon,
                               Ptr            pixMapPtr,
                               unsigned long  rowBytes  )
{
  long      i;
  short     dx1, dx2;    /* x length of sides */
  short     dy1, dy2;    /* y length of sides */
  short     topVertex;
  short     edgeCount;   /* Edges remaining to draw */
```

```
short       polygonColor;
Vertex3D  **polyVertexList; /* Local pointer to the polygon vertices */

/* These variables define which two segments (1 & 2) we're
 * drawing between. start1 and end1 are the starting and
 * ending indices of line #1, xStart1, yStart1, xEnd1,
 * and yEnd1 are the coordinates of line #1. Each of these
 * has a counterpart for line #2.
 */
short       start1, end1;
short       xStart1, yStart1;
short       xEnd1, yEnd1;
short       start2, end2;
short       xStart2, yStart2;
short       xEnd2, yEnd2;
Ptr         pixelPtr1, pixelPtr2;
Ptr         linePixelPtr;

edgeCount = polygon->numOfVertices;
polygonColor = polygon->color;
polyVertexList = polygon->polyVertex;

/* Figure out which vertex is at the top of the polygon */
{
  short  minVertexY;

  /* Start by assuming the first vertex is on top */
  topVertex = 0;
  minVertexY = polyVertexList[0]->sy;

  /* loop through all of the vertices */
  for (i = 1; i < polygon->numOfVertices; i++) {
    /* Check to see if this vertex is higher
     * than the current one.
     */
    if (polyVertexList[i]->sy < minVertexY) {
      /* It is. Remember it for later */
      topVertex = i;
      minVertexY = polyVertexList[i]->sy;
    }
  }
}

/* Find the starting and ending vertices for the first
 * two edges
 */
start1 = topVertex;
start2 = topVertex;  /* They both start from the same vertex */
xStart1 = xStart2 = polyVertexList[start1]->sx;
yStart1 = yStart2 = polyVertexList[start1]->sy;
```

Continued on next page

Continued from previous page

```
/* Get the end of vertex 1 - check for wrap */
end1 = start1 - 1;
if (end1 < 0)
  end1 = polygon->numOfVertices - 1;
xEnd1 = polyVertexList[end1]->sx;
yEnd1 = polyVertexList[end1]->sy;

/* Get the end of vertex 2 */
end2 = start2 + 1;
if (end2 == polygon->numOfVertices)
  end2 = 0;
xEnd2 = polyVertexList[end2]->sx;
yEnd2 = polyVertexList[end2]->sy;

/* Our setup is done. Start the drawing */

/* Set up the offsets for both edges */
pixelPtr1 = (rowBytes * yStart1) + xStart1 + pixMapPtr;
pixelPtr2 = (rowBytes * yStart2) + xStart2 + pixMapPtr;

while (edgeCount > 0) {  /* Draw until we're out of edges */
  short    errorTerm1, errorTerm2;
  short    xUnit1, yUnit1;
  short    xUnit2, yUnit2;
  short    count1, count2;
  short    length;

  /* Initialize error terms */
  errorTerm1 = errorTerm2 = 0;

  /* Find the x length of edges */
  dx1 = xEnd1 - xStart1;

  /* If the line is going to the left, set the
   * xUnit to -1 and make dx positive
   */
  if (dx1 < 0) {
    dx1 = -dx1;
    xUnit1 = -1;
  } else {
    xUnit1 = 1;
  }

  /* Do the same for edge 2 */
  dx2 = xEnd2 - xStart2;
  if (dx2 < 0) {
    dx2 = -dx2;
    xUnit2 = -1;
  } else {
    xUnit2 = 1;
  }
```

```
/* Find the y length of the edges */
dy1 = yEnd1 - yStart1;
yUnit1 = rowBytes;

dy2 = yEnd2 - yStart2;
yUnit2 = rowBytes;

/* Use one of four different methods for drawing between
 * these edges
 */
if (dx1 > dy1) {  /* Edge 1 slope is < 1 */
  if (dx2 > dy2) {  /* Case 1 */
    /* Edge 2 slope is < 1 */
    /* Figure out how many pixels to draw in each edge */
    count1 = dx1;
    count2 = dx2;

    /* Draw until one of the edges is done */
    while (count1 && count2) {
      /* Draw the wireframe portion of the line
       * until we're ready to jump down a pixel
       */

      while ((errorTerm1 < dx1) && (count1 > 0)) {
        count1--;   /* Count off this pixel */
        pixelPtr1 += xUnit1;  /* Point to next pixel */
        xStart1 += xUnit1;

        /* Increase the error term */
        errorTerm1 += dy1;

        /* Check to see if we're ready to move in y */
        if (errorTerm1 < dx1) {
          /* Nope, we're not ready yet. Plot a pixel for
           * this line
           */
          *pixelPtr1 = polygonColor;
        }
      }
      /* Reset the error term */
      errorTerm1 -= dx1;

      /* Now do the same thing to edge 2 */

      while ((errorTerm2 < dx2) && (count2 > 0)) {
        count2--;      /* Count off this pixel */
        pixelPtr2 += xUnit2;  /* Point to next pixel */
        xStart2 += xUnit2;

        /* Increase the error term */
        errorTerm2 += dy2;
```

Continued on next page

Continued from previous page

```
          /* Are we ready to move in y? */
          if (errorTerm2 < dx2) {
            /* We're not ready yet. Plot a pixel */
            *pixelPtr2 = polygonColor;
          }
        }

        /* Reset the error term */
        errorTerm2 -= dx2;

        /* Draw the line from edge 1 to edge 2 */

        length = (pixelPtr2 - pixelPtr1)+1;
        if (length < 0) {   /* If negative... */
          length = -length;  /* make it positive */
          linePixelPtr = pixelPtr2;
        } else {
          linePixelPtr = pixelPtr1;
        }

        while (length--)
          *linePixelPtr++ = polygonColor;

        /* Advance to next line */
        pixelPtr1 += yUnit1;
        yStart1++;
        pixelPtr2 += yUnit2;
        yStart2++;
      }
    } else {   /* Case 2 */
    /* Edge 2 slope is >= 1 */

    /* Increment edge 1 on x and edge 2 on y */
    count1 = dx1;
    count2 = dy2;

    /* Draw until one of the edges is done */
    while (count1 && count2) {
      /* Draw the wireframe portion of the line
       * until we're ready to jump down a pixel
       */

      while ((errorTerm1 < dx1) && (count1 > 0)) {
        count1--;  /* Count off this pixel */
        pixelPtr1 += xUnit1;  /* Point to next pixel */
        xStart1 += xUnit1;

        /* Increase the error term */
        errorTerm1 += dy1;

        /* Check to see if we're ready to move in y */
```

```
        if (errorTerm1 < dx1) {
          /* Nope, we're not ready yet. Plot a pixel for
           * this line
           */
          *pixelPtr1 = polygonColor;
        }
      }
      /* Reset the error term */
      errorTerm1 -= dx1;

      /* Now handle edge 2 */

      errorTerm2 += dx2;  /* Increment error term */

      /* Check to see if it's time to move in the x
       * direction. If so, reset the error term
       * and increment the pixelOffset
       */
      if (errorTerm2 >= dy2) {
        errorTerm2 -= dy2;
        pixelPtr2 += xUnit2;
        xStart2 += xUnit2;
      }
      count2--;

      /* Draw a line from edge 1 to edge 2.
       * Find the length of the line:
       */
      length = (pixelPtr2 - pixelPtr1)+1;
      if (length < 0) {  /* If negative... */
        length = -length;  /* make it positive */
        linePixelPtr = pixelPtr2;
      } else {
        linePixelPtr = pixelPtr1;
      }

      while (length--)
        *linePixelPtr++ = polygonColor;

      /* Advance to next line */
      pixelPtr1 += yUnit1;
      yStart1++;
      pixelPtr2 += yUnit2;
      yStart2++;
    }
  }
} else{
  /* Edge 1 slope is >= 1 */
  if (dx2 > dy2) {  /* Case 3 */
    /* Edge 2 slope is < 1 */
```

Continued on next page

Continued from previous page

```
                /* Increment edge 1 on y and edge 2 on x */
                count1 = dy1;
                count2 = dx2;

                /* Draw until one edge is done */
                while (count1 && count2) {
                  /* Process edge 1 */

                  /* Initialize edge 1 errorterm */
                  errorTerm1 += dx1;

                  /* If it's time to move in the x dimension, reset
                   * error term and move offset to the next pixel
                   */
                  if (errorTerm1 >= dy1) {
                    errorTerm1 -= dy1;
                    pixelPtr1 += xUnit1;
                    xStart1 += xUnit1;
                  }

                  count1--;

                  /* Handle the second edge */

                  while ((errorTerm2 < dx2) && (count2 > 0)) {
                    count2--;       /* Count off this pixel */
                    pixelPtr2 += xUnit2;  /* Point to next pixel */
                    xStart2 += xUnit2;

                    /* Increase the error term */
                    errorTerm2 += dy2;

                    /* Are we ready to move in y? */
                    if (errorTerm2 <= dx2) {
                      /* We're not ready yet. Plot a pixel */
                      *pixelPtr2 = polygonColor;
                    }
                  }

                  /* Reset the error term */
                  errorTerm2 -= dx2;

                  /* Draw the line from edge 1 to edge 2 */
                  length = (pixelPtr2 - pixelPtr1)+1;
                  if (length < 0) {  /* If negative... */
                    length = -length; /* make it positive */
                    linePixelPtr = pixelPtr2;
                  } else {
                    linePixelPtr = pixelPtr1;
                  }
```

```
      while (length--)
        *linePixelPtr++ = polygonColor;

      /* Advance to next line */
      pixelPtr1 += yUnit1;
      yStart1++;
      pixelPtr2 += yUnit2;
      yStart2++;
    }
} else {  /* Case 4 */
  /* Edge 2 slope >= 1. Increment edge 1
   * and edge 2 on y
   */
  count1 = dy1;
  count2 = dy2;

  /* Draw until one edge is done */

  while (count1 && count2) {
    /* Handle edge 1 */

    /* Initialize edge 1 errorterm */
    errorTerm1 += dx1;

    /* If it's time to move in the x dimension, reset
     * error term and move offset to the next pixel
     */
    if (errorTerm1 >= dy1) {
      errorTerm1 -= dy1;
      pixelPtr1 += xUnit1;
      xStart1 += xUnit1;
    }

    count1--;

    /* Now handle edge 2 */

    errorTerm2 += dx2;  /* Increment error term */

    /* Check to see if it's time to move in the x
     * direction. If so, reset the error term
     * and increment the pixelOffset
     */
    if (errorTerm2 >= dy2) {
      errorTerm2 -= dy2;
      pixelPtr2 += xUnit2;
      xStart2 += xUnit2;
    }
    count2--;

    /* Draw a line from edge 1 to edge 2.
```

Continued on next page

Continued from previous page

```
         * Find the length of the line:
         */
        length = (pixelPtr2 - pixelPtr1)+1;
        if (length < 0) {  /* If negative... */
          length = -length;  /* make it positive */
          linePixelPtr = pixelPtr2;
        } else {
          linePixelPtr = pixelPtr1;
        }

        while (length--)
          *linePixelPtr++ = polygonColor;

        /* Advance to next line */
        pixelPtr1 += yUnit1;
        yStart1++;
        pixelPtr2 += yUnit2;
        yStart2++;
      }
    }
  }

  /* An edge is done. Start another edge, if there are any remaining */
  if (count1 == 0) {
    /* Edge 1 is complete. Decrement the edgecount */
    edgeCount--;

    /* Make the ending vertex into the starting vertex */
    start1 = end1;

    /* Get a new ending vertex */
    end1 -= 1;

    /* Check to see if this vertex wraps to the beginning */
    if (end1 < 0) {
      end1 = polygon->numOfVertices-1;
    }

    /* Get the x & y of the new ending vertex */
    xEnd1 = polyVertexList[end1]->sx;
    yEnd1 = polyVertexList[end1]->sy;
  }

  if (count2 == 0) {
    /* Edge 2 is complete. Decrement the edge count */
    edgeCount -= 1;

    /* Make ending vertex 2 into starting vertex 2 */
    start2 = end2;

    /* Get a new ending vertex */
```

```
     end2++;

     /* Check to see if this vertex wraps to the beginning */
     if (end2 == polygon->numOfVertices) {
       end2 = 0;
     }

     /* Get the x & y of new ending vertex */
     xEnd2 = polyVertexList[end2]->sx;
     yEnd2 = polyVertexList[end2]->sy;
   }
  }
 }
```

The Speed of the New Polygon-Fill Routine

Running the application using the optimized polygon-fill function gives you a frame rate of between 29 and 30 fps. Looking at the profiling statistics, the timing of PolygonFillDrawPolygon() is now 2.55 milliseconds, down from the 3.48 millisecond timing done at the beginning of the chapter, approximately a 40 percent speed increase. Although this increase isn't huge, as I mentioned before this algorithm was pretty fast to begin with.

The CopyBits() call has been a spectre haunting you throughout this process. With the optimizations in the rest of the program, CopyBits() now consumes almost 71 percent of the CPU time. The next chapter will tackle this problem and present you with ways of bypassing QuickDraw and writing directly to the window.

13

Accelerating and Bypassing QuickDraw

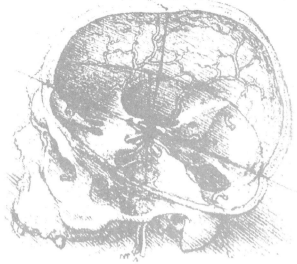

Accelerating and Bypassing QuickDraw

In the last chapter, you saw that your application originally spent about half its time in its own code, and half in CopyBits(). Through a series of optimizations, by the end of the chapter, you had reduced the functions of the application to use about 30 percent of the CPU time, whereas CopyBits() uses approximately 70 percent. If you want to increase the speed of your application even more, it's clear that you have to start attacking the CopyBits() function and find a faster way of copying images onto the screen.

In this chapter, you'll be replacing the CopyBits() function with one that is faster. However, you're not going to stop at improving the bit-copying routine but you'll also be looking at ways to bypass the remainder of QuickDraw (because CopyBits is only a small portion of QuickDraw as a whole). In fact, you'll end up with an application that doesn't use *any* QuickDraw functions under certain circumstances. You'll also be creating a routine that will take advantage of a feature found only on 68040 processors. However, there is something to discuss first that is more important than how to get around QuickDraw: when and why you *should not* do this.

Why Not to Bypass QuickDraw

As any Apple QuickDraw engineer can tell you, this chapter treads on dangerous ground. However, this is the way it's always been for games—if programmers didn't break the rules, you wouldn't have any of the incredible creations you see today. Marathon, F/A-18 Hornet, A-10—they all work behind the operating system's back when it's necessary. The key is knowing which rules to break and when.

Perhaps the greatest consideration to take into effect is compatibility. The techniques documented in this chapter are not guaranteed to work on all future Macintosh models. In fact, there are several older models with which they are already incompatible (more about that later). Apple has been known to change the structure of basic parts of the Macintosh. If you write directly to the screen, your game might not work in a future Macintosh.

The second consideration is that it's very difficult to write routines that are faster than QuickDraw's. Despite the lamentations of some programmers, QuickDraw is not slow. However, it is very general purpose, and every time it is called, it has some overhead as it checks its parameters to see if they're valid. QuickDraw goes through great pains not to crash with invalid inputs to help ensure a stable platform.

QuickDraw can also function under many environments—if you bypass it, you lose several of its features, including the following:

▸ Clipping to a port: If you write directly to the screen, you must ensure that you don't write outside the bounds of the window.

▸ Drawing across several monitors: Don't try to do this by hand—it's much more complicated than it looks.

▸ Automatically adjusting for different monitor bit depths: You must write code specifically for each bit depth you support.

▸ Drawing to windows in the background: If you write directly to the screen, you'll either have to limit yourself to drawing on foreground windows or calculating complicated intersections to avoid drawing over the wrong areas.

▸ Drawing over balloon help: In drawing to the screen, you'll copy over any balloon help that's being displayed. However, this is a relatively minor problem because balloon help is rarely used in games.

If nothing else, attempting to write routines for handling these cases should give you great respect for Apple's engineers. It would take a superhuman programmer to write a routine that did everything that CopyBits() did, only faster.

Why You Should Bypass QuickDraw

OK, sure, you've probably heard all the reasons not to bypass QuickDraw before. In spite of those concerns, it's part of a hacker's spirit to do it anyway, and with good reason: Under limited constraints, you can write a routine that works faster than CopyBits() does.

The reason you can beat CopyBits() is that you know certain things about your environment that QuickDraw doesn't. You know that most of the time you're going to be copying from an 8-bit offscreen image onto an 8-bit monitor. You know that both images use the same color table and you know how large the offscreen image and the window are. You can build special routines that are optimized for these conditions and perform extremely well under them.

At the same time, you should be aware that the user's environment may not always support the features you require for custom routines. I'll include two versions of offscreen functions—one that uses QuickDraw and one that uses custom functions.

This provides several benefits. If future Macintoshes do not support custom routines or the user's machine does not have the necessary features, the game can fall back on QuickDraw. According to Apple's guidelines, you should *always* include a QuickDraw version of your routines.

A New Drawing System

Let's look at how you're handling your QuickDraw offscreen images right now. As Figure 13-1 shows, the offscreen is created by calling NewGWorld(). The GWorld is then erased and the object is drawn into it using DrawObject(). You then use CopyBits() to transfer it to the screen. This process provides a smooth animation with very little flickering.

There are two ways you can go about drawing directly onto the screen. The first method is to force DrawObject() to draw onto the screen instead of onto a GWorld and directly erase the screen for each frame. This is the fastest method because you're only writing the image information once, but there is a big problem with flickering. Because the screen has to be erased before the object is drawn, there is a certain amount of time when there is nothing being shown in the window and then the object is drawn line by line. The effect is similar to looking through a fan; and it is unacceptable for game animation.

The second method is to do everything the same as for QuickDraw, except replace the CopyBits() routine with your own. This isn't as fast, but it provides an animation as smooth (or even smoother) than that obtained from QuickDraw.

Environment Restrictions

Before you start to build your routines, you must accept a few restrictions that will allow you to make good optimizations:

 Both the offscreen image and the monitor must be in 8-bit mode. This allows you to copy quickly, with no color translation, and with only 1 byte per pixel.

 The destination window must be the same size as the offscreen image, but that's easy to control within the code. In addition, the width of the window must be a multiple of 16 (you'll see why later). You're going to optimize your drawing to a window of 480x300 pixels, but the routines can easily be modified to handle a different size.

 For the fastest techniques you'll be using, the x coordinate of the destination window must be a multiple of 16. This lines it up on a 16-byte memory boundary that allows you to take a few shortcuts, as you'll soon see.

FIGURE 13-1

ⓐ ⓐ ⓐ ⓐ ⓐ ⓐ

The object-drawing sequence

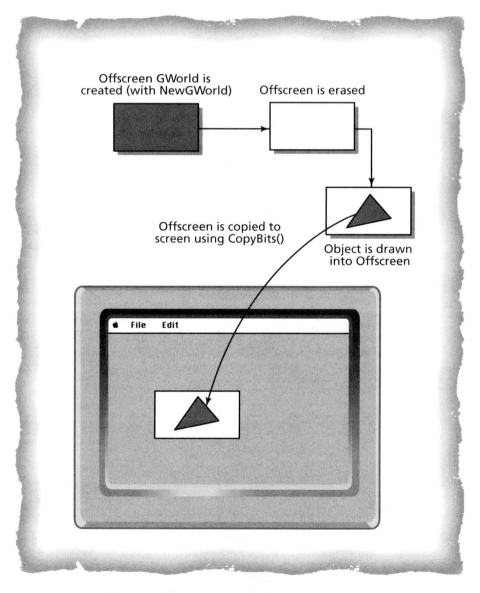

Offscreen GWorld is created (with NewGWorld)

Offscreen is erased

Offscreen is copied to screen using CopyBits()

Object is drawn into Offscreen

🍎 File   Edit

Finding the Screen

The first step to drawing onto the screen is to find its address in memory. The Macintosh screen is nothing more than a glorified PixMap. And this PixMap is contained in each and every window on the screen. So to gain access to the screen, you can just look at the fields of any window being shown on that screen.

Normally, you declare windows to be a WindowPtr. A WindowPtr holds a BitMap instead of a PixMap (a BitMap is only black and white), but if you typecast the window to a CGrafPtr (or a color window), you can access its PixMapHandle.

Once you have the PixMapHandle, you can call GetPixBaseAddr() (just as for GWorlds) and it returns the address of the upper-left-hand pixel of the screen. Like any other PixMap, the screen also has a rowbytes value, which is obtained in the same way as for any pixmap. Here is some code that obtains the screen's information from a window:

```
screenPixMapHandle = ((CGrafPtr)myWindow)->portPixMap;
screenBaseAddress = GetPixBaseAddr(screenPixMapHandle);
screenRowBytes = (**screenPixMapHandle).rowBytes & 0x3FFF;
```

Unlike a normal PixMapHandle, the screen's PixMap does not need to be locked down with LockPixels() before you do any drawing.

Because you want to draw directly into the window and the address you've obtained actually points to the upper-left-hand corner of the *screen*, you have to offset the address to find the upper-left-hand corner of the *window*, like this:

```
windowBaseAddress = screenBaseAddress +
                    (windowYCoordinate * screenRowBytes) +
                    windowXCoordinate;
```

Copying onto the Screen

Now that you have the address of the window's pixel data, you can copy an image into it from an offscreen GWorld. The easiest way to do this is to loop through the height of the image and then loop through the width, copying each pixel as you go along, like this:

```
src = offscreenPixMapBaseAddress;
dst = screenPixMapBaseAddress;

/* Loop through the y pixels */
for (i = 0; i < height; i++) {
  /* Loop through the x pixels */
  for (j = 0; j < width; j++) {
    /* Copy one pixel */
    *dst++ = *src++;
  }
```

Continued on next page

Continued from previous page

```
/* Move from the right-hand side of the pixmap to the left-hand
 * side of the next row
 */
src += (offscreenPixMapRowBytes - width);
dst += (screenRowBytes - width);
}
```

This loop will do the job, but will do it much slower than CopyBits() will. Because you're so concerned about speed, let's look at how to speed up this loop.

The most obvious measure would be to unroll the inner loop, which will give you a modest speed enhancement. However, even more speed could be realized by copying 4 bytes at a time instead of just 1 because the pixmap's width will be a multiple of 16 (and, consequently, a multiple of 4 as well). This will significantly enhance the loop's speed.

The *src* and *dst* pointers are defined as pointers to bytes. To copy a longword at a time, you must first typecast the longword to a long pointer (long *). If you use the increment operator, it will get incremented by 4 pixels each time.

It's also a little tricky to add the rowbytes value onto the source and destination pixels. Because they're defined as long pointers, adding the rowbytes will actually cause the pointer to be incremented by *four times* the rowbytes value. To solve this problem, fool the compiler into thinking that, for this task, the pointers are just 32-bit integer values by typecasting them.

Listing 13-1 is the improved loop.

Listing 13-1 *The improved loop routine*

```
/* Use a loop to copy a longword at a time to the screen.
 * Typecast the data pointers to (long *)'s, so that
 * a longword is copied every time, plus it gets
 * incremented by 4 instead of 1.
 */
longsrc = (long*)offscreenPixMapBaseAddress;
longdst = (long*)screenPixMapBaseAddress;

/* Set the rowbytes values up so they only move from the right-hand
 * side of the pixmap to the left-hand side of the next row.
 */
srcRowBytes = offscreenPixMapRowBytes - width;
dstRowBytes = screenRowbytes - width;

/* Start the loop */
do {
  /* (kWindowWidth / 4) longwords need to be copied per
   * row, and there are 8 copied per iteration of the
   * inner loop, so we want to loop (kWindowWidth / 32) times.
   * In this case, it's OK to use a divide, because
   * you're dividing a constant - this will get evaluated
   * at compile-time, not at run-time.
   */
```

```
    i = kWindowWidth / 32;
    do {
      /* Do the copy */
      *longdst++ = *longsrc++;
      *longdst++ = *longsrc++;
      *longdst++ = *longsrc++;
      *longdst++ = *longsrc++;
      *longdst++ = *longsrc++;
      *longdst++ = *longsrc++;
      *longdst++ = *longsrc++;
      *longdst++ = *longsrc++;
    } while (--i);

    /* Jump down a row. This is a little tricky, since if
     * we just add dstRowBytes to the long pointer, it will
     * get incremented by 4*dstRowBytes. Instead, we
     * fool the compiler into thinking it's a just a long
     * value, add the rowbytes to it, then typecast it back
     * to a long pointer.
     */
    longdst = (long *)((long)longdst + dstRowBytes);
} while (--height);
```

This improved loop is a fair amount faster than CopyBits() and it's what you'll be using on most Macintoshes. However, if you're using a Macintosh with a 68040 processor, you can take advantage of a special feature that will give you some incredible performance benefits.

An Image Copier Just for the 68040

A special instruction called MOVE16 was added to the 68040 chip; it wasn't in any previous 68k CPU nor is it in the PowerPC chip. MOVE16 is a machine code instruction that can move 16 bytes at a time from one memory location to another. However, if you want to take advantage of it, you'll need to write an assembly language routine to do it; none of the available Macintosh C compilers currently takes advantage of this instruction when compiling C code (and they probably never will).

There are a few catches to using MOVE16. First of all, any code that uses this instruction will not run on a 68000, 68020, or 68030 processor (although it will run in emulation on the Power Macintosh). You'll have to build code that will detect the type of processor being used and, if the processor is an 040, it will use the new routine.

The second catch is that both the source and destination addresses used for MOVE16 must be 16-byte aligned. This little catch is what really makes MOVE16 more difficult to use and it's why my original list of restrictions said that the x coordinate of the window must be a multiple of 16. Forcing the window to that location ensures that the destination address will be on a 16-byte boundary.

The source address, however, is a different story. When you call NewGWorld(), you have absolutely no control over whether the resulting pixmap will be on a 16-byte boundary. You're guaranteed that it'll fall on a 4-byte boundary, but that's it.

If you don't want your image-copying routines to get too complicated, this is the end of the story—the MOVE16 instruction is unusable. However, if you're willing to make your offscreen image a little bit more abstract, you can make this work (and, as you'll see, it'll be worth it for the speed).

Abandoning QuickDraw

You're not going to be creating a GWorld. In fact, the offscreen image will be created by allocating a huge pointer that will hold all the pixel data. Because it's not a pixmap, the rowbytes value will be the same as the width. And you'll notice that all the routines you've created for drawing into an image have required only a pointer to the first pixel and a rowbytes value. The DrawObject() routines will remain untouched—they don't need to know that they're not drawing into a GWorld.

Creating your own offscreen buffer will require you to write your own routine for erasing the pixmap, but that won't be too hard (although, as you'll soon find out, it takes a long time just to *erase* an image). In fact, you won't be able to use *any* QuickDraw routines on the new offscreen image. In this case, that doesn't really matter, but that fact may make this technique a little less appealing for some tasks.

Creating a new pointer, however, does not ensure that pointer address will be on a 16-byte boundary. Therefore, you'll create a pointer that is 16 bytes larger than what you really need. Then you'll offset that pointer so that your image data will start on the first 16-byte boundary. You need to keep the original pointer around so you can dispose of the image at a later time. Here is some code to accomplish this task:

```
gCustomImagePtr = NewPtr((kWindowRowBytes * kWindowHeight) + 16);

/* We want the beginning of our image to start on a 16-byte boundary,
 * but pointers aren't always allocated that way. So we allocate
 * a normal pointer, then add enough onto that value to force it
 * to start on the correct boundary. We keep around the original
 * pointer so we can dispose of it when necessary.
 */
imageData = gCustomImagePtr + ((long)gCustomImagePtr % 16);
```

Drawing into the New Offscreen

Using the existing routines to draw into the new offscreen image (to distinguish it from a GWorld, I'll refer to it as an offscreen memory map) is a very simple task. When calling DrawObject, just pass in a pointer to the image data and its rowbytes value (which is identical to its width), like this:

```
DrawObject( theObject,
            kRender_PolygonFill,
            offscreenImagePtr,
            offscreenRowBytes   );
```

DrawObject() then draws into the memory map correctly because all it needs to know is where the image starts and how wide it is.

Copying from the New Offscreen

Each time a block of data is moved onto the screen, the source and destination pointers are incremented by 16. One row in the 480-pixel-wide image can be copied with just 30 instructions. You can use the inline assemblers in Metrowerks and Think C to create the 040 image copier.

Unfortunately, here is where you run into another problem. Neither the Metrowerks nor the Think C assembler can handle 68040-specific instructions. However, if you figure out how that instruction will be assembled, you can enter it in that form. Here is the instruction you will use for copying:

```
MOVE16 (A0)+, (A1)+
```

This instruction, when assembled, will become this code:

```
0xF6209000
```

You can force the assembler to put this instruction directly into the code by using the DC.L assembler instruction along with the code:

```
dc.l 0xF6209000
```

DC.L is assembly shorthand for Declare Longword. This instruction allows you to put hexadecimal codes directly into the assembled instructions. You're using it to tell the compiler "Don't worry about this code; I know what I'm doing."

As with the profiler, Metrowerks and Think C use different methods for declaring inline assembly functions. Let's examine the Metrowerks version first.

The Metrowerks Inline Assembler

Metrowerks requires that the entire function be declared as an assembly language function. This is done by including asm in the function declaration, like this:

```
asm void myFunction(void) {
...assembly instructions...
}
```

The first instruction of the assembly routine has to be fralloc, which sets up the routine's structure. When you finish the routine, use frfree, and then rts to return to the calling routine. Note that fralloc and frfree are not true 68k assembly instructions, but rather macros that are specific to CodeWarrior.

The Think C Assembler

Think C's assembler is slightly different. Its instructions are located within a normal C routine by using an asm{} instruction, like this:

```
void myFunction(void) {
  asm {
    ...assembly instructions...
  }
}
```

No additional instructions are needed for the assembly routine; the C portion of the routine takes care of initialization and returning to the caller.

An Assembly Setup for Both Compilers

By using #ifdef instructions, you can write a routine that will work for both compilers, just as you did for the profiler. Here is how it's set up:

```
#ifdef __MWERKS__
asm void myFunction(void) {
  fralloc
#else
void myFunction(void) {
  asm {
#endif
    ...assembly instructions...
#ifdef THINK_C
  }
}
#else
  frfree
  rts
}
```

Because you are directly embedding 68k machine code, you must be careful to be sure that this function is not compiled for a PowerPC processor by typing

```
#ifndef powerc
...
#endif
```

Creating the Function

The specialized 040 image-copying routine is called Blit040Screen(). It takes three parameters: pointers to the screen and offscreen images and the rowbytes value for the screen. You don't need the rowbytes value for the offscreen image because you know it will always be 480 (the window width). In addition, because there is no padding at the end of each row, you know that once you're done copying one row, the image pointer will automatically be positioned at the next row. This is very convenient and saves a little time.

The first thing the function does is copy the offscreen image pointer into A0 and the screen image pointer into A1. Both the Metrowerks and Think C compilers have implemented their inline assembly in such a way that you don't need to restore the A0, A1, D0, D1, or D2 registers. Because you'll be using only these registers, you'll save a little time because you don't need to save and restore them.

Next, the rowBytes value is placed into D1 and you stuff the value of 300 into D0, which you will use for counting down as you finish each row of the image. This is accomplished like this:

```
movea.l  src, a0;
movea.l  dst, a1;
move.l   #0x012c, d0;
move.l   dstRowBytes, d1;
```

Following this are 30 MOVE16 instructions, all declared using DC.L. These 30 instructions move an entire row of the image at a time. After the row has been moved, add the screen rowbytes value to the screen's pointer, wrapping it around to the other side:

```
add.l  d1, a1;        /* dst += dstRowBytes */
```

Then loop back to the beginning, decrementing the D0 register as you do:

```
subq.w #0x0001, d0;  /* loop -= 1 */
bne    @loop;         /* } while (loop) */
```

That's the entire routine. The comments are there to equate these instructions to C statements. Listing 13-2 shows the complete function.

Listing 13-2 *The 040 image-copying routine*

```
/**
 ** Blit040Screen()
 **
 ** Uses the 68040 instruction MOVE16 to quickly copy data from
 ** a custom offscreen memory map to a window. Since Metrowerks
 ** does not (yet) support 040 inline instructions, we have to
 ** manually encode the MOVE16 instruction in a dc.l statement.
```

Continued on next page

Continued from previous page

```
**    This could be used normally in a Think C application,
**    however.
**
**    Metrowerks and Think C define inline assembler routines
**    differently, so we must compensate for that as well.
**
**    This routine will NOT compile for the PowerPC.
***/
#ifndef powerc

#if __MWERKS__    /* If we're compiling for metrowerks, declare the routine
as asm */
asm void Blit040Screen( char *src,
          char *dst,
          long dstRowBytes  )
{
  fralloc;

#else  /* Otherwise, set it up for Think C */
void Blit040Screen( char *src,
        char *dst,
        long dstRowBytes  )
{
  asm {
#endif  /* The rest of the routine is the same for both compilers */
  movea.l  src, a0;
  movea.l dst, a1;
  move.l  #0x012c, d0;
  move.l  dstRowBytes, d1;

@loop:                    /* do { */
  dc.l 0xF6209000         /* Move16 (a0++, a1++) */
  dc.l 0xF6209000
  dc.l 0xF6209000
  dc.l 0xF6209000
  dc.l 0xF6209000
  dc.l 0xF6209000
  dc.l 0xF6209000
  dc.l 0xF6209000
  dc.l 0xF6209000
  dc.l 0xF6209000
  dc.l 0xF6209000
  dc.l 0xF6209000
  dc.l 0xF6209000
  dc.l 0xF6209000
  dc.l 0xF6209000
  dc.l 0xF6209000
  dc.l 0xF6209000
  dc.l 0xF6209000
  dc.l 0xF6209000
```

```
        dc.l 0xF6209000
        dc.l 0xF6209000
        dc.l 0xF6209000
        dc.l 0xF6209000
        dc.l 0xF6209000
        dc.l 0xF6209000
        dc.l 0xF6209000
        dc.l 0xF6209000
        dc.l 0xF6209000
        dc.l 0xF6209000

        add.l  d1, a1;        /* dst += dstRowBytes */

        subq.w  #0x0001, d0;  /* loop -= 1 */
        bne     @loop;        /* } while (loop) */
/* We must now balance each of the closing brackets for both compilers.
 * Metrowerks also needs two more statements (frfree and rts)
 */
#ifdef THINK_C
  }
}
#else
  frfree
  rts
}
#endif

#endif /* #ifndef powerc */
```

Mixing QuickDraw and Custom Routines

Because of all the limitations you're imposing on the offscreen images, it would be a good idea to keep QuickDraw routines around in case you need to fall back on them. To manage the two systems, put both offscreen definitions in one file; the routines in that file will be the only ones that will know which method you're using. The main function calls a routine in this file that figures out whether to create a QuickDraw GWorld or a custom offscreen image. This function then stores the results in global variables and passes back a pointer to the beginning of the image data and a rowbytes value.

Two other routines are necessary for managing the offscreen buffer—one for erasing it and one for copying it to the screen. All these routines are in a file called Custom Offscreen.c.

Creating the Offscreen Image

The routine for creating the offscreen image is called CreateOffscreenImage(). It is responsible for figuring out whether to create a QuickDraw GWorld or a custom offscreen and whether it is being run on a 68040 processor.

The conditions for creating a custom offscreen are as follows:

 The screen must be in 8-bit color.

 The window must be a specified size (kWindowWidth and kWindowHeight, stored in Screen Assumptions.h so it can be included by any other file).

 A flag passed into the function for allowing a custom offscreen must be True.

If any of these conditions are not met, a GWorld is created instead. As the offscreen is created, it is stored in several global variables so you'll know what you're dealing with later. Here is a list of the globals you'll be using:

```
Boolean        gUsingCustomOffscreen; /* Are we using custom routines? */
Boolean        gUsing040Processor; /* Are we on an 040? */
Ptr            gImageDataPtr;      /* Pointer to the image data */
unsigned long  gImageRowBytes;     /* RowBytes of image data */
PixMapHandle   gQuickDrawImage;    /* The Quickdraw image - only valid
                                    * if we're not using custom routines
                                    */
GWorldPtr      gQuickDrawGWorld;   /* Quickdraw's offscreen image */
Ptr            gCustomImagePtr;    /* The allocated pointer to our custom
                                    * offscreen. This variable only needs
                                    * to be remembered so we can dispose
                                    * of the pointer - the gImageDataPtr
                                    * value does not necessarily point to
                                    * the beginning of the allocated
                                    * pointer.
                                    */
```

The rest of the application doesn't need access to any of these variables except for gImageDataPtr, which is passed back to the main() function. In fact, any routine that is not in this file does not know if a custom offscreen or a GWorld is being used.

The first part of the function figures out whether or not to use a custom offscreen. The bit depth of the monitor can be obtained by grabbing the portPixMap from the WindowPtr that has been passed in, then dereferencing the PixMap and looking at *pixelSize*:

```
/* Get the screen's PixMapHandle from the WindowPtr. */
screenPixMap = ((CGrafPtr)window)->portPixMap;

/* Check to see if it's 8-bit */
if ((**screenPixMap).pixelSize != 8) {
  /* If not, we can't use custom routines */
```

```
      useCustomRoutine = FALSE;
   }
```

If a custom offscreen is used, it is allocated by calling NewPtr() and passing in the size of the image (width times height) plus 16 so you can align it on the correct boundary. It also checks for an error and returns if there is one:

```
if (useCustomRoutine) {
  /* Create a custom offscreen */
  gCustomImagePtr = NewPtr((kWindowRowBytes * kWindowHeight) + 16);
  if (gCustomImagePtr == NULL) {
    err = MemError();
    return err;
  }
```

The next step is to align that pointer on a 16-byte boundary. You can't just add bytes to the original pointer because then you wouldn't be able to dispose of it later (the *original* pointer must be used when you call DisposePtr()). Calculate the distance this pointer is from a 16-byte boundary and add that to the pointer, assigning it to another variable:

```
imageData = gCustomImagePtr + ((long)gCustomImagePtr % 16);
```

Allocate the GWorld the same way as before; extract the base address and rowbytes from it and assign them to global variables:

```
/* Create a GWorld */
err = NewGWorld( &gQuickDrawGWorld,
                 8,
                 &bounds,
                 NULL,
                 NULL,
                 0  );

/* Check for an error */
if (err)
  return err;

/* Get its pixmap handle */
gQuickDrawImage = GetGWorldPixMap(gQuickDrawGWorld);

/* Lock the pixmap */
LockPixels(gQuickDrawImage);

/* Get the pixmap's base address */
imageData = GetPixBaseAddr(gQuickDrawImage);

/* Get the pixmap's rowbytes */
rowBytes = (**gQuickDrawImage).rowBytes & 0x3FFF;
```

The last task of CreateOffscreenImage() is to determine what kind of processor it is running on. Apple provides a toolbox routine that can be used to gain access to this type of information. The routine is called Gestalt() and it can give you information on everything ranging from the system software version to the current Macintosh model. The only information you're interested in is the processor type, which is represented by the constant gestaltProcessorType. Here is the prototype for Gestalt():

```
OSErr GestaltType(long selectorCode, long *gestaltResult);
```

To find out the processor type, call Gestalt() using the constant gestaltProcessorType and examine the result passed back in gestaltResult. The result can be compared against several gestalt constants:

```
enum {
        gestalt68000                    = 1,
        gestalt68010                    = 2,
        gestalt68020                    = 3,
        gestalt68030                    = 4,
        gestalt68040                    = 5
};
```

These constants are defined in Gestalt.h, part of Apple's headers. This gestalt listing does not include the PowerPC processor; to check for that, use the gestalt type gestaltNativeCPUtype.

Listing 13-3 is the complete CreateOffscreenImage() routine.

Listing 13-3 *The CreateOffscreenImage() routine*

```
/**
 **    CreateOffscreenImage()
 **
 **    This routine figures out whether it can use its custom routines,
 **    and, if so, creates an offscreen memory map. If not, it creates
 **    a GWorld. It stores the results in global variables and passes
 **    back a pointer to the beginning of the pixmap data.
 **    It also figures out whether it's running on an
 **    040 macintosh and, if so, sets a flag so we can use the
 **    faster blitting routine.
 **
 **    Returns an error if there wasn't enough memory.
 **/
OSErr   CreateOffscreenImage(    WindowPtr         window,
                                 Ptr               *pixelDataPtr,
                                 unsigned long     *rowBytesValue,
                                 Boolean           canUseCustomRoutines   )
{
  unsigned long rowBytes;
  PixMapHandle  screenPixMap;
  Boolean       useCustomRoutine;
```

```
Rect        bounds;
Ptr         imageData;
OSErr       err = noErr;
Long        gestaltResponse;

bounds = window->portRect;
/* First figure out if we can use custom routines. First see if
 * the calling routine will let us use the routines. If so,
 * check the rest of the conditions (8-bit screen, a fixed
 * window size).
 */
useCustomRoutine = canUseCustomRoutines;

if (canUseCustomRoutines) {
  /* Get the screen's PixMapHandle from the WindowPtr. */
  screenPixMap = ((CGrafPtr)window)->portPixMap;

  /* Check to see if it's 8-bit */
  if ((**screenPixMap).pixelSize != 8) {
    /* If not, we can't use custom routines */
    useCustomRoutine = FALSE;
  }

  /* Make sure the image is the same dimensions that our
   * routines are optimized for.
   */
  if (((bounds.right - bounds.left) != kWindowWidth) ||
      ((bounds.bottom - bounds.top) != kWindowHeight))
  {
    /* If not, use quickdraw's routines */
    useCustomRoutine = FALSE;
  }
}

/* Now create the image - either the quickdraw GWorld, or
 * just a large pointer if we're using custom routines.
 */
if (useCustomRoutine) {
  /* Create a custom offscreen */
  gCustomImagePtr = NewPtr((kWindowRowBytes * kWindowHeight) + 16);
  if (gCustomImagePtr == NULL) {
    err = MemError();
    return err;
  }
  /* We want the beginning of our image to start on a 16-byte boundary,
   * but pointers aren't always allocated that way. So we allocate
   * a normal pointer, then add enough onto that value to force it
   * to start on the correct boundary. We keep around the original
   * pointer so we can dispose of it when necessary.
   */
  imageData = gCustomImagePtr + ((long)gCustomImagePtr % 16);
```

Continued on next page

Continued from previous page

```
      /* Remember the offscreen's rowbytes value */
      rowBytes = kWindowRowBytes;
   } else {
     /* Create a GWorld */
     err = NewGWorld( &gQuickDrawGWorld,
                      8,
                      &bounds,
                      NULL,
                      NULL,
                      0  );

     /* Check for an error */
     if (err)
       return err;

     /* Get its pixmap handle */
     gQuickDrawImage = GetGWorldPixMap(gQuickDrawGWorld);

     /* Lock the pixmap */
     LockPixels(gQuickDrawImage);

     /* Get the pixmap's base address */
     imageData = GetPixBaseAddr(gQuickDrawImage);

     /* Get the pixmap's rowbytes */
     rowBytes = (**gQuickDrawImage).rowBytes & 0x3FFF;
   }

   /* Set up the global variables */
   gImageRowBytes = rowBytes;
   gUsingCustomOffscreen = useCustomRoutine;
   gImageDataPtr = imageData;


   /* Now check to see if we're running with an 040 processor */
   Gestalt(gestaltProcessorType, &gestaltResponse);

   /* Compare the gestalt response to a toolbox constant */
   if (gestaltResponse == gestalt68040) {
     gUsing040Processor = TRUE;
   } else {
     gUsing040Processor = FALSE;
   }

   /* Pass back the image data and rowbytes */
   *pixelDataPtr = imageData;
   *rowBytesValue = rowBytes;

   /* Return the error code (most likely noErr) */
   return err;
}
```

Erasing the Offscreen Image

When the offscreen needs to be erased, a different process is used depending on whether it is a QuickDraw image or a custom image. QuickDraw images can be erased with a simple EraseRect() routine, but you have to use a loop for erasing the custom offscreen image.

The routine for erasing the QuickDraw image involves setting the port to the GWorld, calling EraseRect(), and restoring the port to its original settings:

```
/**
 **   EraseOffscreenImage()
 **
 **   Figures out whether we're using a custom offscreen, or a quickdraw
 **   offscreen - if we're using a custom one, uses EraseMemoryMap() to
 **   erase it, otherwise uses EraseRect() to do it.
 **/
void EraseOffscreenImage(void)
{
  if (gUsingCustomOffscreen == TRUE)
    EraseMemoryMap(gImageDataPtr);
  else {
    /* Using quickdraw */
    GWorldPtr    savePort;
    GDHandle     saveDevice;

    GetGWorld(&savePort, &saveDevice);
    SetGWorld(gQuickDrawGWorld, NULL);

    EraseRect(&gQuickDrawGWorld->portRect);

    SetGWorld(savePort, saveDevice);
  }
}
```

The custom offscreen erasing routine is faster than erasing with the QuickDraw routine, but unfortunately not by much. Use a technique similar to the non-040 copying algorithm: erase a longword at a time with an unrolled loop. Don't worry about looping through the width and then the height of the image because all you're dealing with is essentially a huge block of memory. Here is the routine:

```
/**
 **   EraseMemoryMap()
 **
 **   Erases all of the entries in the offscreen memory map. The memory
 **   map must be a predetermined size, indicated in kWindowRowBytes and
 **   kWindowHeight.
 **/
void EraseMemoryMap(Ptr  memoryMap)
{
```

Continued on next page

```
Continued from previous page
long        loopIterations;
long        *longdst;

longdst = (long*)memoryMap;
loopIterations = (kWindowRowBytes * kWindowHeight) / 32;

do {
  *longdst++ = 0; /* Clear 32 bytes at a time */
  *longdst++ = 0;
  *longdst++ = 0;
  *longdst++ = 0;
  *longdst++ = 0;
  *longdst++ = 0;
  *longdst++ = 0;
  *longdst++ = 0;
} while (--loopIterations);
}
```

CopyImageOntoScreen()

The CopyImageOntoScreen() function is called whenever the rest of the application has finished drawing the current frame to the offscreen and wants it displayed. This routine uses one of three methods for drawing the image: QuickDraw, Custom, and Custom 68040. If it detects it has a QuickDraw image, it will dispatch to QDCopyOntoScreen() (which you'll see shortly). If it's running on an 040 *and* the window is aligned on a 16-byte boundary, it dispatches to Blit040Screen() (which you saw earlier). Otherwise, it handles the custom drawing moving a longword at a time.

Shielding the Cursor

Before any drawing can be done to the screen, it must call a function named ShieldCursor(). This function will prevent the cursor from leaving ghost images on the screen as the copying is being done (in fact, it will hide the cursor if it is located in the area that's being copied). Here is its prototype:

```
void ShieldCursor( Rect *shieldRect, Point offsetPoint);
```

shieldRect is the area into which you'll be copying. It can be in either global or local coordinates. If you use local coordinates, however, you need to provide the offset from local to global coordinates (i.e., the location of the window on the screen) in *offsetPoint*.

Once you're done copying, call ShowCursor() to balance the call to ShieldCursor():

```
void  ShowCursor(void);
```

Remembering the Last Destination

Because the same pixmap, base address, and rowbytes are generally used for the destination (i.e., the screen) each time this routine is called, you can use static variables to remember their values. The first time the function is called, the variables are set to those of the screen. Then instead of being recalculated, they are remembered through each call. This saves a little time because you don't have to make these toolbox calls each time.

Checking for a 16-Byte Boundary

Before the 040-specific copying routine is called, you must ensure that the window is located on a 16-byte boundary. Normally, you would do this by checking to see if the remainder of (windowX / 16) is 0, but because 16 is expressed in hexadecimal as 0x10, all you need to do is check to see if the last hexadecimal digit is 0. You can do this with a simple & instruction, like this:

```
if ((windowX & 0x000F) == 0) {
        ....code....
}
```

The Copy Function

Listing 13-4 is the complete source for CopyImageOntoScreen().

Listing 13-4 *The CopyImageOntoScreen() routine*

```
/**
 **   CopyImageOntoScreen()
 **
 **   Copies the image onto the screen. Uses custom routines
 **   or quickdraw, depending what was allocated by
 **   CreateOffscreenImage().
 **/
void CopyImageOntoScreen( WindowPtr    mainWindow,
                          short        windowX,
                          short        windowY )
{
  unsigned long          dstRowBytes;
  char                   *src, *dst;
  long                   *longsrc, *longdst;
  Point                  thisPoint;
  register short         i;
  PixMapHandle           windowPixMap;
  Rect                   windowRect;
  short                  height;
```

Continued on next page

Continued from previous page

```
/* These static variables save the last pixmap used for copying. If
 * the same pixmap is used again (which will generally be the
 * case), we don't need to figure out the base address or rowbytes
 * again.
 */
static char            *screenImagePtr = NULL;
static PixMapHandle     screenPixMap = NULL;
static unsigned long    screenRowBytes = 0;

/* Get the window's boundary */
windowRect = mainWindow->portRect;

/* First check to see if we're using custom blitting routines. If
 * we're not, just use the quickdraw version to display the image.
 */
if (gUsingCustomOffscreen == FALSE) {
  /* Not using custom routines - use CopyBits(). */
  QDCopyOntoScreen(gQuickDrawImage, mainWindow, &mainWindow->portRect);
} else{
  /* We're using our own custom routines */

  /* Find the window's pixmap */
  windowPixMap = ((CGrafPtr)mainWindow)->portPixMap;

  /* See if we've already saved the window's pixmap information. If
   * not, save it now.
   */
  if (screenPixMap != windowPixMap) {
    screenPixMap = windowPixMap;
    screenImagePtr = GetPixBaseAddr(windowPixMap);

    screenRowBytes = ((**windowPixMap).rowBytes & 0x3FFF);
  }

  /* Shield the cursor so we don't draw over it. This must be done
   * any time you draw directly to the screen.
   */
  thisPoint.h = windowX;
  thisPoint.v = windowY;
  ShieldCursor(&windowRect, thisPoint);

  /* Grab the offscreen's image pointer and position a pointer at
   * the upper left-hand corner of the window on the screen.
   */
  src = gImageDataPtr;
  dst = screenImagePtr + ((long)windowY * screenRowBytes) + windowX;

  /* Reduce the screen's rowbytes value by the
   * width of the window - we want to know how much to
   * add to the data pointer to jump from the
```

```
    * right-hand side of the window to the
    * left-hand side of the next row.
    */
   dstRowBytes = screenRowBytes - 480;

   /* Figure out which copying method to use. If we are running
    * on an 040, use a function that takes advantage of special
    * instructions on that chip. Otherwise, use an unrolled loop
    * for doing the copying.
    *
    *  For the 040 version to work, the window MUST be on a
    *  16-byte boundary. Otherwise, use the other custom routine.
    *
    *  A fast MOD can be achieved by masking out the lowest
    *  4 bits of the variable.
    *
    *  Also ensure that the routine will not be called on a
    *  PowerPC processor. By using #ifdef instructions,
    *  these lines won't even be compiled on a PowerPC.
    */
#ifndef powerc
   if (gUsing040Processor && ((windowX & 0x000F) == 0)) {
     /* Use the 040 routine to copy the image */
     Blit040Screen(src, dst, dstRowBytes);
   }
   else
#endif
   {
     /* Use a loop to copy a longword at a time to the screen.
      * Typecast the data pointers to (long *)'s, so that
      * a longword is copied every time, plus it gets
      * incremented by 4 instead of 1.
      */
     longsrc = (long*)src;
     longdst = (long*)dst;

     /* Get the window's height */
     height = kWindowHeight;

     /* Start the loop */
     do {
       /* (kWindowWidth / 4) longwords need to be copied per
        * row, and there are 8 copied per iteration of the
        * inner loop, so we want to loop (kWindowWidth / 32) times.
        * In this case, it's OK to use a divide, because
        * you're dividing a constant - this will get evaluated
        * at compile-time, not at run-time.
        */
       i = kWindowWidth / 32;
       do {
         /* Do the copy */
         *longdst++ = *longsrc++;
```

Continued on next page

Continued from previous page

```
            *longdst++ = *longsrc++;
            *longdst++ = *longsrc++;
            *longdst++ = *longsrc++;
            *longdst++ = *longsrc++;
            *longdst++ = *longsrc++;
            *longdst++ = *longsrc++;
            *longdst++ = *longsrc++;
        } while (--i);

        /* Jump down a row. This is a little tricky, since if
         * we just add dstRowBytes to the long pointer, it will
         * get incremented by 4*dstRowBytes. Instead, we
         * fool the compiler into thinking it's just a long
         * value, add the rowbytes to it, then typecast it back
         * to a long pointer.
         */
        longdst = (long *)((long)longdst + dstRowBytes);
    } while (--height);
}

    /* Show the cursor again. */
    ShowCursor();
 }
}
```

QDCopyOntoScreen()

The QuickDraw copying routine calls CopyBits() to move the image onto the screen:

```
/**
** QDCopyOntoScreen()
**
** Copies an offscreen pixmap to the window. This has been
** broken off to its own routine so its speed can be measured.
**/
void QDCopyOntoScreen( PixMapHandle   offscreen,
                       WindowPtr      mainWindow,
                       Rect           *bounds  )
{
  CopyBits( (BitMap *)*offscreen,
            (BitMap *)&mainWindow->portBits,
            bounds,
            bounds,
            srcCopy,
            NULL );
}
```

You now have all the functions that go into CustomScreenUtils.c. To take advantage of these features, some modifications must be made to the main() function. Let's take a look at those.

Taking Advantage of Custom Offscreens

Few modifications need to be made to the main() function. CreateOffscreenImage() returns an image pointer and a rowbyte value, which are then passed on to DrawObject(), but other than that, it doesn't need to worry about the offscreen image. The other thing to note is that the window is now created with an x value of 32 (on a 16-byte boundary) and it's created to the size specified in Screen Assumptions.h.

Listing 13-5 is the new main() routine.

Listing 13-5 The new main() routine

```
/**
** main()
**
**/
void main(void)
{
  Rect            windowRect;
  WindowPtr       mainWindow;
  Ptr             offscreenImagePtr;    /* A pointer to our image data */
  unsigned long   offscreenRowBytes;    /* The image's rowbytes */
  OSErr           err;
  short           xAngle, yAngle;       /* Angles expressed in degrees */
  Fixed24         transformMatrix[4][4];
  Object3D        *theObject;
  long            thisTickCount, originalTickCount;
  long            framesSoFar;
  long            framesPerSecond;
  Str255          fpsText;

  /* Initialize everything we need */
  InitGraf(&qd.thePort);
  InitWindows();
  InitCursor();

  /* Initialize the sin/cos look-up tables */
  InitializeSinCosTable();

  /* Set the window size */
  SetRect(&windowRect, 0, 0, kWindowWidth, kWindowHeight);

  /* Offset the window rect so that the window does not appear
   * under the menubar.
   */
  OffsetRect(&windowRect, 32, 40);
```

Continued on next page

Continued from previous page

```
  /* Create the window */
  mainWindow = CreateWindow(&windowRect);

  SetPort(mainWindow);

  /* Create the offscreen image */
  err = CreateOffscreenImage(  mainWindow,
                               &offscreenImagePtr,
                               &offscreenRowBytes, TRUE);

  if (err || offscreenImagePtr == NULL)  /* Quit if there was an error */
    ExitToShell();

  /* Read the resource in from disk */
  theObject = LoadObjectFromRsrc(128);

  /* Test for failure */
  if (theObject == NULL) {
    ExitToShell();
  }

  /* Start the rotations off at 0 */
  xAngle = 0;
  yAngle = 0;

  /* Initialize the timing variables */
  framesSoFar = 0;
  originalTickCount = TickCount();

#if __MWERKS__   /* If we're using the metrowerks compiler... */
#if __profile__
  /* Initalize the metrowerks profiler */
  ProfilerInit(collectSummary, bestTimeBase, 100, 20);
#endif
#else      /* Otherwise, we must be using the Think C compiler */
#if __option(profile)
  /* Initialize the Think C profiler */
  InitProfile(100, 20);

  /* Open a file for the Think C profile output to go into */
  freopen("Optimization TC Report", "w", stdout);
#endif
#endif

  /* Wait until the user clicks before quitting */
  while (!Button())
  {
    /* Erase the offscreen memory map */
    EraseOffscreenImage();

    /* Fiddle with the rotation values */
    xAngle += 5;
```

```
        yAngle += 8;

        /* If either angle has passed 360 degrees, reset it.
         */
        if (xAngle >= 360)
          xAngle -= 360;

        if (yAngle >= 360)
          yAngle -= 360;

        /* Initialize our transformation matrix */
        InitMatrix(transformMatrix);

        /* Apply the rotations to the matrix */
        RotateMatrix(transformMatrix, xAngle, yAngle, 0);

        /* Transform the shape */
        TransformObject3D(theObject, transformMatrix);

        /* Convert the shape to world coordinates */
        ObjectToWorldCoordinates(theObject);

        /* Project the shape into screen coordinates */
        ProjectObject(theObject);

        /* Draw the shape */
        DrawObject(  theObject,
                     kRender_PolygonFill,
                     offscreenImagePtr,
                     offscreenRowBytes   );

        /* Copy the offscreen image to the screen */
        CopyImageOntoScreen(mainWindow, 32, 40);

      /* Increment the framecount, calculate fps and draw it on the screen */
        framesSoFar += 1;
        thisTickCount = TickCount();
        framesPerSecond = ((float)framesSoFar /
                           (float)(thisTickCount - originalTickCount)) * 60;

        /* Convert that fps number into text so we can show it */
        NumToString(framesPerSecond, fpsText);

        /* Draw the string */
        MoveTo(10, 30);
        DrawString(fpsText);

    }

#if __MWERKS__
#if __profile__
```

Continued on next page

Continued from previous page
```
    /* Dump out the profiler data to a file */
    ProfilerDump("\pOptimization Profiler Info");

    /* Stop the profiler */
    ProfilerTerm();
#endif
#endif
}
```

Reaping the Benefits

After compiling and running the new polygon-fill application, look at the frame rate. On the Quadra 700, not using the 040 routines, the frame rate is 31 fps. If the 040 routine is used, the frame rate jumps up to 36 fps! Clearly, the work you have done has been worth it.

The timing of the original CopyBits() routine averages 14.32 milliseconds per frame. When the custom routines are used, the timing drops to 13.70 milliseconds; the 040 routine takes a mere 9.55 milliseconds per frame. In fact, if you look at profiler results from a 68040 Macintosh, you'll notice that erasing the memory map takes longer than copying it does!

This will assist you greatly in achieving an admirable frame rate for animations; the techniques demonstrated in this chapter can be applied to many types of games. It is very important, however, to remember the guidelines behind using custom routines and to remember that sometimes it's better just to use QuickDraw.

The next chapter will focus on Apple's newest platform, the PowerPC processor. Because of the many changes brought on by this chip, there are different techniques to use when attempting to optimize for it. I'll discuss things like specific optimization tricks and debates over using assembly language for the PowerPC. As the 68k platform dies out, the PowerPC chip will be the one you want to shoot for.

14

Optimizing Power Macintosh

ome trili fare i manubelle le quali puis obano i laiga
a grape si i auri le meno di o gonj o lato grano debono
ergari nella mano o la puis quella mesa manubelle peg; quin
a forga o pib i lomo peb ibal.

14

Optimizing Power Macintosh

The final topic on optimization centers around Apple's latest technology, the Power Macintosh line of computers. In creating this line, Apple has taken a large departure from any previous Macintosh. Instead of using one of Motorola's 68000 line of microprocessors Apple switched to an entirely new architecture in a chip called the PowerPC.

From CISC to RISC

Unlike the 68k processor, the PowerPC is based on a different design paradigm. Whereas the 68k processor attempts to get as much done as possible using just one instruction called complex instruction set computing (CISC), the PowerPC's instructions do very specific tasks. This way, more instructions are required to do something than on a CISC processor, but each instruction can be executed much faster. This model is called reduced instruction set computing (RISC) and its ultimate goal is to break each of its instructions down until they all take one cycle to complete. Although this has not been entirely achieved in the current design, the PowerPC has succeeded in providing tremendous speed enhancements over the 68k line.

465

Optimizing for the New Platform

As you no doubt know, this transition has meant that software must be recompiled to take advantage of the PowerPC's speed. Just feeding your code through a PowerPC compiler will offer you a 200 percent to 300 percent speed enhancement; after seeing this boost, most programmers stop there, satisfied with the performance of their applications.

However, some untapped potential still remains. For 10 years, Macintosh programmers have learned how to tweak their code to work the best under the 68k line. Although many of these techniques still hold true for the PowerPC, a good deal of them have to be unlearned. Many optimizations that are typically done for the 68k line, including some explained in Chapter 11, will either produce no performance enhancement for the PowerPC or slow it down.

Likewise, you can make several optimizations to an application to tweak it for the PowerPC that hurt performance on the 68k line. In almost every case, the huge performance boost on one chip outweighs a small penalty on the other chip, or vice versa, so your decision will usually be easy. In addition, as the number of Power Macintosh owners begins to eclipse that of 68k owners, you may want to focus exclusively on RISC chip optimizations and deliver a Power Macintosh-only game.

The Structure of the PowerPC Chip

The PowerPC chip is composed of a branch unit, an integer unit, a floating-point unit, and sometimes a load/store unit. The different generations of the PowerPC chip (i.e., 601, 603, 604, etc.) can have multiple integer and floating-point units (I'll examine the structure of the individual processors in a bit). Each unit is capable of processing one instruction at the same time, so a chip with one branch unit, one integer unit, and one floating-point unit (like the 601) is capable of executing three instructions at the same time under ideal circumstances.

The Branch Unit

The branch unit of the PowerPC chip is used to process a branch instruction and is responsible for predicting which instruction should be executed next. In most cases, the result of a particular instruction will already have decided the direction of the branch. Thus in most cases, a branch does not use any processing time, which is a large departure from the CISC architecture. I'll look at how this affects code later in this chapter.

The Load/Store Unit

The load/store unit is responsible for loading data from the memory banks into the PowerPC's registers and storing it back again. If a particular PowerPC chip does not have a separate load/store unit (which, for the Macintosh line, currently includes only the 601), the integer unit must perform this task.

The Processing Units

The integer and floating-point units are known as *processing units* and they are responsible for the real work. When an instruction enters one of these units, the unit goes through four steps as it processes the instruction:

1. It fetches the instruction.

2. It decodes the instruction and fetches operands.

3. It performs the operation.

4. It stores the results.

A separate portion of the chip is designed to handle each of these stages. The steps are done independently, allowing the unit to do all four at the same time. For example, while the unit is decoding an instruction, it can also fetch the next instruction. During the next cycle, it is performing the first instruction while decoding the second and fetching a third, as shown in Figure 14-1. This process is known as *pipelining* and it is one of the major strengths of the RISC processor design.

Although each instruction requires four cycles to be completely executed, by taking advantage of pipelining, the unit can execute instructions at a rate of one per cycle. However, this speed can be obtained only if the unit doesn't have to wait for the results of one instruction before executing the next one. If it does, the earlier stages of the unit stay idle while the first instruction passes through, which is known as a *pipeline stall*. Take this C code fragment, for example:

```
i = i + 1;
if (i > j)
  k = k + 1;
```

The unit will begin to execute the first instruction (i = i + 1), but it can't begin the second instruction (if (i > j)) until it knows the result of the first. The compiler is responsible for attempting to eliminate processor stalls by reordering the instructions and interleaving the portions that don't rely on each other.

Under ideal circumstances (i.e., no pipeline stalls), each unit of the processor can finish one instruction per cycle. Because the processor has multiple units, the average time per instruction can actually drop below one cycle.

FIGURE 14-1
◎ ◎ ◎ ◎ ◎ ◎
*Pipelining on a
PowerPC*

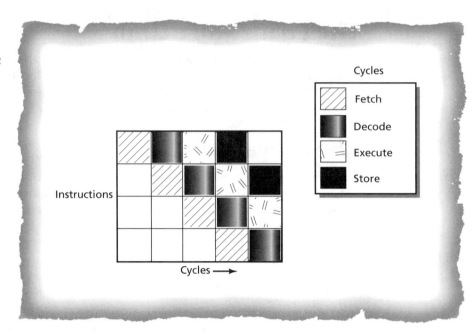

The PowerPC Family

Let's look at the characteristics of the individual members of the PowerPC family.

The PowerPC 601

The PowerPC 601 chip is based on IBM's POWER architecture, which was used in its RS/6000 systems. The 601 was designed to be a transitional chip and thus does not exploit the full potential of the PowerPC architecture. It contains one integer unit, one floating-point unit, one branch unit, and 32k of cache used for both data and instructions.

The PowerPC 603

The 603 processor is in the second generation of PowerPC technology. Like the 601, it has one integer, one floating-point unit, and one branch unit, but also has a separate load/store unit, which the 601 lacks. Also, unlike the 601, it has only 16k of cache, split into 8k for instructions and 8k for data. Its performance is slightly less than that of the 601, but it requires less power and is significantly less expensive.

The PowerPC 603e

The 603e was designed when Apple realized that the 603 couldn't achieve the performance Apple expected, particularly for the 68k emulator. Like the 603, the 603e has one integer unit, one floating-point unit, one branch unit, and one load/store unit, but it also has 32k of cache—16k for data and 16k for instructions. It consumes slightly more power than the 603 does, making it a little less ideal for notebook computers. The 603e's performance is about equal to the 601's in most cases, but at a lower price.

The PowerPC 604

The PowerPC 604 begins to take full advantage of the RISC architecture. It has three integer units, one floating-point unit, one branch unit, one load/store unit, and 32k of on-chip cache (16k for data, 16k for instructions). The 604 is about 50 percent faster than the 601 at the same clock speed and can execute up to four instructions for each clock cycle.

The PowerPC 620

The 620 chip is the first 64-bit PowerPC processor. It contains three general-purpose integer units and one floating-point unit, plus 64k of cache split evenly between data and instructions. It's estimated to be well over twice as fast as the 601 at the *same* clock speed, but its architecture will allow for far greater clock speeds.

PowerPC Assembly Language

Ever since the release of the PowerPC processor, programmers have been arguing over the merits of writing assembly language for the PowerPC. Many of these people have been writing 68k assembly for years to optimize specific routines because CISC compilers have never been able to work as intelligently as a good assembly language engineer.

RISC processors, however, are much more difficult to write assembly for. They have a smaller instruction set, meaning the programmer has to use more instructions to get the same job done. In addition, the instructions are much more cryptic (if you've ever looked at PowerPC assembly code, you no doubt understand this) and you can't do the same sort of memory operations possible with the 68k.

Also, many people have argued that a RISC compiler writes *better* code than a programmer can. Indeed, a RISC compiler has to be quite a bit more intelligent than its CISC counterpart. To gain maximum performance, it uses *instruction scheduling*, meaning it rearranges the instructions to take advantage of all the PowerPC units by interleaving floating-point and integer operations. When your C source code is compiled into an application, all your commands get jumbled together, making the code almost impossible for a human to decipher. By contrast, it is very difficult for a programmer to schedule his or her code effectively for a particular processor.

The argument about whether to write assembly language or not continues today and it will probably continue throughout the existence of RISC technology. Some programmers resent the fact that they are told not to mess around with assembly, whereas others want to leave the dirty work to the compiler. Another thing to keep in mind is that when Apple moved from the 68k line to PowerPC, programmers who had a lot of 68k assembly routines had the hardest time porting their code, whereas C code is very portable.

This book does not include any PowerPC assembly routines because not many people can understand them and neither compiler used in this book supports PowerPC assembly language. If you're feeling brave, you may want to try learning it; the bibliography of this book lists some references to help you.

Changes in Optimization Strategy between 68k and PowerPC

As I mentioned earlier, some of the optimization tricks you've learned up to now don't have the same effect on the PowerPC processor as they do on the 68k processor. Let's take a look at what you're going to have to change.

Unrolling Loops

Loop unrolling is still very important on the PowerPC, but for a different reason. Because the PowerPC processor will predict the direction a branch will take (e.g., at the end of a loop), the looping operation is usually handled for "free." However, if the code within the loop is very simple, the processor may not be able to take advantage of its parallel processing capabilities. It is also important not to unroll a loop so far that the code no longer fits inside the CPU's cache.

Generally, on the PowerPC you only want to unroll a loop if each loop iteration is performing a simple operation. If the routine is very speed critical, you may want to do some timing tests to determine the best strategy to use.

Fixed-Point Numbers

On the PowerPC 601 chip, integer calculations are actually slower than their floating-point counterparts due to the large floating-point unit on the chip. On the later PowerPC processors, such as the 604, integer and floating-point calculations are almost identical in speed.

Because fixed-point calculations require you to use bitshift operations with multiplies and divides, the speed for fixed-point can be a bit slower than that for floating-point, plus fixed-point loses a good deal of precision. But on a 68k processor, floating-point is *much* slower, so if you write a game to be compiled on both platforms, you're probably better off using fixed-point. If you write a PowerPC-only game, use floating-point numbers wherever it makes sense.

Long vs. Short

Whereas the 68k processor can handle short (16-bit) integers faster than long (32-bit) ones, the PowerPC is the other way around. Take this code fragment, for example:

```
short   i;
short   j;
short   k;

j = 10000;
for (i = 0; i < j; i++)
  k += i + j;
```

By changing i, j, and k to 32-bit values, you can speed up this loop by around 30 percent. In addition, it's faster to use unsigned values than signed values because the compiler doesn't have to worry about sign extensions.

Coding Style for the PowerPC Processor

The PowerPC processor has quite a few quirks that you should know about in order to write the best C code possible. Most of these style issues will not affect the speed on a 68k machine, so you can safely use them in an application compiled for both platforms.

The PowerPC Memory Structure

The PowerPC chips have an on-chip cache of 16k, 32k, or 64k depending on the model. This cache, although not as fast as registers, is faster than main memory or even a Level 2 cache. Figure 14-2 illustrates each of the levels of memory on the PowerPC 601, in increasing order of size and decreasing order of speed. The later PowerPC processors split the cache into two parts, as shown in Figure 14-3. This change shouldn't affect the way you write your code much, but you should be aware of it.

When operating in an inner loop, you want your memory accesses to stay as close to the left (toward the registers) as possible. This means you want as many variables as possible to go into the registers (usually not too difficult, since there are 32 registers). Ideally, the data you operate on should be in the data cache and secondary information should reside in the Level 2 cache or in main memory. Unfortunately, you don't have

FIGURE 14-2

◉ ◉ ◉ ◉ ◉ ◉

*Memory
structure on a
601*

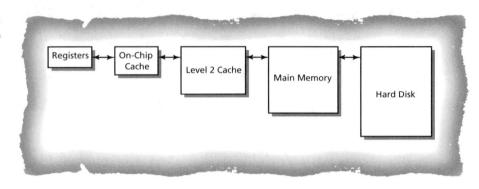

a large amount of control over where your data ends up because it's all decided during runtime; however, you can take some steps to encourage your code to act the way you want.

Locality

Locality, which was briefly mentioned in Chapter 12, is the most important way you can influence your code's behavior. Locality is much more important on PowerPC processors than it is on the 68k. It comes in two flavors: spatial locality and temporal locality. Spatial locality means that if a memory location was just accessed, chances are that another memory location close to that one will be accessed next. Temporal locality means that if a memory location has been accessed recently, it is likely to be accessed again soon. Data and instructions are kept in the caches based on these two assumptions, and organizing your code to reflect this will do wonders for its speed.

The 603 and later processors have separate caches for instructions and data and slightly different techniques are used to encourage proper use of them.

Code Locality

Code locality helps make the instruction cache on the chip effective. The easiest way to use code locality is by always keeping similar routines grouped together in the same

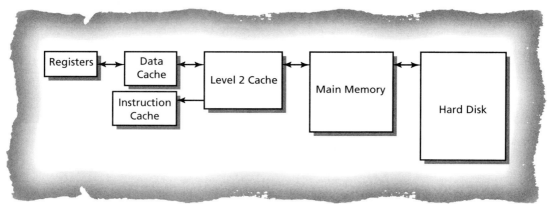

FIGURE 14-3 ◉ *Memory structure on the 603 and 604*

file. In general, your functions are placed in the assembled code in the same order as they appear in the source file. Let's look at an example where a time-critical function (I'll call it MyFunction1()) is calling a subroutine in the middle of a tight loop (I'll call the subroutine MyFunction2()), where MyFunction2() is in a different file, like this:

```
MySourceFile1.c:
void MyFunction1() {
  unsigned long i;
  for (i = 0; i < 10000; i++) {
    MyFunction2();
  }
}
```

```
MySourceFile2.c:
void MyFunction2() {
  ..do something...
}
```

Every time MyFunction2() is called, the processor must jump to a completely different address. Although this function follows temporal locality (because MyFunction2() is being called in a short timespan), it doesn't work well for spatial locality. Temporal locality would *probably* be enough to put both routines in the cache in this example, but it's best not to count on it.

A better solution would be to declare MyFunction2() just above MyFunction1(). Even better, declare MyFunction2() as *static* so the compiler knows that it is only being called from this file, like this:

```
MySourceFile1.c:
static void MyFunction2() {
  ..do something...
}

void MyFunction1() {
  unsigned long i;
  for (i = 0; i < 10000; i++) {
    MyFunction2();
  }
}
```

It may seem that you can optimize this function even more by not calling MyFunction2() at all, but instead placing its code inside the *for()* loop. This technique will help greatly for a 68k processor, but it won't have much effect on the PowerPC. MyFunction2() is what is known as a *leaf function*: it takes no parameters. This means the processor doesn't have to waste any time pushing parameters onto the stack. Instead, the Branch Unit will automatically do the jump without any effort from the other units.

Data Locality

Data locality attempts to keep the information you're working on in the data cache of the PowerPC. In Chapter 12, you saw an example where an array was accessed by indexing through the rows first. On a 68k processor, this results in a slight speed penalty, but on a PowerPC, if the array was large enough, the penalty would be huge. Each time through the loop, the beginning of the array would have to be reloaded into the cache from the memory banks.

Depending on the circumstances, this penalty can be as much as 10 times as slow or even more, if the actual operation is simple.

PowerPC Branching

When the PowerPC branch unit encounters a conditional expression (e.g., an If...Else or a while() statement), sometimes it doesn't yet know what the result is going to be (because the other two units are still working on the previous instructions). It could wait until it knows where to go (which would involve waiting until the other two units' pipelines emptied out), causing a pipeline stall. That would work, but we'd be wasting processor cycles. Although it doesn't seem like it would make much difference for performance, the processor can encounter branch conditionals millions of times per second, so every cycle counts.

Instead of waiting, the branch unit will attempt to "guess" which direction the branch is going to take. Its guessing mechanism is rather simple—if the branch is forward, it will guess that it won't be taken; if the branch is backward, it guesses that it *will* be taken.

This means that loops (which involve instructions to branch backward) will be assumed to continue and conditional expressions (e.g., If...Else) will be assumed to be true. The branch unit will then continue to feed instructions to the processing units. If the branch unit was wrong, it will flush out everything that has taken place in the pipeline and feed it the correct instructions.

How does this affect your code? Take this example:

```
for (i = 0; i < 1000; i++) {
  if (i == 0) {
    ....complicated instructions....
  } else {
    ....simple instruction....
  }
}
```

This code segment is an example of handling branching poorly. The case where i is equal to 0 is very rare (1 in 1000), but the branch unit will always assume it will be true until it finds out otherwise.

The example also displays poor code locality. In most cases, the processor will have to jump over the complicated instructions for i being equal to 0, possibly causing cache problems. In general, it is preferable to put the more likely case first.

Accessing Video Memory

Unlike general memory where data is cached, any data written to video memory is written immediately. However, as I said earlier in this chapter, memory is comparatively slow, especially many types of video memory. If you try to write to video memory several times in a row, the processor will be stalled as it waits for the previous writes to complete, which can take from 6 to 18 cycles. In the middle of a blitting loop, this time can be critical.

If you manage to find something to do between copies, you'll be able to fill up the pipeline and prevent wasted cycles. However, this is very difficult to do without preemptive multitasking.

The PowerPC works very well when you copy 8 bytes at a time instead of 4 (the size of a longword). To accomplish this, you can use the *double* data type, which is a 64-bit value. The double type is normally reserved for floating-point numbers, but by typecasting the source and destination pointers to (double *), the data is copied as one large 64-bit block. You'll use this method to increase the speed of your blitting routine later in the chapter.

Memory Alignment

In Chapter 11, I briefly mentioned that the PowerPC chip can access aligned data much more efficiently than misaligned data. This means that, for maximum speed, if a 2-byte shortword is accessed, its address should be a multiple of 2; if a 4-byte longword is accessed, its address should be divisible by 4, and so on.

This is a characteristic of most RISC processors. The speed difference isn't too large on a 601 chip because it has some hardware support for misaligned access. The 603 chip and later, however, pay a huge penalty for accessing misaligned data. In most cases on the PowerPC, data loaded into a register cannot be used for the cycle after it has been loaded (a characteristic known as a *load latency*). If the data is misaligned, however, this latency can increase to three or four cycles, making it an expensive operation.

Misaligned floating-point accesses are even more expensive on the 603 and 604 processors; a misaligned load or store can cost up to 50 cycles.

Most of the time, you don't have to worry about memory alignment. It only comes into play when you're accessing fields in a structure or copying a block of memory. Your PowerPC compiler has a switch that will allow you to generate code using 68k alignment or PowerPC alignment; unless you need to load misaligned structures from disk, you should always set the alignment to PowerPC for best performance. With the methods you used for defining your object's resource, PowerPC data alignment will work fine.

Chapter 11 talks about the pros and cons of data alignment and how to make it work with your structures, but you also need to be aware of alignment when copying blocks of data. In this case, it won't matter what type of structure alignment you use, all that matters is whether your data pointers are aligned correctly. With the steps you took in Chapter 13 to align your offscreen memory map and your window (which have been aligned on 16-byte boundaries), you've already guaranteed that you'll have aligned data for the blitting routine.

Passing Parameters

The PowerPC processor has 32 general-purpose 32-bit registers and 32 floating-point registers, each 64 bits wide. If you're familiar with the 68k architecture, this seems like a huge number—the 68k has only 16 general-purpose registers and may not have any floating-point ones.

However, not all of these registers can be used for passing parameters into a function. The architecture allows 8 general-purpose and 13 floating-point registers to be used for this purpose. Any parameters that won't fit in these registers are passed to the function via the stack. Floating-point values exhibit a strange quirk in this respect. If a floating-point value is passed into a function, it will always use a floating-point register (assuming one is still available). If there are any general-purpose registers remaining, however, two of them will also be reserved for the value. Therefore, to get the best performance, you should pass all the necessary integer values into a function *before* the floating-point ones.

68k Code Emulation and the Mixed-Mode Manager

The PowerPC system software has a component called the *Mixed-Mode Manager* that allows it to execute 68k code transparently to the user. It operates as a layer between the object code and the processor, translating the 68k instructions into something the PowerPC processor can understand.

A good deal of the Macintosh toolbox is still in 68k and it won't be entirely native at least until System 8.0 ships. Whenever your code calls a toolbox function that is in 68k code, the Mixed-Mode Manager has to intervene and emulate that function.

Obviously, 68k emulated code is slower than native PowerPC code. However, this is not the only price you pay when you call a 68k function. Whenever the Mixed-Mode Manager has to switch between executing PowerPC code and executing 68k code, it goes through a process called a *context switch* in which it sets up the 68k registers and memory environment. A context switch is very expensive, requiring hundreds of cycles to resolve.

You already know from Chapter 12 that you shouldn't call toolbox functions from within a tight loop. On the Power Macintosh, this goes for calling emulated functions as well.

PowerTracer

So how can you tell which toolbox functions are emulated and which are native? There is no easy answer to this question. Apple doesn't maintain a central public list of the native functions of the toolbox because it would change so often as Apple releases system updates that progressively make the toolbox more completely native.

However, Apple has provided a tool that will, as a side effect, tell you which calls are native and which aren't. The tool is called PowerTracer and it falls in a second category of performance monitoring tools (the first being a profiler) called *tracers*. Like a passive profiler, a tracer will monitor the execution of your application and record what it's doing. Unlike a profiler, however, a tracer will also record the *order* in which the functions are called, giving you a bit more information.

The output of a profiler can be useful if, for example, you have a function that is called from two different routines. When it is called by the first routine, it doesn't consume much processor time, but if it's called by the second routine, it bogs down. Looking at the results from the profiler, you would see that this routine is expensive, but you wouldn't know that it is actually rather efficient given one particular set of data.

Whereas the output from the tracer can sometimes be more useful than that of a profiler, tracers generally produce much more data than a profiler does. This may sound attractive because of the increased information you gain, but it actually becomes a problem when you attempt to sort out the useful information from the useless. A majority of the time, you'll want to stick with a profiler because it is so much easier to understand.

The Metrowerks Profiler/Tracer

The Metrowerks profiler actually has the capabilities of a tracer if you turn on the *detailed* profiling information. When the output file is opened by the profiler application, the function call chains can be examined to find the calling order and relative speed.

Obtaining PowerTracer

PowerTracer is a free utility from Apple, and it can be downloaded via FTP from ftp.info.apple.com. Its pathname is

```
Apple.Support.Area/Developer_Services/Tool_Chest/Testing_&_Debugging/Tracer
```

The PowerTracer Interface

To use PowerTracer, drop the PowerTracer control panel into the system folder of your Power Macintosh and restart it. Open the control panel and you'll see a window like the one in Figure 14-4.

Clicking on Preferences will give you the window shown in Figure 14-5. Here you can see the size of the buffers used by PowerTracer. The Event Buffer is allocated from main memory when the computer starts up. Whatever size you specify here will be eaten up from your available memory.

When PowerTracer runs out of space in memory, it will start to save information on the hard disk. Max Dump File Size allows you to specify the maximum size for the hard disk buffer file.

PowerTracer produces a lot of data. For every second that PowerTracer monitors an application, it will produce approximately 650k of data. This means that if you monitor your application for 1 minute, you will have 38 *megabytes* of data to wade through. Because you probably don't have enough memory to hold more than a few seconds of tracer data, PowerTracer will start to write the information it gathers to the hard disk. The Preferences dialog lets you set the maximum size of the hard disk buffer. If the tracer encounters this limit, it automatically stops collecting data.

FIGURE 14-4

◎ ◎ ◎ ◎ ◎ ◎

The PowerTracer control panel

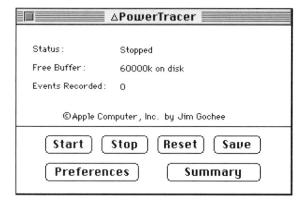

FIGURE 14-5

◎ ◎ ◎ ◎ ◎ ◎

The PowerTracer Preferences dialog

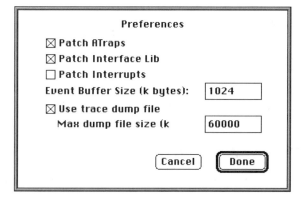

▨ Leaving Enough Space for PowerTracer

It is important not to let PowerTracer fill up your entire hard drive. If you don't have much space free, you may want to be cautious about using it, as some versions of PowerTracer can corrupt the hard drive if they run out of space. Consult the documentation for PowerTracer for more information.

The other options in the Preferences dialog let you specify which types of calls you want to monitor. ATraps are toolbox functions residing in ROM, Interface Lib includes functions that are linked with the code by the compiler, and Interrupts are functions that are called independently of your code's execution.

Going back to the control panel window, notice that there are five other buttons: Start, Stop, Reset, Save, and Summary. Start and Stop begin and end the trace, respectively. Reset causes the tracer information to be purged, and Save will create a file containing the data from the last trace.

The last button, Summary, will save the accumulated data into a more compact form that is much easier to digest. I'll examine this option in a bit.

Starting and Stopping a Trace

You can start a trace by clicking on the Start button, but after the trace has begun you have to start your application and jump to the portion you want to test. Because the tracer is collecting data at a phenomenal rate, you can't spend too much time collecting data on an application's performance (if you have a large hard drive, you *might* be able to get 5 minutes of data; a more common figure would be 15-30 seconds). The time you spend getting the application to run both allows less time for collecting the data you want and skews the results.

Controlling PowerTracer from MacsBug

Fortunately, there is a better way to control PowerTracer. The PowerTracer package includes several DCMDS (or *debugger commands*) that can be used in MacsBug. Debugger commands are small programs that MacsBug can execute through a simple instruction.

▣ Installing MacsBug

MacsBug is a low-level debugger that is indispensable for any Macintosh programmer. It provides detailed information about an application and allows you to do assembly level debugging. MacsBug has been included on the source code disc with this book (in the folder Utilities). Once it's installed, you'll see a message saying *MacsBug Installed* each time your machine boots up.

From then on, when your Macintosh crashes, it will usually invoke MacsBug. You'll know that MacsBug is running because your entire screen will turn white and you'll see a text-based interface reminiscent of DOS. You can also bring up MacsBug by pressing COMMAND-POWERKEY (which works on most Macintoshes) or by pressing the interrupt switch on the front or back of your computer.

Don't feel intimidated by MacsBug's interface—you'll get used to it. For now, I'll just be using it to execute some commands provided by PowerTracer. For an excellent introduction and tutorial on MacsBug, read *Debugging Macintosh® Software with MacsBug®* by Konstantin Othmer and Jim Straus (Addison-Wesley, Inc., 1991.)

The DCMDS PowerTracer provides are stored in the resource fork of the control panel. To use them in MacsBug, you have to copy them into MacsBug's preferences folder. This folder is named MacsBug Preferences and is located in your system folder (this holds true for MacsBug version 6.5.2 and later). If this folder does not exist, create a new folder with that name. Open the PowerTracer control panel in ResEdit, highlight the MXBM, MXWT, and DCMD resources, and copy them. Then use ResEdit to create a new file named PowerTracer Dcmds and save it in the MacsBug Preferences folder. Paste the resources into the file and save it.

After restarting your computer, you will be able to break into MacsBug whenever you want to and turn PowerTracer on or off. This allows much more precise control over the execution of PowerTracer.

To turn PowerTracer on, use the MacsBug DCMD PTStart; to end the trace, use PTStop. After you issue the PTStart instruction, PowerTracer immediately begins to collect data on whatever is running, so it also records the time between when you press Return and when you're able to leave MacsBug, which skews the results. In addition, when you break into MacsBug to give the PTStop command, that data will also be added to the trace.

Fortunately, MacsBug provides the capability to issue multiple commands at the same time by separating them with a semicolon (;). You can create a command that will immediately start PowerTracer running, return to the application, and then stop the trace when MacsBug is entered again by typing "PTStart; g; PTStop".

Tracing the Polygon-Fill Application

To perform a trace on any application, all you need to do is run it and then break into MacsBug. Once you're at the MacsBug prompt, type "PTStart;g;PTStop" and control will immediately switch back to the application. Let it run for a few seconds (depending on how much hard drive space you have free and how much space you allocated in the control panel's Preferences dialog). Then break into MacsBug again. PowerTracer will automatically stop gathering information and you can continue the application's execution by pressing COMMAND-G.

Obtaining PowerTracer's Output

To see what PowerTracer has produced, open the control panel and press the Summary button. This gives you a summary of your application's trace, which you can open using a word processor or your development environment (the file will probably be too large to open in SimpleText).

The file will look something like this (only a partial listing is shown below; the most expensive routines are listed at the top):

```
# Time in the profile #
    Total time for entire profile: 9295 msecs,        9 secs
    Total time spent in the toolbox:      7014 msecs,  7 secs,  75% of total time
    Total time spent at application level: 2281 msecs,  2 secs,  25% of total time
```

Continued on next page

Continued from previous page

Total time spent in interrupts: 0 msecs,   0 secs,   0% of total time

Totals
    Total Functions called   :76979   (8280 per second)
    Transition Summary (MM = MixedMode)
        ( )68k   -> ( )68k   :14055   (1511 per second)
        (·)PowerPC -> (·)PowerPC   :3171   (341 per second)
        (·)PowerPC -> ( )MM PowerPC :0   (0 per second)

        ( )68k   -> ( )PowerPC   :59753   (6427 per second)
        (·)PowerPC -> ( )68k   :0   (0 per second)

        MM Context Switches   :59753   (6427 per second)

Profile sorted by percent based on level 1 calls:

Function Name	Trap:Selector	Count	Avg	FuncΣ	Acc %	Func %	TotalΣ	Level 1 %
±CopyBits	A8EC:0	634	5987	3616738	38.907	38.907	3795807	40.833
±EraseRect	A8A3:0	633	3766	2354925	64.240	25.333	2383896	25.645
±DrawString	A884:0	634	481	8793	64.335	0.095	305360	3.285
SetGWorld	AB1D:80006	1268	216	272052	67.261	2.927	274304	2.951
GetGWorld	AB1D:80005	634	177	110325	68.448	1.187	112495	1.210
Button	A974:0	634	69	44080	68.922	0.474	44264	0.476
PBControlSync	A004:0	5	7892	37985	69.331	0.409	39461	0.284
±MoveTo	A893:0	634	31	11357	69.453	0.122	19990	0.215
BlockMoveData	A22E:0	1932	15	30542	69.781	0.329	30542	0.163
PBWriteAsync	A403:0	11	2349	11370	69.904	0.122	25845	0.093
PBControlAsync	A404:0	27	547	10270	70.014	0.110	14788	0.060
·EraseRect	A8A3:0	1	4358	4294	70.060	0.046	4358	0.047
·NumToString	0:0	634	5	3667	70.100	0.039	3667	0.039
·TickCount	A975:0	634	5	3490	70.137	0.038	3490	0.038
UnlockMemory	A05C:3	33	327	10797	70.254	0.116	10797	0.037
PrimeTime	A05A:0	48	115	5558	70.313	0.060	5558	0.013

This profile was taken on a Power Macintosh 7100/66. It used the QuickDraw version of the spinning cube, achieving about 75 fps (about 2.1 times as fast as the 040 Custom Cube application you built in Chapter 13). As you can see from the top of the report, the test was performed for 9 seconds, producing about 5.4 megabytes of data. PowerTracer will track only time spent in toolbox functions, so none of your routines will be listed in the report.

The next few lines tell you how much time the CPU spent executing toolbox routines and how much it spent in the application. Typical programs spend 80 percent of their time in the toolbox and only 20 percent in their own code. However, games are not typical; if you've written a lot of code to bypass toolbox functions (like the custom blitter you wrote in Chapter 13), the balance will be significantly different, as you'll see in a bit. This version of the Spinning Cube application spent about 75 percent of its time in the toolbox and 25 percent in the application.

The PowerTracer data will also tell you how much time was spent in interrupt routines. The spinning cube doesn't have any interrupt-level routines, and you're not monitoring them anyway (they can be traced by turning that option on in PowerTracer's preferences dialog). One caveat to monitoring interrupt-level routines is that you can't use the Power Macintosh DebugServices application at the same time (which is necessary for both the Metrowerks and Think C 8 debuggers).

The next section of the profile tells you that a total of 76,979 functions were called at a rate of 8,280 per second. This should start to give you an appreciation for the work the PowerPC processor is doing.

Below that, the profile shows how many context switches were performed. In this case, 14,055 entries were 68k functions being called by other 68k functions. Although the code is emulated, a context switch does not need to be done, so those functions aren't too expensive.

Only 3,171 functions were native, but fortunately this number includes the most expensive ones, as you'll see shortly.

The next few lines give you information on how many times the Mixed-Mode Manager had to perform a context switch. Because context switches are very expensive, this is the most important information PowerTracer gives you. In this case, 59,753 context switches were made when 68k code called PowerPC code; that's 6,427 per second.

The last section tells you how much time was spent in each of the toolbox calls the application made. Because it's such a simple application and you've already closely examined how it spends its time, this information won't be a big surprise. However, it will prove to be very important when your game starts to grow in size and complexity.

As you can see, 40 percent of the application's time is spent in CopyBits() and 25 percent is spent in EraseRect(). It also spends some time in DrawString() when it draws the fps figure on the window, but that amounts to only 3.2 percent of the time. If you look to the left of the function names, you'll see some symbols that represent the type of toolbox call it is. The first three have a ± symbol, which means that the system software has both a native and a 68k version of the function. A • means that the call is native only, and no symbol means it's 68k.

In general, for native code, you should try to reduce the number of calls to 68k toolbox functions. Not only are those functions emulated, they require a context switch. In the example here, there's not much you can do that would produce significant enhancements because so little time is being spent in 68k functions. As your game grows, however, you should use PowerTracer again to examine its habits and make improvements.

The PowerMac Optimized Cube

The Power Macintosh's video memory is relatively slow compared to main memory. As I mentioned earlier, when an application writes to the video memory several times, the application is stalled until the earlier writes are completed. If you enable the custom screen code you developed in Chapter 13 (not including the MOVE16 version, because that won't work on a PowerPC), you achieve a frame rate of 65 fps. This is actually *slower* than the CopyBits() version because CopyBits() has been specially optimized for the PowerPC.

Improving the Screen Copier

You can do a few PowerPC optimizations of your own. The custom code is now writing a longword (32 bits) at a time to the video memory, which requires a total of 36,000 copies (assuming a 480x300 window).

A major improvement would be to copy 64 bits at a time instead of 32. Because a *double* is 64 bits long, you can conveniently fool the compiler into thinking you're copying a double-precision floating-point number. This is surprisingly similar to the longword-copying version you've been using up to this point, which looks like this:

```
i = kWindowWidth / 32;
do {
        /* Do the copy */
        *longdst++ = *longsrc++;
        *longdst++ = *longsrc++;
        *longdst++ = *longsrc++;
        *longdst++ = *longsrc++;
        *longdst++ = *longsrc++;
        *longdst++ = *longsrc++;
        *longdst++ = *longsrc++;
        *longdst++ = *longsrc++;
} while (--i);
```

The *longdat* and *longsrc* variables are defined as longword pointers (long *). To do 64-bit copies, define two *double pointers* (double *), like this:

```
const double *doubleSrc;
      double *doubleDst;

/* Typecast the pointers to (double *)'s */
doubleSrc = (const double*)src;
doubleDst = (double*)dst;
```

Then use a similar loop for copying the data (there are half as many statements inside the loop because you're copying twice as much per instruction):

```
i = kWindowWidth / 32;
do {
        /* Do the copy */
        *doubleDst++ = *doubleSrc++;
        *doubleDst++ = *doubleSrc++;
        *doubleDst++ = *doubleSrc++;
        *doubleDst++ = *doubleSrc++;
} while (--i);
```

You also probably want to put conditional statements around the PowerPC copying code, because it doesn't work very well on 68k Macintoshes—for those machines, continue to use the methods from Chapter 13. It's also helpful to define a constant that is checked before using the PowerPC blitting routine so you can easily turn it on or off.

Listing 14-1 is the new CopyImageOntoScreen() function.

Listing 14-1 *The new CopyImageOntoScreen() routine*

```
void CopyImageOntoScreen( WindowPtr    mainWindow,
                          short        windowX,
                          short        windowY  )
{
    unsigned long    dstRowBytes;
    char             *src, *dst;
    const long       *longsrc;
    long             *longdst;
    Point            thisPoint;
    register short   i;
    PixMapHandle     windowPixMap;
    Rect             windowRect;
    short            height;

    /* These static variables save the last pixmap used for copying. If
     * the same pixmap is used again (which will generally be the
     * case), we don't need to figure out the base address or rowbytes
     * again.
     */
    static char            *screenImagePtr = NULL;
    static PixMapHandle    screenPixMap = NULL;
    static unsigned long   screenRowBytes = 0;

    /* Get the window's boundary */
    windowRect = mainWindow->portRect;

    /* First check to see if we're using custom blitting routines. If
     * we're not, just use the quickdraw version to display the image.
     */
    if (gUsingCustomOffscreen == FALSE) {
      /* Not using custom routines - use CopyBits(). */
      QDCopyOntoScreen(gQuickDrawImage, mainWindow, &mainWindow->portRect);
    } else{
      /* We're using our own custom routines */

      /* Find the window's pixmap */
      windowPixMap = ((CGrafPtr)mainWindow)->portPixMap;

      /* See if we've already saved the window's pixmap information. If
       * not, save it now.
       */
      if (screenPixMap != windowPixMap) {
```

Continued on next page

Continued from previous page

```
        screenPixMap = windowPixMap;
        screenImagePtr = GetPixBaseAddr(windowPixMap);

        screenRowBytes = ((**windowPixMap).rowBytes & 0x3FFF);
    }

    /* Shield the cursor so we don't draw over it. This must be done
     * any time you draw directly to the screen.
     */
    thisPoint.h = windowX;
    thisPoint.v = windowY;
    ShieldCursor(&windowRect, thisPoint);

    /* Grab the offscreen's image pointer and position a pointer at
     * the upper left-hand corner of the window on the screen.
     */
    src = gImageDataPtr;
    dst = screenImagePtr + ((long)windowY * screenRowBytes) + windowX;

    /* Reduce the screen's rowbytes value by the
     * width of the window — we want to know how much to
     * add to the data pointer to jump from the
     * right-hand side of the window to the
     * left-hand side of the next row.
     */
    dstRowBytes = screenRowBytes - 480;

    /* Figure out which copying method to use. If we are running
     * on an 040, use a function that takes advantage of special
     * instructions on that chip. Otherwise, use an unrolled loop
     * for doing the copying.
     *
     *   For the 040 version to work, the window MUST be on a
     *   16-byte boundary. Otherwise, use the other custom routine.
     *
     *   A fast MOD can be achieved by masking out the lowest
     *   4 bits of the variable.
     *
     *   Also ensure that the routine will not be called on a
     *   PowerPC processor. By using #ifdef instructions,
     *   these lines won't even be compiled on a PowerPC.
     */
#ifndef powerc /* If we're not using a PowerPC... */
    if (gUsing040Processor && ((windowX & 0x000F) == 0)) {
        /* Use the 040 routine to copy the image */
        Blit040Screen(src, dst, dstRowBytes);
    }
    else
#else  /* If we are using a PowerPC... */
    /* Copy 8 bytes at a time to the screen by putting the
     * data into doubles (64-bits each).
```

```
       */
    if (kUsePowerPCDoubleBlit) {
      const double    *doubleSrc
      const double    *doubleDst;

      /* Typecast the pointers to (double *)'s */
      doubleSrc = (const double*)src;
      doubleDst = (double*)dst;

      /* Get the window's height */
      height = kWindowHeight;

      /* Start the loop */
      do {
        /* (kWindowWidth / 8) doubles need to be copied per
         * row, and there are 4 copied per iteration of the
         * inner loop, so we want to loop (kWindowWidth / 32) times.
         */
        i = kWindowWidth / 32;
        do {
          /* Do the copy */
          *doubleDst++ = *doubleSrc++;
          *doubleDst++ = *doubleSrc++;
          *doubleDst++ = *doubleSrc++;
          *doubleDst++ = *doubleSrc++;
        } while (--i);

        /* Jump down a row. */
        doubleDst = (double *)((long)doubleDst + dstRowBytes);
      } while (--height);
    } else
#endif
    {
      /* Use a loop to copy a longword at a time to the screen.
       * Typecast the data pointers to (long *)'s, so that
       * a longword is copied every time, plus it gets
       * incremented by 4 instead of 1.
       */
      longsrc = (const long*)src;
      longdst = (long*)dst;

      /* Get the window's height */
      height = kWindowHeight;

      /* Start the loop */
      do {
        /* (kWindowWidth / 4) longwords need to be copied per
         * row, and there are 8 copied per iteration of the
         * inner loop, so we want to loop (kWindowWidth / 32) times.
         * In this case, it's OK to use a divide, because
         * you're dividing a constant - this will get evaluated
```

Continued on next page

Continued from previous page

```
         * at compile-time, not at run-time.
         */
        i = kWindowWidth / 32;
        do {
          /* Do the copy */
          *longdst++ = *longsrc++;
          *longdst++ = *longsrc++;
          *longdst++ = *longsrc++;
          *longdst++ = *longsrc++;
          *longdst++ = *longsrc++;
          *longdst++ = *longsrc++;
          *longdst++ = *longsrc++;
          *longdst++ = *longsrc++;
        } while (--i);

        /* Jump down a row. This is a little tricky, since if
         * we just add dstRowBytes to the long pointer, it will
         * get incremented by 4*dstRowBytes. Instead, we
         * fool the compiler into thinking it's a just a long
         * value, add the rowbytes to it, then typecast it back
         * to a long pointer.
         */
        longdst = (long *)((long)longdst + dstRowBytes);
      } while (--height);
    }

    /* Show the cursor again. */
    ShowCursor();
  }
}
```

Improving the Memory Eraser

The routine for clearing out memory—EraseMemoryMap()—also consumes a lot of the CPU's resources. Examining it, you can see that it is also erasing memory a longword at a time. By applying the same optimization technique to it that you did to the screen copier, you can give it a small performance boost (the boost won't be quite as great because writing longwords to main memory is faster than writing them to video memory).

Here is the new memory eraser:

```
void EraseMemoryMap(Ptr  memoryMap)
{
#ifndef powerc  /* 68k Code */
  long      loopIterations;
  long      *longdst;

  longdst = (long*)memoryMap;
  loopIterations = (kWindowRowBytes * kWindowHeight) / 32;

  do {
```

```
      *longdst++ = 0;
      *longdst++ = 0;
      *longdst++ = 0;
      *longdst++ = 0;
      *longdst++ = 0;
      *longdst++ = 0;
      *longdst++ = 0;
      *longdst++ = 0;
   } while (--loopIterations);

#else   /* PowerPC Code */

   long        loopIterations;
   double      *doubledst;

   doubledst = (double*)memoryMap;
   loopIterations = (kWindowRowBytes * kWindowHeight) / 64;

   do {
     *doubledst++ = 0;
     *doubledst++ = 0;
     *doubledst++ = 0;
     *doubledst++ = 0;
     *doubledst++ = 0;
     *doubledst++ = 0;
     *doubledst++ = 0;
     *doubledst++ = 0;
   } while (--loopIterations);
#endif
}
```

Timing the New Routines

After compiling these improved routines and running the application, you'll notice a rather large performance boost—you're now running at 85 fps, which is 13 percent faster than the QuickDraw version and 30 percent faster than the longword copying version. The speed of CopyImageOntoScreen has improved by approximately 50 percent over the longword copier, so you've been quite successful.

Because the application is still so simple, there aren't many other optimizations you could make to increase the speed dramatically. In any case, 85 fps on a low-end 601 chip gives you plenty of room to experiment with some better rendering techniques.

Taking Advantage of the Speed

Asteroids or Centipede wouldn't be any more exciting if they ran more quickly (although your game would be over sooner). The *real* reason to optimize your code is so you can use the speed to increase the realism and quality of your game. Adding better rendering modes and more detailed objects is one way to make a game more interesting; I'll be examining ways to do this over the course of the next several chapters.

I will begin by developing methods of bringing a fully three-dimensional universe onto the screen. An important part of this process is knowing which parts of that universe are actually visible to the user and throwing away the rest. There are two parts to this task. The first, known as *hidden surface removal,* involves figuring out which polygons are obscured by other objects in the foreground. The other involves showing only polygons that lie within the boundary of the screen and is known as *clipping.* The next two chapters are devoted to these two tasks.

15

Hidden Surface Removal

come tuttili pori le manovelle ... le quali promovano e laiga
no sgrappi ... meritumenti ... pesso sapograno ti bone
esgare nellama e lapera ... nella manovella pregi quin
aforça ... più ...uomo più val.

15

Hidden Surface Removal

Sometimes when creating a virtual world with three-dimensional graphics, you find it is difficult to do something that you take for granted in the real world. In the real world, objects that are far away can be obscured by objects that are closer. However, the polygon-drawing routines you've built up to now don't care how far away a polygon is—they just draw all of the polygons as they find them. This means that an object in the foreground may get obscured by one in the background, clearly not a desirable effect.

Unfortunately, showing everything in the scene in the proper way is not a trivial task for a computer. In this chapter, I'll develop a method of showing the foreground objects on *top* of those in the background, providing a more convincing three-dimensional world.

A few techniques typically are used to achieve this effect. In this chapter, I'll look at two of them: the Painter's algorithm and the z-Buffer algorithm. However, neither of these techniques is perfect, so you'll have to settle for some compromises.

Why Hidden-Line Removal Is Difficult for Computers

The polygons that are shown on the computer screen represent objects that are a specific distance from the viewer, as represented by their z coordinate. Polygons with higher z coordinates are farther from the viewer, whereas those with lower z coordinates are closer.

The actual polygons that are drawn, however, have no z coordinate; they are distinguished only by varying x and y coordinates. But as the screen has no depth, it has no way of knowing which polygons are closer than others. Therefore, it's up to the drawing algorithm to decide how the polygons are drawn.

In Chapter 11, I examined a method of eliminating any polygons that are facing away from the viewer. If you're working with an object that has only convex surfaces (i.e., none of the angles between its polygons is larger than 180°), this method will take care of the polygons within one object, but it won't help if you have any objects that are overlapping. The methods I'll look at in this chapter will solve this problem as well.

Painter's Algorithm

If you've ever taken a painting class, you may have been taught to paint the background of the image first, then use additional layers as the rest of the scene is created. For example, Figure 15-1 shows a landscape in which the artist has begun by painting distant mountains. In Figure 15-2, the nearby trees have been added, followed by the foreground objects in Figure 15-3.

One of the techniques for hidden surface removal uses a similar approach. First you determine how far away each object is from the viewer (indicated by its z coordinate),

FIGURE 15-1

◉ ◉ ◉ ◉ ◉ ◉

The Painter's algorithm draws the distant parts of the scene first

FIGURE 15-2
◎ ◎ ◎ ◎ ◎ ◎
Next, the closer trees are drawn on the scene, obscuring part of the mountains

FIGURE 15-3
◎ ◎ ◎ ◎ ◎ ◎
Finally, the nearby house is drawn onto the scene, obscuring parts of the trees and mountains

FIGURE 15-4

◎ ◎ ◎ ◎ ◎ ◎

These two poly-
gons would not
be sorted in the
proper order by
comparing their
z extents

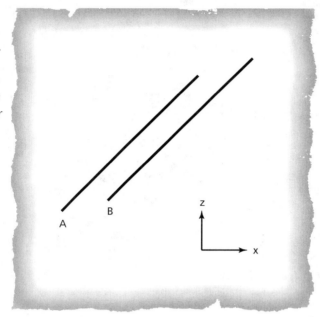

then you draw each object, starting with the farthest and working toward the closest. This method solves the problem of hidden surface removal, but it brings up another problem. How do you determine the order in which to draw these polygons? The answer may seem trivial, but it's more difficult than it sounds.

The obvious method for sorting polygons is to look at their z coordinates and use a standard sorting algorithm to put them in back-to-front order. This is called a depth sort, and it's the first step of the Painter's algorithm.

But which z coordinate of the polygon do you use? After all, each polygon is represented by at least three vertices, and each vertex has its own z coordinate. Do you sort by the minimum z or the maximum z or some average of these values?

For most purposes, it doesn't make much difference which of these methods you use, as long as it's used consistently throughout all your polygons.

Ensuring the Proper Order

Once the polygons have been sorted, can you just start drawing them onto the screen? Not necessarily. Just because the polygons have been sorted with one of the methods just described, it doesn't mean they are in the proper order for the Painter's algorithm. Figure 15-4 shows two polygons from a top-down view. The viewer is positioned at the bottom of the image, looking up.

Although polygon A has a smaller maximum z coordinate, polygon B extends in front of it. In addition, polygon A has a smaller minimum z coordinate *and* a smaller average z coordinate. So if you use any of the sorting methods previously discussed, the polygons will always end up sorted in the wrong order.

This might convince you that none of those sorting methods should be used because they don't always give the correct result. Although you could throw these methods out, the cases where they turn out to be incorrect are actually relatively uncommon. Instead, what you can do is sort using any one of the z extents and then perform some additional checks on each of the polygons to ensure that you have them in the correct order.

There is a standard algorithm to test if any two polygons are in the correct order. It involves four separate tests on each pair of polygons in the scene, in a fixed order, after the initial depth sort is complete. In the paragraphs that follow, I'll refer to the two polygons in the pair as A and B, where A is the polygon determined in the initial sort to be the closer of the two and B is the one determined to be the farther of the two. The actual order may turn out to be the reverse, of course, but that's why you're performing these tests.

The four tests are designed so that if a pair of polygons passes any one of them, you know that the pair is in the proper order and doesn't need to be swapped. Thus once a successful result is returned from a test, the rest of the tests don't need to be performed. Only if the pair flunks all four tests must their order be swapped.

These four tests *could* be performed on every pair of polygons in the scene. If there are five polygons in a scene, then pairs 1 and 2 would need to be compared, followed by 1 and 3, 1 and 4, 1 and 5, 2 and 3, 2 and 4, and so forth. Fortunately, in practice, the comparison doesn't need to be that exhaustive. Only polygons that overlap in the z extent, where the range between the maximum z coordinates and the minimum z coordinates of the polygons overlap, need to be compared (see Figure 15-5). If two polygons don't overlap in the z extent, you are assured that these two polygons were sorted correctly by the z-sort.

Determining whether the z extents of the polygons overlap is simple. Polygon A is determined by the initial depth sort to be closer to the viewer. Polygon B is then presumed to be farther away. If the maximum z coordinate of polygon A is less than the minimum z coordinate of polygon B, then there is no z overlap. The polygons must be in the correct order.

The Four Tests

If the z extents *do* overlap, you need to perform additional tests to determine if the polygons need to be swapped. Using the same convention of referring to the allegedly nearer polygon as polygon A and the other as polygon B, here are the four tests that help make that determination.

FIGURE 15-5

These polygons overlap in the z extent

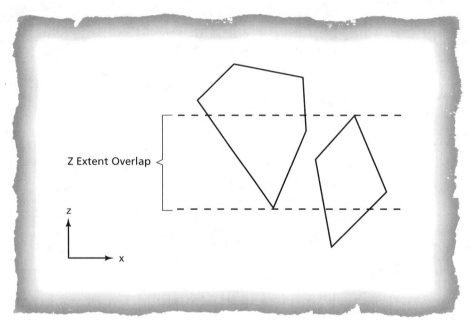

Test 1

Do the x extents of the two polygons overlap (see Figures 15-6a and b)? If not, it does-n't matter whether the two polygons are in the wrong order or not because they don't overlap and can't possibly obscure each other on the screen. This can be determined by comparing the minimum and maximum x coordinates of the two polygons. If the minimum x of B is larger than the maximum x of A or vice versa, the x extents don't overlap. No more tests need be performed.

Test 2

Do the y extents of the two polygons overlap? (See Figure 15-7.) This works exactly like the previous test, except that the minimum and maximum y coordinates are com-pared. If the two polygons don't overlap in the y extent, it doesn't matter if they're in the wrong order because they can't obscure each other on the screen. No more tests need be performed.

It may help, in performing tests 1 and 2, to imagine the polygon as being surrounded by a rectangle—known technically as a *bounding rectangle*—with one corner at the min-imum x and y of the polygon and the opposite corner at the maximum x and y of the

FIGURE 15-6a

◎ ◎ ◎ ◎ ◎ ◎

Do the polygons overlap in the x extent?
These polygons do not overlap in the x extent

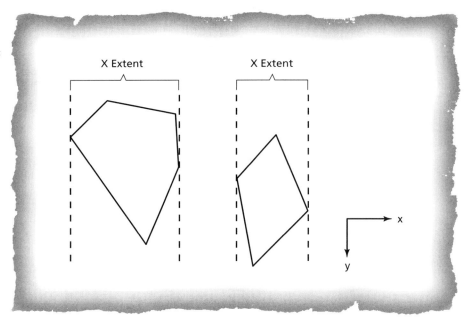

FIGURE 15-6b

◎ ◎ ◎ ◎ ◎ ◎

These polygons do overlap in the x extent

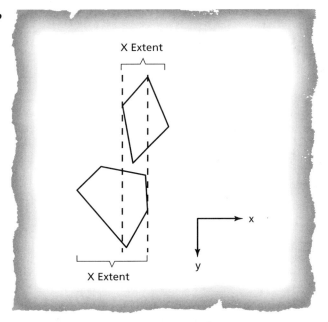

FIGURE 15-7
◉ ◉ ◉ ◉ ◉ ◉
These polygons overlap in the y extent

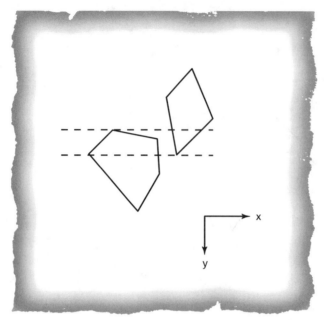

polygon. If the bounding rectangles of the two polygons don't overlap, then the polygons can't possibly obscure one another on the screen.

Test 3

Is polygon B entirely on the far side (i.e., the correct side) of A (see Figure 15-8)? This is a rather complicated test and involves some fairly esoteric mathematics. Later in this chapter, you'll see a standard formula for performing this test and I will explain mathematics in considerably more detail. For now, simply imagine that polygon A is part of an infinite plane that extends to all sides of it and that you must test to see if polygon B is entirely on the far side of that plane. If so, the polygons pass the test and no more tests need be performed.

Test 4

Is polygon A entirely on the nearer side of polygon B (see Figure 15-9)? This test is much like test 3, except it is checking to see if polygon A is on the near side of the plane of polygon B. If the two polygons pass either one of these tests, they are in the correct order.

Only tests 3 and 4 are necessary to show that the two polygons are in the wrong order. The other two tests check to see if the polygons actually obscure each other on the screen. The advantage of checking the overlap conditions first is that those tests are fast,

FIGURE 15-8
◉ ◉ ◉ ◉ ◉ ◉
Polygon B, as seen from above, is entirely on the far side of polygon A

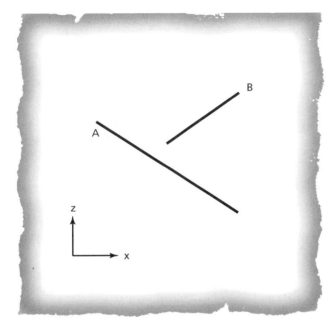

FIGURE 15-9
◉ ◉ ◉ ◉ ◉ ◉
Polygon A, as seen from above, is entirely on the near side of polygon B

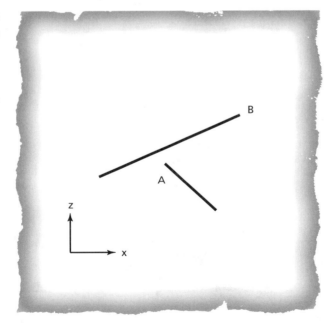

whereas tests 3 and 4 take much more time. By testing for overlap, you can process most polygons with two very fast boundary checks instead of the time-consuming planar checks.

If all the tests up to this point have failed, the two polygons are in the incorrect order so they should be swapped in the polygon list. You can then continue with the remaining polygons in the list.

Mutual Overlap and Bisecting

Once you've performed the extensive list ordering, can the polygons be safely drawn in polygon list order without any hidden surfaces showing through? Not necessarily. There are two situations that even a depth sort followed by these four tests can't handle. The first is called *mutual overlap* or *cyclical overlap*. It occurs when three or more polygons overlap in a circular fashion, with each polygon overlapping the next and the last overlapping the first. In Figure 15-10, for instance, polygon A is overlapped by polygon B, which is overlapped by polygon C, which, in turn, is overlapped by polygon A. If these polygons were being prepared for the Painter's algorithm, there would be no correct order in which they could be sorted. No matter what order you draw them in, at least one polygon will show through at least one other polygon.

The second situation occurs when one polygon goes through another one, as shown in Figure 15-11. Again, no matter which of these polygons is drawn first, the resulting image won't be correct.

FIGURE 15-10

◎ ◎ ◎ ◎ ◎ ◎

Three polygons mutually overlapping each other

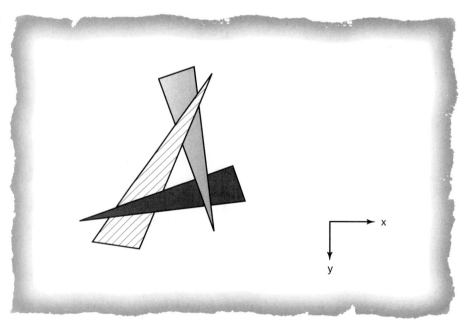

What can be done about these two problems? The only fully satisfactory solution is to split one of the polygons into two polygons. There would then be a correct order into which the polygons could be placed. But this approach brings a number of problems of its own, not the least of which is the need to allocate memory on the fly for the new polygon.

This is a major drawback to the Painter's algorithm and is enough to preclude its use in any situation that demands very accurate graphics. I'll look at how this drawback affects the decision to use the Painter's algorithm for games later in this chapter.

Time Considerations

As you can see, the Painter's algorithm can result in many calculations. In particular, the four sorting tests can be quite time consuming.

In a worst-case situation, execution time can go up as the *square* of the number of polygons in the scene (which makes it a $O(n^2)$ algorithm, in computer science terms). Fortunately, it's not necessary to compare *every* pair of polygons in the scene, just those with overlapping z extents.

Considering the potential time demands of the Painter's algorithm—and, more specifically, the way those time demands can increase almost exponentially as the number of polygons increases—you might wonder if there is a method that does not increase its time demands as rapidly as this algorithm does when additional polygons are added.

FIGURE 15-11

◎ ◎ ◎ ◎ ◎ ◎

A polygon crossing through another

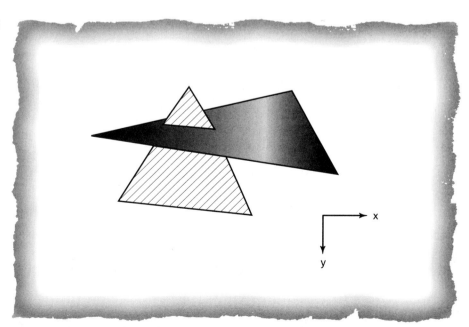

In fact, there is. Furthermore, it's an extremely straightforward algorithm, without the complications inherent in the Painter's algorithm, and is therefore easier to implement.

Let's take a look at this algorithm, called the z-Buffer algorithm.

The z-Buffer Algorithm

As far as the Painter's algorithm is concerned, the problem with polygons is that they can have more than one vertex—and each of these vertices can have a different z coordinate. In fact, not only can the vertices of polygons have varying z coordinates, but every *point* on the surface of a polygon can have a different z coordinate. The only truly exhaustive way to perform a depth sort would involve determining the depth of every point on the surface of every polygon on the screen and drawing only the points nearest to the viewer.

But clearly that's not possible. After all, there are an infinite number of points in a plane, or even in a section of a plane, and a polygon is a section of a plane. There's no way you can sort an infinite number of points and determine which is nearest to the viewer.

Fortunately, it's not necessary to sort an infinite number of points. It's only necessary to sort those points that are going to be *drawn*—that is, those that correspond to the pixels on the screen. Unlike the number of points on the surface of a polygon, the number of pixels on the screen is finite. If you had some way of keeping track of what's being drawn at each pixel position on the screen, you could assure yourself that only those pixels representing the points closest to the viewer would get displayed. In effect, you would be performing a separate depth sort for every pixel in the viewport area of the screen.

That's exactly what the z-Buffer algorithm does. It determines which points on which polygons are closest to the viewer for *every pixel in the viewport* so that only those points get displayed. It requires that the programmer set aside an integer array in which each element corresponds to a pixel in the viewport. Every time a point on the surface of a polygon is drawn in the viewport, the z coordinate of that point is placed into this array. The next time a pixel is to be drawn to that same position, the z coordinate of the point represented by the new pixel is compared with the value currently in the array. If the z coordinate in the buffer is smaller than that of the new point, the new pixel is not drawn because that point would be farther away than the old point and is therefore part of a hidden surface. If the z coordinate in the buffer is larger than that of the new point, the new pixel is drawn over the old one and the z coordinate of the *new* point is put in the buffer, replacing the old one.

The z-Buffer algorithm, if correctly implemented, works perfectly: No hidden surfaces will show through. The algorithm is also straightforward, so it is not difficult to implement. An efficiently written z-Buffer algorithm requires relatively few lines of code; it is certainly easier to implement than the Painter's algorithm.

The z-Buffer algorithm has two drawbacks: time and memory. To implement the z-Buffer algorithm, the polygon-fill routine would have to be modified, and the new version would unquestionably be slower than the original. This is because to draw a horizontal line, you have to keep track of a z coordinate for each pixel (which will require at least one division per scanline, and one addition per pixel), and then do a comparison and a branch for every pixel. As discussed in Chapter 14, a loop that uses so many branches is difficult to pipeline by the processor, leaving it much slower than a simple tight plotting loop.

The z-Buffer algorithm can also consume a great deal of memory. A full-screen display on a 13-inch monitor consists of 307,200 pixels. If you use a 32-bit value for each z coordinate, the buffer alone will consume 1200k of memory. You could probably safely use 16-bit values instead for the z coordinates, but you're still eating up 600k of memory.

Memory concerns are certainly less of a problem with today's machines than they were in the past, but a significant number of Macintosh owners still have only 4 megabytes of memory. A game in this environment can safely expect only about 1.5 to 2 megabytes, and instantly reserving a quarter or a half of the available memory can be problematic.

Yet the z-Buffer algorithm has a rather large advantage over just about all other methods of hidden surface removal. As new polygons are added to the scene, the amount of time consumed by the algorithm increases linearly, not exponentially—so if you double the number of polygons in the polygon list, the time required to perform the z-Buffer algorithm also doubles (on the average). With other algorithms, including the Painter's algorithm, the time might well quadruple. Thus, above a certain number of polygons, the z-Buffer is actually faster than the Painter's algorithm. Alas, that "certain number" of polygons is probably well into the thousands, far more than you'll be using for any scene in this book. (The actual break-even point between the Painter's algorithm and the z-Buffer algorithm is impossible to determine precisely because it would depend on how well the two algorithms were implemented by their programmers.)

There is another reason to be aware of the z-Buffer algorithm. Some of the newer dedicated graphics cards that are available for the Macintosh support the z-Buffer algorithm in hardware. This hardware support for hidden surface removal is generally much faster than any software version, including the Painter's algorithm, so if you decide to take advantage of this hardware, you'll almost certainly find that using a z-Buffer algorithm provides the best speed and quality.

At the present time, there is probably no real-time 3D game that uses the z-Buffer algorithm without hardware support. However, as computer speed increases, as it always will, and memory-rich configurations become more widespread, using a z buffer will become much more feasible.

As noted a few paragraphs back, if you want to implement this algorithm, it would be done in the polygon-drawing routine. The variation on Bresenham's algorithm that you use to draw the edges of the polygon would need to be extended to three dimensions so that the second error term could keep track of the z coordinate at each point on the edge. Then, when drawing the horizontal lines from the left edge to the right edge, you could use another variation on Bresenham's to calculate the changing z coordinate. This z value would be the one placed into the z buffer to determine whether the pixels are drawn or ignored.

For this chapter, however, I'm going to stick with the Painter's algorithm. Despite its problems, a game environment is usually not demanding enough to make these limitations noticeable. Let's get back to the sorting technique you'll be using for this hidden surface algorithm.

Building the Hidden Surface Removal System

As you learned, the Painter's algorithm is an awkward algorithm to implement for hidden surface removal because of all the special cases that need to be handled. But inelegance is not always the same as inefficiency. As awkward as it is, the Painter's algorithm is the fastest thing you've got.

To implement this algorithm, you will have to treat the three-dimensional world in a slightly different manner. Up until now, you have organized this world as a list of objects with specific positions and orientations. These objects, in turn, were defined as lists of polygons. But the Painter's algorithm, as you'll implement it here, doesn't care about objects. All that matters to it is polygons. The code you create to perform the Painter's algorithm will sort and compare polygons, which will then be drawn on the display by the unmodified polygon-fill routine.

It's still going to be necessary to treat the world as a list of objects, though. As you'll see when the final game is put together, this is the most logical way to treat a world if you want it to resemble your own. So at some point before the Painter's algorithm is executed, the database representing the world will need to be rearranged from a list of objects into a list of polygons, containing all polygons potentially visible in the viewport.

Linked Lists

To assist in organizing objects and polygons, you're going to take advantage of a programming concept called a *linked list*. A linked list is a series of structures connected together by pointers. Every element in this list contains a pointer to the next element (and optionally another pointer to the previous element, which creates a *doubly linked list*, as shown in Figure 15-12). The list is terminated by putting a Null value in the *next* field of the endmost element. If the list is doubly linked, the first element also has Null in its *prev* field.

A linked list can then be traversed by using a very simple *while()* loop. First you set a pointer to the first element; then you set the pointer to the next element each time through the loop. Here is an example of how you might do this:

```
MyStructure      *structPtr;

structPtr = linkedListFirstElement;
while (structPtr != NULL) {
   ....process the structure.....
   structPtr = structPtr->next;
}
```

You're going to be creating two linked lists: one for all the objects in a scene and the other for all the polygons in the scene. The advantage of creating a linked list of objects is that it allows you to move easily between all the objects in the scene, transforming and projecting them. A linked list also allows you to easily add or remove objects from the scene easily.

A linked list of polygons is also advantageous for another reason: Elements in a linked list are very easy to sort. Instead of moving memory around, you can simply redirect a few pointers and the list is suddenly rearranged (see Figures 15-13a and 15-13b).

To form a linked list out of the object and polygon structures, you need to add two pointers to each. One points to the next element in the list; the other points to the previous element. By forming a doubly linked list, you can gain access to every

FIGURE 15-12

◉ ◉ ◉ ◉ ◉ ◉

A doubly linked list

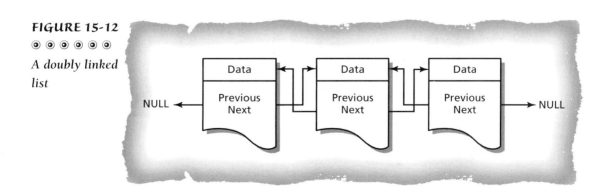

FIGURE 15-13a

◉ ◉ ◉ ◉ ◉ ◉

A simple linked list before rearranging

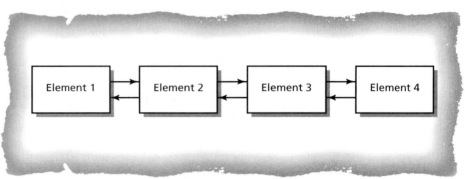

FIGURE 15-13b

◉ ◉ ◉ ◉ ◉ ◉

The linked list after elements 2 and 3 have been swapped

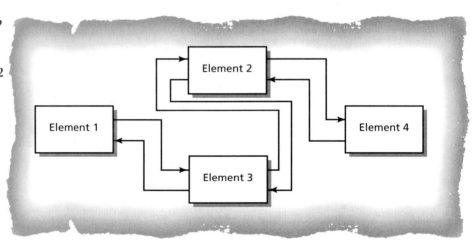

element in the list by having a pointer to only one element. Here is the new object structure:

```
typedef struct Object3D {
  short           numOfVertices;
  short           numOfPolygons;
  short           originX, originY, originZ;
  Vertex3D        vertex[kMaximumVertices];
  Polygon3D       polygon[kMaximumPolys];

  /* nextObject and prevObject form a linked list for
   * the virtual world
   */
  struct Object3D    *nextObject, *prevObject;
} Object3D;
```

The polygon structure has a few additional fields besides the linked list pointers for keeping track of its maximum and minimum x, y, and z coordinates:

```
typedef struct Polygon3D {
  short              numOfVertices;
  unsigned char      color;
  Vertex3D           *polyVertex[kMaxPolygonSize];

  /* nextPolygon and prevPolygon form a linked list for
   * the Painter's Algorithm
   */
  struct Polygon3D  *nextPolygon, *prevPolygon;

  /* Next are the minimum and maximum coordinates for the
   * polygon, forming a bounding box.
   */
  short              xmin, xmax, ymin, ymax, zmin, zmax;
} Polygon3D;
```

A Structure for the World

Because you're now going to be dealing with multiple objects in a scene, it would be helpful to create a structure that handles this. Call this structure World3D; one instance of it will be declared as a global variable in a new file called World Utilities.c. The structure itself only has to hold two variables: a pointer to the beginning of the object linked list and a pointer to the beginning of the polygon linked list. Here is the definition for World3D:

```
typedef struct {
  Object3D        *objectList;
  Polygon3D       *paintersList;
} World3D;
```

Notice that you don't need to keep track of how many objects are in the object list or how many polygons are in the Painter's list. This is because you can just traverse the list until you find a *next* field that is set to Null, indicating the end of the list.

Loading in the World's Objects

You can easily store all of your objects in OBJ3 resources and then load them all at the same time when the world is created. All you need is a routine that will take as parameters the first and last resource IDs of the series of objects. The function will then load each of these objects and place them in a linked list in a global World3D structure (which I'll call gWorld3D).

Once the objects are loaded, the function will step through all the objects and form a linked list out of their polygons. At this point, it doesn't matter that the polygons are not sorted by their z coordinates (in fact, you couldn't sort them even if you wanted to—they haven't been transformed and projected yet). They'll get sorted the first time through the sorting routine. The polygons will always stay in this linked list—the list is built only once, but it is sorted for every frame.

Listing 15-1 shows the function that will accomplish this task.

Listing 15-1 *The LoadWorldFromRsrc() routine*

```
/**
** LoadWorldFromRsrc()
**
** Initializes the world by loading in all objects from disk between
** the two provided resource IDs (e.g. pass in 100, 120 to load all
** objects with resource IDs from 100 to 120).
**
** This routine returns a pointer to the base object.
**/
Object3D  *LoadWorldFromRsrc(short objectStartID, short objectEndID)
{
  short       i;
  Object3D    *baseObject;
  Object3D    *thisObject;
  Object3D    *prevObject;
  Polygon3D   *basePolygon;
  Polygon3D   *thisPolygon;
  Polygon3D   *prevPolygon;

  /* Load the first object into memory, keep it as the base object */
  baseObject = LoadObjectFromRsrc(objectStartID);

  /* Test for failure */
  if (baseObject == NULL)
    return baseObject;

  /* Start the object chain */
  baseObject->prevObject = NULL;
  prevObject = baseObject;

  /* If we have more objects to load, continue loading them */
  if (objectStartID < objectEndID) {
    for (i = objectStartID + 1; i <= objectEndID; i++) {
      /* Load the object */
      thisObject = LoadObjectFromRsrc(i);

      /* If the object was successfully loaded, add it to the chain */
      if (thisObject != NULL) {
        /* Connect them together */
        prevObject->nextObject = thisObject;
        thisObject->prevObject = prevObject;

        /* Advance the prevObject pointer */
```

```
      prevObject = thisObject;
    }
  }
}

/* Finish off the chain with a NULL value */
prevObject->nextObject = NULL;

/* Now build a list of polygons. We don't bother sorting them at this
 * point, since they'll be sorted the first time through the Painter's
 * algorithm.
 */
thisObject = baseObject;
prevPolygon = NULL;

/* Loop until we reach the end of the object linked list */
while (thisObject != NULL) {
  short    numOfPolygons;

  /* Gather all of the polygons in this object */
  numOfPolygons = thisObject->numOfPolygons;

  /* Loop through all of those polygons */
  for (i = 0; i < numOfPolygons; i++) {
 /* If we're at the start of the list, use this polygon as the base. */
    if (prevPolygon == NULL) {
      basePolygon = prevPolygon = &thisObject->polygon[i];
      basePolygon->prevPolygon = NULL;
    } else {
      /* Add this polygon to the chain */
      thisPolygon = &thisObject->polygon[i];
      prevPolygon->nextPolygon = thisPolygon;
      thisPolygon->prevPolygon = prevPolygon;

      /* Advance the prevPolygon pointer */
      prevPolygon = thisPolygon;
    }
  }
  thisObject = thisObject->nextObject;
}

/* Finish off the polygon chain with a NULL value */
prevPolygon->nextPolygon = NULL;

/* Place the base pointers into the world structure */
gWorld3D.objectList = baseObject;
gWorld3D.paintersList = basePolygon;

/* Return the base object */
return baseObject;
}
```

Depth Sorting

The next step is to sort the polygon list using the Painter's algorithm. You'll start out with a simple routine that dispatches to several other functions that calculate the polygon extents. Next you'll sort the polygons based on their maximum z coordinates, and then you'll do some final sorting based on the Painter's algorithm:

```
/**
 **   SortPolygonList()
 **
 **   Applies a simple z-minimum sort on the polygons in the polygon
 **   linked list, then uses the Painter's algorithm to ensure that
 **   they are in the proper order.
 **/
void  SortPolygonList(void)
{
  /* Calculate the extents for each of the polygons */
  CalculatePolygonExtents();

  /* Sort the polygons based on their z values */
  ZSortPolygonList();

  /* Apply the Painter's algorithm to make sure they're
   * in the right order
   */
  PaintersProcessPolygonList();
}
```

Determining the Polygon's Extents

This step is rather easy. All you need to do is figure out the maximum and minimum x, y, and z coordinates of each of the polygon's vertices. The results are then stored in the polygon structure, as shown in Listing 15-2.

Listing 15-2 *The CalculatePolygonExtents() routine*

```
/**
 **   CalculatePolygonExtents()
 **
 **   Takes each of the polygons in the painters list and calculates their
 **   extents, storing the results back into the polygon structure.
 **/
static void  CalculatePolygonExtents(void)
{
  short       i;
  short       numOfVertices;
  short       xmin, xmax, ymin, ymax, zmin, zmax;
  Polygon3D   *thisPolygon;
```

```
/* Calculate the extents for each of the polygons */
thisPolygon = gWorld3D.paintersList;

while (thisPolygon != NULL) {
  /* Initialize the extent variables to the first polygon vertex.
   * We use the screen coordinates for x and y, but there is
   * no screen coordinate for z (the z term has already
   * been eliminated through projection). So, for the z term,
   * we take it from the world coordinate.
   */
  xmin = xmax = thisPolygon->polyVertex[0]->sx;
  ymin = ymax = thisPolygon->polyVertex[0]->sy;
  zmin = zmax = thisPolygon->polyVertex[0]->wz;

  /* Continue with the remainder of the vertices */
  numOfVertices = thisPolygon->numOfVertices;
  for (i = 1; i < numOfVertices; i++) {
    if (xmin > thisPolygon->polyVertex[i]->sx)
      xmin = thisPolygon->polyVertex[i]->sx;
    if (xmax < thisPolygon->polyVertex[i]->sx)
      xmax = thisPolygon->polyVertex[i]->sx;

    if (ymin > thisPolygon->polyVertex[i]->sy)
      ymin = thisPolygon->polyVertex[i]->sy;
    if (ymax < thisPolygon->polyVertex[i]->sy)
      ymax = thisPolygon->polyVertex[i]->sy;

    if (zmin > thisPolygon->polyVertex[i]->wz)
      zmin = thisPolygon->polyVertex[i]->wz;
    if (zmax < thisPolygon->polyVertex[i]->wz)
      zmax = thisPolygon->polyVertex[i]->wz;

  }
  /* Store the results in the polygon structure */
  thisPolygon->xmin = xmin;
  thisPolygon->xmax = xmax;
  thisPolygon->ymin = ymin;
  thisPolygon->ymax = ymax;
  thisPolygon->zmin = zmin;
  thisPolygon->zmax = zmax;

  thisPolygon = thisPolygon->nextPolygon;
 }
}
```

z-Sorting the Polygon List

The next step is to sort the polygon list based on each polygon's maximum z coordinates. If two polygons are found to be in the incorrect order, call the routine

SwapPolygons(), which I'll look at shortly. Then move back one step in the list and compare the freshly swapped polygon with the one that is now before it. For example, say you have three polygons, A, B, and C, that are linked together in that order. You find that C has a smaller maximum z coordinate than B does, so they need to be swapped. After you call SwapPolygons(), the list order is A, C, B. At this point, compare A and C to see if they are in the correct order and swap them if they are not.

This sorting technique is more efficient than a simple Bubble Sort because you don't need to start over traversing the list every time you have a swap. Because this routine is going to be called for every frame, it has to be efficient.

Listing 15-3 is the code for the polygon z-sorter.

Listing 15-3 *The ZSortPolygonList() routine*

```
/**
**   ZSortPolygonList()
**
**   Sorts each of the polygons based on their z-minimum values.
**
**/
static void  ZSortPolygonList(void)
{
  Polygon3D    *thisPolygon;
  Polygon3D    *prevPolygon;

  /* Start out with the second polygon */
  prevPolygon = gWorld3D.paintersList;
  thisPolygon = prevPolygon->nextPolygon;

  /* Loop until we're out of polygons */
  while (thisPolygon != NULL) {
    /* Compare this polygon with the previous one to see if they
     * should be swapped. If so, start looping as we move this polygon
     * backwards in the list (i.e. towards the top of the list).
     */
    while ( (prevPolygon != NULL) &&
            (thisPolygon->zmax > prevPolygon->zmax)) {
      /* Swap the polygons in the list */
      SwapPolygons(prevPolygon);

      /* Move the prevPolygon pointer back one step */
      prevPolygon = thisPolygon->prevPolygon;

      /* Check to see if we've moved this polygon to the front of the
       * list. If so, point the global base list to this polygon.
       */
      if (prevPolygon == NULL)
        gWorld3D.paintersList = thisPolygon;
    }

    /* Advance thisPolygon to the next polygon */
```

```
        prevPolygon = thisPolygon;
        thisPolygon = thisPolygon->nextPolygon;
    }
}
```

Painter's Polygon Test

The last sorting step is to compare each of the adjacent polygons using the Painter's algorithm. Before going into the Painter's algorithm, however, you must first check to see if the z extents of the polygons overlap. If they don't, you already know that these polygons are sorted correctly. Otherwise, you must continue into the Painter's algorithm.

As mentioned earlier, this algorithm involves four steps. You'll be performing steps 1 and 2 with the same function, which checks to see if the x or y extents overlap. Steps 3 and 4 are performed with separate, but similar, functions. I'll look at each of these functions more closely in a bit.

If all these tests fail, the polygon must be swapped, which is done using exactly the same technique as the z-sort function used. Then step back by one polygon and perform the test again. Listing 15-4 shows the function.

Listing 15-4 The PaintersProcessPolygonList() routine

```
/**
**  PaintersProcessPolygonList()
**
**  Checks to see if any of the polygons were incorrectly sorted.
**  If so, it swaps them around.
**/
static void  PaintersProcessPolygonList(void)
{
  Polygon3D     *thisPolygon;
  Polygon3D     *prevPolygon;
  Boolean       shouldBeSwapped;

  /* Start with the second polygon */
  prevPolygon = gWorld3D.paintersList;
  thisPolygon = prevPolygon->nextPolygon;

  /* Loop until we're out of polygons */
  while (thisPolygon != NULL) {
    /* OK, start to do our tests. Start by assuming that we will
     * want to swap them; allow our tests to disprove this idea.
     */
    shouldBeSwapped = TRUE;

    /* Do we even need to perform any checks with these polygons? */
    if (PolygonZOverlap(prevPolygon, thisPolygon) == FALSE) {

      /* They overlap in z. Do they overlap in x and y?
```

Continued on next page

Continued from previous page

```
        * (tests 1 and 2)
        */
       if (PolygonXYOverlap(prevPolygon, thisPolygon) == FALSE) {
         /* No, stop checking */
         shouldBeSwapped = FALSE;
       }

       /* If we haven't failed the test yet, check to see
        * if the second polygon is entirely on the far side of
        * the first (test 3).
        */
       if (shouldBeSwapped == TRUE) {
         if (PolygonSurfaceInside(prevPolygon, thisPolygon) == TRUE) {
           /* Yes, it is; stop checking */
           shouldBeSwapped = FALSE;
         }
       }

       /* Finally, check to see if the first polygon is
        * entirely on the near side of the second (test 4).
        */
       if (shouldBeSwapped == TRUE) {
         if (PolygonSurfaceOutside(prevPolygon, thisPolygon) == TRUE) {
           /* Yes, it is; stop checking */
           shouldBeSwapped = FALSE;
         }
       }
     } else
       shouldBeSwapped = FALSE;

     /* If we passed all of those tests, swap the polygons.
      */
     if (shouldBeSwapped) {
       /* Swap the polygons in the list */
       SwapPolygons(prevPolygon);

       /* Check to see if we've moved this polygon to the beginning of the
        * list. If so, point the main painter list at the polygon.
        */
       if (thisPolygon->prevPolygon == NULL) {
         gWorld3D.paintersList = thisPolygon;
       }
       /* Move to the next polygon */
       thisPolygon = prevPolygon->nextPolygon;
     } else {
       /* If we didn't do a swap, just proceed to the next
        * polygon in the list
        */
       prevPolygon = thisPolygon;
       thisPolygon = thisPolygon->nextPolygon;
     }
   }
 }
}
```

Polygon z Overlap

The z-overlap function is very simple. It just checks the extents of the polygons to see if the minimum z-extent of the first polygon is greater than the maximum z-extent of the second polygon, or vice versa:

```
/**
 ** PolygonZOverlap()
 **
 ** Compares two polygons to see if they overlap in the z coordinate.
 **/
static Boolean  PolygonZOverlap(Polygon3D *p1, Polygon3D *p2)
{
  /* If the minimum of p1 is greater than the maximum of p2, or
   * vice-versa, return FALSE, otherwise return TRUE.
   */
  if ((p1->zmin >= p2->zmax) || (p2->zmin >= p1->zmax))
    return FALSE;
  else
    return TRUE;
}
```

Polygon xy Overlap

This function is very similar to PolygonZOverlap(), except that it performs checks against two coordinates instead of one:

```
/**
 ** PolygonXYOverlap()
 **
 ** Checks to see if the bounding box of two polygons intersects.
 **/
static Boolean  PolygonXYOverlap(Polygon3D *p1, Polygon3D *p2)
{
  /* If the x minimum of p1 is greater than the x maximum of p2, or
   * vice versa, return FALSE.
   */
  if ((p1->xmin >= p2->xmax) || (p2->xmin >= p1->xmax))
    return FALSE;

  /* If the y minimum of p1 is greater than the y maximum of p2, or
   * vice versa, return FALSE.
   */
  if ((p1->ymin >= p2->ymax) || (p2->ymin >= p1->ymax))
    return FALSE;

  return TRUE;
}
```

Polygon Surface Inside

The surface inside and surface outside functions are rather complicated. They use the *plane equation* to determine whether the polygon pair is in the correct order. This equation can be expressed like this:

```
Ax + By + Cz + D
```

The variables x, y, and z are the x, y, z coordinates of a point. The variables A, B, C, and D are called the *coefficients of the plane,* which can be derived from the coordinates of any three points on the surface of a plane (as long as all three points don't happen to fall on a single line). If the coordinates of those three points are represented by the variables (x^1, y^1, z^1), (x^2, y^2, z^2), and (x^3, y^3, z^3), then the coefficients of the plane can be derived through these four formulas:

```
A = y1(z2 - z3) + y2(z3 - z1) + y3(z1 - z2)
B = z1(x2 - x3) + z2(x3 - x1) + z3(x1 - x2)
C = x1(y2 - y3) + x2(y3 - y1) + x3(y1 - y2)
D = -x1(y2z3 - y3z2) - x2(y3z1 - y1z3) - x3(y1z2 - y2z1)
```

Now that you know both the plane equation and the formulas necessary for determining the coefficients of a plane, you can use these tools to determine if a point lies on a particular plane (and, if not, on which side of the plane the point lies). Plug the coefficients of the plane into the A, B, C, and D variables of the plane equation and the x, y, and z coordinates of the point into the x, y and z variables and solve the equation. If the result is zero, the point lies on the plane. If the result is negative, the point lies on the counterclockwise side of the plane, the side from which the three points that you used to calculate the coefficients appear to be arranged in a counterclockwise manner. (Remember that these points cannot be on a single line; they must form the vertices of a triangle.) If the result is positive, the point lies on the opposite side of the plane—what you might call the clockwise side of the plane.

Now you can determine if polygon B (the polygon determined by the depth sort to be the more distant of the pair) is on the far side of polygon A, where it belongs. How? By using the plane equation to determine on which side of the plane of polygon A each of the vertices of polygon B lies. (Each vertex, remember, is simply a point in space with x, y, and z coordinates that can be plugged into the plane equation.)

The logic of the process is a bit complicated, however. Recall that the vertices of all the polygons in the world database have been designed so that, when viewed from outside the object of which they are a part, they are arranged in a counterclockwise manner. This makes the backface removal operate correctly.

The only polygons you care about ordering correctly are those that will be facing the viewer. Therefore, if a point lies on the clockwise side of one of the polygons, you can assume it is on the opposite side from the viewer.

It follows that you can tell whether polygon B is on the opposite side of polygon A from the viewer (which is where it's supposed to be after the depth sort) by testing to see if all its vertices are on the clockwise side of the *plane* of polygon A. Here's the procedure: First calculate the coefficients of the plane of polygon A using the x, y, and z coordinates of the first three vertices of polygon A as the three points on the plane. Next plug the resulting coefficients into the A, B, C, and D variables of the plane equation. Then use a *for* loop to step through all of the vertices of polygon B, plugging the x, y and z coordinates of each into the x, y, and z variables of the plane equation. If the resulting plane equations evaluate to positive numbers *for every one of the vertices of polygon B* then they are all on the clockwise side of polygon A. Because this is the far side of the polygon, the two polygons are in the correct order and don't need to be swapped. No more tests need to be performed.

Let's look at the actual code that performs the test. The function PolygonSurfaceInside() performs test 3, checking to see if polygon A is on the far (clockwise) side of polygon B. It returns True if it is.

```
static Boolean  PolygonSurfaceInside(Polygon3D *p1, Polygon3D *p2)
```

Before you can use the plane equation, you must calculate the coefficients of the plane of p2. For the three points on the plane, use the first three vertices of p2:

```
/* Get the coefficients of polygon 2 */
x1 = p2->polyVertex[0]->wx;
y1 = p2->polyVertex[0]->wy;
z1 = p2->polyVertex[0]->wz;
x2 = p2->polyVertex[1]->wx;
y2 = p2->polyVertex[1]->wy;
z2 = p2->polyVertex[1]->wz;
x3 = p2->polyVertex[2]->wx;
y3 = p2->polyVertex[2]->wy;
z3 = p2->polyVertex[2]->wz;
a = y1 * (z2 - z3) + y2 * (z3 - z1) + y3 * (z1 - z2);
b = z1 * (x2 - x3) + z2 * (x3 - x1) + z3 * (x1 - x2);
c = x1 * (y2 - y3) + x2 * (y3 - y1) + x3 * (y1 - y2);
d = -x1 * (y2 * z3 - y3 * z2) -
  x2 * (y3 * z1 - y1 * z3) -
  x3 * (y1 * z2 - y2 * z1);
```

The numbers can get pretty large when making these calculations, so use variables of type *long* to guard against integer overflow, which can create difficult-to-find bugs in the code.

Now you need to loop through the vertices of p1, plugging the x, y, and z coordinates of each into the plane equation along with the coefficients you just calculated. If the plane equations using these numbers evaluate to anything except a positive result, the test has been flunked and False is returned to indicate that the polygons may be in the incorrect order. If only positive values are detected, True is returned to indicate that p1 is indeed on the far side of p2:

```
/* Plug the vertices of p1 into the plane equation of p2 */
isOK = TRUE;
```

Continued on next page

Continued from previous page

```
   for (i = 0; i < p1->numOfVertices; i++) {
     if ( ((a * p1->polyVertex[i]->wx) +
         (b * p1->polyVertex[i]->wy) +
         (c * p1->polyVertex[i]->wz) + d) < 0) {
       isOK = FALSE;
       /* Break out of the loop, since we already know we flunked */
       break;
     }
   }


   /* Return the result */
   return isOK;
```

Listing 15-5 is the complete listing of PolygonSurfaceInside().

Listing 15-5 The PolygonSurfaceInside( ) routine

```
/**
 **   PolygonSurfaceInside()
 **
 **   Checks to see if p2 is entirely on the far side of p1.
 **/
static Boolean  PolygonSurfaceInside(Polygon3D *p1, Polygon3D *p2)
{
   long      x1, x2, x3;
   long      y1, y2, y3;
   long      z1, z2, z3;
   long      a,b,c,d;
   short     i;
   Boolean   isOK;

   /* Get the coefficients of polygon 2 */
   x1 = p2->polyVertex[0]->wx;
   y1 = p2->polyVertex[0]->wy;
   z1 = p2->polyVertex[0]->wz;
   x2 = p2->polyVertex[1]->wx;
   y2 = p2->polyVertex[1]->wy;
   z2 = p2->polyVertex[1]->wz;
   x3 = p2->polyVertex[2]->wx;
   y3 = p2->polyVertex[2]->wy;
   z3 = p2->polyVertex[2]->wz;
   a = y1 * (z2 - z3) + y2 * (z3 - z1) + y3 * (z1 - z2);
   b = z1 * (x2 - x3) + z2 * (x3 - x1) + z3 * (x1 - x2);
   c = x1 * (y2 - y3) + x2 * (y3 - y1) + x3 * (y1 - y2);
   d = -x1 * (y2 * z3 - y3 * z2) -
     x2 * (y3 * z1 - y1 * z3) -
     x3 * (y1 * z2 - y2 * z1);

   /* Plug the vertices of p1 into the plane equation of p2 */
   isOK = TRUE;
   for (i = 0; i < p1->numOfVertices; i++) {
     if ( ((a * p1->polyVertex[i]->wx) +
```

```
            (b * p1->polyVertex[i]->wy) +
            (c * p1->polyVertex[i]->wz) + d) < 0) {
        isOK = FALSE;
        /* Break out of the loop, since we already know we flunked */
        break;
      }
   }

   /* Return the result */
   return isOK;
}
```

Polygon Surface Outside

Test 4, PolygonSurfaceOutside(), is pretty much the same as test 3, except that you are now checking to see if polygon A is entirely on the near (counterclockwise) side of polygon B. To do this, simply reverse the role of the two polygons, taking the coefficients of p1 instead of p2 and using the *for* loop to step through the vertices of p2 instead of p1. Listing 15-6 is the source code for this function.

Listing 15-6 *The PolygonSurfaceOutside( ) routine*

```
/**
 ** PolygonSurfaceOutside()
 **
 ** Checks to see if p1 is entirely on the near side of p2.
 **/
static Boolean  PolygonSurfaceOutside(Polygon3D *p1, Polygon3D *p2)
{
    long     x1, x2, x3;
    long     y1, y2, y3;
    long     z1, z2, z3;
    long     a,b,c,d;
    short    i;
    Boolean  isOK;

    /* Get the coefficients of polygon 1 */
    x1 = p1->polyVertex[0]->wx;
    y1 = p1->polyVertex[0]->wy;
    z1 = p1->polyVertex[0]->wz;
    x2 = p1->polyVertex[1]->wx;
    y2 = p1->polyVertex[1]->wy;
    z2 = p1->polyVertex[1]->wz;
    x3 = p1->polyVertex[2]->wx;
    y3 = p1->polyVertex[2]->wy;
    z3 = p1->polyVertex[2]->wz;
    a = y1 * (z2 - z3) + y2 * (z3 - z1) + y3 * (z1 - z2);
    b = z1 * (x2 - x3) + z2 * (x3 - x1) + z3 * (x1 - x2);
    c = x1 * (y2 - y3) + x2 * (y3 - y1) + x3 * (y1 - y2);
    d = -x1 * (y2 * z3 - y3 * z2) -
```

Continued on next page

Continued from previous page

```
      x2 * (y3 * z1 – y1 * z3) –
      x3 * (y1 * z2 – y2 * z1);

   /* Plug the vertices of p2 into the plane equation of p1 */
   isOK = TRUE;
   for (i = 0; i < p2->numOfVertices; i++) {
     if ( ((a * p2->polyVertex[i]->wx) +
         (b * p2->polyVertex[i]->wy) +
         (c * p2->polyVertex[i]->wz) + d) > 0) {
       isOK = FALSE;
       /*  Break out of the loop, since we already know we flunked */
       break;
     }
   }

   return is OK;
}
```

Polygon Swapping

You now have all the functions necessary for performing the Painter's algorithm tests on the polygon list. All you need are a few utility routines to do some menial tasks and a routine that will draw the new polygon list.

You've already seen calls to SwapPolygons() in ZSortPolygonList() and PaintersProcessPolygonList(). SwapPolygons() takes a pointer to a polygon and swaps it with the next polygon in the list (you don't want to pass it the last polygon in the list). All that's necessary for this function are a few pointer swaps to get everything rearranged. This routine could easily be changed to operate on any type of linked list.

```
/**
 **    SwapPolygons()
 **
 **    Takes a polygon from a linked list and swaps it with its
 **    next polygon
 **/
static void  SwapPolygons(Polygon3D *firstPolygon)
{
  Polygon3D    *p1, *p2;

  p1 = firstPolygon;
  p2 = p1->nextPolygon;

  /* Update the polygon before the first one, and after the second one */
  p1->prevPolygon->nextPolygon = p2;
  p2->nextPolygon->prevPolygon = p1;

  /* Update the contents of the polygons we're swapping */
  p2->prevPolygon = p1->prevPolygon;
  p1->nextPolygon = p2->nextPolygon;
```

```
    p2->nextPolygon = p1;
    p1->prevPolygon = p2;
}
```

Retrieving the Linked Lists

The last two routines that round out World Utilities.c provide access to the contents of the gWorld3D global variable. The first returns a pointer to the object linked list:

```
/**
 **  GetObjectList()
 **
 **  Returns the object list.
 **/
Object3D  *GetObjectList(void)
{
  return gWorld3D.objectList;
}
```

The second returns a pointer to the Painter's polygon linked list:

```
/**
 **  GetSortedPolygonList()
 **
 **  Returns the sorted painters polygon list.
 **/
Polygon3D  *GetSortedPolygonList(void)
{
  return gWorld3D.paintersList;
}
```

Drawing the Polygon List

The polygon-drawing routine must be slightly modified to draw a linked list of polygons. Like the other linked list functions, it uses a *while()* loop to go through each of the elements of the linked list and draw each polygon. In fact, it is less complicated than the DrawObject() routine it is replacing:

```
/**
 **  DrawPolygonList()
 **
 **  Draws a polygon list using one of the available rendering modes.
 **/
void  DrawPolygonList( short          renderingMode,
                       Ptr            pixMapPtr,
                       unsigned long  rowBytes  )
{
  Polygon3D  *thisPolygon;
```

Continued on next page

Continued from previous page

```
thisPolygon = GetSortedPolygonList();

/* Loop through the polygons until we run out of them */
while (thisPolygon != NULL) {
  if (!BackfacePolygon(thisPolygon))
  {

    /* Figure out what rendering mode to use for this polygon */
    switch (renderingMode) {

      case kRender_Wireframe:  /* Wireframe rendering */
        WireframeDrawPolygon(thisPolygon, pixMapPtr, rowBytes);
        break;

      case kRender_PolygonFill:
        PolygonFillDrawPolygon(thisPolygon, pixMapPtr, rowBytes);
        break;
    }
  }
  thisPolygon = thisPolygon->nextPolygon;
 }
}
```

The sample program provided for this chapter does not look any different than the one for Chapter 14. Because you're still working with only one object, its hidden surface removal is taken care of by the BackfacePolygon() routine. Before you can start making the scene more complicated, you need to address another very important concern: removing pixels that would be drawn outside of the window. You haven't encountered this problem yet in the sample programs because all the animations have been within the boundary of the window, but if you want to start looking at more complicated scenes, clipping is a vital part of the process.

16

Polygon Clipping

come tristi . sono le manouelle . e . le quali . si muoueuano . la iqu
no i grauissi . suni . le nostri . a . gonio . saseyrano di boni
orgare . nellamano . i laperma . nella . nella . manouella . pigi . quo ti
aforga . a . pib . i somo . peb . boi.

si po . . . .
. . . .
. . . .

16

Polygon Clipping

Literally and figuratively, the *animation window*, or viewport, on the screen provides a window into the world inside the computer. Like a real window, the animation window gives you a clear view of that world. But, also like a real window, the animation window lets you see only a part of what's in that world—the part that's in front of the window. A lot of things may be going on in the world inside the computer, but if it isn't happening in front of the window, you have no view of it.

I've avoided this limitation up until now by deliberately placing all the action in the 3D world directly in front of the window. You haven't missed seeing anything yet because there hasn't been anything to miss. What you saw was all there was to see.

To be fully realistic, however, the three-dimensional world must include features that are not in front of the window. You aren't putting on a stage production here, where the only real action takes place within the confines of a proscenium arch. Neither are you making a movie, where the only action going on beyond the reach of the camera is a crowd of bored crew members standing around drinking stale coffee. You're building an entire world—and creating a window into that world.

As in the real world, objects will be moving in and out of view. This means that the program must somehow decide which parts of this simulated world appear in the window and which do not. This is a relatively trivial problem.

To determine which polygons are fully within the window and which are not, you need merely check to see if their maximum and minimum x, y, and z coordinates, as calculated in the previous chapter, fall within the maximum and minimum x, y, and z coordinates of the window (I'll deal with the concept of a window having maximum and minimum z coordinates in a moment, when I discuss view volumes). The real problem arises when you must deal with a polygon that falls partially inside the animation window and partially outside of it. You must find a way to draw only that part of the polygon that falls within the window.

Determining which part of a polygon is inside the window is called *polygon clipping*. Like the hidden surface problem discussed in the last chapter, this is not a trivial problem. Fortunately, unlike the hidden surface problem, it has an elegant solution. Before I get to that solution, however, let's examine the problem in more detail.

The View Volume

If you are indoors at the moment and there's a window in the room where you are, open it and look through it from a distance of three or four feet, so you see something like the scene shown in Figure 16-1. What are the dimensions of the window, roughly speaking? For the sake of argument, let's say that the window is 3 feet wide. Does that mean

FIGURE 16-1
◎ ◎ ◎ ◎ ◎ ◎
A view of the outside world through a window

that the view through the window is 3 feet wide? Not necessarily. If someone has bricked up your window prior to condemning your building, then your view is probably only 3 feet wide, provided the bricks are immediately on the other side of the window (see Figure 16-2a). On the other hand, if the view through your window is of an apartment building on the opposite side of the street, your view is likely to be several hundred feet wide, as in Figure 16-2b. Better still, if you are able to see to the horizon, your view is probably several miles wide, as in Figure 16-2c. And if it's night and you can see the stars, your view is probably several thousand light years wide, encompassing a fairly large chunk of the galaxy, as in Figure 16-2d.

As a rule, then, you can say that your view becomes wider with distance. You have a relatively narrow view of things that are close to the window, but a wide view of things that are distant from the window. This is a result of the perspective I discussed in Chapter 10. The rays of light that carry the images of objects seen through your window are converging toward your eyes, so that the rays of light from objects at opposite ends of the window come together at an angle when they reach your eyes. The farther away the objects reflecting (or producing) those rays of light are, the greater the area encompassed by this angle and the farther apart the objects are in reality. Needless to say, all this is

FIGURE 16-2a

◉ ◉ ◉ ◉ ◉ ◉

If your window has been bricked over, your view will be very limited

FIGURE 16-2b

◉ ◉ ◉ ◉ ◉ ◉

Facing a building across the street will give you a broader view, perhaps several hundred feet

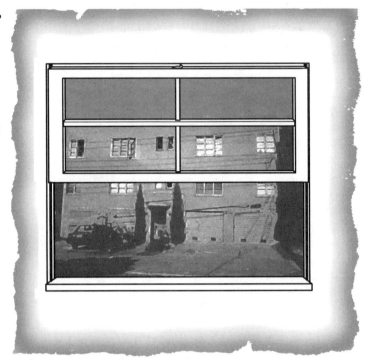

FIGURE 16-2c

◉ ◉ ◉ ◉ ◉ ◉

If you have a view of the horizon, your view is probably several miles wide

true of the vertical dimension of your view field as well, though this is probably less obvious because the world is arranged in a relatively horizontal fashion.

Now imagine that you've been transported into the sky and are looking down at your building from far above. Further, imagine that you can see a beam of light shining out your window representing the area you can see *through* your window. This beam will grow wider with distance, as in Figure 16-3a. If you examine the beam from the side, you'll see that it grows wider in the vertical dimension, too, as in Figure 16-3b. The beam takes the form of a cone, with its point at your eyes and its bottom at the farthest distance you are capable of seeing. (In theory, this distance is infinite, or at least many light years in length. In practice, however, you can treat the bottom of the pyramid as being about 10 miles away, the distance of the horizon viewed from near the ground.) The part of the pyramid that is entirely outside your window (and is truncated by your window pane, giving it a flat top) is called a *frustum* and represents your *view volume*— the volume of space within which you can see things through your window. Anything that is completely outside the view volume is invisible from your window even though it might be clearly visible to viewers on the outside. Anything that is completely inside

FIGURE 16-3a
ⓐ ⓐ ⓐ ⓐ ⓐ ⓐ
The view from your window extends out in a cone as it gets farther away

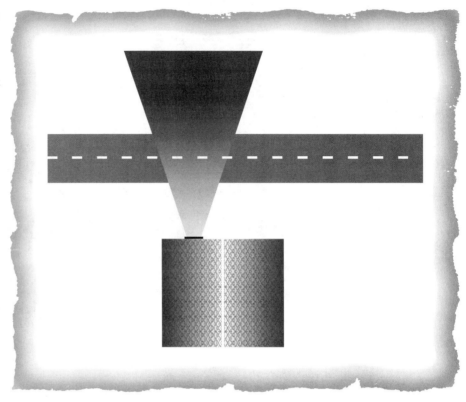

FIGURE 16-3b
ⓐ ⓐ ⓐ ⓐ ⓐ ⓐ
Your vertical view also extends in the same fashion

the view volume is potentially visible through your window, though it may be blocked by other objects—the hidden surface problem again. Objects that are partially inside the view volume will appear to be clipped off at the edge of the window if they are not blocked by nearer objects.

Clipping against the View Volume

The animation window on the computer display works exactly like the window in your room. It allows you to see a cone- (or frustum-) shaped view volume within the numerically described world that you are creating in the computer. Up to now, you have carefully placed objects so that they are always within this view volume. Eventually, however, you must allow objects to lie outside the view volume as well.

Clipping can get especially tricky because a) when a polygon is clipped, it can become either more or less complex (i.e., it may gain several new edges or lose some that it already has) and b) when clipping, you can't share vertices between different polygons in the same object like you've been able to do up to now.

Let's look at why these two points are true. Figure 16-4a shows a three-sided polygon against the edge of the viewport. After it has been clipped, as in Figure 16-4b, it gains an extra edge (the edge that goes along the side of the screen), which turns it into

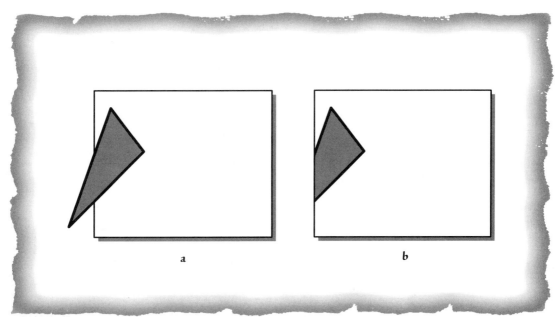

         a   **b**

FIGURE 16-4a ◉ *A triangle that is partially out of the viewport*
FIGURE 16-4b ◉ *After the triangle has been clipped, it has four sides*

a four-sided polygon. This can also go the other way; in Figure 16-5a, a four-sided polygon is barely on the screen. After it's clipped, as shown in Figure 16-5b, it is composed of just three sides. Because the edges are changing in this manner, it is impossible to share vertex information between different polygons in an object.

Up to this point, you've been storing all the vertices in the object structure and then referencing them by using pointers from within each polygon. This way, for a cube, you could transform, project, and draw only six vertices. If the polygons didn't share vertices, you would be processing (6 polygons x 4 vertices/polygons) = 24 vertices. But just because you can no longer share the vertices when performing the clipping, that doesn't mean you have to discard the advantages of this approach entirely. Instead, process all the vertices of an object together and copy them into their respective polygons only when performing the clipping (which happens later in the process).

To make this work, you'll have to add a few more fields to the polygon structure. One is an array of vertices for holding the clipped vertices; another keeps track of how many vertices are formed from the clipping process. You need to allocate more space for the clipped vertex array than you did for the original vertex array because a four-sided polygon could potentially turn into an eight-sided polygon or even more. Just to be safe (and because, for this demonstration, you're not *too* worried about memory consumption), you're going to be allocating space for 12 clipped vertices. This

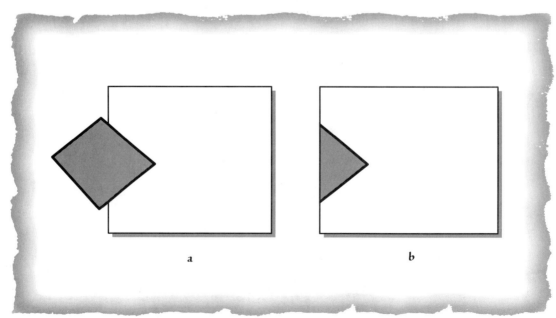

a

b

FIGURE 16-5a ◉ *A parallelogram that is mostly out of the viewport*
FIGURE 16-5b ◉ *After the polygon is clipped, it has only three sides*

may be slightly more than you need for polygons that start out with four sides, but the memory won't really matter unless you start using polygons numbering in the thousands.

One additional field must be added to specify the rendering mode to use for drawing the polygon. This relieves the higher-level routines (such as main()) from deciding how to render the polygon.

Here is the new Polygon3D structure:

```
typedef struct Polygon3D {
  short             numOfVertices;
  unsigned char     color;
  Vertex3D          *polyVertex[kMaxPolygonSize];

  /* renderingMode is one of several constants defining how
   * to render this polygon
   */
  short             renderingMode;

  /* nextPolygon and lastPolygon form a linked list for
   * the Painter's Algorithm
   */
  struct Polygon3D  *nextPolygon, *lastPolygon;

  /* Next are the minimum and maximum coordinates for the
   * polygon, forming a bounding box.
   */
  short             xmin, xmax, ymin, ymax, zmin, zmax;

  /* clippedList is a list of vertices after the polygon is
   * clipped, then projected, then clipped again.
   */
  short             numOfClippedVerts;
  ClippedVertex     clippedList[12];

  /* Rejected means that we won't be drawing this polygon because
   * it is backfacing, or it falls outside the view frustum
   */
  Boolean           rejected;
} Polygon3D;
```

The standard Vertex3D structure stores much more data than you need for the clipping array, so I've designed a structure called ClippedVertex especially for the clipped vertex array:

```
typedef struct {
  short x,y,z;       /* Clipped coordinates */
} ClippedVertex;
```

To perform the clipping, you need a new routine that will take a Polygon3D as input, clip each of its vertices, and place the result in the ClippedList array. If this function were to take the three-dimensional data of the object and attempt to clip it against a pyramid, the math could get very tricky indeed. Fortunately, when clipping against the left, right, top, and bottom edges of the viewport, you don't have to do this. Because the object's 3D data gets turned into 2D data when it is projected, you can take the projected data and clip it against the extents of the viewport, which is a much simpler operation.

But what about clipping against the bottom and the tip of the view frustum? After the vertices are projected, their z coordinates lose any real meaning and, in any case, the reason you're clipping against the z coordinates is so the projection code doesn't get messed up with negative z values (or, even worse, a z value of 0).

To work around this problem, you're going to break up the clipping into two separate parts. The first part will clip against the z coordinates of the polygon *before* it's projected. The second part will clip against the x and y extents of the viewport *after* the polygon has been projected.

The New 3D Pipeline

At this point, it's helpful to step back and look at the larger picture of the entire 3D engine. Figure 16-6 illustrates what the 3D process will look like by the end of this chapter. The only real change in the process for this chapter is the addition of the z clipping before and the x/y clipping after the projection process, plus a routine for rejecting polygons (I'll talk about this in more detail in a bit). As a matter of fact, each of these steps used to be more or less controlled from the main *event* loop. In this chapter, you'll be changing the DrawPolygonList routine to control steps 5 through 11. This revision simplifies the code for the main *event* loop and it places a majority of the process in one easy-to-locate place. In later chapters, I'll be moving these steps around a little bit more, but this structure will do for now.

Let's look at the new DrawPolygonList routine. Basically, it calls a routine for clipping the z extents of the polygon list, projects the polygon list, clips the x and y extents of the polygons, calls a trivial rejection routine, calls the SortPolygonList() routine, and then draws each polygon to the screen.

DrawPolygonList() doesn't take a renderingMode constant any more. As you saw earlier, the rendering mode is now stored in the polygon structure and is loaded in from disk along with the rest of the object when the program starts up (I'll talk more about this later in this chapter).

Listing 16-1 is the code for the new DrawPolygonList() routine.

FIGURE 16-6

◉ ◉ ◉ ◉ ◉ ◉

*The graphics
process you'll
develop in this
chapter*

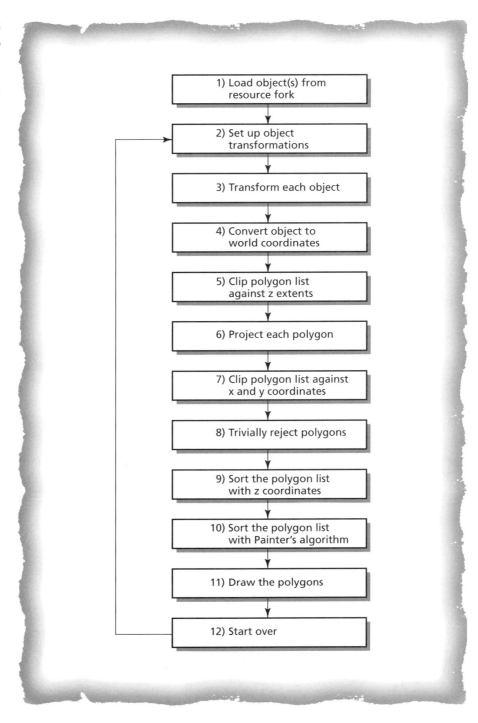

Listing 16-1 *The DrawPolygonList() routine*

```
/**
** DrawPolygonList()
**
** Draws a polygon list using one of the available rendering modes.
**/
void  DrawPolygonList( Ptr          pixMapPtr,
                       unsigned long  rowBytes  )
{
  Polygon3D      *polygonList;
  Polygon3D      *thisPolygon;

  /* Obtain the polygon list */
  polygonList = GetPaintersPolygonList();

  /* Clip against the Z extents */
  ZClipPolygonList();

  /* Project all of the vertices of all of the objects */
  ProjectPolygonList(polygonList);

  /* Clip against the X and Y extents */
  XYClipPolygonList();

  /* Get rid of any polygons that are outside the view frustum or are
   * backfacing
   */
  TrivialPolygonReject();

  /* Sort the polygon list */
  SortPolygonList();

  /* Get the painter's list again, since it has been rearranged
   * during the sort
   */
  polygonList = GetPaintersPolygonList();

  /* Loop through the polygons until we run out of them */
  thisPolygon = polygonList;

  while (thisPolygon != NULL) {
    if (thisPolygon->rejected == FALSE)
    {
      /* Figure out what rendering mode to use for this polygon */
      switch (thisPolygon->renderingMode) {

        case kRender_Wireframe:  /* Wireframe rendering */
          WireframeDrawPolygon(thisPolygon, pixMapPtr, rowBytes);
          break;

        case kRender_PolygonFill:
```

```
        PolygonFillDrawPolygon(thisPolygon, pixMapPtr, rowBytes);
        break;
    }
  }
  thisPolygon = thisPolygon->nextPolygon;
}
}
```

The Sutherland-Hodgman Algorithm

As for hidden surface removal, you have an array of choices for a clipping algorithm. Among the more popular ones are the Sutherland-Hodgman algorithm and the Liang-Barsky algorithm (named after their respective inventors). The Sutherland-Hodgman algorithm is a little longer but it is less complex overall and somewhat faster than the Liang-Barsky algorithm, so that's what you'll use for your 3D engine.

There are two distinct parts to the clipping process. The first is clipping against the front of the view volume (i.e., the z coordinate); the second is clipping against the right, left, top, and bottom edges of the viewport (i.e., the x and y coordinates). You're not actually going to be clipping against the back of the view volume. Instead, if a polygon gets far enough away from the viewer (meaning that the minimum z coordinate is above some arbitrary value), you can simply choose not to draw it at all.

The two clipping processes are a little different because clipping against the front of the view volume requires that you clip in three dimensions and clipping against the edges requires that you clip in only two dimensions. (You'll also be preserving a z coordinate, but only to do a polygon sort, and you'll just be making an estimate for it because you won't need precise information).

In one sense, clipping against the front is a bit more complicated because it's in three dimensions; on the other hand, it doesn't handle as many cases as the edge-clipping routine does.

The front-clipping algorithm will take a polygon, which I'll call polygon A, that extends past the minimum z coordinate (which I arbitrarily chose) and clip its edge, as shown in Figure 16-7, producing polygon B.

After polygon B has been projected, the second part of the clipping algorithm breaks its task into four parts that involve clipping against the left, right, top, and bottom edges of the viewport. Instead of writing four separate routines for this, combine them into one that is structured like this:

1. Clip polygon B against the left edge of the viewport, producing polygon C (see Figure 16-8a).

2. Clip polygon C against the right edge of the viewport, producing polygon D (see Figure 16-8b).

3. Clip polygon D against the top edge of the viewport, producing polygon E (see Figure 16-8c).

FIGURE 16-7
◎ ◎ ◎ ◎ ◎ ◎

Clipping polygon A against the front of the view volume, producing polygon B

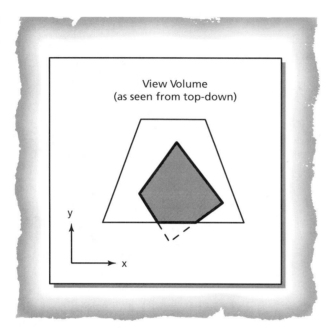

FIGURE 16-8a
◎ ◎ ◎ ◎ ◎ ◎

Clipping polygon B against the left side of the view volume, producing polygon C

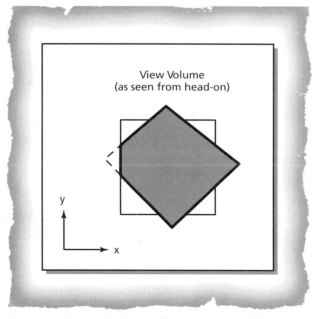

4. Clip polygon E against the bottom edge of the viewport, producing polygon F (see Figure 16-8d).

The result of these operations is polygon F (see Figure 16-9), the end product of the clipping algorithm applied to polygon A.

FIGURE 16-8b

ⓞ ⓞ ⓞ ⓞ ⓞ ⓞ

Clipping polygon C against the right side of the view volume, producing polygon D

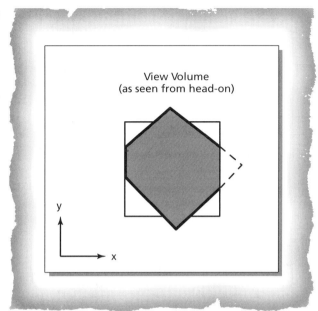

FIGURE 16-8c

ⓞ ⓞ ⓞ ⓞ ⓞ ⓞ

Clipping polygon D against the top of the view volume, producing polygon E

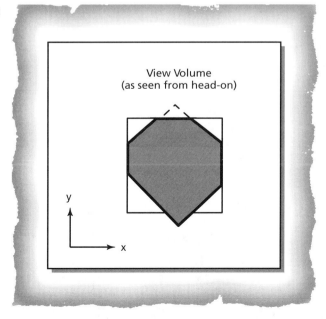

Clipping a polygon against an edge is a matter of building up, edge by edge, a new polygon that represents the clipped version of the old polygon. You can think of this as a process of replacing the unclipped edges of the old polygon with the clipped edges of the new polygon. To determine the coordinates of the vertices of the new polygon,

FIGURE 16-8d

◎ ◎ ◎ ◎ ◎ ◎

Clipping polygon E against the bottom of the view volume, producing polygon F

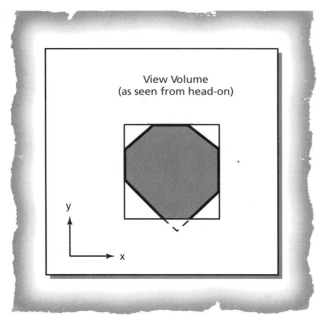

FIGURE 16-9

◎ ◎ ◎ ◎ ◎ ◎

Polygon F, the outcome of the clipping algorithm applied to polygon A

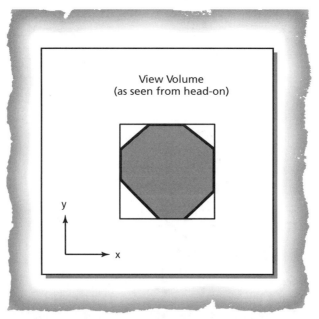

each edge of the old polygon must be examined and classified by type, depending on where it falls relative to the side of the view volume against which it is being clipped.

Four Types of Edges

There are four types of edges the clipping function will encounter. All four are illustrated by the polygon in Figure 16-10, which overlaps the left edge of the animation window (and thus the left side of the view volume). The arrows show the direction in which the algorithm will work around the edges of the polygon, which is the same as the order in which the vertices are stored in the polygon's vertex array. The four types of edges are:

1. Edges that are entirely inside the view volume (such as edge a in Figure 16-10)

2. Edges that are entirely outside the view volume (such as edge c)

3. Edges that are leaving the view volume—that is, edges in which the first vertex (in the order indicated by the arrows) is inside the view volume and the second vertex is outside (such as edge b)

4. Edges that are entering the view volume—that is, edges in which the first vertex is outside the view volume and the second vertex is inside (such as edge d)

FIGURE 16-10

◎ ◎ ◎ ◎ ◎ ◎

The four types of polygon edges considered by the Sutherland-Hodgman algorithm

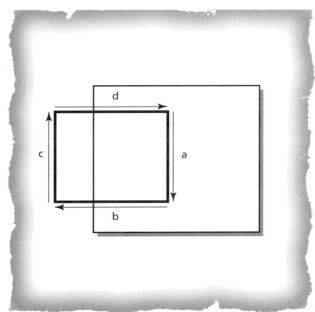

Each type of edge will be replaced by a clipped edge in a different way, as follows:

1. Edges that are entirely inside the view volume will be replaced by identical edges. In effect, these edges will be copied unchanged to the new polygon.

2. Edges that are entirely outside the view volume will be eliminated. No new edge will be added to the clipped polygon for such edges in the old polygon.

3. Edges that are leaving the view volume will be clipped at the edge of the view volume. The first vertex of such an edge will be copied unchanged to the clipped edge, but the second vertex will be replaced by a new vertex having the coordinates of the point at which the edge intersects the side of the view volume.

4. Edges that are entering the view volume will be replaced by two edges. One of these will be the old edge clipped at the point where it intersects the side of the view volume. The other will be a new edge that connects the first vertex of this edge with the last vertex of the previous type 3 edge—the one that was clipped at the side of the view volume.

If you start with edge 1 of the polygon in Figure 16-10 and clip each polygon mentally according to the procedures outlined above, you should eventually wind up with the clipped polygon shown in Figure 16-11. As you can see, edge c, which was entirely outside the view volume, has been eliminated, whereas the type 4 replacement

FIGURE 16-11

◎ ◎ ◎ ◎ ◎ ◎

What remains after the polygon in Figure 16-10 has been clipped against the left side of the viewport

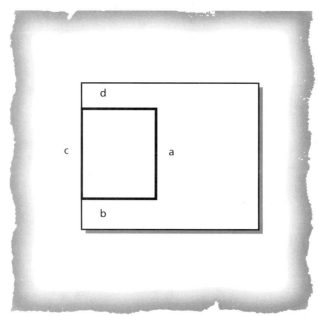

has generated a new edge. The rough skeleton of the procedure for clipping against an individual edge is as follows:

```
for (every edge of the polygon) {
        if type 1 edge, perform type 1 replacement else
        if type 2 edge, perform type 2 replacement else
        if type 3 edge, perform type 3 replacement else
        if type 4 edge, perform type 4 replacement
}
```

The complete z-clipping function consists of one such loop, whereas the x and y-clipping function consists of four loops in this sequence (one for each edge).

The Point-Slope Equation

Implementing this algorithm in C is a straightforward, if somewhat tedious, task. About the only part that might prove troublesome is determining the x, y coordinates where an edge of the polygon intersects a side of the view volume. Becasue, for the most part, you'll be treating the edges of the polygons as two-dimensional lines and clipping them against the two-dimensional edges of the viewport, which are *also* two-dimensional lines, you can determine the point of intersection using the mathematical formula known as the *point-slope equation*.

Using the Point-Slope Equation for the x and y Boundaries

Say you're clipping a line with starting vertices (x1, y1) and ending vertices (x2, y2) against a window with minimum coordinates (xmin, ymin) and maximum coordinates (xmax, ymax). When you clip this line against the right or left edge of the window, you already know the x coordinate at which the line crosses the edge of the window because it's always the same as the x coordinate of the edge. Thus you can find the x coordinate at which the line crosses the left edge of the window with the statement

```
clipped_x = xmin;
```

because xmin is the x coordinate of the left edge. And you can find the x coordinate at which a line crosses the right edge of the window with the statement

```
clipped_x = xmax;
```

because xmax is the x coordinate of the right edge.

Finding the y coordinate at which a line crosses the left and right edges is trickier, but you can figure it out using the point-slope equation. First you must calculate the slope of the line, which I discussed in Chapter 9. To recap briefly, the slope of a line is a real number that represents a ratio of the change in x coordinates to the change in y coordinates along equal portions of the line. It can be calculated with the formula

```
slope = (y2 - y1) / (x2 - x1);
```

Once you know the slope, the formula for finding the y coordinate at which the line crosses the left edge of the window is

```
clipped_y = y1 + (slope * (xmin - x1));
```

Similarly, the formula for finding the y coordinate at which a line crosses the right edge of a window is

```
clipped_y = y1 + (slope * (xmax - x1));
```

Clipping against the top and bottom edges works much the same way, except instead of knowing the x coordinate of the point of intersection you now know the y coordinate and must calculate the x coordinate using a slightly different version of the same point-slope formula. You find the y coordinate at which the line crosses the top edge of the window with the statement

```
clipped_y = ymin;
```

because ymin is the y coordinate of the top edge. Finally, you find the y coordinate at which a line crosses the bottom edge of the window with the statement

```
clipped_y = ymax;
```

To find the x coordinate at which the line crosses the top edge of the window, use this formula:

```
clipped_x = x1 + (ymin - y1) / slope;
```

Similarly, find the x coordinate at which the line crosses the bottom edge of the window with the formula

```
clipped_x = x1 + (ymax - y1) / slope;
```

You may have noticed that one of the differences between left/right clipping and top/bottom clipping is that you use multiplication to find the y coordinate of a left/right clip, but division to find the x coordinate of a top/bottom clip. As you know from Chapter 12, it is much more expensive to do division, so it would be advantageous to find a way of using a multiplication for both versions.

Notice that you're dividing by the slope of the line. The slope is also determined by a division (y length divided by x length). If you reverse the terms of the slope calculation (x length divided by y length), you get the inverse of the slope, which can be multiplied to the rest of the formula, like this:

```
clipped_x = x1 + (ymin - y1) * inverse_slope;
clipped_x = x1 + (ymax - y1) * inverse_slope;
```

The formula for the inverse slope is:

```
inverse_slope = (x2 - x1) / (y2 - y1);
```

Another thing that may have caught your eye is that it looks as if you could get some invalid results if you attempt to do a division by zero. The slope formulas involve a division by the x length and the y length, respectively, and if this length is zero when you calculate the slope, you'll get an error (i.e., the computer will crash). However, this is not a problem. Because you calculate the slope only when the line crosses the left or right edge of the viewport, the x length *has* to be nonzero (if it wasn't, the line couldn't cross a vertical edge). When you cross the top or bottom of the viewport, you calculate the inverse slope, which requires a nonzero y length, which you are also guaranteed to have.

Using the Point-Slope Equation for Clipping against z

Clipping against the front of the view volume is a bit more complicated because you must determine both the x and y coordinates of the point at which a line intersects a plane at a known z coordinate, which I'll call zmin. And you must take into account the z coordinates of the starting and ending points of the line, which I'll call z1 and z2. To calculate the new coordinates, use a three-dimensional extension of the point-slope equation. The formulae for determining the x and y points of intersection are:

```
clipped_x = (x2 - x1) * t + x1;
clipped_y = (y2 - y1) * t + y1;
```

The factor t is similar to the slope factor in the two-dimensional equations, which can be calculated thus:

```
t = (zmin - z1) / (z2 - z1);
```

The z coordinates will be the same as zmin.

The z-Clipping Function

Because you're performing the z clipping and the x and y clipping separately, you're going to build a different routine for each. The first, called ZClipPolygonList(), clips against the front of the view volume and is responsible for moving the polygon's vertices from the object's list into the polygon structure itself (in the ClippedList structure).

The first thing that ZClipPolygonList does is grab the polygon list and copy a global zmin value into a local variable (because, as I discussed before, local variables are faster than globals). It then starts to run through each of the polygons in a *while()* loop:

```
Polygon3D    *polygonBase, *thisPolygon;
short        zMin;

polygonBase = gWorld.paintersList;
thisPolygon = polygonBase;

/* Copy globals into local variables, where they will be faster */
zMin = gClipZMin;
while (thisPolygon != NULL) {
  ClippedVertex  *clipList;
  short          v1,v2;
  Vertex3D       *pv1, *pv2;
  float          t;
  short          numOfClippedVerts;
```

The Front of the View Volume

Now set up a pointer to the beginning of the clipped vertex list and initialize the number of clipped vertices to 0:

```
/* Point the clipList pointer at the first clipped vertex */
clipList = thisPolygon->clippedList;
numOfClippedVerts = 0;
```

The variable v1, which represents the first vertex of the edge to be clipped, is initialized to the last vertex of the polygon:

```
/* Initialize v1 to the last vertex */
v1 = thisPolygon->numOfVertices;
```

Similarly, the variable v2 represents the second vertex of the edge you're working on. Set up a *for* loop with v2 so that it works through each vertex of the polygon:

```
/* Loop through all of the edges of the polygon */
for (v2 = 0; v2 < thisPolygon->numOfVertices; v2++) {
```

Because you'll be accessing these two vertices often, set two variables, pv1 and pv2, to point at them:

```
/* Get pointers to both vertices */
pv1 = thisPolygon->polyVertex[v1];
```

```
pv2 = thisPolygon->polyVertex[v2];
```

You're now ready to act upon this edge depending on which type it is.

Type 1 Edge

If the z coordinates of both the first vertex and the second vertex are greater than zmin, the entire edge is inside the front of the view volume, so copy this edge into the clipped vertex list:

```
/* Categorize edges by type */
if ((pv1->wz >= zMin) && (pv2->wz >= zMin)) {
  /* Entirely inside front */
  clipList->x = pv2->wx;
  clipList->y = pv2->wy;
  clipList->z = pv2->wz;

  /* Advance clipped list pointer */
  clipList++;
  numOfClippedVerts++;
}
```

Type 2 Edge

If the z coordinates of both the first and second vertices are less than zmin, the entire edge is outside the front of the view volume, so ignore this edge:

```
else if ((pv1->wz < zMin) && (pv2->wz < zMin)) {
  /* Edge is entirely past front; do nothing */
}
```

Type 3 Edge

If the z coordinate of the first vertex is greater than zmin and the z coordinate of the second vertex is less than zmin, then the edge is leaving the view volume. Calculate the value of t and then apply the point-slope formula to the x and y coordinates of the edge:

```
else if ((pv1->wz >= zMin) && (pv2->wz < zMin)) {
  /* Edge is leaving view volume */
  t = (float)(zMin - pv1->wz) /
      (float)(pv2->wz - pv1->wz);
  clipList->x = pv1->wx + (pv2->wx - pv1->wx) * t;
  clipList->y = pv1->wy + (pv2->wy - pv1->wy) * t;
  clipList->z = zMin;

  /* Advance the clipped list pointer */
  clipList++;
  numOfClippedVerts++;
}
```

Type 4 Edge

If the z coordinate of the first vertex is less than zmin and the z coordinate of the second vertex is greater than zmin, the edge is entering the view volume. Again, calculate the t value and use it for the point-slope formula. However, in this case, you must also create a second edge by copying the second vertex of the line into the clipped-edge list:

```
else if ((pv1->wz < zMin) && (pv2->wz >= zMin)) {
    /* Edge is entering view volume */
    t = (float)(zMin - pv1->wz) /
        (float)(pv2->wz - pv1->wz);

    clipList->x = pv1->wx + (pv2->wx - pv1->wx) * t;
    clipList->y = pv1->wy + (pv2->wy - pv1->wy) * t;
    clipList->z = zMin;
    clipList++;

    clipList->x = pv2->wx;
    clipList->y = pv2->wy;
    clipList->z = pv2->wz;
    clipList++;
    numOfClippedVerts += 2;
}
```

Now that you've checked all of the cases, advance v1 to point to the second vertex of the current edge, which is also the first vertex of the second edge:

```
    /* Advance to next vertex */
    v1 = v2;
}
```

That's the heart of the z-clipping routine; the polygon has now been clipped against the front of the view volume. Store the number of clipped vertices in the polygon and then move on to the next polygon in the linked list:

```
    /* Put number of clipped vertices in poly structure */
    thisPolygon->numOfClippedVerts = numOfClippedVerts;

    /* Advance to next polygon */
    thisPolygon = thisPolygon->nextPolygon;
  }
}
```

The ZClipPolygonList Function

Listing 16-2 is the complete code for the ZClipPolygonList() function.

Listing 16-2 The ZClipPolygonList() function

```
/**
**  ZClipPolygonList()
**
**  Clips all of the polygons against the front of the view volume
**/
void  ZClipPolygonList(void)
{
  Polygon3D    *polygonBase, *thisPolygon;
  short        zMin;

  polygonBase = gWorld.paintersList;
  thisPolygon = polygonBase;

  /* Copy globals into local variables, where they will be faster */
  zMin = gClipZMin;

  while (thisPolygon != NULL) {
    ClippedVertex  *clipList;
    short          v1,v2;
    Vertex3D       *pv1, *pv2;
    float          t;
    short          numOfClippedVerts;

    /* Point the clipList pointer at the first clipped vertex */
    clipList = thisPolygon->clippedList;
    numOfClippedVerts = 0;

    /* Initialize v1 to the last vertex */
    v1 = thisPolygon->numOfVertices;

    /* Loop through all of the edges of the polygon */
    for (v2 = 0; v2 < thisPolygon->numOfVertices; v2++) {
      /* Get pointers to both vertices */
      pv1 = thisPolygon->polyVertex[v1];
      pv2 = thisPolygon->polyVertex[v2];

      /* Categorize edges by type */
      if ((pv1->wz >= zMin) && (pv2->wz >= zMin)) {
        /* Entirely inside front */
        clipList->x = pv2->wx;
        clipList->y = pv2->wy;
        clipList->z = pv2->wz;

        /* Advance clipped list pointer */
        clipList++;
        numOfClippedVerts++;
      }

      else if ((pv1->wz < zMin) && (pv2->wz < zMin)) {
        /* Edge is entirely past front; do nothing */
      }
```

Continued on next page

Continued from previous page

```
        else if ((pv1->wz >= zMin) && (pv2->wz < zMin)) {
    /* Edge is leaving view volume */
    t = (float)(zMin - pv1->wz) /
        (float)(pv2->wz - pv1->wz);
    clipList->x = pv1->wx + (pv2->wx - pv1->wx) * t;
    clipList->y = pv1->wy + (pv2->wy - pv1->wy) * t;
    clipList->z = zMin;

    /* Advance the clipped list pointer */
    clipList++;
    numOfClippedVerts++;
  }

    else if ((pv1->wz < zMin) && (pv2->wz >= zMin)) {
    /* Edge is entering view volume */
    t = (float)(zMin - pv1->wz) /
        (float)(pv2->wz - pv1->wz);

    clipList->x = pv1->wx + (pv2->wx - pv1->wx) * t;
    clipList->y = pv1->wy + (pv2->wy - pv1->wy) * t;
    clipList->z = zMin;
    clipList++;

    clipList->x = pv2->wx;
    clipList->y = pv2->wy;
    clipList->z = pv2->wz;
    clipList++;
    numOfClippedVerts += 2;
  }

  /* Advance to next vertex */
  v1 = v2;
}

/* Put number of clipped vertices in poly structure */
thisPolygon->numOfClippedVerts = numOfClippedVerts;

/* Advance to next polygon */
thisPolygon = thisPolygon->nextPolygon;
  }
}
```

The Rest of the View Volume

The second part of the clipping process handles the left, right, top, and bottom of the view volume. This makes this part of the process significantly longer, but a great deal of the code is virtually identical to the z-clipping function.

One of the main differences is that you must create a second array for holding temporary vertex values as you're clipping an edge. This is because, while processing one edge, you can't start writing back to the same data you're reading from (because the output data may be longer or shorter than the input).

Once you finish with the first edge, the polygon's vertices will be contained in the temporary vertex array. You could copy those vertices back into the polygon's internal vertex array and then continue with the next clipping operation. You could also just write the next clipping operation to copy from the temporary list back into the polygon's list. This is a little more efficient because it eliminates a wasteful copying operation. This process will happen twice (once for the left and right clipping and again for the top and bottom clipping).

The first portion of XYClipPolygonList() looks similar to the z-clipping routine. The only things to note are that you copy all four extent globals into local variables and you're declaring a temporary vertex array (tempClipList) into which you'll copy them.

```
void  XYClipPolygonList(void)
{
  Polygon3D    *polygonBase, *thisPolygon;
  short        xMin, xMax, yMin, yMax;

  polygonBase = gWorld.paintersList;
  thisPolygon = polygonBase;

  /* Copy globals into local variables, where they will be faster */
  xMin = gClipXMin;
  xMax = gClipXMax;
  yMin = gClipYMin;
  yMax = gClipYMax;

  while (thisPolygon != NULL) {
    ClippedVertex  *clipList;
    ClippedVertex  tempClipList[20];
    short          clipRef;
    short          v1,v2;
    float          slope, inverseSlope;

    clipList = thisPolygon->clippedList;
```

Before you clip against a particular polygon, make sure that it still has at least three vertices (because some or all of its vertices could have been eliminated by the z-Clipping algorithm):

```
    if (thisPolygon->numOfClippedVerts > 2) {
```

Begin the clipping by first handling the left side (xmin) of the viewport. Initialize a reference number to keep track of the number of clipped vertices and an index for the starting and ending vertices of the edges:

```
/*** Part 1: Clip against the left side of the viewport */
/***           Clip from the regular list into the temp list */

clipRef = 0;
v1 = thisPolygon->numOfClippedVerts-1;

for (v2 = 0; v2 < thisPolygon->numOfClippedVerts; v2++) {
```

Now, as you did in to the z-clipping routine, check to see what type of edge you're dealing with and handle it appropriately. The first type is a vertex whose x coordinates are both greater than xmin, so just copy it to the temporary list:

```
/* Categorize edges by type */
if ((clipList[v1].x >= xMin) && (clipList[v2].x >= xMin)) {
  /* Edge isn't off right side of viewport; copy it over */
  tempClipList[clipRef].x = clipList[v2].x;
  tempClipList[clipRef].y = clipList[v2].y;
  tempClipList[clipRef].z = clipList[v2].z;
  clipRef++;
}
```

In the second case, both vertices are off the left edge of the viewport, so ignore this edge:

```
else if ((clipList[v1].x < xMin) && (clipList[v2].x < xMin)) {
  /* Edge is entirely off viewport; do nothing */
}
```

The third case occurs when an edge is leaving the viewport. Calculate a slope value and use the point-slope formula to determine the y value of the edge:

```
else if ((clipList[v1].x >= xMin) && (clipList[v2].x < xMin)) {
  /* Edge is leaving viewport */
  slope = (float)(clipList[v2].y - clipList[v1].y) /
          (float)(clipList[v2].x - clipList[v1].x);
  tempClipList[clipRef].x = xMin;
  tempClipList[clipRef].y =
    clipList[v1].y + slope * (xMin - clipList[v1].x);
  tempClipList[clipRef].z = clipList[v1].z;
  clipRef++;
}
```

In the fourth case, an edge is entering the viewport. Again, the point-slope formula is used to calculate the y value; copy a second point into the clipped-vertex array:

```
else if ((clipList[v1].x < xMin) && (clipList[v2].x >= xMin)) {
  /* Edge is entering viewport */
  slope = (float)(clipList[v2].y - clipList[v1].y) /
          (float)(clipList[v2].x - clipList[v1].x);
  tempClipList[clipRef].x = xMin;
```

```
          tempClipList[clipRef].y =
            clipList[v1].y + slope * (xMin - clipList[v1].x);
          tempClipList[clipRef].z = clipList[v2].z;
          clipRef++;

          tempClipList[clipRef].x = clipList[v2].x;
          tempClipList[clipRef].y = clipList[v2].y;
          tempClipList[clipRef].z = clipList[v2].z;
          clipRef++;
        }
```

Finally, advance to the next edge:

```
        v1 = v2;
      }
```

Once you have finished clipping this polygon against the left edge of the viewport, store the new size of the clipped-vertex list in the polygon:

```
      thisPolygon->numOfClippedVerts = clipRef;
    }
```

The other three cases are very similar. The right-side clipping segment copies from the temporary clipping list back into the polygon's clipping list and compares the values with xmax instead of xmin, as shown in Listing 16-3.

Listing 16-3 Copying the right-side clipping segment

```
  if (thisPolygon->numOfClippedVerts > 2) {
    /*** Part 2: Clip against the right edge of the viewport */
    /***         Clip from the temp list back into the regular list */

    clipRef = 0;
    v1 = thisPolygon->numOfClippedVerts-1;

    for (v2 = 0; v2 < thisPolygon->numOfClippedVerts; v2++) {
      /* Categorize edges by type */
      if (   (tempClipList[v1].x <= xMax) &&
             (tempClipList[v2].x <= xMax))
      {
        /* Edge isn't off right side of viewport; copy it over */
        clipList[clipRef].x = tempClipList[v2].x;
        clipList[clipRef].y = tempClipList[v2].y;
        clipList[clipRef].z = tempClipList[v2].z;
        clipRef++;
      }

      else if (   (tempClipList[v1].x > xMax) &&
                  (tempClipList[v2].x > xMax)) {
        /* Edge is entirely off viewport; do nothing */
```

Continued on next page

Continued from previous page

```
    }

    else if (  (tempClipList[v1].x <= xMax) &&
               (tempClipList[v2].x > xMax)) {
      /* Edge is leaving viewport */
      slope = (float)(tempClipList[v2].y - tempClipList[v1].y) /
              (float)(tempClipList[v2].x - tempClipList[v1].x);
      clipList[clipRef].x = xMax;
      clipList[clipRef].y =
        tempClipList[v1].y + slope * (xMax - tempClipList[v1].x);
      clipList[clipRef].z = tempClipList[v1].z;
      clipRef++;
    }

    else if (   (tempClipList[v1].x > xMax) &&
                (tempClipList[v2].x <= xMax))
    {
      /* Edge is entering viewport */
      slope = (float)(tempClipList[v2].y - tempClipList[v1].y) /
              (float)(tempClipList[v2].x - tempClipList[v1].x);
      clipList[clipRef].x = xMax;
      clipList[clipRef].y =
        tempClipList[v1].y + slope * (xMax - tempClipList[v1].x);
      clipList[clipRef].z = tempClipList[v2].z;
      clipRef++;

      clipList[clipRef].x = tempClipList[v2].x;
      clipList[clipRef].y = tempClipList[v2].y;
      clipList[clipRef].z = tempClipList[v2].z;
      clipRef++;
    }
    v1 = v2;
  }
  thisPolygon->numOfClippedVerts = clipRef;
}
```

When clipping against the upper side of the viewport, compare the vertices against ymin and use an inverse slope for the point-slope formulas to avoid an extra division. Like the left-clipping portion, you're again copying from the polygon's clipped vertex array into the temporary array, as shown in Listing 16-4.

Listing 16-4 *Clipping against the upper side of the viewport*

```
if (thisPolygon->numOfClippedVerts > 2) {
  /*** Part 3: Clip against the top side of the viewport */
  /***          Clip from the regular list into the temp list */

  clipRef = 0;
  v1 = thisPolygon->numOfClippedVerts-1;
```

```
      for (v2 = 0; v2 < thisPolygon->numOfClippedVerts; v2++) {
        /* Categorize edges by type */
        if ((clipList[v1].y >= yMin) && (clipList[v2].y >= yMin)) {
          /* Edge isn't off top side of viewport; copy it over */
          tempClipList[clipRef].x = clipList[v2].x;
          tempClipList[clipRef].y = clipList[v2].y;
          tempClipList[clipRef].z = clipList[v2].z;
          clipRef++;
        }

        else if ((clipList[v1].y < yMin) && (clipList[v2].y < yMin)) {
          /* Edge is entirely off viewport; do nothing */
        }

        else if ((clipList[v1].y >= yMin) && (clipList[v2].y < yMin)) {
          /* Edge is leaving viewport */
          inverseSlope =   (float)(clipList[v2].x - clipList[v1].x) /
                           (float)(clipList[v2].y - clipList[v1].y);
          tempClipList[clipRef].x =
            clipList[v1].x + (yMin - clipList[v1].y) * inverseSlope;

          tempClipList[clipRef].y = yMin;
          tempClipList[clipRef].z = clipList[v1].z;
          clipRef++;
        }

        else if ((clipList[v1].y < yMin) && (clipList[v2].y >= yMin)) {
          /* Edge is entering viewport */
          inverseSlope =   (float)(clipList[v2].x - clipList[v1].x) /
                           (float)(clipList[v2].y - clipList[v1].y);
          tempClipList[clipRef].x =
            clipList[v1].x + (yMin - clipList[v1].y) * inverseSlope;

          tempClipList[clipRef].y = yMin;
          tempClipList[clipRef].z = clipList[v2].z;
          clipRef++;

          tempClipList[clipRef].x = clipList[v2].x;
          tempClipList[clipRef].y = clipList[v2].y;
          tempClipList[clipRef].z = clipList[v2].z;
          clipRef++;
        }

      v1 = v2;
    }
    thisPolygon->numOfClippedVerts = clipRef;
  }
```

Clipping against the bottom of the viewport utilizes the ymax parameter and places the clipped vertices back into the polygon's structure, as shown in Listing 16-5.

Listing 16-5 *Clipping against the bottom of the viewport*

```
if (thisPolygon->numOfClippedVerts > 2) {
  /*** Part 4: Clip against the bottom edge of the viewport */
  /***          Clip from the temp list back into the regular list */

  clipRef = 0;
  v1 = thisPolygon->numOfClippedVerts-1;

  for (v2 = 0; v2 < thisPolygon->numOfClippedVerts; v2++) {
    /* Categorize edges by type */
    if (   (tempClipList[v1].y <= yMax) &&
           (tempClipList[v2].y <= yMax)) {
      /* Edge isn't off edge side of viewport; copy it over */
      clipList[clipRef].x = tempClipList[v2].x;
      clipList[clipRef].y = tempClipList[v2].y;
      clipList[clipRef].z = tempClipList[v2].z;
      clipRef++;
    }

    else if (   (tempClipList[v1].y > yMax) &&
                (tempClipList[v2].y > yMax)) {
      /* Edge is entirely off viewport; do nothing */
    }

    else if (   (tempClipList[v1].y <= yMax) &&
                (tempClipList[v2].y > yMax))
     {
      /* Edge is leaving viewport */
      inverseSlope =  (float)(tempClipList[v2].x -
                                 tempClipList[v1].x) /
                         (float)(tempClipList[v2].y -
                                 tempClipList[v1].y);
      clipList[clipRef].x = tempClipList[v1].x +
                    (yMax - tempClipList[v1].y) * inverseSlope;
      clipList[clipRef].y = yMax;
      clipList[clipRef].z = tempClipList[v1].z;
      clipRef++;
    }

    else if (   (tempClipList[v1].y > yMax) &&
                (tempClipList[v2].y <= yMax))
     {
      /* Edge is entering viewport */
      inverseSlope =  (float)(tempClipList[v2].x -
                                 tempClipList[v1].x) /
                         (float)(tempClipList[v2].y -
                                 tempClipList[v1].y);
      clipList[clipRef].x = tempClipList[v1].x +
                    (yMax - tempClipList[v1].y) * inverseSlope;
      clipList[clipRef].y = yMax;
      clipList[clipRef].z = tempClipList[v2].z;
```

```
        clipRef++;

        clipList[clipRef].x = tempClipList[v2].x;
        clipList[clipRef].y = tempClipList[v2].y;
        clipList[clipRef].z = tempClipList[v2].z;
        clipRef++;
      }

      v1 = v2;
    }
    thisPolygon->numOfClippedVerts = clipRef;
  }
```

You can now move on to the next polygon in the linked list to complete the x and y clipping:

```
    thisPolygon = thisPolygon->nextPolygon;
  }
}
```

The XYClipPolygonList() Function

Listing 16-6 is the complete source code for the XYClipPolygonList() routine.

Listing 16-6 *The XYClipPolygonList() routine*

```
/**
** XYClipPolygonList()
**
** Clips the polygon's x and y extents against the edge of the screen
**/
void XYClipPolygonList(void)
{
  Polygon3D    *polygonBase, *thisPolygon;
  short        xMin, xMax, yMin, yMax;

  polygonBase = gWorld.paintersList;
  thisPolygon = polygonBase;

  /* Copy globals into local variables, where they will be faster */
  xMin = gClipXMin;
  xMax = gClipXMax;
  yMin = gClipYMin;
  yMax = gClipYMax;

  while (thisPolygon != NULL) {
    ClippedVertex  *clipList;
    ClippedVertex  tempClipList[20];
    short          clipRef;
    short          v1,v2;
```

Continued on next page

Continued from previous page

```
float              slope, inverseSlope;

clipList = thisPolygon->clippedList;

if (thisPolygon->numOfClippedVerts > 2) {
  /*** Part 1: Clip against the left side of the viewport */
  /***          Clip from the regular list into the temp list */

  clipRef = 0;
  v1 = thisPolygon->numOfClippedVerts-1;

  for (v2 = 0; v2 < thisPolygon->numOfClippedVerts; v2++) {
    /* Categorize edges by type */
    if ((clipList[v1].x >= xMin) && (clipList[v2].x >= xMin)) {
      /* Edge isn't off right side of viewport; copy it over */
      tempClipList[clipRef].x = clipList[v2].x;
      tempClipList[clipRef].y = clipList[v2].y;
      tempClipList[clipRef].z = clipList[v2].z;
      clipRef++;
    }

    else if ((clipList[v1].x < xMin) && (clipList[v2].x < xMin)) {
      /* Edge is entirely off viewport; do nothing */
    }

    else if ((clipList[v1].x >= xMin) && (clipList[v2].x < xMin)) {
      /* Edge is leaving viewport */
      slope = (float)(clipList[v2].y - clipList[v1].y) /
              (float)(clipList[v2].x - clipList[v1].x);
      tempClipList[clipRef].x = xMin;
      tempClipList[clipRef].y =
        clipList[v1].y + slope * (xMin - clipList[v1].x);
      tempClipList[clipRef].z = clipList[v1].z;
      clipRef++;
    }

    else if ((clipList[v1].x < xMin) && (clipList[v2].x >= xMin)) {
      /* Edge is entering viewport */
      slope = (float)(clipList[v2].y - clipList[v1].y) /
              (float)(clipList[v2].x - clipList[v1].x);
      tempClipList[clipRef].x = xMin;
      tempClipList[clipRef].y =
        clipList[v1].y + slope * (xMin - clipList[v1].x);
      tempClipList[clipRef].z = clipList[v2].z;
      clipRef++;

      tempClipList[clipRef].x = clipList[v2].x;
      tempClipList[clipRef].y = clipList[v2].y;
      tempClipList[clipRef].z = clipList[v2].z;
      clipRef++;
    }
```

```
      v1 = v2;
    }
  thisPolygon->numOfClippedVerts = clipRef;
}

if (thisPolygon->numOfClippedVerts > 2) {
  /*** Part 2: Clip against the right edge of the viewport */
  /***          Clip from the temp list back into the regular list */

  clipRef = 0;
  v1 = thisPolygon->numOfClippedVerts-1;

  for (v2 = 0; v2 < thisPolygon->numOfClippedVerts; v2++) {
    /* Categorize edges by type */
    if (   (tempClipList[v1].x <= xMax) &&
           (tempClipList[v2].x <= xMax))
    {
      /* Edge isn't off right side of viewport; copy it over */
      clipList[clipRef].x = tempClipList[v2].x;
      clipList[clipRef].y = tempClipList[v2].y;
      clipList[clipRef].z = tempClipList[v2].z;
      clipRef++;
    }

    else if (  (tempClipList[v1].x > xMax) &&
               (tempClipList[v2].x > xMax)) {
      /* Edge is entirely off viewport; do nothing */
    }

    else if (  (tempClipList[v1].x <= xMax) &&
               (tempClipList[v2].x > xMax)) {
      /* Edge is leaving viewport */
      slope = (float)(tempClipList[v2].y - tempClipList[v1].y) /
              (float)(tempClipList[v2].x - tempClipList[v1].x);
      clipList[clipRef].x = xMax;
      clipList[clipRef].y =
        tempClipList[v1].y + slope * (xMax - tempClipList[v1].x);
      clipList[clipRef].z = tempClipList[v1].z;
      clipRef++;
    }

    else if (  (tempClipList[v1].x > xMax) &&
               (tempClipList[v2].x <= xMax))
    {
      /* Edge is entering viewport */
      slope = (float)(tempClipList[v2].y - tempClipList[v1].y) /
              (float)(tempClipList[v2].x - tempClipList[v1].x);
      clipList[clipRef].x = xMax;
      clipList[clipRef].y =
        tempClipList[v1].y + slope * (xMax - tempClipList[v1].x);
      clipList[clipRef].z = tempClipList[v2].z;
      clipRef++;
```

Continued on next page

Continued from previous page

```
        clipList[clipRef].x = tempClipList[v2].x;
        clipList[clipRef].y = tempClipList[v2].y;
        clipList[clipRef].z = tempClipList[v2].z;
        clipRef++;
      }
      v1 = v2;
    }
    thisPolygon->numOfClippedVerts = clipRef;
  }

  if (thisPolygon->numOfClippedVerts > 2) {
    /*** Part 3: Clip against the top side of the viewport */
    /***          Clip from the regular list into the temp list */

    clipRef = 0;
    v1 = thisPolygon->numOfClippedVerts-1;

    for (v2 = 0; v2 < thisPolygon->numOfClippedVerts; v2++) {
      /* Categorize edges by type */
      if ((clipList[v1].y >= yMin) && (clipList[v2].y >= yMin)) {
        /* Edge isn't off top side of viewport; copy it over */
        tempClipList[clipRef].x = clipList[v2].x;
        tempClipList[clipRef].y = clipList[v2].y;
        tempClipList[clipRef].z = clipList[v2].z;
        clipRef++;
      }

      else if ((clipList[v1].y < yMin) && (clipList[v2].y < yMin)) {
        /* Edge is entirely off viewport; do nothing */
      }

      else if ((clipList[v1].y >= yMin) && (clipList[v2].y < yMin)) {
        /* Edge is leaving viewport */
        inverseSlope =   (float)(clipList[v2].x - clipList[v1].x) /
                         (float)(clipList[v2].y - clipList[v1].y);
        tempClipList[clipRef].x =
          clipList[v1].x + (yMin - clipList[v1].y) * inverseSlope;

        tempClipList[clipRef].y = yMin;
        tempClipList[clipRef].z = clipList[v1].z;
        clipRef++;
      }

      else if ((clipList[v1].y < yMin) && (clipList[v2].y >= yMin)) {
        /* Edge is entering viewport */
        inverseSlope =   (float)(clipList[v2].x - clipList[v1].x) /
                         (float)(clipList[v2].y - clipList[v1].y);
        tempClipList[clipRef].x =
          clipList[v1].x + (yMin - clipList[v1].y) * inverseSlope;
```

```
                tempClipList[clipRef].y = yMin;
                tempClipList[clipRef].z = clipList[v2].z;
                clipRef++;

                tempClipList[clipRef].x = clipList[v2].x;
                tempClipList[clipRef].y = clipList[v2].y;
                tempClipList[clipRef].z = clipList[v2].z;
                clipRef++;
            }

        v1 = v2;
    }
    thisPolygon->numOfClippedVerts = clipRef;
}

if (thisPolygon->numOfClippedVerts > 2) {
    /*** Part 4: Clip against the bottom edge of the viewport */
    /***          Clip from the temp list back into the regular list */

    clipRef = 0;
    v1 = thisPolygon->numOfClippedVerts-1;

    for (v2 = 0; v2 < thisPolygon->numOfClippedVerts; v2++) {
        /* Categorize edges by type */
        if (      (tempClipList[v1].y <= yMax) &&
                  (tempClipList[v2].y <= yMax)) {
            /* Edge isn't off edge side of viewport; copy it over */
            clipList[clipRef].x = tempClipList[v2].x;
            clipList[clipRef].y = tempClipList[v2].y;
            clipList[clipRef].z = tempClipList[v2].z;
            clipRef++;
        }

        else if ( (tempClipList[v1].y > yMax) &&
                  (tempClipList[v2].y > yMax)) {
            /* Edge is entirely off viewport; do nothing */
        }

        else if ( (tempClipList[v1].y <= yMax) &&
                  (tempClipList[v2].y > yMax))
        {
            /* Edge is leaving viewport */
            inverseSlope =  (float)(tempClipList[v2].x -
                                    tempClipList[v1].x) /
                            (float)(tempClipList[v2].y -
                                    tempClipList[v1].y);
            clipList[clipRef].x = tempClipList[v1].x +
                        (yMax - tempClipList[v1].y) * inverseSlope;
            clipList[clipRef].y = yMax;
            clipList[clipRef].z = tempClipList[v1].z;
            clipRef++;
```

Continued on next page

Continued from previous page

```
         }

    else if (   (tempClipList[v1].y > yMax) &&
                (tempClipList[v2].y <= yMax))
     {
       /* Edge is entering viewport */
       inverseSlope =   (float)(tempClipList[v2].x -
                                tempClipList[v1].x) /
                        (float)(tempClipList[v2].y -
                                tempClipList[v1].y);
       clipList[clipRef].x = tempClipList[v1].x +
                      (yMax - tempClipList[v1].y) * inverseSlope;
       clipList[clipRef].y = yMax;
       clipList[clipRef].z = tempClipList[v2].z;
       clipRef++;

       clipList[clipRef].x = tempClipList[v2].x;
       clipList[clipRef].y = tempClipList[v2].y;
       clipList[clipRef].z = tempClipList[v2].z;
       clipRef++;
     }

     v1 = v2;
    }
    thisPolygon->numOfClippedVerts = clipRef;
   }
  thisPolygon = thisPolygon->nextPolygon;
 }
}
```

Rejecting Polygons

You can perform some simple tests on a polygon to tell you whether or not it might be
drawn on the screen. You've already seen one of these tests, backface removal. You can
also test to see whether the polygon has any vertices at all (it may not, if the clipping
routines have removed them all) or if the polygon's z coordinates place it closer than
the minimum z coordinate (i.e., the front of the viewing pyramid) or farther than an
arbitrary maximum z coordinate (which means it's too far away to see).

TrivialPolygonReject() will take the entire polygon list and check it against each of
these tests. If a polygon fails any of them, it can't be seen by the viewer and a flag is set
in the *rejected* field of the polygon structure indicating this fact.

TrivialPolygonReject() is responsible for calling the CalculatePolygonExtents() routine, which I looked at in Chapter 15. Because the polygon extents are also used by the
sorting function, it is important that TrivialPolygonReject() be called *before* the Painter's
sorting routines are performed.

```
/**
 **  TrivialPolygonReject()
 **
 **  Scans through all of the polygons in the list and checks
 **  to see if they are inside the view frustum, and if
 **  they face forward. If not, it marks them for rejection.
 **/
void  TrivialPolygonReject(void)
{
  Polygon3D  *thisPolygon;

  /* Calculate the polygon extents first */
  CalculatePolygonExtents();

  thisPolygon = gWorld.paintersList;
  while (thisPolygon != NULL) {
    if ((thisPolygon->zmax < gClipZMin) ||
        (thisPolygon->zmin > gClipZMax) ||
        (thisPolygon->numOfClippedVerts < 3) ||
        (BackfacePolygon(thisPolygon))) {

      thisPolygon->rejected = TRUE;
    } else
      thisPolygon->rejected = FALSE;

    thisPolygon = thisPolygon->nextPolygon;
  }
}
```

Any routines that occur later in the process can check the *rejected* field to see if they should even bother to process this polygon.

View Volume Extent Values

You've seen several references to a few global variables that indicate the minimum and maximum extents of the view volume. These variables are declared at the top of World Utilities.c:

```
short    gClipXMin, gClipXMax;
short    gClipYMin, gClipYMax;
short    gClipZMin, gClipZMax;
```

There is also a function to initialize these variables when the application starts up:

```
/**
 **  InitializeWorldBounds()
 **
 **  Sets up the clipping boundary for our polygons
```

Continued on next page

```
Continued from previous page
**/
void  InitializeWorldBounds(  short  xMin,
                              short  xMax,
                              short  yMin,
                              short  yMax,
                              short  zMin,
                              short  zMax  )
{
  gClipXMin = xMin;
  gClipXMax = xMax;
  gClipYMin = yMin;
  gClipYMax = yMax;
  gClipZMin = zMin;
  gClipZMax = zMax;
}
```

If the size of the view volume ever changes (e.g., if the user can change the size of the window), this routine should be called again to set up the new values.

Changes in the Polygon-Drawing Routines

The two polygon-drawing routines, WireframeDrawPolygon() and PolygonFillDrawPolygon(), have been changed slightly to handle the new polygon format. However, because the changes are so minor and these routines are so large, the complete new functions are not reproduced here (you can find them in the Polygon Render.c file in the Chapter 16 folder on the source code disc).

The changes to these routines simply involve reading the vertices from the polygon's *clipList* array instead of from the *polyVertex* pointer array.

Changes to the Polygon Resource

The polygon rendering mode is now stored in the polygon's resource file. To handle this, the OBJ3 resource template has been expanded to hold another 16-bit word value and the LoadObjectFromRsrc() routine loads that value when reading the polygons. Unfortunately, because the size of the object resource has been altered, this change renders objects created with any previous templates incompatible with the new template.

Viewing the Clipped Polygon

To see polygon clipping in action, simple define one of your objects with an x or y value that places it halfway off of the viewport, as in Figure 16-12. (For example, the

Spinning Cube animation included for this chapter places the cube at an x coordinate of 200, which leaves it halfway off the right side of the window.) Although the result may not be breathtaking, you've just achieved a major step in creating a 3D graphics engine.

So far, the polygons have been pretty much stationary. Although you could add some code to animate the positions of each object, in the final game you're going to want to be able to walk around the scene interactively. In the next chapter, I'll look at how to manipulate your view of the world, which (unlike clipping and hidden surface removal) is easier than it sounds.

FIGURE 16-12

◎ ◎ ◎ ◎ ◎ ◎

The spinning cube, clipped against the right side of the viewport

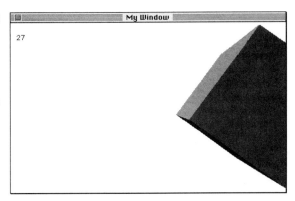

17

Viewing the World

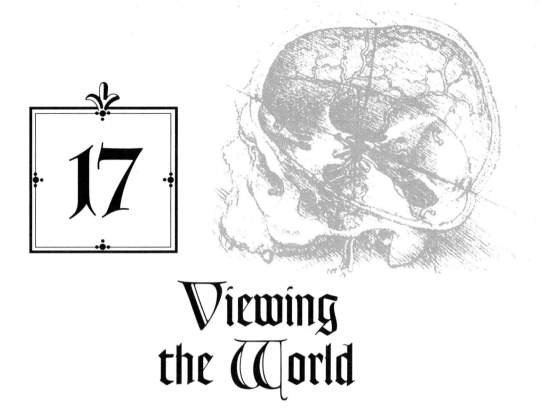

17

Viewing
the World

You now have almost everything you need for your 3D engine. You have the components of code necessary to create, transform, project, clip, and finally draw a virtual 3D world. However, you're still missing one critical part. In all the examples you've looked at so far, the objects in the world are moving but the *view* of the world is not. The objects drawn in the window are being seen from the world coordinate (0, 0, 0) and looking down the z axis. You can picture a video camera positioned at the origin of the window, pointing down the z axis (as in Figure 17-1).

In these games, you want the user to be able to move around in the world. It won't do to have the user merely *watching* the action; he or she must *participate*. To do this, you need to find a way of moving the virtual camera around the world. When the player moves forward, the camera moves forward. When the player turns to the left or right, the camera rotates to the left or right (i.e., around the y axis). The player can then look at the world through the new orientation of the camera. This is what you'll accomplish in this chapter.

Once you have created this camera, or *view system*, you'll have the entire 3D graphics engine and I'll devote the remainder of the book to taking advantage of this engine.

This chapter will also involve changing part of the structure of the routines you've built so far. These changes will make the engine's structure better suited to your purposes.

Moving Around inside the Computer

Using the view system to move the camera around inside the world is an illusion. This shouldn't be surprising—a great deal of computer graphics is an illusion, including the final rendered result. All the formulas behind projection and viewing are based on the world being viewed from the origin looking down the z axis. But a 3D game depends on the player being able to move to *anywhere* within the world (or at least within the confines of the game). How can you move the camera around without messing up these formulas?

It's very difficult to get projection routines to work when the camera is not on the origin. So you're not going to change them. Instead, you're going to move the *world*. If you take the position of the virtual camera in the world and subtract it from the position of every object in the world, everything will appear as it would from the camera.

You can also extend this to rotation. If you take the camera's rotation values and apply the *inverse* rotations to all the objects in the world, you can simulate the rotation of the camera.

Moving the world in this fashion may sound like an expensive task, but you've already got a tool that makes it simple—the matrix. Because you can multiply matrices together to apply a series of transformations, you can perform both the object's internal transformations and the viewing transformation at the same time.

FIGURE 17-1
◎ ◎ ◎ ◎ ◎ ◎
By default, the camera is positioned at the origin and points down the z axis

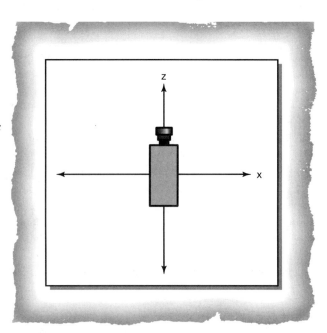

View Translations

The idea that you can fake the camera's movements around the world by moving the world instead may seem a little odd at first. Let's see why it works.

The first step to understanding this concept is to realize that all motion is relative. For example, have you ever had the experience of sitting in a car at a stoplight, looking at the car waiting next to you, and hitting the brake because you thought your car was moving backward—only to discover that you were actually standing still while the other car was moving forward?

When you were looking at the other car, the only frame of reference you had for your car's position was that of the other car. Your mind assumed that the other car was stationary and when you saw its position changing relative to your own, your instinct told you that you were moving backward. In fact, relative to the other car, you were moving backward.

Now say you want to travel from New York to Los Angeles. In a normal world, you would board a plane, which would fly the distance, moving you in relation to the earth, like the airplane in Figure 17-2. When you think about moving from one place to another on the earth, you assume in our minds that the earth is stationary. Thus your frame of reference becomes the earth.

But what if, instead of flying across the earth's surface, you floated in the air and someone moved the earth around until you were above L.A.? (This idea is shown in Figure 17-3.) The same basic effect would be achieved using a very different method.

FIGURE 17-2

◉ ◉ ◉ ◉ ◉ ◉

Normally, to travel from New York to Los Angeles, you move in an airplane

FIGURE 17-3
◉ ◉ ◉ ◉ ◉ ◉

*If practical,
you could stand
still while the
planet moved
underneath
you; the result
would be the
same*

Of course, moving the entire planet just for the sake of getting one person to a different city would be impractical, not to mention impossible. But in your 3D world, you're not dealing with solid objects that have mass. You're dealing with electronic illusions without substance.

So in a flight simulator, according to the 3D game engine, you're not flying at all. You're floating in the air and the game engine moves the entire world around you. Although this sounds very difficult to do, it's really no harder to accomplish than the rotating cube—and that wasn't so hard, was it? All you need to do is take the player's position in the world (which I'll refer to as the camera's position) and subtract it from the position of every object in the world. It's that simple.

Rotating the World

Rotating the camera is very similar in concept to moving it. Imagine you are walking down a street looking forward when a friend suddenly shouts to you from your left. Normally, you would turn to look, changing your own direction of view (see Figures 17-4a and b).

What if, instead of looking to your left, you continue to look forward and the entire planet is rotated underneath you (see Figure 17-5)? It sounds ludicrous to do this and in the real world it is, but now you're dealing with a virtual world. These things are not only possible, they're easy to do.

FIGURE 17-4a

◎ ◎ ◎ ◎ ◎ ◎

If you are walking down the street and a friend calls to you from your left…

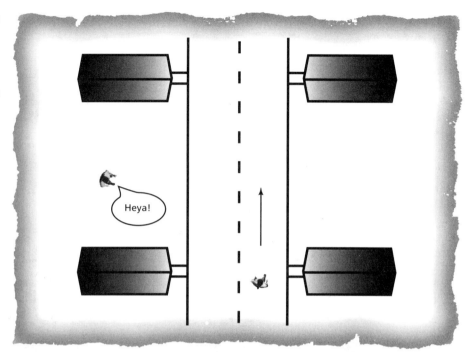

FIGURE 17-4b

◎ ◎ ◎ ◎ ◎ ◎

…normally, you will turn to face your friend.

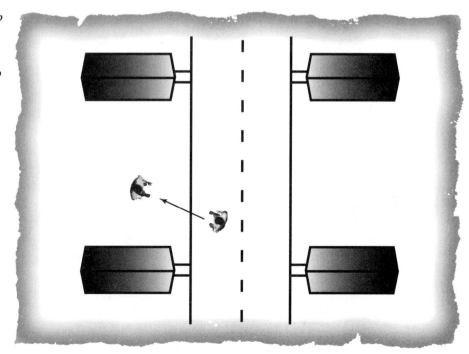

FIGURE 17-5

◉ ◉ ◉ ◉ ◉ ◉

You could also stand still and have the planet rotate underneath you (theoretically speaking, of course)

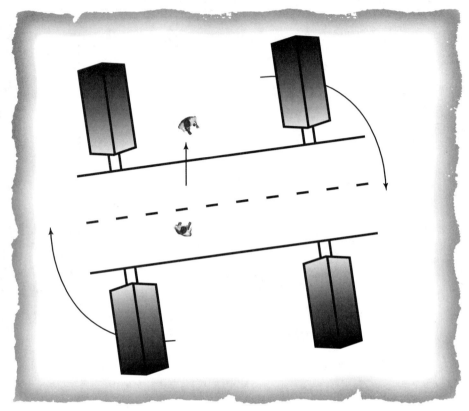

As with the translation, you rotate the world using the inverse of the camera's angle. When expressed in degrees, the inverse can be calculated simply by subtracting the angle from 360. This is done for each of the three camera angles (x, y, and z rotations) and concatenated together in one matrix, as you've done for your objects.

Before you start adding these transformations to code, let's talk about creating a camera that will represent the player's position in the world.

Adding the Camera to the World

You're going to treat the viewing camera as an object in the world. You won't be using the Object3D structure because the camera has no shape (you only care about its position and rotation and you will never be drawing it). Instead, you'll create a new structure for the view and declare one instance of it as a global variable in a new file, called View System.c. This structure will hold the position and rotation of the camera, and several new functions will modify these fields.

When the camera's transformations are applied to the world, they will be combined in a transformation matrix. The matrix is then multiplied to the transformation matrix of each object. But you don't want to be constantly regenerating this matrix. What if the camera doesn't move during one frame? In some games, this case would be rare, but in others, it would be quite a common occurrence. Why waste time creating the view matrix if it hasn't changed? Instead, you can store the viewing matrix inside the view structure. You also can store a variable in the structure indicating whether the matrix is valid or not. Each time the position or rotation of the camera is changed, this variable is changed to indicate that the structure needs regeneration. Once the new matrix is created, this variable is reset.

Let's take a look at this structure:

```
typedef struct {
  /* These fields hold the current stats of the view camera */
  short    viewXAngle, viewYAngle, viewZAngle;
  short    viewXPos, viewYPos, viewZPos;

  /* This is the transformation that is applied to all of the objects
   * in the scene. It is constructed by taking the inverse values
   * of each of the above parameters and forming a matrix
   */
  Matrix4    viewTransformation;

  /* update is true if the parameters have changed since we last
   * updated the view matrix.
   */
  Boolean    update;
} ViewInfo;
```

Then declare a global variable in View System.c to hold the camera's parameters:

```
ViewInfo    gCameraViewData;
```

Initializing the View Camera

You need a simple routine to initialize the viewing camera. The default values place the camera at the origin of the world with no rotation angles. It also sets *update* to True so that the matrix is regenerated:

```
/**
 ** InitializeView()
 **
 ** Sets the global view structure to its default
 ** values (camera at 0,0,0 with a rotation of 0,0,0,
 ** which points it directly down the z axis).
 **/
void  InitializeView(void)
{
```

Continued on next page

Continued from previous page

```
  gCameraViewData.viewXAngle = 0;
  gCameraViewData.viewYAngle = 0;
  gCameraViewData.viewZAngle = 0;

  gCameraViewData.viewXPos = 0;
  gCameraViewData.viewYPos = 0;
  gCameraViewData.viewZPos = 0;

  gCameraViewData.update = TRUE;
}
```

Moving the Camera around the World

You can now create a couple simple routines for moving the camera around the world. The first routine will move the camera to a specific x, y, and z coordinate by replacing the camera's position values:

```
/**
 **  MoveViewToPosition()
 **
 **  Moves the view camera to a specific location.
 **/
void  MoveViewToPosition(short xPos, short yPos, short zPos)
{
  /* Set the structure's fields */
  gCameraViewData.viewXPos = xPos;
  gCameraViewData.viewYPos = yPos;
  gCameraViewData.viewZPos = zPos;

  /* Set the view's update flag so the matrix is recalculated */
  gCameraViewData.update = TRUE;
}
```

MoveViewToPosition() is useful for setting the camera's position when the game begins or when starting a new level. However, the position values are stored in the view structure so that you don't *have* to keep track of them elsewhere. Therefore, let's create another routine that will move the camera by a specified distance. This will be helpful if you want to move the player by, say, 5 units in x.

```
/**
 **  MoveViewByDistance()
 **
 **  Move the view a specifed distance in x, y, and z.
 **/
void  MoveViewByDistance(short xDist, short yDist, short zDist)
{
  /* Set the structure's fields */
  gCameraViewData.viewXPos += xDist;
  gCameraViewData.viewYPos += yDist;
  gCameraViewData.viewZPos += zDist;
```

```
    /* Set the view's update flag so the matrix is recalculated */
    gCameraViewData.update = TRUE;
}
```

Rotating the Camera

Just as important as moving, the player's viewing rotation must change. These routines are very similar to those for changing the camera's position, with one major difference. Because you use a look-up array to determine sine and cosine values, the rotation values always have to be between 0 and 359. Therefore, check to see if the angle is within this range and, if it is not, find its *complement*, or equivalent value that *is* within this range.

The first routine, RotateViewToAngle(), sets the object's rotation to a specific value:

```
/**
 ** RotateViewToAngle()
 **
 ** Rotates to specified x, y, and z angles. Also makes sure the
 ** angles are between 0 and 359 degrees, and adjusts them if they
 ** aren't.
 **/
void  RotateViewToAngle(short xAngle, short yAngle, short zAngle)
{
  /* Check to see if the angle is less than 0 or
   * greater than 359. If so, find the equivalent
   * angle.
   */
  while (gCameraViewData.viewXAngle >= 360)
    gCameraViewData.viewXAngle -= 360;
  while (gCameraViewData.viewXAngle < 0)
    gCameraViewData.viewXAngle += 360;
  while (gCameraViewData.viewYAngle >= 360)
    gCameraViewData.viewYAngle -= 360;
  while (gCameraViewData.viewYAngle < 0)
    gCameraViewData.viewYAngle += 360;
  while (gCameraViewData.viewZAngle >= 360)
    gCameraViewData.viewZAngle -= 360;
  while (gCameraViewData.viewZAngle < 0)
    gCameraViewData.viewZAngle += 360;

  /* Set the structure's fields */
  gCameraViewData.viewXAngle = xAngle;
  gCameraViewData.viewYAngle = yAngle;
  gCameraViewData.viewZAngle = zAngle;

  /* Set the view's update flag so the matrix is recalculated */
  gCameraViewData.update = TRUE;
}
```

The second routine changes the camera's rotation angles by a specified angle. After adding to the camera's angle, it checks to see if the result is between 0 and 359:

```
/**
 **   RotateViewByAngle()
 **
 **   Rotates the view by specified x, y, and z angles. Also checks
 **   to see if the results are between 0 and 359 degrees, and, if
 **   not, changes them to equivalent angles.
 **/
void  RotateViewByAngle(short xAngle, short yAngle, short zAngle)
{
  /* Set the structure's fields */
  gCameraViewData.viewXAngle += xAngle;
  gCameraViewData.viewYAngle += yAngle;
  gCameraViewData.viewZAngle += zAngle;

  /* Check to see if the view's angle values are all still between
   * 0 and 359. If not, adjust them.
   */
  while (gCameraViewData.viewXAngle >= 360)
    gCameraViewData.viewXAngle -= 360;
  while (gCameraViewData.viewXAngle < 0)
    gCameraViewData.viewXAngle += 360;
  while (gCameraViewData.viewYAngle >= 360)
    gCameraViewData.viewYAngle -= 360;
  while (gCameraViewData.viewYAngle < 0)
    gCameraViewData.viewYAngle += 360;
  while (gCameraViewData.viewZAngle >= 360)
    gCameraViewData.viewZAngle -= 360;
  while (gCameraViewData.viewZAngle < 0)
    gCameraViewData.viewZAngle += 360;

  /* Set the view's update flag so the matrix is recalculated */
  gCameraViewData.update = TRUE;
}
```

Moving the Camera Forward

Changing the position of the camera by separate x, y, and z values is useful, but most of the time you want to move the camera based on the direction it is facing at the time. For example, if the camera is facing at an angle between the x and y axes, you want to move the camera in both directions at the same time. To assist with this, let's create a routine that will move the camera by a specified distance in the direction it is facing at the time.

This process involves some trigonometry. The first step is to create a *unit vector* that points in the same direction as the camera. A unit vector is a vector that has a length of one; if you multiply a *distance* factor by each element of the vector, you find the correct x, y, and z distances to move the camera.

This unit vector can be formed by taking a vector facing down the z axis or with coordinates of (0, 0, 1). Then apply the camera's rotation vectors to this vector.

As you may remember from Chapter 4, rotation around the z axis is equivalent to performing a roll in an aircraft. Although this rotation will affect the view from the camera, it won't affect the directional vector at all. Imagine pointing a pencil away from you, as in Figure 17-6. If you rotate it around the z axis, the direction in which the pencil is pointing won't change at all.

FIGURE 17-6

◎ ◎ ◎ ◎ ◎ ◎

If you hold a pencil facing away from you and rotate it, its orientation will not change

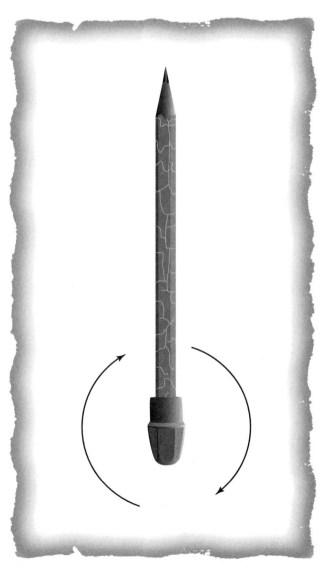

So you don't need to apply the z rotation to the unit vector. Also, because you know what direction the vector was originally facing, you can streamline the rotation process. The rotation can be reduced to this formula:

```
unit_x = cos(x_angle) * -sin(y_angle);
unit_y = sin(x_angle);
unit_z = cos(x_angle) * cos (y_angle);
```

Let's write a function that will return a unit vector pointing in the same direction as the camera. Because the sine and cosine look-up tables are stored as 24.8 fixed-point numbers, this function will also return this unit vector using the same fixed-point numbering system. Here is the complete AngleVectorsToXYZ() function:

```
/**
 **    AngleVectorsToXYZ()
 **
 **    Rotates a [0,0,1] vector by 3 input angles
 **    Actually, the z rotation won't have any effect since
 **    the vector starts out pointing down the z axis.
 **    This routine expects the angles to be between 0 and 359.
 **/
void  AngleVectorsToXYZ( short     xAngle,
                         short     yAngle,
                         short     zAngle,
                         Fixed24   *x,
                         Fixed24   *y,
                         Fixed24   *z  )
{
  Fixed24     ySin, yCos;
  Fixed24     xSin, xCos;

  /* Ignore z axis rotation, go directly to x */

  /* Take the inverse of the x rotation */
  if (xAngle > 0)
    xAngle = 360-xAngle;
  xSin = gSinTable[xAngle];
  xCos = gCosTable[xAngle];

  /* Handle the y axis rotation */
  if (yAngle > 0)
    yAngle = 360-yAngle;
  ySin = gSinTable[yAngle];
  yCos = gCosTable[yAngle];

  *x = (-ySin * xCos) >> 8;
  *y = xSin;
  *z = (xCos * yCos) >> 8;
}
```

Now let's take advantage of this new function. It is a simple matter to write a function that will take one input, *distance*, and move the camera forward or backward by that distance. It calls AngleVectorsToXYZ() and then multiplies the movement distance by each of the values it receives to determine the distance to move the camera in each dimension. This function is rather simple; most of the work has already been done by other routines.

```
/**
 **   MoveViewForwardAndBack()
 **
 **   Moves the view by a specified distance forward or backward,
 **   based on the view's rotation values.
 **/
void  MoveViewForwardAndBack(short distance)
{
  short    movementInX, movementInY, movementInZ;
  Fixed24  unitX, unitY, unitZ;
  /* Convert the view's direction into three fixed numbers
   * representing a unit vector facing in the direction of
   * the view's rotation.
   */
  AngleVectorsToXYZ( gCameraViewData.viewXPos,
                     gCameraViewData.viewYPos,
                     gCameraViewData.viewZPos,
                     &unitX,
                     &unitY,
                     &unitZ  );

  /* Find the distance in each dimension that we're moving */
  movementInX = (distance * unitX) >> 8;
  movementInY = (distance * unitY) >> 8;
  movementInZ = (distance * unitZ) >> 8;

  /* Move the view */
  MoveViewByDistance(movementInX, movementInY, movementInZ);
}
```

Retrieving the View Transformation

Just like the object transformations you've been performing since Chapter 9, the view transformation is created by sending a matrix through several operations to build a series of mathematical procedures. Fortunately, you can use the same matrix routines for the view transformation. However, there are some differences. As I mentioned earlier in this chapter, the rotation and translation operations have to be applied in *inverse*. So when creating the transformations, you use the negative of the translation values and subtract the rotation values from 360. A scale value has no real application for a view translation.

The next routine will return the current view transformation to the caller. Before this transformation is returned, however, the routine checks to see if the matrix is current. If it isn't, the routine will regenerate the matrix using standard matrix routines. The routine then stores the result in the view structure, changes the *update* flag, and returns the matrix:

```
/**
 **  GetCurrentViewTransformation()
 **
 **  Updates the view's transformation matrix if necessary and returns
 **  a pointer to it.
 **/
Matrix4Ptr GetCurrentViewTransformation(void)
{
  short    xRot, yRot, zRot;
  /* Check to see if the matrix is current. */
  if (gCameraViewData.update == TRUE) {
    /* Update the view matrix */

    /* Initialize the matrix */
    InitMatrix(&gCameraViewData.viewTransformation);

    /* Apply the rotation. Remember that for the view
     * system, the transformations must be applied as
     * an inverse. Start with translation.
     */
    TranslateMatrix( &gCameraViewData.viewTransformation,
                     -gCameraViewData.viewXPos,
                     -gCameraViewData.viewYPos,
                     -gCameraViewData.viewZPos  );

    /* Now apply the negative rotation values */
    xRot = gCameraViewData.viewXAngle;
    if (xRot != 0) xRot = 360 - xRot;
    yRot = gCameraViewData.viewYAngle;
    if (yRot != 0) yRot = 360 - yRot;
    zRot = gCameraViewData.viewZAngle;
    if (zRot != 0) zRot = 360 - zRot;

    RotateMatrix( &gCameraViewData.viewTransformation,
                  xRot, yRot, zRot  );

    /* Set the update flag to FALSE - the matrix is current */
    gCameraViewData.update = FALSE;
  }

  /* Return the matrix */
  return &gCameraViewData.viewTransformation;
}
```

Applying the View Changes to the 3D Engine's Structure

All that needs to be done to hook this view system into the 3D virtual world is to multiply this view transformation matrix with the object's matrix before applying it to the individual vertices of the object. Despite how complicated it seems, implementing the view system is one of the easiest parts of creating a 3D game engine.

However, I've also taken this opportunity to revamp other parts of the engine's structure. The pipeline illustration shown in Chapter 16 remains pretty much the same, but the individual steps are now performed by other functions.

Here is a basic outline of the changes implemented in this chapter:

- Each object's rotation and scaling values are now stored in the Object3D structure. The object's position was already being stored (originX, originY, and originZ). Now the object's complete transformation matrix is also stored in the structure and is treated similarly to the matrix stored in the view structure.

- A new routine, TransformObjectList(), is now responsible for several steps in preparing an object to be drawn. Among these steps are creating the object transformation matrix, combining that matrix with the view transformation matrix, and transforming each of the object's vertices.

- ObjectToWorldCoordinates() has been eliminated. Instead, the object's translation is now part of its transformation matrix.

- A Matrix4 structure has been added and all the matrix routines have been modified to operate on it.

- Several routines, similar to those to change the object's position, rotation, and scale, have been added for the view system.

- The wx, wy, wz, wt, sx, sy, and st fields have been eliminated from the Vertex3D structure. The objects are now translated into the tx, ty, and tz fields directly and then projected after they are converted to ClippedVertices.

- The remaining fields of the Vertex3D structure and those of the ClippedVertex structure are now defined as *long* instead of *short*. This extra precision is needed to avoid overflow errors along the way.

- LoadObjectFromRsrc() now initializes the new fields of the Object3D structure with default values.

- A new file, User Input.c, has been added to demonstrate the capabilities of the view system. This file checks the keyboard for keys that are pressed and moves the view camera in response.

Let's begin with the new structure for the objects, because you will be using it throughout the rest of the chapter.

A New Structure for Objects

The Object3D structure has several new fields to keep track of its rotation, scale, and current transformation matrix. You'll recognize most of the fields from the view structure you recently looked at, and their use is almost identical.

```
typedef struct Object3D {
  short           numOfVertices;
  short           numOfPolygons;
  short           originX, originY, originZ;
  Vertex3D        vertex[kMaximumVertices];
  Polygon3D       polygon[kMaximumPolys];

  /* Here we have the rotation and scaling information for the
   * object, which will be applied as a transformation each time
   * the object is drawn. The angles are in degrees, from 0 to 359.
   */
  short           xAngle, yAngle, zAngle;
  float           scalingFactor;

  /* objectTransformation is a matrix that holds the transformation
   * for the last calculated transformation. If the transformation
   * values are changed, the 'update' flag must be set to TRUE
   * so this matrix is recalculated.
   */
  Matrix4         objectTransformation;
  Boolean         update;

  /* nextObject and lastObject form a linked list for
   * the virtual world
   */
  struct Object3D    *nextObject, *lastObject;
} Object3D;
```

A little later in the chapter, I'll discuss routines for modifying the position, rotation, and scaling fields of the structure. But first let's see how those fields are applied to the object's transformation matrix, along with those of the viewing system.

Transforming the Object List

With this chapter, I add a translation factor to the object's transformation and follow that up with the view transformation. The new function, TransformObjectList(), must check to see if each object's transformation matrix is current and, if it is not, regenerate it using the familiar matrix-manipulation routines. The function then multiplies that matrix with the one from the view system and applies it to the object's vertex list. It then moves to the next object and repeats the process, as shown in Listing 17-1.

Listing 17-1 The TransformObjectList( ) routine

```
/**
** TransformObjectList()
**
** Takes each of the objects in the object list and applies a
** transformation to them based on their current scale and
** rotation parameters. It also translates the
** object to world coordinates.
**/
void TransformObjectList(void)
{
  Object3D      *thisObject;
  Matrix4Ptr    transMatrixPtr;
  Matrix4Ptr    viewTransformation;
  Matrix4       objectAndViewingMatrix;

  /* Get the current view information */
  viewTransformation = GetCurrentViewTransformation();

  /* Run through each object in the list */
  thisObject = GetObjectList();
  while (thisObject != NULL) {
    /* Get a pointer to this object's transformation matrix */
    transMatrixPtr = &thisObject->objectTransformation;

    /* Check to see if this object's transformation array needs to be
     * updated.
     */
    if (thisObject->update == TRUE) {
      /* Update this object's transformation matrix */
      InitMatrix(transMatrixPtr);

      /* Add in the rotation values */
      if ( (thisObject->xAngle != 0) ||
           (thisObject->yAngle != 0) ||
           (thisObject->zAngle != 0) ) {
        RotateMatrix( transMatrixPtr,
                      thisObject->xAngle,
                      thisObject->yAngle,
                      thisObject->zAngle );
      }

      /* Add in the scaling factor */
      if (thisObject->scalingFactor != 1.0) {
        ScaleMatrix(transMatrixPtr, thisObject->scalingFactor);
      }
```

Continued on next page

Continued from previous page

```
        /* Add in the translation factor */
        if ((thisObject->originX != 0) ||
            (thisObject->originY != 0) ||
            (thisObject->originZ != 0)) {
          TranslateMatrix( transMatrixPtr,
                           thisObject->originX,
                           thisObject->originY,
                           thisObject->originZ  );
        }


        /* The object's matrix has been updated */
        thisObject->update = FALSE;
      }

      /* Add in the viewing matrix to the whole mess */
      MatrixMultiply( transMatrixPtr,
                      viewTransformation,
                      &objectAndViewingMatrix);

      /* Apply it to this object */
      TransformObject3D(thisObject, &objectAndViewingMatrix);

      /* Move to the next object in the list */
      thisObject = thisObject->nextObject;
    }
}
```

The New Matrix Structure

So far you've seen several references to a new matrix type, called Matrix4. To facilitate passing matrices between different routines more easily, the matrix has now been defined as a structure, like this:

```
typedef struct {
  Fixed24      m[4][4];
} Matrix4, *Matrix4Ptr;
```

This change has been made because C places some rather large restrictions on passing matrices between routines, especially two-dimensional ones. The way the matrix is used hasn't changed much, except that now, when referencing the elements of the array, you must tack on a field (m) to the statement.

In addition, all the matrix creation and manipulation routines have been added to a new file, Matrix.c. The changes to the individual routines are rather simple, and because there are several of these functions, I won't document them here. To see the new matrix routines, look in Matrix.c in the Chapter 17 folder of the source code disc.

The routine that applies a matrix to the vertices of just one object, TransformObject3D(), has also been modified to handle the new matrix type. The modifications are rather simple and the routine is shown in Listing 17-2 as an example of the changes necessary for all of the matrix routines.

Listing 17-2 *The TransformObject3D() routine*

```
/**
** TransformObject3D()
**
** Takes an object's local coordinates and transforms them
** with the provided transformation matrix, placing
** the result in the tx,ty,tz, and tt fields of the
** vertices.
**/
void TransformObject3D( Object3D    *theObject,
                        Matrix4Ptr  transformMatrix  )
{
  short     i;
  short     numOfVertices;

  numOfVertices = theObject->numOfVertices;

  /* Transform the object's vertices with the matrix */
  for (i = 0; i < numOfVertices; i++) {
    /* Declare some temporary variables */
    short      temp0, temp1, temp2, temp3;
    Vertex3D  *vertexRef;

    /* Get a pointer to the current vertex */
    vertexRef = &theObject->vertex[i];

    /* Multiply against the matrix. The vertices are integers,
     * not fixed-point, so we can do straight multiplication
     * and shift the result back when we're done.
     */
    temp0 = (vertexRef->lx * transformMatrix->m[0][0] +
             vertexRef->ly * transformMatrix->m[1][0] +
             vertexRef->lz * transformMatrix->m[2][0] +
             transformMatrix->m[3][0]) >> 8;

    temp1 = (vertexRef->lx * transformMatrix->m[0][1] +
             vertexRef->ly * transformMatrix->m[1][1] +
             vertexRef->lz * transformMatrix->m[2][1] +
             transformMatrix->m[3][1]) >> 8;

    temp2 = (vertexRef->lx * transformMatrix->m[0][2] +
             vertexRef->ly * transformMatrix->m[1][2] +
             vertexRef->lz * transformMatrix->m[2][2] +
             transformMatrix->m[3][2]) >> 8;

    temp3 = (vertexRef->lx * transformMatrix->m[0][3] +
             vertexRef->ly * transformMatrix->m[1][3] +
```

Continued on next page

Continued from previous page

```
                vertexRef->lz * transformMatrix->m[2][3] +
                transformMatrix->m[3][3]) >> 8;

    /* Put the results into the vector's
     * transformed coordinates
     */
    vertexRef->tx = temp0;
    vertexRef->ty = temp1;
    vertexRef->tz = temp2;
    vertexRef->tt = temp3;
  }
}
```

Changing the Object's Parameters

As with the View structure, you need a set of routines to change the object's position and rotation. These routines are very similar to those for the view structure except that there are two new routines for modifying an object's scale (remember, the view system does not have a *scale* field). Also, for the object structure, there is no equivalent to the view's MoveForwardAndBack() function. Because you won't have any objects in the database that will be changing position (except, of course, the camera), you have no need to move an object forward and backward. If you want to add a routine that will move an object in this fashion, it shouldn't be very difficult.

The first pair of routines I'll look at are MoveObjectToPosition() and MoveObjectByDistance(). Like the position modifying routines for the view system, MoveObjectToPosition() replaces the object's *originX*, *originY*, and *originZ* fields:

```
/**
 ** MoveObjectToPosition()
 **
 ** Sets the object's position.
 **/
void MoveObjectToPosition( Object3D  *theObject,
                           short     xPos,
                           short     yPos,
                           short     zPos  )
{
  /* Set the fields of the object */
  theObject->originX = xPos;
  theObject->originY = yPos;
  theObject->originZ = zPos;

  /* Mark the object to be updated */
  theObject->update = TRUE;
}
```

MoveObjectByDistance() adds three distance values onto the object's current coordinates:

```
/**
 **  MoveObjectByDistance()
 **
 **  Changes the object's position by a specified distance.
 **/
void  MoveObjectByDistance( Object3D  *theObject,
                            short     xDist,
                            short     yDist,
                            short     zDist )
{
  /* Move the object */
  theObject->originX += xDist;
  theObject->originY += yDist;
  theObject->originZ += zDist;

  /* Mark the object to be updated */
  theObject->update = TRUE;
}
```

The rotation functions should also be familiar. RotateObjectToAngle() sets the object's rotation angles to those specified:

```
/**
 **  RotateObjectToAngle()
 **
 **  Sets the object's rotation values to those specified.
 **/
void  RotateObjectToAngle( Object3D   *theObject,
                           short      xAngle,
                           short      yAngle,
                           short      zAngle )
{
  /* Check to see if the angle is less than 0 or
   * greater than 359. If so, find the complementary
   * angle.
   */
  while (xAngle >= 360)    xAngle -= 360;
  while (xAngle < 0)       xAngle += 360;
  while (yAngle >= 360)    yAngle -= 360;
  while (yAngle < 0)       yAngle += 360;
  while (zAngle >= 360)    zAngle -= 360;
  while (zAngle < 0)       zAngle += 360;

  /* Set the fields in the object structure */
  theObject->xAngle = xAngle;
  theObject->yAngle = yAngle;
  theObject->zAngle = zAngle;
```

Continued on next page

Continued from previous page

```
  /* Set a flag so the transformation matrix is recalculated
   * in the next frame.
   */
  theObject->update = TRUE;
}
```

RotateObjectByAngle() adds three angle values onto the object's current rotation angles and then checks to make sure that the result is in a range between 0 and 359 degrees:

```
/**
 **   RotateObjectByAngle()
 **
 **   Rotates an object by a specific distance. This routine is similar
 **   to RotateObjectToAngle(), except that it adds the input angles
 **   to the object's current values instead of replacing them.
 **/
void  RotateObjectByAngle( Object3D  *theObject,
                           short      xAngle,
                           short      yAngle,
                           short      zAngle  )
{
  /* Add the angles onto the object's current settings */
  theObject->xAngle += xAngle;
  theObject->yAngle += yAngle;
  theObject->zAngle += zAngle;

  /* Check to see if the object's angle values are all still between
   * 0 and 359. If not, adjust them.
   */
  while (theObject->xAngle >= 360)    theObject->xAngle -= 360;
  while (theObject->xAngle < 0)       theObject->xAngle += 360;
  while (theObject->yAngle >= 360)    theObject->yAngle -= 360;
  while (theObject->yAngle < 0)       theObject->yAngle += 360;
  while (theObject->zAngle >= 360)    theObject->zAngle -= 360;
  while (theObject->zAngle < 0)       theObject->zAngle += 360;

  /* Mark the object to be updated */
  theObject->update = TRUE;
}
```

You also have two new routines to modify the scale of the object. The first simply replaces the object's current scale value with the one provided by the caller:

```
/**
 **   SetObjectScale()
 **
 **   Sets the object's scale value to a specified value.
 **/
void  SetObjectScale(  Object3D  *theObject,
                       float      scale  )
{
```

```
  /* Change the scale */
  theObject->scalingFactor = scale;

  /* Mark the object to be updated */
  theObject->update = TRUE;
}
```

The second scaling routine, however, does not add a value to the current scaling factor, as the position or rotation function does. Instead, the provided scaling factor is *multiplied* by the object's current scale. This enables you to change the object's size by a certain percentage (e.g., to increase the object's size by 10 percent, you would pass a scaling value of 1.10 to this routine).

```
/**
 ** ChangeObjectScale()
 **
 ** Multiplies the object's scaling factor by a specified value.
 **/
void ChangeObjectScale(  Object3D *theObject,
                         float     scaleMultiplier  )
{
  /* Change the scale */
  theObject->scalingFactor *= scaleMultiplier;

  /* Mark the object to be updated */
  theObject->update = TRUE;
}
```

A Demonstration of the View System

You now have enough code to move a camera around the scene interactively, so let's look at a sample program that demonstrates this new capability. The scene will consist of two spinning cubes and you can move around that scene using the keyboard. Keys will rotate the view to the left or right (i.e., around the y axis), as well as forward and backward and up and down.

Responding to User Input

The best key combinations to use for moving lie on the numeric keypad. 8 moves forward, 5 (or 2) moves backward, 4 turns left, and 6 turns right. In addition, 7 moves up and 1 moves down.

However, if you have a computer that does not have a keypad (such as a PowerBook), you can use an alternate set of keys. In this case, the four arrow keys move forward, back, left, and right, and the A and Z keys move up and down, respectively.

The code can be compiled to use either set of key codes. Here is the code that defines the constants for the keys:

```
#if 1
/* Keypad movement keys */
#define kKeyMoveForward    0x5B  /* keypad '8' */
#define kKeyMoveBack       0x57  /* keypad '5' */
#define kKeyTurnLeft       0x56  /* keypad '4' */
#define kKeyTurnRight      0x58  /* keypad '6' */
#define kKeyMoveUp         0x59  /* keypad '7' */
#define kKeyMoveDown       0x53  /* keypad '1' */

#else
/* Arrow movement keys */
#define kKeyMoveForward    0x7E  /* up arrow key */
#define kKeyMoveBack       0x7D  /* down arrow key */
#define kKeyTurnLeft       0x7B  /* left arrow key */
#define kKeyTurnRight      0x7C  /* right arrow key */
#define kKeyMoveUp         0x00  /* 'a' key */
#define kKeyMoveDown       0x06  /* 'z' key */
#endif
```

Here the code is defined to use the numeric keypad. If you want to use the arrow keys instead, change the line that says "#if 1" to "#if 0." When the file is compiled, the second set of constants will be used.

In the previous examples where you've responded to several types of keypresses during each frame, you called the routine IsKeyPressed() several times to check each key that could be pressed. This meant that, if the game could respond to six different keys, IsKeyPressed() would be called six times each frame. IsKeyPressed(), in turn, calls the Toolbox function GetKeys(), which can be an expensive call.

There is a much more efficient way to handle this process. Instead of calling GetKeys() several times per frame, it's called just once. The same key map is then checked for each key you are interested in.

I had to rewrite IsKeyPressed(). The only difference is that instead of calling GetKeys(), this new routine takes a key map as a parameter, checks it for the desired key code, and returns a Boolean result. Here is the new routine:

```
/**
**   CheckKeyMap()
**
**   Looks in the provided key map to see if the indicated key is
**   pressed. Similar to CheckKeyDown(), except takes an input
**   of a KeyMap instead of calling a toolbox routine to
**   retrieve it.
```

```
**/
static Boolean  CheckKeyMap(unsigned char *keyMap, unsigned short theKey)
{
  Long        keyMapIndex;
  Boolean     isKeyPressed;
  short       bitToCheck;

  keyMapIndex = keyMap[theKey / 8];
  /* compute the individual bit to check */
  bitToCheck = theKey % 8;
  /* Calculate the status of the individual key */
  isKeyPressed = (keyMapIndex >> bitToCheck) & 0x01;

  return isKeyPressed;
}
```

A routine called HandleUserInput() handles all keyboard input. If the user presses the forward or backward movement keys, the view's MoveForwardOrBackward() routine
is called. If the upward or downward movement keys are pressed, the view is modified using MoveViewByDistance() (because you know that the view's z coordinate is the
only one that will be modified by this movement). If either rotation key is pressed, the
view is modified using RotateViewByAngle().

Currently, the movement keys modify the view's position by 10 units and rotations
are done in 3-degree increments. This gives a fairly realistic response to the user's keypresses.

Here is the source code for HandleUserInput():

```
/**
 **  HandleUserInput()
 **
 **  Checks the keyboard for any keys held down and moves the camera
 **  accordingly.
 **/
void  HandleUserInput(void)
{
  unsigned char  ourKeyMap[16];

  /* Get the key map */
  GetKeys((unsigned long *)ourKeyMap);

  /* Check for moving the camera forward */
  if (CheckKeyMap(ourKeyMap, kKeyMoveForward))
    MoveViewForwardAndBack(10);  /* Move camera forward 10 units */
  if (CheckKeyMap(ourKeyMap, kKeyMoveBack))
    MoveViewForwardAndBack(-10);  /* Move camara back 10 units */
  if (CheckKeyMap(ourKeyMap, kKeyMoveUp))
    MoveViewByDistance(0, 10, 0);  /* Move camera up 10 units */
  if (CheckKeyMap(ourKeyMap, kKeyMoveDown))
    MoveViewByDistance(0, -10, 0);    /* Move camera down 10 units */
```

Continued on next page

Continued from previous page

```
   if (CheckKeyMap(ourKeyMap, kKeyTurnLeft))
     RotateViewByAngle(0, -3, 0);  /* Rotate camera -3 degrees on y */
   if (CheckKeyMap(ourKeyMap, kKeyTurnRight))
     RotateViewByAngle(0, 3, 0);    /* Rotate camera 3 degrees on y */
 }
```

A Revised main() Routine

Now that you've looked at all these changes to the 3D engine's pipeline, it's time to examine some modifications to the main() routine. Most of the object's transformations are handled in separate routines, so the only two routines you need to call to draw the polygons on the offscreen image are TransformObjectList() and DrawPolygonList().

Because the two cubes are rotating, change their rotation angles by making calls to RotateObjectByAngle() during each frame. To handle the user input to change the view, call HandleUserInput().

There is also one additional initialization call for the view system—InitializeView(), which sets up all the default variables for the view.

An advantage to the work you've been doing is that, although other parts of the engine have been getting more complicated, the main() function has actually gotten simpler. This is because most of the work of the 3D game engine has been handed off to other, more specialized, routines. In fact, in many large applications, the main() function is one of the shortest routines in the entire project.

Listing 17-3 is the modified main() routine.

Listing 17-3 *The modified main() routine*

```
void main(void)
{
  Rect           windowRect;
  WindowPtr      mainWindow;
  Ptr            offscreenImagePtr;
  unsigned long  offscreenRowBytes;
  OSErr          err;
  Object3D       *baseObject;
  long           thisTickCount, originalTickCount;
  long           framesSoFar;
  long           framesPerSecond;
  Str255         fpsText;

  /* Initialize everything we need */
  InitGraf(&qd.thePort);
  InitWindows();
  InitCursor();

  /* Initialize the sin/cos look-up tables */
  InitializeSinCosTable();
```

```
/* Set the window size */
SetRect(&windowRect, 0, 0, kWindowWidth, kWindowHeight);

/* Offset the window rect so that the window does not appear
 * under the menu bar.
 */
OffsetRect(&windowRect, 32, 40);

/* Create the window */
mainWindow = CreateWindow(&windowRect);

/* Set the clipping boundaries */
InitializeWorldBounds(0, kWindowWidth-1, 0, kWindowHeight-1, 2, 10000);

SetPort(mainWindow);

/* Create the offscreen image */
err = CreateOffscreenImage(mainWindow, &offscreenImagePtr,
&offscreenRowBytes, TRUE);

if (err || offscreenImagePtr == NULL)  /* Quit if there was an error */
  ExitToShell();

/* Read all of the objects in from the disk and return the base of the list */
baseObject = LoadWorldFromRsrc(128, 129);

/* Test for failure */
if (baseObject == NULL) {
  ExitToShell();
}

/* Initialize the view */
InitializeView();

/* Initialize the timing variables */
framesSoFar = 0;
originalTickCount = TickCount();

#if __MWERKS__   /* If we're using the metrowerks compiler... */
#if __profile__
  /* Initalize the metrowerks profiler */
  ProfilerInit(collectSummary, bestTimeBase, 100, 20);
#endif
#else       /* Otherwise, we must be using the Think C compiler */
#if __option(profile)
  /* Initialize the Think C profiler */
  InitProfile(100, 20);

  /* Open a file for the Think C profile output to go into */
  freopen("Optimization TC Report", "w", stdout);
```

Continued on next page

Continued from previous page

```
#endif
#endif

   /* Wait until the user clicks before quitting */
   while (!Button())
   {
     /* Erase the offscreen memory map */
     EraseOffscreenImage();

     /* Rotate both objects slightly */
     RotateObjectByAngle(baseObject, 5, 8, 0);
     RotateObjectByAngle(baseObject->nextObject, 4, 12, 3);

     /* Allow for user input */
     HandleUserInput();

     /* Transform the entire object list */
     TransformObjectList();

     /* Draw the objects */
     DrawPolygonList( offscreenImagePtr,
              offscreenRowBytes   );

     /* Copy the offscreen image to the screen */
     CopyImageOntoScreen(mainWindow, 32, 40);

     /* Increment the framecount, calculate fps and draw it on the screen */
     framesSoFar += 1;
     thisTickCount = TickCount();
     framesPerSecond = ((float)framesSoFar / (float)(thisTickCount -
originalTickCount)) * 60;

     /* Convert that fps number into text so we can show it */
     NumToString(framesPerSecond, fpsText);

     /* Draw the string */
     MoveTo(10, 30);
     DrawString(fpsText);

   }

#if __MWERKS__
#if __profile__
   /* Dump out the profiler data to a file */
   ProfilerDump("\pOptimization Profiler Info");

   /* Stop the profiler */
   ProfilerTerm();
#endif
#else
#if __option(profile)
```

```
    /* Dump the profile statistics */
    DumpProfile();
#endif
#endif
}
```

Experiencing the 3D World

Now that you can move around within the 3D world, you can actually begin to "experience" the environment. When you run the application, you'll see a 3D world like the one shown in Figure 17-7.

By using the movement keys, you can move these cubes around and examine them from any direction. You can even move through them, but because backfacing polygons are not being drawn, the cube will seem to disappear as soon as the camera sees "inside" the polygon.

In the next chapters, I'm going to examine interesting ways to use the 3D viewing routines. You'll be creating a walk-through 3D maze similar to those in popular action games. This will be followed by a texture-mapped maze and will culminate in a full working flight simulator. By then, you'll be well on your way to creating the next generation of Macintosh computer games!

FIGURE 17-7

◎ ◎ ◎ ◎ ◎ ◎

The scene consisting of two rotating cubes

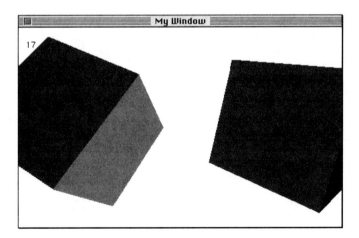

Three-Dimensional Mazes

18

Three-Dimensional Mazes

You hear a chittering from around the corner. Your blood freezes as you ready your laser pistol and slide silently along the wall. You wait until you hear the creature heading away, then you leap around the edge. The green buglike alien hasn't heard you yet, but the lumbering monster behind it has. You scream in surprise, getting off a few shots before you duck behind the edge and out of the reach of your hairy nemesis.

Quick, what kind of game were you just playing? A board game? A 2D sprite game? An Ultima-style adventure game? Not likely. Games that can evoke this kind of fear and excitement are usually of the first-person perspective (3D) variety, the newest and one of the most popular styles of computer game.

In the chapters leading up to this one, you've built all the components you need for a 3D computer game. Now it's time to take advantage of them. In this chapter, you're going to develop a 3D maze that you can walk through. The walls will be created using the polygon-fill routine, so it won't look like a Marathon or Wolfenstein 3D game, but it'll give you a good feel for the techniques necessary for such a game. In the next chapter I'll expand the game to include texture mapping so you can get these effects.

The Maze Layout

The maze will be a simple one, but not because of limitations to the rendering engine; you could create pretty much *any* world using the rendering engine; one with multiple levels, curved passageways, and anything else you can imagine. I'm keeping the maze simple to aid in another problem I haven't dealt with yet: collision detection. (I discussed collision detection in Chapter 8 for the Invaders! game, but 3D collision detection is an entirely different matter.)

To aid in collision detection, you'll design the maze in a grid. The grid can be any size to accommodate a detailed world, but you're going to make yours 10 columns wide and 10 rows deep. Each of these 100 squares can either be occupied by a wall or be empty.

Because you're in the design stage here, you can take a sheet of graph paper and mark off a 10x10 block of squares. Then begin filling in the areas you want to be occupied by walls. Every square must be entirely filled or entirely empty—a wall cannot cut through a square diagonally or fill in just a few edges. Figure 18-1 shows the maze configuration you're going to use in this chapter, but if you want to it shouldn't be difficult to create your own maze.

FIGURE 18-1
◎ ◎ ◎ ◎ ◎ ◎

Before constructing your maze, draw what you want it to look like on a sheet of graph paper

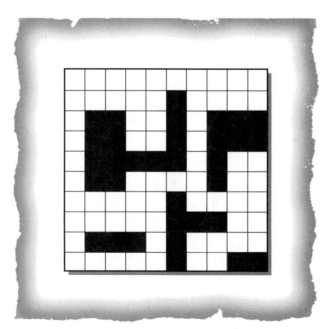

Defining the Maze Objects

The next step is to create the object resources that will be used to render the maze. You can do this very easily using the OBJ3 resource template and a resource editor such as ResEdit or Resourcerer. Before you start defining objects, however, think about how they will be laid out.

Take a look at the sheet of graph paper and choose one edge of the block to be at the "bottom." This edge now becomes the x axis of the maze. In other words, the x coordin.aes of your objects increase as you look from left to right.

That would mean that the other coordinate would be y, right? Well, no. Because you're looking at the map from the top down (i.e., not the same perspective you'll see when it appears on the screen), the y coordinate leads into and out of the page and the z coordinate goes up and down.

This discrepancy can cause some real confusion, because the user is going to be traveling around the maze in the x and z coordinates. In fact, you could even limit the user to not traveling in the y (up and down) coordinate at all.

The next thing you need to resolve before creating the objects is how much area each square takes up. In the previous chapters, each edge of the spinning cube was 160 units wide (I use a generic term *units* because its size is not really defined in pixels). That worked fairly well, so let's stick to it.

The Outer Walls

Let's begin by creating the outer walls of the maze. You can define all four walls as one object, but this presents an interesting problem. All the cubes you've created up to now have been viewed from outside the object. This allowed the backface removal to work correctly since any polygon facing away (i.e., its vertices were defined clockwise) was discarded. If you moved the view inside the cube, the cube would seem to disappear.

But for this maze, it'll be normal to be inside the wall object. If you define this object the same way you define the cube, the walls will always be invisible as long as you are inside them.

To solve this problem, define the walls so that they appear counterclockwise when viewed from inside the object or clockwise when viewed from outside. Because you're not going to allow the user to move outside the object, it'll look correct all the time.

The other question, is how large are the walls? Because the walls have to encompass 10 blocks in each dimension (and you are already decided on 160 units per block), the walls will be 1600 units wide.

In this example, you're not going to have floors or ceilings. Drawing these large polygons that take up most of the screen slows down the 040 processor significantly, and produces abysmal results on an 030 or earlier processor. You still have eight vertices for the object, but only four polygons. If you have a faster processor or you want to see what the environment looks like with floors and ceilings, you can easily add the extra two polygons.

Figure 18-2 shows the definitions for each of the wall's vertices and the ordering of those vertices to create the polygons. In the 3D Maze.rsrc file on the source code disc, you can find the wall object's definition in the OBJ3 #128 resource.

The Inner Walls

Each of the inner walls (which I'll call *barriers* to avoid confusion with the other walls) also has only four polygons because from the user's perspective, the tops or the bottoms of the barriers will never be visible. The barriers are defined using the normal polygon ordering because they'll be viewed from the outside. I'll define each of these objects based on a point at its center. This way, if you have two barriers that are the same shape, you can just create the first barrier, make a copy of it, and change the position of the copy to produce the second barrier.

Before you start defining these objects, however, it would be advantageous to break down the inner walls of the maps into as few objects as possible. For example,

FIGURE 18-2

◎ ◎ ◎ ◎ ◎ ◎

The vertices defining the outer wall

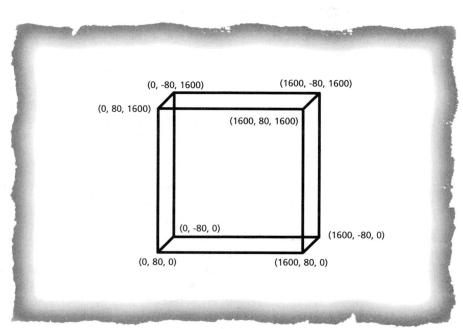

if there is a wall that is three blocks long, instead of creating three objects one block wide, you can create one object that is three blocks wide. However, avoid creating a concave object. In fact, to keep things simple, design each of your objects to have eight vertices. Figure 18-3 shows the map broken down into individual objects, with each of them numbered.

As you can see, the map can be created using only nine barrier objects. Many of them are exact duplicates with only their origin fields changed. To aid in the placement of the objects on this grid, it is helpful to number each line of the grid at an interval of 160 units. But you're placing objects *between* the grid lines so it would be even more helpful to number the *middle* of each grid box. Such a numbering would begin at 80 for the first box in each dimension and increase by 160 for each subsequent box, up to 1520 for the last box, as shown in Figure 18-4.

You can now define the barrier objects. Here are the vertices for the first one:

```
Vertex 0:   -240,    80,    80
Vertex 1:    240,    80,    80
Vertex 2:    240,   -80,    80
Vertex 3:   -240,   -80,    80
Vertex 4:   -240,    80,   -80
Vertex 5:    240,    80,   -80
Vertex 6:    240,   -80,   -80
Vertex 7:   -240,   -80,   -80
```

FIGURE 18-3

◎ ◎ ◎ ◎ ◎ ◎

The inner walls are broken down into individual objects

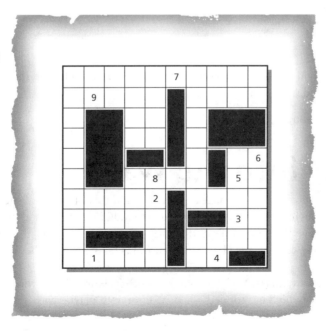

Its polygons are then defined as follows:

```
Polygon 1:  0, 1, 2, 3
Polygon 2:  0, 3, 7, 4
Polygon 3:  1, 5, 6, 2
Polygon 4:  7, 6, 5, 4
```

Its origin is placed where the center of the polygon lies on the map, as easily seen by the grid numbering:

```
Origin: 400, 0, 240
```

Running into the Walls

You now have the entire maze defined, but it's still not very realistic. If you attempt to walk through the maze now, you are able to walk right through each of the barrier walls and through the outer walls of the maze. When this happens, the entire object disappears from view because backface removal is taking care of the polygon on the other side.

Obviously, this isn't what happens in the real world. If you run into something, you expect that you'll be stopped—gently or forcibly, maybe with a broken nose. So now you have to develop some sort of system where you can figure out whether the player has run into another object. This is called *collision detection*. I briefly covered its sprite equivalent in Chapter 8 when you created the Invaders! game.

A Two-Dimensional Picture of a Three-Dimensional World

Although you are now in a three-dimensional environment, you're still going to be using only two-dimensional collision detection. This detection will be similar to that found in Wolfenstein 3D. Because the user can travel only in the x and z coordinate planes, he or she can only run into objects that lie on the same plane.

This makes the algorithm much easier to deal with, but you can go one more step. All the objects defined in the database are rectangular (when viewed from top-down). Better still, the rectangles are formed from evenly spaced squares.

You need a way to keep track of where the objects lie in the world. You could do this through some complex manipulations of the polygons that would tell you what is "inside" and what is "outside" an object. Not only would this be mathematically difficult, it would take a significant amount of CPU time.

An Array of Walls

Instead, you're going to use a simple way of keeping track of objects. All you need to do is define a two-dimensional array as large as the original map. In this case, it'll be 10 rows by 10 columns, or 100 elements. In each position in the array, simply store a Boolean variable telling you whether the square is occupied or vacant.

Then, when you need to figure out if the position coincides with that of a barrier, you can just figure out what square you're standing in (with a simple division) and then do a look-up in the array for that position. If that entry of the array comes back True, you know you've stepped on a wall. If it comes back False, the coast is clear.

Building the Array

Let's look at how to build the array first. Scanning the polygon database to determine which polygons are in which positions would be possible but difficult. Instead, you're going to build an array by hand that mirrors the set up of the polygons. It is important to get each entry correct, because otherwise the player won't be able to move in areas where there is no wall and will be able to walk straight through other walls.

The array is defined as a global in a new file called Map.c. It's just a simple two-dimensional array of Boolean values:

```
Boolean  gBarrierMap[10][10];
```

During the initialization process, go through each element of the array and initialize it to False (i.e., no barrier). Then go through it again and set just those that are occupied to True. It's not a difficult routine, but be careful about typos; they can have drastic effects on gameplay:

```
/**  InitializeMap()
 **
 **  Fills in the global barrier map with the locations of all of the
 **  walls.
 **/
void  InitializeMap(void)
{
  short  i, j;

  /* First initialize them all to FALSE to clear the map */
  for (i = 0; i < 10; i++) {
    for (j = 0; j < 10; j++) {
      gBarrierMap[i][j] = FALSE;
    }
  }

  /* Set up the individual boxes */
  gBarrierMap[0][5] = TRUE;  gBarrierMap[0][8] = TRUE;
  gBarrierMap[0][9] = TRUE;  gBarrierMap[1][1] = TRUE;
  gBarrierMap[1][2] = TRUE;  gBarrierMap[1][3] = TRUE;
  gBarrierMap[1][5] = TRUE;  gBarrierMap[2][5] = TRUE;
  gBarrierMap[2][6] = TRUE;  gBarrierMap[2][7] = TRUE;
  gBarrierMap[3][5] = TRUE;  gBarrierMap[4][1] = TRUE;
  gBarrierMap[4][2] = TRUE;  gBarrierMap[4][7] = TRUE;
  gBarrierMap[5][1] = TRUE;  gBarrierMap[5][2] = TRUE;
  gBarrierMap[5][3] = TRUE;  gBarrierMap[5][4] = TRUE;
  gBarrierMap[5][5] = TRUE;  gBarrierMap[5][7] = TRUE;
  gBarrierMap[6][1] = TRUE;  gBarrierMap[6][2] = TRUE;
  gBarrierMap[6][5] = TRUE;  gBarrierMap[6][7] = TRUE;
  gBarrierMap[6][8] = TRUE;  gBarrierMap[6][9] = TRUE;
  gBarrierMap[7][1] = TRUE;  gBarrierMap[7][2] = TRUE;
  gBarrierMap[7][5] = TRUE;  gBarrierMap[7][7] = TRUE;
  gBarrierMap[7][8] = TRUE;  gBarrierMap[6][9] = TRUE;
  gBarrierMap[8][5] = TRUE;
}
```

Checking against the Array

In the simplest incarnation, checking to see if the player has hit a wall involves indexing into the gBarrierMap array to the square that the player is standing on. However, you have to beware of one more thing. Not only can you not allow a player to walk through a wall, you must also prevent him or her from getting too close to it. If the wall's z coordinate extends to less than 2, the ZClip() function will clip it off, leaving a partial wall drawn in front of the player, which is clearly not good.

It is to this end that I introduce a *slop factor*. This factor is the distance you'll keep the player away from the wall. When the collision detection routine is called, add this slop factor to the player's position before doing the detection, then subtract it and try again. If either case ends up in a collision, treat it as though the player were standing inside a barrier and return True.

I have defined the slop factor as 5, but this is an arbitrary value; if you notice problems with players getting too close to walls, feel free to adjust it.

```
#define kCollisionSlopFactor    5
```

To detect which square the user is standing in, divide the x and z coordinates by the size of each square, which I've defined below:

```
#define kGridSize              160
```

Begin by adding the slop factor to the x and z coordinates and then dividing the result by the grid size:

```
/* Add the slop factor to the coordinates and
 * convert them to fit within the confines
 * of the map (which is 1/160 scale).
 */
mapX = (x + kCollisionSlopFactor) / kGridSize;
mapZ = (z + kCollisionSlopFactor) / kGridSize;
```

Then compare the coordinates with the array to see if you have a hit:

```
/* Check to see if this position intersects a barrier */
if (gBarrierMap[mapZ][mapX])
  return TRUE;
```

Next, repeat the process, this time by subtracting the slop factor from the coordinate:

```
/* Now subtract the slop factor from the coordinates
 * and try again
 */
mapX = (x - kCollisionSlopFactor) / kGridSize;
mapZ = (z - kCollisionSlopFactor) / kGridSize;

/* Check to see if this position intersects a barrier */
if (gBarrierMap[mapZ][mapX])
  return TRUE;
```

There is another case you have to beware of. Not only can you not allow the player to go through the barriers in the middle of the world, you can't let him or her go through the walls along the outside. You can't check the array for this, but you can check to see if the position is less than 0 or greater than 1600 (the world's size) in either the x or z dimension. If it is, tell the calling function that a collision was found.

This process is actually done before you check for collisions against barriers and it also involves adding and subtracting the slop factor from the x and z coordinates:

```
/* See if the position is outside the bounds of the map */
if (  (x < kCollisionSlopFactor) ||
      (x > (kGridSize * 10) + kCollisionSlopFactor) ||
      (z < kCollisionSlopFactor) ||
      (z > (kGridSize * 10) + kCollisionSlopFactor))
    return TRUE;
```

Here is the complete code for CheckBarrierCollision():

```
/**
 **   CheckBarrierCollision()
 **
 **   Checks to see if the view position is intersecting one of the
 **   barriers.
 **/
Boolean  CheckBarrierCollision(short x, short z)
{
  short  mapX, mapZ;

  /* See if the position is outside the bounds of the map */
  if (  (x < kCollisionSlopFactor) ||
        (x > (kGridSize * 10) + kCollisionSlopFactor) ||
        (z < kCollisionSlopFactor) ||
        (z > (kGridSize * 10) + kCollisionSlopFactor))
      return TRUE;

  /* Add the slop factor to the coordinates and
   * convert them to fit within the confines
   * of the map (which is 1/160 scale).
   */
  mapX = (x + kCollisionSlopFactor) / kGridSize;
  mapZ = (z + kCollisionSlopFactor) / kGridSize;

  /* Check to see if this position intersects a barrier */
  if (gBarrierMap[mapZ][mapX])
    return TRUE;

  /* Now subtract the slop factor from the coordinates
   * and try again
   */
  mapX = (x - kCollisionSlopFactor) / kGridSize;
  mapZ = (z - kCollisionSlopFactor) / kGridSize;

  /* Check to see if this position intersects a barrier */
  if (gBarrierMap[mapZ][mapX])
    return TRUE;
```

```
/* No collision was detected */
return FALSE;
}
```

Checking Collision while Moving

The best place to hook in the detection is while you're moving the player, in the MoveViewForwardAndBack() function. You're not going to worry about detecting for collision in the other view-moving functions (MoveViewToPosition() and MoveViewByDistance()) because you are assuming those functions aren't going to be used directly in response to the user's movements.

One way you could handle the detection is to calculate the new location of the user and, if he or she is positioned too close to a barrier, not move the view at all. This would work, but it would leave a peculiar situation. Figure 18-5 shows the player walking toward a wall at an angle. When the view reaches that wall, the player might expect that the x movement would stop, but the z movement would continue, and the view would start "sliding" along the wall. This is a situation that is found in many 3D games and, although it may not be entirely realistic, players have come to expect, if not depend, on it.

To account for this, test the x and z movement separately. After the movementInX and movementInZ variables are calculated, perform a couple of tests. First add the movementInX value to the view's position and test for a collision. If there is a collision, assume the user is too close to a wall in the x dimension so you set the movementInX value to 0.

FIGURE 18-5

◉ ◉ ◉ ◉ ◉ ◉

The player slides along the z dimension

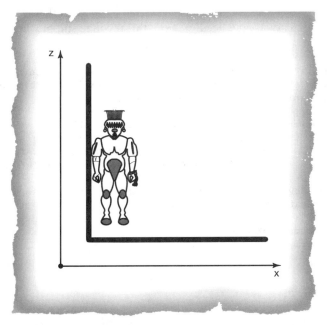

```
/* Check to see if movement in X would intersect us with
 * a barrier
 */
if ( CheckBarrierCollision(
            gCameraViewData.viewXPos + movementInX,
            gCameraViewData.viewZPos  ))
{
  /* Moving this distance in X would run into a wall.
   * Eliminate this movement.
   */
  movementInX = 0;
}
```

Then check to see if a movement in the z dimension will run up against an inner wall:

```
/* Check to see if movement in Z would intersect us with
 * a barrier
 */
if ( CheckBarrierCollision(
            gCameraViewData.viewXPos,
            gCameraViewData.viewZPos + movementInZ  ))
{
  /* Moving this distance in Z would run into a wall.
   * Eliminate this movement.
   */
  movementInZ = 0;
}
```

Finally, check the movement in *both* x and z to see if that leads you into an inner wall. Note that you only need to check this if you're still moving in both the x and z directions:

```
/* If we're still moving in both dimensions, add _both_ values
 * onto the camera's position, and test again. If this one fails,
 * we want to set both movement values to 0.
 */
if ((movementInZ != 0) && (movementInX != 0)) {
  if ( CheckBarrierCollision(
              gCameraViewData.viewXPos + movementInX,
              gCameraViewData.viewZPos + movementInZ  ))
  {
    /* Moving this distance in X and Z would run into a
     * wall. Eliminate this movement.
     */
    movementInX = 0;
    movementInZ = 0;
  }
}
```

At this point, move the view (if any movement is left):

```
/* If we've still got somewhere to go, move the view */
if ((movementInX != 0) && (movementInZ != 0))
  MoveViewByDistance(movementInX, movementInY, movementInZ);
```

Listing 18-1 is the complete MoveViewForwardAndBack() function.

Listing 18-1 The MoveViewForwardAndBack() routine

```
/**
 ** MoveViewForwardAndBack()
 **
 ** Moves the view by a specified distance forward or backward,
 ** based on the view's rotation values.
 **/
void MoveViewForwardAndBack(short distance)
{
  short  movementInX, movementInY, movementInZ;
  Fixed24  unitX, unitY, unitZ;
  /* Convert the view's direction into three fixed numbers
   * representing a unit vector facing in the direction of
   * the view's rotation.
   */
  AngleVectorsToXYZ( gCameraViewData.viewXAngle,
                     gCameraViewData.viewYAngle,
                     gCameraViewData.viewZAngle,
                     &unitX,
                     &unitY,
                     &unitZ );

  /* Find the distance in each dimension that we're moving */
  movementInX = (distance * unitX) >> 8;
  movementInY = (distance * unitY) >> 8;
  movementInZ = (distance * unitZ) >> 8;

  /* Check to see if movement in X would intersect us with
   * a barrier
   */
  if ( CheckBarrierCollision(
            gCameraViewData.viewXPos + movementInX,
            gCameraViewData.viewZPos ))
  {
    /* Moving this distance in X would run into a wall.
     * Eliminate this movement.
     */
    movementInX = 0;
  }

  /* Check to see if movement in Z would intersect us with
   * a barrier
```

Continued on next page

Continued from previous page

```
  */
  if (  CheckBarrierCollision(
              gCameraViewData.viewXPos,
              gCameraViewData.viewZPos + movementInZ  ))
  {
    /* Moving this distance in Z would run into a wall.
     * Eliminate this movement.
     */
    movementInZ = 0;
  }

  /* If we're still moving in both dimensions, add _both_ values
   * onto the camera's position, and test again. If this one fails,
   * we want to set both movement values to 0.
   */
  if ((movementInZ != 0) && (movementInX != 0)) {
    if (  CheckBarrierCollision(
                gCameraViewData.viewXPos + movementInX,
                gCameraViewData.viewZPos + movementInZ  ))
    {
      /* Moving this distance in X and Z would run into a
       * wall. Eliminate this movement.
       */
      movementInX = 0;
      movementInZ = 0;
    }
  }

  /* If we've still got somewhere to go, move the view */
  if ((movementInX != 0) || (movementInZ != 0))
    MoveViewByDistance(movementInX, movementInY, movementInZ);
}
```

Limitations of This Collision
Detection Routine

It is worth noting that this collision detection routine will work only for the case I've designed: a flat two-dimensional maze with square objects. It won't work for the flight simulator, so when you reach that point, you'll be going back to the old MoveViewForwardAndBack() function.

The collision detection routine could be expanded to work on walls that are not always perpendicular, but it would involve a little more math when the player is in a square that has a partial polygon in it. With a little more work, you could also modify the routine to handle polygons that are triangles.

Realistic Walking

Most of the popular games in the 3D maze genre have an interesting effect when the player is walking—the view bobs up and down, giving the illusion of walking. The effect isn't very hard to implement in a 3D environment, so let's take a stab at it and see what you come up with.

▓ The Confused Brain

Most of us don't really notice that the world bobs up and down as you walk, but that's because our minds compensate for this effect. However, if you're sitting still and playing a game, your mind *knows* that you're not actually moving and thus no compensation occurs.

Because this disparity between games and the real world exists, your mind can get confused and some people experience dizziness or nausea when watching a game that bobs up and down. Nonetheless, it is a popular effect and it does make the walking feeling a little more complete. If you implement the "walking bob" into your game, it's a good idea to include a preference that allows the user to turn it off if he or she doesn't react well to it.

One very simple way to go about it is to define a constant "bobbing speed" and adjust the view's y coordinate between two extremes at this speed. This produces the type of motion illustrated in Figure 18-6. As you can see, it's not very smooth and it doesn't mirror real motion very well.

A better solution is to develop a way of giving the user a smooth transition between going up and going down. In other words, turn the motion into a path that looks more like a sine wave.

A Motion Table

This motion could be calculated by actually using the sine wave function and doing some math to figure out the player's y position at any moment. But if you think about it for a moment, there is a much more elegant solution. You can store a table of values indicating the y direction and speed the user is traveling. Then whenever the user moves forward, the next value in this table will be retrieved and the view's y position will be changed by that amount. When the table is exhausted, just start again from the beginning.

The key to getting a smooth curve is to provide slow changes when the view is close to its maximum or minimum y value and fast changes in between. This will, in effect,

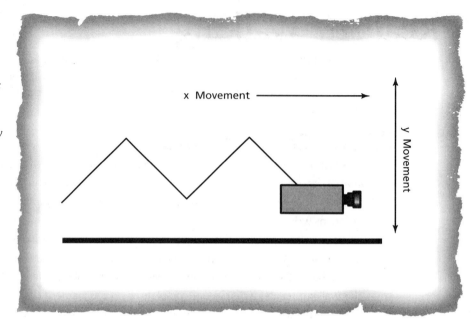

emulate the sine wave table but without any complex calculations. Here is a sample motion table that I'll use for this chapter:

```
short    gBounceDistance[18] = {
  -1, -2, -4, -5, -6, -5, -4, -2, -1, 1, 2, 4, 5, 6, 5, 4, 2, 1
};
```

Figure 18-7 shows what the motion will look like using this array. As you can see, it is much more realistic than before.

Implementing the Bob

Probably the best place to implement view bobbing is in the HandleUserInput() function. It's easy to hook in code here that reacts when the player moves forward or backward.

This routine will need to keep track of which element in the motion table it accessed last time; the best way to do this is through a static variable. You could initialize it to start at the beginning of the motion table, but that would start the view moving up immediately, which could be a little strange. Instead, start the index at a later point in the table—entry 15 was chosen arbitrarily.

```
static short        currentBounceEntry = 15;
```

FIGURE 18-7

◉ ◉ ◉ ◉ ◉ ◉

By using a pseudo-sine table, you get much smoother movement in the y dimension

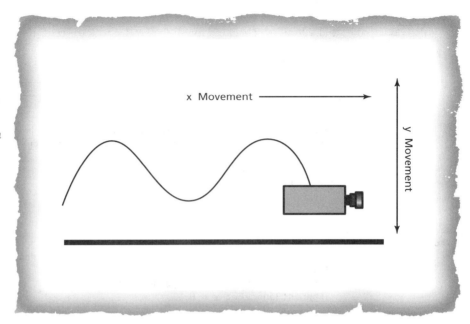

You'll also want to know if the user did something in this turn that would warrant changing the view's height. To this end, declare a Boolean variable called doTheBounce:

```
Boolean        doTheBounce;
```

Before any of the keys are checked, doTheBounce is initialized to False, indicating that the player shouldn't bounce:

```
/* Start off by assuming that we won't be bouncing the player
 * in this frame
 */
doTheBounce = FALSE;
```

If the player then moves forward or backward, the doTheBounce variable is set to True:

```
/* Check for moving the camera forward */
if (CheckKeyMap(ourKeyMap, kKeyMoveForward)) {
  MoveViewForwardAndBack(15);  /* Move camera forward 15 units */
  doTheBounce = TRUE;  /* Bounce the player */
}
if (CheckKeyMap(ourKeyMap, kKeyMoveBack)) {
  MoveViewForwardAndBack(-15);  /* Move camera back 15 units */
  doTheBounce = TRUE;  /* Bounce the player */
}
```

After you finish checking for all the keys, check to see if the player is bouncing:

```
/* Handle the player bounce, if appropriate */
if (doTheBounce) {
```

Then retrieve the bounce distance from the motion array and advance the array index:

```
  /* How far are we changing the player's height this turn? */
  bounceDistance = gBounceDistance[currentBounceEntry];

  /* Advance the array entry */
  currentBounceEntry++;
```

Next, make sure the array index hasn't exceeded the array's size and reset it to 0 if it has:

```
  /* Check to see if we've reached the end of the array */
  if (currentBounceEntry == kBounceArraySize) {
    /* Start over from the beginning */
    currentBounceEntry = 0;
  }
```

Now all you need to do is to add the bounce distance onto the view's current y position with a simple call to MoveViewByDistance():

```
  /* Change the view's y coordinate by the bounce distance */
  MoveViewByDistance(0, bounceDistance, 0);
}
```

Footsteps in the Dark

Another thing you can do to add to motion is sound. Once again, the asynchronous sound player comes to the rescue. The user makes one complete step each time through the motion array. If you play the footstep sound each time the array's index is reset, the sound will be synchronized with the motion of the user.

To send a sound to the asynchronous player, you need to load it into memory first. Because you don't want to load the sound every time through this loop, you can declare the sound handle as a static variable and initialize it to Null:

```
  static SndListHandle  footstepSound = NULL;
```

Then, each time through the loop, check to see if the footstepSound variable is still Null. If it is, load the sound resource and attach it to this variable. Because the footstepSound variable is now non-Null, the resource will be loaded only once.

```
/* Check to see if our sound has been initialized yet. If it
 * hasn't, load it in now.
 */
if (footstepSound == NULL) {
  footstepSound = (SndListHandle)GetResource('snd ', 128);
}
```

Now whenever you've reached the end of the motion array, you can play the asynchronous sound, like this:

```
/* Check to see if we've reached the end of the array */
if (currentBounceEntry == kBounceArraySize) {
  /* Start over from the beginning */
  currentBounceEntry = 0;

  /* When the player bounces, play the footsteps
   * sound.
   */
  PlayAsyncSound(footstepSound, 0);
}
```

This is all that's necessary to implement both the motion bob and realistic footsteps into the maze game. Listing 18-2 is the complete source code for the new HandleUserInput() routine.

Listing 18-2 *The HandleUserInput()*

```
/**
 ** HandleUserInput()
 **
 ** Checks the keyboard for any keys held down and moves the camera
 ** accordingly.
 **/
void HandleUserInput(void)
{
  unsigned char       ourKeyMap[16];
  static short        currentBounceEntry = 15;
  Boolean             doTheBounce;
  static SndListHandle footstepSound = NULL;

  /* Check to see if our sound has been initialized yet. If it
   * hasn't, load it in now.
   */
  if (footstepSound == NULL) {
    footstepSound = (SndListHandle)GetResource('snd ', 128);
  }

  /* Get the key map */
  GetKeys((unsigned long *)ourKeyMap);
```

Continued on next page

Continued from previous page

```
/* Start off by assuming that we won't be bouncing the player
 * in this frame
 */
doTheBounce = FALSE;

/* Check for moving the camera forward */
if (CheckKeyMap(ourKeyMap, kKeyMoveForward)) {
  MoveViewForwardAndBack(15);  /* Move camera forward 15 units */
  doTheBounce = TRUE;  /* Bounce the player */
}
if (CheckKeyMap(ourKeyMap, kKeyMoveBack)) {
  MoveViewForwardAndBack(-15);  /* Move camera back 15 units */
  doTheBounce = TRUE;  /* Bounce the player */
}
if (CheckKeyMap(ourKeyMap, kKeyTurnLeft))
  RotateViewByAngle(0, -5, 0);  /* Rotate camera -5 degrees on y */
if (CheckKeyMap(ourKeyMap, kKeyTurnRight))
  RotateViewByAngle(0, 5, 0);    /* Rotate camera 5 degrees on y */

/* Handle the player bounce, if appropriate */
if (doTheBounce) {
  short     bounceDistance;

  /* How far are we changing the player's height this turn? */
  bounceDistance = gBounceDistance[currentBounceEntry];

  /* Advance the array entry */
  currentBounceEntry++;

  /* Check to see if we've reached the end of the array */
  if (currentBounceEntry == kBounceArraySize) {
    /* Start over from the beginning */
    currentBounceEntry = 0;

    /* When the player bounces, play the footsteps
     * sound.
     */
    PlayAsyncSound(footstepSound, 0);
  }

  /* Change the view's y coordinate by the bounce distance */
  MoveViewByDistance(0, bounceDistance, 0);
}
}
```

For a humorous variation, which you might call "Walking on Fowl," try changing the GetResource() call to load in sound ID 5 instead of 128.

Hooking It All In

You've now designed all the elements of the 3D maze game. The only remaining routine is main(), where you have a few more things to initialize now.

Because none of the objects is moving, you can eliminate the RotateObjectByAngle() calls. The asynchronous sound package has to be initialized now, along with the new maze file. Lastly, the view is placed at the coordinate (80, 0, 80)—you can't have it starting out at (0, 0, 0) any more because that's now the intersection of two walls.

Listing 18-3 is the complete new main() function.

Listing 18-3 *The new main( ) routine*

```
/**
** main()
**
**/
void main(void)
{
  Rect          windowRect;
  WindowPtr     mainWindow;
  Ptr           offscreenImagePtr;
  unsigned long offscreenRowBytes;
  OSErr         err;
  Object3D      *baseObject;
  long          thisTickCount, originalTickCount;
  long          framesSoFar;
  long          framesPerSecond;
  Str255        fpsText;

  /* Initialize everything we need */
  InitGraf(&qd.thePort);
  InitWindows();
  InitCursor();

  /* Initialize the sin/cos look-up tables */
  InitializeSinCosTable();

  /* Set the window size */
  SetRect(&windowRect, 0, 0, kWindowWidth, kWindowHeight);

  /* Offset the window rect so that the window does not appear
   * under the menu bar.
   */
  OffsetRect(&windowRect, 32, 40);

  /* Create the window */
  mainWindow = CreateWindow(&windowRect);

  /* Set the clipping boundaries */
```

Continued on next page

Continued from previous page

```
     InitializeWorldBounds( 0,
                            kWindowWidth-1,
                            0,
                            kWindowHeight-1,
                            2,
                            10000);

  /* Initialize the maze map */
  InitializeMap();

  /* Initialize the async sound player */
  InitializeAsyncSoundPlayer();

  SetPort(mainWindow);

  /* Create the offscreen image */
  err = CreateOffscreenImage( mainWindow,
                              &offscreenImagePtr,
                              &offscreenRowBytes,
                              TRUE       );

  if (err || offscreenImagePtr == NULL)  /* Quit if there was an error */
    ExitToShell();

  /* Read all of the objects in from the disk and return
   * the base of the list
   */
  baseObject = LoadWorldFromRsrc(128, 137);

  /* Test for failure */
  if (baseObject == NULL) {
    ExitToShell();
  }

  /* Initialize the view */
  InitializeView();

  /* Initialize the timing variables */
  framesSoFar = 0;
  originalTickCount = TickCount();

#if __MWERKS__   /* If we're using the metrowerks compiler... */
#if __profile__
  /* Initialize the metrowerks profiler */
  ProfilerInit(collectSummary, bestTimeBase, 100, 20);
#endif
#else      /* Otherwise, we must be using the Think C compiler */
#if __option(profile)
  /* Initialize the Think C profiler */
  InitProfile(100, 20);

  /* Open a file for the Think C profile output to go into */
  freopen("Optimization TC Report", "w", stdout);
```

```
#endif
#endif

   MoveViewToPosition(80, 0, 80);

   /* Wait until the user clicks before quitting */
   while (!Button())
   {
     /* Erase the offscreen memory map */
     EraseOffscreenImage();

     /* Allow for user input */
     HandleUserInput();

     /* Transform the entire object list */
     TransformObjectList();

     /* Draw the objects */
     DrawPolygonList( offscreenImagePtr,
             offscreenRowBytes   );

     /* Copy the offscreen image to the screen */
     CopyImageOntoScreen(mainWindow, 32, 40);

     /* Increment the framecount, calculate fps
      * and draw it on the screen
      */
     framesSoFar += 1;
     thisTickCount = TickCount();
     framesPerSecond = ((float)framesSoFar /
                     (float)(thisTickCount - originalTickCount)) * 60;

     /* Convert that fps number into text so we can show it */
     NumToString(framesPerSecond, fpsText);

     /* Draw the string */
     MoveTo(10, 30);
     DrawString(fpsText);

   }

#if __MWERKS__
#if __profile__
   /* Dump out the profiler data to a file */
   ProfilerDump("\pOptimization Profiler Info");

   /* Stop the profiler */
   ProfilerTerm();
#endif
#else
#if __option(profile)
```

Continued on next page

Continued from previous page

```
  /* Dump the profile statistics */
  DumpProfile();
#endif
#endif
}
```

Moving around the Maze

When you run the maze application, use the standard control keys (either the keypad or the arrow keys) to navigate. When moving around, you may still notice some hidden surface problems. The Painter's algorithm doesn't work well with many polygons cramped in a small area, but some tweaking would probably resolve these problems. In the next chapter, I'll be looking at a new method of hidden surface removal that is more effective for your purposes.

Figure 18-8 shows two views of the user navigating around the maze. Despite the impressive nature of the maze you've created, you're not making very full use of the

FIGURE 18-8

Two views of the 3D maze

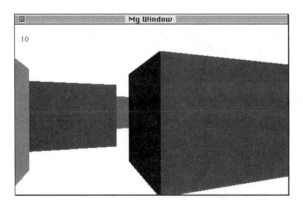

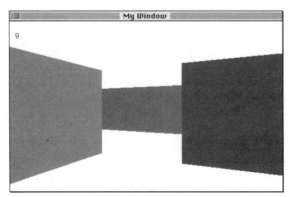

3D engine because you're dealing with only two dimensions of movement and the engine can deal with three.

You can now go in two directions. You can stay with this type of maze layout and reduce the complexity of the 3D engine or you can create a world that *does* take advantage of the engine's nature.

In the next two chapters, you're actually going to be doing both. In Chapter 19, you'll be adding an impressive feature to the maze—texture mapping. You'll be designing a texture-mapping algorithm that can deal with true three-dimensional surfaces and using it to improve the maze game.

In Chapter 20, you'll be using the 3D engine to create a flight simulator. Flight simulators require a true 3D engine because you can move in any direction and rotate to any angle (at least until your plane stalls), so they are well suited to the work you've done on the graphics engine so far.

19

Texture Mapping

come tutti sono i manuelli... li quali... bono... a sia
e i gra... si... le... ti a... a... e fa a... ano di bo ni
... a... e... la... la... permane... la... manubella pegi que...
a for... e più i... omo... bi...

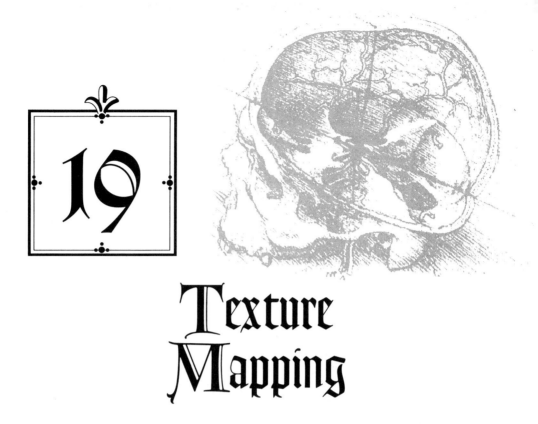

19

Texture Mapping

Although the process of texture mapping has been around for years in computer graphics and rendering, it is a relatively new concept in games. This is primarily because texture mapping is computationally expensive and requires a great deal of memory. However, as you are no doubt aware, personal computers that are used for games have been gaining both speed and memory, so the time for texture mapping has finally come to the gaming industry.

Although not the first, the legendary DOOM is certainly the most popular texture-mapping game that ushered in the next generation. If you're not familiar with DOOM, it involves running around a maze with texture-mapped walls and floors and shooting anything that moves.

The Macintosh answer to DOOM was Marathon, which I've mentioned several times in this book as a prime example of a well-designed game. The primary feature that makes these games both technically amazing and incredibly exciting is that they are *fast*. Both these games exhibit texture-mapping speed that, until they came out, was thought to be impossible.

Tricks and Cheats

Both Marathon and DOOM, as well as countless other games of the same genre, cheat. That is to say, they don't use true texture mapping to create their environment. The entire DOOM or Marathon world consists of walls, floors, and ceilings, plus a few bitmap sprites here and there. You can turn side to side and, in Marathon, you can look up and down, but only a limited distance. In neither game can you *roll*, or rotate yourself on the z axis. Therefore, every floor and every ceiling is always perfectly horizontal and every wall is always perfectly vertical.

This isn't to say that these two games are poorly designed. In fact, they succeed in submersing you so deeply in their environment that you don't even notice the limitations. The mark of a good game is not what it *can't* do but what it convinces you it *can* do.

In this chapter, I'm going to look at how these games achieve their environment but I'm also going to look at a different kind of texture mapping in more detail. This is *freeform* texture mapping and it is truly three dimensional.

Raycasting

The basic graphics engine of DOOM or Marathon is very different from the one you've been building. In your graphics engine, when you want to draw a frame, you look through the database of polygons and draw each polygon that is facing the viewer in a specific order. This technique is called *raycasting*.

The pseudo-texture-mapping engine instead draws the scene by scanning across the viewport one column at a time. For every column it has to draw, it checks the polygon database to see if any polygons are visible within this strip. It then calculates which polygon is the closest, pulls the texture from that polygon, and stretches a row of it out until it fills the proper height on the viewport.

The principle components of this engine's operation are as follows:

 It calculates which polygons are visible within each row of the viewport.

It calculates the height of the polygon when viewed from a specific distance.

It finds which column of the polygon's texture map will be shown on the screen.

It stretches the texture map to fill the correct height.

Ray Tracing

The first step taken by the pseudo-texture-mapping engine involves a process similar to the photorealistic raytracing function found in high-end 3D rendering packages. Ray tracing is done by taking each pixel on the screen and "casting" a virtual ray from that pixel into the world behind it. The angle of that ray can be changed, but typically the span from the left to the right side of the screen covers approximately a 30° field of view.

The ray is then compared to each polygon in the database to see if it hit any of them. When the engine has determined which, if any, polygons the ray has intersected, it calculates which one is closest to the viewer, finds the color on that polygon, and draws it on the screen (in a ray tracing engine, the polygon could also be transparent or reflective, in which case the engine would have to continue tracing until it hit another polygon). Of course, in high-end graphics programs, the process is much more involved than this, but this description will suffice for now.

Ray tracing produces excellent results, but it's *slow*. The pseudo-texture-mapping engine, instead of casting a ray for every pixel on the viewport, casts one for every *column* on the viewport. This technique has come to be known as *raycasting*, although raycasting originally meant the same thing as ray tracing.

Casting through the Viewport

Figure 19-1 shows a series of rays being cast through the viewport. If the viewport is 640 pixels wide (a common Macintosh screen width), then 640 rays will be cast for each frame drawn. If the game expects to draw 30 fps, it's clear that the raycasting will have to be fast.

Each ray that is cast is then compared with every polygon in the database (or, more likely, every polygon that hasn't already been rejected by some previous operation). In most games, the ray will always have to hit at least one polygon because the player is normally surrounded by walls (even when looking into outer space; the space is simulated by texturing a wall with stars).

All the intersected polygons are then compared to see which is the closest. From there, it is a relatively simple process to see how tall the polygon is and then to stretch it out and draw it on the current column.

Wolfenstein 3D comprises this process. DOOM and Marathon have additional enhancements to the engine that allow them to have walls that do not reach entirely to the ceiling or floor. When one of these polygons is hit, a partial column is drawn on the screen and the next polygon the ray hits is also processed to draw anything that extends above or below behind the shorter polygon.

FIGURE 19-1

◎ ◎ ◎ ◎ ◎ ◎

*Rays being cast
through the
viewport; one
ray per column*

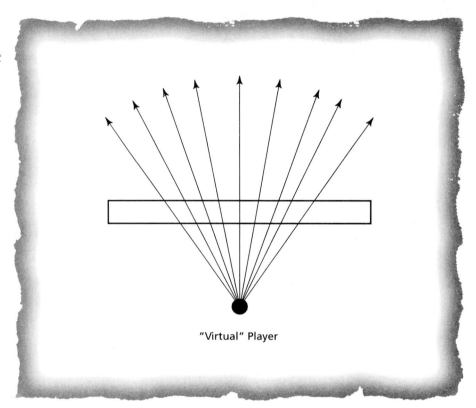

"Virtual" Player

Database Organization

An important aspect of Marathon and similar games is how the database is organized. Figure 19-2 shows a top-down view of the player standing inside a Marathon environment. The player is always inside a two-dimensional polygon that stretches along the x and z coordinate planes. When the rays are cast, each ray *must* hit one of the edges of this polygon. In Marathon, however, many of the polygons' edges do not have any height or depth. So the polygon the player is standing in may have a wall along two or three of its edges, but the other edges may be entirely open or may have a partial wall.

If some of the rays hit an edge that does not have a wall, the engine can check to see which polygons in the database share that particular edge. Because there is no wall here, the engine will always find at least one polygon that shares the edge and it can continue to look for polygon intersections from there until it finally does encounter a wall, which it then draws.

Each of the polygons can also have a floor and a ceiling height. If, while casting, the ray enters a polygon that has a higher floor or a lower ceiling than the previous poly-

FIGURE 19-2

◎ ◎ ◎ ◎ ◎ ◎

*Marathon's
database is
organized so
that the player
is always inside
a polygon and
adjacent
polygons can
easily be found
to cut down on
the ray-polygon
intersection
work*

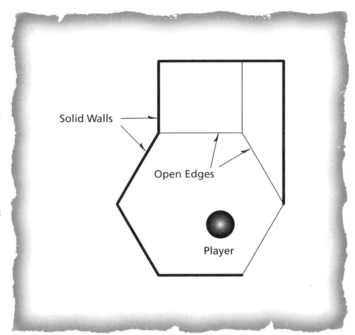

gon (i.e., the floor or ceiling changes height at that point), a segment from the first poly-gon is drawn to fill in the gap.

Other elements in the game, such as monsters or items the player can pick up, are then drawn on top of the completed image. These items have been prerendered in a 3D package in each of their possible orientations and are stored in a bitmap look-up table. They are scaled to the proper size before being drawn into the scene.

Freeform Texture Mapping

If you have ever played a game called Descent, you know that it does not use raycast-ing for its texture-mapping engine. In Descent, the player can roll, twist, turn, and anything else you can imagine in a true three-dimensional environment. And the complete environment—walls, floors, and ceilings—is texture mapped.

Games like Descent use a 3D engine like the one you've been developing in this book, but instead of filling each polygon with a solid color, they apply a bitmapped image to each pixel. This is called *freeform texture mapping* and it is based on the idea that each of the polygon's vertices corresponds to a single point on a two-dimensional texture map.

For example, look at Figure 19-3. A single polygon has been defined in three-dimensional space, but each of its vertices is associated with a corner of the texture map. When you draw the polygon on the screen, you stretch and deform the two-dimensional texture map so that its corners match up with the polygon's vertices and you get the result shown in Figure 19-4. Although the figures do not show it, this also applies to polygons that have fewer or greater than four vertices. The corresponding points in the texture map do not necessarily have to be placed at the corners.

If you continue to draw all the polygons in your scene using this texture mapping, you end up with a complete texture-mapped environment that you can fly through at full tilt (assuming the processor can keep up).

Affine Texture Mapping

In the texture-mapping engine you're going to be using in this chapter, you use a method called *interpolation* to map the entire texture map onto the surface of the polygon. Interpolation is a method of estimating a series of values between two known values; you will use it repeatedly throughout the texture-mapped drawing routine.

The 3D engine has been built to allow for additional polygon rendering methods easily. The texture mapping will merely be one more rendering method tacked on to the engine; call the new routine TextureMapDrawPoly().

TextureMapDrawPoly() will use many of the same polygon methods created in PolygonFillDrawPolygon(). It draws the polygon one scanline (or row) at a time, constantly drawing between two edges. In this case, however, you're going to be filling in the pixels with a bitmapped image instead of a solid color.

Because each of the vertices of the polygon is associated with a point on the texture map, as you're drawing an edge between vertices (as you do using the polygon-fill drawing algorithm), you know the corresponding line being drawn on the texture map. In most cases, the edges of the polygon will correspond to the four corners of the texture map, but there is no reason why this must be the case. You can map the vertices to any place in the texture map you like.

Let's look at how you're going to perform this texture mapping. Figure 19-5 shows a polygon to be drawn on the screen along with its corresponding texture map. As you begin to draw this polygon, start with the edge between vertex 0 and 1 and the edge between vertex 3 and 0. The next step is to imagine a line on the texture map between vertex 0 and 1 and another line between 3 and 0. In this case, because the vertices are mapped to the corners of the texture map, it's easy, because the first edge corresponds to the left edge of the map and the second edge corresponds to the top.

Now as you're drawing each scanline between the polygon edges, you're also going to be figuratively drawing a line between the two edges on the texture map. In Figure

FIGURE 19-3
◉ ◉ ◉ ◉ ◉ ◉
Each of the polygon's vertices has an associated point on the texture map

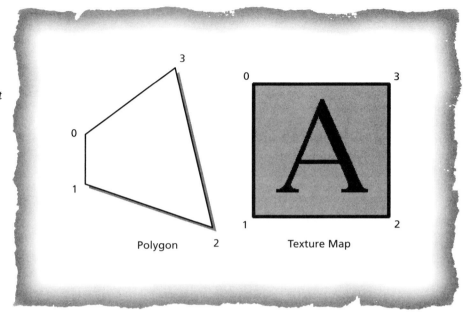

FIGURE 19-4
◉ ◉ ◉ ◉ ◉ ◉
The texture-mapped polygon

FIGURE 19-5

Preparing to
texture map a
polygon

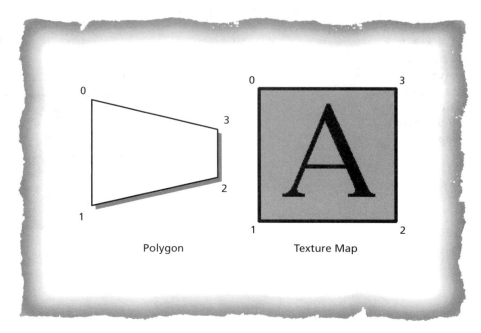

19-6, the scanline has reached a point halfway between edges 3 and 0. However, at this point, the beginning of the scanline is only about one-sixth of the way between edges 0 and 1. As you're drawing this line, you need to know what pixels to pull from the texture map, so draw an imaginary line on the texture map corresponding to the same points. As you can see, this line touches the black edges of the texture map at the beginning and end and a light gray in the middle, so this line of pixels is stretched out to draw this scanline.

When the scanline hits edge 3, begin drawing lines between edge 0-1 and 2-3 on the polygon. At the same time, shift the line on the texture map to the same orientation, as shown in Figure 19-7. As you can see, at this point, you've started to draw the top of the A in the texture map.

Now the right side of the scanline will work its way down the texture map much more quickly than the left side, which will stretch out the left side of the A and compress the right edge, giving you the proper result. Figure 19-8 shows the final result of texture mapping this polygon.

This form of texture mapping, called *affine texture mapping*, works very well and is the method you'll be using in this chapter. It does, however, have problems.

Perspective Texture Mapping

When a polygon is viewed at an angle, some of the vertices will be farther from the viewer than others. If you look at a set of lines that are perpendicular to you but parallel

FIGURE 19-6

◎ ◎ ◎ ◎ ◎ ◎

The scanline has reached halfway between edges 0 and 3, so the corresponding texture-map line is at the same place

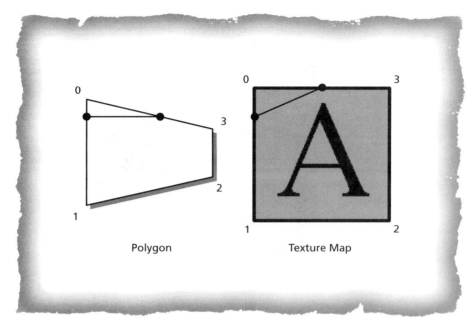

Polygon Texture Map

FIGURE 19-7

◎ ◎ ◎ ◎ ◎ ◎

When edge 3-0 has finished, switch to edge 2-3 on the polygon and at the same time switch to edge 2-3 on the texture map

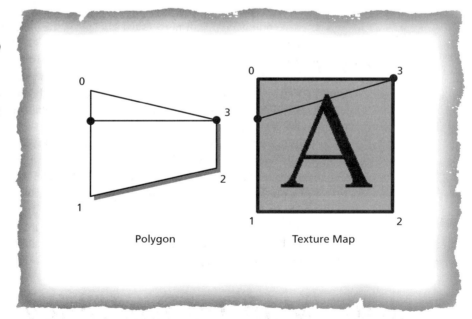

Polygon Texture Map

FIGURE 19-8

◉ ◉ ◉ ◉ ◉ ◉

*The final result
of the texture-
mapped
polygon*

to each other extending into the distance (such as a fence), the more distant lines appear to be closer together than the closer ones, as shown in Figure 19-9. The Texture-Mapping algorithm, however, will draw each of these lines the same distance apart.

A technique called *perspective texture mapping* attempts to resolve this problem by accounting for the z coordinate of the vertices farther from the viewer. However, this process takes additional processor time and for most games, affine texture mapping will produce an effect that is good enough.

Affine texture mapping's limitations become most apparent when viewing large polygons, especially ones that are very close to the viewer. If you can manage to keep most texture mapping a certain distance away from the viewer (which is easy for a flight simulator—if the player is flying that low, he or she is going to crash!), these limitations shouldn't be too bad.

You are going to be doing a form of compensation for the limitations of affine texture mapping, but it's not as involved as perspective texture mapping. I'll examine this compensation later in the chapter.

Texture Map Transparency

You gain one bonus from texture mapping: *transparency*. Because the algorithm is already expensive, you can add this feature without slowing down the texture mapping very

FIGURE 19-9

◉ ◉ ◉ ◉ ◉ ◉

If you view parallel lines from a perspective, they appear to get closer together as the distance increases

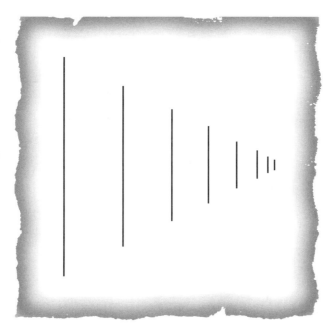

much. While copying the texture map data, the routine can first check to see if the current texture map pixel is a certain value and, if it is, just not copy it. You're going to use the value of 0, or pure white. Although this does keep you from using a solid white color in your textures, if this became a problem, you can simply choose another color.

As an example of this feature, look at Figure 19-10. It's a texture that consists of vertical bars with white between them. When you use this texture on one of your objects, you'll be able to see through the white area and the polygons behind it.

Transparency is useful for walls that are partially see-through or for windows. If you don't want to use this feature, it's easy to turn off, which will give you a slightly faster texture-mapping routine. For now, however, keep it in.

The Texture-Mapping Algorithm Revealed

To accommodate the texture map, you need to add a few fields to some of the structures. First of all, add fields to the Polygon3D structure so you can associate each of its

FIGURE 19-10

◎ ◎ ◎ ◎ ◎ ◎

The white areas of this texture will appear to be transparent when rendered by the Texture-Mapping algorithm

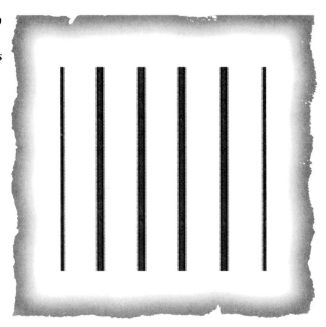

vertices with a point on the texture map. A point on the texture map will be defined with this structure:

```
typedef struct {
        short   x,y;
} TextureVert;
```

Polygon3D Structure

Then include an array in the Polygon3D structure that is the same size as its vertex array:

```
TextureVert     textureVertices[kMaxPolygonSize];
```

The textures will be stored as PICT resources in the application. The Polygon3D structure has a field telling you which resource ID holds the texture for this polygon:

```
short           textureMap;
```

Listing 19-1 is the complete new Polygon3D structure.

Listing 19-1 *The Polygon3D structure*

```
typedef struct Polygon3D {
    short               numOfVertices;
    unsigned char       color;
    Vertex3D            *polyVertex[kMaxPolygonSize];
```

```
/* renderingMode is one of several constants defining how
 * to render this polygon
 */
short               renderingMode;

/* nextPolygon and lastPolygon form a linked list for
 * the Painter's Algorithm
 */
struct Polygon3D  *nextPolygon, *lastPolygon;

/* Next are the minimum and maximum coordinates for the
 * polygon, forming a bounding box.
 */
short               xmin, xmax, ymin, ymax, zmin, zmax;

/* clippedList is a list of vertices after the polygon is
 * clipped, then projected, then clipped again.
 */
short               numOfClippedVerts;
ClippedVertex       clippedList[12];

/* TextureVertices maps the polygon's points onto a texture
 * map.
 */
TextureVert         textureVertices[kMaxPolygonSize];

/* TextureMap is the resource ID of the texture to use in
 * painting this polygon
 */
short               textureMap;

/* Rejected means that we won't be drawing this polygon because
 * it is backfacing, or it falls outside the view frustum
 */
Boolean             rejected;
} Polygon3D;
```

ClippedVertex Structure

When the polygon's vertices are clipped, the corresponding texture coordinates must also be clipped at the same relative position. I'll discuss this process in more detail later, but for now, you need to add a few fields to the ClippedVertex structure to hold the texture coordinate corresponding to that vertex:

```
typedef struct {
  long  x,y,z;              /* Clipped coordinates */
  long  tx, ty;             /* Texture coordinates */
} ClippedVertex;
```

These are the fields you'll be using to draw the polygon.

Texture Bitmap Structure

You're going to be defining your textures to be 128x128 pixels:

```
#define kTextureMapSize        128
```

In the future, it'll also be helpful to know how many bits you would need to shift a number to get the texture map size. In the case of a 128-pixel texture, the shift is 7:

```
#define kTextureMapShift       7
```

You'll see the uses for this soon. I've chosen the 128x128 size here because it provides a moderately good-looking texture without consuming too much memory. If you want to get better (or smaller) textures, all you need to do is change kTextureMapSize, but it always has to be a power of 2. An interesting fact about this algorithm is that increasing the texture map size won't significantly affect the speed of the algorithm, only its memory requirements.

You also need a structure to hold the texture bitmap information. You could use a pixmap for this, but you don't want to deal with the additional overhead of rowbytes and all the extra information a pixmap provides that you don't need. Instead, as you did for the custom screen blitter, just declare one large structure to hold everything. You know that each row is kTextureMapSize bytes wide and there are kTextureMapSize rows in the entire image.

```
typedef struct {
        char    data[kTextureMapSize*kTextureMapSize];
} TextureRec, *TexturePtr, **TextureHandle;
```

Dissecting the Drawing Routine

The texture map routine begins just like the other polygon-drawing routines do:

```
void  TextureMapDrawPoly(  Polygon3D      *poly,
                           Ptr            pixMapPtr,
                           unsigned long  rowBytes  )
```

You'll need quite a few variables for this routine. You'll recognize several of them from PolygonFillDrawPolygon(); I'll explain the others when I get to them:

```
{
  long          dstRowBytes;
  char          *src, *dst;
  char          *pixMapStartAddr;
  char          *textureMapStartAddr;
```

```
short        firstVert, minAmt;
short        xStart1, yStart1, xStart2, yStart2;
short        xEnd1, yEnd1, xEnd2, yEnd2;
short        startVert1, startVert2, endVert1, endVert2;
long         lineStartX, lineStartY, lineEndX, lineEndY;
short        lineLength;
long         startDeltaX, endDeltaX;
short        i;
long         dx1, dx2, dy1, dy2;
short        yHeight1, yHeight2;
short        totalEdges;

long         A;    /* A = Fraction of scanline start between
                    * startVert1 & endVert1
                    */
long         B;    /* B = Fraction of scanline end between
                    * startVert2 & endVert2
                    */
long         ax,ay; /* a = Fraction of texture line start */
long         bx,by; /* b = Fraction of texture line end */
short        edgeCount;
TextureHandle texture;
long         txStart1, tyStart1, txStart2, tyStart2;
long         txEnd1, tyEnd1, txEnd2, tyEnd2;
ClippedVertex *vertexList;
```

The first thing to do is load the texture bitmap data from the hard disk. You'll see the routine that accomplishes this a little later; for now it will suffice to know that it fills out a TextureHandle with the bitmap data for this texture:

```
/* Find the texture image data */
texture = GetTextureHandle(poly->textureMap);
```

Next, process some standard information for drawing—the starting address for the texture map, the pointer to the offscreen image, and the rowbytes:

```
/* Set up the pix map for writing */
pixMapStartAddr = pixMapPtr;
textureMapStartAddr = (**texture).data;
dstRowBytes = rowBytes;
```

As with the polygon-drawing routine, you need to find the topmost vertex of the polygon:

```
/* Remember how many edges we are dealing with */
totalEdges = edgeCount = poly->numOfClippedVerts-1;

/* Get a pointer to the polygon's clipped vertex list */
vertexList = poly->clippedList;
```

Continued on next page

Continued from previous page
```
/* Scan to find out which vertex is the topmost */

firstVert=0;                /* Start by assuming vertex 0 is at top */
minAmt=vertexList[0].y;          /* Find y coordinate of vertex 0 */
for (i=1; i <= totalEdges; i++) {        /* Search thru vertices */
  if ((vertexList[i].y) < minAmt) {  /* Is another vertex higher? */
    firstVert=i;              /* If so, replace previous top vertex */
    minAmt=vertexList[i].y;
  }
}
```

The next step is to set up the starting and ending vertices of the right and left edges you're going to be processing. At the same time, copy over the corresponding coordinates for the texture map. The polygon coordinates are stored in the variables xStart1, yStart1, xEnd1, yEnd1, xStart2, yStart2, xEnd2, and yEnd2. The respective texture coordinates are stored in txStart1, tyStart1, txEnd1, tyEnd1, txStart2, tyStart2, txEnd2, and tyEnd2. Here you initialize the starting coordinates of both vertices:

```
/* Finding starting and ending vertices of first two edges: */
startVert1=firstVert;     /* Get starting vertex of edge 1 */
startVert2=firstVert;     /* Get starting vertex of edge 2 */
xStart1=vertexList[startVert1].x;
yStart1=vertexList[startVert1].y;
txStart1 = vertexList[startVert1].tx;
tyStart1 = vertexList[startVert1].ty;
xStart2=vertexList[startVert2].x;
yStart2=vertexList[startVert2].y;
txStart2 = vertexList[startVert2].tx;
tyStart2 = vertexList[startVert2].ty;
```

Next, initialize the ending coordinates of the first line while checking to see if you wrap around to the last vertex in the list:

```
endVert1=startVert1-1;              /* Get ending vertex of edge 1 */
if (endVert1<0)
  endVert1=totalEdges;                      /* Check for wrap */
xEnd1=vertexList[endVert1].x;         /* Get x & y coordinates */
yEnd1=vertexList[endVert1].y;              /* of ending vertices */
txEnd1 = vertexList[endVert1].tx;
tyEnd1 = vertexList[endVert1].ty;
```

Next, you need to handle the second edge, checking to see if you wrap around to the first vertex:

```
endVert2=startVert2+1;              /* Get ending vertex of edge 2 */
if (endVert2 == totalEdges+1)
  endVert2=0;                              /* Check for wrap */
xEnd2=vertexList[endVert2].x;         /* Get x & y coordinates */
yEnd2=vertexList[endVert2].y;              /* of ending vertices */
```

```
txEnd2 = vertexList[endVert2].tx;
tyEnd2 = vertexList[endVert2].ty;
```

You're just about ready to start working your way down the polygon a scanline at a time, but a few things are left to initialize. dx1 and dx2 tell you how far the first and second edge travels in x, and dy1 and dy2 are the y lengths of the edges, respectively.

You also need to initialize two variables called startDeltaX and endDeltaX. These two fixed-point numbers represent the x distance the line is traveling for every pixel moved in y. This value is added onto the current x position each time the scanline is finished to determine the next x value:

```
/* Set up the loop parameters */
dx1 = xEnd1 - xStart1;
dy1 = yEnd1 - yStart1;
yHeight1 = dy1;
if (dy1)
  startDeltaX = (dx1 << 8) / dy1;

dx2 = xEnd2 - xStart2;
dy2 = yEnd2 - yStart2;
yHeight2 = dy2;
if (dy2)
  endDeltaX = (dx2 << 8) / dy2;
```

Then initialize the starting and ending x and y values for the current scanline. These values are updated after each scanline has been processed:

```
/* lineStart and lineEnd are 24.8 fixed-point numbers for remembering
 * the beginning and ending coordinates of the current scanline.
 * Because we're scanning across each row, lineStartY and lineEndY will
 * always be the same, but we keep them in separate variables just
 * for clarity.
 */
lineStartX = ((long)xStart1) << 8;
lineStartY = ((long)yStart1) << 8;
lineEndX = ((long)xStart2) << 8;
lineEndY = ((long)yStart2) << 8;
```

The *main* loop looks similar to the one used for the polygon-fill routine. The loop continues until all the edges have been processed:

```
/* Begin the main loop. This loop will continue until all of the
 * edges of the current polygon have been drawn.
 */
while (edgeCount > 0) {
```

You can ignore the current scanline if one of the edges does not travel any distance in y (i.e., if it is a horizontal line). If both edges are nonhorizontal, you can continue:

```
/* Only process these edges if they are both traveling some distance
 * in y.
 */
if (dy1 && dy2) {
```

Now start tracing down the polygon scanline by scanline until either the left or right edge runs out, just as you did in the Polygon-Fill algorithm:

```
/* Now begin processing scanline by scanline on our polygon
 * until one of our edges runs out.
 */
do {
```

Calculate the length of every scanline

```
/* Calculate the length of this scanline */
lineLength = (lineEndX - lineStartX) >> 8;
```

and continue only if it's greater than 0:

```
/* Only continue further if this scanline's length is greater
 * than 0
 */
if (lineLength > 0) {
```

At this point, you need to declare several more variables for the actual texture mapping. These variables keep track of the current position on the texture map and the distance to move per pixel on the polygon:

```
unsigned long  textureX, textureY;
long           textureDeltaX, textureDeltaY;
long           textureXErrorTerm, textureYErrorTerm;
short          textureXDirection, textureYDirection;
```

For the interpolation, you need to find out how far you've traveled so far between the starting and ending vertices of edge 1 and how far you've traveled on edge 2. This is done simply by taking the current y position minus the y coordinate of the ending coordinates and dividing that by the total height of the scanline. Then, to make the result work in the formulas, take its absolute value and subtract it from 1 (which is expressed as 256 in 24.8 fixed-point notation):

```
/* How far are we between the start1 and end1 vertices? A holds
 * this ratio.
 */
A = (lineStartY - (((long)yEnd1) << 8)) / dy1;
/* Take the opposite of A */
A = 256 - ABS(A);
```

Then do the same thing for the second edge:

```
/* Now do the same thing for start2 and end2, and place the
 * result in B.
 */
B = (lineEndY - (((long)yEnd2) << 8)) / dy2;
/* Take the opposite of B */
B = 256 - ABS(B);
```

Next, you want to find coordinates on the texture map that correspond to the starting and ending points of the scanline. Edge 1 can be processed by finding the total distance that edge 1 travels along the texture and then using A to interpolate the distance for both the x and y coordinates. txStart1 and tyStart1 are normal integer numbers, but the rest of the variables you're dealing with here are fixed-point, so you must also shift them so they match up:

```
/* Find the x and y coordinate on the texture that
 * corresponds to the beginning of the scanline.
 */
ax = (txStart1 << 8) - ((txStart1 - txEnd1) * A);
ay = (tyStart1 << 8) - ((tyStart1 - tyEnd1) * A);
```

Then do the same thing for edge 2:

```
/* Find the coordinate that corresponds to the
 * end of the scanline.
 */
bx = (txStart2 << 8) - ((txStart2 - txEnd2) * B);
by = (tyStart2 << 8) - ((tyStart2 - tyEnd2) * B);
```

You have just a few things left to set up before you can start texture mapping. The address of the first destination (offscreen image) pixel is calculated the same way you calculated it for the Polygon-Fill algorithm. However, lineStartX and lineStartY are both fixed-point, so you must convert them to normal integer numbers first:

```
/* Calculate the address of the first scanline pixel
 * on the screen.
 */
dst = pixMapStartAddr +
      (dstRowBytes * (lineStartY >> 8)) +
      (lineStartX >> 8);
```

textureX and textureY represent the current position on the texture map and they're initialized to the initial ax and ay values:

```
/* Start out the texture map coordinate */
textureX = ax;
textureY = ay;
```

You have one more interpolation to do for this routine. You know the starting and ending coordinates of the current line on the texture map and you know how long that line is going to be on the screen. You can now calculate how far you're going to be moving in x and y on the texture map for every pixel plotted in the scanline by dividing the difference between the two texture coordinates by the scanline length:

```
/* Calculate how far we'll be moving along the texture
 * for every pixel we move on the screen
 */
textureDeltaX = (bx - ax) / (lineLength+1);
textureDeltaY = (by - ay) / (lineLength+1);
```

You'll be adding these values to two error term variables and incrementing the current texture coordinate whenever either one of them is incremented past 1 (or, in the case of 24.8 fixed-point numbers, 256). The textureDelta values, however, can also be negative. It'll be easier if they're always positive, so ensure that they are. However, you must remember if they used to be negative so set a flag at the same time:

```
/* If we're moving backwards, reverse the textureDelta
 * and set a flag indicating so.
 */
if (textureDeltaX < 0) {
  textureXDirection = -1;
  textureDeltaX = -textureDeltaX;
} else
  textureXDirection = 1;

if (textureDeltaY < 0) {
  textureYDirection = -1;
  textureDeltaY = -textureDeltaY;
} else
  textureYDirection = 1;
```

Next, initialize the error terms:

```
/* Initialize the texture error terms */
textureXErrorTerm = textureYErrorTerm = 0;
```

Finally, the last thing to do before you begin the *pixel-plotting* loop is calculate the address of the first pixel you'll be taking from the texture map. In this case, you'll see some shortcuts because you know how large the texture map is and the fact that the size is always a power of 2. The textureY value is a 24.8 fixed-point number, so normally, you would need to shift it to the right by 8 places before multiplying it by the rowbytes value. And because the rowbyte value is always a power of 2, you can use a right-shift instead of a multiplication.

But why shift left if you're just going to shift right again immediately afterward? Instead, you can just shift left by (8 - kTextureMapShift), right? This is true, but there is also the issue of the left over fractional bits in the textureY variable you need to get rid of.

This can be done by performing a bitwise AND operation (with the C operator &) with the top (32 - kTextureMapShift) bits set to 1.

Then shift the textureX value to the right by eight places and add it to the result. Here is the complete statement that will accomplish this:

```
/* Find the address of the pixel on the texture map
 * corresponding to the first pixel of the scanline
 */
src = textureMapStartAddr +
    ((textureY >> (8 - TEXTURE_MAP_SHIFT)) &
    (0xFFFFFFFF << TEXTURE_MAP_SHIFT)) +
    (textureX >> 8);
```

Now begin the innermost loop of the pixel-plotting. Everything in this loop is extremely time-critical because it will be executed once for every pixel in the polygon:

```
/* This is the innermost loop of the texture mapping
 * engine. As you can see, it has quite a bit of code
 * inside it, which is why it's significantly slower than
 * the polygon-fill routine. Everything in this loop
 * is extremely time-critical, because it's processed once
 * for every pixel in the polygon.
 */
while (lineLength >= 0) {
```

Now check to see if the current pixel on the texture map is 0 or not. If the texture map's entry is 0, the pixel is not copied, giving you transparency. Otherwise, go ahead and copy the pixel:

```
/* Check to see if the current pixel in the texture map
 * is non-white. If so, plot it from the texture map.
 */
if(*src)
{
  *dst = *src;
}
```

Now check to see if you're going to be moving along the texture in the x dimension by adding the textureDeltaX value to the error term variable:

```
/* Increment the texture's X error term */
textureXErrorTerm += textureDeltaX;
```

If the error term is greater than 255, move the texture's x value. You may be moving it by more than 1 pixel at a time, so shift the error term to the right by eight places to find the change in x. Also check to see if you're supposed to be moving to the left or right along the texture:

```
/* If it's time to move by one or more pixels on the
 * texture map, calculate the new address of src.
 */
if (textureXErrorTerm > 255) {
```

Continued on next page

Continued from previous page

```
    if (textureXDirection == 1)
      src += (textureXErrorTerm >> 8);
    else
      src -= (textureXErrorTerm >> 8);
    textureXErrorTerm &= 0xFF;
  }
```

Now do the same for the y coordinate. Because you'll be moving by the texture's rowBytes value, you have to use the same shifting techniques used when originally calculating the texture's address:

```
/* Increment the texture's Y error term */
textureYErrorTerm += textureDeltaY;
/* If it's time to move by one or more pixels on the
 * texture map, calculate the new address of src.
 */
if (textureYErrorTerm > 255) {
  if (textureYDirection == 1)
    /* We must change src by multiplying the change in y
     * by the texture map's rowBytes value. While the method
     * we use to do this looks cumbersome and slow, it's
     * actually much faster than a multiplication operation.
     */
    src += (textureYErrorTerm >> (8 - TEXTURE_MAP_SHIFT)) &
        (0xFFFFFFFF << TEXTURE_MAP_SHIFT);
  else
    src -= (textureYErrorTerm >> (8 - TEXTURE_MAP_SHIFT)) &
        (0xFFFFFFFF << TEXTURE_MAP_SHIFT);
  textureYErrorTerm &= 0xFF;
}
```

Before finishing the loop, increment the destination pointer and decrement the line length:

```
    /* Increment the destination address */
    dst++;
    lineLength--;
  }
}
```

You're now ready to move to the next scanline. lineStartY and lineEndY are both 24.8 fixed-point numbers, so add 1.0 in 24.8 fixed-point (which is 256 in integer form) to each. Also add the startDeltaX and endDeltaX values to the scanline's lineStartX and lineEndX variables, respectively:

```
/* Increment the scanline (which is a fixed-point number) */
lineStartY += 256;
lineEndY += 256;
```

```
/* Change the scanline's starting and ending x values */
lineStartX += startDeltaX;
lineEndX += endDeltaX;
```

You're now finished with this scanline. Loop around until you're finished with one of the two sides:

```
} while (((lineStartY >> 8) < yEnd1) && ((lineEndY >> 8) < yEnd2));
}
```

The remainder of the routine looks very similar to the end of the PolygonFillDrawPolygon() routine. Check to see which side has finished and fill out the variables with the new coordinates for the next side.

```
if (((lineStartY >> 8) == yEnd1) || (!dy1)) {
  /* Line 1 ended. Fill in the info for the next line */

  startVert1 = endVert1;
  xStart1 = xEnd1;
  yStart1 = yEnd1;
  txStart1 = txEnd1;
  tyStart1 = tyEnd1;

  endVert1=startVert1-1;              /* Get ending vertex of edge 1 */
  if (endVert1<0) endVert1=totalEdges;         /* Check for wrap */
  xEnd1 = vertexList[endVert1].x;      /* Get x & y coordinates */
  yEnd1 = vertexList[endVert1].y;       /* of ending vertices */
  txEnd1 = vertexList[endVert1].tx;
  tyEnd1 = vertexList[endVert1].ty;

  /* Calculate the info necessary for this scanline */
  dx1 = xEnd1 - xStart1;
  dy1 = yEnd1 - yStart1;
  yHeight1 = dy1;
  if (dy1)
    startDeltaX = (dx1 << 8) / dy1;

  lineStartX = ((long)xStart1) << 8;
  lineStartY = ((long)yStart1) << 8;

  /* We have one less edge to draw */
  edgeCount--;
}

if (((lineEndY >> 8) == yEnd2) || (!dy2)) {
  /* Line 2 ended. Fill in the info for the next line */

  startVert2 = endVert2;
  xStart2 = xEnd2;
  yStart2 = yEnd2;
```

Continued on next page

Continued from previous page

```
      txStart2 = txEnd2;
      tyStart2 = tyEnd2;

      endVert2=startVert2+1;              /* Get ending vertex of edge 2 */
      if (endVert2==(totalEdges+1))              /* Check for wrap */
        endVert2=0;
      xEnd2=vertexList[endVert2].x;           /* Get x & y coordinates */
      yEnd2=vertexList[endVert2].y;             /* of ending vertices */
      txEnd2 = vertexList[endVert2].tx;
      tyEnd2 = vertexList[endVert2].ty;

      /* Calculate the info necessary for this scanline */
      dx2 = xEnd2 - xStart2;
      dy2 = yEnd2 - yStart2;
      yHeight2 = dy2;
      if (dy2)
        endDeltaX = (dx2 << 8) / dy2;

      lineEndX = ((long)xStart2) << 8;
      lineEndY = ((long)yStart2) << 8;

      /* We have one less edge to draw */
      edgeCount--;
    }
  }
}
```

There you have it: the entire texture-mapping routine. Listing 19-2 is the complete source code for TextureMapDrawPoly().

Listing 19-2 *The TextureMapDrawPoly() routine*

```
void  TextureMapDrawPoly( Polygon3D     *poly,
                          Ptr           pixMapPtr,
                          unsigned long rowBytes  )
{
  long      dstRowBytes;
  char      *src, *dst;
  char      *pixMapStartAddr;
  char      *textureMapStartAddr;
  short     firstVert, minAmt;
  short     xStart1, yStart1, xStart2, yStart2;
  short     xEnd1, yEnd1, xEnd2, yEnd2;
  short     startVert1, startVert2, endVert1, endVert2;
  long      lineStartX, lineStartY, lineEndX, lineEndY;
  short     lineLength;
  long      startDeltaX, endDeltaX;
  short     i;
  long      dx1, dx2, dy1, dy2;
  short     yHeight1, yHeight2;
  short     totalEdges;
```

```
long            A;      /* A = Fraction of scanline start between
                         * startVert1 & endVert1
                         */
long            B;      /* B = Fraction of scanline end between
                         * startVert2 & endVert2
                         */
long            ax,ay; /* a = Fraction of texture line start */
long            bx,by; /* b = Fraction of texture line end */
short           edgeCount;
TextureHandle   texture;
long            txStart1, tyStart1, txStart2, tyStart2;
long            txEnd1, tyEnd1, txEnd2, tyEnd2;
ClippedVertex   *vertexList;

/* Find the texture image data */
texture = GetTextureHandle(poly->textureMap);

/* Set up the pix map for writing */
pixMapStartAddr = pixMapPtr;
textureMapStartAddr = (**texture).data;
dstRowBytes = rowBytes;

/* Remember how many edges we are dealing with */
totalEdges = edgeCount = poly->numOfClippedVerts-1;

/* Get a pointer to the polygon's clipped vertex list */
vertexList = poly->clippedList;

/* Scan to find out which vertex is the topmost */

firstVert=0;                /* Start by assuming vertex 0 is at top */
minAmt=vertexList[0].y;          /* Find y coordinate of vertex 0 */
for (i=1; i <= totalEdges; i++) {        /* Search thru vertices */
  if ((vertexList[i].y) < minAmt) {  /* Is another vertex higher? */
    firstVert=i;             /* If so, replace previous top vertex */
    minAmt=vertexList[i].y;
  }
}

/* Finding starting and ending vertices of first two edges: */
startVert1=firstVert;      /* Get starting vertex of edge 1 */
startVert2=firstVert;      /* Get starting vertex of edge 2 */
xStart1=vertexList[startVert1].x;
yStart1=vertexList[startVert1].y;
txStart1 = vertexList[startVert1].tx;
tyStart1 = vertexList[startVert1].ty;
xStart2=vertexList[startVert2].x;
yStart2=vertexList[startVert2].y;
txStart2 = vertexList[startVert2].tx;
tyStart2 = vertexList[startVert2].ty;
```

Continued on next page

Continued from previous page

```
  endVert1=startVert1-1;                    /* Get ending vertex of edge 1 */
  if (endVert1<0)
    endVert1=totalEdges;                           /* Check for wrap */
  xEnd1=vertexList[endVert1].x;              /* Get x & y coordinates */
  yEnd1=vertexList[endVert1].y;               /* of ending vertices */
  txEnd1 = vertexList[endVert1].tx;
  tyEnd1 = vertexList[endVert1].ty;

  endVert2=startVert2+1;                    /* Get ending vertex of edge 2 */
  if (endVert2 == totalEdges+1)
    endVert2=0;                                    /* Check for wrap */
  xEnd2=vertexList[endVert2].x;              /* Get x & y coordinates */
  yEnd2=vertexList[endVert2].y;               /* of ending vertices */
  txEnd2 = vertexList[endVert2].tx;
  tyEnd2 = vertexList[endVert2].ty;

  /* Set up the loop parameters */
  dx1 = xEnd1 - xStart1;
  dy1 = yEnd1 - yStart1;
  yHeight1 = dy1;
  if (dy1)
    startDeltaX = (dx1 << 8) / dy1;

  dx2 = xEnd2 - xStart2;
  dy2 = yEnd2 - yStart2;
  yHeight2 = dy2;
  if (dy2)
    endDeltaX = (dx2 << 8) / dy2;


  /* lineStart and lineEnd are 24.8 fixed-point numbers for remembering
   * the beginning and ending coordinates of the current scanline.
   * Because we're scanning across each row, lineStartY and lineEndY will
   * always be the same, but we keep them in separate variables just
   * for clarity.
   */
  lineStartX = ((long)xStart1) << 8;
  lineStartY = ((long)yStart1) << 8;
  lineEndX = ((long)xStart2) << 8;
  lineEndY = ((long)yStart2) << 8;

  /* Begin the main loop. This loop will continue until all of the
   * edges of the current polygon have been drawn.
   */
  while (edgeCount > 0) {
    /* Only process these edges if they are both travelling some distance
     * in y.
     */
    if (dy1 && dy2) {
      /* Now begin processing scanline-by-scanline on our polygon
       * until one of our edges runs out.
       */
      do {
```

```
/* Calculate the length of this scanline */
lineLength = (lineEndX - lineStartX) >> 8;

/* Only continue further if this scanline's
 * length is greater than 0
 */
if (lineLength > 0) {
  unsigned long  textureX, textureY;
  long           textureDeltaX, textureDeltaY;
  long           textureXErrorTerm, textureYErrorTerm;
  short          textureXDirection, textureYDirection;

  /* How far are we between the start1 and end1 vertices? A holds
   * this ratio.
   */
  A = (lineStartY - (((long)yEnd1) << 8)) / dy1;
  /* Take the opposite of A */
  A = 256 - ABS(A);

  /* Now do the same thing for start2 and end2, and place the
   * result in B.
   */
  B = (lineEndY - (((long)yEnd2) << 8)) / dy2;
  /* Take the opposite of B */
  B = 256 - ABS(B);

  /* Find the x and y coordinate on the texture that
   * corresponds to the beginning of the scanline.
   */
  ax = (txStart1 << 8) - ((txStart1 - txEnd1) * A);
  ay = (tyStart1 << 8) - ((tyStart1 - tyEnd1) * A);

  /* Find the coordinate that corresponds to the
   * end of the scanline.
   */
  bx = (txStart2 << 8) - ((txStart2 - txEnd2) * B);
  by = (tyStart2 << 8) - ((tyStart2 - tyEnd2) * B);

  /* Calculate the address of the first scanline pixel
   * on the screen.
   */
  dst = pixMapStartAddr +
      (dstRowBytes * (lineStartY >> 8)) +
      (lineStartX >> 8);

  /* Start out the texture map coordinate */
  textureX = ax;
  textureY = ay;

  /* Calculate how far we'll be moving along the texture
   * for every pixel we move on the screen
   */
```

Continued on next page

Continued from previous page

```
        textureDeltaX = (bx - ax) / (lineLength+1);
        textureDeltaY = (by - ay) / (lineLength+1);

        /* If we're moving backwards, reverse the textureDelta
         * and set a flag indicating so.
         */
        if (textureDeltaX < 0) {
          textureXDirection = -1;
          textureDeltaX = -textureDeltaX;
        } else
          textureXDirection = 1;

        if (textureDeltaY < 0) {
          textureYDirection = -1;
          textureDeltaY = -textureDeltaY;
        } else
          textureYDirection = 1;

        /* Initialize the texture error terms */
        textureXErrorTerm = textureYErrorTerm = 0;

        /* Find the address of the pixel on the texture map
         * corresponding to the first pixel of the scanline
         */
        src = textureMapStartAddr +
            ((textureY >> (8 - TEXTURE_MAP_SHIFT)) &
             (0xFFFFFFFF << TEXTURE_MAP_SHIFT)) +
            (textureX >> 8);

        /* This is the innermost loop of the texture mapping
         * engine. As you can see, it has quite a bit of code
         * inside it, which is why it's significantly slower than
         * the polygon-fill routine. Everything in this loop
         * is extremely time-critical, because it's processed once
         * for every pixel in the polygon.
         */
        while (lineLength >= 0) {
          /* Check to see if the current pixel in the texture map
           * is non-white. If so, plot it from the texture map.
           */
          if(*src)
          {
            *dst = *src;
          }

          /* Increment the texture's X error term */
          textureXErrorTerm += textureDeltaX;

          /* If it's time to move by one or more pixels on the
           * texture map, calculate the new address of src.
           */
```

```
          if (textureXErrorTerm > 255) {
            if (textureXDirection == 1)
              src += (textureXErrorTerm >> 8);
            else
              src -= (textureXErrorTerm >> 8);
            textureXErrorTerm &= 0xFF;
          }

          /* Increment the texture's Y error term */
          textureYErrorTerm += textureDeltaY;
          /* If it's time to move by one or more pixels on the
           * texture map, calculate the new address of src.
           */
          if (textureYErrorTerm > 255) {
            if (textureYDirection == 1)
              /* We must change src by multiplying the change in y
               * by the texture map's rowBytes value. While the method
               * we use to do this looks cumbersome and slow, it's
               * actually much faster than a multiplication operation.
               */
              src += (textureYErrorTerm >> (8 - TEXTURE_MAP_SHIFT)) &
                  (0xFFFFFFFF << TEXTURE_MAP_SHIFT);
            else
              src -= (textureYErrorTerm >> (8 - TEXTURE_MAP_SHIFT)) &
                  (0xFFFFFFFF << TEXTURE_MAP_SHIFT);
            textureYErrorTerm &= 0xFF;
          }

          /* Increment the destination address */
          dst++;
          lineLength--;
        }
      }

      /* Increment the scanline (which is a fixed-point number)*/
      lineStartY += 256;
      lineEndY += 256;

      /* Change the scanline's starting and ending x values */
      lineStartX += startDeltaX;
      lineEndX += endDeltaX;

    } while (((lineStartY >> 8) < yEnd1) && ((lineEndY >> 8) < yEnd2));
  }

  if (((lineStartY >> 8) == yEnd1) || (!dy1)) {
    /* Line 1 ended. Fill in the info for the next line */

    startVert1 = endVert1;
    xStart1 = xEnd1;
    yStart1 = yEnd1;
```

Continued on next page

Continued from previous page

```
        txStart1 = txEnd1;
        tyStart1 = tyEnd1;

        endVert1=startVert1-1;                /* Get ending vertex of edge 1 */
        if (endVert1<0) endVert1=totalEdges;          /* Check for wrap */
        xEnd1 = vertexList[endVert1].x;         /* Get x & y coordinates */
        yEnd1 = vertexList[endVert1].y;          /* of ending vertices */
        txEnd1 = vertexList[endVert1].tx;
        tyEnd1 = vertexList[endVert1].ty;

        /* Calculate the info necessary for this scanline */
        dx1 = xEnd1 - xStart1;
        dy1 = yEnd1 - yStart1;
        yHeight1 = dy1;
        if (dy1)
          startDeltaX = (dx1 << 8) / dy1;

        lineStartX = ((long)xStart1) << 8;
        lineStartY = ((long)yStart1) << 8;

        /* We have one less edge to draw */
        edgeCount--;
      }

      if (((lineEndY >> 8) == yEnd2) || (!dy2)) {
        /* Line 2 ended. Fill in the info for the next line */

        startVert2 = endVert2;
        xStart2 = xEnd2;
        yStart2 = yEnd2;
        txStart2 = txEnd2;
        tyStart2 = tyEnd2;

        endVert2=startVert2+1;                /* Get ending vertex of edge 2 */
        if (endVert2==(totalEdges+1))               /* Check for wrap */
          endVert2=0;
        xEnd2=vertexList[endVert2].x;           /* Get x & y coordinates */
        yEnd2=vertexList[endVert2].y;            /* of ending vertices */
        txEnd2 = vertexList[endVert2].tx;
        tyEnd2 = vertexList[endVert2].ty;

        /* Calculate the info necessary for this scanline */
        dx2 = xEnd2 - xStart2;
        dy2 = yEnd2 - yStart2;
        yHeight2 = dy2;
        if (dy2)
          endDeltaX = (dx2 << 8) / dy2;

        lineEndX = ((long)xStart2) << 8;
        lineEndY = ((long)yStart2) << 8;
```

```
        /* We have one less edge to draw */
        edgeCount--;
      }
    }
  }
```

Clipping and the Texture Map

Clipping provides an interesting problem for texture mapping. No longer can you just lop off the edge of the polygon and be done with it—otherwise, you would be drawing the texture map into a polygon much smaller than it used to be, and if you walked along the polygon, the texture map would appear to "crawl" along its surface.

To solve this problem, whenever you clip a polygon edge, calculate the percentage of that edge that is still remaining. The texture coordinates are then interpolated to find the coordinates for the clipped vertex. If the edge is not clipped, the texture coordinates are just copied over from the old edge to the new one.

Clipping Textures against z

Let's examine the changes to the ZClip() function first. When an edge is clipped by the near z plane, a t value is calculated to determine where to clip the x and y components of the line. It so happens that this t value can also easily be used to clip the texture coordinates, like this:

```
/* Calculate the texture coordinates */
clipList->tx = ((textureX2 - textureX1) * t) +
        textureX1;
clipList->ty = ((textureY2 - textureY1) * t) +
        textureY1;
clipList++;
```

In cases where you aren't clipping an edge, the texture coordinates are copied over, like this:

```
clipList->tx = textureX2;
clipList->ty = textureY2;
```

The solution to clipping against the z plane turns out to be rather simple. Listing 19-3 is the complete code for the new ZClip() function.

Listing 19-3 *The ZClipPolygonList() routine*

```
/**
 **    ZClipPolygonList()
 **
 **    Clips all of the polygons against the front of the view volume
 **/
```

Continued on next page

Continued from previous page

```
void  ZClipPolygonList(void)
{
  Polygon3D     *polygonBase, *thisPolygon;
  long          zMin;

  polygonBase = gWorld.paintersList;
  thisPolygon = polygonBase;

  /* Copy globals into local variables, where they will be faster */
  zMin = gClipZMin;

  while (thisPolygon != NULL) {
    ClippedVertex  *clipList;
    short          v1,v2;
    Vertex3D       *pv1, *pv2;
    float          t;
    short          numOfClippedVerts;
    short          textureX1, textureX2, textureY1, textureY2;

    /* Point the clipList pointer at the first clipped vertex */
    clipList = thisPolygon->clippedList;
    numOfClippedVerts = 0;

    /* Initialize v1 to the last vertex */
    v1 = thisPolygon->numOfVertices-1;

    /* Loop through all of the edges of the polygon */
    for (v2 = 0; v2 < thisPolygon->numOfVertices; v2++) {
      /* Get pointers to both vertices */
      pv1 = thisPolygon->polyVertex[v1];
      pv2 = thisPolygon->polyVertex[v2];

      /* Find the texture points corresponding to these points */
      textureX1 = thisPolygon->textureVertices[v1].x;
      textureY1 = thisPolygon->textureVertices[v1].y;
      textureX2 = thisPolygon->textureVertices[v2].x;
      textureY2 = thisPolygon->textureVertices[v2].y;

      /* Categorize edges by type */
      if ((pv1->tz >= zMin) && (pv2->tz >= zMin)) {
        /* Entirely inside front */
        clipList->x = pv2->tx;
        clipList->y = pv2->ty;
        clipList->z = pv2->tz;

        /* Copy the texture coordinates */
        clipList->tx = textureX2;
        clipList->ty = textureY2;

        /* Advance clipped list pointer */
        clipList++;
        numOfClippedVerts++;
      }
```

```
        else if ((pv1->tz < zMin) && (pv2->tz < zMin)) {
  /* Edge is entirely past front; do nothing */
}

else if ((pv1->tz >= zMin) && (pv2->tz < zMin)) {
  /* Edge is leaving view volume */
  t = (float)(zMin - pv1->tz) /
    (float)(pv2->tz - pv1->tz);
  clipList->x = pv1->tx + (pv2->tx - pv1->tx) * t;
  clipList->y = pv1->ty + (pv2->ty - pv1->ty) * t;
  clipList->z = zMin;

  /* Calculate the texture coordinates */
  clipList->tx = ((textureX2 - textureX1) * t) +
          textureX1;
  clipList->ty = ((textureY2 - textureY1) * t) +
          textureY1;

  /* Advance the clipped list pointer */
  clipList++;
  numOfClippedVerts++;
}

else if ((pv1->tz < zMin) && (pv2->tz >= zMin)) {
  /* Edge is entering view volume */
  t = (float)(zMin - pv1->tz) /
    (float)(pv2->tz - pv1->tz);

  clipList->x = pv1->tx + (pv2->tx - pv1->tx) * t;
  clipList->y = pv1->ty + (pv2->ty - pv1->ty) * t;
  clipList->z = zMin;

  /* Calculate the texture coordinates */
  clipList->tx = ((textureX2 - textureX1) * t) +
          textureX1;
  clipList->ty = ((textureY2 - textureY1) * t) +
          textureY1;
  clipList++;

  /* Copy the vertex coordinates */
  clipList->x = pv2->tx;
  clipList->y = pv2->ty;
  clipList->z = pv2->tz;

  /* Copy the texture coordinates */
  clipList->tx = textureX2;
  clipList->ty = textureY2;
  clipList++;
  numOfClippedVerts += 2;
}
```

Continued on next page

Continued from previous page

```
    /* Advance to next vertex */
    v1 = v2;
  }

  /* Put number of clipped vertices in poly structure */
  thisPolygon->numOfClippedVerts = numOfClippedVerts;

  /* Advance to next polygon */
  thisPolygon = thisPolygon->nextPolygon;
  }
}
```

Clipping Textures against x and y

Clipping a texture-mapped polygon against the x and y screen extents presents an additional problem, which occurs when the perspective transformation is applied to the polygon. Figure 19-11 shows a top-down view of a polygon in the viewport before it has been projected into screen space. If the texture map were applied to this polygon, about half of the texture would actually appear on the screen and the other half would fall off the edge of the screen.

Figure 19-12 shows the polygon *after* it has been projected. Because the projection function involves multiplying each vertex by some large value (in this case, 350) and then dividing it by the vertex's z coordinate, distant points that are inside the viewport will move closer to the middle of the screen, but closer points that are outside the viewport will be multiplied by a huge value. As Figure 19-12 shows, points that are slightly to the left of the viewport will suddenly have a large negative value and points to the right of the viewport will suffer a similar effect.

If you now texture map this polygon, only about 20 percent of the texture shows up on the screen; the remaining 80 percent falls to the left of the viewport. If you clip the polygons using the same interpolation you used for ZClip(), walls along the edge of the screen will become very stretched out and the texture will quickly become unrecognizable. This problem is even more extreme when larger polygons are projected.

Perspective texture mapping eliminates this problem because it takes into account the z coordinate of each of the pixels. Because you're using affine texture mapping, however, you need to approach the problem from a different direction.

In effect, you're going to be "removing" the projection function when calculating the new texture coordinates. Because the coordinates have been divided by their z coordinates and you know what those z coordinate are, you can remove the projection by multiplying the coordinates by the same z value. The magnitudes of the coordinates will still be much larger than they were originally (because they were multiplied by 350 during the projection), but because you're just looking for a ratio, that doesn't matter.

FIGURE 19-11

◎ ◎ ◎ ◎ ◎ ◎

A top-down view of a polygon before it is projected; at this point, about half of the polygon is inside the view volume

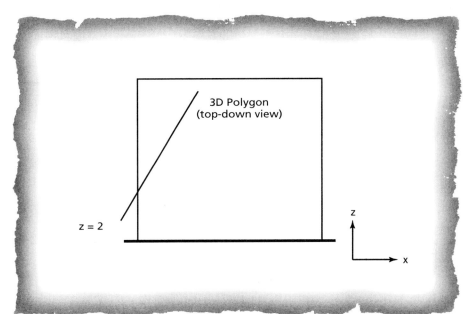

FIGURE 19-12

◎ ◎ ◎ ◎ ◎ ◎

The polygon after it has been projected; at this point, only about 1/5 of the polygon remains on the screen

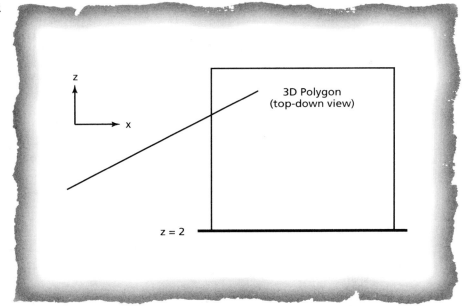

Here is how you would remove the projection from the x coordinate of a pair of vertices that leave the left edge of the viewport and then calculate the new percentage to use in the texture calculation:

```
pt0x = clipList[v1].x * clipList[v1].z;
pt1x = clipList[v2].x * clipList[v2].z;

texturePos = (((float)(pt0x)) /
              (float)(pt0x - pt1x));
```

Compensating for the right edge of the viewport is slightly more complicated. The x coordinate must be subtracted from the maximum x coordinate of the viewport, or xMax. This allows the ratio calculation to be based around 0, like the calculation you used for the left edge. Here is the code to use for this operation:

```
pt0x = (xMax - tempClipList[v1].x) * tempClipList[v1].z;
pt1x = (xMax - tempClipList[v2].x) * tempClipList[v2].z;

texturePos = (((float)(pt0x)) /
              (float)(pt0x - pt1x));
```

You can easily interpolate the new tx and ty values for the edges with this formula:

```
tempClipList[clipRef].tx = ((clipList[v2].tx -
                             clipList[v1].tx) * texturePos) +
                             clipList[v1].tx;
tempClipList[clipRef].ty = ((clipList[v2].ty -
                             clipList[v1].ty) * texturePos) +
                             clipList[v1].ty;
```

This operation has to be applied when the edge leaves the viewport and when it enters. In the end, the XYClip() routine is significantly longer, but not much more computationally expensive than it was before. Listing 19-4 is the complete source code for the new XYClip() routine.

Listing 19-4 The XYClipPolygonList() routine

```
/**
** XYClipPolygonList()
**
** Clips the polygon's x and y extents against the edge of the screen
**/
void  XYClipPolygonList(void)
{
  Polygon3D   *polygonBase, *thisPolygon;
  long        xMin, xMax, yMin, yMax;

  polygonBase = gWorld.paintersList;
  thisPolygon = polygonBase;
```

```
/* Copy globals into local variables, where they will be faster */
xMin = gClipXMin;
xMax = gClipXMax;
yMin = gClipYMin;
yMax = gClipYMax;

while (thisPolygon != NULL) {
  ClippedVertex  *clipList;
  ClippedVertex  tempClipList[20];
  short          clipRef;
  short          v1,v2;
  float          t;
  float          texturePos;
  long           pt0y, pt1y;
  long           pt0x, pt1x;

  clipList = thisPolygon->clippedList;

  if (thisPolygon->numOfClippedVerts > 2) {
    /*** Part 1: Clip against the left side of the viewport */
    /***         Clip from the regular list into the temp list */

    clipRef = 0;
    v1 = thisPolygon->numOfClippedVerts-1;

    for (v2 = 0; v2 < thisPolygon->numOfClippedVerts; v2++) {
      /* Categorize edges by type */
      if ((clipList[v1].x >= xMin) && (clipList[v2].x >= xMin)) {
        /* Edge isn't off right side of viewport; copy it over */
        tempClipList[clipRef].x = clipList[v2].x;
        tempClipList[clipRef].y = clipList[v2].y;
        tempClipList[clipRef].z = clipList[v2].z;

        /* Copy over the texture vertices */
        tempClipList[clipRef].tx = clipList[v2].tx;
        tempClipList[clipRef].ty = clipList[v2].ty;

        clipRef++;
      }

      else if ((clipList[v1].x < xMin) && (clipList[v2].x < xMin)) {
        /* Edge is entirely off viewport; do nothing */
      }

      else if ((clipList[v1].x >= xMin) && (clipList[v2].x < xMin)) {
        /* Edge is leaving viewport */
        t = (float)(xMin - clipList[v1].x) /
            (float)(clipList[v2].x - clipList[v1].x);

        tempClipList[clipRef].x = xMin;
        tempClipList[clipRef].y = clipList[v1].y +
```

Continued on next page

Continued from previous page

```
                                     (clipList[v2].y - clipList[v1].y) * t;
            tempClipList[clipRef].z = clipList[v1].z +
                                     (clipList[v2].z - clipList[v1].z) * t;

            /* Calculate the texture coordinates */
            {
              pt0x = clipList[v1].x * clipList[v1].z;
              pt1x = clipList[v2].x * clipList[v2].z;

              texturePos = (((float)(pt0x)) /
                      (float)(pt0x - pt1x));

              tempClipList[clipRef].tx = ((clipList[v2].tx -
                                      clipList[v1].tx) * texturePos) +
                                      clipList[v1].tx;
              tempClipList[clipRef].ty = ((clipList[v2].ty -
                                      clipList[v1].ty) * texturePos) +
                                      clipList[v1].ty;
            }

            clipRef++;
          }

          else if ((clipList[v1].x < xMin) && (clipList[v2].x >= xMin)) {
            /* Edge is entering viewport */
            t = (float)(xMin - clipList[v1].x) /
              (float)(clipList[v2].x - clipList[v1].x);
            tempClipList[clipRef].x = xMin;
            tempClipList[clipRef].y = clipList[v1].y +
                                      (clipList[v2].y - clipList[v1].y) * t;
            tempClipList[clipRef].z = clipList[v1].z +
                                      (clipList[v2].z - clipList[v1].z) * t;

            /* Calculate the texture coordinates */
            {
              pt0x = clipList[v1].x * clipList[v1].z;
              pt1x = clipList[v2].x * clipList[v2].z;

              texturePos = (((float)(pt0x)) /
                          (float)(pt0x - pt1x));

              tempClipList[clipRef].tx = ((clipList[v2].tx -
                                      clipList[v1].tx) * texturePos) +
                                      clipList[v1].tx;
              tempClipList[clipRef].ty = ((clipList[v2].ty -
                                      clipList[v1].ty) * texturePos) +
                                      clipList[v1].ty;
            }

            clipRef++;
```

```
                /* Copy the next vertex over */
                tempClipList[clipRef].x = clipList[v2].x;
                tempClipList[clipRef].y = clipList[v2].y;
                tempClipList[clipRef].z = clipList[v2].z;

                /* Copy the texture coordinates */
                tempClipList[clipRef].tx = clipList[v2].tx;
                tempClipList[clipRef].ty = clipList[v2].ty;

                clipRef++;
            }

            v1 = v2;
        }
        thisPolygon->numOfClippedVerts = clipRef;
    }

    if (thisPolygon->numOfClippedVerts > 2) {
        /*** Part 2: Clip against the right edge of the viewport */
        /***          Clip from the temp list back into the regular list */

        clipRef = 0;
        v1 = thisPolygon->numOfClippedVerts-1;

        for (v2 = 0; v2 < thisPolygon->numOfClippedVerts; v2++) {
            /* Categorize edges by type */
            if ((tempClipList[v1].x <= xMax) && (tempClipList[v2].x <= xMax))
{

                /* Edge isn't off right side of viewport; copy it over */
                clipList[clipRef].x = tempClipList[v2].x;
                clipList[clipRef].y = tempClipList[v2].y;
                clipList[clipRef].z = tempClipList[v2].z;

                /* Copy the texture coordinates */
                clipList[clipRef].tx = tempClipList[v2].tx;
                clipList[clipRef].ty = tempClipList[v2].ty;

                clipRef++;
            }

            else if ((tempClipList[v1].x > xMax) &&
                     (tempClipList[v2].x > xMax)) {
                /* Edge is entirely off viewport; do nothing */
            }

            else if ((tempClipList[v1].x <= xMax) &&
                     (tempClipList[v2].x > xMax)) {
                /* Edge is leaving viewport */
                t = (float)(xMax - tempClipList[v1].x) /
                    (float)(tempClipList[v2].x - tempClipList[v1].x);
                clipList[clipRef].x = xMax;
```

Continued on next page

Continued from previous page

```
            clipList[clipRef].y = tempClipList[v1].y +
                        (tempClipList[v2].y - tempClipList[v1].y) * t;
            clipList[clipRef].z = tempClipList[v1].z +
                        (tempClipList[v2].z - tempClipList[v1].z) * t;


        /* Calculate the texture coordinates */
        {
          pt0x = (xMax - tempClipList[v1].x) * tempClipList[v1].z;
          pt1x = (xMax - tempClipList[v2].x) * tempClipList[v2].z;

          texturePos = (((float)(pt0x)) /
                        (float)(pt0x - pt1x));

          clipList[clipRef].tx = ((tempClipList[v2].tx -
                                tempClipList[v1].tx) * texturePos) +
                                tempClipList[v1].tx;
          clipList[clipRef].ty = ((tempClipList[v2].ty -
                                tempClipList[v1].ty) * texturePos) +
                                tempClipList[v1].ty;
        }
        clipRef++;
    }

    else if ((tempClipList[v1].x > xMax) &&
            (tempClipList[v2].x <= xMax)) {
      /* Edge is entering viewport */
      t = (float)(xMax - tempClipList[v1].x) /
        (float)(tempClipList[v2].x - tempClipList[v1].x);
      clipList[clipRef].x = xMax;
      clipList[clipRef].y = tempClipList[v1].y +
                    (tempClipList[v2].y - tempClipList[v1].y) * t;
      clipList[clipRef].z = tempClipList[v1].z +
                    (tempClipList[v2].z - tempClipList[v1].z) * t;

      /* Calculate the texture coordinates */
      {
        pt0x = (xMax - tempClipList[v1].x) * tempClipList[v1].z;
        pt1x = (xMax - tempClipList[v2].x) * tempClipList[v2].z;

        texturePos = (((float)(pt0x)) /
                      (float)(pt0x - pt1x));

        clipList[clipRef].tx = ((tempClipList[v2].tx -
                              tempClipList[v1].tx) * texturePos) +
                              tempClipList[v1].tx;
        clipList[clipRef].ty = ((tempClipList[v2].ty -
                              tempClipList[v1].ty) * texturePos) +
                              tempClipList[v1].ty;
      }

      clipRef++;
```

```
                   clipList[clipRef].x = tempClipList[v2].x;
                   clipList[clipRef].y = tempClipList[v2].y;
                   clipList[clipRef].z = tempClipList[v2].z;

                   /* Copy the texture coordinates */
                   clipList[clipRef].tx = tempClipList[v2].tx;
                   clipList[clipRef].ty = tempClipList[v2].ty;

                   clipRef++;
               }

               v1 = v2;
           }
           thisPolygon->numOfClippedVerts = clipRef;
       }

       if (thisPolygon->numOfClippedVerts > 2) {
           /*** Part 3: Clip against the top side of the viewport */
           /***          Clip from the regular list into the temp list */

           clipRef = 0;
           v1 = thisPolygon->numOfClippedVerts-1;

           for (v2 = 0; v2 < thisPolygon->numOfClippedVerts; v2++) {
               /* Categorize edges by type */
               if ((clipList[v1].y >= yMin) && (clipList[v2].y >= yMin)) {
                   /* Edge isn't off top side of viewport; copy it over */
                   tempClipList[clipRef].x = clipList[v2].x;
                   tempClipList[clipRef].y = clipList[v2].y;
                   tempClipList[clipRef].z = clipList[v2].z;

                   /* Copy the texture coordinates */
                   tempClipList[clipRef].tx = clipList[v2].tx;
                   tempClipList[clipRef].ty = clipList[v2].ty;

                   clipRef++;
               }

               else if ((clipList[v1].y < yMin) && (clipList[v2].y < yMin)) {
                   /* Edge is entirely off viewport; do nothing */
               }

               else if ((clipList[v1].y >= yMin) && (clipList[v2].y < yMin)) {
                   /* Edge is leaving viewport */
                   t = (float)(yMin - clipList[v1].y) /
                       (float)(clipList[v2].y - clipList[v1].y);
                   tempClipList[clipRef].x = clipList[v1].x +
                                       (clipList[v2].x - clipList[v1].x) * t;

                   tempClipList[clipRef].y = yMin;
                   tempClipList[clipRef].z = clipList[v1].z +
                                       (clipList[v2].z - clipList[v1].z) * t;
```

Continued on next page

Continued from previous page

```
        /* Calculate the texture coordinates */
        {
          pt0y = clipList[v1].y;
          pt1y = clipList[v2].y;

          texturePos = (((float)(pt0y)) /
                  (float)(pt0y - pt1y));

          tempClipList[clipRef].tx = ((clipList[v2].tx -
                                  clipList[v1].tx) * texturePos) +
                                  clipList[v1].tx;
          tempClipList[clipRef].ty = ((clipList[v2].ty -
                                  clipList[v1].ty) * texturePos) +
                                  clipList[v1].ty;
        }

        clipRef++;
      }

      else if ((clipList[v1].y < yMin) && (clipList[v2].y >= yMin)) {
        /* Edge is entering viewport */
        t = (float)(yMin - clipList[v1].y) /
            (float)(clipList[v2].y - clipList[v1].y);
        tempClipList[clipRef].x = clipList[v1].x +
                              (clipList[v2].x - clipList[v1].x) * t;

        tempClipList[clipRef].y = yMin;
        tempClipList[clipRef].z = clipList[v1].z +
                  (clipList[v2].z - clipList[v1].z) * t;

        /* Calculate the texture coordinates */
        {
          pt0y = clipList[v1].y;
          pt1y = clipList[v2].y;

          texturePos = (((float)(pt0y)) /
                  (float)(pt0y - pt1y));

          tempClipList[clipRef].tx = ((clipList[v2].tx -
                                  clipList[v1].tx) * texturePos) +
                                  clipList[v1].tx;
          tempClipList[clipRef].ty = ((clipList[v2].ty -
                                  clipList[v1].ty) * texturePos) +
                                  clipList[v1].ty;
        }

        clipRef++;

        tempClipList[clipRef].x = clipList[v2].x;
        tempClipList[clipRef].y = clipList[v2].y;
        tempClipList[clipRef].z = clipList[v2].z;
```

```
                    /* Copy the texture coordinates */
                    tempClipList[clipRef].tx = clipList[v2].tx;
                    tempClipList[clipRef].ty = clipList[v2].ty;

                    clipRef++;
                }

                v1 = v2;
            }
            thisPolygon->numOfClippedVerts = clipRef;
        }

        if (thisPolygon->numOfClippedVerts > 2) {
          /*** Part 4: Clip against the bottom edge of the viewport */
          /***          Clip from the temp list back into the regular list */

          clipRef = 0;
          v1 = thisPolygon->numOfClippedVerts-1;

          for (v2 = 0; v2 < thisPolygon->numOfClippedVerts; v2++) {
            /* Categorize edges by type */
            if ((tempClipList[v1].y <= yMax) && (tempClipList[v2].y <= yMax))
{

                /* Edge isn't off edge side of viewport; copy it over */
                clipList[clipRef].x = tempClipList[v2].x;
                clipList[clipRef].y = tempClipList[v2].y;
                clipList[clipRef].z = tempClipList[v2].z;

                /* Copy the texture coordinates */
                clipList[clipRef].tx = tempClipList[v2].tx;
                clipList[clipRef].ty = tempClipList[v2].ty;

                clipRef++;
            }

            else if ((tempClipList[v1].y > yMax) &&
                     (tempClipList[v2].y > yMax)) {
                /* Edge is entirely off viewport; do nothing */
            }

            else if ((tempClipList[v1].y <= yMax) &&
                     (tempClipList[v2].y > yMax)) {
                /* Edge is leaving viewport */
                t = (float)(yMax - tempClipList[v1].y) /
                    (float)(tempClipList[v2].y - tempClipList[v1].y);
                clipList[clipRef].x = tempClipList[v1].x +
                            (tempClipList[v2].x - tempClipList[v1].x) * t;

                clipList[clipRef].y = yMax;
                clipList[clipRef].z = tempClipList[v1].z +
                            (tempClipList[v2].z - tempClipList[v1].z) * t;
```

Continued on next page

Continued from previous page

```
                    /* Calculate the texture coordinates */
                    {
                      pt0y = (yMax - tempClipList[v1].y);
                      pt1y = (yMax - tempClipList[v2].y);

                      texturePos = (((float)(pt0y)) /
                                    (float)(pt0y - pt1y));

                      clipList[clipRef].tx = ((tempClipList[v2].tx -
                                               tempClipList[v1].tx) * texturePos) +
                                               tempClipList[v1].tx;
                      clipList[clipRef].ty = ((tempClipList[v2].ty -
                                               tempClipList[v1].ty) * texturePos) +
                                               tempClipList[v1].ty;
                    }

                  clipRef++;
                }

                else if ((tempClipList[v1].y > yMax) &&
                        (tempClipList[v2].y <= yMax)) {
                  /* Edge is entering viewport */
                  t = (float)(yMax - tempClipList[v1].y) /
                    (float)(tempClipList[v2].y - tempClipList[v1].y);
                  clipList[clipRef].x = tempClipList[v1].x +
                              (tempClipList[v2].x - tempClipList[v1].x) * t;

                  clipList[clipRef].y = yMax;
                  clipList[clipRef].z = tempClipList[v1].z +
                              (tempClipList[v2].z - tempClipList[v1].z) * t;

                  /* Calculate the texture coordinates */
                  {
                    pt0y = (yMax - tempClipList[v1].y);
                    pt1y = (yMax - tempClipList[v2].y);

                    texturePos = (((float)(pt0y)) /
                                  (float)(pt0y - pt1y));

                    clipList[clipRef].tx = ((tempClipList[v2].tx -
                                             tempClipList[v1].tx) * texturePos) +
                                             tempClipList[v1].tx;
                    clipList[clipRef].ty = ((tempClipList[v2].ty -
                                             tempClipList[v1].ty) * texturePos) +
                                             tempClipList[v1].ty;
                  }

                  clipRef++;

                  clipList[clipRef].x = tempClipList[v2].x;
                  clipList[clipRef].y = tempClipList[v2].y;
                  clipList[clipRef].z = tempClipList[v2].z;
```

```
        /* Copy the texture coordinates */
        clipList[clipRef].tx = tempClipList[v2].tx;
        clipList[clipRef].ty = tempClipList[v2].ty;

        clipRef++;
      }

      v1 = v2;
    }
    thisPolygon->numOfClippedVerts = clipRef;
  }
  thisPolygon = thisPolygon->nextPolygon;
}
}
```

Texture-Mapped Rendering Mode

Because you now have the capability to render texture-mapped polygons, you need to add a new rendering mode to Poly Render.h. The new mode is called kRender_PolygonTextureMap and its ID is 3. This code segment has also been added to DrawPolygonList() to handle the new mode:

```
case kRender_PolygonTextureMap:
  TextureMapDrawPoly(thisPolygon, pixMapPtr, rowBytes);
  break;
```

Loading the Texture

All the hard work is done. All that's missing are routines to load the texture from disk, and you need to modify the OBJ3 resource again to hold a field for the texture ID, and for the coordinates of the texture.

The texture map handling is done in a new file called Texture.c. You want to achieve several goals by handling the texture data. First, you don't want to have to load a texture every time it is referenced. Second, if two polygons use the same texture map (which happens very often), you don't want to have to load two copies of the same texture.

All the textures are stored in PICT resources in the application's resource fork. You can declare an array of TextureHandles that will hold each texture as it's loaded and retrieve it when it is referenced the next time:

```
TextureHandle   TextureArray[kTextureArraySize];
```

Declare the kTextureArraySize large enough to hold every different texture you're going to need during the course of the game. Each texture consumes 16k of data when loaded, but because you store the textures in handles, you don't have to allocate this memory until the texture is actually loaded from disk. Thus, the array takes up only 4 bytes for every element in the texture array (because a handle is 4 bytes long).

For now, limit yourself to 30 textures, but that's far more than you'll use during the course of this book.

```
#define kTextureArraySize        30
```

The PICT resources will begin at ID 128; the first element of this array holds texture ID 128, the second holds 129, and so on:

```
#define kFirstTextureID          128
```

The first thing you want to do with this array is initialize each element to Null. This is so you can tell whether a texture has been loaded or not simply by looking at its entry in the array. If the entry is Null, you still need to load it; otherwise, you can just pass back the existing handle.

InitializeTextureArray() simply loops through each element and sets it to Null. It should be called once when the program starts up, just like the other initialization routines.

```
/**
 **   InitializeTextureArray()
 **
 **   Sets all of the entries of the texture array to NULL
 **   so they can be loaded in when first referenced.
 **/
void  InitializeTextureArray() {
  short    i;

  for (i = 0; i < kTextureArraySize; i++) {
    TextureArray[i] = NULL;
  }
}
```

The next routine, GetTexture(), loads the PICT resource, creates a 128x128 GWorld, copies the texture into the GWorld, and finally copies the individual pixels into a new TextureHandle. The intermediate step of the GWorld is necessary because a PICT resource isn't necessarily stored as a bitmap and you don't necessarily know the format of the PICT resource.

Texture Scaling

An additional advantage of copying the texture into an intermediate GWorld is that it is automatically scaled to the current texture size. Thus you could paste PICT images that aren't necessarily 128x128 into the resource fork. However, putting in textures of a lower resolution will defeat the purpose of using high-resolution textures. You should also be careful that the texture isn't too large to load into memory.

This process may sound needlessly complicated, but it's only called once for each texture in the database so it can afford to be a little slow. The routine is somewhat long (Listing 19-5), but it doesn't do anything you haven't seen before.

Listing 19-5 *The GetTexture() routine*

```
/**
** GetTexture()
**
** Loads a PICT texture from disk, draws it into a GWorld,
** then allocates a TextureHandle and copies the image data
** into that.
**/
TextureHandle  GetTexture(short  id) {
  GWorldPtr      gw;
  PixMapHandle   pm;
  PicHandle      pict;
  long           srcRowBytes;
  Rect           textureRect;
  char           *src, *dst;
  TextureHandle  texture = NULL;
  OSErr          theErr;
  short          i;

  /* Load the PICT resource */
  pict = GetPicture(id);

  /* If it was successful... */
  if (pict != NULL) {
    /* Create a new GWorld the size of our texture. If the PICT
     * happens to be a different size, it will be scaled to the
     * texture map size when it's drawn into this GWorld.
     */
    SetRect(&textureRect, 0, 0, kTextureMapSize, kTextureMapSize);
    theErr = NewGWorld(&gw, 8, &textureRect, nil, nil, 0);

    if (theErr == noErr) {
      GWorldPtr  curPort;
      GDHandle   curDev;

      /* Draw the PICT into the GWorld */
      GetGWorld(&curPort, &curDev);
      SetGWorld(gw, NULL);
      DrawPicture(pict, &textureRect);
      SetGWorld(curPort, curDev);

      /* We don't need the PICT any more */
      ReleaseResource((Handle)pict);

      /* Allocate the TextureHandle's memory */
      texture = (TextureHandle)NewHandle(sizeof(TextureRec));
```

Continued on next page

Continued from previous page

```
    if (texture != NULL) {
      /* Get the basic information about the GWorld's
       * image.
       */
      pm = GetGWorldPixMap(gw);
      LockPixels(pm);
      src = GetPixBaseAddr(pm);
      dst = (char*)(**texture).data;

      srcRowBytes = (**pm).rowBytes & 0x3FFF;

      /* Copy the image from the pixmap into the
       * TextureHandle
       */
      for (i = 0; i < kTextureMapSize; i++) {
        BlockMove(src, dst, kTextureMapSize);
        src += srcRowBytes;
        dst += kTextureMapSize;
      }
      UnlockPixels(pm);
    }
    /* Get rid of the GWorld */
    DisposeGWorld(gw);
  }
}
return texture;
}
```

Finally, you need a routine to deliver the texture handle to TextureMapDrawPoly(). This routine, called GetTextureHandle(), checks the texture array entry to see if it's Null. If it *is* Null, the routine loads the texture into memory. In any case, it then returns the texture handle to the calling routine:

```
/**
 ** GetTextureHandle()
 **
 ** If the requested texture has already been loaded, this
 ** routine just returns a handle to it. Otherwise, it calls
 ** GetTexture() to load the texture from disk.
 **/
TextureHandle  GetTextureHandle(short id) {
  short  arrayIndex = id - kFirstTextureID;

  if (TextureArray[arrayIndex] == NULL) {
    TextureArray[arrayIndex] = GetTexture(id);
  }
  return TextureArray[arrayIndex];
}
```

OBJ3 and Texture Mapping

A few new fields have to be added to the OBJ3 resource to correspond to the new fields in the Polygon3D structure. In addition to the vertex index in each polygon, there is now a Texture X and Texture Y, which represent points on the surface of the texture map. For example, the upper-left point of a polygon should receive 0 in both of these fields and the lower-right point receives 127 in both fields.

In addition, each polygon now has a field for the Texture ID. This field is ignored if the polygon's rendering mode is not set to kRender_PolygonTextureMap, but otherwise it corresponds to a PICT resource ID.

You can see the redesigned polygon database in the Object Template.rsrc file in the folder for this chapter on the source code disc.

Loading the Texture-Mapped Objects

In response to the changes to the OBJ3 resource, the LoadObjectFromRsrc() function has to be modified. When loading the polygon vertices, this function also loads the polygon's texture map information (although not the actual texture bitmap). Listing 19-6 is the new source.

Listing 19-6 *The LoadObjectFromRsrc() routine*

```
/**
**   LoadObjectFromRsrc()
**
**   Fetches an object from an 'obj3' resource, converts it
**   to a Object3D type, processes the object, and sends
**   it back.
**/
Object3D *  LoadObjectFromRsrc(short resourceID)
{
  Object3D     *newObject;
  short        numOfVertices;
  short        numOfPolygons;
  short        currentVertice;
  short        currentPolygon;
  Handle       objectResourceHandle;
  long         resourceDataOffset;
  Ptr          resourceData;

  /* Load the resource from the disk */
  objectResourceHandle = GetResource('Obj3', resourceID);
```

Continued on next page

Continued from previous page

```
      /* Check to make sure the resource was loaded correctly */
      if (objectResourceHandle == NULL)
        return NULL;

      /* Alloate memory for the new object */
      newObject = (Object3D *)NewPtr(sizeof(Object3D));

      /* Lock the resource handle */
      HLock(objectResourceHandle);

      /* Dereference the handle into a pointer */
      resourceData = *objectResourceHandle;

      /* Initialize the offset. This offset indicates the last
       * byte of the resource data that we read. The data
       * parsing routines will automatically increase this
       * value as they read the data.
       */
      resourceDataOffset = 0;

      /* Begin reading from the object data. The first word
       * of the data is the number of vertices in the object.
       */
      numOfVertices = ReadDataWord(resourceData, &resourceDataOffset);

      /* Make sure that the object does not have too many vertices */
      if (numOfVertices > kMaximumVertices) {
        DebugStr("\pThe resource data has too many vertices. Increase
    kMaximumVertices if you want to load this object.");
        return NULL;
      }


      newObject->numOfVertices = numOfVertices;

      /* Read all of the vertices in */
      for (currentVertice = 0; currentVertice < numOfVertices;
    currentVertice++)
      {
        short     verticeX, verticeY, verticeZ;

        verticeX = ReadDataWord(resourceData, &resourceDataOffset);
        verticeY = ReadDataWord(resourceData, &resourceDataOffset);
        verticeZ = ReadDataWord(resourceData, &resourceDataOffset);

        /* Put this vertex into the object */
        newObject->vertex[currentVertice].lx = verticeX;
        newObject->vertex[currentVertice].ly = verticeY;
        newObject->vertex[currentVertice].lz = verticeZ;
        newObject->vertex[currentVertice].lt = 1;
      }
```

```
      /* Read the number of polygons in the object */
      numOfPolygons = ReadDataWord(resourceData, &resourceDataOffset);

      /* Make sure the object doesn't have too many polygons */
      if (numOfVertices > kMaximumPolys) {
        DebugStr("\pThe resource data has too many polygons. Increase
    kMaximumPolys if you want to load this object.");
        return NULL;
      }

      newObject->numOfPolygons = numOfPolygons;

      /* Read all of the polygons in */
      for (currentPolygon = 0; currentPolygon < numOfPolygons;
    currentPolygon++)
      {
        short      numOfPolygonVerts;
        short      currentPolygonVert;
        Polygon3D  *polygonRef;

        /* Obtain a pointer to the current polygon in the new object */
        polygonRef = &newObject->polygon[currentPolygon];

        /* Read the polygon color */
        polygonRef->color = ReadDataWord(resourceData, &resourceDataOffset);

        /* Read in the polygon rendering mode */
        polygonRef->renderingMode = ReadDataWord(resourceData,
    &resourceDataOffset);

        /* Read in the polygon texture ID */
        polygonRef->textureMap = ReadDataWord(resourceData,
    &resourceDataOffset);

        /* Read the number of vertices in this polygon */
        numOfPolygonVerts = ReadDataWord(resourceData, &resourceDataOffset);

        /* Make sure that this polygon doesn't have too many vertices */
        if (numOfPolygonVerts > kMaxPolygonSize) {
          DebugStr("\pThe resource data has too many vertices in a polygon.
    Increase kMaxPolygonSize if you want to load this object.");
          return NULL;
        }

        polygonRef->numOfVertices = numOfPolygonVerts;

        /* Read each of the vertices */
        for (  currentPolygonVert = 0;
               currentPolygonVert < numOfPolygonVerts;
               currentPolygonVert++  )
        {
```

Continued on next page

Continued from previous page

```
        short    vertexIndex;
        Vertex3D *vertexPtr;
        short    textureCoordinate;

        vertexIndex = ReadDataWord(resourceData, &resourceDataOffset);

        /* Verify that the vertex index is valid */
        if (vertexIndex >= numOfVertices) {
          DebugStr("\pOne of the polygon vertex indices is invalid.");
          return NULL;
        }

        /* Find a pointer to this vertex and put it into the polygon */
        vertexPtr = &newObject->vertex[vertexIndex];
        polygonRef->polyVertex[currentPolygonVert] = vertexPtr;

        /* Read in the texture X for this vertex */
        textureCoordinate = ReadDataWord(resourceData,
&resourceDataOffset);
        /* Store it in the polygon */
        polygonRef->textureVertices[currentPolygonVert].x =
textureCoordinate;

        /* Read in the texture Y for this vertex */
        textureCoordinate = ReadDataWord(resourceData,
&resourceDataOffset);
        /* Store it in the polygon */
        polygonRef->textureVertices[currentPolygonVert].y =
textureCoordinate;

    }

    /* We're done with the polygon - we'll calculate the polygon
     * normal later.
     */
  }

  /* Read the origin of the object */
  newObject->originX = ReadDataWord(resourceData, &resourceDataOffset);
  newObject->originY = ReadDataWord(resourceData, &resourceDataOffset);
  newObject->originZ = ReadDataWord(resourceData, &resourceDataOffset);

  /* We're done reading the object. Unlock the data handle and release
   * the resource.
   */
  HUnlock(objectResourceHandle);
  ReleaseResource(objectResourceHandle);

  /* Initialize the transformation fields of the object */
  newObject->xAngle = newObject->yAngle = newObject->zAngle = 0;
  newObject->scalingFactor = 1.0;
  newObject->update = TRUE;
```

```
                    /* Return the new object */
                    return newObject;
                }
```

Other Miscellaneous Changes

To demonstrate the texture-mapping techniques, you're going to change the 3D maze you created in the last chapter so that the walls are texture mapped. In the last chapter, you were restricted to moving along the x-z plane. However, to really show off what texture mapping can do, I'm going to remove that restriction. Now you can not only turn left and right, you can also pitch forward and backward or roll left and right. However, these view rotations don't correspond directly with changing the view's x, y, and z coordinates. As with the MoveForwardAndBack() function, you must write a routine that uses trigonometry to convert what I'll refer to as yaw, pitch, and roll movements to simple x, y, and z rotations.

The MoveForwardAndBack() routine also simplifies certain rotations. For example, if you pitch up past 90° (i.e., straight up), you can get the equivalent by changing both the yaw and roll by 180° and changing pitch to a value less than 90. Although this may sound complicated, it doesn't really affect the calculation speed and it offers two advantages: It will make the maneuvers easier to visualize and it will help you move to airplane terms in the next chapter.

Listing 19-7 is a routine that changes the view's x, y, and z rotations based on yaw, pitch, and roll values.

Listing 19-7 The RotateViewWithRelativeAngles( ) routine

```
/**
 **    RotateViewWithRelativeAngles()
 **
 **    Changes the view's rotation using roll,
 **    pitch, and yaw values.
 **/
void  RotateViewWithRelativeAngles(   short roll,
                                      short pitch,
                                      short yaw  )
{
  /* Add the roll & yaw values onto the view's angles */
  gCameraViewData.viewZAngle += roll;
  gCameraViewData.viewYAngle += yaw;

  /* Check to see if roll is between 0 and 359 */
  if (roll < 0) roll += 360;
  if (roll > 359) roll -= 360;

  /* Calculate the change to pitch (xAngle) based on
   * the pitch and roll values
   */
```

Continued on next page

684   Chapter 19   ✦✦✦✦✦

Continued from previous page

```
  gCameraViewData.viewXAngle += (pitch * gCosTable[roll]) >> 8;

  /* Calculate the additional change to yaw (yAngle)
   * based on the pitch and roll values.
   */
  gCameraViewData.viewYAngle -= (pitch * gSinTable[roll]) >> 8;

  /* Handle bounds checking on the angles */
  while (gCameraViewData.viewXAngle < 0)
    gCameraViewData.viewXAngle += 360;
  while (gCameraViewData.viewXAngle > 359)
    gCameraViewData.viewXAngle -= 360;
  while (gCameraViewData.viewYAngle < 0)
    gCameraViewData.viewYAngle += 360;
  while (gCameraViewData.viewYAngle > 359)
    gCameraViewData.viewYAngle -= 360;
  while (gCameraViewData.viewZAngle < 0)
    gCameraViewData.viewZAngle += 360;
  while (gCameraViewData.viewZAngle > 359)
    gCameraViewData.viewZAngle -= 360;

  /* Handle a special case when the pitch loops around */
  if ( (gCameraViewData.viewXAngle > 90) &&
       (gCameraViewData.viewXAngle < 270)  ) {

    /* Flip the roll around by 180 degrees */
    if (gCameraViewData.viewZAngle < 180)
      gCameraViewData.viewZAngle += 180;
    else
      gCameraViewData.viewZAngle -= 180;

    /* Flip the yaw around by 180 degrees */
    if (gCameraViewData.viewYAngle < 180)
      gCameraViewData.viewYAngle += 180;
    else
      gCameraViewData.viewYAngle -= 180;

    /* Mirror the pitch to the adjacent quadrant */
    if (gCameraViewData.viewXAngle <= 180)
      gCameraViewData.viewXAngle = 180 -
          gCameraViewData.viewXAngle;
    else
      gCameraViewData.viewXAngle = 540 -
          gCameraViewData.viewXAngle;
  }
  gCameraViewData.update = TRUE;
}
```

HandleUserInput() must also be changed to handle the new degree of freedom. To allow the user to control rotation with his or her left hand, control the roll with the Q and W keys and the pitch with A and Z.

HandleUserInput() (Listing 19-8) simply monitors for these keys and calls RotateViewWithRelativeAngle() with the proper parameters when one of the keys has been pressed. In addition, I've removed the bouncing motion and the footsteps sound because the player is no longer "walking" on a two-dimensional surface.

Listing 19-8 The HandleUserInput( ) routine

```
/**
**   HandleUserInput()
**
**   Checks the keyboard for any keys held down and moves the camera
**   accordingly.
**/
void  HandleUserInput(void)
{
  unsigned char        ourKeyMap[16];

  /* Get the key map */
  GetKeys((unsigned long *)ourKeyMap);

  /* Check for moving the camera forward */
  if (CheckKeyMap(ourKeyMap, kKeyMoveForward)) {
    MoveViewForwardAndBack(20);  /* Move camera forward 20 units */
  }
  if (CheckKeyMap(ourKeyMap, kKeyMoveBack)) {
    MoveViewForwardAndBack(-20);  /* Move camara back 20 units */
  }
  if (CheckKeyMap(ourKeyMap, kKeyTurnLeft))
    /* Change the camera's yaw by 5 degrees */
    RotateViewWithRelativeAngles(0, 0, -5);
  if (CheckKeyMap(ourKeyMap, kKeyTurnRight))
    /* Change the camera's yaw by 5 degrees */
    RotateViewWithRelativeAngles(0, 0, 5);

  if (CheckKeyMap(ourKeyMap, kKeyRollLeft))
    /* Change the camera's roll by 5 degrees */
    RotateViewWithRelativeAngles(-5, 0, 0);
  if (CheckKeyMap(ourKeyMap, kKeyRollRight))
    /* Change the camera's roll by 5 degrees */
    RotateViewWithRelativeAngles(5, 0, 0);

  if (CheckKeyMap(ourKeyMap, kKeyPitchDown))
    /* Change the camera's pitch by 5 degrees */
    RotateViewWithRelativeAngles(0, -5, 0);
  if (CheckKeyMap(ourKeyMap, kKeyPitchUp))
    /* Change the camera's pitch by 5 degrees */
    RotateViewWithRelativeAngles(0, 5, 0);
}
```

Running the Texture-Mapped World

If you now compile and run your new texture-mapped virtual world, you'll be greeted with a scene similar to the one in Figure 19-13. So far, it looks like something you might see from a typical raycast environment. However, if you press one of the roll keys (Q or W), the entire world will rotate around (Figure 19-14), giving you a scene you'll never get from a raycasting engine!

Try turning to the right. You'll see a sample texture map that has been designed with a transparent texture map (see Figure 19-15). Because the texture map and the polygon surface are two dimensional, transparent texture maps don't work for creating objects with depth but they do work for simple barriers, plants, or similar items.

Despite the compensation you performed when clipping the polygons, there are some limitations to affine texture mapping. The textures tend to start distorting when polygons are viewed from very close, which doesn't exactly make it ideal for a 3D maze-rendering engine. You can reduce or even eliminate this phenomenon by using smaller polygons. This algorithm is also not yet fast enough to handle full-screen texture mapping.

However, the engine has been designed to mix different types of polygon rendering easily and it will be put to good use for the flight simulator in the next chapter. You can use it to render simple objects, especially those that will be viewed from a distance. This way, the slower rendering speed won't hurt you much and you can get a fairly decent-looking world to fly around in.

FIGURE 19-13

◎ ◎ ◎ ◎ ◎ ◎

The initial view from the texture-mapped maze

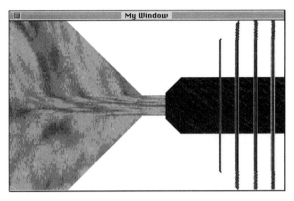

FIGURE 19-14

◎ ◎ ◎ ◎ ◎ ◎

Turning sideways within the world still texture maps correctly

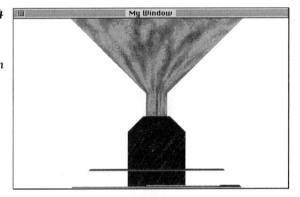

FIGURE 19-15

◎ ◎ ◎ ◎ ◎ ◎

A demonstration of the transparent textures

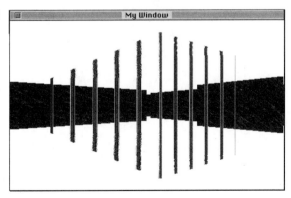

Graphics in Flight

ome trsibli fiore iemanouelle . diquali piuobano ilaisa
o igrapesi . mure lcommetti o genso saseranoteBono .
rsari nellamade rsapermaquibla alsa manobelle pesi qui n
aforsa . o pib isomo pib bal.

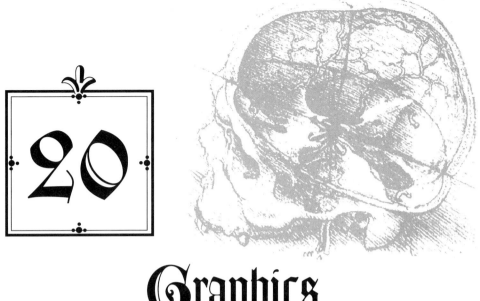

20

Graphics in Flight

Finally it's time to build the flight simulator. You have the necessary components: a basic application shell, a sound package, and a 3D polygon renderer. Although these three parts will form most of the simulator, a significant amount of code still must be written to support the characteristics of the airplane.

The new code will primarily do three things: create a flight model that approximates that of a real airplane, draw the instrument panel on the screen, and draw the horizon. You also need a routine that will allow you to change the pitch of the engine's sound (which will be created using the Continuous Sound package you built earlier), but this routine is very simple.

The most technically challenging task you face is creating an environment that feels like a real airplane, and that's the problem I'll tackle first.

The Flight Model

The flight model is the part of the flight simulator that stands between the user's input and the view system. It is one of the most important parts in attempting to make the simulation believable, but it is buried beneath the surface of the simulator so that many users may not even be aware of its existence.

The flight model determines how the airplane reacts to its environment. For example, when the airplane is pitched upward (so its nose points up into the air), the flight model determines that the plane should be gaining altitude (assuming, of course, its speed is sufficient). The flight model is also responsible for detecting things like whether the airplane has crashed or landed when it reaches the ground.

The flight models of games such as A-10 or F/A-18 Hornet are extremely complicated, which partially accounts for why these games are so popular. In fact, A-10 goes beyond calculating the flight model for the airplane and attempts to model the physics affecting everything else in the world, going so far as to cause debris to roll down a hillside.

The flight model you'll be creating in this chapter is quite simple. It attempts to model only the simplest characteristics of an airplane, but it is a good basis to start from. A large portion of this flight model was originally written by Mark Betz for Flights of Fantasy, but it's been modified to fit with the structures you've already created.

How an Airplane Flies

A large number of flight simulator games come with huge manuals that explain every little detail about the physics of flight, designed either to curtail the number of technical support calls from people wondering why the airplane stalls when they try to fly it straight up or to make the players feel they're getting more for their money. The physics of flight are not too overwhelming, however.

Every airplane's flight is affected by four principle forces, each emanating from a different direction. These forces are *lift*, *gravity*, *thrust*, and *drag*, and Figure 20-1 shows their effects. The forces are paired and each counters the effect of its opposite. Lift pushes the airplane upward as gravity pulls it down, and thrust pushes it forward as drag slows it down.

The trick of flying is to balance these forces. This can be a little dicey because thrust and lift are closely related—the more thrust is generated, the more lift is attained.

Two of these four forces arise from nature. Gravity will always pull an object toward the earth as long as you're at a low enough altitude, and drag will always occur as you travel through the atmosphere.

The other two forces are more or less under your control. You control thrust directly using a propeller or a jet engine and you control lift by changing the wing's shape or orientation. Let's look at these two forces in more detail.

Thrust

You may remember from your high school physics class that "for every action, there is an equal and opposite reaction," otherwise known as Sir Isaac Newton's First Law

FIGURE 20-1

ⓐ ⓐ ⓐ ⓐ ⓐ ⓐ

*The four forces
that dictate the
airplane's flight*

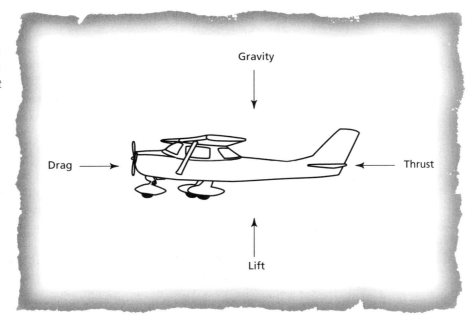

of Motion. This means that when you push something, it pushes back. If you can apply enough pressure to the object, either you or the object is going to have to move. If you're pushing a car that's in neutral, chances are that the car will give way first, moving away from you. However, if you happen to be wearing roller skates, you'll instead be pushed backward.

A jet or rocket engine operates by superheating a gas and forcing it out the back. This creates a large force pressing outwards, which also applies forward pressure. Because the airplane (or rocket) is relatively light compared to the force the engine is producing, it moves forward.

A propeller operates slightly differently. The propeller blades are shaped similarly to those of a fan and when they spin quickly, the air pressure on the front side of the propeller decreases. The propeller is then *pulled* into the low-pressure area (along with the rest of the airplane), creating thrust.

While the atmosphere allows the propeller-driven aircraft to pull itself along, it also applies an opposite pressure back onto the airplane's body called *drag*. This is the same effect you experience in automobiles: the faster a car travels, the harder it has to work to maintain that speed (which causes it to consume more fuel). This is the main reason modern cars are rounded: By changing the car's shape, you can reduce the atmosphere's drag. (It is interesting to note that, if you created a spacecraft that never entered the atmosphere, its shape would have no effect on its speed. In fact, you could design a huge flying space *box*. like the Borgs'.)

Thrust can be used to create lift, which is how rockets and missiles operate, as when the Space Shuttle first takes off. In fact, commercial airliners use thrust to create lift directly as they take off: They point their noses up and let the engines push the plane up. However, most of the altitude these airliners achieve is gained using another, more fuel-efficient method.

Lift

At some point in your life, you were probably unable to resist the temptation to stick your hand out the window of your car as you were traveling along at slightly over the speed limit. You probably noticed that if you tilt your hand downward into the wind, your entire arm is pressed down, and if you tilt it the other way, you feel a force pulling it up. This pressure is the same basic force used to fly an airplane.

This force is created similarly to the one generated by an airplane's propellers. If the air pressure on one side of an object is greater than the pressure on the opposite side, the object is going to be pushed toward the lower pressure.

The airplane's wings operate by creating a higher pressure on one side than the other. Figure 20-2 shows air flowing over the surface of a wing. However, the wing does not move as your hand does. It remains parallel to the ground, but the top of the wing is shaped so that it has more surface area than the bottom. Because the air on top has more

FIGURE 20-2
◎ ◎ ◎ ◎ ◎ ◎
The airflow over a wing

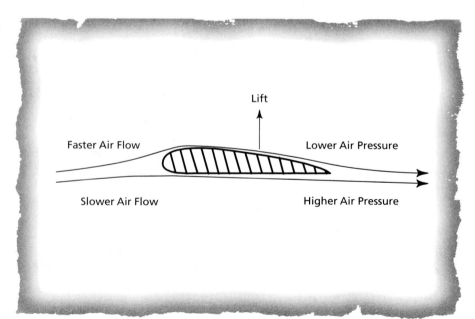

surface to travel over, it has to move faster, and the increased speed causes the air pressure above the wing to drop. This, in turn, pushes the wing upward.

It may be hard to believe that this small difference could generate enough force to lift an entire airplane. However, if you consider that the force applied to your hand when you stick it out your window is probably a few pounds and the airplane's wings are 20 times as wide and several hundred times longer than your hand, thousands of pounds of lift could be generated, more than enough to put a small plane into the air.

The lift generated can also be affected by tilting the wings forward and back, much the same as when you tilt your hand. Because the wings of most airplanes are firmly attached to the body, the only way to tilt the wings is to tilt the entire airplane (ignoring flaps and ailerons for the moment). The airplane's tilt is known as the *angle of attack*, which is essentially a rotation around the craft's x axis.

Tilting the front end of the airplane upward so the undersides of the wings are exposed to the oncoming air increases lift. However, doing this also creates drag, slowing the airplane down (because it's less aerodynamic in this position), which in turn can *decrease* lift (see Figure 20-3). If the angle of attack is too great, the airplane's speed can decrease to such a point that it starts to fall, a condition known as a *stall*. The airplane's lift can be regained once enough speed has been achieved, but gaining this speed requires a good deal of altitude to begin with. Countless airplane crashes have been caused by an airplane stalling when it is too close to the ground (which you're surely able to attest to if you're an avid fan of flight simulators).

Controlling the Airplane's Flight

With all these forces operating on the surface of the plane, it's a wonder the plane can remain in the air and under control. The trick is to balance the two forces that are under the pilot's control (thrust and lift) with those that are not (drag and gravity).

Thrust is easy to control. Thrust starts out in the form of some sort of fuel, such as a high-grade gasoline. From there, it is either burned to heat air (in the case of a jet engine) or exploded in a piston engine (in the case of a propeller engine) or some combination of the two (in a turboprop engine). The thrust can be controlled by changing the amount of fuel flowing to the engine, which is done using a *throttle*.

The thrust controls the lift, albeit in a complicated fashion. Because lift is a function of the speed of the airplane, it makes sense that reducing the throttle will reduce the lift of the plane. This is true to some extent, but it isn't quite that simple. Reducing the throttle does reduce the airplane's speed and it begins to lose lift. But as it falls under the influence of gravity and begins to lose altitude, it also gains speed—which, in turn, increases lift. Getting an airplane to go back down after it is in the sky is not a trivial matter and requires some experience. In fact, landing is probably the single most difficult thing a pilot must do. Taking off and maneuvering are simple in comparison.

FIGURE 20-3
ⓞ ⓞ ⓞ ⓞ ⓞ ⓞ

The angle of attack affects the airplane's lift

(a) A slight angle of attack produces a small amount of lift

(b) A large angle of attack produces more lift

(c) If the angle of attack is too great, the plane will stall

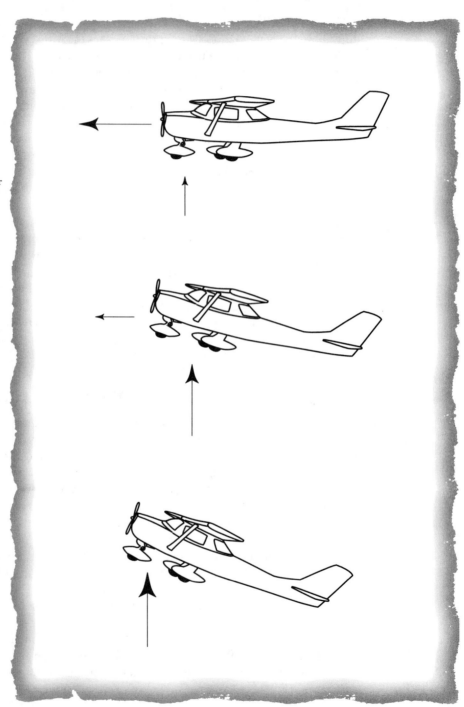

To simplify these matters and to give pilots the added ability to steer, airplanes have control surfaces. These are external features of the plane that can be manipulated with controls placed in the cockpit, effectively allowing the pilot to change the shape of the plane dynamically while flying to speed it up, slow it down, gain or lose altitude, or steer left and right.

The three major airplane control surfaces are the *ailerons*, the *elevators*, and the *rudder*. They are controlled from the cockpit by two controls: the *stick* and the *pedals*. When moved to the left or right, the stick controls the ailerons. When moved forward and back, it controls the elevators. The pedals control the rudder.

But how do these actually affect the airplane's movement? Basically, these control the plane's rotations (just like the rotations you've been applying to three-dimensional objects). As you know, an object can rotate in three directions: along the x axis, the y axis, and the z axis. On the airplane, however, these axes have different terms, as you might expect.

An airplane's rotation around its x axis is known as its *pitch* (see Figure 20-4a) because the airplane pitches forward and back relative to the perspective of the pilot. Rotation around the y axis determines its *yaw* (Figure 20-4b), which changes the airplane's compass heading. Finally, rotating around the z axis is called *roll* because the airplane appears to roll over (see Figure 20-4c).

You now have a very basic idea of the physics affecting an airplane. Now let's look at how you can simulate them in code.

The Airplane State

To make things a little easier on yourself, store all the information related to the virtual airplane in one structure. Although it ends up being a rather large structure, the advantage is you can pass just a single structure to most of the routines and they'll have everything they need.

```
typedef struct {
    short       aileronPosition;    /* Aileron position from -100 to 100 */
    short       elevatorPosition;   /* Elevator position from -100 to 100*/
    short       throttlePosition;   /* Throttle position from 0 to 100 */
    short       rudderPosition;     /* Rudder position from -100 to 100 */

    Boolean     ignitionOn;         /* Ignition state (on/off) */
    Boolean     engineOn;           /* Engine state (on/off) */
    short       engineRPM;          /* Speed of the engine */
    float       fuel;               /* Airplane fuel level */
    float       fuelConsumption;    /* Fuel consumption in units/minute */

    Fixed24     xPosition;          /* x, y, and z position of the */
    Fixed24     yPosition;          /* plane in the world */
    Fixed24     zPosition;

    float       pitch;              /* Pitch, yaw, and roll of */
```

Continued on next page

Continued from previous page

```
float      yaw;                /* the plane (x, y, and z */
float      roll;              /* rotations, respectively) */

float      deltaPitch;       /* deltaPitch, deltaYaw, and */
float      deltaYaw;         /* deltaRoll represent the speed at which */
float      deltaRoll;        /* the plane is turning */

float      airspeed;         /* The horizontal speed of the */
                             /* plane (mph) */
float      verticalSpeed;    /* How far the airplane climbs */
                             /* per timeslice */
float      feetPerTimeslice; /* How far the airplane moves (in */
                             /* any dimension) */
                             /* per timeslice */
float      angleOfFlight;    /* The effective angle of flight */
float      climbRate;        /* Same as verticalSpeed, except */
                             /* expressed in feet per minute */
short      altitude;         /* Altitude in feet */

Boolean    airborne;         /* Are we in the air? */
Boolean    stalled;          /* Is the plane currently stalled? */
Boolean    brake;            /* Is the brake on? */

short      viewDirection;    /* Which way the view is facing */
} AirplaneStatusRec;
```

The comments are fairly self-explanatory and you'll soon see each of these elements used in the flight model code.

Receiving Input

In Chapter 8, you implemented several methods of receiving input for the Invaders! game. Most of these methods can still be used for the flight simulator, but there is one that you're going to discontinue: mouse relative. This method of control is counterintuitive in a flight simulator because you expect the stick to go wherever the mouse goes.

You're going to create one routine that determine the airplane's control surfaces no matter what the input method is. As in the Invaders! game, the preferred input method will be chosen from the menu and the current setting will be passed on to User Input.c, where the functions in that file can take advantage of it.

In addition to the stick control, the user can directly control several other settings: ignition, brakes, throttle, rudder, and which direction the user is currently looking. You'll map all of these keys to the keyboard, but you can also take advantage of the capabilities of joysticks. The ThrustMaster joystick has five extra buttons plus a "hat" switch that can be used for changing the view; the ThrustMaster add-ons provide a throttle (on the ThrustMaster WCS) and rudders (on the ThrustMaster rudder control). Table 20-1 shows how you'll map the controls to both the keyboard and the ThrustMaster joystick.

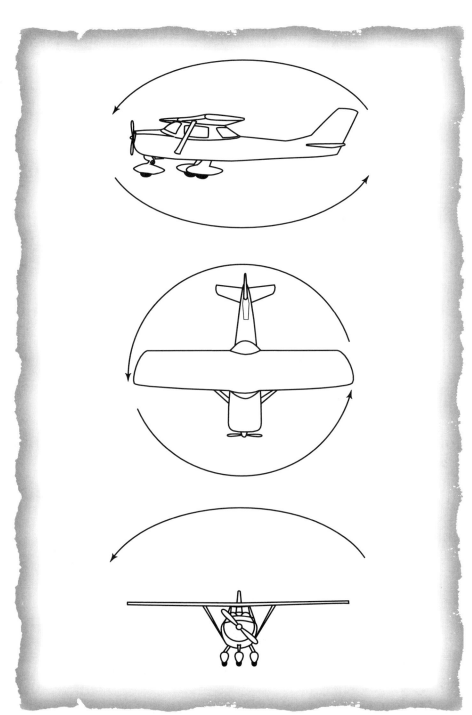

FIGURE 20-4

⊚ ⊚ ⊚ ⊚ ⊚ ⊚

*The three
rotations of the
airplane*

(a) Pitch

(b) Yaw

(c) Roll

Function	Keyboard	ThrustMaster
Ignition	i	Upper Thumb
Brakes	b	Lower Thumb
Rudders	< and >	Rudder Controls
Throttle	- and +	WCS Throttle Control
View Forward	w	Hat Forward
View Left	a	Hat Left
View Right	s	Hat Right
View Back	z	Hat Back

TABLE 20-1 ◈ *Control Mapping to the Keyboard and the ThrustMaster Joystick*

These keyboard controls will always be active and the ThrustMaster controls will be active if the ThrustMaster joystick is selected and the appropriate extra equipment is found.

After the stick, throttle, and rudder control positions are calculated, the *aileronPosition, elevatorPosition, throttlePosition,* and *rudderPosition* fields of the airplane's status are updated along with the additional controls. The next time the flight model is calculated, these controls will be acted upon.

Listing 20-1 shows the HandleUserInput() function.

Listing 20-1 *The HandleUserInput() function*

```
/**
**  HandleUserInput()
**
**  Checks the keyboard for any keys held down and moves the camera
**  accordingly.
**/
void  HandleUserInput(AirplaneStatusRec  *airplaneStatus)
{
  unsigned char  ourKeyMap[16];
  short          stickX, stickY, rudder, throttle;
  Boolean        ignitionToggle, brakeToggle;
  short          viewDirection;

  /* Get the current stick settings */
  stickX = airplaneStatus->aileronPosition;
  stickY = airplaneStatus->elevatorPosition;
  rudder = airplaneStatus->rudderPosition;
  throttle = airplaneStatus->throttlePosition;
  viewDirection = airplaneStatus->viewDirection;
```

```
ignitionToggle = brakeToggle = FALSE;

/* Get the key map */
GetKeys((unsigned long *)ourKeyMap);

/* Which input method are we using? This portion only
 * checks for stick-specific items, like the x and y
 * positions. The throttle, rudder, and other items
 * are checked after this loop (because they are always
 * controlled by the keyboard). The joysticks
 * can affect these things, but we're still going to check
 * the keyboard, to give the user more control.
 */
switch (gUserInputMethod) {
  case kKeyboardInput:
  {
    if (CheckKeyMap(ourKeyMap, kKeyRollLeft))
      stickX -= kKeyboardSensitivity;
    else if (CheckKeyMap(ourKeyMap, kKeyRollRight))
      stickX += kKeyboardSensitivity;
    else
      stickX = 0;
    if (CheckKeyMap(ourKeyMap, kKeyPitchDown))
      stickY += kKeyboardSensitivity;
    else if (CheckKeyMap(ourKeyMap, kKeyPitchUp))
      stickY -= kKeyboardSensitivity;
    else
      stickY = 0;
  }
  break;

  case kAbsoluteWindowInput:
  case kAbsoluteScreenInput:
  {
    Point     mouseLoc;
    Rect      outerMouseBounds;
    GrafPtr   windowPort;

    /* Where is the mouse's location? */
    GetMouse(&mouseLoc);

    /* Get the rectangle that represents the maximum bounds of
     * the mouse.
     */
    if (gUserInputMethod == kAbsoluteScreenInput) {
      outerMouseBounds = qd.screenBits.bounds;
    } else {
      GlobalToLocal(&mouseLoc);
      GetPort(&windowPort);
      outerMouseBounds = windowPort->portRect;
    }
```

Continued on next page

Continued from previous page

```
    /* Find the relative position of the mouse */
    stickX = (((float)(mouseLoc.h - outerMouseBounds.left) /
              (float)outerMouseBounds.right) * 30) - 15;
    stickY = -(((float)(mouseLoc.v - outerMouseBounds.top) /
              (float)outerMouseBounds.bottom) * 30) - 15;
  }
  break;

  case kThrustMaster:
  {
    /* ThrustMaster stick ranges are from -127 to 127, so
     * we need to scale these to be within our own ranges
     * (-15 to 15).
     */
    stickX = ((long)gThrustMasterInfo->roll * 15) / 127;
    stickY = -((long)gThrustMasterInfo->pitch * 15) / 127;

    /* We can also handle some other things with the
     * thrustmaster, like the thrust and the rudder
     */
    if (gThrustMasterInfo->throttleAttached)
      throttle = ((long)gThrustMasterInfo->thrust * 100) / 255;

    if (gThrustMasterInfo->rudderAttached)
      rudder = ((long)gThrustMasterInfo->yaw * 15) / 255;

    /* We'll map the ignition to the thumb-high, the
     * brake to the thumb-low, and the view to the hat
     */
    if (gThrustMasterInfo->thumbHigh)
      ignitionToggle = TRUE;

    if (gThrustMasterInfo->thumbLow)
      brakeToggle = TRUE;

    if (gThrustMasterInfo->hatUp)
      viewDirection = kViewForward;
    else if (gThrustMasterInfo->hatDown)
      viewDirection = kViewBackward;
    else if (gThrustMasterInfo->hatLeft)
      viewDirection = kViewLeft;
    else if (gThrustMasterInfo->hatRight)
      viewDirection = kViewRight;
  }
  break;

  case kMouseStick:
  {
    /* MouseStick stick ranges are from -127 to 127, so
     * we need to scale these to be within our own ranges
     * (-15 to 15).
     */
```

```
      stickX = ((long)gMouseStickInfo->stick1_xIn * 15) / 127;
      stickY = ((long)gMouseStickInfo->stick1_yIn * 15) / 127;
    }
    break;
}

/* Now handle the keyboard input for things like brake,
 * rudder, ignition, and view changes
 */
if (CheckKeyMap(ourKeyMap, kKeyRudderLeft))
  rudder -= kKeyboardSensitivity;
if (CheckKeyMap(ourKeyMap, kKeyRudderRight))
  rudder += kKeyboardSensitivity;
if (CheckKeyMap(ourKeyMap, kKeyThrottleUp))
  throttle += kKeyboardSensitivity;
if (CheckKeyMap(ourKeyMap, kKeyThrottleDown))
  throttle -= kKeyboardSensitivity;

if (CheckKeyMap(ourKeyMap, kKeyIgnition))
  ignitionToggle = TRUE;
if (CheckKeyMap(ourKeyMap, kKeyBrake))
  brakeToggle = TRUE;

if (CheckKeyMap(ourKeyMap, kKeyViewForward))
  viewDirection = kViewForward;
else if (CheckKeyMap(ourKeyMap, kKeyViewBackward))
  viewDirection = kViewBackward;
else if (CheckKeyMap(ourKeyMap, kKeyViewLeft))
  viewDirection = kViewLeft;
else if (CheckKeyMap(ourKeyMap, kKeyViewRight))
  viewDirection = kViewRight;

/* Check to see if each element is within its intended range */
if (stickX < -15)  stickX = -15;
if (stickX > 15)   stickX = 15;
if (stickY < -15)  stickY = -15;
if (stickY > 15)   stickY = 15;
if (throttle < 0)  throttle = 0;
if (throttle > 100)  throttle = 100;
if (rudder < -15)  rudder = -15;
if (rudder > 15)   rudder = 15;

/* Update the plane's status with the new info */
airplaneStatus->aileronPosition = stickX;
airplaneStatus->elevatorPosition = stickY;
airplaneStatus->throttlePosition = throttle;
airplaneStatus->rudderPosition = rudder;
airplaneStatus->viewDirection = viewDirection;

if (ignitionToggle)
  airplaneStatus->ignitionOn = !airplaneStatus->ignitionOn;
```

Continued on next page

Continued from previous page

```
  if (brakeToggle)
    airplaneStatus->brake = !airplaneStatus->brake;
}
```

Running the Flight Model

At this point, you know the current settings of each of the airplane's control surfaces. Now you need to have those surfaces affect the basic operation of the airplane, which is the heart of the flight model.

The flight model will be broken down into five parts, each modeling a form of physics affecting the airplane:

1. Calculating the airplane's power dynamics, such as engine speed

2. Calculating the airplane's flight dynamics; this is probably the most complicated portion of the flight model, as it attempts to model thrust, lift, gravity, and drag as they relate to each other

3. Calculating the momentum of the plane's movements

4. Calculating how quickly the plane is changing orientation based on the current control surfaces

5. Applying the changes to the roll, pitch, and yaw of the airplane calculated in step 4

These five steps are broken down into six functions (step 4 has one supporting function); once viewed in this fashion, the daunting math calculations become a little easier to handle.

Most of these routines make use of a global variable called gLastFrameTiming. This longword holds the number of milliseconds (one-thousandth of a second) that have passed since the last frame was drawn on the screen. If you adjust your calculations based on this number, the actual movement of the plane won't change when you use a faster or slower machine, even though the overall frame rate increases. This is very important for today's games because computing power is changing so rapidly—a machine that is unbelievably fast today will be a low-end system tomorrow.

The gLastFrameTiming variable is calculated before any of the six functions that you're using to model the physics of flight are called. I'll look at the process of calculating this variable in a bit. For now, however, just assume that it's accurate.

Calculating Power Dynamics

The first step of the flight model is very simple. CalculatePowerDynamics() checks to see if the ignition is turned on. If so, it also checks to see if the engine has been started and, if not, the function turns the engine on. Next, it compares the airplane's current engine RPM to the throttle setting. Because you have 100 throttle settings and the airplane's maximum RPM is somewhere around 2000, calculate the RPM for a particular throttle setting like this: RPM = (throttle * 17) + 300. This formula also forces the engine to have a minimum RPM setting of approximately 300.

If the engine's RPM does not match the throttle setting, CalculatePowerDynamics() will adjust the RPM slightly. By gradually changing the RPM in this fashion, the engine will appear to spin up to the throttle setting slowly.

This function is also responsible for changing the current engine sound pitch based on its RPM. This is accomplished using a function called AdjustSoundPitch(), which I'll examine later in this chapter. The function also starts or stops the engine sound if appropriate.

Listing 20-2 is the complete source code for CalculatePowerDynamics().

Listing 20-2 *The CalculatePowerDynamics( ) routine*

```
/**
 **   CalculatePowerDynamics()
 **
 **   Adjusts the engine RPM for the flight model. It also toggles
 **   the engine on/off. Part 1 of our flight model.
 **/
static void  CalculatePowerDynamics(void)
{
  long  idealRPM;

  /* Is the ignition on? */
  if (gAirplaneStatus.ignitionOn) {
    /* Has the engine been started? If not, start it. */
    if (gAirplaneStatus.engineOn == FALSE) {
      gAirplaneStatus.engineOn = TRUE;
      /* At this point, start the engine sound */
      if (!gEngineSoundIsPlaying)
        StartContinuousSound(128, 1, 0);
      gEngineSoundIsPlaying = TRUE;
    }


    /* Increment or decrement the RPM if it doesn't match the
     * engine's throttle setting.
     */
    idealRPM = (300 + (gAirplaneStatus.throttlePosition * 17));
    if (gAirplaneStatus.engineRPM < idealRPM) {
      gAirplaneStatus.engineRPM += gLastFrameTiming * 0.5;
      if (gAirplaneStatus.engineRPM > idealRPM)
        gAirplaneStatus.engineRPM = idealRPM;
    }
    else if (gAirplaneStatus.engineRPM > idealRPM) {
      gAirplaneStatus.engineRPM -= gLastFrameTiming * 0.5;
      if (gAirplaneStatus.engineRPM < idealRPM)
        gAirplaneStatus.engineRPM = idealRPM;
    }
```

Continued on next page

Continued from previous page

```
  /* Set the pitch to match the engine's RPM */
  AdjustSoundPitch((long)(gAirplaneStatus.engineRPM + 375) * 40);
} else {
  /* In this case, the ignition is not on. Check to see if
   * the engine is on - if it is, turn it off.
   */
  if (gAirplaneStatus.engineOn)
    gAirplaneStatus.engineOn = FALSE;


  /* Is the engine still turning? If so, slow it down */
  if (gAirplaneStatus.engineRPM > 0) {
    gAirplaneStatus.engineRPM -= gLastFrameTiming * 0.5;
    AdjustSoundPitch((long)(gAirplaneStatus.engineRPM + 375) * 40);
  } else {
    if (gEngineSoundIsPlaying)
      StopContinuousSound(TRUE);
    gEngineSoundIsPlaying = FALSE;
  }
}

/* Make sure the engine RPM doesn't go negative */
if (gAirplaneStatus.engineRPM < 0)
  gAirplaneStatus.engineRPM = 0;
}
```

Calculating Flight Dynamics

The second stage of the flight model is significantly more complex. It's responsible for calculating the thrust, lift, drag, and gravity forces acting upon the airplane, which are generally explained with fairly complicated physics equations. But instead of being based on actual physics, the formulas used in this routine are based more on arbitrary calculations obtained through experimentation and tweaking. It doesn't do a perfect job of describing the movements of an airplane, but it does it well enough to create a feeling of flight.

If you wanted to add additional physics effects, such as wind or ice, to the flight simulator world, this would be the routine to modify and it provides a good basis for such experimentation.

The first portion of the routine calculates the current airspeed of the plane by examining its current RPM. The airspeed is also modified by the airplane's pitch; a negative pitch indicates the nose is facing into the air and the airspeed will be decreased; a positive pitch indicates the airplane is accelerating as it heads toward the ground.

The lift being applied to the plane is then calculated. It's based mainly on the plane's speed and pitch (because a steeper pitch results in greater lift). A gravitational constant is then applied to the lift, simulating the effects of the earth's gravity on any flying object.

The last thing this routine does is calculate the angle of attack of the airplane. As you may recall, the angle of attack represents how steeply the plane is climbing. If the angle of attack becomes too great and the plane doesn't have enough speed, it will stall, causing it to pitch forward. The plane's recovery from the stall, which happens automatically when its pitch exceeds 30 degrees, is also considered.

Listing 20-3 is the source code for CalculateFlightDynamics().

Listing 20-3 *The CalculateFlightDynamics() routine*

```
/**
 ** CalculateFlightDynamics()
 **
 ** Model things like lift, speed, and acceleration. This function
 ** doesn't attempt to model actual physics, it just uses some
 ** very rough formulas. Part 2 of our flight model.
 **/
static void  CalculateFlightDynamics(void)
{
  float  idealSpeed;    /* Speed ideally set by the RPM */
  float  liftSpeed;     /* Modified speed for lift calculation */
  float  horizAccel;    /* Horizontal acceleration (thrust) */
  float  lVelocity;     /* Vertical velocity from lift */
  float  gVelocity;     /* Vertical velocity from gravity */
  float  angleOfAttack;

  /* Calculate the ideal speed of the airplane */
  idealSpeed = gAirplaneStatus.engineRPM / 17.5;
  /* Modify the ideal speed based on the airplane's pitch */
  idealSpeed += gAirplaneStatus.pitch * 1.5;

  /* Calculate the horizontal acceleration */
  horizAccel = ((gAirplaneStatus.engineRPM *
              (idealSpeed - gAirplaneStatus.airspeed)));
  /* Scale it back to a reasonable number */
  horizAccel *= ((float)gLastFrameTiming / 10000000);

  /* Handle the brake if we're on the ground */
  if ((gAirplaneStatus.brake) &&
     (gAirplaneStatus.airborne == FALSE))
  {
    if (gAirplaneStatus.airspeed > 0)
      gAirplaneStatus.airspeed -= 1;
    else
      gAirplaneStatus.airspeed = 0;
  } else
    /* Accelerate normally */
    gAirplaneStatus.airspeed += horizAccel;

  /* Force the speed to a range of -1..1 */
  liftSpeed = (gAirplaneStatus.airspeed / 65) - 1;

  /* Truncate it at 1 */
```

Continued on next page

Continued from previous page

```
   if (liftSpeed > 1) liftSpeed = 1;

   /* Lift curve: L = arctan(V) */
   lVelocity = atan(liftSpeed) * kDegreesToRadians;
   /* Change lift to be between 0 and 90 degrees */
   lVelocity += 45;
   /* Shift range to 0..~17 */
   lVelocity /= 5.29;
   /* Multiply by pitch modifier */
   lVelocity *= (-(gAirplaneStatus.pitch * 0.157) + 1);
   /* Modify by the timeslice */
   lVelocity *= ((float)gLastFrameTiming / 1000);

   /* Calculate gravitational pull */
   gVelocity = ((float)gLastFrameTiming * kGravitationalConstant) / 1000;
   /* Find the entire vertical velocity */
   gAirplaneStatus.verticalSpeed = gVelocity + lVelocity;

   /* If we're on the ground, our vertical speed will be 0 */
   if ((gAirplaneStatus.airborne == FALSE) &&
      (gAirplaneStatus.verticalSpeed < 0))
        gAirplaneStatus.verticalSpeed = 0;

   /* Convert the vertical speed to feet/minute */
   gAirplaneStatus.climbRate = gAirplaneStatus.verticalSpeed /
                          ((float)gLastFrameTiming * 60000);

   /* Change the horizontal speed to feet/timeslice */
   gAirplaneStatus.feetPerTimeslice =
      (gAirplaneStatus.airspeed / 682) * gLastFrameTiming;

   /* Find the effective angle of flight */
   if (gAirplaneStatus.feetPerTimeslice > 0)
     angleOfAttack = -(atan((float)gAirplaneStatus.verticalSpeed /
                     gAirplaneStatus.feetPerTimeslice));
   else
     angleOfAttack = -(atan(gAirplaneStatus.verticalSpeed));

   /* atan() returns radians, so convert them to degrees */
   angleOfAttack *= kRadiansToDegrees;

   /* See if we're stalling */
   if (((gAirplaneStatus.pitch < angleOfAttack) &&
      (angleOfAttack < 0)) &&
      (gAirplaneStatus.airspeed < 40))
   {
     /* We've stalled. */
     gAirplaneStatus.stalled = TRUE;
   }

   /* If we've stalled, check to see if we've recovered yet */
   if (gAirplaneStatus.stalled) {
```

```
      if (gAirplaneStatus.pitch > 30)
        gAirplaneStatus.stalled = FALSE;
      else
        /* Let the stall take its toll */
        gAirplaneStatus.pitch += 1;
  }
}
```

Calculating the Airplane's Momentum

If you pull the stick to the left and the airplane starts rolling, then you center the stick again, don't expect the airplane to stop turning immediately. Because the airplane is not a light machine, its momentum will carry it for a little bit. The next function, InertialDamp() does this for you. For each frame, it lessens the deltaPitch, deltaYaw, and deltaRoll values slightly to slow the plane's rotations down. It's not the best simulation, but it starts to give you a realistic feeling of the plane's characteristics.

```
/**
 **   InertialDamp()
 **
 **   This function attempts to simulate the inertial damping of
 **   angular rates of change. It needs a lot of work, but
 **   you can see its effects in the momentum effect when the
 **   airplane is rolled. Part 3 of our flight model.
 **/
static void  InertialDamp(void)
{
  if (gAirplaneStatus.deltaPitch != 0) {
    gAirplaneStatus.deltaPitch *= 0.7;

    if ((gAirplaneStatus.deltaPitch > -0.1) &&
        (gAirplaneStatus.deltaPitch < 0.1))
      gAirplaneStatus.deltaPitch = 0;
  }

  if (gAirplaneStatus.deltaYaw != 0) {
    gAirplaneStatus.deltaYaw *= 0.7;

    if ((gAirplaneStatus.deltaYaw > -0.1) &&
        (gAirplaneStatus.deltaYaw < 0.1))
      gAirplaneStatus.deltaYaw = 0;
  }

  if (gAirplaneStatus.deltaRoll != 0) {
    gAirplaneStatus.deltaRoll *= 0.7;

    if ((gAirplaneStatus.deltaRoll > -0.1) &&
        (gAirplaneStatus.deltaRoll < 0.1))
      gAirplaneStatus.deltaRoll = 0;
  }
}
```

Handling the Airplane's Control Surfaces

Next, check the airplane's control surfaces to see how they affect the airplane's rotations. For example, if the ailerons are down, the plane is going to pitch upward at a speed relative to the aileron positions. While this function calculates the effect the rudders are having on the airplane's yaw, it also calls the "helper" function CalculateTurnRate() to see the effect its roll is having (because, to execute a tight turn, airplanes usually roll to the left or right instead of relying on rudders). The result of CalculateTurnRate() is then added to the deltaYaw value, as shown in Listing 20-4.

Listing 20-4 *The CalculateRateOfChange() routine*

```
/**
**    CalculateRateOfChange()
**
**    This function finds the current rates of change for
**    the aircraft's motion in the three axes, based on
**    control surface deflection, airspeed, and elapsed time.
**    Part 4 of our flight model.
**/
static void CalculateRateOfChange(void)
{
  float   torque;

  /* Change the airplane's delta-rotations based on
   * control positions and airspeed
   */
  if (gAirplaneStatus.airborne) {
    if (gAirplaneStatus.aileronPosition != 0) {
      /* The airplane is rolling */
      torque = (gAirplaneStatus.airspeed *
            gAirplaneStatus.aileronPosition) / 10000;
      if (((torque > 0) && (gAirplaneStatus.deltaRoll <
                          (torque * gLastFrameTiming))) ||
        ((torque < 0) && (gAirplaneStatus.deltaRoll >
                          (torque * gLastFrameTiming))))
        gAirplaneStatus.deltaRoll += torque * 6;
    }
  }

  if (gAirplaneStatus.elevatorPosition != 0) {
    /* The airplane is pitching */
    torque = (gAirplaneStatus.airspeed *
            gAirplaneStatus.elevatorPosition) / 10000;

    /* If we're on the ground, we have to rely on pure lift
     * to get us into the air
     */
    if ((gAirplaneStatus.airborne == FALSE) && (torque > 0))
      torque = 0;
```

```
      if (((torque > 0) && (gAirplaneStatus.deltaPitch <
                          (torque * gLastFrameTiming))) ||
        ((torque < 0) && (gAirplaneStatus.deltaPitch >
                          (torque * gLastFrameTiming))))
        gAirplaneStatus.deltaPitch += torque * 1.5;
    }

    if (gAirplaneStatus.airspeed > 0) {
      torque = 0.0;
      if (gAirplaneStatus.rudderPosition != 0)
        torque = (gAirplaneStatus.airspeed *
                  gAirplaneStatus.rudderPosition) / 10000;

      torque += CalculateTurnRate();

      if (((torque > 0) && (gAirplaneStatus.deltaYaw <
                          (torque * gLastFrameTiming))) ||
        ((torque < 0) && (gAirplaneStatus.deltaYaw >
                          (torque * gLastFrameTiming))))
        gAirplaneStatus.deltaYaw += torque * 1.5;
    }
}
```

CalculateTurnRate does a simple calculation based on the airplane's roll; a steep roll will result in a faster turn, but only to a maximum of 90 degrees on either side:

```
/**
 **  CalculateTurnRate()
 **
 **  Calculates the turn rate based on the plane's roll
 **/
static float  CalculateTurnRate(void)
{
  float   torque = 0;
  float   roll;

  roll = gAirplaneStatus.roll;
  if (roll <= 180) {
    if (roll > 90)
      roll = 180 - roll;
    torque = roll * 0.0005;
  } else {
    if (roll < 270)
      roll = 540 - roll;
    torque = (roll - 360) * 0.0005;
  }
  return torque;
}
```

Rotating the Airplane

The fifth and final step of the flight model is to apply the rotational speed to the airplane's facing angles. This process should look familiar to you; you used the same formulas in Chapter 19 for the RotateViewWithRelativeAngles() function. It has to take into account the current rotations of the airplane, which involves a little trigonometry.

This function (Listing 20-5) also checks for special conditions, such as the airplane's pitch exceeding + or - 90 degrees (which correspond respectively to the airplane facing straight down or straight up). Such a rotation can also be expressed by changing both the airplane's yaw and roll angles by 180 degrees and flipping around the pitch. Although this sounds like I'm making things more complicated, it will actually simplify some of your calculations later in this chapter, plus it makes it easier for you to visualize the airplane's orientation.

Listing 20-5 The ApplyRotations() routine

```
/**
 **   ApplyRotations()
 **
 **   This function applies the current angular rates of
 **   change to the current aircraft rotations, and checks
 **   for special case conditions such as pitch exceeding
 **   +/- 90 degrees.  Part 5 of our flight model.
 **/
static void  ApplyRotations(void)
{
  /* Make some local variables for yaw, pitch, and
   * roll so that our code is a little more clean
   */
  float  roll, pitch, yaw;

  /* Add the roll & yaw values onto the view's angles */
  roll = gAirplaneStatus.roll + gAirplaneStatus.deltaRoll;
  yaw = gAirplaneStatus.yaw + gAirplaneStatus.deltaYaw;

  /* Check to see if roll is between 0 and 359 */
  if (roll < 0) roll += 360;
  if (roll > 359) roll -= 360;

  /* Calculate the change to pitch based on
   * the delta pitch and roll values
   */
  pitch = gAirplaneStatus.pitch +
        (gAirplaneStatus.deltaPitch *
         (((float)gCosTable[(short)roll]) / 256));

  /* Calculate the additional change to yaw
   * based on the pitch and roll values.
   */
```

```
yaw -= (gAirplaneStatus.deltaPitch *
    (((float)gSinTable[(short)roll]) / 256));

/* Handle bounds checking on yaw between -180 and 180 */
while (yaw < 0)
  yaw += 360;
while (yaw > 359)
  yaw -= 360;

/* Handle a special case when the pitch loops around */
if ((pitch > 90) || (pitch < -90)) {

  /* Flip the roll around by 180 degrees */
  if (roll >= 0)
    roll -= 180;
  else
    roll += 180;
  if (yaw >= 180)
    yaw -= 180;
  else
    yaw += 180;
  if (pitch > 0)
    pitch = (180 - pitch);
  else
    pitch = (-180 - pitch);
}

/* Dampen everything out to 0 if they get close enough */
if ((pitch > -0.5) && (pitch < 0.5))
  pitch = 0;
if ((roll > -0.5) && (roll < 0.5))
  roll = 0;
if ((yaw > -0.5) && (yaw < 0.5))
  yaw = 0;

/* Put these variables back into the airplane status */
gAirplaneStatus.pitch = pitch;
gAirplaneStatus.roll = roll;
gAirplaneStatus.yaw = yaw;
}
```

Running the Flight Model

The entire flight model can be processed through one function. This function will be responsible for calling each of the five parts of the flight model and then updating the position of the airplane based on its rotations. It also calculates the gLastFrameTiming variable you've been seeing so much of over the last few functions and checks to see if the airplane has landed or crashed during the course of the last frame.

The movement calculations are accomplished using a routine you've had for a while: AngleVectorsToXYZ(). Using the unit vector returned from this function, the new position of the airplane is calculated, as shown in Listing 20-6.

Listing 20-6 *The RunFlightModel() routine*

```
/**
** RunFlightModel()
**
** Processes one frame of action for the flight simulator. Moves
** the plane to its new position, calculates things like whether
** or not the plane has stalled, and whether it is airborne
**/
static void  RunFlightModel(void)
{
  Fixed24      xMovement;  /* These variables are used */
  Fixed24      yMovement;  /* to calculate a vector */
  Fixed24      zMovement;  /* representing the airplane's */
                           /* facing */

  /* Find how long it took to draw the last frame
   * (in thousandths of a second)
   */
  gLastFrameTiming = ElapsedMicroseconds() / 1000;

  /* Make sure we don't have a 0 timing, because that
   * would cause divide-by-zero errors
   */
  if (gLastFrameTiming == 0)
    gLastFrameTiming = 1;

  /* Start updating the airplane's parameters through several
   * flight model calls.
   */

  /* Calculate power dynamics for the airplane - essentially
   * the engine speed.
   */
  CalculatePowerDynamics();

  /* Calculate flight dynamics for the airplane - things like
   * lift, airspeed, and acceleration.
   */
  CalculateFlightDynamics();

  /* Simulate the inertial damp of the airplane */
  InertialDamp();

  /* Find how fast the airplane's motion is changing */
  CalculateRateOfChange();

  /* Applies the angular rates of change to the airplane */
```

```
ApplyRotations();

/* Calculate the airplane's movement unit vector */
AngleVectorsToXYZ(  gAirplaneStatus.pitch,
                    gAirplaneStatus.yaw,
                    gAirplaneStatus.roll,
                    &xMovement,
                    &yMovement,
                    &zMovement  );

/* Scale the unit vector into an x,y, and z distance */
xMovement *= gAirplaneStatus.feetPerTimeslice;
yMovement *= gAirplaneStatus.feetPerTimeslice;
zMovement *= gAirplaneStatus.feetPerTimeslice;

/* Move the plane based on this distance. */
gAirplaneStatus.xPosition += xMovement >> 8;
gAirplaneStatus.yPosition += yMovement >> 8;
gAirplaneStatus.zPosition += zMovement >> 8;

/* Calculate the airplane's altitude */
gAirplaneStatus.altitude = (gAirplaneStatus.yPosition -
                            kSeaLevelAltitude);

/* Check to see if we're airborne */
if ((gAirplaneStatus.airborne == FALSE) &&
    (gAirplaneStatus.altitude > 0))
    gAirplaneStatus.airborne = TRUE;

/* Check to see if we've landed (or crashed) */
if ((gAirplaneStatus.airborne) &&
    (gAirplaneStatus.altitude <= 0))
{
  /* We've approached the ground. Is the plane able to land? */
  if ( ((gAirplaneStatus.pitch > 10)||(gAirplaneStatus.pitch < -10)) ||
       ((gAirplaneStatus.roll > 10)||(gAirplaneStatus.roll < -10)) ||
       ((gAirplaneStatus.airspeed > 120)))
  {
    /* The airplane was not positioned correctly (i.e. its pitch,
     * roll, or airspeed was unacceptable for landing). Show
     * a "Crashed!" dialog box.
     */
    if (gEngineSoundIsPlaying)
      StopContinuousSound(TRUE);
    gEngineSoundIsPlaying = FALSE;
    ShowCrash();
    ResetAircraftControls();
  } else {
    /* The conditions were favorable. Land the aircraft. */
    LandAircraft();
  }
}
}
```

Processing a Complete Frame

Looking one level higher, you can build a function that does *everything* necessary for the flight simulator except handing the menu interface and drawing the rendered frame to the window (both of which are still handled by the main() function). You've already seen most of the functions called by this routine; the rest will be explained in the next section, which covers drawing the cockpit:

```
/**
 **   ProcessAirplane()
 **
 **   Updates the entire airplane for one frame, handling input,
 **   flight model, drawing the world, and drawing the
 **   cockpit over the top.
 **/
void  ProcessAirplane(void)
{
  static long    lastUserInputTime = 0;
  long           thisTick;

  /* Check for user input only once per four ticks */
  thisTick = TickCount();
  if (thisTick - lastUserInputTime > 4) {
    /* Handle user input */
    HandleUserInput(&gAirplaneStatus);
    lastUserInputTime = thisTick;
  }

  /* Process the flight model for the airplane */
  RunFlightModel();

  /* Update the view system to handle the new position of the plane */
  SetAirplaneToView(&gAirplaneStatus);

  /* Draw the horizon onto the image */
  DrawHorizonWithViewSettings(gOffscreenPtr, gOffscreenRowBytes);

  /* Apply any animations to the objects in the world */
  AnimateObjectList();

  /* Transform all of the objects in the world */
  TransformObjectList();

  /* Draw the polygon list into the offscreen image */
  DrawPolygonList(gOffscreenPtr, gOffscreenRowBytes);

  /* Draw the cockpit over the top */
  DrawCockpit();
}
```

The Airplane Cockpit

Drawing the bitmapped cockpit on the screen is a little bit more tricky than it might sound at first. As you know, copying an image the size of the window is an expensive operation: The CopyBits() replacement routine, although not the most expensive function, takes a significant amount of CPU time. If you try to copy a bitmapped image of an airplane cockpit onto the offscreen, surely it would be equally expensive, if not more so.

But let's examine what the cockpit is going to look like. Figure 20-5 shows what you'll see when you're facing forward in the airplane. The bottom of the image contains the details of the airplane's gauges, whereas most of the top is transparent. However, you can't just copy the bottom third of the image—portions of the plane's wings and supports can still be seen in the top two-thirds of the screen.

You can take advantage of the fact that large portions of the cockpit image are transparent. If, when copying the cockpit, you can determine beforehand that there is a long transparent strip where you're not going to be copying any data, it'll speed up the process significantly. You will therefore be using a special copy routine that works from a compressed image and copies only nontransparent pixels.

Compressing the Cockpit

This determination will be made with some preprocessing of the cockpit image. When the program starts up, you can scan through the bitmap and remember where you have sequences of transparent pixels (which I'll define as having a color of 0, or pure white). Wherever you encounter such a strip, you can store it as a single number, representing how many 0s there are.

FIGURE 20-5

◎ ◎ ◎ ◎ ◎ ◎

The front view of the cockpit

You go through a similar process with the opaque pixels. First determine how many opaque pixels you have in a row and then store that number, along with those pixels' values, in the memory area.

Figure 20-6 shows this process. The bitmap shows a sequence of 5 opaque pixels, followed by 8 transparent pixels, followed by 3 opaque pixels. As the figure shows, you store a 5, followed by the opaque pixel data, then an 8, for the transparent pixels, then a 3, followed by the remaining opaque pixels.

This works fairly well, but when you encounter a pixel count, how do you know whether you're dealing with a run of opaque pixels or a run of transparent pixels? To solve this problem, add a value of 128 to the run of transparent pixels. Then, when copying the image to the screen, if you encounter a run that is greater than 128, you'll know it's a run of transparent pixels (and you can determine how many by subtracting 128). A side effect of this is that a run can be, at most, 127 pixels long. Of course, you can store longer runs by breaking them into multiple smaller runs.

This encoding process is similar to RLE compression and the ending image (if it has a great deal of white in it) should actually be slightly smaller than what you started with. Ironically, although compression usually slows things down, you're going to be using it to speed up the drawing code!

Let's look at a function that will take an image (stored as raw data in a pointer) and compress all the occurrences of 0. This routine isn't very optimized, but it's called only once for each of the cockpit images when the application starts up.

The routine starts out by creating a pointer that is twice the size of the original image. This is because RLE compression can theoretically *double* the size of an image (if every pixel is a different color or, in this case, if you have an image that alternates transparent and opaque pixels). Although this case is rare, you should account for it anyway. You'll be decreasing the buffer size later on when you figure out just how big the ending image is.

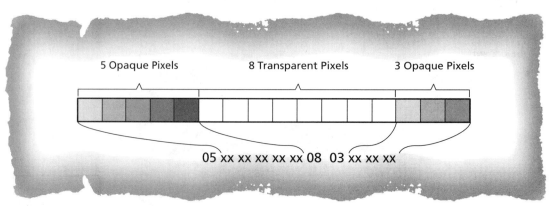

5 Opaque Pixels   8 Transparent Pixels   3 Opaque Pixels

05 xx xx xx xx xx 08 03 xx xx xx

FIGURE 20-6 ◉ *Compressing the image*

```
compressedBuffer = NewPtr(*dataSize * 2);
```

Then loop through the entire image until you reach the end:

```
/* Loop through the entire image */
while (dataPosition < dataLength) {
```

If the next pixel contains 0, begin counting how many 0s you have in a row. This continues until you reach an opaque pixel:

```
/* Does the next pixel contain 0? */
if (*uPtr == 0) {
```

Start the run counter off at 0:

```
/* Set the run length to 0 */
runLength = 0;
```

Next, loop until you encounter a pixel that is not 0, adding to the runLength counter each time. At the same time, keep track of where you are in the image data to make sure you don't reach the end. Break out if the run length reaches 127.

```
/* Loop while the next byte is 0 */
while (*uPtr == 0) {
  /* Move the pointer to the next byte */
  uPtr++;
  /* Add one to the run length */
  runLength++;
  /* Add one to the data position */
  dataPosition++;
  /* If we've reached a run of 127 pixels,
   * break out (because we can only handle
   * runs of 127 at a time)
   */
  if (runLength == 127) break;

  /* If we've reached the end of the image,
   * break out.
   */
  if (dataPosition == dataLength)
    break;
}
```

Then put this run length into the compressed image data, after adding 128:

```
/* Set the next byte of the uncompressed image to
 * the run length. We add 128 to the run length to
 * indicate that it's a run of zeros.
 */
*cPtr++ = 128 + runLength;
```

The other case is for opaque pixels. Copy over each pixel as you encounter it because you need to save this data. However, as you're advancing the compressed image pointer, remember what position to put the run length data into:

```
/* We won't know how long the run is until we've
 * copied over the data into the compressed
 * image. So we want to save a pointer to the
 * current position of the compressed data, so
 * we can shove the datalength into it later,
 * when we know how long it is.
 */
dataLengthPtr = cPtr;
/* Advance the cPtr to the next byte */
cPtr++;
```

The loop is very similar to the *transparent-pixel* loop:

```
/* Loop while the next byte is not zero */
while (*uPtr != 0) {
  /* Put the current byte into the compressed image */
  *cPtr++ = *uPtr++;
  /* Add one to the run length */
  runLength++;
  /* Add one to the data position */
  dataPosition++;
  /* If we've reached a run of 127 pixels,
   * break out (since we can only handle
   * runs of 127 at a time)
   */
  if (runLength == 127) break;

  /* If we've reached the end of the image,
   * break out.
   */
  if (dataPosition == dataLength)
    break;
}
```

Finally, the run length is stored the compressed image data:

```
/* Now that we know the run length, stuff
 * it back into the compressed image data
 */
*dataLengthPtr = runLength;
```

Listing 20-7 is the complete source code for the Compression algorithm.

Listing 20-7 The RLEZeroCompressBuffer() routine

```
/**
 **   RLEZeroCompressBuffer()
 **
 **   Takes a buffer of 8-bit values and compresses all of the
 **   runs of 0 with an RLE algorithm
 **/
OSErr   RLEZeroCompressBuffer(Ptr inputData, Ptr *compressedData, long
*dataSize)
{
  long      runLength;
  Ptr       uPtr;      /* Pointer to the uncompressed data */
  Ptr       cPtr;      /* Pointer to the compressed data */
  Ptr       compressedBuffer;
  Ptr       dataLengthPtr;
  long      dataPosition;
  long      dataLength;
  long      compressedDataLength;
  OSErr     err = noErr;

  dataLength = *dataSize;
  dataPosition = 0;

  /* Set both the uncompressed data pointer
   * to the beginning of the data.
   */
  uPtr = inputData;

  /* In the absolute worst case, RLE compression can actually double the
   * size of the image. To account for this, allocate a buffer
   * twice as big as the uncompressed data. We'll take care of making it
   * smaller later.
   */
  compressedBuffer = NewPtr(*dataSize * 2);

  /* Check to see if this succeeded */
  if (compressedBuffer == NULL) {
    err = MemError();
    return err;
  }

  /* Start off our compressed pointer at the beginning of this data */
  cPtr = compressedBuffer;

  /* Loop through the entire image */
  while (dataPosition < dataLength) {
    /* Does the next pixel contain 0? */
    if (*uPtr == 0) {
      /* Set the run length to 0 */
      runLength = 0;
```

Continued on next page

Continued from previous page

```
/* Loop while the next byte is 0 */
while (*uPtr == 0) {
  /* Move the pointer to the next byte */
  uPtr++;
  /* Add one to the run length */
  runLength++;
  /* Add one to the data position */
  dataPosition++;
  /* If we've reached a run of 127 pixels,
   * break out (because we can only handle
   * runs of 127 at a time)
   */
  if (runLength == 127) break;

  /* If we've reached the end of the image,
   * break out.
   */
  if (dataPosition == dataLength)
    break;
}

/* Set the next byte of the uncompressed image to
 * the run length. We add 128 to the run length to
 * indicate that it's a run of zeros.
 */
*cPtr++ = 128 + runLength;
} else {
/* In this case, we have a run of non-zeros */
runLength = 0;

/* We won't know how long the run is until we've
 * copied over the data into the compressed
 * image. So we want to save a pointer to the
 * current position of the compressed data, so
 * we can shove the datalength into it later,
 * when we know how long it is.
 */
dataLengthPtr = cPtr;

/* Advance the cPtr to the next byte */
cPtr++;
    /* Loop while the next byte is not zero */
while (*uPtr != 0) {
  /* Put the current byte into the compressed image */
  *cPtr++ = *uPtr++;
  /* Add one to the run length */
  runLength++;
  /* Add one to the data position */
  dataPosition++;
  /* If we've reached a run of 127 pixels,
   * break out (since we can only handle
   * runs of 127 at a time)
   */
```

```
          if (runLength == 127) break;

        /* If we've reached the end of the image,
         * break out.
         */
        if (dataPosition == dataLength)
          break;
      }
      /* Now that we know the run length, stuff
       * it back into the compressed image data
       */
      *dataLengthPtr = runLength;
    }
  }
  /* Set the last byte of the compressed data to 0, so we
   * know where to stop uncompressing it.
   */
  *cPtr++ = 0;

  /* Find the total size of the compressed image */
  compressedDataLength = (long)cPtr - (long)compressedBuffer;

  /* Resize the pointer to the new size of the compressed data.
   * We use SetPtrSize() to do this. If SetPtrSize() is asked
   * to increase the size of a pointer, it will frequently
   * fail (since it can't move a pointer around in
   * memory), but it will always succeed when asked to shrink
   * one. One must be careful when using it, still, since
   * shrinking pointers can cause heap fragmentation. It
   * shouldn't be too bad in this case, however.
   */
  SetPtrSize(compressedBuffer, compressedDataLength);

  /* Pass back this info to the caller */
  *compressedData = compressedBuffer;

  *dataSize = compressedDataLength;

  /* Return the error condition */
  return err;
}
```

Drawing the Compressed Image

Although it seems like you've made your bitmapped image more complicated, drawing it will actually be faster now because you can skip over large portions of the destination
image. Like the Compression algorithm, the drawing routine is essentially broken into
two parts: one for transparent pixels, the other for opaque ones.

The process begins by reading the first pixel in the compressed data. If the value is greater than 128, you have a run of transparent pixels. Otherwise, it's a run of opaque pixels.

```
/* Start a loop until we're out of compressed image */
while (*src != 0) {
  runLength = *src++;

  /* If the runlength is >= 128, it's a run of zeros. Just advance
   * the dst pointer by that many
   */
  if (runLength >= 128) {
```

In the case of transparent pixels, subtract 128 from the run length to get the true run size:

```
    runLength -= 128;
```

Now simply add the run length to the destination image pointer. However, there is one problem. If the destination is a Macintosh PixMap, it may have a RowBytes value that is different from the row's actual length due to row padding (which I covered in Chapter 4). If you advance the pointer past the end of one row, you have to be sure to add the additional row padding value onto the destination pointer:

```
    /* Check to see if we're going to go past the edge
     * of the source image. If so, include the row padding
     * in the total run length.
     */
    currentRowLength += runLength;
    if (currentRowLength > dstWidth) {
      runLength += rowPadding;
      currentRowLength -= dstWidth;
    }
```

Finally, add the run length to the destination pointer:

```
    /* Move the dst pointer forward by the run length */
    dst += (unsigned char*)runLength;
```

In the case of opaque pixels, you have to break the copying into two parts in case the run goes past the edge of the screen. The first part is for pixels that are on the current row and the second part is for those that fall on the next row. The first part of the algorithm calculates how long each part is going to be:

```
    /* Check to see if we're going to go past the edge
     * of the source image
     */
    if (currentRowLength + runLength < dstWidth) {
```

```
      extraRunLength = 0;
    } else {
      extraRunLength = (currentRowLength + runLength) - dstWidth;
      runLength -= extraRunLength;
    }
    currentRowLength += runLength;
```

Then copy data over from the compressed image onto the offscreen image:

```
/* Start filling the dst with data from the source */
while (runLength--) {
  *dst++ = *src++;
}
```

Then, add in the row padding (if you have indeed reached the end of the row):

```
/* If we've reached the end, add the row padding to the pointer */
if (currentRowLength == dstWidth) {
  dst += (unsigned char*)rowPadding;
  currentRowLength = 0;
}
currentRowLength += extraRunLength;
```

Finally, fill out the remainder of the row:

```
/* If we've got extra data to fill out, continue */
if (extraRunLength) {
  while (extraRunLength--) {
    *dst++ = *src++;
  }
}
```

This code is contained within the DrawCockpit() function. In addition to copying over the cockpit image, it calls additional routines to draw the instrument gauges onto the offscreen image, which I'll examine in the next section. Listing 20-8 is the complete source code for DrawCockpit().

Listing 20-8 *The DrawCockpit() routine*

```
/**
** DrawCockpit()
**
** Draws the cockpit image over the screen and, if the view is
** facing forwards, also draws the instruments.
**/
static OSErr  DrawCockpit(void)
{
  unsigned char    *cockpitImage;
  unsigned char    *src, *dst;
  long             rowPadding;
```

Continued on next page

Continued from previous page

```
    short               currentRowLength;
    short               runLength, extraRunLength;
    short               dstWidth;

    /* Get the proper image for our view direction */
    switch(gAirplaneStatus.viewDirection) {
      case kViewForward: cockpitImage = gForwardCockpit; break;
      case kViewLeft: cockpitImage = gLeftCockpit; break;
      case kViewRight: cockpitImage = gRightCockpit; break;
      case kViewBackward: cockpitImage = gBackwardCockpit; break;
    }

    /* Decompress the image directly onto the offscreen buffer */
    src = cockpitImage;
    dst = (unsigned char *)gOffscreenPtr;

    /* Calculate just the rowbyte padding for the offscreen image */
    dstWidth = gOffscreenWidth;
    rowPadding = gOffscreenRowBytes - dstWidth;
    currentRowLength = 0;
    extraRunLength = 0;

    /* Start a loop until we're out of compressed image */
    while (*src != 0) {
      runLength = *src++;

      /* If the runlength is >= 128, it's a run of zeros. Just advance
       * the dst pointer by that many
       */
      if (runLength >= 128) {
        runLength -= 128;

        /* Check to see if we're going to go past the edge
         * of the source image. If so, include the row padding
         * in the total run length.
         */
        currentRowLength += runLength;
        if (currentRowLength > dstWidth) {
          runLength += rowPadding;
          currentRowLength -= dstWidth;
        }

        /* Move the dst pointer forward by the run length */
        dst += (unsigned char*)runLength;
      } else {
        /* We've got a run of non-zeros. Copy them from the src to dst */

        /* Check to see if we're going to go past the edge
         * of the source image
         */
```

```
      if (currentRowLength + runLength < dstWidth) {
        extraRunLength = 0;
      } else {
        extraRunLength = (currentRowLength + runLength) - dstWidth;
        runLength -= extraRunLength;
      }

      currentRowLength += runLength;

      /* Start filling the dst with data from the source */
      while (runLength--) {
        *dst++ = *src++;
      }

      /* If we've reached the end, add the row padding to the pointer */
      if (currentRowLength == dstWidth) {
        dst += (unsigned char*)rowPadding;
        currentRowLength = 0;
      }

      currentRowLength += extraRunLength;

      /* If we've got extra data to fill out, continue */
      if (extraRunLength) {
        while (extraRunLength--) {
          *dst++ = *src++;
        }
      }
    }
  }

  /* If we're facing forward, draw the instruments */
  if (gAirplaneStatus.viewDirection == kViewForward) {
    SetFuelGauge(gAirplaneStatus.fuel);
    SetAltimeter(gAirplaneStatus.altitude);
    SetKPHDial(gAirplaneStatus.airspeed);
    SetRPMGauge(gAirplaneStatus.engineRPM);
    SetSlipGauge(-gAirplaneStatus.aileronPosition);
    SetCompass(gAirplaneStatus.yaw);
    SetIgnitionSwitch(gAirplaneStatus.ignitionOn);

    /* Draw the brake light */
    if (gAirplaneStatus.brake)
      BresenhamLine(  37,258,37,251,
                      gOffscreenPtr,
                      gOffscreenRowBytes,
                      215);
  }
}
```

Aircraft Instruments

Now that the cockpit image has been drawn onto the screen, you need to handle the various switches, gauges, and instruments the player will be able to see. In the flight simulator, you're going to include eight separate airplane instruments:

- A fuel gauge
- An RPM (engine speed) gauge
- An altitude gauge (which really has three separate needles; one for feet, one for hundreds of feet, and one for thousands of feet)
- An airspeed gauge
- A slip gauge, which indicates how fast the airplane is rolling to either side; the slip gauge is a small metal ball that rolls along a curved strip
- A compass
- An ignition switch
- A brake light

All but one of these instruments will be handled in a new file called Instruments.c (the only one that's not handled there is the brake light because it's so simple). To handle the information necessary for each of these gauges, a GaugeRec structure has been created. This structure holds not only the common information needed by all the instruments but also a few fields that are specific to some. These instrument-specific fields are ignored by the other instruments.

```
typedef struct {
   short          scrOrigX;
   short          scrOrigY;
   char           needleColor;
   short          centerX;
   short          centerY;

   /* For any gauge that has an image
    * associated with it
    */
   Ptr            gaugeImage;

   /* For the fuel gauge */
   short          sizeOfTank;

   /* For the compass gauge */
   short          framWid;
   short          framDep;
   short          stripWid;
   short          stripDep;
   unsigned char  lastDir;
} GaugeRec;
```

The *scrOrigX* and *scrOrigY* fields locate the position of the gauge on the instrument panel, whereas *centerX* and *centerY* find the instrument center point from there.

The *gaugeImage* field is used only in the controls that have a bitmapped image associated with them; that is, in the compass, the slip gauge, and the ignition switch. This data area holds the raw image data with no row byte padding. The pointer is allocated when the gauge is initialized. Only the fuel gauge and the compass gauge use the remaining fields.

Needle Gauges

The first set of instruments I'll look at are those that consist of only a needle, which are the fuel, RPM, airspeed, and altimeter gauges. At the top of the Instruments.c file, several arrays have been defined that hold every possible position of each of these needles. Although these values could be calculated on the fly as the gauge is drawn, storing them in tables avoids some complicated trigonometric calculations.

When the gauge is drawn, the proper entry of this array is calculated and the BresenhamLine() function is called to draw the line. Here is how the RPM gauge is drawn:

```
/**
 **   SetRPMGauge()
 **
 **   Updates the RPM gauge to reflect the airplane's engine speed.
 **/
void  SetRPMGauge(short rpms)
{
  short  pX, pY;
  if (rpms >= 0) {
    rpms = rpms / 125;
    pX = rpmPoints[rpms][0];
    pY = rpmPoints[rpms][1];
    BresenhamLine( gRPMGauge.scrOrigX +
                   gRPMGauge.centerX,
                   gRPMGauge.scrOrigY +
                   gRPMGauge.centerY,
                   gRPMGauge.scrOrigX + pX,
                   gRPMGauge.scrOrigY + pY,
                   gOffscreenData,
                   gOffscreenRowBytes,
                   gRPMGauge.needleColor  );
  }
}
```

Bitmapped Gauges

The gauges that have an image associated with them are a little more complicated. Of these, the compass gauge is the most complicated because it simulates a round strip turning inside the airplane's instrument panel.

The Slip Gauge

Drawing the slip gauge is a simple matter of determining the gauge position (which is done with the help of an array of constants, just like the needle gauges) and then calling a simple routine that actually draws the image:

```
/**
 **   SetSlipGauge()
 **
 **   Updates the airplane's slip gauge to reflect the airplane's
 **   current deflection.
 **/
void  SetSlipGauge(short deflection)
{
  int pX, pY;

  if (deflection < -9) deflection = -9;
  if (deflection > 9) deflection = 9;

  deflection = deflection + 9;
  pX = slipPoints[deflection][0];
  pY = slipPoints[deflection][1];
  DrawLinearImageOnOffscreen( gSlipGauge.gaugeImage,
                              gOffscreenData,
                              gOffscreenRowBytes,
                              (gSlipGauge.scrOrigX + pX),
                              (gSlipGauge.scrOrigY + pY),
                              (gSlipGauge.scrOrigX + pX + 8),
                              (gSlipGauge.scrOrigY + pY + 8)  );
}
```

The Ignition Switch

The ignition switch is the easiest bitmapped gauge of the three. You need to copy the image only if the switch is on because the cockpit panel image already shows the switch in the "off" position.

```
/**
 **   SetIgnitionSwitch()
 **
 **   Copies the proper ignition switch image to the offscreen. Since the
 **   'off' switch is already on the offscreen, we only need to copy an
 **   image if the switch is 'on'.
 **/
void  SetIgnitionSwitch(Boolean on)
{
  if (on) {
    DrawLinearImageOnOffscreen( gIgnitionSwitch.gaugeImage,
                                gOffscreenData,
                                gOffscreenRowBytes,
                                446, 283, 464, 309  );
```

```
  }
  return;
}
```

The Compass Gauge

The compass gauge is significantly more complicated. The gauge will be represented as a continuous strip constantly turning around within the instrument panel. In the code, however, the compass strip is a simple rectangular bitmap, as shown in Figure 20-7. You're going to draw a small portion of this strip onto the screen, with the middle of the strip representing the current orientation of the airplane. The tricky part is handling the case when the portion shown on the screen overlaps from the right side to the left side of the strip (e.g., if the airplane is flying south, the S, which is positioned at the edge of the strip, would need to be drawn in the middle of the compass gauge on the cockpit). In this case, you need to break the copying into two parts: one to handle the left edge, one to handle the right.

The first part of the compass-copying routine figures out where on this strip you're going to start copying from. fWinStart represents this position:

```
fWinStrt = gCompassGauge.lastDir - (gCompassGauge.framWid / 2);
if (fWinStrt < 0)                    /* calculate left edge of strip */
  fWinStrt = gCompassGauge.stripWid + fWinStrt;
```

Next, check to see if you're going to be wrapping around the compass strip. If so, calculate where the split occurs and set a flag telling you that you have to do two copies:

```
/* if it extends past end of strip... */
if ((fWinStrt + gCompassGauge.framWid) > gCompassGauge.stripWid)
{
  /* roll back line length  */
  lineLen = gCompassGauge.stripWid - fWinStrt;
  /* set two-blit flag */
  blit2 = true;
  /* calculate second line length */
  blit2Len = gCompassGauge.framWid - lineLen;
}
else
  lineLen = gCompassGauge.framWid;
```

FIGURE 20-7

◎ ◎ ◎ ◎ ◎ ◎

The compass strip

Then find the appropriate pointers to the correct positions on the compass image and on the offscreen image:

```
/* Find the address of the src compass strip */
src = gCompassGauge.gaugeImage + fWinStrt;

/* Find the address of the top-left of the compass
 * area on the offscreen
 */
dst = gOffscreenData +
    (gCompassGauge.scrOrigY * gOffscreenRowBytes) +
    gCompassGauge.scrOrigX;
dstWrap = gOffscreenRowBytes - lineLen;
srcWrap = gCompassGauge.stripWid - lineLen;
```

Next, blit (or copy) the first portion of the compass strip:

```
/* Work our way down the rows of the image */
for (i = 0; i < gCompassGauge.framDep; i++)
{
  for (j = 0; j < lineLen; j++)        /* cycle through pixels */
  {
    *(dst++) = *(src++);
  }
  dst += dstWrap;                      /* wrap to the next line */
  src += srcWrap;
}
```

If you need only one blit, you're done. However, if the compass image is wrapping around to the other side of the strip, you now need to do the second blit. The code for this is very similar to that for the first blit:

```
if (blit2)                      /* do the second blit, if any, */
{                               /* the same way */
  src = gCompassGauge.gaugeImage;
  dst = gOffscreenData +
      (gCompassGauge.scrOrigY * gOffscreenRowBytes) +
      gCompassGauge.scrOrigX + lineLen;
  dstWrap = gOffscreenRowBytes - blit2Len;
  srcWrap = gCompassGauge.stripWid - blit2Len;
  for (i = 0; i < gCompassGauge.framDep; i++)
  {
    for (j = 0; j < blit2Len; j++)
    {
      *(dst++) = *(src++);
    }
    dst += dstWrap;
    src += srcWrap;
  }
}
```

Listing 20-9 is the complete source code for the compass-blitting function.

Listing 20-9 *The CompassBlitBox( ) routine*

```
/**
**   CompassBlitBox()
**
**   Copies the compass image into the offscreen. This
**   routine is special, since we're going to be copying
**   a portion of the compass image based on what
**   direction the plane is flying, and we also need to
**   wrap around to the beginning of the compass image
**   if we reach the edge.
**/
void  CompassBlitBox(void)
{
    short       fWinStrt;          /* left x of strip blit window        */
    short       i, j;              /* counters                           */
    short       lineLen;           /* length of line copied from strip   */
    Boolean     blit2 = false;     /* true if need to blit twice         */
    short       blit2Len;          /* length of 2nd line if any          */
    char        *src;              /* pointer into strip                 */
    char        *dst;              /* pointer into compass window        */
    long        dstWrap;           /* value to wrap to next dst line     */
    short       srcWrap;           /* value to wrap to next src line     */

    fWinStrt = gCompassGauge.lastDir - (gCompassGauge.framWid / 2);
    if (fWinStrt < 0)              /* calculate left edge of strip */
      fWinStrt = gCompassGauge.stripWid + fWinStrt;

    /* if it extends past end of strip... */
    if ((fWinStrt + gCompassGauge.framWid) > gCompassGauge.stripWid)
    {
      /* roll back line length  */
      lineLen = gCompassGauge.stripWid - fWinStrt;
      /* set two-blit flag */
      blit2 = true;
      /* calculate second line length */
      blit2Len = gCompassGauge.framWid - lineLen;
    }
    else
      lineLen = gCompassGauge.framWid;

    /* Find the address of the src compass strip */
    src = gCompassGauge.gaugeImage + fWinStrt;

    /* Find the address of the top-left of the compass
     * area on the offscreen
     */
    dst = gOffscreenData +
        (gCompassGauge.scrOrigY * gOffscreenRowBytes) +
```

Continued on next page

Continued from previous page

```
        gCompassGauge.scrOrigX;
    dstWrap = gOffscreenRowBytes - lineLen;
    srcWrap = gCompassGauge.stripWid - lineLen;

    /* Work our way down the rows of the image */
    for (i = 0; i < gCompassGauge.framDep; i++)
    {
      for (j = 0; j < lineLen; j++)          /* cycle through pixels */
      {
        *(dst++) = *(src++);
      }
      dst += dstWrap;                        /* wrap to the next line */
      src += srcWrap;
    }

    if (blit2)                               /* do the second blit, if any, */
    {                                        /* the same way */
      src = gCompassGauge.gaugeImage;
      dst = gOffscreenData +
          (gCompassGauge.scrOrigY * gOffscreenRowBytes) +
          gCompassGauge.scrOrigX + lineLen;
      dstWrap = gOffscreenRowBytes - blit2Len;
      srcWrap = gCompassGauge.stripWid - blit2Len;
      for (i = 0; i < gCompassGauge.framDep; i++)
      {
        for (j = 0; j < blit2Len; j++)
        {
          *(dst++) = *(src++);
        }
        dst += dstWrap;
        src += srcWrap;
      }
    }
}
```

Updating the View System

So far, you've been changing the settings within the airplane status structure but you haven't been sending those settings to the view system. Conceptually, this is a very simple thing to do—simply copy the x, y, and z position and the yaw, pitch, and roll parameters of the airplane structure into the view structure.

However, this routine has a few more responsibilities. Because the player can be viewing in any one of four directions (forward, back, left, or right), you must also account for that here. This is done by adding or subtracting from the airplane's yaw, and switching around the pitch and roll components.

In addition, this routine (Listing 20-10) must ensure that each of the angles is within the proper range of 0 to 359 degrees and then mark the view system's matrix to be updated.

Listing 20-10 The SetAirplaneToView( ) routine

```
/**
** SetAirplaneToView()
**
** Takes the airplane's status and sets up all of the
** view structures to reflect that status.
**/
void  SetAirplaneToView(AirplaneStatusRec *airplaneInfo)
{
  /* Set the view's position to that of the plane */
  gCameraViewData.viewXPos = airplaneInfo->xPosition;
  gCameraViewData.viewYPos = -airplaneInfo->yPosition;
  gCameraViewData.viewZPos = airplaneInfo->zPosition;

  /* Set the view's rotation to that of the plane */
  gCameraViewData.viewXAngle = airplaneInfo->pitch;
  gCameraViewData.viewYAngle = airplaneInfo->yaw;
  gCameraViewData.viewZAngle = airplaneInfo->roll;

  /* Adjust the view's rotation based on the direction
   * that the player is looking. This can easily be
   * modified so that the player has more angles that
   * he or she can look out.
   */
  switch(airplaneInfo->viewDirection) {
    short    tempAngle;

    case kViewForward:
      /* No changes need to be made */
      break;

    case kViewLeft:
      tempAngle = gCameraViewData.viewZAngle;
      gCameraViewData.viewZAngle =
        gCameraViewData.viewXAngle;

      if ((tempAngle > 90) ||
          (tempAngle < -90))
        gCameraViewData.viewZAngle = -gCameraViewData.viewZAngle;

      if ((gCameraViewData.viewXAngle > 90) ||
          (gCameraViewData.viewXAngle < -90))
        gCameraViewData.viewZAngle = -gCameraViewData.viewZAngle;

      gCameraViewData.viewXAngle = -tempAngle;

      gCameraViewData.viewYAngle += 90;
      break;

    case kViewRight:
      tempAngle = gCameraViewData.viewZAngle;
```

Continued on next page

Continued from previous page

```
          gCameraViewData.viewZAngle =
            -gCameraViewData.viewXAngle;

          if ((tempAngle > 90) ||
              (tempAngle < -90))
            gCameraViewData.viewZAngle = -gCameraViewData.viewZAngle;

          if ((gCameraViewData.viewXAngle > 90) ||
              (gCameraViewData.viewXAngle < -90))
            gCameraViewData.viewZAngle = -gCameraViewData.viewZAngle;

          gCameraViewData.viewXAngle = tempAngle;

          gCameraViewData.viewYAngle -= 90;
          break;

        case kViewBackward:
          tempAngle = gCameraViewData.viewZAngle;
          gCameraViewData.viewZAngle =
            -gCameraViewData.viewZAngle;
          gCameraViewData.viewXAngle =
            -gCameraViewData.viewXAngle;

          gCameraViewData.viewYAngle += 180;
          break;
    }

    /* Reverse the x angle */
    gCameraViewData.viewXAngle = -gCameraViewData.viewXAngle;

    /* Handle bounds checking and force all angles to
     * between 0 and 359.
     */
    while (gCameraViewData.viewXAngle < 0)
      gCameraViewData.viewXAngle += 360;
    while (gCameraViewData.viewXAngle > 359)
      gCameraViewData.viewXAngle -= 360;

    while (gCameraViewData.viewYAngle < 0)
      gCameraViewData.viewYAngle += 360;
    while (gCameraViewData.viewYAngle > 359)
      gCameraViewData.viewYAngle -= 360;

    while (gCameraViewData.viewZAngle < 0)
      gCameraViewData.viewZAngle += 360;
    while (gCameraViewData.viewZAngle > 359)
      gCameraViewData.viewZAngle -= 360;

    /* Flag the view transformation to be updated */
    gCameraViewData.update = TRUE;
}
```

Drawing the Horizon

Drawing the horizon on the screen is surprisingly complicated. Although a horizon may not seem to be a terribly important feature to you on the ground (especially if you live in a city, where you can rarely even *see* the horizon), it's one of the most dominant features from an airplane cockpit window.

At first look, it may not seem necessary to write special code to draw the horizon. After all, the horizon is nothing more than the edge of a large object that is usually found directly beneath us—the earth itself. But the earth doesn't lend itself well to inclusion within a polygon database. Mainly, it is too large, and if you include it as part of your polygon database, you could be facing some overflow problems plus it would take too long to draw. You will be representing the earth as a polygon, but it won't be treated the way you treat the other polygons in the database.

The simplest way to represent a horizon is as a line that can intersect the view window with the area on one side of that line filled with pixels of one color and the area on the other side of that line filled with pixels of a different color. In most flight simulators, one of these colors is green (representing ground) and the other is blue (representing sky). Some flight simulators (Out of the Sun is a good example) may blend the two colors near the horizon for realism.

How the Horizon Works

Let's consider some of the problems inherent in drawing the horizon. Imagine you're standing in the middle of a vast plain, without buildings or trees to obstruct your view of the land. About 8 miles away is the horizon, a seemingly straight line that stretches all the way around your field of view. Turn as much as you want on your y axis (yaw) and it's still there. Furthermore, it looks the same in every direction.

In fact, as much as the horizon looks like a straight line, it really isn't. It's a circle, of which you happen to be standing in the middle, and it extends out so far from where you're standing that you can't get out of its center far enough to make it look like anything other than a straight line. The only way to see it for what it is would be to climb high into the earth's atmosphere, almost into outer space.

So how do you represent this in the view window? You could draw a line across the center of the display and paint the area underneath it green and the area above it blue. But that won't do you much good because the moment the viewer moves, you'll have to change the representation. The way in which the representation changes, however, depends on how the viewer is moving. Going upward doesn't make much difference to the way the horizon looks, unless you're writing a spacecraft simulator. Moving left, right, forward, and back won't make any difference, either. Rotation, on the other hand, makes a big difference. Rotating on the z axis causes the horizon to spin around and rotating on the x axis causes it to move up and down (see Figures 20-8a and b). What happens when the viewer rotates 180 degrees on his or her x axis? Another horizon appears from behind, but upside down!

With all this in mind, treat the horizon as a straight line across the middle of the screen that can rotate around the viewer's position depending on the viewer's rotation relative to the world's axes. But restrict these rotations to 180 degrees. After that, treat the rotations as mirrors of smaller rotations, but with the positions of sky and ground reversed. The actual colors will be drawn using the polygon-fill routines, which means you'll have to fill in polygon structures for both the ground and the sky. Let's look at the code.

FIGURE 20-8a

◎ ◎ ◎ ◎ ◎ ◎

Rotating the airplane causes the horizon to change

Airplane roll rotates the horizon

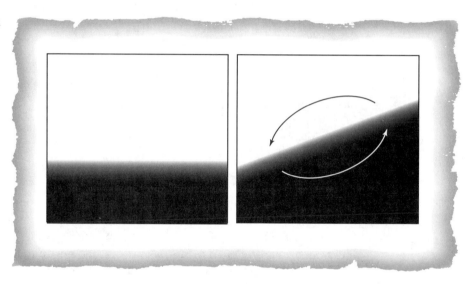

FIGURE 20-8b

◎ ◎ ◎ ◎ ◎ ◎

Pitch causes the horizon to move up and down

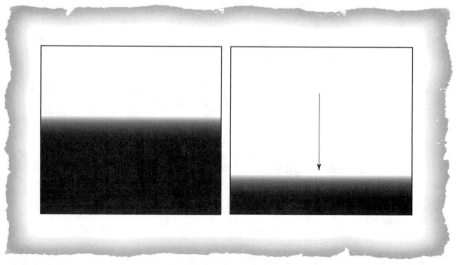

The Horizon Code

Start by filling out some of the vertices of the temporary polygons with preliminary values. Because you're not building an object structure, create an array of four Vertex3D structures to which you'll point the polygon vertices:

```
Vertex3D          vert[4];
```

The polygon is then initialized to point at the elements of this array and the array's z coordinates are initialized to some arbitrary large value, representing the horizon's distance:

```
/* Initialize the polygon and its vertices */
horizonPolygon.polyVertex[0]=&vert[0];
horizonPolygon.polyVertex[1]=&vert[1];
horizonPolygon.polyVertex[2]=&vert[2];
horizonPolygon.polyVertex[3]=&vert[3];
vert[0].tz=kHorizonDistance;
vert[1].tz=kHorizonDistance;
vert[2].tz=kHorizonDistance;
vert[3].tz=kHorizonDistance;
```

Then initialize some of the remaining polygon values, such as the linked-list structure and the rendering mode:

```
/* Initialize the linked list pointers for this polygon */
horizonPolygon.nextPolygon = NULL;
horizonPolygon.lastPolygon = NULL;

/* Set the rendering mode */
horizonPolygon.renderingMode = kRender_PolygonFill;
```

You need to reverse the roll angle because the horizon will actually be rolled in the opposite direction as the view:

```
/* Reverse the roll so the polygons are
 * rotated in the opposite direction
 */
roll = -roll;
```

Next, make sure the angles are between 0 and 359. Also, because you don't want to view rotation angles greater than 180 degrees on the x axis, mirror any x rotation that is larger. However, this rotation also means that the sky and ground need to be reversed. To indicate this, set a variable called *flip*.

A z rotation of between 90 and 270 degrees will also set the flip variable. However, if both these conditions are true, they cancel each other out.

```
/* Check all angles to make sure they're between 0 and 359 */
if (pitch < 0) pitch += 360;
if (pitch > 359) pitch -= 360;
if (roll < 0) roll += 360;
if (roll > 359) roll -= 360;

/* Map rotation angle to remove backward wrap-around. If the
 * pitch is between 90 and 270, the airplane is facing
 * backwards, so set the flip flag to indicate this. Also,
 * if the roll is between 90 and 270, the airplane is
 * upside-down, so also set the flip flag. If both are true,
 * they cancel each other out, so we're safe.
 */
flip=0;
if ((pitch > 90) && (pitch < 270)) {
  if (pitch < 180)
    pitch += 180;
  else
    pitch -= 180;
  flip = !flip;
}

if ((roll>90) && (roll<270)) {
  flip = !flip;
}
```

Rotating the Horizon

Next, perform three-dimensional rotations on the horizon lines. You won't use the standard rotational matrices for this purpose; you don't need much of the functionality it provides. Instead, just use the standard rotational formulas I looked at in Chapter 4 to rotate a 3D line from coordinates rx1, ry1, rz1 to rx2, ry2, rz2. All you're looking for here is the slope of this rotated line so you need to create a line long enough to obtain an accurate slope:

```
rx1=-100;  ry1=0;  rz1=kHorizonDistance;
rx2=100;   ry2=0;  rz2=kHorizonDistance;
```

The rotation code uses the cosine and sine tables developed in Chapter 12 as well as fixed-point calculations. Only the x and z rotations need be performed because the y rotation will have no effect:

```
/* Rotate around viewer's X axis: */
temp_ry1=(ry1*gCosTable[pitch] - rz1*gSinTable[pitch]) >> 8;
temp_ry2=(ry2*gCosTable[pitch] - rz2*gSinTable[pitch]) >> 8;
temp_rz1=(ry1*gSinTable[pitch] + rz1*gCosTable[pitch]) >> 8;
temp_rz2=(ry2*gSinTable[pitch] + rz2*gCosTable[pitch]) >> 8;
ry1=temp_ry1;
```

```
ry2=temp_ry2;
rz1=temp_rz1;
rz2=temp_rz2;

/* Rotate around viewer's Z axis: */
temp_rx1=(rx1*gCosTable[roll] - ry1*gSinTable[roll]) >> 8;
temp_ry1=(rx1*gSinTable[roll] + ry1*gCosTable[roll]) >> 8;
temp_rx2=(rx2*gCosTable[roll] - ry2*gSinTable[roll]) >> 8;
temp_ry2=(rx2*gSinTable[roll] + ry2*gCosTable[roll]) >> 8;
rx1=temp_rx1;
ry1=temp_ry1;
rx2=temp_rx2;
ry2=temp_ry2;
```

Next, perform the perspective adjustments on the line, dividing the x and y coordinates of the vertices by the z coordinate. First, though, make sure the z is never less than 10, which could cause some minor problems in the horizon appearance:

```
/* Adjust for perspective */
z=rz1;
if (z<10) z=10;
/* Divide world x,y coordinates by z coordinates
 * to obtain perspective:
 */
rx1=(float)kHorizonDistance*((float)rx1/(float)z)+kHalfWindowWidth;
ry1=(float)kHorizonDistance*((float)ry1/(float)z)+kHalfWindowHeight;
rx2=(float)kHorizonDistance*((float)rx2/(float)z)+kHalfWindowWidth;
ry2=(float)kHorizonDistance*((float)ry2/(float)z)+kHalfWindowHeight;
```

Creating the Polygons

Now you're ready to create the two polygons that represent sky and ground. Calculate the slope of the horizon line and then create a large polygon that has an upper edge (for the ground) or a lower edge (for the sky) with the same slope as the horizon line. First you'll need to get the change in the x and y coordinates in the horizon line:

```
dx = rx2 - rx1;
dy = ry2 - ry1;
```

So that you won't get an error if the line is vertical (which would generate a divide-by-zero error in the slope equation), cheat by checking for a 0 change in the x coordinate and resetting it to 1 if this change occurs:

```
/* Cheat to avoid divide error: */
if (!dx) dx++;
```

Now obtain the slope:

```
/* Obtain slope of line: */
slope = (float)dy/(float)dx;
```

Use the first two vertices of the vert structure to hold the upper line of the first polygon, which will be a line with the slope of the horizon and the width of the viewport:

```
/* Calculate line of horizon: */
vert[0].tx=gClipXMin;
vert[0].ty=slope*(gClipXMin-rx1)+ry1;
vert[1].tx=gClipXMax;
vert[1].ty=slope*(gClipXMax-rx1)+ry1;
```

You can determine whether this first polygon will be the color of the ground or the sky by checking the flip variable you set earlier. If it's False, you want the color of the ground; otherwise, you want the color of the sky:

```
/* Create the first polygon. If the airplane has not rolled over, this
 * is the ground polygon, otherwise it'll be the sky polygon. The only
 * thing that differentiates the two are the color, so determine
 * the status of the plane and set the color appropriately.
 */
if (!flip)
  horizonPolygon.color=kGrassColor;
else
  horizonPolygon.color=kSkyColor;
```

Now set the other two vertices to the extreme coordinates so you can be sure that they fit properly in the viewport and there will be no problems drawing the proper line slope:

```
/* Set vertex coordinates: */
vert[2].tx=32767;
vert[2].ty=32767;
vert[3].tx=-32767;
vert[3].ty=32767;
```

At this point, you need to clip the polygon. However, the clipping routine works on the global polygon list, a list that does not include this polygon. You're going to cheat a little here and temporarily replace the global polygon list with just this one pointer so that the clipping routine will function on it. Set the global list back to normal before you leave the function.

```
/* Save the current painter's polygon list */
tempPaintersList = gWorld.paintersList;

/* Replace the list with our polygon */
gWorld.paintersList = &horizonPolygon;

/* Clip the polygon */
ZClipPolygonList();
XYClipPolygonList();
```

If the polygon hasn't been clipped out of existence, now draw it:

```
/* Draw the polygon: */
if (horizonPolygon.numOfClippedVerts > 0)
  PolygonFillDrawPolygon( &horizonPolygon,
                          offscreenData,
                          offscreenRowBytes );
```

Next, repeat the process for the other polygon:

```
/* Now we repeat the process with the second polygon. If it's
 * not flipped, give it the sky color. If it's flipped, give
 * it the ground color:
 */
if (!flip)
  horizonPolygon.color=210;
else
  horizonPolygon.color=161;

/* Set vertex coordinates: */
vert[2].tx=32767;
vert[2].ty=-32767;
vert[3].tx=-32767;
vert[3].ty=-32767;

/* Clip this polygon. We've already got horizonPolygon
 * in the painter's list, so all we need to do is
 * call the clipping routines again.
 */
ZClipPolygonList();
XYClipPolygonList();

/* And finally draw the second polygon */

if (horizonPolygon.numOfClippedVerts > 0)
  PolygonFillDrawPolygon( &horizonPolygon,
                          offscreenData,
                          offscreenRowBytes );
```

Finally, you need to put the Painter's polygon list back where it belongs:

```
/* Restore the painter's polygon list */
gWorld.paintersList = tempPaintersList;
```

DrawHorizon()

Listing 20-11 is the complete DrawHorizon() function.

Listing 20-11 *The DrawHorizon() routine*

```
/**
**   DrawHorizon()
**
**   Draws the sky and ground onto the screen
**/
void DrawHorizon(  Ptr       offscreenData,
                   long      offscreenRowBytes,
                   short     pitch,
                   short     roll  )
{
   long          rx1,rx2,temp_rx1,temp_rx2;
   long          ry1,ry2,temp_ry1,temp_ry2;
   long          rz1,rz2,temp_rz1,temp_rz2;

   Vertex3D      vert[4];
   Polygon3D     horizonPolygon;
   Polygon3D     *tempPaintersList;
   short         flip;
   short         dx,dy;
   short         line_ready;
   short         z;
   float         slope;

   /* Initialize the polygon and its vertices */
   horizonPolygon.polyVertex[0]=&vert[0];
   horizonPolygon.polyVertex[1]=&vert[1];
   horizonPolygon.polyVertex[2]=&vert[2];
   horizonPolygon.polyVertex[3]=&vert[3];
   vert[0].tz=kHorizonDistance;
   vert[1].tz=kHorizonDistance;
   vert[2].tz=kHorizonDistance;
   vert[3].tz=kHorizonDistance;

   /* Initialize the linked list pointers for this polygon */
   horizonPolygon.nextPolygon = NULL;
   horizonPolygon.lastPolygon = NULL;

   /* Set the rendering mode */
   horizonPolygon.renderingMode = 2;

   /* Reverse the roll so the polygons are
    * rotated in the opposite direction
    */
   roll = -roll;

   /* Check all angles to make sure they're between 0 and 359 */
   if (pitch < 0) pitch += 360;
   if (pitch > 359) pitch -= 360;
   if (roll < 0) roll += 360;
   if (roll > 359) roll -= 360;
```

```
/* Map rotation angle to remove backward wrap-around. If the
 * pitch is between 90 and 270, the airplane is facing
 * backwards, so set the flip flag to indicate this. Also,
 * if the roll is between 90 and 270, the airplane is
 * upside-down, so also set the flip flag. If both are true,
 * they cancel each other out, so we're safe.
 */
flip=0;
if ((pitch > 90) && (pitch < 270)) {
  if (pitch < 180)
    pitch += 180;
  else
    pitch -= 180;
  flip = !flip;
}

if ((roll>90) && (roll<270)) {
  flip = !flip;
}

/* Create initial horizon line: */

rx1=-100;  ry1=0; rz1=kHorizonDistance;
rx2=100;   ry2=0; rz2=kHorizonDistance;

/* Rotate around viewer's X axis: */
temp_ry1=(ry1*gCosTable[pitch] - rz1*gSinTable[pitch]) >> 8;
temp_ry2=(ry2*gCosTable[pitch] - rz2*gSinTable[pitch]) >> 8;
temp_rz1=(ry1*gSinTable[pitch] + rz1*gCosTable[pitch]) >> 8;
temp_rz2=(ry2*gSinTable[pitch] + rz2*gCosTable[pitch]) >> 8;
ry1=temp_ry1;
ry2=temp_ry2;
rz1=temp_rz1;
rz2=temp_rz2;

/* Rotate around viewer's Z axis: */
temp_rx1=(rx1*gCosTable[roll] - ry1*gSinTable[roll]) >> 8;
temp_ry1=(rx1*gSinTable[roll] + ry1*gCosTable[roll]) >> 8;
temp_rx2=(rx2*gCosTable[roll] - ry2*gSinTable[roll]) >> 8;
temp_ry2=(rx2*gSinTable[roll] + ry2*gCosTable[roll]) >> 8;
rx1=temp_rx1;
ry1=temp_ry1;
rx2=temp_rx2;
ry2=temp_ry2;

/* Adjust for perspective */
z=rz1;
if (z<10) z=10;

/* Divide world x,y coordinates by z coordinates
 * to obtain perspective:
 */
```

Continued on next page

Continued from previous page

```
rx1=(float)kHorizonDistance*((float)rx1/(float)z)+kHalfWindowWidth;
ry1=(float)kHorizonDistance*((float)ry1/(float)z)+kHalfWindowHeight;
rx2=(float)kHorizonDistance*((float)rx2/(float)z)+kHalfWindowWidth;
ry2=(float)kHorizonDistance*((float)ry2/(float)z)+kHalfWindowHeight;

/* Create sky and ground polygons, then clip to screen window

/* Obtain delta x and delta y: */
dx = rx2 - rx1;
dy = ry2 - ry1;
line_ready = 0;
horizonPolygon.numOfVertices=4;

/* Cheat to avoid divide error: */
if (!dx) dx++;

/* Obtain slope of line: */
slope = (float)dy/(float)dx;

/* Calculate line of horizon: */
vert[0].tx=gClipXMin;
vert[0].ty=slope*(gClipXMin-rx1)+ry1;
vert[1].tx=gClipXMax;
vert[1].ty=slope*(gClipXMax-rx1)+ry1;

/* Create the first polygon. If the airplane has not rolled over, this
 * is the ground polygon, otherwise it'll be the sky polygon. The only
 * thing that differentiates the two are the color, so determine
 * the status of the plane and set the color appropriately.
 */
if (!flip)
  horizonPolygon.color=161;
else
  horizonPolygon.color=210;

/* Set vertex coordinates: */
vert[2].tx=32767;
vert[2].ty=32767;
vert[3].tx=-32767;
vert[3].ty=32767;

/* At this point, we need to clip this polygon. Unfortunately,
 * the clipping lists work on the global polygon list, and this
 * polygon isn't part of that list. So, in order to get this
 * polygon processed, we're going to cheat a litle bit. We're
 * going to fool the clipping routine into thinking that this
 * polygon is the only polygon in the list by temporarily swapping
 * it with the painter's list, and immediately restoring
 * it afterwards.
 */
```

```
/* Save the current painter's polygon list */
tempPaintersList = gWorld.paintersList;

/* Replace the list with our polygon */
gWorld.paintersList = &horizonPolygon;

/* Clip the polygon */
ZClipPolygonList();
XYClipPolygonList();

/* Draw the polygon: */

if (horizonPolygon.numOfClippedVerts > 0)
  PolygonFillDrawPolygon( &horizonPolygon,
                          offscreenData,
                          offscreenRowBytes );

/* Now we repeat the process with the second polygon. If it's
 * not flipped, give it the sky color. If it's flipped, give
 * it the ground color:
 */
if (!flip)
  horizonPolygon.color=210;
else
  horizonPolygon.color=161;

/* Set vertex coordinates: */
vert[2].tx=32767;
vert[2].ty=-32767;
vert[3].tx=-32767;
vert[3].ty=-32767;

/* Clip this polygon. We've already got horizonPolygon
 * in the painter's list, so all we need to do is
 * call the clipping routines again.
 */
ZClipPolygonList();
XYClipPolygonList();

/* And finally draw the second polygon */

if (horizonPolygon.numOfClippedVerts > 0)
  PolygonFillDrawPolygon( &horizonPolygon,
                          offscreenData,
                          offscreenRowBytes );

/* Restore the painter's polygon list */
gWorld.paintersList = tempPaintersList;
}
```

The Engine Sound

You're almost finished. The last problem to investigate is playing the sound of the airplane's engine.

In Chapter 7, you learned how to create continuous sounds. Although the sound package you created there is almost perfect for the airplane's engine sound, it's missing one critical part. You don't want the engine to sound exactly the same while the player is changing its RPM, and it wouldn't be an acceptable solution to store a separate sound resource for every conceivable RPM setting. Instead, you need a simple way of changing the pitch of the current sound. Fortunately, this is rather easy to do through the use of a sound command.

The command you want to use is rateCmd. In the sound command structure, you only need to fill out *param2* with a 16.16 fixed-point number indicating the new pitch. Using a pitch of 1 (which is expressed as 1 << 16, or 65536, because it's a 16.16 fixed-point number) sets the sound to play at the same frequency it was originally recorded at. A pitch of 2 will play the sound twice as fast, whereas a pitch of 0.5 will play it at half-speed. The engine RPM sounds will have a range of approximately 0.2 to 1.5, which provides a full range of sound.

The function sets up a sound command structure with the rateCmd instruction and the pitch in *param2*. SndDoImmediate() sends the command to the current sound channel, where the pitch is immediately changed.

```
/**
 **   AdjustSoundPitch()
 **
 **   Changes the frequency of the currently playing continuous sound.
 **   A value of 65536 will play it at the original speed; anything
 **   higher than that will speed it up, and anything lower will
 **   slow it down.
 **/
void  AdjustSoundPitch(long  newPitch)
{
  SndCommand     soundCommand;

  /* Set up the command structure */
  soundCommand.cmd = rateCmd;
  soundCommand.param1 = 0;
  soundCommand.param2 = newPitch;

  /* Send the command to our channel */
  SndDoImmediate(gContinuousSoundChannel, &soundCommand);
}
```

Learning to Fly

You now have all the pieces of the flight simulator and you're ready to fly! When you run the application, there will be a slight delay after the window appears as the program is loading all of the needed images and compressing them. After a moment, however, the screen will be drawn and you'll be ready to begin (see Figure 20-9).

Press ⬚ to start the plane's engines. You should hear the engine turn on (it appears this plane has no muffler!). To increase the throttle, press the ⬚ key until you reach 100 percent RPM. Disengage the brake by pressing ⬚ and you should begin taxiing down the runway. Pull back on the stick (using whichever input method you prefer), and you'll climb into the air, where you can fly around to your heart's content (see Figure 20-10).

Although you can fly into the ground and crash, running into any of the other objects currently won't do you any harm. On your tour, be sure to fly by the airport control

FIGURE 20-9

◎ ◎ ◎ ◎ ◎ ◎

Preparing for takeoff

FIGURE 20-10

◎ ◎ ◎ ◎ ◎ ◎

Looking back after becoming airborne

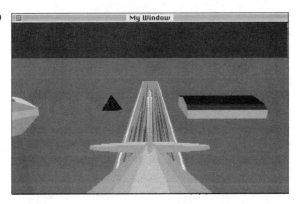

tower, complete with a spinning radar on top (see Figure 20-11). The radar tower, along with all the rest of the items in the polygon database, is courtesy of Brendan Donohoe. It's an excellent example of how such a simple polygon engine can be used to create realistic-looking models.

Looking Ahead

Now that you've built a very basic flight simulator, the next step is up to you. Several parts of the simulator lend themselves to improvements, and what you've built will work very well as a basis of future enhancements. Share what you learn, and soon we'll all be writing better games.

What happens when you've built your masterpiece game, however? Do you give it away as freeware, attempt to sell it yourself as shareware, or try to sell it to a commercial software house? In the next chapter, I'll examine these possibilities, as well as discuss the recommendations of some industry giants.

FIGURE 20-11
◎ ◎ ◎ ◎ ◎ ◎
The airport's
control tower

21

Game
Marketing and
Distribution

come terbi dare o manutelle ... li quali provobano e l'aiga
o grapo si muove comunti o pone so fa zozzano li bono
orgare nelle mali rrfa permanze alla manubella pegi quin
aforza o piu i sromo pibibal.

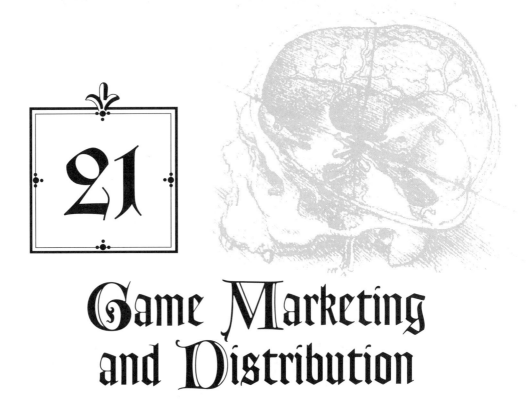

21

Game Marketing and Distribution

So you've been spending 24 hours a day in front of your computer, you've solved a billion different programming glitches, and your friends think you've either died or moved to Canada. But you don't care—your game is finally done! And this isn't any ordinary game; it's the next DOOM and it could make you filthy stinkin' rich.

But how? What do you do now? Do you sell it to some mega-corporation? Do you license it to the same corporation and hope to collect fat royalty checks? Do you attempt to market it yourself as shareware? Or, out of the goodness of your heart, do you give the game away for free?

In this chapter, I'll examine these options and look at some of their advantages and disadvantages. I'll look at some of the costs that may be involved and what you might expect your financial gains to be. Let's start out with the most modest choice you have, giving the game away for free.

Freeware

Many games are released into the general public without any thought of compensation; they are collectively grouped under the category of *freeware*. In most cases, freeware means that the author is not asking for any monetary payment for the software, although some authors request a postcard or an interesting regional item (like small denominations of foreign currency).

Freeware should not be confused with material in the *public domain*. If an author releases a piece of software (or any other intellectual property) in the the public domain, he or she is explicitly giving up all copyrights to it. With freeware, however, the author retains the copyright (which means that someone cannot legally change the name and startup screen of the game and sell it as commercial software, among other things.)

Although it may not seem very appealing to not receive any compensation for your work, there are several advantages to it. First of all, you are under no obligation to write bugfixes or upgrades to the product. You can do them in your spare time, but nobody in their right minds will send you e-mail demanding you fix that bug that erases their hard drive every time they play. Some people will anyway, but because they owe you nothing for the game, you don't owe them an upgrade. (Please note, however, that writing a game that erases a person's hard drive will probably not put you in good standing with your users.)

The second advantage of freeware is that it costs you absolutely nothing to distribute the game. All you need to do is upload it to an online service or one of the helpful Internet sites and the game is distributed for you. You also don't have the bother of keeping a database of registered users and sending disks of the current version or bugfixes.

A third advantage of choosing freeware is all the e-mail you'll get from people telling you how happy they are with the game (and mentioning this bug about erasing the hard drive at the same time). If the game were being distributed as shareware, these same people wouldn't speak up, for fear of letting you know that they're enjoying the game without registering it.

Finally, freeware is a good way to establish yourself in the gaming community and gain recognition in anticipation of future software releases.

Most games distributed as freeware are those that didn't take too much time to develop. Although there are some notable exceptions, this category is largely dominated by games created from construction kits or HyperCard or as a first programming project. (This is not to say that *no* construction kit or HyperCard games had a significant amount of effort put into them, just that a majority are in this category.) If you're looking for a little spending money, it would be best to try a different distribution method.

Shareware

The shareware concept was started many years ago in the early days of the personal computer. The concept is simple: Give your program to as many people as you can and ask them to give you some money if they like it. In theory, it works as a try-before-you-buy system. The users benefit because they don't end up buying things they can't use and the developers benefit because they get revenue from the product plus happy customers.

There are two types of shareware developers. The first type is looking for a little income from the product, enough to go out for ice cream once in a while. The second type is attempting to live off of the income generated. Although the developer may not expect a six-digit income, he or she needs more than $15 or $20 a week to survive.

To a lesser extent, there are two extremes of shareware games. On one end is the game that is extremely polished and could easily be mistaken for some of the best commercial software you can find. On the opposite extreme is the game that was written in one weekend, has poorly drawn graphics, and couldn't hold a monk's attention for more than a minute.

Unfortunately, the two types of developers don't always match up with the two extremes of games. Although a few developers create incredibly slick games and don't expect much in return, many more create a Tetris clone on Friday night and expect to retire on the income.

Does It Work?

The entire shareware concept has generated a great deal of discussion in the developer community. Many shareware authors have complained bitterly that the system doesn't work, that they've received three registrations for software that has been downloaded 3,000 times.

Other shareware authors have displayed very impressive results, some making enough to start their own companies and prosper on the income. They claim that the shareware system does work and computer users are generally an honest lot.

Who is right? Well, obviously both types of authors have hard evidence to support their claims. And both are correct, to some degree. Although it is true that many disillusioned shareware authors are actually asking far too much for almost worthless software, some authors have invested considerable time into a quality product that just doesn't pull in any money. On the other hand, some shareware software has people beating down the doors to register.

So the shareware concept can work, but it isn't easy. It isn't a matter of writing the software, uploading it to your local online service, and collecting payment checks. If you expect to receive any income, you'll have to work for it.

Setting a Price

Choosing a price for your software can be tricky. Any business course will teach you that the more you charge for widgets, the fewer widgets people will buy. This holds true in shareware as well, but with an interesting twist. If you charge too little for your software, it can actually cause *fewer* people to register the product. If you ask for $5.00 to register, users may assume that you aren't that serious about getting revenue. Who will actually get around to writing a check for $5.00, writing the address out, putting the stamp on, and mailing it? This may be casting users as a lazy lot, but price can significantly affect the way a product is viewed.

Of course, charging too much also cuts down the number of registrations. For example, a recent popular shareware game asks $30.00 for a registration. Because that price approaches the cost of a commercial game, there have been some protests and the author has probably received fewer registrations that he might have. This isn't to say the product isn't *worth* the $30.00, but will users pay that price?

An important idea to keep in mind when comparing shareware prices with commercial software prices is that shareware authors receive every bit of the registration price from the users. Although the author has some costs involved in sending out disks or other distribution, almost all the revenue is profit.

On the other hand, commercial software distributors have a much higher overhead to contend with. For the $45.00 you pay for a game in the store, probably about $2.00 actually goes to the author. Commercial software has to hit *much* higher sales to break even than shareware does; advertising is not cheap!

For shareware games, the standard registration fee ranges between $10.00 and $25.00 (US). If the game is particularly well polished (and addictive), you may want to charge more; if the game is worth anything less, you'd probably be better off just sending it out as freeware.

Convincing Users to Register

As any salesperson can tell you, getting a customer to take out his or her checkbook and pay for a product isn't easy. However, it's even more difficult when you're not there to convince them. Your only contact with the user is your product, and too much or too little prodding can lose the registration.

One of the greatest turn-offs users can experience from shareware is practically being yelled at every time they use the product, especially if it accuses them of ripping the author off. In fact, some shareware programs begin this tirade the first time a user runs their program, which hardly inspires the user to send money. More likely, the program will end up in the trash can.

Some shareware programs are so meek in announcing the author's wishes that users don't even know that they are *supposed* to register. There may be a comment somewhere at the bottom of the Read-Me file that registration might be nice, if the user isn't too busy or doesn't mind being bothered. These pieces of software may be used by the most noble of people without ever being paid for.

Many of the more successful shareware games, such as those offered by Ambrosia Software, Inc., put up a dialog box each time the software is run asking for a registration code and letting the user push Not Yet if he or she hasn't registered yet (see Figure 21-1). When the user chooses to register, he or she prints out a registration form (either as a separate text file or printed directly from the application), fills it out, and mails it with a check. When the author receives it, he or she creates a serial number and mails it back to the user. The user then types the number into the application and the dialog box no longer appears.

A second technique is to distribute either a demo or a "crippled" version of the game. A demo typically has one to three levels of the real game; a crippled version typically has a critical feature disabled, such as saving or more powerful weapons. When the user sends in the money, he or she receives the full version in the mail. This technique can also be combined with a registration number—when the user types in the registration number, the extra levels or features become available. This method is more persuasive than the simple dialog box, but it has a few disadvantages. First of all, the developer has to mail out disks for every registration received, which can be expensive and time consuming. Secondly, because the full capabilities are within the program, just disabled, a more knowledgeable player can use debugging tools to fool the program into thinking that it's already registered and receive the extra levels or features for free.

Sending out a demo version with limited levels also has some success stories. Perhaps the most famous is that of Id Software, the creators of DOOM; however, in fact, it is unclear whether DOOM was actually shareware or a commercial game with a widely distributed demo version.

Testing Your Game

A critical step in the development of your game that should not be ignored is testing. History has shown many a game released before its time and buggy software does not make an author rich. Because so many operating system versions, monitor sizes, and extensions now exist, just because the game works on your machine doesn't necessarily mean it'll work on anyone else's. Fortunately for you, teeming masses out there are dying to help you in testing. Just post a message to a bulletin board and you're almost

FIGURE 21-1

◎ ◎ ◎ ◎ ◎ ◎

The Registration dialog for Apeiron, an Ambrosia product

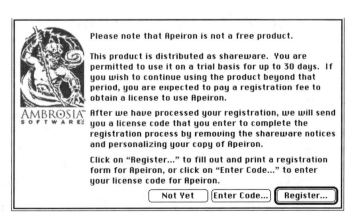

Please note that Apeiron is not a free product.

This product is distributed as shareware. You are permitted to use it on a trial basis for up to 30 days. If you wish to continue using the product beyond that period, you are expected to pay a registration fee to obtain a license to use Apeiron.

AMBROSIA™
SOFTWARE℠

After we have processed your registration, we will send you a license code that you enter to complete the registration process by removing the shareware notices and personalizing your copy of Apeiron.

Click on "Register..." to fill out and print a registration form for Apeiron, or click on "Enter Code..." to enter your license code for Apeiron.

[Not Yet]   [Enter Code...]   [[Register...]]

guaranteed to have your mailbox flooded for weeks with letters begging to have a crack at your game.

There is a downside to this, however. Most beta testers don't provide feedback to you once they have the game in their hands. Getting bug reports back is akin to pulling teeth, and the process can become very frustrating. Fortunately, there are a few people who will keep in regular contact and inform you of any little problem they find.

Distributing Your Game

Before people can start sending you buckets of money, they need to see your game. You have several methods to get your game into the hands of users. The easiest and most obvious is to hop on the Internet and upload it to the major ftp sites, or even to create your own Web page. Online services, like America Online and CompuServe, are also popular distribution mediums.

But this will reach only about 20 percent of the Macintosh computer market. The majority of your target is in homes without resident computer experts, usually homes with children between 13 and 18. Unfortunately, this is also the market least likely to register their copies of shareware.

David Richards of Ambrosia Software, Inc., had this to say about distributing Ambrosia's products and informing users of what they had to offer: "We also put the product in our color brochure which is sent out to anyone who requests one, and to everyone who registers as a response. The brochure contains the license code for the individual, and also informs him of the other products we offer. There is also an order form within the brochure that can be used to order more products. This really helps to reach the Mac owners that are not online."

Of course, this also means that you'll be putting more money into your distribution. Ambrosia invests this money because it is making a living off of shareware distribution— you have to decide how serious you want to be about shareware.

Accepting Registrations

You have a few choices about how to accept payment from your users. The most basic is to accept personal checks. This works well if you're in the United States and you expect to receive registrations only from other citizens. However, if you live outside the United States, converting personal checks to your local currency may be expensive; possibly expensive enough to eliminate your profits. Although you could request that users send money only in your particular currency, the bother of doing this will probably discourage most users.

An alternative would be to set yourself up to receive credit card orders. This makes it very simple for users to submit payments and the credit card company will automatically convert your currency based on the current rates, usually for no charge. There are several obstacles to this path, however. First of all, most banks are reluctant to process credit card orders from small businesses, much less a person working out of his or her home. If you talk to banks, be sure to describe yourself as a business (of course, you'll need a business name). Banks generally don't want to deal with mail-order businesses, but it might help if you stress that you're selling to a very specific market. Reports from shareware authors also indicate that small banks are more willing than larger ones. In any case, it'll probably be a difficult task, and you can expect to give up some of your profits to the bank: somewhere between 5 and 10 percent. On the plus side, a credit card account can significantly improve your profits; many people find sending a credit card number easier than writing a check.

Once you start accepting registrations, it is vitally important to enter them into a customer database. This database will allow you to keep track of who has received materials from you and how many people you have registered. In addition, it will give you a mailing list to send announcements to when you release your next game.

Additional Materials

Many shareware authors send printed manuals to users who register. Although this is a nice touch and probably increases the number of registrations, it's not strictly necessary for a game. After all, most games should be fairly self-explanatory.

If you don't limit yourself to electronic distribution, you'll have more problems to contend with. Some users that can't download the game may want a copy of the newest version of the software sent to them when they register, and you may want to let people order trial copies for the cost of the disk and then register if they like the game.

The cost of the disks, labels, and postage should all be considered when planning your distribution.

Technical Support

You probably don't have the resources to answer phone calls from your customers for technical support. Probably, your only option is to field e-mail messages from users, but if your product does well, you may end up spending a significant amount of time answering questions.

For this reason, it is very important that your software be relatively bugfree and easy to understand before you send it out. Many shareware developers have released unstable, beta-quality products and their registrations reflect this fact.

One more thing to note is that the unavailability of telephone technical support is another reason for pricing shareware software significantly below its commercial counterparts.

Your Responsibility for Upgrades

If you release a game that turns out to have several glaring bugs, your customers are going to be annoyed. If the bugs are immediately apparent, users won't register the product. However, if users run into the problems only after they are far into the game, you're under a moral obligation to fix the bugs and send them a new version. Many shareware authors let customers download updates from electronic networks; that is considered an adequate response. If you really want to impress your customers, you can mail them updates on disks. However, this may prove to be too expensive.

Making Shareware Work

Shareware will work for you if your software is of good quality and reasonably priced. Don't expect to push together a product in 3 hours and get rich off of it, and don't assume that your work is done once your product has been completed. If you want to turn shareware into a source of income, you'll have to invest much of your time and effort, as any entrepreneur does.

Unless you are very artistically talented, don't try to draw the game's artwork yourself. Programmers traditionally make horrible artists. If you have talented friends, talk them into helping you. Otherwise, if you're serious about making money off the game, hire a professional graphical artist.

Although with shareware there will always be a significant number of people using the software without paying for it (some estimate 90 percent, but this may be a bit high), there are two important facts to keep in mind. First, the total number of people using the software may be greater than if it were commercial (so you have a smaller percentage of a greater number). Second, you need far fewer registrations to break even (because you, the author, actually make much more money per unit sold).

Even if shareware does work for you, it won't happen quickly. Experienced shareware authors say it takes at least 6 months to start making any profit from the software.

Shareware authors also point out that one of the biggest mistakes you can make is to wait until significant profits start to accumulate before doing bug fixes or product improvements. Let your love of writing software, not the anticipation of profit, drive you. If you write your game only to make money, you will probably be disappointed.

In support of shareware over commercial distribution, David Richard of Ambrosia had this to say: "With the rush to get online, electronic distribution is fast becoming a viable medium of distribution. But what shareware has over other means of distribution is that you can receive the product in literally a matter of minutes, direct to your hard drive. You can also try the product before you buy it. These are very positive points for the consumer. But there are more reasons that are positive for the developer as well. Releasing a product becomes very efficient. I release a product in about 5 hours. It's done after that. Also, distribution is rather inexpensive and there are no middlemen to deal with. No printers, packagers, designers, duplicators, labelers, distributors or retailers to go through. Besides, with all that work being done by all those people, the price of the product is sure to go up (along with the amount of work needed to get the product out the door)."

Commercial Distribution

In some ways, choosing to distribute your software commercially can take less effort on your part than shareware, but it also can result in smaller financial returns. Commercial distribution is less forgiving than shareware, and your game has to have not only top-notch programming but also professional artwork, music, and design. Although to the programmer it may seem that these elements are trivial to produce, don't be fooled. Many of today's games have more artists than programmers on the credits, and it's not because programmers are more productive. If you have to hire someone to do the art (and you probably will), you can take heart in one unfortunate fact: graphic artists usually work for less than programmers (i.e., they are vastly underpaid).

In general, you have three choices for commercial distribution: The first is selling the rights to your program outright, taking a single check, and leaving. This is a drastic measure, and it's one that isn't done very often. The second option is more common, and more complicated. You keep the rights to the game, but you allow another company with more resources to advertise, distribute, and promote it. You then receive a percentage of the sales, and you're responsible for fixing bugs and writing newer versions. The last choice is the most overwhelming and risky option: attempting your own commercial distribution. This is not an option for the faint of heart; it will require a significant investment of your time and money.

Selling the Rights to Your Game

Software rights are rarely sold outright and usually only for already well-established products. The most difficult part is convincing a company to buy your game and to pay the right price. Usually you'll give up your source code, and you might be expected to provide some technical support or minor upgrades. However, this option probably won't be open to you until your product is well established.

Finding a Distributor

Arranging for a company to distribute your game isn't nearly as hard as the previous option, as long as your game is of sufficient quality. In general, a percentage of the game's sales will be paid to you as royalties, and you'll retain most of the rights to the product. You will almost certainly be limited to dealing with only one distributor, so choose well.

You want a company that has enough money to invest in advertising—without advertising, your product will go nowhere. Look for a proven track record of other successful products and make sure that the outfit is reputable; it's far from unheard of for a company to misrepresent its sales and attempt to cheat the author.

You'll have to be willing to invest time in polishing your product and ensuring that it's bugfree. Your distributor will probably handle technical support, but the game has to have a good interface and be easy to describe in a manual (which you may or may not have to write).

Selling Your Game on Your Own

This is by far the most exciting and risky choice you can make. And as these things go, it can also provide the biggest return. Despite the hazards involved, it can work, as shown by companies like Bungie, Graphic Simulations, and Parsoft.

Starting your own company requires a large amount of money. If you aren't wealthy, you'll need to find some friends or colleagues to invest in your company. Keep in mind, however, that the more money they put in, the less of the company you own.

Advertising will be by far your greatest expense. Having a mail-order company like MacWarehouse or Mac's Place list your game in its catalog can cost several thousand dollars per month. Advertising in a magazine such as *MacUser* or *MacWorld* is even more expensive: a full-page ad can cost around $30,000 per month.

To cover expenses like these, your product has to sell extremely well. You can also take advantage of mediums that are much more cost-efficient for you, such as advertising in *Inside Mac Games,* an excellent CD-ROM game magazine. Press releases distributed via the Internet are also very helpful and free.

Other forms of advertising you can consider are setting up a World Wide Web page about your game or talking about it on online services, such as America Online. Although these methods of advertising are relatively cheap, they reach only a small audience: people who are connected online. The more expensive options are required to reach the rest of the population.

Other things you'll need to consider include creating manuals and boxes, duplicating disks, handling technical support, and setting up an office; the list goes on and on. A college class on business management (or at *least* a book) is highly recommended if you're interested in this approach.

Copy Protection

Protecting your product is a voraciously discussed topic and it's a major source of contention between game players and game writers. The first form of copy protection involved affecting the master disks in such a way that they couldn't be copied with the software provided by the computer. This required the player to use only the original disks, which wasn't too much of a problem because nobody had hard drives at that time.

When players started to want their programs on the hard drive instead of floppy disks, writers switched to a form of password protection. This approach requires the user to look up a word in the game manual and type it in each time the game starts up. It assumes that the player won't lose the manual and will lug it around if he or she plays on a PowerBook.

Game players have always objected to copy protection and some won't buy a game that uses this device. However, the problem of software piracy still exists today and many developers want to protect their work.

Most recent games don't have copy protection, mainly because developers fear that their game's sales would suffer if it were protected. However, with the popularization of CD-ROM games, many developers have gone back to requiring that the original disk be present before running the game and there hasn't been much, if any, protest. This is because it's reasonable to expect that the CD-ROM, with a few hundred megabytes of data on it, always be present because few users have the storage space to copy this much information onto their hard drives. Also, because CD-ROMs can't be written on, users don't have to worry about the disc being damaged. Recent CD-ROM games that have used this copy protection include World of Xeen and Dark Forces.

Choosing a Direction

Just when you've finished your program and thought you were all done, there's clearly a lot more work to be done. Unless you plan on releasing your software as freeware, you've got to figure out a way to handle distribution and advertising. Although these tasks can be daunting, they're also extremely rewarding, and many authors feel that this stage is the best part of the whole process. You'll have to decide for yourself.

22

The Future
of 3D
Games

22

The Future
of 3D Games

Throughout this book, I've tried to make the best of the machines available today. Many of the programming techniques game programmers use now depend heavily on the speed of today's computers—games like Marathon or Descent would simply not have been possible on the machines available 5 years ago. Likewise, the newest games today will be child's play 5 years from now.

We know what used to amaze us and we're enjoying some incredible games today, but what will we be playing tomorrow? What could we do given a computer that's two, five, or ten times as fast as the ones we're using now?

Improved Techniques

Usually when presented with a faster computer, game programmers don't create new rendering techniques. You already know about many realistic techniques that create 3D graphics, it's just that they're too slow to use for a real-time game. For example, software packages have done texture mapping and advanced shading techniques for years, but today games use those procedures to create an incredible user experience.

Polygon Shading

One technique that has come into common use recently is shading a polygon based on its facing a local light source. A polygon that is pointing directly at a light will appear to be brighter, whereas one facing away will be completely dark. The shading calculation is a simple matter of determining the cosine of the polygon's angle to the light, but the problem comes when drawing the polygon on the screen. Because most games are now run in 8-bit color, there may not be enough colors in the palette to draw the polygon well. With some palette manipulation, a respectable result can be obtained, but a better solution lies around the corner.

Most Power Macintosh machines shipped today are capable of 16- or 24-bit color, which gives the user just over 32,000 colors or 16 million colors, respectively. Unfortunately, with this increased color capacity, it takes the computer longer to update the screen. The screen's image is usually stored in a type of memory called *video RAM*; this memory is not terribly fast. So while the processor gains speed rapidly, the rest of the computer improves much more slowly. Still, we should start seeing computers fast enough for 24-bit games in the near future. Already, at least one 3D game uses 16-bit color: Marathon uses it for shading textures.

Smoothing Polygons

Shading can also be used to produce smoother-looking objects. Normally, a rounded object can be represented only with several flat polygons. Unless you use a huge number of polygons, the object won't look completely smooth. However, you can take the edges of each polygon and blend them together to make the polygon look more realistic.

Gouraud Shading

I discussed one of these shading techniques, gouraud shading, in Chapter 9. If you remember, gouraud shading involves calculating the correct shading color at each of the polygon's vertices and then interpolating these colors as the polygon is drawn. Figure 22-1 shows an example of gouraud shading. The result is a fairly smooth object, but if a light shines in the middle of a polygon (as opposed to near its vertices), the effect of the light can be lost.

Phong Shading

Phong shading solves this problem by calculating the shading at *every pixel* on the polygon. Although this is significantly more expensive (because you're performing a cosine calculation and several multiplies at each pixel), the results are remarkable, as shown in Figure 22-2. This technique can also produce specular highlights, which can make the surface of an object appear to be shiny.

Shadows

If your game takes place in the outdoors, you can draw shadows underneath any air-borne objects across the ground; F/A-18 and A-10 both do this. If you feel particularly adventurous, you can adjust the shadows based on the time of day in the game. For example, at 8 in the morning, the shadows would fall far to the west of the object, plus they would be stretched. Figure 22-3 shows the walking man from Chapter 5 with phong shading and shadows.

Currently, many of the shadows shown in these games have hard edges. In the future, it may be possible for them to be more realistic "soft" shadows. Soft shadows are very

FIGURE 22-1

◎ ◎ ◎ ◎ ◎ ◎

A gouraud-shaded landscape

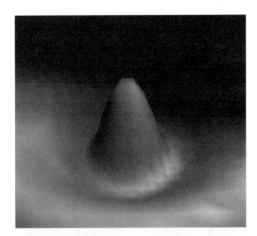

FIGURE 22-2

◎ ◎ ◎ ◎ ◎ ◎

The same landscape, only phong shaded

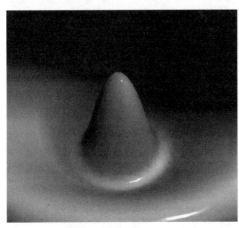

FIGURE 22-3
◉ ◉ ◉ ◉ ◉ ◉
*The walking
man, phong
shaded with
shadows*

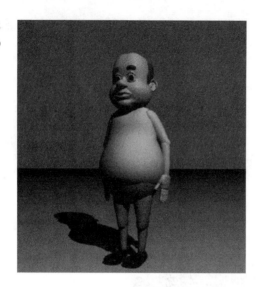

difficult to obtain even with professional 3D packages because the calculations they require are very expensive.

As you often do for games, you can cheat. You can simply blur the edges of the shadow as you cast it down, producing a realistic shadow without a lot of calculations.

Ray Tracing

You've probably seen ray-traced games. They became popular along with CD-ROM games and include such titles as MYST, Journeyman Project, and Iron Helix. The ray-traced scenes of these games are prerendered, which may take hours or even days to complete. I talked briefly about ray tracing in Chapter 9, but let's take a closer look at it now.

A raytracer takes each pixel of the window and traces a ray (hence the name) backward from the viewer's eye until it hits an object in the scene or misses everything. If an intersection is detected, all the scene's light sources are taken into account and the color of that point on the object is calculated (by a process similar to phong shading). If the ray misses everything in the scene, the color is taken from the scene's background (which is most commonly black).

Reflections can also be calculated when ray tracing. If the object is defined as reflective, a new angle is calculated for the ray and the tracing continues. If the object isn't *completely* reflective, the object's color is combined with whatever the additional ray tracing comes up with. Because raytracing is recursive in this way, it can be very time consuming.

Another advantage of ray tracing is that you no longer have to stick with polygonal objects. All you need to do is detect when and where a ray intersects an object and then calculate the object's color at that point. To make an object appear perfectly smooth, you can define it as a set of curves, usually *bezier* curves. When four curves intersect, they form a *patch*, which is a two-dimensional curved surface.

However, ray-patch intersections are very mathematically expensive and although there are a few shortcuts, this technique will probably stay out of reach of games for many years.

Texture mapping is relatively easy to do when ray tracing. Because you already know where the ray fell on the object, you can easily calculate where to find the correct color on the texture map.

Another thing to note with ray tracing is that it automatically solves the problem of hidden surface removal because it's essentially doing the same thing as an efficient z-buffer algorithm.

It's ironic that ray tracing, one of the most realistic and expensive rendering effects available, is conceptually very simple. Other than the shortcuts and optimizations employed by professional ray-tracing packages, you now know how to perform most of the techniques involved.

What We're Likely to See

In a few years, we'll see texture mapping used in many more games. There is already a flight simulator called Flight Unlimited that uses texture mapping to draw the entire landscape; the effect is astonishing. Mountains look like mountains, not big pyramids of green; rivers flow across the landscape; and you can even fly into sheer cliffs. Not surprisingly, this game requires the newest processor technology and it lacks a good frame rate even so. Nevertheless, it does what any good game should do: makes the most of the best computers available.

It won't be too long before flight simulators and other games are *expected* to be fully texture mapped. However, graphics are not the only thing that flight simulators are judged on. You should also start seeing more laws of physics implemented, something A-10 has already started to do. Imagine a virtual world where temperature, climate, and seasons have a large effect on the operations of the player's craft. For example, a heat-seeking missile would have a much easier time tracking its target in an arctic climate than it would in the Sahara desert. The missile's guidance systems might also be affected by the burning tank the player just destroyed. The fire might spread to the local forest, causing a large-scale conflagration, and so on.

Artificial intelligence is something that can go a long way toward making a realistic game. When is the last time your enemies ran for cover when you fired on them? Or how about your wingman doing something other than flying into a mountainside? Artificial intelligence may or may not improve in the coming years—it has historically consumed little processor time, so theoretically intelligent enemies are more a function of programming adeptness than processing power. It's definitely a field that needs more work.

Another thing that would improve the gaming experience is modeling a more complete world for the player to function in. A flight simulator called Flying Nightmares from Domark Software models an entire squadron, and the player is responsible for controlling ground troops as well as his or her own aircraft. When the player destroys a building or military emplacement in one battle, the destruction remains (and affects the enemy's actions) during the next battle.

With extra processor time, an entire army could be commanded by the player, who could witness the movements of ground and air troops even as he or she participates in the action. In a way, this scenario would combine the large-scale action of a wargame with the realistic small-scale action of a flight or tank simulator.

Input and Output Devices

Future technology is not limited to the processor. Many companies are scrambling to create realistic input devices. ThrustMaster, Inc., is already selling input devices that simulate those on a military aircraft, including a flight stick, a throttle, and a rudder. It also sells a complete set to model an automobile: a brake/gas pedal and a steering wheel.

Some arcades have moving platforms that pitch and roll to simulate the gravitational effects a pilot would feel when flying. They also have monitors strategically placed around the player so he or she can see not only ahead but to the sides as well.

Although companies might scramble to come up with such a device to be sold to individuals, most users would hesitate to buy a two-ton platform that takes up most of the living room and costs a quarter of a million dollars. On the bright side, we may start to see more of these platforms in local arcades.

A few of the more recent flight simulators, namely F/A-18 and A-10, can take advantage of multiple monitors, showing side views out of the additional screens. This is a feature that probably won't become much more popular than it already is, because very few machines are equipped with more than one monitor. It certainly isn't a feature that you're likely to see on the Intel platform, where it's difficult to connect more than one monitor.

Movies have idolized the concept of virtual reality. You often see the hero wearing a pair of glasses that has two miniature displays to show a stereo image. When a player wearing these glasses looks left and right or up and down, the computer receives a signal so it can update the view.

Although they're still exotic in the real world, a few of these glasses are available for the Intel platform and at least one company makes them for the Macintosh. These glasses don't support motion detection yet, but that'll probably happen eventually. If a standard is reached for their interface and the price is reasonable (around $200 per pair), you can be sure that almost every major 3D game will eventually support virtual reality glasses.

Graphics Acceleration

Apple has recently released a 3D graphics package called QuickDraw 3D. Although QuickDraw 3D is a complete polygon and spline rendering package that'll give you the same capability of the engine you've developed in this book, the software-based engine is a bit slow to use in games. The real beauty of the package is that you can use QuickDraw 3D to render the world and it will automatically take advantage of 3D acceleration boards that are offered by several companies.

These boards have a built-in z-buffering system and handle the rendering of texture-mapped and gouraud-shaded polygons at speeds of up to 30 fps.

The main disadvantage of using QuickDraw 3D for rendering your game is that it's available only on Power Macintosh computers and it's not fast enough for many games unless a hardware accelerator is available. Until these accelerator cards become standard fare, you would have to implement your own 3D rendering system plus support the QuickDraw 3D standard and be able to switch between them.

It's possible that Apple will start offering QuickDraw 3D cards as part of a standard computer configuration in the future, and it's probable that some Power Macintosh machines will soon be fast enough to support QuickDraw 3D in software for some games.

The Speed of Technology

Most of us have experienced buying a computer that quickly becomes obsolete. Suddenly what you paid $3,000 for is worth just over $1,000 and you're looking hungrily at the latest and greatest. We're constantly progressing in every aspect of computers, and rather quickly. Let's take a look at what might happen to the various components of the Macintosh over the next few years.

The Processor

Several years ago, Gordon Moore, one of the founders of Intel, stated that processor speed doubles every 18 months. If you look at this trend over several years, it really starts to add up. In 3 years, processors will theoretically be four times as fast as they are today. In 6 years, they should be 16 times as fast.

Let's take an example that seems preposterous today. Say it takes 10 minutes to ray-trace a particular scene on a Power Macintosh. If we wanted this scene to be drawn 20 times a second, our processor would have to be 10 minutes * 60 secs/minute * 20 frames per second; let's see, that's 12,000 times as fast as it is today. Because $2^{13} = 8192$ and $2^{14} = 16,384$, we'll need between 13 and 14 iterations of processor speed-doubling before machines will be fast enough for this. That number equates to about 20 years of progress, according to Moore's estimations.

So if you can imagine a full-screen raytraced game 20 years from now, that *might* be what we'll have. Unfortunately, Moore also predicted that processor speed will peak out around the turn of the century, leaving us with machines that are about 10 times as fast as a Power Macintosh 9500/132. Still, that's not too bad.

Memory

All the other parts of the computer have progressed much more slowly than the processor. The minimum configuration for a new Macintosh recently went from 4 megabytes to 8 megabytes and many are configured with 16 megabytes. Because memory is greatly affected by the relatively high price of RAM chips, it'll probably be at *least* 2 or 3 years before 16 megabytes becomes the minimum configuration.

Secondary Storage

When CD-ROMs flooded the market a few years ago, games were revolutionized. Suddenly, they were no longer limited by being distributed on a few small floppy disks and needing to reside on the player's hard drive, where they consumed valuable space. Today, it's not uncommon for a game to use several hundred megabytes of space for graphics and sound, all distributed on a CD-ROM that costs less than two floppy disks.

Several new standards are in the works that will increase the storage of CD-ROMs even more. Today, they are capable of storing just over 600 megabytes of data, but one standard would place multiple layers of data on the same disc, bringing the capacity to 1.2 gigabytes; some manufacturers are considering putting data on both sides of the disc.

It is unlikely that increased storage capabilities will significantly affect tomorrow's games. Although a few games use more than one CD-ROM, usually because of many cut-scene movies, most don't even fill a single disc yet.

Hard disk space is also increasing. The last few years have seen the price of gigabyte drives fall significantly, and it won't be long before gigabyte drives become standard on any computer.

Monitors

The Macintosh started out with 9-inch black-and-white monitors with a resolution of 512x342. When the Macintosh II was introduced, the monitor standard went to 640x480 in 8-bit color. Essentially, this is where it has remained ever since, although many of the newer machines can handle 16-bit color. Many PowerBook computers support only 640x400 with 4-bit grayscale, and this is likely to remain true in the near future.

Most games continue to support 640x480 at 8-bit color as the standard, not functioning on any smaller size and not taking advantage of any larger size. A growing number of users have Apple's 15-inch multisync monitor, which is capable of 832x624 resolution, and they want their games to take advantage of it. There is a chance that the standard will move to 832x624 in a few years, but for the short term 640x480 will reign.

A True Virtual Reality

The term virtual reality has been so hyped by the media that it's unclear what is really possible and probable compared to movies like *Lawnmower Man*. Some aspects of this virtual reality are within grasp, whereas others remain a distant dream.

As I mentioned earlier, we already have virtual reality glasses that present a stereo image to the user; these will probably enter the mainstream within a few years. We also have devices to detect the user's head and arm movements, but it's unclear whether or when these items will become popular.

We are quite a long way from being able to slip a plug in the back of our heads and have an entire experience projected upon us, including sight, sound, smell, taste, and feeling. We're learning more about the brain, but we don't know *that* much yet. Still, it's important to imagine what might be possible in the future; science fiction retains a healthy domain. As time progresses, aggressive programmers like you will bring the realm of science fiction into science fact as you create the next great gaming revolution.

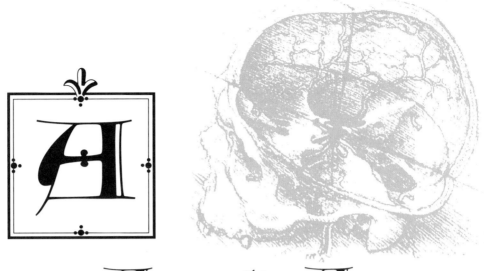

Appendix A: Recommended Reading

The following books were valuable resources in the writing of *Black Art of Macintosh Game Programming* and are highly recommended for further information on Mac programming and 3D animation.

Macintosh-related Books

How To Write Macintosh Software, Scott Knaster; New York: Addison-Wesley, 1992.
Inside Macintosh Series, Apple Computer, Inc.; New York: Addison-Wesley, 1992–.

Books on Three-Dimensional Animation

Computer Graphics, Principles and Practice, J.D. Foley, A. Van Dam, Steven Feiner, and John Hughes; New York: Addison-Wesley, 1992.
Fundamentals of Interactive Computer Graphics, Alan Watt; New York: Addison-Wesley, 1989.

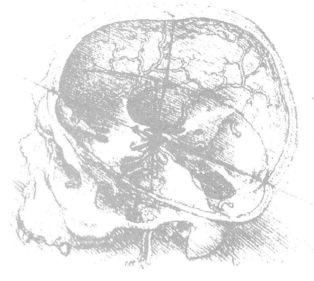

Index

N

NOTES

NOTES

NOTES

NOTES

NOTES

NOTES

NOTES

NOTES

NOTES

NOTES

NOTES

NOTES

NOTES

Books have a substantial influence on the destruction of the forests of the Earth. For example, it takes 17 trees to produce one ton of paper. A first printing of 30,000 copies of a typical 480-page book consumes 108,000 pounds of paper, which will require 918 trees!

Waite Group Press™ is against the clear-cutting of forests and supports reforestation of the Pacific Northwest of the United States and Canada, where most of this paper comes from. As a publisher with several hundred thousand books sold each year, we feel an obligation to give back to the planet. We will therefore support organizations which seek to preserve the forests of planet Earth.

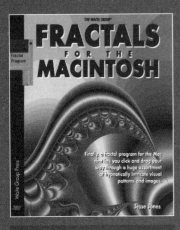
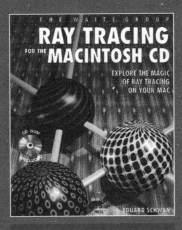

LIMITED WARRANTY

The following warranties shall be effective for 90 days from the date of purchase: (i) The Waite Group, Inc. warrants the enclosed disk to be free of defects in materials and workmanship under normal use; and (ii) The Waite Group, Inc. warrants that the programs, unless modified by the purchaser, will substantially perform the functions described in the documentation provided by The Waite Group, Inc. when operated on the designated hardware and operating system. The Waite Group, Inc. does not warrant that the programs will meet purchaser's requirements or that operation of a program will be uninterrupted or error-free. The program warranty does not cover any program that has been altered or changed in any way by anyone other than The Waite Group, Inc. The Waite Group, Inc. is not responsible for problems caused by changes in the operating characteristics of computer hardware or computer operating systems that are made after the release of the programs, nor for problems in the interaction of the programs with each other or other software.

THESE WARRANTIES ARE EXCLUSIVE AND IN LIEU OF ALL OTHER WARRANTIES OF MERCHANTABILITY OR FITNESS FOR A PARTICULAR PURPOSE OR OF ANY OTHER WARRANTY, WHETHER EXPRESS OR IMPLIED.

EXCLUSIVE REMEDY

The Waite Group, Inc. will replace any defective disk without charge if the defective disk is returned to The Waite Group, Inc. within 90 days from date of purchase.

This is Purchaser's sole and exclusive remedy for any breach of warranty or claim for contract, tort, or damages.

LIMITATION OF LIABILITY

THE WAITE GROUP, INC. AND THE AUTHORS OF THE PROGRAMS SHALL NOT IN ANY CASE BE LIABLE FOR SPECIAL, INCIDENTAL, CONSEQUENTIAL, INDIRECT, OR OTHER SIMILAR DAMAGES ARISING FROM ANY BREACH OF THESE WARRANTIES EVEN IF THE WAITE GROUP, INC. OR ITS AGENT HAS BEEN ADVISED OF THE POSSIBILITY OF SUCH DAMAGES.

THE LIABILITY FOR DAMAGES OF THE WAITE GROUP, INC. AND THE AUTHORS OF THE PROGRAMS UNDER THIS AGREEMENT SHALL IN NO EVENT EXCEED THE PURCHASE PRICE PAID.

COMPLETE AGREEMENT

This Agreement constitutes the complete agreement between The Waite Group, Inc. and the authors of the programs, and you, the purchaser.

Some states do not allow the exclusion or limitation of implied warranties or liability for incidental or consequential damages, so the above exclusions or limitations may not apply to you. This limited warranty gives you specific legal rights; you may have others, which vary from state to state.

SATISFACTION REPORT CARD

Please fill out this card if you wish to know of future updates to
Black Art of Macintosh Game Programming or to receive our catalog.

First Name: _____   **Last Name:** _____

Address: _____

City: _____   **State:** _____   **Zip:** _____

Daytime Telephone: (_____) _____

E-mail Address: _____

Date product was acquired: Month _____   **Day** _____   **Year** _____   **Your Occupation:** _____

Overall, how would you rate *Black Art of Macintosh Game Programming?*

☐ Excellent   ☐ Very Good   ☐ Good
☐ Fair   ☐ Below Average   ☐ Poor

What did you like MOST about this book? _____

_____

What did you like LEAST about this book? _____

_____

_____

Please describe any problems you may have encountered with installing or using the disk: _____

_____

How did you use this book (problem-solver, tutorial, reference...)?

_____

What is your level of computer expertise?

☐ New   ☐ Dabbler   ☐ Hacker
☐ Power User   ☐ Programmer   ☐ Experienced Professional

What computer languages are you familiar with? _____

_____

Please describe your Macintosh:

Computer _____   Hard disk _____
Modem _____   3.5" disk drives _____
Video card _____ Monitor _____
Printer _____   Peripherals _____
Sound board _____ CD-ROM _____

Where did you buy this book?

☐ Bookstore (name): _____
☐ Discount store (name): _____
☐ Computer store (name): _____
☐ Catalog (name): _____
☐ Direct from WGP   ☐ Other _____

What price did you pay for this book? _____

What influenced your purchase of this book?

☐ Recommendation   ☐ Advertisement
☐ Magazine review   ☐ Store display
☐ Mailing   ☐ Book's format
☐ Reputation of Waite Group Press   ☐ Other

How many computer books do you buy each year? _____

How many other Waite Group books do you own? _____

What is your favorite Waite Group book? _____

_____

Is there any program or subject you would like to see Waite Group Press cover in a similar approach? _____

_____

Additional comments? _____

_____

_____

Please send to: **Waite Group Press**
                       200 Tamal Plaza
                       Corte Madera, CA 94925

☐ **Check here for a free Waite Group catalog**

BEFORE YOU OPEN THE DISK OR CD-ROM PACKAGE ON THE FACING PAGE, CAREFULLY READ THE LICENSE AGREEMENT.

Opening this package indicates that you agree to abide by the license agreement found in the back of this book. If you do not agree with it, promptly return the unopened disk package (including the related book) to the place you obtained them for a refund.